I0112458

Reckoning and Renewal: The World Trade Organization and Its Dispute Settlement System at 30

Reckoning and Renewal: The World Trade Organization and Its Dispute Settlement System at 30

Essays in Honour of Valerie Hughes

EDITED BY

Nicolas Lamp

UNIVERSITY OF TORONTO PRESS

Toronto Buffalo London

Irwin UTP Publishing
An imprint of University of Toronto Press
Toronto Buffalo London
utppublishing.com
© University of Toronto Press 2025
Printed in Canada

ISBN 978-1-4875-7089-7 (paper)   ISBN 978-1-4875-7090-3 (OA)

All rights reserved. The use of any part of this publication reproduced, transmitted
in any form or by any means, electronic, mechanical, photocopying, recording,
or otherwise, or stored in a retrieval system, without prior written consent of the
publisher – or in the case of photocopying, a licence from Access Copyright, the
Canadian Copyright Licensing Agency – is an infringement of the copyright law.

Library and Archives Canada Cataloguing in Publication

Title: Reckoning and renewal : the World Trade Organization and its dispute
    settlement system at 30 : essays in honour of Valerie Hughes / edited by
    Nicolas Lamp.
Names: Lamp, Nicolas, 1982- editor | Hughes, Valerie (Professor of law), honoree
Description: Includes bibliographical references and index.
Identifiers: Canadiana (print) 20250229501 | Canadiana (ebook) 20250229528 |
    ISBN 9781487570897 (paper) | ISBN 9781487570903 (OA PDF)
Subjects: LCSH: World Trade Organization. | LCSH: International commercial
    arbitration. | LCSH: Foreign trade regulation. | LCGFT: Festschriften.
Classification: LCC K2400 .R43 2025 | DDC 341.5/22—dc23

Cover design: Sidra Nadim

We welcome comments and suggestions regarding any aspect of our
publications – please feel free to contact us at news@utorontopress.com or
visit us at utppublishing.com.

Every effort has been made to contact copyright holders; in the event of an error
or omission, please notify the publisher.

We wish to acknowledge the land on which the University of Toronto Press
operates. This land is the traditional territory of the Wendat, the Anishnaabeg, the
Haudenosaunee, the Métis, and the Mississaugas of the Credit First Nation.

University of Toronto Press acknowledges the financial support of the
Government of Canada and the Ontario Arts Council, an agency of the
Government of Ontario, for its publishing activities.

Canada Council **Conseil des Arts**
for the Arts **du Canada**

ONTARIO ARTS COUNCIL
CONSEIL DES ARTS DE L'ONTARIO
an Ontario government agency
un organisme du gouvernement de l'Ontario

Funded by the   Financé par le
Government   gouvernement
of Canada   du Canada

Canadä

Table of Contents

Table of Contents

Table of Contents

Foreword*

RECKONING AND RENEWAL: THE WORLD Trade Organization and Its Dispute Settlement System at 30 is a timely and vital volume that not only surveys the evolution and current state of World Trade Organization (WTO) dispute settlement—warts and all—but also honours Valerie Hughes, one of its most dedicated architects. Her distinguished career spans roles as panelist, Canadian government official, and senior member of the WTO Secretariat. I am especially proud that several chapters in this book were written by WTO Secretariat staff members, showing the continued importance of the role of the Secretariat in serving WTO Members.

One of the foundational pillars of the WTO is its dispute settlement mechanism—a rules-based system established by WTO Members to ensure the stability, predictability, and fairness of the global trading order. The Dispute Settlement Understanding (DSU) was designed and established by Members not only to encourage mutually agreed solutions but also to provide for binding adjudication, strict timelines, and a two-tiered review—features that, collectively, make it one of the most advanced dispute resolution mechanisms in international law. Over the years, it has enabled the peaceful resolution of hundreds of disputes, providing a forum through which Members can assert and defend their rights within a legal framework, beginning with consultations to resolve differences, and, if necessary, proceeding through the full dispute settlement process. These achievements were not automatic or inevitable—they were the result of vision, determination, and meticulous legal craftsmanship. The formative years of the dispute settlement mechanism are examined in the first section of the book, which traces the evolution of

---

* The views expressed in this Foreword are mine and do not represent the positions or opinions of the WTO or its Members. Nor do I endorse any particular views expressed in this book. I wish to extend my thanks to my trusted advisor, Iryna Polovets, for her able assistance on this project, especially in working with the contributions from WTO Secretariat staff.

WTO dispute settlement into a widely used and highly regarded mechanism within the international legal landscape.

Today, as the WTO and the broader multilateral trading system confront unprecedented challenges, the dispute settlement system continues to face its own reckoning. Over the years, the system has come under increasing strain, most importantly through the paralysis of the Appellate Body since 2019 due to blockage of appointment of Appellate Body Members and the inability of WTO Members to agree on a way forward. Unquestionably, the fact that a Member can appeal a panel decision to a non-functioning Appellate Body has undermined the "finality" of the system, leaving some cases unresolved and creating uncertainty. Say what you want about whether there should be an Appellate Body or not, whether there should be appeal and review at all or not, or whether the system should be somewhere in between, the reality is that an Appellate Body that is on the books but nonfunctional, as it is now, gives Members a loophole to avoid "finality" of outcomes simply by appealing. Accordingly, unless it is addressed one way or another, as Members decide, it will continue to leave cases in limbo if a party chooses to appeal.

The existential crisis of the Appellate Body has brought to light highly divergent views among Members on several fundamental issues: the proper scope of judicial interpretation, the role of precedent, the nature of the procedures used, and even the broader purpose of dispute settlement within a multilateral framework. The second part of the book engages directly on these themes, offering a range of perspectives on the political, institutional, and jurisprudential tensions that have brought the system to its current impasse.

However, while the system is battered, it is not broken. Even in the absence of a functioning Appellate Body, WTO Members continue to use the system to resolve disputes and reach mutually agreed solutions. We can back this up with data. Since 2019, when the Appellate Body ceased to operate, Members have filed forty-seven new requests for consultations, and thirty-two panels have been established by the dispute settlement body (DSB). During this period, forty-one disputes have been resolved, settled, or suspended, surpassing the twenty-five cases that have been appealed into the void. Of those forty-one disputes, twenty-eight disputes were resolved either by mutually agreed solutions (fourteen); withdrawal of the complaint (five); or suspension of proceedings at the request of the complainant (nine). This analysis demonstrates that Members continue to find value in the consultation and panel process for resolving disputes.

In addition, efforts have been underway to rebuild consensus and restore trust in the system, most recently through rigorous and intensive reform discussions conducted at the WTO, which have led to many valuable proposals for improving the system concerning appeal and review. In addition, these interest-based negotiations have yielded significant concepts and ideas to make the dispute settlement more accessible for developing Members.

In the meantime, Members have also demonstrated creativity and adaptability by developing alternative approaches within the DSU framework, most notably through the use of Article 25 arbitrations as well as the Multi-Party Interim Appeal Arbitration Arrangement (MPIA), to which twenty-seven Members[1] are party. This continued engagement reflects a shared recognition among many Members that an effective dispute settlement mechanism is an essential component of the WTO's credibility and long-term viability. The third part of the book explores these developments, focusing on pathways to revitalization of dispute settlement. The exploration of dispute settlement mechanisms under preferential trade agreements adds a further layer of opportunity, reminding us that innovation and adaptation are not foreign to the multilateral system but integral to its evolution.[2]

As part of its rebirth, the WTO dispute settlement system must, to remain relevant, respond to the evolving and often divergent priorities of WTO Members. Such issues include how and whether to address unilateral approaches to trade policy, the complexity of supply chains, the role of national security, and the nature of overdependence in various forms. In addition, pressing challenges such as the role of digital trade, economic and environmental sustainability, development, and artificial intelligence are relevant to reform. In short, the system must be equipped to address not only traditional trade disputes but also the increasingly complex and cross-cutting issues that characterize contemporary global governance. The final section of the book looks ahead—not only to the future of dispute settlement but to the evolution of WTO governance as a whole.

And of course, it should go without saying that the WTO is about more than dispute settlement. Administering trade agreements, providing a forum for trade negotiations, monitoring domestic trade policies, and assisting developing countries to build trade capacity are other essential functions geared towards liberalizing trade and raising living standards within the economic rule of law. The WTO's vibrant committee structure, as well as

---

1   Counting the EU as one Member.

2   At the same time, it is noteworthy that no preferential trade agreement contains an appellate review mechanism, with the exception of the *African Continental Free Trade Agreement*, which incorporates all elements of the WTO DSU without change.

the trade policy review mechanism, provide the opportunity to address trade concerns and give meaning to the rules established by Members. In addition, Members have been able to negotiate new rules, by consensus, although the process is admittedly slow. The latest example of success is the WTO *Agreement on Fisheries Subsidies*, agreed by ministers at the WTO's 12th Ministerial Conference in 2022, which will enter into force as soon as only fourteen more out of 111 required Members (as of this writing) deposit their instruments of acceptance. Technical assistance and capacity building help developing Members implement WTO agreements and provide important tools for sustainable economic development. The sheer impact of all of these elements of the multilateral trading system cannot be forgotten.

At the same time, we must acknowledge "reforming" the WTO is essential. Although reform means different things to different people and encompasses substantive, process, and governance components, it is unquestionable that the WTO must reposition itself to address today's challenges. And reform of the dispute settlement system must be part of that repositioning.

As the book makes clear, reforming the dispute settlement system will require more than technical adjustments. It demands a clear-eyed acknowledgment and understanding of past shortcomings, a renewed political commitment to multilateralism, and recognition of the importance of predictability in global trade. Just as critically, it will require thoughtful and principled leadership. While rules and procedures are essential, the book reminds us that it is also the dedication of individuals—their professionalism, integrity, and perseverance—that breathes life into these structures.

And to that end, this collection casts a happy note by paying well-deserved tribute to Valerie Hughes, who has been an essential part of the development and stewardship of the WTO dispute settlement system throughout her career. As Director at different times of both the Appellate Body Secretariat and the Legal Affairs Division of the WTO Secretariat—an unparalleled dual achievement—she provided leadership and guidance that shaped generations of Secretariat lawyers. Her invaluable contributions before and after her Secretariat tenure are also noteworthy for their impact and foresight. The presence of contributors she mentored or inspired throughout this book stands testament to her enduring influence and legacy.

I extend my appreciation to the contributors and editor of this collection, and particularly to Nicolas Lamp for driving such a valuable project. May it serve as a source of insight, inspiration, and resolve as we confront the challenges ahead, seek to reposition the WTO, and revitalize the vision of a rules-based multilateral trading system.

Angela Ellard,
Deputy Director-General of the World Trade Organization
Geneva, May 2025

Acknowledgements

THE IDEA OF BRINGING TOGETHER a group of authors to write in honour of Valerie Hughes about the World Trade Organization (WTO) and its dispute settlement system came to me when I was co-teaching with Valerie at the Queen's University Faculty of Law after Valerie's retirement from the WTO. Valerie accompanied me and the students in Queen's Law's international law summer program on field trips to Brussels and Geneva, she supervised the students on the Jackson moot team, and she helped us to establish a TradeLab clinic in international trade law at Queen's Law. The students and I were struck by the universal admiration and adoration that trade lawyers expressed towards Valerie wherever we went. The sheer number of distinguished trade experts who had been hired, trained, mentored, and taught by Valerie was awe-inspiring. I realized that the enormous amount of goodwill that Valerie had accrued over the course of her astonishing career could be used to motivate a uniquely broad and diverse set of authors to write in her honour. The forty-four contributors to this book—and many others who, for one reason or another, would have liked to contribute but were unable to do so—are a testament to the profound impact that Valerie has had on the work, careers, and lives of so many in the trade law community in Canada, Geneva, and beyond.

In bringing this project to fruition, I have relied on a group of stellar research assistants, all of them JD students at Queen's Law. Conor Alexander and Alara Once helped me get the project off the ground and took on the enormous task of bringing the entire book into conformity with the McGill guide; Kyla Velonic helped out during the final stretch before the submission of the manuscript. Sierra Wild proofread and corrected the entire copyedited manuscript with astonishing attention to detail, and Megan Coulter helped her to bring it over the finish line.

I am grateful to the WTO's Deputy Director-General (DDG) Angela Ellard for supporting the project from the outset, contributing the foreword, and for overseeing the review of the contributions by WTO Secretariat staff members. I owe special thanks to DDG Ellard's amazing advisor Iryna Polovets for her tireless work in support of the book. I am grateful to Dmitry Grozoubinski and his team at the Geneva Trade Platform, as well as to Jorge Castro and Leslie Stephenson at the WTO, for hosting a book workshop, at which the book started to take shape, in June 2024.

Publishing the book with the University of Toronto Press was a wonderful experience. Josephine Mo and her team shepherded the book to publication with unfailing kindness and enthusiasm.

I am grateful to the contributors for their confidence in me and for their fantastic contributions, from which I have learned so much and I hope many others will as well. I am grateful to my spouse, Jean Thomas, for believing in me in moments of doubt and for sharing moments of joy. I am grateful to Valerie's wonderful partner Anne for her help in keeping the project a secret from Valerie until we could reveal it to her at the right moment. And, first and foremost, I am grateful to Valerie Hughes for being a dear friend to me and my family, a mentor, a sounding board, and someone I can always look up to as a shining example of professionalism, integrity, work ethic, and commitment to higher ideals.

CHAPTER 1

Introduction: Taking Stock of the World Trade Organization and Its Dispute Settlement System at 30

Nicolas Lamp

A. Introduction

THERE IS PERHAPS NO BETTER emblem for the rise and fall of the post-Cold War order than the fate of the World Trade Organization (WTO) and its dispute settlement system. In 1994, WTO Members large and small not only adopted an extensive set of legal rules but also agreed to resolve their differences about each other's trade measures through a process of binding third-party dispute settlement—a commitment to international co-operation that ranks among the more improbable achievements in the history of humanity's attempts to govern itself.

Over the subsequent decades, WTO dispute settlement developed into the most productive multilateral forum of inter-state adjudication in history, building up a vast body of practice and jurisprudence. From cases with high political stakes involving human health and environmental protection to the arcana of trade remedy systems, the WTO dispute settlement system resolved or at least tempered disputes touching on a broad array of economic and regulatory concerns. As it grew in prestige and impact, WTO adjudication also became a focal point of public interest, professional ambition, and academic study.

And yet, the seeds of the system's unravelling were sown not long after it was established, as the evolving practices and jurisprudence of the WTO's

Appellate Body increasingly antagonized the United States. In the late 2010s, against the backdrop of rising superpower rivalry and driven by mounting frustration with the course the system had taken, the United States decided to end the Appellate Body and with it the system of binding dispute settlement. The United States' actions have forced a deep reckoning with the system's merits and faults but have also spurred efforts to preserve and renew the system as it marks its thirtieth anniversary.

This book takes stock of the WTO and its dispute settlement system as it hits that milestone. As the book's title signals, it is an attempt both to survey the system's achievements and shortcomings and to chart a way forward. In this introduction, I will set the scene by reviewing the key developments affecting the WTO and its dispute settlement system over the past ten years. I will then ask what there is to celebrate and introduce the person whom the contributors to this book have chosen to celebrate—the legendary Canadian trade lawyer and WTO official Valerie Hughes. I conclude with a survey of the structure and chapters of the book.

B. A Somber Anniversary, or: How the WTO Looks Different Than Ten Years Ago

IT IS SAFE TO SAY that the festivities marking the third decade of the WTO will be more subdued than the celebrations of previous milestones. The WTO's ten-year anniversary saw the publication of several books that took stock of the rapidly evolving practice and jurisprudence of the dispute settlement system (the WTO's legislative arm was limping along even then).[1] The WTO's Appellate Body took its twenty-year anniversary as an occasion to host conferences in the home countries of each of the seven Appellate Body Members.[2] Critical voices had become louder by then, especially in the

---

1   Merit E Janow, Victoria Donaldson, & Alan Yanovich, eds, *The WTO: Governance, Dispute Settlement & Developing Countries* (Huntington, NY: Juris Publishing, 2008); Rufus Yerxa & Bruce Wilson, eds, *Key Issues in WTO Dispute Settlement: The First Ten Years* (Cambridge: Cambridge University Press, 2005); Giorgio Sacerdoti, Alan Yanovich, & Jan Bohanes, eds, *The WTO at Ten: The Contribution of the Dispute Settlement System* (Cambridge: Cambridge University Press, 2006). The WTO also commissioned a book on its first ten years: Peter Gallagher, *The First Ten Years of the WTO 1995–2005* (Cambridge: Cambridge University Press, 2005).

2   Conferences were held in Florence, Italy (15 May 2015); Beijing, Shanghai, and Shenzhen, China (2–6 July 2015); Seoul, Korea (28 August 2015); Cancún, Mexico (2 to 4 December 2015); Cambridge, Massachusetts, USA (28–29 April 2016); and Delhi,

United States, but few imagined that the Appellate Body would no longer be around ten years later. That is the most striking difference at the WTO's thirty-year anniversary: the Appellate Body is no more. In its absence, appeals "into the void," which prevent panel reports from attaining legal force, have piled up; they stand at thirty-one panel reports and counting.[3] A temporary replacement agreed to by a subgroup of WTO Members has so far ruled on only two appeals, though several additional disputes are in the pipeline.

But the disappearance of the Appellate Body is not the only way in which the WTO at thirty differs fundamentally from its twenty-year-old version. At least two other developments could scarcely have been imagined by the trade experts that gathered at the conferences all over the world for that anniversary. One is the fact that WTO Members have become increasingly willing to invoke the security exceptions in the *Marrakesh Agreement Establishing the World Trade Organization* (WTO Agreement) and to challenge such invocations by other WTO Members in the WTO's dispute settlement system. This represents the breach of a major taboo in WTO practice and litigation and has exposed a deep fault line about the interpretation of the exceptions that WTO Members have so far been unable to resolve. The United States's decision to invoke the security exception to justify the imposition of "reciprocal" tariffs on virtually all its trading partners and of separate sectoral tariffs on an ever-increasing number of goods represents exactly the nightmare scenario that the long-standing taboo was meant to avoid: a situation in which a WTO Member who treats the exception as non-justiciable uses it to disregard its most fundamental WTO obligations and thereby effectively allows the exception to swallow the rules.[4] Another major development of the past ten years is the outbreak of the trade war between the United States and China, which has seen both protagonists disregard their WTO obligations towards

---

India (16–18 February 2017). See WTO, *Appellate Body Annual Report for 2015*, WTO Doc WT/AB/26 (2016), online (pdf): docs.wto.org [perma.cc/Y77S-NTN3]; WTO, *Appellate Body Annual Report for 2016*, WTO Doc WT/AB/27 (2017), online (pdf): docs. wto.org [perma.cc/N5HT-2N5A]; WTO, *Appellate Body Annual Report for 2017*, WTO Doc WT/AB/28 (2018), online (pdf): docs.wto.org [perma.cc/NS55-3CDN].

3   For an up-to-date list of unresolved appeals, see WTO, "Appellate Body" (last visited 4 February 2025), online: wto.org [perma.cc/XX7F-68AN]. Of the thirty-one unresolved appeals, seven were filed while the Appellate Body was still operational, but they could not be decided during the terms of the remaining Appellate Body Members.

4   See US Mission Geneva, "Statement by the United States at the WTO on Reciprocal Tariffs" (10 April 2025), online (pdf): geneva.usmission.gov [perma.cc/X5XT-ZPJR].

each other on a hitherto unfathomable scale. Effectively, the trade war has taken significant parts of the United States-China trade relationship outside the scope of the multilateral trade regime.[5]

Taken together, these developments have shaken the WTO and its dispute settlement system to its core. Apart from decapitating the WTO dispute settlement system and effectively depriving it of its binding character, they mark the breakdown of both formal and informal norms that had sustained the WTO system during its first two decades.

The most important formal norm that has been broken is the obligation to resolve disputes over the violation of WTO law and to impose trade retaliation exclusively through resort to the WTO's dispute settlement procedures.[6] Both in the context of invocations of the security exception and of the United States-China trade war, WTO Members have resorted to immediate trade retaliation without awaiting authorization to do so from the WTO's Dispute Settlement Body. The increased willingness of some WTO Members to disregard the commitment to use the WTO dispute settlement system as the *exclusive* remedy for violations of WTO law puts into question one of the key bargains underlying that system, namely, the acceptance by the WTO Membership of a powerful dispute settlement system in return for the end of the unilateral use of trade sanctions, especially by the United States.[7]

In addition, the rise of litigation around the security exception reflects the breakdown of informal norms that had previously restrained WTO Members both from challenging other WTO Members' invocations of the exception and from abusing the exception. It was Ukraine's decision to use WTO dispute settlement to defend itself against Russia's attempts to strangle its exports in the wake of the revolution of 2014 and Russia's subsequent

---

5   It is important to note that the United States did not justify most of the tariffs imposed on China during the first Trump administration and maintained by the Biden administration (under Section 301 of the *Trade Act of 1974*) on national security grounds; instead, the United States (unsuccessfully) invoked the public morals exception in Article XX of the GATT 1994 to justify those tariffs in the WTO. See *United States—Tariff Measures on Certain Goods from China (Complaint by China)* (2020), WTO Doc WT/DS543/R (Panel Report), online (pdf): docs.wto.org [perma.cc/LT6G-MZ9K].

6   This obligation is codified in Article 23 of the Dispute Settlement Understanding (DSU).

7   At an event at the WTO at which the author was present, the former foreign minister of Brazil, Celso Amorim, remarked that, for Brazil, Article 23 of the DSU was the single most important provision of the WTO Agreement.

invasion and occupation of Crimea and parts of the Donbas that shattered the first taboo. And it was the first Trump administration's perceived abuse of the exception to impose tariffs on steel and aluminum from most of its trading partners that did away with the second taboo, prompting fears that all restraints on the invocation of the exception would be gone. These fears took time to materialize: while there was a marked uptick in invocations of the exception, there were initially no signs of widespread abuse. In fact, the increasing willingness of other WTO Members to litigate invocations of the exception may have helped to discipline invocations of the exception. For some time, it seemed like we had reached a new equilibrium; instead of the old equilibrium in which both the invocation and challenges to the invocation of the exception were policed by informal norms, we now had an equilibrium policed by formal norms. This equilibrium was always unstable, both because some WTO Members disagreed fundamentally with the interpretation of the exception that had been developed by WTO panels and because WTO Members invoking the exception without legal justification could avoid facing the full legal consequences of doing so (since they could appeal panel reports into the void of a defunct Appellate Body). And whatever equilibrium there was, it was no match for the United States under the second Trump administration, which has shown no restraint whatsoever in invoking the exception.

This brings us to the last informal norm—or perhaps it was only an expectation—that has been shattered in the crisis of WTO dispute settlement, namely, the informal norm that WTO Members would work to reach consensus on matters vital to the functioning of the WTO dispute settlement system. Given the experience of the *General Agreement on Tariffs and Trade* (GATT), in which the contracting parties could simply block the establishment of panels and the adoption of panel reports, the WTO dispute settlement system was built to allow almost all steps in the dispute settlement process to occur automatically, with one exception: the appointment of Appellate Body Members. Presumably, negotiators regarded it as vital that WTO Members maintained some level of political control over the adjudicators that would have the final say in the resolution of their disputes.[8] They must nonetheless have presupposed that no WTO Member would exploit this control to fundamentally change the nature of the system by effectively abolishing the

---

8   See Richard H Steinberg, "Judicial Lawmaking at the WTO: Discursive, Constitutional, and Political Constraints" (2004) 98:2 *American Journal of International Law* 247.

Appellate Body. The fact that the United States has exposed this Achilles heel of the dispute settlement system means that WTO Members are unlikely to again rely on each other's goodwill in designing a reformed system—they must now account for the possibility that other WTO Members will exploit any vulnerability in the system in the same way the United States has done.

Ironically, the demise of the Appellate Body has so far masked the full explosive potential of the rise of the security exception and of the United States-China trade war, since the parties to those disputes could appeal them into the void and thereby avoid facing the full legal consequences for their actions. The flipside is that the restoration of a binding dispute settlement system is hard to imagine without these underlying issues being resolved. The challenge for the WTO at thirty thus cannot simply be to restore the dispute settlement system to its supposed former glory; rather, WTO Members must design a system that reflects the ways in which the political, economic, and legal ground has shifted under their feet over the past ten years.

C. And Yet: Reasons to Celebrate

AMID THE GLOOMY HEADLINES AND the attempts to grapple with a series of overlapping crises, it is easy to lose sight of the crucial role that the WTO continues to fulfill and of the important work that is being done at the WTO every day. None other than the United States Trade Representative under the first Trump administration, Robert Lighthizer, who has been a fierce critic of the WTO, has said that, if the WTO did not exist, it would have to be invented.[9] It stands to reason that other WTO Members agree, though potentially for very different reasons than the United States. No WTO Member has ever withdrawn from the organization, and new Members continue to negotiate for accession. A large majority of international trade, including some of the largest trading relationships in the world (for most countries in the world, the European Union and China are the largest trading partners), are conducted on WTO terms. Even in its present, somewhat diminished state, WTO Members derive myriad benefits from the organization.

A first reason to celebrate is thus the persistence, relatively intact, of the WTO *acquis* and the important work that continues to be done by WTO

---

9   US, *Approaching 25: The Road Ahead for the World Trade Organization: Hearing Before the Committee on Finance*, 115th Cong (Washington, DC: United States Government Printing Office, 2019) at 51 (Hon Robert E Lighthizer).

Members in the organization and by the WTO's highly competent staff. This work includes running the committees overseeing the implementation of the various parts of the WTO Agreement, supporting new negotiations and discussions (more on that below), and assisting the first stage of the dispute settlement process—the panel process, which remains operational. Much of this work takes place under the radar of the public. An important part of the reckoning that this book undertakes is therefore to bring to the fore these ongoing achievements of the organization.

A second reason to celebrate is the renewed energy in the WTO's rule-making activities. Whereas the picture today is almost uniformly bleaker on the dispute settlement side than it was ten years ago, the picture is more positive on the negotiations front. WTO negotiations had reached a new low in 2015; while the Nairobi Ministerial Conference in December of that year concluded with some notable results—most significantly, the abolition of agricultural export subsidies—the year also marked the unofficial end of the Doha Round of trade negotiations, as the United States announced that it was abandoning the moribund round. It was entirely unclear how the WTO would move forward from that point.

Ten years later, two themes have emerged that allow us to imagine the future of the WTO's legislative function: plurilateralism and work on sustainability issues. Starting in 2017, subgroups of WTO Members embarked on several "joint statement initiatives" which have since crystallized into concluded agreements in three areas—domestic regulation in services, investment facilitation, and e-commerce. While some WTO Members are resisting the move towards plurilateralism,[10] the initiatives represent an infusion of energy and optimism into the WTO's legislative function. A second theme is a shift in activity towards sustainability topics, reflected most notably in the conclusion of an *Agreement on Fisheries Subsidies* in 2022. The increasing recognition of the WTO's role in combating climate change, including by potentially serving as a forum for developing disciplines on fossil fuel subsidies, is another important development of the past ten years.[11]

But even in the dispute settlement area, where the WTO has experienced its greatest setback compared to ten years ago, there are reasons to celebrate. Pride of place must go to the speedy establishment of the Multi-Party

---

10   See Andrew Stoler's contribution to this volume (Chapter 32).
11   See Jennifer Hillman's and Ronald Steenblik's contributions to this volume (Chapters 29 and 30).

Interim Appeal Arbitration Arrangement (MPIA), which takes the place of the Appellate Body for those WTO Members who have accepted it—a group that includes mid-size powers, such as Canada, Brazil, and Australia, but also heavyweights, such as the European Union and Japan and, most strikingly, China. China, as the world's largest trader, could easily have taken advantage of the dysfunction sown by the United States' move to block appointments to the Appellate Body to insulate itself from effective challenges in the WTO dispute settlement process, as other major traders with problematic trade records, such as India and Russia, have done. Instead, in what can be understood as a remarkable vote of confidence in the rules-based trading system, China chose to join the replacement mechanism spearheaded by Canada and the European Union. While the MPIA has only decided two cases so far, its existence enlarges the options that its members have in dealing with China and has most likely contributed to the continued use of WTO dispute settlement *vis-à-vis* China by WTO Members such as Canada, Australia, and the European Union.

The other remarkable, though so far incomplete, reform effort has been the negotiating process led, until February 2024, by the Guatemalan diplomat Marco Tulio Molina Tejeda.[12] Within a very short time, the process has led to a comprehensive outcome document that only leaves the most controversial issues—the possible restoration of appellate review and the institutional implementation of the reforms—unresolved. The process relied on an innovative "interest-based" approach to negotiations that shows great promise, especially when contrasted with the sclerotic and inconclusive Dispute Settlement Understanding (DSU) review negotiations that had been held, on and off, since 2001.

A final innovative development in the dispute settlement field has been the strong growth of dispute settlement activity under preferential trade agreements (PTAs). Only ten years ago, it was common to dismiss the dispute settlement chapters of PTAs as a dead letter, since their parties seemed to prefer to resolve their disputes under the WTO dispute settlement system.[13]

---

12 See Marco Tulio Molina Tejeda's contribution to this volume (Chapter 28).

13 For example, a 2013 study of dispute settlement mechanisms in PTAs noted that "RTA partners continue to have recourse to the WTO dispute settlement mechanism to resolve disputes between them." The report also highlighted the shorter deadlines for dispute settlement proceedings in PTAs but noted dryly that "it is difficult to determine whether these shorter deadlines are not aspirational until such deadlines are tested in actual cases." Claude Chase et al, "Mapping of Dispute

The latter's partial paralysis has awoken the PTA dispute settlement chapters from their slumber;[14] as countries gain experience and become practiced in PTA dispute settlement, they will likely remain active even if the WTO dispute settlement system is eventually restored. This will enlarge the options that WTO Members have available to resolve their disputes, allowing them to choose the avenue that best suits their interests.

D. An Avoidable Tragedy or a Necessary Adjustment? Different Perspectives on the WTO Dispute Settlement Crisis and the Reform Efforts

HOW ONE EVALUATES THESE DEVELOPMENTS, and whether one regards them as a reason for celebration, or at least cautious optimism, depends in large part on one's theory of the causes of the crisis of WTO dispute settlement and on one's vision of the role that international trade law can realistically play in settling inter-state trade disputes in an era of renewed geopolitical competition.

1) The US View: The Appellate Body Did Not Work Out As Intended, and the WTO has Proved Unable to Deal with China, So We're Out (of Binding Dispute Settlement)

For the United States, the *status quo* would seem to come closest to an ideal world—which is unsurprising, since it had a decisive role in bringing it about. The United States can still resort to binding dispute settlement in a regional context, whether to go after Canadian restrictions on dairy imports or the violation of labour rights in Mexican factories. At the same time, the United States' trading relationship with China and most other WTO Members is no longer subject to enforceable legal restraints. Given that there is virtually no prospect that the United States will be willing to abide by its WTO obligations *vis-à-vis* China (and, at least while the Trump administration is

---

Settlement Mechanisms in Regional Trade Agreements – Innovative or Variations on a Theme?" (2013) WTO Economic Research and Statistics Division, Working Paper No ERSD-2013-07.

14   Another important factor was the reform of the *North American Free Trade Agreement's* (NAFTA) defunct panel process in the *United States-Mexico-Canada Agreement* (USMCA); see Anthony VanDuzer's contribution to this volume (Chapter 21).

in power, any other WTO Member) in the foreseeable future, not having binding dispute settlement presumably suits it well. Moreover, by abolishing the Appellate Body, the United States has also rid itself of what it saw as an unaccountable adjudicator set on developing a jurisprudence with little relationship to what US negotiators had agreed to in 1994.

2) The Historical View: The DSU Was a Product of its Time; Maybe the MPIA is a Product of Ours?

Given the ever-deepening rift between the United States and China, the fact that both countries were once part of a quasi-universal, compulsory, exclusive, and binding dispute settlement system appears more of an accident of history with each passing day. From this perspective, the DSU was a product of the very particular historical constellation of the post-Cold War moment, and the current crisis of WTO dispute settlement and the establishment of the MPIA represents a painful but necessary adjustment to a new and messier political reality. A dispute settlement system that gives the parties the opportunity to veto the adoption of unwelcome panel reports and that makes appeals optional may not have the uniformity and elegance of the old system, but maybe it is a better reflection of the times that we live in.

3) The Institutional View: An Opportunity for Institutional Course Correction

Even if one does not regard the current developments as historically inevitable, one can welcome the current moment of crisis as an opportunity for institutional course correction. Even most defenders of the WTO dispute settlement system agree that it did not work entirely as intended and that several pathologies had developed over the decades. One of the most commonly observed structural faults of the WTO was the extent to which the division of labour between the adjudicatory bodies and the WTO Membership had departed from the WTO's "blueprint."[15] According to this blueprint, WTO Members were supposed to be in charge of norm development by exercising their "exclusive authority" to adopt so-called "authoritative interpretations." The current DSU reform process attempts to address this imbalance

---

15   Tomer Broude, *International Governance in the World Trade Organization: Judicial Boundaries and Political Capitulation* (London: Cameron and May, 2004) 147.

head-on by enhancing the opportunities for legislative-judicial feedback and dialogue.[16]

Another pathology is arguably the extent to which the WTO Appellate Body had been treating its own previous rulings as precedents and proved reluctant to reconsider those precedents. The MPIA provides the opportunity of starting with a clean slate, and the DSU reform process also offers additional guidance. The end of the Appellate Body has delivered a shock to the system that will probably mean that any future appellate organ will be extremely cautious in the way it treats its own jurisprudence.

On this view, even the fact that the MPIA has so far been rarely used may be a feature, rather than a bug, of the new *status quo*. It is a well-known piece of WTO lore (not quite accurate, as it turns out[17]) that the Uruguay Round negotiators expected that appeals would be rare, since most cases would be settled or resolved at the panel stage. While this did not prove to be the case while the Appellate Body was in operation, it seems to be the reality among MPIA parties so far.[18]

Finally, one can also regard the non-use of PTA dispute settlement as an unfortunate, or at the very least inefficient, development that is now being corrected.

4) The (Un)avoidable Tragedy View: Bring Back the Appellate Body at any Cost

The most pessimistic view is that the end of the Appellate Body is simply the result of a lack of institutional safeguards against the abuse of power in international economic governance, and that all would be well if only the United States could have been prevented from vetoing the appointment process for new Appellate Body Members.[19] From this perspective, any attempts to design substitutes, such as the MPIA, or use alternatives, such as PTA dispute settlement, are highly imperfect compromises at best and counter-

---

16 See Nicolas Lamp, "Arrested Norm Development: The Failure of Legislative-Judicial Dialogue in the WTO" (2025) *Leiden Journal of International Law* (forthcoming).

17 See Simon Lester's contribution to this volume (Chapter 8).

18 I am indebted to Elaine Feldman for this observation.

19 See Peter Van den Bossche, "The Demise of the WTO Appellate Body: Lessons for Governance of International Adjudication?" (2021) World Trade Institute, Working Paper No 02/2021 at 12, who identifies the ability of a single WTO Member to block appointments of Appellate Body Members as the principal "aspect of malgovernance" in the WTO.

productive at worst, since they could relieve pressure to restore the system to its former glory.[20] For many in this camp, only the restoration of binding, two-tier dispute settlement would be a reason to celebrate.

Depending on which perspective one adopts—and there is arguably some merit to all of them—the current moment of reckoning and renewal will fall on a spectrum between celebration and mourning. For most, it probably feels deeply ambivalent, a mixture of hope for the future and nostalgia for the past. At the same time, the contributors to this book feel no such ambivalence about the Canadian lawyer Valerie Hughes, whose remarkable career they have chosen as a starting point and inspiration for their analyses of the evolution of the WTO and its dispute settlement system in this book.

E. And Someone to Celebrate: A Book in Honour of Valerie Hughes

IT IS HARD TO THINK of anyone who better embodies everything there is to celebrate about the WTO and its dispute settlement system than the Canadian trade lawyer Valerie Hughes.

As an early Director of the Government of Canada's Trade Law Bureau (1996-99), Hughes shaped the development of litigation capacity in one of the system's most active members. She brought her experience representing Canada in disputes before the International Court of Justice to her new role and thereby cemented the role of international legal expertise, and in particular the use of the *Vienna Convention on the Law of Treaties*, in Canada's approach to WTO litigation.

Hughes then became the first and only individual to serve as the Director both of the Appellate Body Secretariat (2001-05) and of the Legal Affairs Division (2010-16)—the sections of the WTO Secretariat that provide legal support to the Appellate Body and panels, respectively. While she was universally admired by both the adjudicators she supported and her staff in both roles, she left each role after five or six years—the maximum amount of time that she believed one should serve in a director role.[21] Among her

---

20 Some WTO Members have used this argument to explain their reluctance to join the MPIA.

21 Some have argued that the system would have been better able to adapt—and survive—if subsequent directors had followed her example, and the introduction of term limits for directors and even secretariat staff has been proposed as part of the dispute settlement reform discussions. See Jennifer Hillman, "A Reset of the

outstanding accomplishments as a Director of the Legal Affairs Division is the introduction of a digital registry for dispute settlement cases, which greatly facilitated the administration of disputes and can serve as a model for other dispute settlement systems. Another hallmark of her tenures are the numerous lawyers whom she trained and supervised, many of whom are contributors to this book.

Hughes has also supported the system as an adjudicator herself, serving as a frequent panelist, including on a highly sensitive dispute involving the security exception.[22] But Hughes also embodies the period of renewal: she recently concluded her term as an arbitrator on the Appellate Body's replacement mechanism, the MPIA. She is the first Canadian to ever have served at the appeal level in the WTO and played a key role in shaping the practices of the fledging MPIA. At the same time, she continues to serve as a panelist under NAFTA's successor agreement, the USMCA/CUSMA.[23]

During her time as Director of the Legal Affairs Division, Hughes also played an important part in supporting the revival of the WTO's lawmaking function by providing advice on the legal aspects of WTO negotiations; the first new multilateral trade agreement negotiated under WTO auspices, the *Agreement on Trade Facilitation*, was concluded during her tenure.

As a frequent speaker, instructor, and academic commentator, Hughes has also shared her experience as a pioneering female lawyer in a male-dominated field and has championed the investigation of the interconnections between trade and gender.

While the celebration of the WTO's thirty-year anniversary may be subdued, Valerie Hughes's career provides unambiguous reasons for celebration. The book draws on the deep bench of Hughes' friends, colleagues, mentees, and students, all of whom have agreed to write in her honour, to trace the trajectory of the WTO and its dispute settlement system to its current moment of reckoning and renewal.

World Trade Organization's Appellate Body" (January 2020), online: cfr.org [perma. cc/7F7G-GUAA].

22   See *United Arab Emirates—Measures Relating to Trade in Goods and Services, and Trade-Related Aspects of Intellectual Property Rights (Complaint by Qatar)* (2018), WTO Doc WT/DS526/3 (Dispute Settlement Body), online (pdf): docs.wto.org [perma. cc/38B9-JT3A]. The dispute was settled after the panel finalized its report, which will thus unfortunately never see the light of day.

23   This latter engagement prevented some of her friends and former colleagues, who are involved in the disputes on which she serves as a panelist, from contributing to this book.

F. Structure and Overview of the Book

THE BOOK IS DIVIDED INTO three parts. The first part provides a reckoning with the WTO dispute settlement system as it has developed over the past thirty years—from its origins in the Uruguay Round to the current crisis. The second part looks at new developments in dispute settlement from a variety of angles: it delves into the reform discussions for WTO dispute settlement, discusses the work of the Appellate Body's replacement mechanisms, the MPIA, and tracks the revival of dispute settlement under PTAs. The final part turns to the rulemaking dimension and explores both the prospects and formats for WTO negotiations generally and the contribution that the WTO can make in specific areas, especially in fighting the climate crisis. The book concludes with reflections on Valerie Hughes as a model for trade lawyers.

In the first part, some contributions take a historical approach: Mark Jewett, Jonathan Fried, and Rambod Behboodi (Chapters 2 and 3) provide first-hand accounts of how Canada built domestic capacity for WTO dispute settlement.[24] Specifically, they discuss the origins of the Canadian government's Trade Law Bureau, which was a joint venture of two departments of the Canadian government: the Department of Foreign Affairs and the Department of Justice. They reflect on how the different cultures of the two departments shaped the Trade Law Bureau and recall the early years of the operation of the Trade Law Bureau, including the first cases that Canada litigated in the NAFTA and the WTO. Behboodi shows how Valerie Hughes' experience litigating cases in the International Court of Justice shaped her approach to WTO litigation when she was Director of the Trade Law Bureau during its early years.

Other contributions review the practice of the WTO's Legal Affairs Division, focusing on aspects that are normally hidden from public view. María Pereyra (Chapter 4) sheds light on the secretive process for the appointment of WTO adjudicators, with a focus on the panel level. In Chapter 5, Daniel Ari Baker, Jenya Grigorova, and Rodd Izadnia provide a unique insight into the selection process for WTO interns in the Legal Affairs Division, explain

---

24 These chapters add to the literature on the build-up of dispute settlement capacity in other major trading countries; see Gregory C Shaffer, *Defending Interests: Public-Private Partnerships in WTO Litigation* (Washington, DC: Brookings Institution Press, 2003) and Gregory Shaffer, *Emerging Powers and the World Trading System: The Past and Future of International Economic Law* (Cambridge: Cambridge University Press, 2021).

the tasks of interns, and provide statistics on the backgrounds and careers of past interns of the division.

One of the key achievements of Valerie Hughes's tenure was overseeing the establishment of a digital registry for the WTO dispute settlement system, which has greatly facilitated the logistics of dispute settlement both for the parties and the WTO Secretariat. In Chapter 6, Marisa Goldstein and Lizzie Medrano, who played key roles in establishing the digital registry, describe the experience of transitioning from paper filing to the digital registry. Gabrielle Marceau and Maria George (Chapter 7) discuss the increasingly contentious role of the WTO Secretariat in dispute settlement and put that role into the context of the practice of other adjudicatory bodies.

Another group of contributors reflect on the fate of the Appellate Body. Simon Lester (Chapter 8) examines the internal discussions among US negotiators regarding the Appellate Body during the Uruguay Round and highlights the ways in which these discussions foreshadowed issues that would later become serious challenges for the dispute settlement system. In Chapter 9, A.V. Ganesan, who was an Appellate Body Member during Valerie Hughes' tenure as Director of the Appellate Body Secretariat, looks back on the important contributions that Hughes made to the operation and practices of the Appellate Body.

The next set of contributions examine the role of developing countries in the dispute settlement system. The lack of "equality of arms" in dispute settlement proceedings under the WTO has been a perennial concern of developing countries. Mateo Diego-Fernández Andrade, who currently serves as the Mexican arbitrator on the MPIA, discusses what it takes in practice for developing countries to successfully participate in WTO dispute settlement (Chapter 10). He critically interrogates the role of the principle of "special and differential treatment" and surveys the strategies of developing countries that have become active participants in trade dispute settlement both in the WTO and under PTAs. In Chapter 11, Henry Gao and Wenhua Ji focus on a country that had to climb the steepest learning curve in WTO dispute settlement after its accession to the WTO and did so with great success: China. They analyze the ingredients of that success, including the institutional and personnel arrangements in the Chinese government, the strategic use of external legal services, the government's support for academic and civil society institutions, and the government's collaboration with private industry.

The next set of contributions dig more deeply into specific topics in WTO dispute settlement. The first two focus on the energy transition and trade and the environment—two topics that are assuming an ever more central spot on the trade agenda, as countries scramble to mitigate the climate crisis. Trade in energy has not traditionally been a prominent conceptual category in discussions of WTO law, but Iain Sandford reframes our understanding of a cross-section of WTO cases as disputes over "trade in energy" and uses them to project into the future (Chapter 12). And Mateo Ferrero takes stock of how the multilateral trade regime interacts with environmental protection policies by examining the key principles that the WTO's dispute settlement organs have developed in landmark trade disputes (Chapter 13). James Flett, who is among the most experienced litigators in the history of WTO dispute settlement, wades into more technical terrain in his discussion of the general standard of review that the WTO dispute settlement panels apply, or should apply, in examining a dispute that is brought before them (Chapter 14). And Geraldo Vidigal takes the reader back into history to examine the WTO Secretariat's role in fashioning the WTO's system of remedies (Chapter 15).

After these contributions that drill deeply on some key issues in WTO dispute settlement, the next set of chapters takes a step back to provide a wider view. Formal dispute settlement is not the only avenue through which the WTO helps its Members to solve their trade disputes—the WTO's councils and committees have long been recognized as playing an important role in preventing disputes from escalating. Roy Santana and Adeet Dobhal provide a pathbreaking statistical analysis of the development of "trade concerns" that are brought to WTO committees and their interaction with dispute settlement activity (Chapter 16). Penelope Ridings, who served as an arbitrator on the MPIA pool of arbitrators, marshals a wealth of data to paint a first comprehensive picture of the role of women in WTO dispute settlement (Chapter 17). The concluding three chapters in the first part provide different angles on the WTO dispute settlement crisis. Sivan Shlomo-Agon examines the delicate interplay between legitimacy and effectiveness in the practice of WTO dispute settlement (Chapter 18). Donald McRae asks what type of dispute settlement mechanism the WTO system was meant to provide—and critically examines the way the Appellate Body understood its function (Chapter 19). Christopher Cochlin, Mallory Felix, and Alexander Hobbs zero in on the key principle that lent WTO dispute settlement its binding character—the adoption of panel and Appellate Body reports by negative consensus (Chapter 20). They ask whether the gain in legal certainty was worth the political cost.

The second part of the book traces the major trends of renewal in trade dispute settlement. December 2019 marked a major turning point for trade dispute settlement in two ways: 11 December 2019 was the day on which the WTO Appellate Body lost its quorum, as the terms of two of the remaining three Appellate Body Members expired. However, just a day earlier, on 10 December, the United States, Canada, and Mexico signed the USMCA, which restored a functioning dispute settlement in the North American context for the first time since the United States had figured out how to sabotage the NAFTA dispute settlement system in the early 2000s. Ever since, USMCA dispute settlement has been fairly active, and it has become the leading example of a turn to dispute settlement under PTAs, especially for the United States, which has not brought a single WTO dispute since July 2019,[25] even as it has launched five disputes under the state-to-state dispute settlement provisions of the USMCA.[26]

The first set of contributions in Part II trace these developments. Anthony VanDuzer provides a detailed record of dispute settlement under the USMCA—or *Canada-United States-Mexico Agreement* (CUSMA), as it is known in Canada—so far (Chapter 21). Kathleen Claussen considers the role that the public has been able to play in disputes under PTAs, focusing on the North American experience (Chapter 22). Michael Solursh traces the impact of the body of WTO jurisprudence in dispute settlement under PTAs (Chapter 23). And Scott Falls asks what role the WTO Secretariat could play in FTA dispute settlement (Chapter 24).

A second set of contributions in Part II looks at the reform efforts in the WTO, including the turn to arbitration and the ongoing dispute settlement reform discussions. Niall Meagher provides a historical perspective on arbitration in Geneva and draws out parallels between the earliest disputes 150 years ago and the issues that have been vexing dispute settlement lawyers in the WTO (Chapter 25). Müslüm Yilmaz examines the role that arbitration plays in WTO dispute settlement and poses the question of whether it is

---

25 The last-ever dispute brought by the United States concerned retaliatory duties that India had imposed on US imports in response to the additional tariffs on steel and aluminum imposed by the Trump administration on security grounds. The dispute was settled in July 2023; see *India—Additional Duties on Certain Products from the United States (Complaint by the United States)* (2023), WTO Doc WT/DS585/R (Panel Report), online (pdf): docs.wto.org [perma.cc/XFD8-HZ2Q].

26 See Office of the United States Trade Representative, "Chapter 31 Disputes" (last visited 4 February 2025), online: ustr.gov [perma.cc/7CVD-M624].

a temporary instrument that Members use to make up for the absence of the Appellate Body or whether the dispute settlement crisis will result in a more permanent course-correction towards a more arbitration-like rather than court-like system (Chapter 26). Jan Bohanes discusses the most tangible effort to restore a functioning dispute settlement system in the absence of an Appellate Body—the MPIA. Bohanes, who represented one of the parties to the first-ever case to be litigated by the MPIA, focuses on some of the systemic features of the MPIA procedures as they played out in that case (Chapter 27). Finally, Marco Tulio Molina Tejeda describes his experience leading the most promising attempt at a wholesale reform of the WTO dispute settlement system: the informal "interest-based" reform discussions that culminated in a document setting out an almost complete range of reforms in February 2024 and that are now being continued under the auspices of the WTO General Council (Chapter 28).

The final part of the book considers the rulemaking dimension in the WTO. In recent years, WTO Members have turned much of their attention to sustainability issues. While the negotiations on fisheries subsidies have absorbed much of the oxygen, the contributors to this part turn their attention to the WTO's role in the climate crisis more broadly. Jennifer Hillman, a former Member of the WTO Appellate Body, asks which concrete contributions the WTO could make to addressing the climate crisis (Chapter 29), and Ronald Steenblik, who was one of the staff members who pioneered research on environmentally destructive subsidies in his work at the Organisation for Economic Co-operation and Development (OECD) and served as the OECD's Special Counselor for Fossil Fuel Subsidy Reform, looks at the prospects for disciplines on fossil fuel subsidies in the WTO (Chapter 30). Margaret Kim turns our attention to another one of the "new" issues: trade and gender (Chapter 31). As a complement to Penelope Riding's chapter on the role of women in dispute settlement, Kim looks at how gender can be mainstreamed into agreements negotiated in the WTO. The next two chapters take a more systemic look at WTO negotiations: Andrew Stoler, a former US trade negotiator and WTO Deputy Director-General, provides historical background to the return to plurilateral formats in WTO negotiations in the form of the Joint Statement Initiatives (Chapter 32), and Ujal Bhatia, a former Indian ambassador to the WTO and Member of the WTO Appellate Body, examines the interrelationship between negotiations and dispute settlement in the WTO (Chapter 33). In the final chapter, Nadia Theodore, the current Canadian ambassador to the WTO, returns the attention to the book's honouree and concludes with reflections on the role of Valerie Hughes as a model and a leader in the multilateral trading system (Chapter 34).

Part I:

Reckoning—The Origins, Functioning and Crisis of WTO Dispute Settlement

Building Domestic Capacity for WTO Dispute Settlement—The Canadian Experience

CHAPTER 2

From Public International Law to International Economic Law: Valerie Hughes and the Development of International Trade Law Expertise in Canada

Mark Jewett and Jonathan Fried

THIS CHAPTER OFFERS BOTH A personal recounting of Valerie Hughes' ascendancy as an internationally recognized leader in trade law and litigation and, paralleling her career, a brief review of the development of international economic law and expertise in the Canadian public sector.

A. From the Department of Justice to the Trade Law Bureau: Valerie Hughes' Ascendancy as an International Lawyer[1]

IN CANADA, MANY PEOPLE WITH different backgrounds have come to trade and economic law over the course of several years, working productively together, gaining experience and expertise while bringing their own particular skills to the table. In this context, permit me to focus on Valerie. I feel well qualified to do so, having known and worked with her for many years. While her personal story is, of course, *sui generis*, it also provides important context for what many have identified as the legalization and judicialization of the international trade regime.

Valerie gained invaluable experience in the 1984 Gulf of Maine maritime boundary case between Canada and the United States before a Chamber of the International Court of Justice (ICJ).[2] There she worked under the tutelage of Léonard Legault, former Legal Adviser and a great international lawyer at what is now Global Affairs Canada and a mentor to Valerie.

During the preparation of that case, she would often hold the pen as the pleadings were developed, and it was obvious that others placed confidence in her to accurately reflect the many inputs, from a multitude of professions, that were required in such an undertaking. This international experience before the ICJ prepared her well for what was to follow.

Following the conclusion of the case, I was able to bring Valerie into the Department of Justice, in the Constitutional and International Law Section, where she undertook a wide variety of assignments, encompassing public and private international law as well as constitutional issues, which in the Canadian context are so often present at the international level.

Within Canada, bearing in mind the assigned roles of the two Departments (Global Affairs and Justice) there have been disagreements from time to time on the conduct of litigation. A good example of Valerie's negotiating skills can be seen, working together with Donald McRae,[3] in mediating these

---

1   This section was written by Mark Jewett.
2   *Delimitation of the Maritime Boundary in the Gulf of Maine Area (Canada v United States)*, [1984] ICJ Rep 246.
3   See Donald McRae's contribution to this volume (Chapter 19).

differences during the La Bretagne Arbitration between France and Canada over fishing rights in the Gulf of St. Lawrence.[4]

Valerie went from the Constitutional and International Law Section to become General Counsel in the Trade Law Division at Global Affairs Canada (then called the Department of External Affairs and International Trade) from 1996 to 1999, a busy and critical period in international dispute settlement for Canada given the establishment of the World Trade Organization (WTO) dispute settlement mechanism in 1995 and the introduction of investor-state dispute settlement under the *North American Free Trade Agreement* (NAFTA), which came into force in 1994.

Among the WTO cases she litigated during that time were *Australia— Salmon*,[5] where Canada challenged an import restriction imposed by Australia on Canadian salmon, and *Canada—Autos*,[6] where Japan and the European Commission challenged the WTO consistency of the 1965 *Canada-United States Auto Pact*. As well, under NAFTA she had a leading role in the Ethyl case (also known as the MMT case),[7] the first investor-state dispute under the NAFTA (involving a challenge by a US company to Canada's legislation banning the importation of a fuel additive) and was lead counsel for Canada in another of the perennial Softwood Lumber cases (this one addressing the legality of British Columbia's stumpage reduction measures under the 1996 *Canada-United States Softwood Lumber Agreement*).[8]

---

4 *Filleting within the Gulf of St. Lawrence (Canada v France)* (1986), XIX RIAA 590 (Arbitrators: Paul de Visscher, Donat Pharand, Jean-Pierre Queneudec).

5 *Australia—Measures Affecting Importation of Salmon (Complaint by Canada)* (1998), WTO Doc WT/DS18/R (Panel Report), online (pdf): docs.wto.org [perma.cc/Y7GW-ZD6K] [*Australia—Salmon*].

6 *Canada—Certain Measures Affecting the Automobile Industry (Complaint by Japan and European Communities)* (2000), WTO Docs WT/DS139/R, WT/DS142/R (Panel Report), online (pdf): docs.wto.org [perma.cc/QFS7-HY43] [*Canada—Autos*]. While there are too many to mention individually, Valerie was involved in over seventy WTO disputes in one way or another, either as Counsel or assisting the Appellate Body and Panels or as a panelist (two cases as a panelist: *United Arab Emirates—Measures Relating to Trade in Goods and Services, and Trade-Related Aspects of Intellectual Property Rights (Complaint by Qatar)* and *European Communities and its Member States— Tariff Treatment of Certain Information Technology Products (Complaint by the United States)*).

7 *Ethyl Corporation v Government of Canada* (1998), 38 ILM 708 (Arbitrators: Dr Karl-Heinz Böckstiegel, Charles N Brower, Marc Lalonde).

8 *In the Matter of BC's 1998 Stumpage Reduction* (1999). See British Columbia Ministry of Forests, "Settlement Reached in Stumpage Arbitration" (24 August 1999), online: archive.news.gov.bc.ca [perma.cc/Z862-EUAA].

I had moved on to the Department of Finance and again was able to persuade her to become the Director and General Counsel in the General Legal Services Division there, which included significant trade law responsibilities.

This in-depth immersion in domestic law, and its relation to international law, prepared her well to become chief legal counsel to the Appellate Body at the WTO and Director of the Appellate Body Secretariat (ABS) in 2001.[9] She was involved in over thirty appeals addressing all manner of trade issues, from subsidies to anti-dumping to labelling to intellectual property, and more. Fortunately for her, Valerie's tenure in the ABS predated the challenges that led eventually to the shuttering of the Appellate Body in 2019.

When Valerie returned to Canada in 2006, following my move from Finance and Justice to the Bank of Canada, I was again able to persuade her to apply for and become the Assistant Deputy Minister and Counsel to the Department of Finance, which she did from 2007 to 2010. After I left the Bank of Canada for private practice, it was my turn to be hired by Valerie, when the Department of Finance retained me to advise the government on the Supreme Court Reference on securities regulation.[10]

However, fortunately for those who have been privileged to work with her in the international sphere, the WTO came calling again, and she became the Director of the Legal Affairs Division at the WTO in September 2010. There, Valerie and her team of lawyers served as Secretariat to the WTO's Dispute Settlement Body, and to more than thirty WTO panels in deciding a variety of WTO disputes, including Canada's legal challenges of Europe's unjustified measures on the sale of seal products[11] and US discriminatory measures on country-of-origin labelling of meat products,[12] as well as a challenge by Mexico of the US dolphin-safe tuna marketing regime and several WTO Members' challenges of Australia's tobacco plain packaging legislation.[13] Valerie was also instrumental in instituting the first digital registry for WTO

---

9   See Simon Lester's contribution to this volume (Chapter 8).
10   2018 SCC 48.
11   *European Communities—Measures Prohibiting the Importation and Marketing of Seal Products (Complaint by Norway)* (2014), WTO Docs WT/DS400/AB/R, WT/DS401/AB/R (Appellate Body Report), online (pdf): docs.wto.org [perma.cc/H4R6-6Q36].
12   *United States—Certain Country of Origin Labelling (COOL) Labelling Requirements (Complaint by Canada and Mexico)* (2012), WTO Docs WT/DS384/AB/R, WT/DS386/AB/R (Appellate Body Report), online (pdf): docs.wto.org [perma.cc/SNA7-AA79].
13   *Australia—Certain Measures Concerning Trademarks, Geographical Indications and Other Plain Packaging Requirements Applicable to Tobacco Products and Packaging (Complaint by Indonesia)* (2018), WTO Docs WT/DS435/R, WT/DS441/R,

disputes as well as in advising the WTO Director-General on a variety of legal issues, including exploring legal avenues for securing the successful addition of the first new multilateral agreement (Trade Facilitation[14]) into the umbrella WTO Agreement. She returned to Canada in 2016 and soon joined me at Bennett Jones LLP, where we both practised until recently.

She is now working independently and has been selected by several countries for their dispute settlement rosters. She is currently serving on three dispute settlement panels under the *Canada-United States-Mexico Agreement* (CUSMA).[15]

Finally, I would mention that, among other recognitions, Valerie received the John E. Read Medal presented by the Canadian Council on International Law "for distinguished contribution to international law and organizations" in November 2016.[16]

I recount all this, not only to underline Valerie's many contributions to international trade and economic law, but as an illustration of the ways in which Canadian lawyers have prepared themselves for the litigation function in the WTO.

There are many, many individual stories of Canadian lawyers involved in international trade law, each worth recounting. In the following section, we mention but a few, but note that they have come from a variety of legal backgrounds, from within Global Affairs Canada, and from the Department of Justice, which has specialized legal services in the various departments of government—Finance, Agriculture and Agri-Food, Fisheries, Transport, and others—bringing their particular expertise to bear on Canada's negotiations and obligations in the world of international trade in concert with the

---

WT/DS458/R, WT/DS467/R (Panel Report), online (pdf): docs.wto.org [perma. cc/6MLZ-LS2S].

14 WTO, *Protocol Amending the Marrakesh Agreement Establishing the World Trade Organization*, WTO Dec WT/L/940 (2014) at 3, online (pdf): docs.wto.org [perma.cc/ X2V5-LUC9].

15 "Certain Softwood Lumber Products from Canada: Final Results of the Countervailing Duty Administrative Review" (2017–18) USMCA Secretariat File No USA-CDA-2020-10.12-01; "Certain Softwood Lumber Products from Canada: Final Results of the Countervailing Duty Administrative Review" (2019) USMCA Secretariat File No USA-CDA-2021-10.12-03; "Certain Softwood Lumber Products from Canada: Final Results of the Antidumping Duty Administrative Review" (2019) USMCA Secretariat File No USA-CDA-2021-10.12-04.

16 Canadian Council on International Law, "Valerie Hughes Awarded John E. Read Medal" (6 July 2016), online: ccil-ccdi.ca [perma.cc/EK49-8DUL].

lawyers in the Trade Law Bureau at Global Affairs, itself a joint venture of Justice and Global Affairs.

B. The Development of International Economic Law Expertise in Canada[17]

AS STATED AT THE OUTSET, Valerie's growing expertise and prominence in WTO and related trade law parallelled the increasing centrality of economic law as an integral part of public international law more generally.

While space does not permit an exhaustive analysis, it is fair to say that consideration of the economic dimensions of international legal issues was evident long before the advent of modern free trade agreements in the mid-1980s and of the *Marrakesh Agreement Establishing the World Trade Organization* (WTO Agreement) in 1994. More broadly, in the post-colonial era, increasing focus on development, economic and social rights along with civil rights, and more recently sustainability, led to recognition of what Professors Mac-Donald, Morris, and Johnston termed the International Law and Policy of Human Welfare in their seminal book first published in 1978.[18] Professor McRae in his 1996 Hague Lectures argued cogently that sovereign imperatives in the post-Second World War era have increasingly focused on facilitating exchanges and intercourse between territories and their peoples (and business), as reflected in support and respect for the international trading system.[19]

In the inter-War period, for example, a dispute between a smelting company and nearby farmers over the damages caused by air pollution grew into a dispute between Canada and the United States. A binational arbitral tribunal established in the 1930s, that issued its final decision in 1941, is credited with setting out the "polluter pays" principle. In 1945, the application of the "effects test" under US antitrust law in the Alcoa case reflected fundamental differences between Canada and the United States over the claimed extra-territorial reach of domestic economic regulation, and in the 1949 Radio

---

17   This section was written by Jonathan Fried.
18   See Ronald S John Macdonald, Douglas M Johnston, & Gerald L Morris, eds, *The International Law and Policy of Human Welfare* (Alphen aan den Rijn, NL: Wolters Kluwer, 1978).
19   Donald M McRae, "The Contribution of International Trade Law to the Development of International Law" in *Collected Courses of the Hague Academy of International Law*, vol 260 (Leiden: Brill, 1996) 103.

Patents case, Canada objected strongly to US court direction to Canadian companies to comply with US laws at odds with Canadian laws and policies. In the 1970s, US litigation surrounding an alleged uranium cartel and foreign orderly marketing arrangements again involved Canada, along with Australia and others, in disputes about the proper reach of domestic regulation and sovereign authority.

The United States' sanctions policy, similarly, has long raised issues of economic law for Canada, from the Chinese embargo in the 1950s, the long-standing Cuban embargo that begin in 1961 and was expanded by the Helms-Burton law in the 1990s, the Siberian pipeline sanctions episode in 1979, through to today's debates about economic security and technology policy.

Against this background, international trade law has evolved over several decades. The conclusion of the Tokyo Round of the *General Agreement on Tariffs and Trade* (GATT) negotiations produced agreements on anti-dumping measures, government procurement, technical barriers to trade, and other non-tariff measures, known as "codes," a quantum leap in the codification of disciplines applying to trade in goods. In Canada, trade law first began to assume a discrete space within a new "Economic Law Division" in the Legal Advisor's office of the then Department of External Affairs.

The launch of the Uruguay Round in 1986, and of the *Canada-United States Free Trade Agreement* (Canada-US FTA) negotiations in 1987, provided accelerated impetus for codification of trade disciplines. Under Canada's lead negotiators in Geneva as legal advisors, Debra Steger, assisted by Serge Frechette, brought public and private sector experience and expertise to the table and were key players in developing what became the dispute settlement regime of the WTO. Concurrently, in Ottawa, a special Trade Negotiations Office under Simon Riesman was created to conduct the Canada-US FTA negotiations. Konrad von Finckenstein from the Department of Justice was appointed General Counsel, and Jonathan Fried, from the then-Department of External Affairs and International Trade, was designated as his deputy. They led negotiations on dispute settlement and advised all other negotiating groups, and Konrad later oversaw the preparation and approval of implementing legislation and regulations.

A similar model was followed following the launch of NAFTA negotiations in 1991. A dedicated Office of Trilateral Trade Negotiations was created within the then-Department of Foreign Affairs and International Trade under Chief Negotiator John Weekes. Jonathan Fried was appointed as Principal Counsel, and he assembled a team of lawyers both from the Legal Advisor's office and from the Department of Justice and its various legal services. Lawyers thus played an active role throughout the negotiations in every area discussed. With the conclusion of negotiations in 1992 and the NAFTA's side agreements on environment and labour the following year, this approach became institutionalized with the creation of the Trade Law unit, with Jonathan Fried as its first head, as also described by Rambod Behboodi in this volume.[20] In Geneva, alongside the adoption of the WTO Agreement the role of a dedicated legal advisor within the Canadian Mission was formalized, to advise on trade and economic law issues arising across the international organizations headquartered there, including in addition to the WTO, the United Nations Conference on Trade and Development, the World Intellectual Property Organization, the World Health Organization, and other forums where international economic law issues may arise.

The Trade Law unit, created by formal agreement between the Department of Justice and the Department of External Affairs and International Trade, merged the domestic and international expertise of the two legal communities.[21] The unit since its inception has been accountable to each of the Minister of Justice and to the Legal Advisor within their respective mandates. From the outset as well, it has provided solicitors' negotiating advice and oversight of implementation throughout government and filled the barrister's role on dispute settlement, encompassing state-to-state, investor-state, and binational panel proceedings. It has grown from an initial complement of twelve lawyers to now over seventy, with the head intended to rotate between an official of the Department of Justice and Global Affairs Canada. Thus, Jonathan Fried was followed by Ellen Beall, Leslie Holland, and then Valerie Hughes in quick succession. After Valerie's long tenure, that pattern has continued, with Denyse McKenzie, Meg Kinnear, Matthew Kronby, Arun Alexander, Robert Brookfield, and Shane Spelliscy.

C. Conclusion

VALERIE HUGHES' REMARKABLE CAREER IS testament to an individual of exceptional talent, legal acumen, scholarship, and team leadership. Her early and growing embrace of trade, economic and financial law, building on a

---

20 See Rambod Behboodi's contribution to this volume (Chapter 3).
21 *Ibid.*

foundation of public international law, embodies and personifies the growth of Canadian leadership in the field. With a remarkable record of achievements in each of the challenging roles she undertook, Valerie is both a role model and inspiration for those following her both in Canada and at the WTO. We have been privileged to have had the opportunity to work closely with, and learn from, her along the way.

CHAPTER 3

Developing a Government Trade Law Office: Canada, the Trade Law Bureau, and Valerie Hughes

Rambod Behboodi

"Happy families are all alike; every unhappy family is unhappy in its own way"—Tolstoy.

A. Introduction

Successful institutions are broadly alike in three interrelated respects: structure, culture, and people. The three prongs do not necessarily need to be harmonious: a particular structure can lead to cultural disharmony but that nevertheless survives and, indeed, thrives. As well, looking at a mature and functioning institution, there is a considerable temptation to consider that its success was inevitable; this is the institutional version of survivor bias in scientific analysis. However, institutional success is not a given. Finally, the inertial forces that maintain institutions do not always guide it in the right direction in achieving their objectives; this is classic, and all too common, institutional drift. At the risk of mixing metaphors, institutional drift can be avoided through two mechanisms: laying down a strong cultural keel at the outset, and active renewal of people over time.

This brief chapter is about Valerie Hughes, the third General Counsel (and Director General) of the Trade Law Bureau of the Government of

Canada (JLT). In my view, she was one of the elements that formed JLT's "strong cultural keel" early in its thirty-year history.

This brief personal observation starts with the global context in which Canada found itself in the early 1990s, the establishment of the Trade Law Division, and the entry into force of a new multilateral organization, the World Trade Organization (WTO). We will then examine the contribution of the new Division, and its first permanent Justice Canada head, to the development of international trade law and the rule of law in international trade relations more broadly, in Canada.

The books of JLT, of Valerie Hughes, and of international trade law in Canada are still being written; this paper does not, yet, have a conclusion.

B. The Global Context

TRADE "LAW" AND "LITIGATION" WAS not always thus.

Until 1989, for Canada, the only game in town for the resolution of trade disputes was the *General Agreement on Tariffs and Trade* (GATT).

The GATT was—for lack of a better word—a peculiar entity in the firmament of international law and organizations. The underlying agreement was applied "provisionally" throughout its life;[1] it did not even have a legal officer until 1975.[2] Its dispute settlement mechanism had developed through a series of evolutionary and incremental changes leading to expert panels that, though quasi-judicial in conception and character, nevertheless viewed trade disputes through a largely diplomatic lens.[3] Canada was not an active participant in formal disputes either as a complainant or a responding party; when it did participate, Canadian delegations comprised trade policy officials who, legend (theirs, recounted with considerable pride) had it, "wrote out the submission on the flight over to Geneva."

---

1   GATT, *Provisional Application of the General Agreement on Tariffs and Trade* (1947), online (pdf): wto.org [perma.cc/N8XR-LD3V].

2   Gabrielle Marceau, ed, *A History of Law and Lawyers in the GATT/WTO: The Development of the Rule of Law in the Multilateral Trade System* (Cambridge: Cambridge University Press, 2015).

3   Rambod Behboodi, "Legal Reasoning and the International Law of Trade: The First Steps of the Appellate Body of the WTO" (1998) 32:4 *Journal of World Trade* 55; Jon Ragnar Johnson, Joel S Schachter, & Goodman & Goodman, *The Free Trade Agreement: A Comprehensive Guide* (Aurora, ON: Canadian Law Book, 1998).

The *Canada-United States Free Trade Agreement* (FTA) entered into force on 1 January 1989.[4] The FTA had two dispute resolution mechanisms: a traditional binational/inter-state panel process, and an innovative trade remedy binational judicial review mechanism, overseen by an "extraordinary challenge committee" review mechanism.[5] Meanwhile, GATT dispute settlement was undergoing its own transformation,[6] although the core elements of GATT dispute resolution, the elements that made it particularly challenging—consensus-driven establishment of panels and adoption of panel reports—were left intact.

As a sign of confidence in their new FTA, the United States and Canada submitted their first cases, essentially disputes under GATT disciplines,[7] to the binational dispute resolution framework.[8] One of the cases was run along traditional dispute settlement lines; the other saw the heavy involvement, for the first time, of a private sector law firm in the development and presentation of Canada's case. Canada lost both.

Given its history in the GATT,[9] the FTA *Salmon and Herring*[10] case was arguably not winnable for Canada. The original GATT case had been about a Canadian export ban on herring and salmon. After Canada lost the GATT case, it advised the United States that it would implement the panel report by removing the export ban and imposing a *landing* requirement. The United States considered that the new requirements would amount to the same thing[11] and brought a case under the FTA. The Panel considered that the new

---

4   Georgetown Law, "US-Canada Free Trade Agreement (FTA)" (last modified 5 November 2024), online: georgetown.edu [perma.cc/8A49-SMAK].

5   For a full explanation of the "Chapter 19" binational process, see Rambod Behboodi, *Industrial Subsidies and Friction in World Trade: Trade Policies or Trade Politics?*, 1st ed (London: Routledge, 1994).

6   GATT, "Mid-Term Review: Final Agreement at Geneva," *GATT Newsletter* (May 1989), online (pdf): docs.wto.org [perma.cc/BN5Q-74EQ].

7   The *Salmon and Herring* case was a continuation of an earlier GATT dispute. See *Canada—Measures Affecting Exports of Unprocessed Herring and Salmon (Complaint by the United States)* (1988), GATT Doc L/6268, 35th Supp BISD (1988) 98, online (pdf): docs.wto.org [perma.cc/M5YJ-QBEL] [*Salmon and Herring*].

8   *Re Canada's Landing Requirement for Pacific Coast Salmon and Herring* (1989), CDA-89-1807-01, (Ch 18 Panel), online (pdf): publications.gc.ca [perma.cc/S8DD-XQ9F].

9   WTO, "US versus Canada: Fish Export Ban" (last visited 21 May 2025), online: wto.org [perma.cc/6NE4-GTQD].

10 *Re Canada's Landing Requirement for Pacific Coast Salmon and Herring* (1989), above note 8.

11 *Ibid* at para 2.02.

landing requirement was an import restriction inconsistent with Article XI of the GATT (incorporated into the FTA under Article 407) and was not justified by Article XX.

The *Lobsters*[12] case was different. The Panel described the measure at issue in the following terms:

> On December 12, 1989, the United States enacted an amendment to the Magnuson Fishery Conservation and Management Act (the "Magnuson Act") to prohibit, among other things, the sale or transport in or from the United States of whole live lobsters smaller than the minimum possession size in effect under U.S. federal law ("subsidized lobsters"). By that amendment (the "1989 amendment" or "U.S. measures"), lobsters originating in foreign countries or in states having minimum lobster size requirements smaller than the minimum limits imposed by U.S. federal law are prohibited, with effect from December 12, 1989, from entering into interstate or foreign commerce for sale within or from the United States (emphasis added).

Canada's sole claim of violation was under Article XI. However, the United States pointed out:

> [U]nder GATT precedent Canada, as the moving party in the dispute, had the burden of proving that the 1989 amendment was inconsistent with Article XI. In the view of the United States, because the 1989 amendment does not fall under Article XI, no exception under Article XX need be invoked. The United States argued that Article III rather than Article XI governs laws like the 1989 amendment, which is an "internal measure" requiring identical minimum   domestic lobsters.[13]

The Panel[14] found:

(a) as a matter of fact, the measure was being enforced internally;[15] and
(b) as a matter of law, the measure fell under Article III and its Interpretive Note.[16]

---

12   *Re Lobsters from Canada* (1990), USA-89-1807-01 (Ch 18 Panel), online (pdf): publications.gc.ca [perma.cc/G6EZ-AUJ8].

13   *Ibid.*

14   The Panel was split; this was the majority finding.

15   *Re Lobsters from Canada* (1990), above note 12.

16   *Ibid.*

Even though the United States had signaled its intention to invoke Article III as a *defence*, Canada had failed to include the provision as a claim in the alternative.[17] Canada's claim failed.

At times like this, Canadian institutions rise to the occasion. Instead of blaming the panel majority, Canada's foreign affairs ministry proceeded to establish an International Economic Law Division, and in the cases that followed under the FTA,[18] the Legal Bureau led the Canadian delegation.

The early 1990s were a momentous period in the history of Canadian international trade law and policy. The *North American Free Trade Agreement* (NAFTA) was negotiated in 1992 and entered into force on 1 January 1994;[19] the gavel was struck on the Uruguay Round negotiations on 15 December 1993, and the *Marrakesh Agreement Establishing the World Trade Organization* (WTO Agreement) was signed on 15 April 1994.[20]

NAFTA maintained the binational panel/Chapter 19 framework of the FTA and added three new dispute settlement frameworks,[21] including—for the first time in a *trade agreement*—an investor-state arbitration mechanism. In parallel, the new WTO Agreement presented what amounted to a quantum leap in international dispute resolution: a quasi-judicial framework with mandatory and binding jurisdiction, an appellate instance, and automatic "adoption" of reports (subject to reverse consensus).

At times like this, having already risen to the occasion, Canadian institutions tend not to rest on their laurels. To a civilian looking from the outside, the Canadian bureaucracy may appear heavy and sclerotic; institutionally, however, it is remarkably supple, innovative, and collaborative.

Enter the Department of Justice.

---

17 *Ibid.* The Panel made no determination as to whether these Article III measures were consistent with the national treatment requirements of that Article, *since such a determination was outside the terms of reference laid down by the Parties* (emphasis added).

18 *Re Article 304 and the Definition of Direct Cost of Processing or Direct Cost of Assembling* (1992), USA-92-1807-01 (Ch 18 Panel), online: sice.oas.org [perma. cc/8CZS-F266].

19 U.S. Customs and Border Protection, "North American Free Trade Agreement" (last modified 6 December 2024), online: cbp.gov [perma.cc/5XUL-7YP3].

20 United Nations Treaty Collection, "Marrakesh Agreement Establishing the World Trade Organization" (1 January 1995), online: treaties.un.org [perma.cc/XG2R-DCEQ].

21 Rambod Behboodi, "The Dog That Did Not Bark: The Mystery of the Missing Dispute Settlement Chapter in NAFTA" (Presentation delivered at the Columbia Law School, New York, New York, 6 April 2013), online (pdf): genevatradelaw.com [perma.cc/A8G3-6HT2].

C. The Letter

CANADA'S DEPARTMENT OF EXTERNAL AFFAIRS began life in 1909[22] as a "glorified colonial post office"[23] in modest offices above a barbershop in Ottawa. Within two decades, Canada's longest-serving Prime Minister considered the Department "the most conspicuous and in some respects the most important department of government."[24] Along the way, and to get there, it had acquired new offices on Parliament Hill and a "brilliant"[25] legal advisor, Loring Christie, and, after the outbreak of the Great War, a whole new, and crucial, *global* mandate through Canada's membership on the Imperial War Cabinet.

The Legal Advisor retained a central role in External Affairs in the interwar and post-war era of global law and institution-making. Even after the 1962 reforms to the Canadian Department of Justice that brought all departmental legal offices under one umbrella, the Legal Bureau continued its independent existence under the Foreign Minister.[26]

With the transformation of the international trade dispute resolution landscape, the traditional institutional incrementalism of both External Affairs and Justice Canada gave way to what amounted to a revolutionary change: the establishment of a *joint* legal services unit responsible for the provision of legal advice on Canada's trade law obligations *to the entire government* and for the conduct of litigation on behalf of Canada before international trade tribunals.

The 1 June 1993 letter signed by the deputy ministers of Trade and Justice that established the Trade Law Division is remarkable in many ways—for one thing, the vast mandate of the new division[27]—but what stands out is the anticipation of *institutional design* and *culture*:

---

22   Government of Canada, "History of Global Affairs Canada" (last modified 1 May 2024), online: international.gc.ca [perma.cc/X7SG-A3YK].

23   Canadian Parliamentary Review, "DFAIT Marks its Centennial" (last modified 14 September 2020), online: revparl.ca [perma.cc/5YQU-V9YH].

24   *Ibid.*

25   *Ibid.*

26   Justice Canada has a domestic legal advisory division housed in Global Affairs Canada, under joint jurisdiction of the Legal Advisor and Justice Canada's Public Law Branch.

27   Letter of DMT Allan Kirkpatrick to DM Justice John Tait:
     The division should embrace the full gamut of international trade law – legal interpretation of existing bilateral and multilateral trade agreements; legal advice on negotiation and conclusion of new trade agreements; coordination of drafting and implementation into domestic law of trade treaty obligations; legal aspects of Free

The division will be accommodated as expeditiously as possible in one location, which shall be as close as possible to the relevant clients and will be staffed in roughly equal numbers by members of the bar from our two Departments, with a starting complement of 12 lawyers. It is understood that this number will include one EX-level position from the Department of External Affairs and one senior-level position from the Department of Justice. The principal counsel's position will rotate between suitable candidates from our two departments and be mutually agreed. The first principal will come from the Department of External Affairs. It is also understood that the head will undertake Justice and External Affairs management training if not done previously. Staffing of other professional positions in the unit must ensure an appropriate mix of solicitor and advocacy skills. Future decisions regarding the size of the division will be taken by mutual agreement of the two Departments.

While the principal counsel is to have maximum flexibility in assigning duties within the division, all lawyers in the unit are to be treated equally, and a balance of interesting work is to be offered to Justice and External lawyers. Departmental programs such as work profiling, mentoring and Legal Awareness in Justice shall be respected. Performance appraisals, rating and other personnel issues must fully accord with the process or practice of the Department of which that officer is a member.

The new Trade Law Division started work on 14 June 1993; Jonathan Fried, then Principal Legal Counsel of the North American Free Trade Negotiations, was named JLT's first Principal Counsel. The author joined JLT as Counsel on the Department of Foreign Affairs and International Trade (DFAIT) side almost two years later; Jonathan Fried moved to the policy side in 1996.

Enter the Department of Justice.

D. The First Rotation

JONATHAN FRIED HAD BEEN A negotiator and a diplomat, with strong academic and professional credentials as a public international lawyer. He had been the driving force for the creation of JLT and, in his three-year tenure,

---

Trade Agreement (FTA) Chapter 18 panels and their NAFTA equivalent, as well as dispute settlement panels under the General Agreement on Tariffs and Trade and its related instruments; FTA Chapter 19 binational panels and their NAFTA equivalent.

had put an indelible stamp on its culture and all its operations. Because he was from DFAIT, he was already a natural fit within the trade policy framework, and as a result of his work on NAFTA, he had an intimate relationship with the senior trade policy management of the Department.

Anyone coming into the position from outside DFAIT faced a formidable challenge, both within the unit and with the client.

This was in 1996. Valerie Hughes had been with Justice Canada for well over a decade. Being a foreign service brat, she was not a stranger to the world of DFAIT; having started her career working on the *Gulf of Maine*[28] case with Léonard Legault (then, and later, Legal Advisor), she was no stranger to international litigation.

By the time Ms. Hughes arrived at JLT in late spring of 1996 as the Justice rotational head, Canada already had two active WTO cases on the go;[29] an investor-state dispute was in the offing; new counsel were arriving, and new cases were to come that summer.[30]

And the first Appellate Body report came out on 20 May 1996.[31]

Arguably, for trade lawyers, this—and not 1 January 1995, or 15 June 1994, or 15 December 1993—is the date at which "trade law" as we know it was born. Before *US—Gasoline*, we were still speaking the language of the negotiators and trade policy specialists—what Hudec called "a diplomat's concept of legal order."[32] After that, with the *Vienna Convention on the Law of Treaties* (Vienna Convention) given new life after decades of relative obscurity and the WTO Agreement no longer in "clinical isolation" from public international law, it was the language of the law that became ascendant in trade dispute resolution. This is not to make a value judgement—it could reasonably be argued that the very success of the "judicialization" of trade policy

---

28   *Delimitation of the Maritime Boundary in the Gulf of Maine Area Case (Canada v United States)*, [1984] ICJ Rep 246 [*Gulf of Maine*].

29   WTO, "European Communities—Trade Description of Scallops" (last visited 16 June 2025), online: wto.org [perma.cc/G752-K7H4] [*EC—Scallops (Chile)*]; WTO, "Japan—Taxes on Alcoholic Beverages" (last visited 16 June 2025), online: wto.org [perma.cc/RDK8-T9LV] [*Japan—Alcoholic Beverages II*].

30   WTO, "Canada—Certain Measures Concerning Periodicals," (last visited 16 June 2025), online: wto.org [perma.cc/WRR2-PANL]; WTO, "Brazil—Export Financing Programme for Aircraft" (last visited 16 June 2025) online: wto.org [perma.cc/ULG8-KP49].

31   *United States—Standards for Reformulated and Conventional Gasoline (Complaint by Venezuela)* (1996), WTO Doc WT/DS2/AB/R (Appellate Body Report), online (pdf): docs.wto.org [perma.cc/RH28-M94H] [*US—Gasoline*].

32   Robert E Hudec, *Enforcing International Trade Law: The Evolution of the Mordern GATT Legal System* (Salem: Butterworth Legal Publishers, 1993) at 12.

is why, in the end, the WTO's principal judicial organ was mothballed—but rather, in my view, a factual observation.[33]

If there was any doubt left about the near-total transformation of trade litigation from policy to law, and its practitioners from policy specialists and negotiators to trade lawyers, the *NAFTA Supply Management Report* released later that year by five professors of public international law resolved the issue for good.

Transformations are difficult affairs; stepping into a changing environment as an outsider can be arduous. For Valerie, it cannot have been a picnic having her predecessor, Jonathan Fried, as her chief client. And it was going to get a lot more challenging.

(1) What do you do when the client calls to inform you of a consultation request, for which they need a lawyer *in* Geneva in three days?

(2) Oh, and the client needs a lawyer in St. Petersburg, Russia, for negotiations on the fur trade?

(3) And all this comes out of your already-strained budget?

(4) And your lead counsel on a politically sensitive case is already knee—soon, neck—deep in another, equally politically sensitive, case?

(5) And the only other available counsel who knows anything about the subject matter has just started work on Canada's first investor-state case (and has to fly to St. Petersburg to negotiate fur)?

You have a sense of humour about it and make sure you recruit additional good counsel.

Now, these were the easier management issues. It was going to get much more difficult.

Inevitably, a new manager proposing any change at any time is faced with objections as to form—"this is how we have always done it"—and substance—"this is the law I have been working under this for three years." In these circumstances, brute force does not always work.

So, you have a sense of humour about that too.

And when a new manager goes into an area that is considered glamorous, expect professional jealousies to flourish. With so many *international* cases

---

33 *Re Tariffs Applied by Canada to Certain US-Origin Agricultural Products (Canada v US)* (2008), CDA-95-2008-01 (Ch 20 Panel), online (pdf): publications.gc.ca [perma. cc/64D8-JJ95].

going on in Geneva, it was inevitable that professional litigators at Justice Canada would want to be engaged.[34]

And yes, again, you have a sense of humour about that.

E. Substantive Contribution to the International Law of Trade

VALERIE WAS AN EXCELLENT MANAGER and mentor; the counsel she hired and advanced went on to achieve great things in the world of trade law, and if that were her only legacy, it would be tough to beat. It was not. Something else was happening in our world—a conceptual revolution—and Valerie had a significant role in driving it.

It is now axiomatic that the WTO Agreement is law, it is international law, and there is nothing that sets it apart from other international law, or indeed other systems of law. It was not always thus. Given the context of the GATT, there was a live, and lively, debate about the nature of the WTO Agreement and its reach into trade and domestic policymaking in Canada.

Where were the conceptual battle lines?

1) Trade Policy and Trade Politics

There were those—like Judith Bello,[35] or even the European Court of Justice in the *Portugal* case[36]—who considered the WTO Agreement a mere commercial agreement, a balance of commercial benefits.

The foundational concepts of a commercial framework are *interest* and *negotiation* over the exchange of concessions.[37] In this paradigm, relative power and not notions of law and legal obligation influence the conduct of adherents to the system. Within this context, pragmatists considered dispute

---

34 Justice Canada co-led the Canadian delegation in *Supply Management* and partici-
    pated in *EC–Hormones (US)*. JLT and Justice Canada eventually agreed to joint dele-
    gations in investor-state cases under Chapter 11 of the NAFTA.

35 Former United States Trade Representative General Counsel. See Judith Hippler Bello,
    "The WTO Dispute Settlement Understanding: Less is More" (1996) 90:3 *American
    Journal of International Law* 416.

36 *Portuguese Republic v Council of the European Union*, C-149/96, [1999] ECR I-08395,
    online: eur-lex.europa.eu [perma.cc/PC5R-6C4A].

37 See Phillip Trimble, "International Trade and the Rule of Law" (1985) 83:1 *Michigan
    Law Review* 1030.

settlement as a natural extension of the negotiation process.[38] That is to say, two countries might have a dispute about "law" and legal obligation, but any such dispute was at best a background to what Hudec called a "negotiated diplomatic approach to all policy conflicts."[39]

Pragmatists could, with some justice, point to the structure of the GATT as support for their contention that law was not central but ancillary to trade relations between the states. The idea was that the rules of the system would be applied on an *ad hoc* basis, in essence through further *negotiation* rather than adjudication as to their application to specific sets of facts. The objective of the GATT was not the punishment of a delict, the imposition of sanctions against an illegal act, or the penalization of a breach of a rule. Rather, the emphasis was throughout on conciliation and resolution. The aim was "to restore, with the minimum interference with trade, the balance of concessions and advantages between the parties in dispute."[40]

This context also implies the possibility of an "efficient breach."

2) Persuasion

John Jackson advanced the proposition that the WTO Agreement was a *system of laws*. What does that mean in concrete terms? Let me illustrate the point using Canada as an example.

Canada as a sovereign state enters into an agreement with other countries to establish *rules* that would govern their conduct *vis-à-vis* one another. Those rules impose limits on Canada's sovereign capacity; Canada agrees to those limits in return for similar limits on other Members' sovereign capacity. Canada abides by the *rules* thus negotiated, by making changes to its domestic legal framework, transposing international law into domestic legislation. Canada does all of this because:

---

38 Ronald A Brand, "Competing Philosophies of GATT Dispute Settlement in the *Oilseeds* Case and the Draft Understanding on Dispute Settlement" (1993) 27:6 *Journal of World Trade* 117 at 121.

39 Hudec, above note 32 at 11.

40 Olivier Long, *Law and its Limitations in the GATT Multilateral Trade System* (Dordrecht: Martinus Nijhof Publishers, 1985) at 76; See also Edwin Vermulst & Bart Driessen, "An Overview of the WTO Dispute Settlement System and its Relationship with the Uruguay Round Agreements: Nice on Paper but Too Much Stress for the System?" (1995) 29:2 *Journal of World Trade* 134; Debra P Steger, "WTO Dispute Settlement: Revitalization of Multilateralism After the Uruguay Round" (1996) 9:2 *Leiden Journal of International Law* 319 at 319.

(1) it is in its national interest that other Members abide by commitments they enter into;

(2) these are rules *it* has negotiated as the very manifestation of its national sovereignty; and

(3) it is in its national, ethical, and moral interest that relations between states are governed by transparent and predictable rules, rather than through secret negotiations governed purely by the economic, political, and military might of one side in the bargain.

In this paradigm, there is no notion of "efficient breach" because there can never be an "efficient" violation of the law.

This is how the "rule of law" gets imprinted upon the consciousness of lawyers and trade policy officials.

Our generation of trade lawyers was fortunate to see the process by which those belonging to a nascent *legal* system begin to accept that system and speak, and think, in terms of *law*. We saw Members *persuade* themselves, and being persuaded, that the system they had created and were living under was one governed by *laws*; we saw Members accept the *rule of law* in their trading relations; we saw Members adopt and assume the philosophical and *psychological* conditioning that is necessary for the functioning of law *as law*.

3) The Trade Law Bureau and Valerie Hughes

Now, this is a long and complex process; no one person or event is responsible for the transition of a Member from a GATT mentality to the world of the WTO. And the argument can be made that Canada being Canada, we would always have ended up where we ended up.

But individuals matter.

It took institutional courage and imagination for certain individuals to conceive of JLT and bring it into existence. Whom you staff your new legal services with, what emphasis you put on their professional education and training, and how you manage scarce resources—these all shape the culture of a place. And, when that place is a legal service providing advice to the government as a whole in respect of its complex web of international obligations, you can see how the influence of one manager can multiply across an entire government.

Valerie Hughes helped deepen and strengthen the centrality of "law" in WTO advice and litigation in Canada's trade relations and in the reception of the treaty in domestic law. Canada was supremely lucky that right when the Appellate Body was shaping not just the treaty, but *the way we look at* the WTO Agreement, it had at the helm of its trade law service a capable public international lawyer with unique insight into international judicial institutions. This is how not just the treaty but the jurisprudence found its way into the firmament of Canada's domestic law.

And what a jurisprudence!

The controversies of the past decade have obscured where we were—and where we might have gone. It is worthwhile to go briefly through those momentous early decisions.

We have seen how in its first-ever decision, the Appellate Body stated that international trade law may not be viewed "in clinical isolation" from public international law. They went further. As if to press the point, they revived what had been a more or less dead letter treaty, the *Vienna Convention on the Law of Treaties*. Remember that neither France nor the United States has ratified it, and many Members had not even signed the Convention; the Appellate Body has applied the Vienna Convention as if it were customary international law.

In *Japan–Alcoholic Beverages II*, its second report, the Appellate Body began with an overarching statement of principle about the rule of law in trade relations:

> It is self-evident that in an exercise of their sovereignty, and in pursuit of their own respective national interests, the Members of the WTO have made a bargain. In exchange for the benefits they expect to derive as Members of the WTO, they have agreed to exercise their sovereignty according to the commitments they have made in the WTO Agreement.

The Appellate Body then sets out another basic feature of a legal system: coherent judicial decision-making. The Appellate Body is ostensibly talking about GATT panel reports and not its own decisions, but it might as well be. And it says that they are not binding but, they "create legitimate expectations among WTO Members, and, therefore, should be taken into account where they are relevant to any dispute."

After it decides the case, the Appellate Body makes another overarching statement. This is a statement aiming *not* at the resolution of the case before it but at *persuading* the Members of the WTO that there is a new game in town: "WTO rules are reliable, comprehensible and enforceable." This is shorthand for, "the WTO Agreement is law."

The next two cases decided by the Appellate Body dealt with an obscure agreement under the WTO Agreement. But the obscurity of the provisions in these cases masked two critical pronouncements, both going to the nature of the WTO Agreement as law, and to the dispute settlement procedures of the WTO Agreement as *legal procedures*.

In *US—Cotton Underwear*,[41] the Appellate Body notes that consultations "must be real and fair, not merely *pro forma* ... grounded on ... due process considerations." Where did the Appellate Body get *due process* from? It is not in the text of the Agreement. It is not in the negotiating history. It was nowhere in the GATT. And no commentator had ever talked about *due process* when referring to GATT dispute settlement.

Of course, the Appellate Body did not invent the concept. And of course, no one was going to argue against it. It is a concept with which every occidental jurist is familiar. More than that: it is a concept—in various forms, it appears in most legal systems—without which it is impossible to consider a legal system with an adjudicatory body even remotely functioning.

In *US—Wool Shirts*,[42] the Appellate Body goes even further: it expresses directly what it had only hinted at before. The case is remarkable because of how clearly and effortlessly the Appellate Body asserts that it is a *judicial* system interpreting and applying a body of *laws*, that is, that the Members are governed by a system of laws.

Valerie Hughes was there at this critical point in the life of JLT and the WTO—that is, the initial phase of creating an *international law of trade* and integrating it into the greater body of public international law. She led our internal debates; her experience in, and understanding and knowledge of, public international law invariably elevated our discussions and sharpened our analyses. She encouraged us to teach and to publish and thus to be *active* participants in both the *interpretive community* of international trade law and the training of the succeeding generations of international trade lawyers. Above all, she guided the Division and advised the client—the government of Canada—in a way that helped Canada ease its way into the new world it might not even have been aware it was creating.

---

41 *United States—Restrictions on Imports of Cotton and Man-made Fibre Underwear (Complaint by Costa Rica)* (1997), WTO Doc WT/DS24/AB/R at 15 (Appellate Body Report) online (pdf): docs.wto.org [perma.cc/R7UU-NPE9] [*US—Cotton Underwear*].

42 *United States—Measures Affecting Imports of Woven Wool Shirts and Blouses from India (Complaint by India)* (1997), WTO Doc WT/DS33/AB/R at 14 (Appellate Body Report) online (pdf): docs.wto.org [perma.cc/M4C5-76CH] [*US—Wool Shirts*].

The Work of the Legal Affairs Division

CHAPTER 4

The Appointment of WTO Adjudicators: Rules and Evolving Practices

María J. Pereyra[*]

A. Introduction

THIS CONTRIBUTION AIMS TO PROVIDE an overview of the relevant rules and practices regarding the appointment of adjudicators[1] in dispute settlement proceedings within the World Trade Organization (WTO).

---

[*] María J. Pereyra is Senior Counsellor in the Legal Affairs Division of the WTO, member of the Executive Council of the Society of International Economic Law (SIEL) (2018–24) and of the Advisory Board of the Master on International Legal Studies at IE Law School. The author wishes to express her gratitude to Carlo M. Cantore, Dispute Settlement Lawyer in the Legal Affairs Division of the WTO, for his valuable comments on earlier drafts of this article. The views expressed are those of the author. They do not represent the positions or opinions of the WTO, its Secretariat, or of WTO Members. They are also without prejudice to Members' rights and obligations under the WTO. Any errors are attributable to the author.

[1] Members of dispute settlement panels, arbitrators, and Members of the currently non-operational Appellate Body. While these categories are not adjudicators in the usual sense of the term, I use the term as a shorthand to refer to them.

Over the years, relevant actors have developed certain practices that effectively complement the rules laid down in the Understanding on Rules and Procedures Governing the Settlement of Disputes (DSU), based on a constructive and open dialogue. More recently, in the context of informal discussions on DSU reform, Members have tabled proposals with the aim of reforming, in part, the panel composition process. In 2024, the process became formalized under the aegis of the General Council. Members have not yet determined how to carry the work forward in 2025.

This chapter is structured as follows. Section B gives account of DSU rules and practices relating the composition of panels, compliance panels under Article 21.5 of the DSU, and arbitrators on the level on nullification or impairment of benefits under Article 22.6 of the DSU. Section C is devoted to the selection of Appellate Body Members and their appointment in disputes. Thereafter, Section D provides information on the selection of arbitrators in arbitrations pursuant to Article 25 of the DSU, be them appeal arbitrations or otherwise. Section E gives account of the appointment of arbitrators tasked with the determination of the reasonable period of time to comply with adverse rulings pursuant to Article 21.3(c) of the DSU. Section F briefly summarizes recent proposals tabled by Members on the reform of the panel composition process. Section G offers concluding remarks.

B. The Composition of Original Panels, Compliance Panels, and Arbitrators on the Level of Nullification or Impairment of Benefits: DSU Rules and Evolving Practices

WTO PANELS ARE COMPOSED ON an *ad hoc* basis for each dispute. Article 8 of the DSU, entitled "Composition of Panels," lays down the rules governing the process of selecting and appointing the individuals who serve on a dispute settlement panel.

Paragraphs 1, 2, 3, 9, and 10 of Article 8 of the DSU relate to the expertise and nationality of prospective panelists. According to these provisions, panels shall be composed of "well-qualified" individuals, including former representatives of WTO Members, former WTO Secretariat officials, and international trade law and policy scholars. Individuals on panels should be selected with a view to ensuring independence, diversity, and a wide spectrum of experience. Unless the parties to a dispute agree otherwise, nationals of main parties or third parties in each dispute shall not serve on the relevant panel. In disputes between a developing WTO Member and a developed WTO Member, at the request of the former, the panel shall include at least one panelist from a developing WTO Member. Panelists serve in their personal capacity and should not receive instructions from Members.[2]

Paragraphs 4 to 7 of Article 8 of the DSU establish rules governing the panel composition process. Paragraph 4 instructs the Secretariat to maintain an "indicative list" of individuals possessing the prescribed qualifications.[3] WTO Members can propose nominations to the indicative list, and such nominations are approved by the Dispute Settlement Body (DSB). Approval of nominations by the DSB is usually a formality, and minutes from DSB meetings show that almost every time names proposed by WTO Members are added to the indicative list without any debate.[4] The DSU does not require that panelists be selected exclusively from the indicative list, and the practice reveals that the majority of the individuals who have served on panels since 1995 was not part of the indicative list.[5]

Paragraph 5 establishes that panels are normally composed of three individuals unless the parties to a dispute agree to a panel composed of five individuals.[6]

---

2   The notion that panelists serve in their personal capacity is reflected in constitution notes (the Secretariat official documents announcing the composition of the panel that is circulated under the WT/DS series) and panel reports. These documents consistently refer to panelists as "Mr" or "Ms," and refrain from using, for instance, diplomatic titles such as "Ambassador" or "H.E."

3   WTO, *Indicative List of Governmental and Non-Governmental Panelists*, WTO Doc WT/DSB/44/Rev.63 (2024), online (pdf): docs.wto.org [perma.cc/U93S-56ZX].

4   To the author's knowledge, the DSB rejected a proposal for addition to the indicative list only in one instance. See WTO, *Minutes of the Meeting (30 September 2019)*, WTO Doc WT/DSB/M/434 (2019) at paras 9.1–9.5, online (pdf): docs.wto.org [perma.cc/69DD-65UE]. In all other instances, nominations to the indicative list have been approved by the DSB substantially without discussions.

5   Interestingly, 68.6 percent of individuals appointed on panels (excluding compliance proceedings under Article 21.5 of the DSU) were not on the indicative list at the time of appointment. See WorldTradeLaw.net, "Count of WTO Panelists, by Appointment Method and Whether on Roster" (last visited 11 April 2025), online: worldtradelaw.net [perma.cc/J8XS-4US6]. The situation is largely the same irrespective of whether the composition of panels is determined by agreement of the parties (72.3 percent) or by the Director-General (67 percent).

6   Whilst a five-person panel technically remains a possibility, this has never happened in WTO dispute settlement. During the GATT era, five-person panels were composed

Paragraphs 6 and 7 are the key provisions regulating the panel composition process. Paragraph 6 entrusts the WTO Secretariat with the task of proposing nominations for the panel to the parties to the dispute. The provision further stipulates that parties can reject proposed nominations for "compelling reasons" only.

The drafters of the DSU did not spell out in greater detail how the Secretariat should identify and propose the names of potential panelists to the parties. Over time, the parties and the Secretariat have developed certain practices for proceeding with panel composition.

After a panel is established by the DSB, the Secretariat invites the parties to a meeting. Depending on the subject matter of the dispute, parties are contacted by either a team from the Legal Affairs Division or from the Rules Division of the WTO Secretariat. These meetings are usually referred to as "criteria" or "preferences" meetings in WTO jargon, as they allow the parties to express their views on the nationality and qualifications that prospective panelists should preferably have.

Criteria meetings are confidential, and no minutes or summaries of the meetings are published after the composition of the panel. The criteria put forward vary from case to case and from party to party. Anecdotally, some parties focus on the expertise of prospective panelists, for instance requesting that at least one individual have experience as a government official or attorney dealing with matters similar to those in dispute. It is not infrequent that parties stress the need for geographical and gender balance.

The Secretariat takes note of the parties' preferences and begins its search for suitable candidates. While the Secretariat is primarily guided by the requirements laid down in the DSU, it also strives to accommodate the parties' preferences, particularly when they are common to both complainant(s) and respondent. Often, this is not possible as parties may put forward opposite criteria. In such circumstances, the Secretariat tries to provide in its recommendations a balance among the parties' preferences.[7]

---

in a handful of disputes. See, e.g., *European Communities—Minimum Import Prices, Licences and Surety Deposits for Certain Processed Fruits and Vegetables (Complaint by the United States)*, GATT Doc L/4687 (1978), online (pdf): docs.wto.org [perma.cc/NR3C-YXBL]; *United States—Tax Legislation (DISC) (Complaint by the European Communities)*, GATT Doc L/4422 (1976), online (pdf): docs.wto.org [perma.cc/WMD8-FPY6].

7   One of the best descriptions of the role of the Secretariat in panel composition was rendered by Valerie Hughes. According to the author, the role of the Secretariat in

The Secretariat then submits for the parties' consideration a "slate" with proposed nominations for the panel. A slate usually comprises two potential chairpersons and four potential members of the panel, although this may vary depending on the parties' preferences and specific requests. For instance, WTO Members might request that a given slate comprise three names only. The Secretariat provides the parties with the CVs of the candidates. At this stage, the Secretariat does not yet verify whether the identified candidates would be available to serve as panelists. When sending the slate, the Secretariat tentatively schedules a meeting to hear the parties' views on the proposed candidates. At that meeting, after reviewing the candidates' profiles, each party expresses its views as to whether it can accept a proposed candidate or not.

The parties may agree on three names after receiving only one slate. In that case, subject to the prospective panelists' confirmation of their availability and the absence of conflict of interest, the panel will be swiftly composed as agreed by the parties. However, it is not uncommon for parties to request that more than one slate be provided because they could agree on only one or two nominations or because they could not agree on any of the proposed nominations.

Panel composition processes are most often conducted as described above, but there may be instances where, based on the parties' positions, events may take a different turn. For example, the parties to a dispute may agree on the appointment of three individuals of their choice, without their names being proposed by the Secretariat. While this scenario is not explicitly envisaged in the DSU, it is not foreclosed either. In these situations, the Secretariat still provides administrative support to the parties. The constitution notes announcing the composition of these panels simply report that the panels have been composed by agreement of the parties.

If there is no agreement between the parties within twenty days after the establishment of a panel, either party can request that the Director-General determine the composition of the panel (Article 8.7 of the DSU). In practice,

panel composition "generally does not involve legal skills; the task is more one of diplomacy, involving utter neutrality and an effort to put forth balanced slates [of candidates] that seek to meet both sides' preferred criteria to some degree." Furthermore, Hughes explained that the Secretariat "will try to guide the discussions and assist the parties in finding a common ground[;] it is not for the [Secretariat] to offer a legal opinion on the rules or on whether one party or the other is right or wrong on its approach." See Valerie Hughes, "The Role of the Legal Adviser in the World Trade Organization" in Andraž Zidar and Jean-Pierre Gauci, eds, *The Role of Legal Advisers in International Law* (Leiden: Brill, 2017) 237 at 246–47.

it is generally the complainant that will choose this path. The Director-General has ten calendar days to complete the composition of the panel, in consultation with the Chairperson of the DSB and the chairpersons of relevant Councils and Committees. Given the strict deadline and the demanding schedule of the WTO Director-General, it is customary for a party seeking the composition of a panel by the Director-General to preliminarily verify the availability of the Director-General to meet with the parties to hear their preferred criteria on composition. Thus, in practice, parties typically file their request on the day before or the same day that the Director-General is available to meet and begin this stage of the composition process, to allow the Director-General ten full days to complete the composition process. The Director-General is briefed by the Secretariat on the composition process to date. This is crucial, as the Director-General is thereby informed of the nominations that have already been turned down by the parties and can thus avoid appointing such a candidate.

Unlike the composition process at the prior stage, once composition is raised at the Director-General's level, the parties are no longer given the possibility to vet different candidates. Furthermore, the Director-General's decision on the appointment of panelists is final, meaning that the parties to the dispute will not have an opportunity to object to the nomination of an individual to a WTO panel.

It is possible that, before requesting the Director-General to complete the composition of a panel, parties had already agreed on one or two names during the composition process at the Secretariat stage. In such instances, the Director-General would take the previously expressed agreement by the parties into account and proceed with the identification of the remaining candidate(s). Until recently, every time either party requested composition by the Director-General, the relevant constitution note would simply indicate that the Director-General had determined the composition of the panel, without specifying whether the parties had previously agreed on the appointment of one or two candidates. In a relatively recent case, marking a departure from previous practice, the composition document noted that the parties had agreed on two names but could not agree on a third one, which was then chosen by the Director-General.[8]

---

8   See the constitution note for the dispute *China—Measures Concerning Trade in Goods (Complaint by the European Union)* (2023), WTO Doc WT/DS610/9, online (pdf): docs. wto.org [perma.cc/N8A9-JKMR].

The DSU contains additional rules that are relevant for this discussion. First, unless the original panelists become unavailable, they are expected to serve as members of a possible compliance panel established pursuant to Article 21.5 of the DSU or as members of the arbitrator tasked with the determination of the level of nullification or impairment of benefits pursuant to Article 22.6 of the DSU.

Moreover, the DSU foresees situations where more than one dispute is brought by different WTO Members with regard to the same matter or measure adopted by another Member. Article 9.3 of the DSU stipulates that when more than one panel is established to examine complaints related to the same "matter," the same persons shall serve as panelists on each of the separate panels "to the greatest extent possible." Also, under Article 10.4 of the DSU, if a third party considers that a measure "already the subject of a panel proceeding" nullifies or impairs the benefits accruing to it under the covered agreements, that WTO Member may resort to dispute settlement and the dispute shall be referred to the original panel wherever possible. These two provisions express a preference for disputes concerning the same matters or measures to be assigned to the same three individuals. While the DSU is silent on the reasons behind these rules, it can be presumed that the drafters intended to promote efficiency and consistency across related disputes and avoid, wherever possible, conflicting outcomes in the event of disputes concerning the very same measures or legal issues. In practice, WTO Members may not always agree on the characterization of certain measures or matters as being the "same" across disputes. In the context of the panel composition process, the parties may eventually reach an agreement among themselves. When that is not possible, the question may ultimately be put to the Director-General in the context of a request for composition under Article 8.7 of the DSU. It would then be for the Director-General to decide on the issue and to determine the composition of the subsequent panel accordingly.

C. The Selection of Appellate Body Members and their Appointment in Disputes

ARTICLES 17.1–17.3 OF THE DSU stipulate that the Appellate Body shall be composed of seven persons to be appointed by the DSB each of them for a four-year term which can be renewed only once and that the Appellate Body membership shall be broadly representative of the Membership in the WTO. Since its establishment, and until it became non-operational at the end of 2019, there has always been one Member of the Appellate Body from the United States and one from the European Union. Since 2008, a third slot was also consistently occupied by a Chinese national. The other four were assigned to nationals of other Members, ensuring a broad geographical balance.[9]

Currently the Appellate Body is not operational due to the lack of consensus at the DSB to launch the selection process for new Appellate Body Members. As a result, since December 2019 the Appellate Body has been unable to review appeals brought by parties in disputes.

In the interest of completeness, I note that pursuant to Article 17.1 of the DSU, Appellate Body Members shall serve on cases "on rotation," and that the details for such rotation are left to the Working Procedures for Appellate Review. In turn, Rule 6 of the Working Procedures for Appellate Review does not add much detail, as it reads as follows: "The Members constituting a division shall be selected on the basis of rotation, while taking into account the principles of random selection, unpredictability and opportunity for all Members to serve regardless of their national origin."[10]

There is no publicly available information regarding how the random selection of Appellate Body Members for a given case was made. The formula was never disclosed to the public, presumably to ensure the unpredictability of the selection process as per Rule 6 of the Working Procedures for Appellate Review.

D. The Appointment of Article 25 Arbitrators

ARTICLE 25 OF THE DSU envisages "expeditious arbitration" as an alternative means of dispute settlement for WTO Members. The provision gives parties the flexibility to agree on tailored rules of procedure for a dispute or a particular segment of a larger dispute. In that context, parties also need to agree on procedures to appoint the arbitrators.

---

9   To select Appellate Body Members, WTO Members developed a practice to establish a Selection Committee composed of the WTO Director-General, the Chairpersons of the General Council, the Council for Trade in Goods, the Council for Trade in Services, the TRIPS Council, and the DSB, to be chaired by the Chairperson of the DSB. WTO Members would submit nominations of candidates, and the Selection Committee would make a recommendation so that the DSB could take a decision to appoint new Appellate Body Members. See WTO, *Appointment/Reappointment of Appellate Body Members*, WTO Dec WT/DSB/70 (2016), online (pdf): docs.wto.org [perma.cc/FT7L-4GBU].

10 See WTO, *Working Procedures for Appellate Review*, WTO Doc WT/AB/WP/6 (2010) at Rule 6, online (pdf): docs.wto.org [perma.cc/MG4G-NYCV].

Although Article 25 of the DSU has not been used frequently, Members have relied on it in different situations. In all these instances, the issue of the appointment of arbitrators naturally arose and relevant actors came up with pragmatic—sometimes creative—solutions, in consultations with each other.

1) Arbitrations under Article 25 Other than Appeal Arbitrations

The first time that Members opted for arbitration under Article 25 of the DSU was in the context of the *US—Section 110(5) Copyright Act* dispute between the (then) European Communities and the United States. In that dispute, the Panel had found that certain aspects of the measure challenged by the European Communities were inconsistent with the United States' obligation under the *Agreement on Trade-Related Aspects of Intellectual Property Rights* (TRIPS).

The parties to that dispute resorted to arbitration under Article 25 of the DSU to determine the level of nullification or impairment of benefits to the European Communities resulting from the WTO-inconsistent measure. In their communication to the Chairperson of the DSB notifying the activation of arbitration procedures, the parties requested that the original panelists be contacted to determine their availability to serve as arbitrators. In the event of unavailability, the parties requested the Chairperson of the DSB to ask the Director-General to assist the parties in selecting alternative panelists.[11] The limited available record reveals that two of the original panelists were not available, and that based on the procedures agreed upon by the parties, the Director-General appointed two individuals to replace them.[12]

More recently, the European Union and the United States resorted to arbitration procedures under Article 25 of the DSU in the context of their reciprocal *US—Steel and Aluminium Products (EU)* and *EU—Additional Duties (US)* disputes. With simultaneous and similarly worded communications, the two Members informed the DSB that they agreed to terminate the existing panel proceedings and that they resorted to arbitration under Article

---

11   See *United States—Section 110(5) of US Copyright Act (Complaint by the European Communities)* (2001), WTO Doc WT/DS160/15 (Agreed Procedures), online (pdf): docs.wto.org [perma.cc/XZ3T-7XR9].

12   See *United States—Section 110(5) of US Copyright Act (Complaint by the European Communities)* (2001), WTO Doc WT/DS160/16, fn 1 (Constitution of the Arbitrator), online (pdf): docs.wto.org [perma.cc/JG2V-DAMX].

25 of the DSU to complete the work in the two disputes.[13] The parties also informed the DSB that, upon composition of the arbitrators, the arbitration proceedings would be immediately suspended for an indefinite period of time.[14] In both disputes, the parties agreed that, if available, the same individuals acting as members of the panels would also serve as arbitrators. All six individuals concerned confirmed their availability.[15]

2) Appeal Arbitrations

Some WTO Members have explored work-around solutions to the current non-operational status of the Appellate Body. One of the avenues chosen by WTO Members is appeal arbitration under Article 25 of the DSU. In the following sub-part, I elaborate on the process followed to appoint arbitrators in the context of appeal arbitrations.

a) Multi-Party Interim Appeal

In April 2020, a group of WTO Members notified the DSB of a Multi-Party Interim Appeal Arbitration Arrangement (MPIA).[16] The group now counts thirty WTO Members (counting the European Union as one Member), and the United Kingdom is the last WTO Member to notify its intention to join the MPIA in June 2025.[17]

Paragraph 4 of the MPIA establishes that appeals are to be heard by three arbitrators selected from a standing pool of ten appeal arbitrators composed

---

13   See *United States—Certain Measures on Steel and Aluminium Products (Complaint by the European Union)* (2022), WTO Doc WT/DS548/19 (Agreed Procedures), online (pdf): docs.wto.org [perma.cc/39UK-2AV4]; *European Union—Additional Duties on Certain Products from the United States (Complaint by the United States)* (2022), WTO Doc WT/DS559/7 (Agreed Procedures), online (pdf): docs.wto.org [perma.cc/NQ9A-K6KJ] [*EU—Additional Duties* (Agreed Procedures)].

14   *Ibid.*

15   See *United States—Certain Measures on Steel and Aluminium Products (Complaint by the European Union)* (2022), WTO Doc WT/DS548/22 (Constitution of the Arbitrator), online (pdf): docs.wto.org [perma.cc/W4R3-4C8F]; *EU—Additional Duties* (Agreed Procedures), above note 13.

16   See WTO, *Multi-Party Interim Appeal Arbitration Arrangement Pursuant to Article 25 of the DSU*, WTO Doc JOB/DSB/1/Add.12 (2020), online (pdf): docs.wto.org [perma.cc/Z72W-ZMFR] [*MPIA*].

17   See WTO, *Multi-Party Interim Appeal Arbitration Arrangement Pursuant to Article 25 of the DSU (Supplement 10)*, WTO Doc JOB/DSB/1/Add.12/Suppl.15 (2025), online (pdf): docs.wto.org [perma.cc/4Z6N-YBEG].

by the participants. Paragraph 4 further requires that the pool of arbitrators comprise persons of "recognized authority, with demonstrated expertise in law, international trade and the subject matter of the covered agreements generally." Under this provision, arbitrators must be unaffiliated with any government and avoid participating in a dispute if their participation would create a direct or indirect conflict of interest. Finally, paragraph 4 requires that the composition of the pool of arbitrators ensure an appropriate overall balance.

Annex 2 of the MPIA ("Composition of the pool of arbitrators pursuant to paragraph 4 of Communication JOB/DSB/1/Add.12") provides detailed rules on the selection of appeal arbitrators for the purposes of composing the pool. According to Annex 2, thirty days after the notification of the communication announcing the establishment of the MPIA, each participating WTO Member can nominate one candidate, notifying other participants. The candidates nominated by the participating WTO Members are requested to undergo a "pre-selection process," to ensure that they met the required qualifications. Such pre-selection process is to be carried out by a pre-selection committee composed of the WTO Director-General, the Chairperson of the DSB, the Chairpersons of the Goods, Services, TRIPS, and General Councils. After consultations, the pre-selection committee is to recommend candidates to the Members, who would then proceed with the composition of the arbitration pool by consensus.

Underscoring the interim nature of the MPIA, the participating WTO Members also committed to partially re-compose the pool of arbitrators periodically, starting two years after composition, following the rules laid down in Annex 2.

On 31 July 2020, participating WTO Members announced the composition of the pool of arbitrators.[18] In July 2022, participating WTO Members informed the DSB that they agreed to keep the pool of ten standing arbitrators unchanged. Participating WTO Members also informed the DSB that, in the event that the impasse of the Appellate Body were to continue, they would "consider a partial re-composition of the pool of arbitrators with effect from 31 July 2024."[19] In July 2024, participating WTO Members announced

---

18   See WTO, *Multi-Party Interim Appeal Arbitration Arrangement Pursuant to Article 25 of the DSU (Supplement 5)*, WTO Doc JOB/DSB/1/Add.12/Suppl.5 (2020), online (pdf): docs.wto.org [perma.cc/47PZ-8D6H].

19   See WTO, *Multi-Party Interim Appeal Arbitration Arrangement Pursuant to Article 25 of the DSU (Supplement 8)*, WTO Doc JOB/DSB/1/Add.12/Suppl.8 (2022), online (pdf): docs.wto.org [perma.cc/B4YN-8T2G].

that the process of partial re-composition of the pool of arbitrators would be launched in March 2025 and on 28 May 2025, the participating WTO Members notified the DSB that the partial re-composition process had been finalized.[20] The pool of arbitrators established in 2020 includes several experts who have previously served as panelists in WTO disputes. For instance, Professor Thomas Cottier, at the time of his appointment to the pool of arbitrators, was the Chairperson of an ongoing dispute in which the three complainants and certain third parties were also MPIA participants. Professor Cottier informed the parties to the dispute about his appointment to the MPIA pool of arbitrators, inviting them to raise concerns, if any. None of the parties raised objections regarding the effect of the appointment to the MPIA pool of arbitrators on Professor Cottier's ability to discharge his functions in the dispute "independently and impartially."[21]

As to the appointment of appeal arbitrators in a given dispute, paragraph 6 transposes to the MPIA, *mutatis mutandis*, the same approach based on random, unpredictable selection of Rule 6(2) of the Working Procedures for Appellate Review, including rotation.[22] A footnote specifies that a party to a dispute may request that any member of the pool of arbitrators who is not a national of one of the participant WTO Members be excluded from the selection process. Currently, there are no arbitrators in the pool who are not nationals of MPIA participants. Finally, the footnote also establishes that two nationals of the same WTO Member may not serve on the same arbitration.

So far, only one case has been adjudicated in the context of an appeal arbitration under the MPIA: *Colombia—Frozen Fries* and another case, *China—IPRs Enforcement (EU)* is pending before MPIA arbitrators. The constitution note on both cases do not reveal details regarding the random selection of the three arbitrators.[23]

---

20   See WTO, *Multi-Party Interim Appeal Arbitration Arrangement Pursuant to Article 25 of the DSU (Supplement 11)*, WTO Doc JOB/DSB/1/Add.12/Suppl.11 (2024), online (pdf): docs.wto.org [perma.cc/47YX-GYFV]. See also WTO, *Multi-Party Interim Appeal Arbitration Arrangement Pursuant to Article 25 of the DSU (Supplement 14)*, WTO Doc JOB/DSB/1/Add.12/Suppl.14 (2025), online (pdf): docs.wto.org [perma.cc/J5YH-TWYF].

21   See *India—Measures Concerning Sugar and Sugarcane (Complaint by Brazil, Australia and Guatemala)* (2021), WTO Docs WT/DS579/R, WT/DS580/R, WT/DS581/R at para 1.15 (Panel Reports), online (pdf): docs.wto.org [perma.cc/C3R9-REN4].

22   See Section C above in this chapter.

23   See *Colombia—Anti-Dumping Duties on Frozen Fries from Belgium, Germany and the Netherlands (Complaint by the European Union)* (2022), WTO Doc WT/DS591/8 (Constitution of the Arbitrator), online (pdf): docs.wto.org [perma.cc/NL29-2ZCA]. See

b) Turkey—Pharmaceutical Products (EU)

In 2022, the European Union (a participant of the MPIA) and Türkiye (not participating in the MPIA) agreed on procedures for appeal arbitrations in two disputes between them: *Turkey—Pharmaceutical Products (EU)* and *EU—Safeguard Measures on Steel (Turkey)*.

In that framework, the parties agreed on detailed rules for the selection of arbitrators in the event either of the parties appealed either of the two panel reports. The parties decided that the arbitrators in both cases should be three persons, randomly selected, "from a combined list of former Appellate Body Members and [MPIA] appeal arbitrators."[24] The parties determined that the selection should take place at the same time for both disputes, to ensure that one of the appeals would be heard by two former Appellate Body Members and one MPIA appeal arbitrator, and the other appeal would be heard by two MPIA appeal arbitrators and one former Appellate Body Member. In addition, the parties stipulated that, in the event that only one of the panel reports was appealed, the appeal would be heard by one former Appellate Body Member, one MPIA appeal arbitrator, and a third person to be drawn at random from those remaining on the combined list of former Appellate Body Members and MPIA arbitrators.[25] Finally, the parties provided for the arbitrators to elect a Chairperson.[26]

Ultimately, only the panel report in *Turkey—Pharmaceutical Products (EU)* was appealed. As set forth in the rules described above, the Arbitrator

---

also WTO, *China—Enforcement of Intellectual Property Rights (Complaint by the European Union)* (2023), WTO Doc WT/DS611/13 (Constitution of the Arbitrator), online (pdf): docs.wto.org [perma.cc/UM48-UZZF].

24 See *Turkey—Certain Measures Concerning the Production, Importation and Marketing of Pharmaceutical Products (Complaint by the European Union)* (2022), WTO Doc WT/DS583/10 (Agreed Procedures for Arbitration) at para 7, online (pdf): docs.wto.org [perma.cc/RC97-NUPH].

25 *Ibid*. The agreed procedures also discipline in detail the composition of the arbitrator in the event of a compliance appeal arbitration, as follows: "In the event of compliance appeal arbitration proceedings the arbitrators shall be the same persons that adjudicated the previous appeal arbitration proceedings, if available. If a person is not available or becomes unavailable in the original or any compliance proceedings, a replacement shall be drawn at random from the combined list of persons who are available. If no persons are available on the combined list, the parties shall agree on a reasonable method for appointing a replacement, taking into account the approach used in the original proceedings. If no agreement can be reached within one month, either party may request the Director-General to appoint a replacement, taking into account the approach used in the original proceedings."

26 *Ibid*.

was composed with one former Appellate Body Member, one MPIA appeal arbitrator, and another individual randomly selected from the combined list.[27] Similarly to what happened in *Colombia—Frozen Fries*, the constitution note announcing the composition of the Arbitrator in *Turkey—Pharmaceutical Products (EU)* does not reveal details on how the random selection was conducted.[28]

E. The Appointment of Arbitrators to Determine the Reasonable Period of Time (RPT) to Implement the Recommendations and Rulings of the DSB

PURSUANT TO ARTICLE 21.3 OF the DSU, at the end of original proceedings, if immediate compliance with the rulings and recommendations of the DSB is impracticable, the losing party in a dispute shall have a reasonable period of time (RPT) to comply. Such a RPT can be: (a) proposed by the WTO Member concerned and approved by the DSB; (b) mutually agreed by the parties to the dispute; or (c) determined through binding arbitration.

Footnote 12 to Article 21 establishes that "[i]f the parties cannot agree on an arbitrator within ten days after referring the matter to arbitration, the arbitrator shall be appointed by the Director-General within ten days, after consulting the parties." Footnote 13 adds that "[t]he expression 'arbitrator' shall be interpreted as referring either to an individual or a group."

Arbitration pursuant to Article 21.3(c) of the DSU has taken place in thirty-eight instances. Despite the language of footnote 13, in all these instances only one individual served as the arbitrator. Furthermore, irrespective of the method for the appointment of the arbitrator (by agreement of the parties or through a request to the Director-General), all Article 21.3(c) arbitrators were chosen among current or former Appellate Body Members or experienced panelists.

---

27 See *Turkey—Certain Measures Concerning the Production, Importation and Marketing of Pharmaceutical Products (Complaint by the European Union)* (2022), WTO Doc WT/DS583/13 (Constitution of the Arbitrator), online (pdf): docs.wto.org [perma. cc/9Z69-W4JB].

28 *Ibid.*

F. Informal Process on Dispute Settlement Reforms and Proposed Changes to the Panel Composition Process

IN FEBRUARY 2023, WTO MEMBERS began to engage in an informal process on dispute settlement reform. One year later, in February 2024, the facilitator of the informal process, Mr. Marco Tulio Molina Tejeda, submitted the text of a Draft Ministerial Decision on Dispute Settlement to the WTO General Council.[29] Chapter II of Title II (Panel proceedings) is entirely dedicated to panel composition.

Chapter II, Section I proposes to remove obstacles to the appointment of third-party nationals on panels by allowing non-governmental third-party nationals to serve as panel members in disputes. The effect of this provision could be to expand the pool of potential panelists in cases with a large number of third parties. At the same time, however, WTO Members would retain the right to object to the appointment of third-party nationals in the event that either party in a dispute requests composition by the Director-General.

In addition, Chapter II, Section II advances the following ideas to revamp the indicative list of governmental and non-governmental panelists:[30] (1) each WTO Member can nominate up to four individuals to the indicative list, including one who is not a national from that WTO Member, keeping in mind the need to ensure respect for gender and geographical balance, (2) the indicative list should be recomposed every four years to make sure that it remains up-to-date, (3) the Secretariat is "encouraged: to draw from the indicative list when proposing nominations for the panel pursuant to Article 8.6 of the DSU, (4) when the Director-General is requested to compose a panel, each party shall submit a list of thirty individuals that are on the indicative list, for the Director-General to verify if there are overlaps, and if so to compose the panel accordingly, or otherwise to determine the composition of the panel keeping in mind the parties' preferred criteria.

Appendix I to Chapter II, Section II seeks to introduce a system to review the qualifications of individuals proposed for inclusion in the indicative list. Under the proposal, the Chairperson of the DSB would be entrusted to review the qualifications of proposed individuals, with assistance from the WTO Secretariat. Should the DSB Chairperson consider that the information

---

29   See WTO, *Special Meeting of the General Council*, WTO Doc JOB/GC/385 (2024) Annex 1, Chapter II, Section II, online (pdf): docs.wto.org [perma.cc/UF2F-4CGP].

30   See Section B above in this chapter.

submitted is inadequate or that a particular candidate is not sufficiently qualified, he or she may recommend to the nominating WTO Member that it abstain from nominating that individual. In that case, the nominating WTO Member may then decide to propose an alternative individual or to nevertheless proceed with the originally proposed nomination.

G. Conclusion

THE PROCESS OF SELECTING AND appointing adjudicators in WTO dispute settlement proceedings is a dynamic one, involving many actors. Practices have evolved to support the formal rules outlined in the DSU, striking a balance between the requirement for impartial and skilled adjudication and flexibility.

Panel composition, primarily defined by Article 8 of the DSU, entails a complex dynamic between the WTO Secretariat and the parties in any given dispute. Although the Secretariat's role defined by the DSU can assist in suggesting potential panelists, the final lineup frequently represents a balancing act by the parties between their interests. Allowing the possibility of the Director-General's participation demonstrates the significance of a flexible procedure that guarantees that panels are composed even when the parties cannot agree in the first instance.

The selection of Appellate Body Members, although currently stalled, historically adhered to principles of geographical representation and expertise. The impasse that exists nowadays has prompted creative solutions such as the MPIA.

New ideas for DSU reform tabled by WTO Members can be viewed as an effort to tackle long-standing issues, especially with regard to panel composition. These recommendations seek to enhance the indicative list's applicability, expedite the appointment procedure, and guarantee that non-governmental third-party nationals are accepted as panelists on a larger scale.

In conclusion, the appointment of WTO adjudicators has evolved throughout time, reflecting a dynamic process characterized by small, continuous improvements, and flexible practices.

CHAPTER 5

Continuity and Renewal: Nurturing WTO Legal Talent through Internships at the Legal Affairs Division

Daniel Ari Baker, Jenya Grigorova, and Rodd Izadnia*

A. Introduction

THE SURVIVAL OF ANY INSTITUTION or field of practice depends on its ability to attract, develop, and retain new talent. In the context of the World Trade Organization (WTO) and of WTO law and dispute settlement in particular, both renewal and continuity have been strengthened by the robust and prestigious internship program run by the Legal Affairs Division (LAD), which brings talented young legal professionals into the Division to gain first-hand experience of and expertise in the multilateral dispute settlement process. The internship program has made significant contributions to both the current composition of the Division and the WTO more broadly (with many staff lawyers having started their careers as legal interns) and the practice of

* Daniel Ari Baker and Jenya Grigorova are Dispute Settlement Lawyers, and Rodd Izadnia is a Counsellor in the Legal Affairs Division of the WTO Secretariat. Rodd and Daniel began their WTO careers as interns during Valerie Hughes' directorship. The views expressed in this chapter are those of the authors in their personal capacities and do not necessarily reflect those of the WTO Secretariat or its Members.

international trade law at the WTO and beyond, with former LAD interns commonly taking up prominent positions in government, private practice, and the civil sector.

Valerie Hughes has always been committed to nurturing young talent, and during her time as Director of the Legal Affairs Division, she was a strong and steadfast supporter of the internship program. In honour of her contribution to the program, and by extension to the international trade careers of so many young lawyers, this chapter provides the first ever detailed consideration of the operation and outcomes of the LAD internship program. It begins by describing the program from initial recruitment through to post-internship employment prospects and provides a factual profile of the individuals that have participated in the program over time, including their geographical origins, gender breakdown, and post-internship employment. The data presented with this chapter give some quantitative sense of the reach of the program and its impact on the career trajectories of its participants, including positions in the WTO Secretariat, law firms, governments, and academia.[1] For many LAD interns, this program is their first opportunity to acquire practical experience in WTO law and intergovernmental dispute settlement.

In addition to providing new insight into an often overlooked aspect of the WTO system, this chapter responds to calls in government and academia for more consideration of how international organizations actually function. By highlighting the role of interns in the dispute settlement system, this chapter offers an insight into an important but underrecognized aspect of the Secretariat's organization, highlighting both the contributions that interns make to LAD's work and the important function of the internship program as an outreach and training tool for generations of WTO lawyers. In so doing, this chapter confirms both the diversity of the LAD internship program and its profound impact not only on WTO dispute settlement but also on the broader fabric of international trade practice globally and across a range of trade-related disciplines and practice areas. This impact is a living

---

1   The data in this chapter are based on information kept by LAD archives (names of interns, gender, nationality, and duration of internship) and on publicly available information (degree at time of internship, occupation immediately after the internship, current occupation, and additional degrees after the internship). The data in this chapter cover the period from 1 January 1996 to 31 December 2024.

testament to Valerie Hughes' dedication to ensuring both continuity and renewal in the multilateral trading system by nurturing the next generation of international trade lawyers.

B. General Background and Description of the Legal Affairs Division Internship

THE LAD INTERNSHIP, IN ITS current form, dates to 2001. Previously it was a two-month program in which interns were primarily involved in non-dispute research work, such as contributing to LAD's flagship publication, the *Analytical Index*. In 2001 on the initiative of LAD lawyer María J. Pereyra, supported by LAD Director Pieter Jan Kuijper, it was overhauled to extend the duration from two to four months (with the possibility of an additional two months depending on performance) and to provide greater compensation (unlike other international organizations in Geneva, the WTO has always paid its interns a daily stipend to support the cost of living in Switzerland). The program also began to increase the substantive responsibilities of interns in the research and support work to Secretariat teams assisting panels. Since then, the program has undergone further changes to the duration and intake process. Most notably, to further professionalize the selection process, Valerie Hughes created the Intern Selection Committee, a group of LAD lawyers that was initially chaired by María J. Pereyra until 2016 and, as described below, continues to operate as a core part of the program. In addition, the period of internship was extended in 2015 from four months, with a possibility of two months' extension, to a set, non-renewable period of six months (Chart 1).[2] Moreover, whereas, in consequence of the variable duration of the internship position, interns prior to 2015 could start at any time of the year provided a vacancy was available,

---

2   Chart 1 traces the average duration of internships.

since 2015 interns begin at set times each year, either in the second week of January or the first week of July.

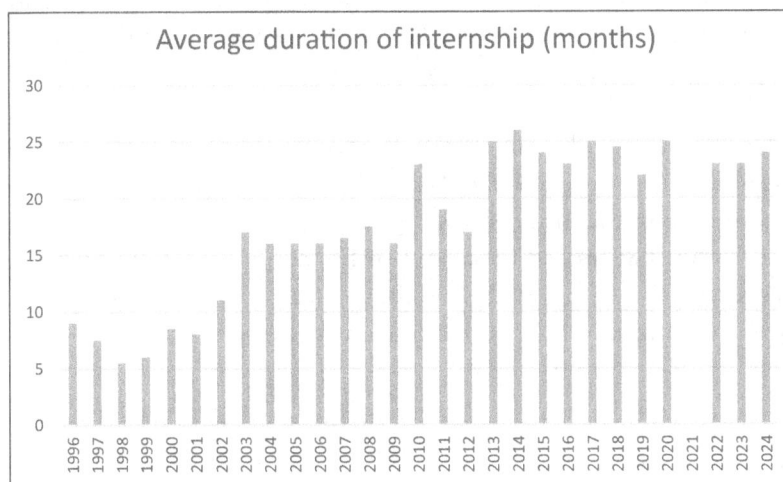

CHART 1. AVERAGE DURATION OF INTERNSHIPS (1996–2024)[3]

In terms of the role and responsibilities of interns, the LAD internship is "substantive" in nature. In other words, LAD interns are invited and expected to make a meaningful contribution to the Division's substantive legal work, including both dispute settlement work and non-dispute-specific research. Their task is not merely to take notes at meetings or copy-edit drafts prepared by others, nor are LAD interns restricted from participating in the active projects and work of the Division. Instead, interns are, from their first day, thrown into the heart (perhaps often experienced, at least initially, as the depths) of the Division's legal work, and encouraged to take part in various projects. We will describe this work in more detail below, but we begin by describing the recruitment and selection process.

C. Internship Requirements

PERSONS WISHING TO INTERN WITH LAD must meet certain minimum requirements in order to be considered for recruitment. There are three essential criteria in this regard. First, all candidates must have completed a law degree resulting in eligibility to practise law. Given the wide variety of legal

---

3   In 2021, due to the COVID-19 pandemic, there was no intake of interns.

education systems around the world, this is an objective criterion that allows for the preselection of candidates who have acquired legal knowledge sufficient to allow them to be eligible to practise law in the jurisdiction where they studied. Candidates need not, however, actually be admitted to practise to qualify. Second, in common with most other internship programs in the WTO, candidates must have completed a program of graduate studies prior to the start date of their internship. For LAD intern candidates, this will usually require completion of a Master's degree (such as an LLM), although in jurisdictions where the first law degree is a graduate degree (for instance, in the United States and Canada), that law degree (e.g., JD) will satisfy this requirement (Chart 2).[4] Finally, the candidate must have demonstrated experience or interest in WTO law and dispute settlement.

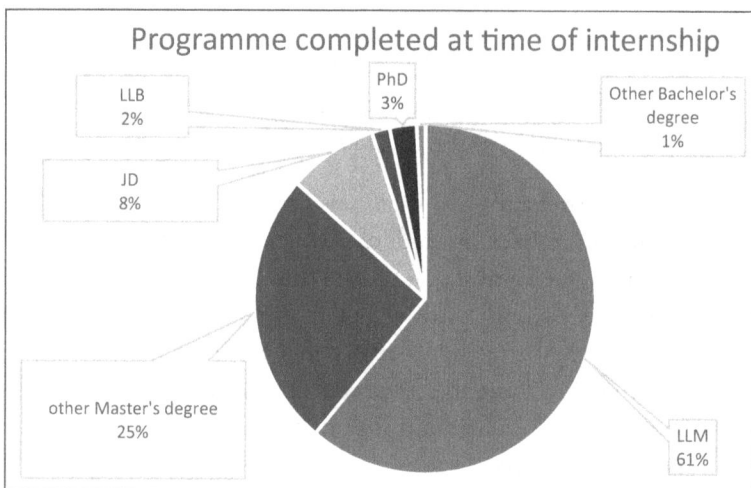

CHART 2. PROGRAMME COMPLETED AT TIME OF INTERNSHIP

This last point is particularly important. The Intern Selection Committee (ISC) recognizes that not all students will have had opportunities in their undergraduate or graduate studies either to study WTO law in a classroom setting or to participate in other WTO-related activities, such as the John H. Jackson Moot Court Competition (formerly the ELSA Moot

---

4   Chart 2 shows the academic studies completed by past LAD interns at the time of their internship, to the extent that this information is publicly available. The Chart does not account for past LAD interns in respect of whom such information is not publicly available.

Court Competition on WTO Law). Accordingly, lack of formal educational engagement with WTO law is not a bar to eligibility, and no particular educational or professional experience is required, provided that the candidate can demonstrate knowledge of and interest in WTO law and dispute settlement. Concomitantly, this requirement means that candidates with a more general interest in public international law, or with a demonstrated interest in another area of international economic law, such as international investment law, are not necessarily considered strong candidates for a LAD internship.

D. Intern Selection

THE PROCESS OF RECRUITING LAD interns is the responsibility of the ISC. The current committee is made up of three LAD staff members: two lawyers and one senior support officer. The ISC is responsible for reviewing applications, shortlisting candidates, carrying out interviews, and, finally, proposing candidates (usually three) for the consideration and approval of the Division's Director.

All candidates must indicate their interest in an internship by submitting an online application through the WTO's recruitment web portal, and twice a year the Human Resources Division sends these applications to the ISC for review. The number of applications varies, but is usually high, and has numbered more than eighty in recent intake cycles. As such, considerable time and effort is required to ensure that all applications receive fair consideration. In reviewing applications, the ISC looks for evidence of required skills and competencies, paying particular attention to demonstrated experience or interest in WTO law and dispute settlement. The ISC is confronted every intake with a significant number of candidates meeting the minimum requirements and deserving of consideration, including many with some prior specialized study of international economic law at a master's or doctoral level.

Candidates may come to the attention of the ISC through referrals, including from current and past staff members (including former interns) and university professors. In any given intake, referrals account for between 10 percent and 20 percent of total applications. Applicants referred to the ISC are required to submit an online application as well, and the process of reviewing their documents is the same as for applicants who apply online only.

Application materials consist of a covering letter, academic or professional references, a CV, academic transcripts, and a writing sample, preferably an academic-style paper on WTO law and dispute settlement. The amount of information submitted with these online applications varies, and often the ISC will reach out to qualified candidates asking them to provide further documentation to complete their applications. Although the WTO works in three official languages (English, French, and Spanish), application materials are generally required to be submitted in English as the working language for much of the dispute settlement activity and legal tasks of the Division. Demonstration of advanced Spanish or French language skills is also considered, particularly where disputes conducted in those languages are anticipated or in progress.

The ISC carefully considers all these materials. There is no required grade-point average, and applications are assessed holistically on the basis of past performance and demonstrated potential. Particular attention is paid to the writing sample, which is assessed on both the depth and accuracy of its substance and the quality of the drafting. This is because, as discussed below, interns are immediately included in the work of teams supporting dispute settlement panels, which involves substantial analytical research and drafting capability. Particular value is placed on papers that are able to explain complex or technical aspects of WTO law and dispute settlement in a clear and concise manner.

Along with demonstrated experience or interest in WTO law and dispute settlement, an applicant's background is also taken into consideration as part of the intake process. The historical data presented in this chapter reflects the broad representation of the WTO Membership in the recruitment of LAD interns and their varied professional and educational experiences. The goal is not simply to select candidates from a certain small group of prestigious universities or programs but to identify talent wherever it may be. As a consequence, individuals from sixty-eight WTO Members have so far been selected as interns at LAD (Chart 3).[5] Approximately half of LAD interns have come from high-income economies (mostly the United States, Canada, and Italy), one-third from upper-middle income economies (mostly Brazil, China, and Colombia), one-fifth from lower-middle income economies (mostly India, Kenya, and Pakistan), and 3 percent from low-income economies (including Uganda, Burundi, Ethiopia, the Gambia,

---

5   Chart 3 shows the nationalities of past LAD interns.

and Madagascar) (Chart 4).[6] The gender distribution of past LAD interns is approximately equal (51 percent male and 49 percent female) (Chart 5).[7]

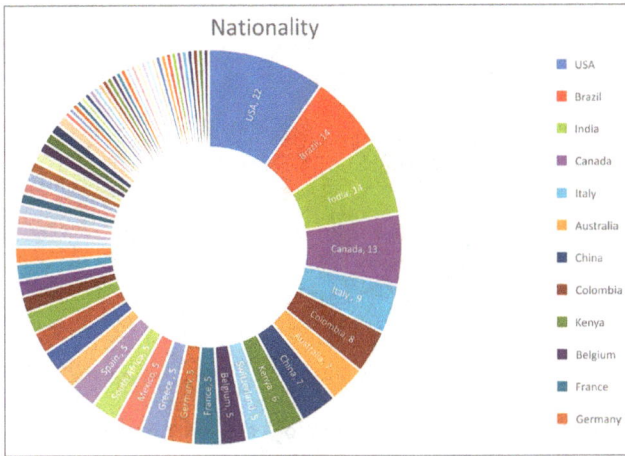

CHART 3. NATIONALITY[8]

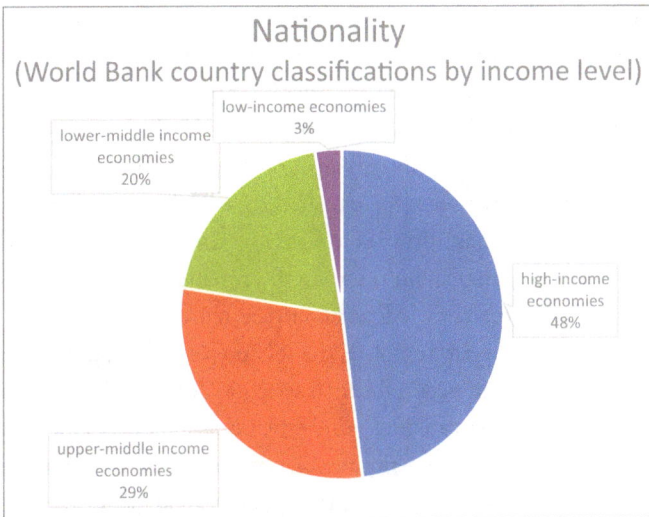

CHART 4. NATIONALITY BASED ON WORLD BANK COUNTRY
CLASSIFICATIONS BY INCOME LEVEL[9]

---

6   Chart 4 shows the nationalities of past LAD interns based on the World Bank country classifications by income level for 2022–23.
7   Chart 5 shows the gender distribution of past LAD interns.
8   For interns with double nationality, both nationalities are counted.
9   For interns with double nationality, both nationalities are counted.

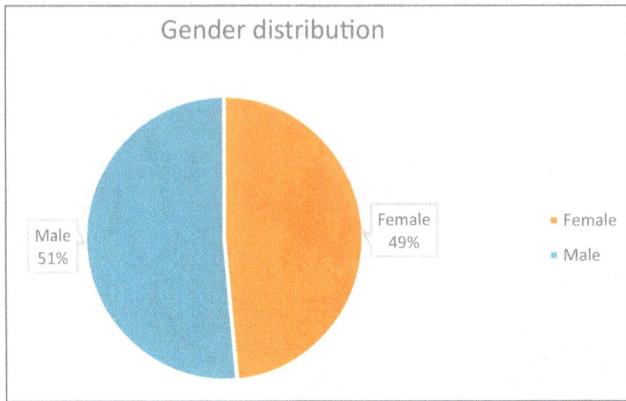

Gender distribution

Male 51%

Female 49%

- Female
- Male

CHART 5. GENDER

From the total pool of candidates for each six-month period, between ten and fifteen are shortlisted and invited to an interview with the ISC. Candidates who are not shortlisted, but who show promise, are kept on file and reconsidered for shortlisting in subsequent rounds. The interview is conducted online and takes the form of an informal, twenty-to thirty-minute conversation divided into two main parts. In the first part, the candidate is asked to describe their educational and professional background, their motivation for applying for a LAD internship, and their career plans and goals in the medium term. In the second part, the ISC asks the candidate a series of substantive questions based on their writing sample. These questions will often seek to challenge or extend the analysis presented in the writing sample to assess the candidate's knowledge and critical reasoning.

Once the interviews are complete, the ISC prepares a recommendation for the Director of LAD, who makes the final selection decision. This recommendation identifies the top three candidates and explains in some detail their academic and work experience and their performance at the interview. It also contains the ISC's reasons for considering the candidates to be a "good fit" for the internship program. The Director then considers the recommendations of the ISC, including the identification of possible alternates, based on the particular needs of the Division at the time and the overall composition of the cohort of interns.

As noted above, in most instances three interns are selected per intake. Fewer may be taken if the ISC does not find three candidates who meet the required standards, but the preference is always to take three wherever possible. Additionally, during the COVID-19 pandemic, the number was reduced, in the light of the difficulty of bringing interns to Switzerland and changes to the Division's workflow caused by the global health crisis (Chart 6).[10]

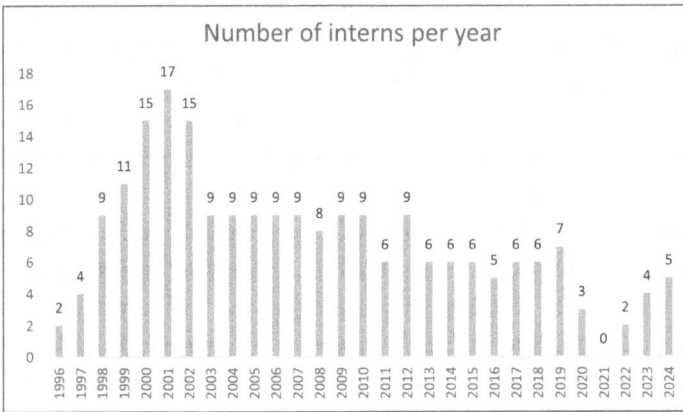

Number of interns per year

CHART 6. NUMBER OF INTERNS PER YEAR[11]

E. Work of Interns

THE SUBSTANTIVE CHARACTER OF THE LAD internship means that interns are invited and expected to take part in all aspects of the Division's work. Interns are integrated into the teams of LAD staff not merely as assistants or adjuncts but rather are expected to contribute as members of the team to which they are assigned. While the learning curve may be steep, induction processes ensure that interns are well acquainted with the tools necessary to their work, including research databases and internal information management systems, and the Dispute Online Registry Application. Given the degree of their integration into the substantive work of LAD, interns also receive instruction on the ethical obligations that are assumed in order to take part in the internship program, including in relation to confidentiality and conflicts of interest.

The primary task of interns is to support a Secretariat team advising a panel in dispute settlement proceedings. Upon arrival at LAD, each intern is typically assigned to a particular dispute team, and this team serves as the focus for the intern's work throughout the internship. Assignment to a case depends on both the needs of the Division and the experience and expressed

10   Chart 6 shows the number of interns per year.
11   In 2021, due to the COVID-19 pandemic, there was no intake of interns.

interests of the particular intern. Under the supervision of LAD lawyers, the intern contributes to the team's work in a number of ways, including by helping to prepare background research on relevant legal issues, analysis of written submissions and evidence, and preparing memos on procedural or other legal questions arising for decision. Interns also read and comment on drafts prepared by other members of the team. Depending on their performance, they may be given increasingly complex assignments and responsibilities over the course of their internship.

A benefit of the LAD internship is the opportunity to interact with Secretariat staff and WTO panelists. Interns' written work is closely supervised by other lawyers in the team who provide written and oral feedback on all work products, both to ensure that the work meets expected standards and to help interns develop their research, analytical, and writing skills. The LAD internship is very much a process of practical learning, and training is done on the go, with interns taking on new tasks as and when they arise in the context of a particular case.

Interns participate with the rest of their team in meetings with the panel and the parties. Thus, they are normally present at all internal meetings with the panel and at meetings of the panel with the parties. Participation in these meetings enables interns to gain a well-rounded and comprehensive understanding of all aspects of the dispute settlement process. The opportunity to observe the conduct of real panel meetings is a particular benefit of the LAD internship, including for those who have participated in the John H Jackson Moot Court Competition. Participation in real panel meetings gives former moot participants an insight into the often restrained and diplomatic atmosphere of panel proceedings, which is not always accurately conveyed in a moot exercise. Exposure to real panel meetings also gives interns an insight into the special style of WTO advocacy and the procedural mechanics of WTO litigation, which can be of use to them in their future careers in international trade law and practice.

In addition to dispute-related work, interns participate in the full range of non-dispute work carried out by the Division. This includes preparing and updating internal research tools and databases and contributing to flagship LAD publications including the Analytical Index and the Handbook on the WTO Dispute Settlement System. Interns also attend a range of meetings throughout the Organization and prepare summaries and minutes to keep other Division members up to date. This is particularly the case for interns in the second half of every year, who have the opportunity to serve as rapporteurs to multiple sessions of the WTO Public Forum.

In recent years, interns have also had the opportunity to conduct a focused research project, unrelated to any ongoing case and usually focused on dispute settlement procedure. These research projects can take a particular procedural rule or issue and explore their legal basis, evolution, and future. In such projects, an intern is invited to present their chosen topic to the Division in an interactive session with LAD lawyers that offers the intern a chance to share their researched conclusions and to elaborate on their own views about possible future developments in WTO law.

F. Compensation of Interns

UNLIKE MANY INTERNATIONAL ORGANIZATIONS, INCLUDING almost all United Nations agencies, LAD interns are paid a *per diem* to help them with the high costs of moving to and living in Geneva. The *per diem*, currently set at 60 CHF per day, is not large, but many interns have noted that without it they would not have been able to participate in the program. Travel costs to Geneva are not covered by the program.

Interns are also entitled to paid leave at the rate of two and a half days per month.

G. After the Internship

AS NOTED ABOVE, LAD INTERNSHIPS are non-renewable and so are never extended beyond six months. Nevertheless, many LAD interns continue on to careers that are closely associated with the WTO (Charts 7 and 8).[12]

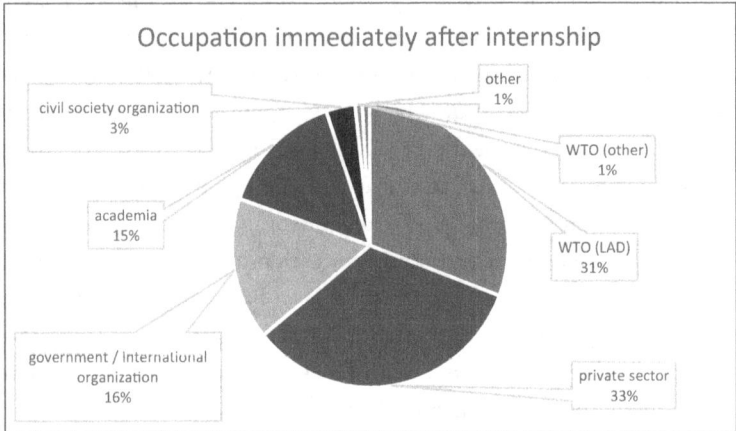

Occupation immediately after internship

- other 1%
- civil society organization 3%
- WTO (other) 1%
- academia 15%
- WTO (LAD) 31%
- government / international organization 16%
- private sector 33%

CHART 7. OCCUPATION IMMEDIATELY AFTER LAD INTERNSHIP

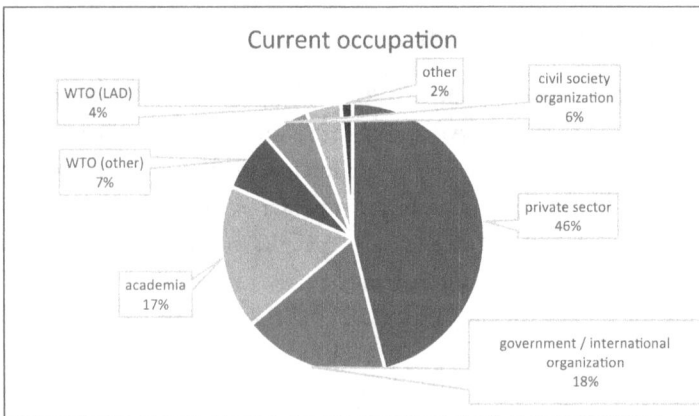

Current occupation

- other 2%
- WTO (LAD) 4%
- civil society organization 6%
- WTO (other) 7%
- private sector 46%
- academia 17%
- government / international organization 18%

CHART 8. CURRENT OCCUPATION

First, some interns may stay on at the WTO, either in LAD or, less commonly, in another Division. Approximately one-third of former interns have

---

12 Chart 7 reflects the different career paths taken by past LAD interns immediately after the end of their internship, to the extent that such information is publicly available. Chart 8 reflects the current occupation of past LAD interns, to the extent that such information is publicly available. These Charts do not account for past LAD interns in respect of whom this information is not publicly available.

remained in LAD immediately after the end of their internship, for various periods of time.[13]

After completion of their internship, some interns may stay on at the WTO on short-term or project contracts. These are contracts of up to a year which may be renewed. Usually, these contracts are given to interns working on a dispute that is still in progress where the intern's contribution has been impactful and their ongoing participation is considered beneficial. The availability of this option is affected by organizational budget constraints and the specific demands of dispute-related work at any given time.

Former interns may also join the WTO as full-term regular staff through the WTO's regular recruitment process. This is a competitive process requiring applicants to sit for a written and oral examination. Former interns are treated as external candidates in these hiring processes, meaning they have no formal advantage over other candidates who have not been LAD interns. However, the LAD internship provides excellent training in the kinds of analytical and drafting skills tested in the hiring exercise, and past interns therefore have a record of successful performance in these competitions. Indeed, currently approximately 10 percent of past LAD interns work at the WTO (in LAD or in other divisions),[14] and about 30 percent of current LAD staff served as interns in LAD before joining the Division as regular staff.

Many interns who do not stay on at the WTO continue to work in the field of international trade or in the adjacent field of international investment law and arbitration law. A little less than half of LAD's past interns are currently employed in the private sector, one-fifth work in government departments of trade and international law or the Secretariats of other international or regional economic organizations, and 17 percent occupy academic posts.

In terms of research, many past interns go on to pursue further academic research with the goal of becoming professors of WTO and public international law. At least 17 percent of past LAD interns proceeded to complete additional degrees after the end of their internship.[15] Many of the most prominent WTO academics currently working have spent as LAD interns.[16]

---

13   See Chart 7.
14   See Chart 8.
15   This figure only takes into account publicly available information about additional degrees completed by past LAD interns after the end of their internship.
16   Former LAD interns include, among others, Ligia Maura Costa (professor, Escola de Administração de Empresas de São Paulo - Fundação Getulio Vargas (FGV EAESP), Federico Ortino (professor, King's College, London), Lorand Bartels (professor,

Others join research institutes or trade-related think-tanks or policy-oriented non-governmental organizations. They thus stay in close touch with developments of the WTO and are often seen at the WTO headquarters at events such as the Public Forum.

Other former interns go on to practise either in other governmental areas or in the private sector. In both cases the specialized training provided by the LAD internship can provide valuable experience, and former LAD interns often go on to represent governments and private parties in a wide range of domestic and international dispute settlement fora, including the WTO dispute settlement system. Charts 8 and 9 show that LAD interns go on to have meaningful and successful careers, very often in fields related to WTO dispute settlement.

H. Future Directions and Challenges

AS THE WTO ENTERS ITS thirtieth year, and LAD enters its fortieth, what are the prospects for the LAD internship? On the whole, they are positive. The value of the internship program is universally recognized both within the Division and at the highest levels of the WTO's administration.

Sustained institutional support and dedication of resources is particularly important to meet challenges facing those who want to pursue a LAD internship. Most notably, as the cost of living increases in Geneva as elsewhere, future attention may be devoted to the sufficiency of the financial support offered to candidates, accounting for the demands of relocating to Geneva and the full diversity of backgrounds from which the internship program draws. Increased support for intern programs may enhance their already significant contribution to the development of skilled professionals in the field and help ensure that WTO internships, the LAD internship among them, remain competitive and accessible for future potential candidates.

University of Cambridge), Walid Ben Hamida (professor, Université de Lille), James Nedumpara (professor, Jindal Global Law School), Denise Prévost (associate professor, Maastricht University), Paolo Farah (professor, West Virginia University), Edna Ramirez Robles (professor, Universidad de Guadalajara), Lukasz Gruszczynski (associate professor, Kozminski University), Gracia Marin Duran (professor, University College London), Antonia Eliason (associate professor, University of Mississippi), Sivan Shlomo-Agon (associate professor, Bar-Ilan University), and Marios Iacovides (associate professor, Uppsala University).

In this connection, a notable recent development concerns the background of interns. Although LAD has always aimed to ensure diversity in its intern cohorts, recent years have seen a very significant increase in the number of candidates and interns from developing countries, particularly from South Asia and Africa. This may be due to the development of specialized academic programs on WTO law in those regions as well as the proven impact of the John H. Jackson Moot Court Competition in introducing aspiring legal professionals into the field of international trade law. This trend is a testament to the continuing relevance of WTO law and dispute settlement in particular across the WTO Membership.

Existing challenges are, in part, tied to challenges facing the WTO dispute settlement system as a whole. As the system faces uncertainty, it seems possible that promising young lawyers may consider other fields of law whose future seems more predictable. Nevertheless, the legal skills and direct experience in intergovernmental dispute settlement offered by the LAD internship program continue to have transferrable value into a broad range of professional endeavours, including the ongoing and future work to meet the manifold challenges facing the multilateral trading system.

I. Conclusion

ALTHOUGH OFTEN OVERLOOKED IN DISCUSSIONS about the WTO dispute settlement system, interns play an important role in the day-to-day work of LAD. Equally importantly, LAD internships provide an invaluable opportunity for promising young lawyers to gain first-hand insight into the dispute settlement system, often preparing participants for a life-long career in the field of international trade.

The LAD internship remains one of the key institutions for training WTO lawyers and spreading awareness in academia, private practice, and the public sector of how the WTO dispute settlement system actually works and the contribution it makes to the security and predictability of the multilateral trading system. As reflected in the trajectories of the many individuals who have passed through the program over time, the LAD internship has a strong legacy of contributing not only to the individual intern's development, but also the broader development of the field of WTO dispute settlement practice.

The fact that LAD's internship program has been a conduit for so many (including two authors of this chapter) into the field of international trade law is a testament to the leadership and support of Valerie Hughes, whose guidance and dedication helped the internship program flourish during her tenure as Director of LAD. All past and present LAD interns, as well as their current colleagues and employers, owe a debt of gratitude to individuals like Valerie who generously invested their time, attention, and expertise to training and nurturing several generations of WTO lawyers.

CHAPTER 6

Bringing WTO Dispute Settlement into the Twenty-First Century: Modernizing the Administration of Disputes to Better Serve Members

Marisa Goldstein and Lizzie Medrano[*]

A. Introduction

WHEN VALERIE HUGHES BECAME DIRECTOR of the Legal Affairs Division of the World Trade Organization (WTO), she brought with her a unique perspective having served as a litigator for Canada in international tribunals, as the Director of the Appellate Body Secretariat, and as a WTO panelist. Valerie was determined to modernize the work of the Legal Affairs Division (LAD) and to ensure that it provided the highest level of service to Members and panelists while increasing the efficiency of the Division's work. Two developments that Valerie instituted are hallmarks of this approach: the

---

[*]   Marisa Goldstein is a Counsellor in the Legal Affairs Division of the WTO Secretariat. Lizzie Medrano is a Training Officer in the WTO Institute for Training and Technical Cooperation; she was previously Dispute Settlement Registrar of the WTO Secretariat. The views expressed in this chapter are those of the authors. They do not represent the positions or opinions of the WTO, its Secretariat or of WTO Members. They are also without prejudice to Members' rights and obligations under the WTO. Any errors are attributable to the authors.

introduction of paralegals into the Legal Affairs Division and the move to a modern digital filing and archiving system for dispute settlement documents.

B. Evolution in Secretariat Support

THE FIRST MAJOR CHANGE THAT Valerie instituted with respect to support for dispute settlement panels was to expand the type of staff members assisting them to include paralegals. Before Valerie's arrival at the Legal Affairs Division, panels were assisted by a team of lawyers, liaison officers from WTO divisions responsible for the administration of the relevant WTO agreement, and sometimes an intern or short-term lawyer.[1] LAD lawyers or the liaison officers from the substantive division would serve as the Panel Secretary responsible for managing all communications between the panel and the parties, such as the distribution of timetables, working procedures, and meeting invitations. WTO disputes have progressively grown more complex, and nowadays cases can involve a high volume of factual information in the form of exhibits as well as legal questions of interpretation involving multiple provisions of the covered agreements. Through the recruitment of paralegals, Valerie added to LAD teams talented staff members with expertise in organizing documents, sorting factual evidence, verifying citations, compiling annexes, as well as preparing spreadsheets, statistical charts, and presentations.[2] This freed up lawyers and other staff to focus more on the substantive issues of the case knowing that their work could now be done more efficiently while at the same time maintaining high quality. Currently there are four paralegals in the WTO Secretariat, with two assigned to the Legal Affairs Division and two to the Rules Division.

C. Electronic Filing

THE NEXT AREA OF MODERNIZATION was to move WTO dispute settlement to electronic filing in a secure, easy-to-use manner. This innovation took longer to implement but has had a profound impact on the way all participants in dispute settlement—from Members, to panelists, to the

---

1   Article 27 of the Dispute Settlement Understanding provides that the WTO Secretariat should assist panels, especially on the legal, historical, and procedural aspects of the matters dealt with and provide secretarial and technical support.

2   WTO, *Vacancy Notice EXT/F/12-07*, WTO Doc OFFICE(12)/19 (2012), online (pdf): docs.wto.org [perma.cc/9NJS-LC3A].

Secretariat—interact with each other and with the documents that make up the panel record.

When the WTO was created and the new Dispute Settlement Understanding (DSU) became operational, there was no Dispute Settlement Registry. Instead, a mailing service was used to send the dispute record to panelists or Appellate Body Members in case of appeal. What was considered part of the official record of the dispute was not defined until 1999, by then Director of the Legal Affairs Division, William Davey and then formalized in Rule 25 of the Working Procedures for Appellate Review as:

> the written submissions, supporting evidence, written arguments submitted at the panel meetings with the parties of the dispute and third parties, the recordings of such panel meetings, and any written answers to questions posed at the meetings, the correspondence relating to the panel dispute between the panel or the WTO Secretariat and the parties or third parties, and any other documentation submitted to the panel.

Rule 25 of the Working Procedures for Appellate Review also requires that

> "[u]pon the filing of a Notice of Appeal, the Director-General of the WTO shall transmit forthwith to the Appellate Body the complete record of the panel proceeding."[3]

It was only in 2001 that a formal Dispute Settlement Registry was created by Pieter Jan Kuijper when he was Director of the Legal Affairs Division. The DS Registrar in its first decade or so largely continued the role of dispatching documents to panelists. However, it gradually took on more responsibilities, including keeping track of documents filed, saving and cataloguing electronic correspondence, and maintaining an organized archive documenting the number of boxes of documents in each dispute. This also included the responsibility to protect the confidentiality of dispute settlement documents particularly in those disputes where additional confidentiality procedures were adopted.

When Valerie Hughes served as Director of the Appellate Body Secretariat, she saw firsthand how the panel record was transferred to the Appellate Body upon appeal as well as how Members effectuated their filings in appeals. When serving as a panelist in *EC—IT Products* in 2009-10, she experienced WTO dispute settlement filing from the panelist perspective. In both panels

---

3   WTO, *Working Procedures for Appellate Review*, WTO Doc WT/AB/WP/6 (2010) at para 25, online (pdf): docs.wto.org [perma.cc/MG4G-NYCV].

and appeals, multiple paper copies were deposited with the Dispute Settlement Registrar in the Legal Affairs Division or with the Appellate Body Secretariat. These documents then had to be processed and mailed to the panelists or Appellate Body members, located in different parts of the world. Members were also required to serve paper copies on the other parties and third parties at their respective missions in Geneva. The amount of paper generated by a single filing could be substantial.

One could argue that the prior filing system mirrored the diplomatic and "quasi-judicial" nature of WTO dispute settlement and avoided being overly formalistic, but this approach had numerous drawbacks. To facilitate the work of the panel and the other party and third parties to the dispute Members would often provide courtesy soft copies over unsecure email channels. Files could be so voluminous that one submission would require multiple emails. This made it difficult to track whether the recipient had received all the relevant documents. There was also a real security risk that confidential documents could be intercepted, forwarded, or simply sent to the wrong email address by mistake. Secretariat teams and the parties maintained distribution lists of the relevant delegates, but these were not systematically updated. As delegates changed, dispute documents could be sent to the wrong people or the intended recipients could be left off email exchanges.

As the courtesy soft copies that Members did provide were not the official filing, the paper copies still needed to be distributed, not only in Geneva but also to wherever in the world the panelists, Appellate Body Members, or scientific experts assisting a panel might be. The shipping costs to send documents exceeded 60,000 CHF per year. This could be even higher in a year where there were a large number of disputes or if there were numerous exhibits in particular cases. In one dispute the documents that needed to be shipped to a wide range of destinations around the globe exceeded twelve kilograms.

In 2010 the Appellate Body sought to formalize filing via email by amending Rule 18 of the Working Procedures for Appellate Review to include the option for Members to file via email by the deadline but still provide the same amount of paper copies twenty as previously required the next day with an additional requirement to certify that the paper and electronic copies were the same and that, in the event of a difference, the electronic copy would prevail. Members were generally receptive to the idea of filing electronically but had objections to the continuation of paper copies and raised concerns about technological security and availability, verification of document receipt times, and the practical implementation of the procedures.[4] In light of these concerns, the Legal Affairs Division, under the leadership of Bruce Wilson, proceeded with exploring the idea of creating a secure database application for e-filing rather than using email.

Other elements of dispute management were also less efficient because of the lack of proper electronic case management. For example, setting the timetable and calculating the number of days between certain deadlines was done manually and without the ability to see the potential dates of holidays into the next calendar year. There was also no place to view all the dates in various disputes at the same time. Parties would often negotiate a timetable with one panel while not realizing that the agreed deadlines overlapped with their commitments in another dispute. From an administrative perspective, the Secretariat would have to maintain three versions of the timetable so that relevant stakeholders (panel, parties, and third parties) could see the dates on the timetable they were supposed to have access to under the DSU.[5] Any changes to the timetable would then have to be transposed three different times and redistributed to the relevant stakeholders.

In addition to using analog filing practices, Members did not follow a systematic nomenclature for dispute settlement documents, which made it difficult for the Registrar to know whether records were complete. All dispute records were maintained physically in cardboard boxes with the DS number of the case on them, and the Registrar knew how many boxes belonged to each dispute but could not always pinpoint the specific box that contained a particular document. Moreover, Members did not have direct access to the archives of their own submissions. They would, instead, have to ask the Secretariat to retrieve boxes from the archive and then search them if they wanted a particular file from an old dispute. During the time the WTO building was under renovation the records were stored off site, so such a search could take days. Records of appealed panels had been transferred to the Appellate Body Secretariat and were not always readily available to the DS Registrar. In some Article 21.5 compliance panel procedures, parties would have to provide

---

4   See WTO, *Proposed Amendments to the Working Procedures for Appellate Review*, WTO Doc WT/AB/WP/W/10 (2010), online (pdf): docs.wto.org [perma.cc/P6BB-D97W]; WTO, *Minutes of Meeting*, WTO Doc WT/DSB/M/283 (2010), online (pdf): docs.wto. org [perma.cc/YCC9-6W65].

5   Article 10 of the DSU provides that third parties are only entitled to the submissions up to the first substantive meeting. They are, therefore, typically not informed of the subsequent relevant dates and deadlines of the proceeding that occur after that date.

again the submissions and evidence from the original panel proceeding. For this reason, Bruce Wilson took the decision to begin the process of scanning and categorizing the old panel and arbitration records so that they could be accessed electronically in a standardized format.

When Valerie returned to the WTO Secretariat as the Director of the Legal Affairs Division in 2010, the decision had already been made to scan and categorize all old dispute settlement documents and to do *something* about the filing system, but the specific modalities of *how* it would be accomplished had not been decided. Valerie quickly advocated for moving forward with an e-filing registry similar to what many national court systems and other multi-national systems were already operating. She also recognized that the project (scanning and development of an e-filing application) would take more than the existing resources in the DS Registry. She saw this moment of transition as an opportunity to professionalize the registry function beyond stamping documents and archiving them in boxes to providing a true service to Members on all aspects of dispute settlement filings.

Valerie's role was more than endorsing an already ongoing project. She provided valuable input, strategic guidance, and support to the Secretariat teams working on various aspects of the project.

Valerie took charge of the process for conducting the requirements assessment and gathering best practices in the area. She spearheaded focus groups of delegates from frequent users of dispute settlement to get their feedback on proposed ideas as well as on their needs. She also created the Working Group on the Digital Registry, which was open to all the Members. This Working Group met periodically to consider policy decisions, view prototypes, and even test them. The Secretariat also instituted regular reporting to the Dispute Settlement Body (DSB) on the ongoing progress in building a digital dispute settlement registry (initially called Digital Dispute Settlement Registry (DDSR), the registry was renamed the Disputes Online Registry Application, or DORA, in 2019). These collaborative efforts, instituted by Valerie, gave Members the assurance that a system was not being imposed on them by the Secretariat. The system was not only being built *for* them but *with* them to make their experience of WTO dispute settlement more efficient and more secure.

Valerie supported the staff members leading the technical aspects of the project in connecting with other adjudicatory bodies that were using e-filing. With Valerie's support and assistance, the team learned from experiences of the International Centre for the Settlement of Investment Disputes (ICSID), the Singapore court system, the US International Trade Commission and US Department of Commerce, and they visited the European Court of Justice to learn about its e-filing system, e-curia. The best practices derived from these visits and conversations were shared with the Working Group of Members.

Valerie moved to provide additional short-term staff to scan and categorize all the archived disputes. The WTO had amassed an impressive amount of documents spanning panels, appeals, compliance panels and appeals, reasonable period of time arbitrations, and arbitrations over the suspension of concessions. By 2019, just before the WTO officially moved to e-filing in all disputes, there were 513 boxes of dispute documents (between the DS Registry and the Appellate Body Secretariat) holding over 2,052 files comprising over 1,285,000 pages, which, laid end-to-end, would amount to approximately 372 kilometres. We could pave the way from Geneva to Zurich with WTO dispute settlement documents! The scanning project was a major endeavour and enabled the WTO to truly know what was in each dispute record and to properly harmonize the categorization of submissions and other types of dispute documents.

Valerie also moved to change the qualifications of the DS Registrar and recruit new staff members to manage the transition. Under Valerie's leadership, the DS Registrar was transformed from a role focused solely on stamping, archiving, and forwarding documents to becoming a central contact point that is the face of the WTO dispute settlement system for delegates and panelists. Now the DS Registrar also coordinates with other Secretariat support services assisting panels such as translators, conference services, security, and—of course—the archive. The Registrar maintains both the physical and electronic records, ensures conformity with applicable procedures, provides case management support to users, and manages the e-filing application (including managing user accounts, generating statistics on dispute activity, and developing user guides and training materials). The DS Registrar is also tasked with developing, under the guidance of senior lawyers, new and improved procedures for the effective maintenance of the DS Registry.[6]

The move to e-filing in WTO dispute settlement did not involve the Legal Affairs Division alone. It necessarily included the Rules Division and the Appellate Body Secretariat on substantive and design issues as well as colleagues in information technology and procurement. The Directors of the three dispute settlement divisions and of the Information Technology and

---

6   WTO, *Vacancy Notice EXT/F/12-24*, WTO Doc OFFICE(13)/38 (2013), online (pdf): docs.wto.org [perma.cc/3GW7-MZ6R].

Solutions Division formed a steering committee for the project to make the ultimate decisions. Managing the staff members working on the day-to-day implementation of the project, as well as the (sometimes differing) interests of internal stakeholders and the concerns of the Members required Valerie's considerable diplomatic and bureaucratic skills. Valerie handled it all with aplomb. She even manned a kiosk at the Nairobi Ministerial demonstrating aspects of the e-filing application on videos and allowing Members to practice e-filing in a fictitious dispute!

The preceding paragraphs may make it seem that Valerie was able to come in, wave her magic wand, and move the WTO to e-filing. If only that were true. The reality reflects a long, hard slog which can provide many lessons for others attempting to go through similar processes. When Valerie left the WTO at the end of 2016, the DDSR had been used as a "pilot" in several disputes, but it could not be said that the WTO had fully transitioned to e-filing.

If fact, after Valerie retired, the WTO Secretariat, under the leadership of the Information Technology Solutions Division and LAD Director John Adank, moved the design and management of the application in-house and transitioned to a different software platform that was more modular and flexible, which resulted in better agility and control over the process. The design and features of the DDSR that had been honed under Valerie's leadership were transposed to the new DORA application. This enabled the WTO to respond more quickly to Member requests for changes and to roll out the application on a minimum viable product basis, building on it as Members grew accustomed to using it and adding new procedures, such as Article 25 arbitrations, as needs arose. The lockdowns of 2020 in response to the COVID-19 pandemic were the type of challenging event that led to a great leap forward in innovation for e-filing. The WTO had to move quickly from a voluntary pilot phase that was used by a few Members in a few disputes to it being the sole mechanism for making dispute settlement filings. Valerie was, in fact one of the first panelists to use the new DORA in a dispute and has used it several times as a panelist and arbitrator since then.

Today all panel filings are done through DORA, as are those for arbitrations conducted pursuant to Articles 22.6 and 25 of the DSU. Authorized users have access to the dispute record—submissions, exhibits, timetables, and communications—in one central and organized place that they can access from anywhere in the world. Members no longer have to worry about sending multiple emails via unsecure means to make submissions or be concerned that their submissions will accidentally end up in the wrong inbox. Members can also used DORA to send documents to the panel and each other even if they do not maintain diplomatic relations or other means of communication with each other. Members and panelists no longer experience delays in receiving documents but instead receive an email notification the moment documents are uploaded into DORA. Access is tightly controlled by the DS Registrar in concert with the account administrators of each Member involved in dispute settlement procedures. Members can see and download all their dispute settlement deadlines into their calendars. Over time, the archive is being uploaded such that Members will have direct access to their old case files without having to go through the Secretariat.

The transition to e-filing is, in a sense, never complete, as the DORA application is constantly evolving to meet the changing needs of Members and the Secretariat. Yet, it would not have happened in the Member-centric and user-friendly way it did without Valerie's diplomacy, leadership, and staunch support for her team.

The move to e-filing involved Valerie's considerable talents in bridging gaps and sheer determination to accomplish her goals. It also required Valerie to acquaint and acclimatize herself to new ways of working and to encourage other Secretariat staff to do the same. For those who know Valerie well, hearing that she was instrumental in developing a software application that required users to move from paper to computer might come as a bit of a surprise. Valerie's own trepidation with respect to "new-fangled" electronic means is a testament to her leadership and ethic—Valerie made the right decision for the dispute settlement system and the WTO Secretariat rather than the decision that would have been easy and comfortable for her.

D. Conclusion

FROM THE DECISION TO RECRUIT paralegals, to fully supporting the development of an e-filing application, to expanding the role of the DS Registrar, Valerie's tenure marked an enormous step forward in ensuring that Members and panels were receiving effective and efficient services from the WTO Secretariat. Without the steps Valerie took in her role as Director, it is unclear how the Secretariat would have managed the increased volume of work that the WTO dispute settlement system experienced in that period as well as being able to pivot quickly to a safe and secure way to conduct WTO disputes when COVID-19 presented new challenges to the way WTO dispute settlement operated.

CHAPTER 7

The Role of the Secretariat in WTO Dispute Settlement: Lessons from Other Adjudicatory Bodies

Gabrielle Marceau and Maria George

A. Introduction

THE DISPUTE SETTLEMENT SYSTEM OF the World Trade Organization (WTO) is a critical aspect of the multilateral trading system, allowing Members to preserve their rights and obligations under the covered agreements.[1] However, the two-tier adjudication system,[2] with panels in the first instance and the Appellate Body at the appeal stage, has been in crisis. In December 2019, as the terms of two out of the three remaining Appellate Body Members ended, and with the appointment processes of new Members blocked, the Appellate Body became effectively defunct as it no longer has the necessary quorum to adjudicate appeals.

---

1   *Marrakesh Agreement Establishing the World Trade Organization*, Annex 2, 15 April 1994, 1869 UNTS 3 at 401, Understanding on Rules and Procedures Governing the Settlement of Disputes, art 3.2 (entered into force 1 January 1995) [*DSU*].

2   For a discussion on the history and development of the two-tier adjudication system, see Petros C Mavroidis, "Taking care of business: The Legal Affairs Division from the GATT to the WTO" in Gabrielle Marceau, ed, *A History of Law and Lawyers in the GATT/WTO: The Development of the Rule of Law in the Multilateral Trading System* (Cambridge: Cambridge University Press, 2015) 236.

We believe this juncture (or crisis) presents an opportunity to address some concerns that have been raised about the role of another important actor in the WTO dispute settlement system: the WTO Secretariat[3] and when it was functional, the Appellate Body Secretariat. This chapter is also well-suited in a book dedicated to Valerie Hughes, who is the only person to have served both as the Director of the Legal Affairs Division (LAD)[4] in the WTO Secretariat and as the Director of the Appellate Body Secretariat.

We start by briefly explaining the institutional framework of the WTO dispute settlement system and the role played by the WTO Secretariat and the Appellate Body Secretariat (when it was functional). Our discussion is restricted to the functions discharged by the Secretariat staff in assisting panelists and Appellate Body Members with their adjudicatory functions. In Section C, we turn to the concerns raised regarding this role of the Secretariat and how they tie into some of the criticisms raised by the United States regarding the Appellate Body. We borrow these concerns from scholars who have raised them over the years and restate them to the best of our understanding. The aim of Section C is not to test these concerns or examine their merits. Instead, we simply identify three broad concerns that have been expressed by others, specifically concerns relating to the influence exercised by Secretariat staff over adjudicators, the lack of transparency in the role and functions of the staff, and the lack of accountability for the staff towards the adjudicators. In the last section, we look to other international adjudicatory bodies (we refer to them as "Institutions" in this chapter) where adjudicators are assisted in their functions by legal assistants (collectively referred to as "Legal Assistants" in this chapter). We believe there is a wealth of practice that can aid the WTO dispute settlement system to benefit from the expertise of the Secretariat staff while also addressing the concerns that have arisen. We focus on two aspects: firstly, the institutional structures that act as checks and balances in the functions of legal assistants; and secondly, the procedural framework in the adjudication process that safeguard against the concerns we identify. We look at the following institutions: the International Court of Justice (ICJ); the Court of Justice of the European Union (CJEU), consisting of the European Court of Justice (ECJ) and the General Court; the Community Court of Justice of the Economic Community of West African

---

3   *Marrakesh Agreement Establishing the World Trade Organization*, Article VI, 15 April 1994, 1869 UNTS 3.

4   We explain the institutional structure further in Section B, below in this chapter.

States (ECOWAS Court); panels for Chapter 31 disputes under the *Agreement between the United States, Mexico, and Canada* (USMCA); and certain other arbitration institutions, such as the Permanent Court of Arbitration (PCA), the International Centre for Settlement of Investment Disputes, and select commercial arbitration institutions. These institutions are by no means exhaustive in terms of practice relating to legal assistants; however, they do offer unique insights that will further our comparative study and inch us closer to addressing concerns arising in the WTO dispute settlement system.

B. Role of the Secretariat in WTO Dispute Settlement: Hiding in Plain Sight?

AS WE WILL ELABORATE FURTHER in the next part, several of the concerns regarding the Secretariat stem from the opacity of the role and functions of its staff in assisting panelists and Appellate Body Members.[5] However, the provisions of the Dispute Settlement Understanding (DSU) paint another picture: the role of the Secretariat is clearly recognized by the Members in two specific provisions.

Panels are *ad hoc* adjudicative bodies established to adjudicate a particular dispute between Members.[6] They make an objective assessment of the factual questions and legal issues referred to them and the conformity of a challenged measure with the covered agreement(s) invoked by the complainant. Thereafter, they make recommendations to the Dispute Settlement Body (DSB).[7] In discharging this function, the WTO Secretariat is tasked with assisting panels in accordance with Article 27.1 of the DSU: "The Secretariat shall have the responsibility of assisting panels, especially on the legal, historical and procedural aspects of the matters dealt with, and of providing secretarial and technical support."[8]

---

5   See Joost Pauwelyn & Krzysztof Pelc, "Who Guards the 'Guardians of the System'?: The Role of the Secretariat in WTO Dispute Settlement" (2022) 116:3 *American Journal of International Law* 534 [Pauwelyn & Pelc, "Who Guards the 'Guardians of the System'?"]; Joost Pauwelyn & Krzysztof Pelc, "The WTO Secretariat's 'Open Secret': Unpacking the Controversy" (18 August 2022), online (blog): ejiltalk.org [perma.cc/D522-2PD8].

6   WTO, *A Handbook on the Dispute Settlement System*, 2nd ed (Cambridge: Cambridge University Press, 2017) at 29 [WTO, *DS Handbook*].

7   The General Council of the WTO convenes as the Dispute Settlement Body (DSB) to deal with disputes between WTO Members in accordance with the DSU.

8   *DSU*, above note 1, art 27.1.

The WTO Secretariat is organized into divisions, each of which is headed by a director who reports to the Director-General (DG) or a Deputy Director-General (DDG) of the WTO. The Secretariat staff of the LAD and the Rules Division (in the case of trade remedy matters) provide assistance to panels.[9] Panels are also assisted by staff who are experts in substantive areas relevant to the dispute (e.g., agriculture specialists or economists), sourced from the respective divisions if the need arises.[10] A team assisting a panel typically comprises one or more junior legal officers (one of whom is appointed as the "secretary" to the panel and who assists with communications between the panel and the disputing parties), one senior legal officer, and other staff depending on the complexity and requirements of the case.[11] The staff report to the Director of the LAD or Rules Division and the DDG in charge of the division. Like all other Secretariat staff, they are appointed by the DG.[12] The panelists do not have direct control over the appointment or annual performance evaluation of the staff. However, they provide feedback on the staff assisting them in a dispute, which may become relevant at the time of appraisal.

The Appellate Body was established as a standing body, acting as the appellate and final stage of the adjudicatory mechanism in the WTO dispute settlement system.[13] Its mandate was to review the legal aspects of the reports issued by panels and to issue an Appellate Body report. The Appellate Body consisted of seven Members, who were working part-time. They were provided a monthly retainer and were additionally paid *per diems* as they worked on appeals. Three Appellate Body Members, selected through random rotation, would be in charge of hearing a case (referred to as a "division").[14] With

---

9   Daniel Ari Baker & Gabrielle Marceau, "The World Trade Organization" in Freya Baetens, ed, *Legitimacy of Unseen Actors in International Adjudication* (Cambridge: Cambridge University Press, 2019) 70 at 83 [Baker & Marceau, *The WTO*].

10 *Ibid*; Valerie Hughes, "Working in WTO Dispute Settlement: Pride Without Prejudice" in Marceau, above note 2.

11 Jasper M Wauters, "The Role of the WTO Secretariat in WTO Disputes – Silent Witness or Ghost Expert?" (2021) 12:S3 *Global Policy* 83 at 84.

12 Pauwelyn & Pelc, "Who Guards the 'Guardians of the System'?" above note 5 at 537.

13 WTO, *DS Handbook*, above note 6 at 31–32. See also, WTO, *Establishment of the Appellate Body*, WTO Doc WT/DSB/1 (1995), online (pdf): docs.wto.org [perma.cc/UA2W-FPVJ] [WTO, *AB Establishment*].

14 *DSU*, above note 1, art 17.1. See also, WTO, *Working Procedures for Appellate Review*, WTO Doc WT/AB/WP/1 (1996) at para 6(2), online (pdf): docs.wto.org [perma.cc/Z66V-LB4Z] [WTO, *AB Working Procedures*].

respect to assistance to Appellate Body Members, Article 17.7 of the DSU reads: "The Appellate Body shall be provided with appropriate administrative and legal support as it requires."[15]

The Appellate Body and its staff (the Appellate Body Secretariat) were established as a separate unit that was independent from the WTO Secretariat, which assisted the panelists.[16] It was composed of lawyers and administrative staff, who were appointed by and reported directly to the DG for all administrative matters.[17] Each Appellate Body division was assisted by a team of junior staff lawyers led by a senior lawyer, reporting to the Director of the Appellate Body Secretariat.[18] In a complex dispute, the Appellate Body also sought advice from staff of the Economic Research and Statistics Division. The staff were not assigned to individual Appellate Body Members but rather reported to the Director of the Appellate Body Secretariat and worked with Appellate Body divisions on appeals as they were filed.

Turning to the functions discharged by the WTO Secretariat and the Appellate Body Secretariat (when it was functional), we briefly recount them in the order of the proceedings. As panels are established *ad hoc* for each dispute, the Secretariat staff play a role in assisting parties with selecting panelists.[19] The WTO Secretariat maintains an indicative list of panelists.[20] With respect to a particular dispute, staff lawyers at LAD consider the requirements of each party relating to the panelists' experience, subject-matter expertise, qualifications, etc., and propose a list of names to the parties.[21] Of course, if the parties can agree between themselves on the panel's composition, the Secretariat does not need to get involved. If the parties cannot agree on the composition of the panel within the prescribed time, either party can request the DG to compose the panel. The senior staff of the Secretariat assist the DG

---

15   *DSU*, above note 1, art 17.7.

16   WTO, *AB Establishment*, above note 13. See also Debra P Steger, "The founding of the Appellate Body" in Marceau, above note 2.

17   WTO, *AB Establishment*, above note 13.

18   *Ibid.*

19   See María Pereyra's contribution to this volume (Chapter 4).

20   *DSU*, above note 1, art 8.4. WTO Members suggest names of individuals for this list, which are added upon approval by the DSB. The list also provides the specific areas of experience or expertise of the individuals in the sectors or subject matter of the covered agreements.

21   *Ibid*, art 8.6. Although the provision states that the parties shall not reject the nominations "except for compelling reasons," there is no mechanism to assess the reasons for rejecting a particular name.

in discharging this function by proposing names of panelists most suited for the dispute in the light of the qualifications identified by the disputing parties.[22]

The WTO Secretariat staff assigned to a particular case assist the panel in drafting the timeline and working procedures, which are approved by the panel and shared with the parties. The staff undertake revisions to these documents under the direction of the panelists. Once the written submissions are filed, the staff prepares an "Issues Paper" summarizing the arguments of the parties, identifying the legal issues that arise, and the various approaches the panel could take to them. The Issues Paper is an advisory note for briefing the panel and does not bind the panelists in any way.[23] Prior to the hearing, the panelists convene a closed briefing session along with the staff. They discuss the issues with each other to understand parties' and third parties' (if any) submissions as well as each panelists' position and request clarifications from the staff on the research in the Issues Paper. Thereafter, the staff undertake various administrative and logistical tasks to prepare for the hearing. The staff are present at the hearing to take notes of the proceedings but do not participate in any manner. During the deliberations of the panel, the staff are present and participate to provide any additional research or inputs regarding the case. Once the panelists have arrived at a decision, they inform the staff about their findings and reasoning and instruct them on the drafting of the report.

The panel report is divided into the descriptive part (factual aspects, claims of the parties, and summary of the factual and legal arguments) and the findings (the panel's reasoning to support its conclusions in upholding or rejecting the complainant's claim).[24] The staff assist in drafting all, or parts of, the report as per the instructions of the panel. Individual members can, and sometimes do, express separate opinions and may be assisted by the staff assigned to the case in drafting them. The panelists discuss the draft between themselves, in order to finalize and share it with the parties for review and comments. This draft is referred to as the "Interim Report." The panelists may

---

22   Giorgio Sacerdoti, "A Critical Reaction to Joost Pauwelyn and Krzysztof Pelc's 'The WTO Secretariat's "Open Secret": Unpacking the Controversy'" (5 September 2022), online (blog): ejiltalk.org [perma.cc/W6PD-44PS].

23   Baker & Marceau, *The WTO*, above note 9 at 83–84.

24   *DSU*, above note 1, art 12.7. The reasoning is a comprehensive discussion of the applicable law in light of the facts established by the panel on the basis of the evidence before it and in the light of the arguments submitted by the parties.

adjust certain aspects of the draft based on such comments before issuing it as the final panel report to the parties, and after translation, circulating it to the DSB.[25]

The panel report is adopted by the DSB by negative consensus,[26] unless a party to the dispute formally notifies its decision to appeal.[27] In case of appeal, the panel report will be considered for adoption by the DSB only after completion of the appeal. Although the Appellate Body is not presently functional, parties can file appeals, effectively halting the adoption of the panel report indefinitely.

When it was operational, the functions of the Appellate Body Secretariat were similar to those discharged by the Secretariat staff assisting panels. The Appellate Body was a permanent body and not an *ad hoc* tribunal, and naturally the Appellate Body Secretariat staff did not play a role in the composition of the Appellate Body or the composition of an Appellate Body division for a particular case. We highlight some important aspects of the functions discharged by the Appellate Body staff: the Working Procedures state that the Members of a division "shall make every effort to take their decisions on the basis of consensus."[28] While little to nothing is known publicly about the role of the Appellate Body staff in specific cases, it has been reported that in some cases the staff can help in bringing about this consensus, by facilitating the process of deliberation and encouraging discussion towards consensus.[29] A final aspect to keep in mind was the role of precedent in Appellate Body cases which eventually became a major concern for the United States. The Appellate Body has stated that although it is not bound to follow precedent, coherent case law is vital in promoting the security and predictability of the multilateral trading system.[30] The Appellate Body Secretariat and the WTO Secretariat staff assisting panelists play a role in achieving this goal by

---

25   *Ibid*, art 16.1.

26   *Ibid*, art 16.2.

27   *Ibid*, art 16.4.

28   WTO, *AB Working Procedures*, above note 14 at para 3(2).

29   Steger, above note 16.

30   *United States—Final Anti-Dumping Measures on Stainless Steel from Mexico (Complaint by Mexico)* (2008), WTO Doc WT/DS344/AB/R at paras 158–12 (Appellate Body Report), online (pdf): docs.wto.org [perma.cc/4CEQ-8M6C]; *United States—Continued Existence and Application of Zeroing Methodology (Complaint by Mexico)* (2009), WTO Doc WT/DS350/AB/R at para 362 (Appellate Body Report), online (pdf): docs.wto.org [perma.cc/WVN6-7GK4].

informing the Appellate Body Members and panelists about how previous panels and Appellate Body divisions have dealt with a specific issue.

Lastly, the WTO Secretariat and Appellate Body Secretariat staff are bound by the Rules of Conduct for the Understanding on Rules and Procedures Governing the Settlement of Disputes[31] and Staff Regulations.[32] These were adopted to promote impartiality and independence by establishing mechanisms for addressing potential conflicts of interest.

C. Concerns and Criticisms Regarding the Role of the Secretariat

THERE IS AN EMERGING LITERATURE on the appropriate role of "legal assistants" in dispute settlement, with some institutions having more robust engagement than others. The conversation regarding the appropriate role of the Secretariat in the WTO dispute settlement system has gained steam since the Appellate Body crisis. The aim of this part is not to relitigate these concerns or examine their veracity. Some other scholars have already undertaken that task.[33] Instead, we seek to distill the core concerns, and in the next section, look to the institutional structure and procedural frameworks of other international dispute settlement bodies for best practices.

In 1995, Alan W. Wolff (who later became a Deputy Director-General of the WTO), made a statement before the Committee on Finance of the United States Senate.[34] He observed that the WTO dispute settlement system is such

---

31 WTO, *Rules of Conduct for the Understanding on Rules and Procedures Governing the Settlement of Disputes*, WTO Doc WT/DSB/RC/1 (1996), online (pdf): docs.wto.org [perma.cc/XKN6-BPQJ].

32 WTO, *Conditions of Service Applicable to the Staff of the WTO Secretariat*, WTO Doc WT/L/282 (1998), online (pdf): docs.wto.org [perma.cc/A8SU-SZ5D].

33 See Gabrielle Marceau & Akshaya Venkataraman, "Unmasking the Phantom of the Opera: Is there a Hidden Secretariat in the WTO Dispute Settlement System?" in Symposium on Joost Pauwelyn & Krzysztof Pelc, "Who Guards the 'Guardian of the System'?: The Role of the Secretariat in Dispute Settlement" (2022) 116 *American Journal of International Law* 395; Wauters, above note 11; Armin Steinbach, "Are the Fingerprints of WTO Staff on Panel Rulings a Problem? A Reply to Joost Pauwelyn and Krzysztof Pelc" (2022) 33:2 *European Journal of International Law* 565; Sacerdoti, above note 22.

34 US, *World Trade Organization (WTO) Dispute Settlement Review Commission Act: Hearing Before the Committee on Finance of the United States Senate*, 104th Cong (1995) at 60 (Alan WM Wolff) [*Alan Wolff Statement*].

that the WTO Secretariat is "going to be very important and influential."[35] He feared that where the Secretariat staff are permanent and the panelists are selected *ad hoc* for a particular dispute,[36] the former may be in a position to exert "substantial influence" on panel decisions. We reproduce the relevant part of DDG Wolff's statement below:

> *Powerful, ensconced staff.* Another troubling procedural aspect of the system is the effective authority of the WTO secretariat. The secretariat advisors may remain the same from year to year while the panelists serve only infrequently. The secretariat, therefore, is in a position where it may exert a substantial influence on the panel decisions. With ad hoc panelists and very limited time, the authority of the secretariat- unelected officials appointed without effective review by WTO member representatives- is likely to grow. The impact of this type of influence on the WTO Appellate Body is also unknown.[37]

Over two decades later, amid the concerns raised by the United States on the functioning of the Appellate Body,[38] the echoes of DDG Wolff's earlier comments are present. We examine how some of DDG Wolff's concerns have been elaborated over the years.

A few years after the establishment of the Appellate Body, Robert Hudec recounted some criticisms of the role played by the Secretariat, specifically that the staff have no mandate to participate in the decision-making function.[39] Further, issues with accountability have also been raised as the staff have no visible responsibility for what is decided.[40] Hudec, however, states that the criticism is misdirected. He claims that the real concern is the legal expertise (or lack thereof) of panelists.[41] Without such expertise from the adjudicators, the Secretariat becomes an important source of legal and insti-

---

35 *Ibid.*

36 Although he does not attach this criticism to the Appellate Body Secretariat, he mentions the impact of this type of influence on the Appellate Body is unknown (at the time, as the Appellate Body had only been functional for over a year).

37 Alan Wolff Statement, above note 34 [emphasis in original].

38 USTR, *Report on the Appellate Body of the World Trade Organization* (Washington, DC: Office of the United States Trade Representative, 2020), online (pdf): ustr.gov [perma. cc/JHU7-JJB9].

39 Robert E Hudec, "The New WTO Dispute Settlement Procedure: An Overview of the First Three Years" (1999) 8:1 *Minnesota Journal of International Law* 1 at 34–35.

40 *Ibid.*

41 *Ibid.*

tutional knowledge. Petros Mavroidis and Bernhard Hoekman have raised a similar point more recently when discussing dispute settlement reform at the WTO.[42] They propose moving to a system with permanent panelists, as opposed to the present *ad hoc* system, which would enable panelists to develop institutional expertise and reduce the support needed from the Secretariat.

In recounting US actions leading up to the Appellate Body crisis, Paul Blustein discusses the role of the Appellate Body Secretariat and its Director at the time, Werner Zdouc. He observes that the Appellate Body Secretariat, and more specifically the Director, undertakes many substantive functions in assisting the Appellate Body Members, including "holding the pen" in the drafting process of decisions.[43] He observes that the criticism of this role, especially from the United States, holds the Secretariat responsible for the adherence of the Appellate Body to precedent (even though the Appellate Body is not legally bound to do so).[44] The underlying assumption is that the staff exert some control over the adjudicators in their decision-making functions owing to their institutional expertise and standing.[45]

Some scholars have argued that the expansive role of the staff raises concerns for the "(external) legitimacy" of the WTO and gives rise to a lack of transparency and accountability. Joost Pauwelyn and Krzysztof Pelc have examined the role of the WTO Secretariat and Appellate Body staff in depth. Their primary concern, as we understand it, stems from the institutional design of the WTO where the staff are permanent while the adjudicators are *ad hoc* or part time. Given this institutional design, they argue that the enhanced role played by the staff at various stages of the dispute resolution process allows them to exercise control over the decision-making function that is beyond their mandate and within the purview of the adjudicators. They are not alone in this claim.[46] Before discussing some of the specific

---

42 Bernard M Hoekman & Petros C Mavroidis, "To AB or Not to AB? Dispute Settlement in WTO Reform" (2020) 23:3 *Journal of International Economics* 703.

43 Blustein admits that this is not uncommon, and judges elsewhere also depend on clerks for assistance with their functions, including research and drafting.

44 Particularly, the United States argued that the Appellate Body's rulings on trade remedies deviated from the wording of the Agreements, and the Appellate Body failed to rectify this through subsequent proceedings.

45 Blustein notes that this position is not undisputed—the power and control alleged may be overstated, and Appellate Body Members who are well-versed with their cases have no difficulty in disagreeing with the staff or the Director.

46 Håkan Nordström, "The WTO Secretariat in a Changing World" (2005) 39:5 *Journal of World Trade* 819; John D Greenwald, "A Comparison of WTO and CIT/AFC

concerns raised by them, we will make one critical observation: the permanent staff of the WTO are not alone in providing substantive assistance to adjudicators; the permanent staff of other adjudicatory bodies plays a very similar role. Although these bodies are not identical in structure to the WTO, we will not focus on these differences. Instead, the question we ask is what the WTO dispute settlement system could learn from the institutional safeguards and procedural frameworks of these institutions that allow legal assistants to work with adjudicators.

A prominent claim made by Pauwelyn and Pelc is that there is a high degree of opacity under which the WTO Secretariat operates. They conclude that although such lack of transparency may not affect the "internal transparency" of the organization relating to its Members, it affects the "external transparency" towards domestic constituencies. They believe that the existence of a "hidden" permanent body with influence over decision-making significantly erodes the image of transparency portrayed to civil society groups. On a related note, they also raise concerns relating to the lack of accountability of Secretariat and Appellate Body staff owing to the absence of any formal qualifications in the DSU for staff. Further, they point to the lack of formal control exercised by the adjudicators over the staff that assist them. As explained earlier, the staff do not report directly to the adjudicators and are assigned cases by their respective staff director. This concern has also been raised by Mavroidis and Hoekman. While our discussion in Section B on the institutional structure of the Secretariat provides some response to these concerns (specifically, the Rules of Conduct and the role played by adjudicators in the review of work undertaken by staff), the comparative exercise could illuminate how other institutions have tackled similar issues more comprehensively.

Another crucial concern raised by Pauwelyn and Pelc relates to the drafting undertaken by the Secretariat staff[47] and its implications for the very nature of dispute settlement at the WTO. This concern rests on the assumption that those who "hold the pen" also influence the decision-making exercise. On this view, drafting cannot be separated from the cognitive task of adjudication. Further, the authorship of the decisions matters *per se*, they

---

Jurisprudence in Review of U.S. Commerce Department Decisions in Antidumping and Countervailing Duty Proceedings" (2013) 21:2 *Tulsa Journal of Comparative and International Law* 261.

47   Joost Pauwelyn & Krzysztof Pelc, "WTO Rulings and the Veil of Anonymity" (2022) 33:2 *European Journal of International Law* 527.

argue, as the findings draw legitimacy from the originator being the chosen adjudicator. We do not seek to venture into the debate on whether drafting encroaches on the adjudicative function[48] or *per se* impacts the legitimacy of the outcome. Rather, we believe concerns like this can be addressed and minimized through procedural and institutional safeguards. This is the aim of our discussion in Section D.

From the above discussion, we distill three broad concerns that will be the focus of our comparative study in Section D:

1) Concerns regarding outsized influence of staff over decision-making. These concerns have arisen in the context of the *ad hoc* nature of the panelists and the part-time nature of Appellate Body Members, in contrast with the permanent role of the respective staff assisting them. This has been most prominently raised with respect to the drafting functions undertaken by the staff. We will call this concern the influence issue.

2) Concerns relating to lack of transparency arising from the opacity surrounding the staff that are involved in a particular dispute, the type of functions discharged by them, and the absence of visible responsibility for what is decided.

3) Concerns relating to the lack of accountability of WTO and Appellate Body Secretariat staff. This is largely owing to lack of formal control exercised by the adjudicators over the staff that assist them, both in terms of appointment and appraisal/review.

D. Lessons from Other Adjudicatory Bodies

BEFORE EMBARKING ON THESE COMPARATIVE exercises, we provide two caveats to the reader. The first relates to the scope of our analysis. As stated above, the influence issue arises primarily from the *ad hoc* nature of panels or the part-time nature of Appellate Body Members, in comparison to the institutional expertise accumulated by the staff. Even with respect to the lack of transparency or accountability, these concerns become more pronounced owing to this difference. While altering the *ad hoc*/part-time nature of the adjudicators is perhaps the most effective solution to these concerns, it requires a fundamental change to the WTO dispute settlement system. Our focus is instead on providing safeguards within the existing institutional

---

48 *Contra* Steinbach, above note 33.

frameworks or procedural steps, that would strengthen the adjudicative functions exercised by panelists/Appellate Body Members. The second caveat relates to the limitation of our comparative exercise. Each international adjudicatory body is different, and consequently, the structures and practices identified below may not be directly transposable in the WTO dispute settlement system. For example, owing to the strict and short timelines for panel reports under the DSU, some of the procedural steps in other institutions may not be feasible without a relaxation of such timelines.[49] We leave it to policymakers and Members to decide how these can be introduced in the WTO. Our aim is to highlight the diversity of practice available with respect to legal assistants that can illuminate solutions for the WTO dispute settlement system.

We look at two types of best practices across institutions: (1) institutional safeguards that provide checks and balances on the functions of legal assistants, and (2) procedural frameworks that strengthen the adjudicative function within the control and mandate of the adjudicators.

1) Institutional Safeguards

The first institutional safeguards introduce various elements of checks and balances that address the three concerns identified in Section C. We examine the framework in the following institutions as illuminating this point.

a) The International Court of Justice

The legal assistants in the ICJ are formally all part of the Registry of the ICJ, however they function very differently than in the WTO. The Department of Legal Affairs of the Registry is responsible for case management, under the overall supervision and control of the Registrar. It consists of the Principal Legal Secretary (D1), who acts as the head of the Department, two First Secretaries (P5), five Secretaries (four P4, one P3) and an Administrative Assistant (OL).[50] Additionally, formally attached to the Department of Legal Affairs are the fifteen Associate Legal Officers ("clerks," P2) and the Special

---

49   For example, the International Court of Justice takes on average four years to complete a case, the International Centre for the Settlement of Investment Disputes (ICSID) takes over three years, the NAFTA state-to-state dispute settlement mechanism about three years, and the NAFTA investor-state system about five years.

50   International Court of Justice, "The Registry" (last visited 28 March 2025), online: icj-cij.org [perma.cc/GM7E-66F9].

Assistant to the President (P3). They are, however, assigned to individual judges. They answer to their judges, and it is the judges and the President (or vice-president in the case of the assistants of the President) that evaluate them. Even for administrative matters like leaves, the approval is first received from the respective judge and thereafter communicated to the Registry. Additionally, even physically, the Associate Legal Officers, Special Assistant to the President and the Judicial Fellows work out of the wing for judges, while the Registry staff operate out of the Peace Palace. Therefore, the institutional framework of the ICJ creates a system of checks and balances, where two sets of actors assist the adjudicators: one that works for the institution as a whole and the other that is under the supervision and control of the individual adjudicator. This addresses both the influence issue as well as the lack of accountability issue.

b) The Economic Community of West African States Court

We see a similar system employed in other adjudicatory bodies like the ECO-WAS Court, which is the principal legal organ of ECOWAS. The essential role of the court is to ensure observance of law and justice in the interpretation and application of the *Treaty of the Economic Community of West African States*, as well as other matters identified therein, including adjudicating cases alleging the violation of human rights in any Member State from 2005.[51] The Registry of ECOWAS consists of five divisions,[52] with the Judicial Process and Case Management Division responsible for the receipt, processing, and service of court processes. In addition to the Registry, the Court has a Research and Documentation Department that performs the bulk of the judicial assistance work in the Court. The department comprises four non-lawyers who work in the library and five lawyers, reporting to the Director who is also a lawyer. The Director allocates work between the team, and the staff is not assigned to a particular judge. The Department also prepares and updates an index of cases, categorized based on subject matter, that may be used in their research and drafting. The Director reports to the President of the Court, including for administrative matters like leaves and performance evaluations, etc. These two sets of actors are legal assistants that work for the institution as a whole.

---

51   *Protocol on the Community Court of Justice as amended by Supplementary Protocol,* Economic Community of West African States, 6 July 1991, art 9.

52   Judicial Process & Case Management; Judicial Certified Translation & Interpretation; Verbatim Reports; Judicial Records, Archives & Publications; and Appeals, Arbitration & Enforcement.

Additionally, the ECOWAS Court judges also have an Executive Assistant (EA) who works for them individually and forms a part of the judge's chambers. The EAs are lawyers with at least seven years of relevant experience and are given a P4 grade level. The judge has complete discretion in selecting their EA, with minimal intervention from the institution, restricted to verifying that the person chosen by the judge is a qualified lawyer and possesses the minimum experience and qualifications for the role. As the EA is attached to the judge, they assist the judge during their tenure.

In a similar manner to the ICJ, the ECOWAS Court institutional framework addresses the influence issue through a balance between assistants working for the institution as a whole and those working exclusively with a single judge. Such a framework ensures that judges are not exclusively reliant on the institutional staff and safeguards against such staff exerting influence over the decision-making. One crucial difference between the framework of the ICJ and that of ECOWAS can be highlighted: in the ECOWAS Court, the head of the institutional office is eventually reporting to the President of the Court. This creates an additional level of oversight that is exercised by adjudicators over the institutional legal assistants and further addresses the accountability issue.

c) The Court Justice of the European Union

Another prominent institution where such checks and balances are present is the CJEU. The CJEU consists of the General Court and the ECJ. The General Court is responsible, *inter alia*, for handling direct actions by individuals (natural and legal persons) against the acts adopted by the institutions of the European Union,[53] including disputes between the Union and its staff,[54] some direct actions brought by Member States, mostly against the Commission, and claims for compensation of damages against the European Union.[55] The ECJ, on the other hand, has jurisdiction over appeals against decisions of the General Court,[56] actions brought by the Commission or a Member State against another Member State for failure to fulfill its obligations under

---

53   *Treaty on the Functioning of the European* Union, 25 March 1957, art 260(4) read with
     art 256(1) at sub-para 1, online (pdf): eur-lex.europa.eu [perma.cc/QHY6-KXBP]
     [*TFEU*]. This includes for example challenges against determinations made by the
     Commission on competition law.
54   *Ibid*, art 270 read with 256(1) at sub-para 1.
55   *Ibid*, art 268 read with 256(1) at sub-para 1.
56   *Ibid*, art 256(1) at sub-para 2.

European Union law,[57] actions brought by a Member State or an institution of the European Union against another institution of the European Union for acting unlawfully, that do not fall within the jurisdiction of the General Court,[58] and requests for a preliminary ruling on the interpretation or validity of European Union law by a court in a Member State (70 percent of its case load consists of these preliminary ruling proceedings).[59] In addition to judges, there are eleven Advocates General in the ECJ, whose function is to present their Opinion in specific cases[60] (though the Advocates General do not present an Opinion in every case). The position in the General Court is different. The President of the General Court may appoint a judge of the General Court as an Advocate General for a particular case on an *ad hoc* basis.[61] At this level itself, there is another actor, i.e., the Advocate General, that is introduced to strengthen the position of adjudicators, *vis-à-vis* the legal assistants, reducing concerns relating to influence by legal assistants.

Now, turning to the legal assistants in the CJEU, a considerable number of actors assist the judges and Advocate General in the judicial work. We highlight some of the key actors that demonstrate the institutional framework of checks and balances. The ECJ and General Court have separate Registries, each headed by their Registrar, appointed by their respective Court,[62]

---

57 *Ibid*, arts 258(2) and 259(1).

58 *Ibid*, art 263 read with Protocol No 3 of the *Statute of the Court of Justice of the European Union*, art 51. Actions can also be brought for failure to act if there was an obligation to, see *Treaty on European Union*, 13 December 2007, art 265, online (pdf): eur-lex.europa.eu [perma.cc/DAL6-KVY7] [*TEU*].

59 TFEU, above note 53, art 267. A proposed amendment made in December 2022 of the Treaty on the Functioning of the European Union (proposed Article 50b) seeks to give the General Court the jurisdiction to hear and determine requests for a preliminary ruling exclusively relating to VAT, excise duties, customs, etc. The request submitted by the Court of Justice pursuant to the second paragraph of Article 281 of the Treaty on the Functioning of the European Union, with a view to amending Protocol No 3 on the Statute of the Court of Justice of the European Union is available online (pdf): curia.europa.eu [perma.cc/4B87-LHFS] [*Proposed Amendment Request*].

60 TFEU, above note 53, art 252(2).

61 There are currently no permanent Advocates General in the General Court. *Ad hoc* appointments of Advocate Generals have been rare, although this might change soon. See Proposed Amendment Request, above note 59. See also, Rafal Mańko, *Amending the Statute of the Court of Justice of the EU* (European Parliamentary Research Service, 2024), online (pdf): europarl.europa.eu [perma.cc/X95S-MAPZ].

62 EU, *Rules of Procedure of the General Court*, [2015] OJ, L 105/1 art 32; EU, *Rules of Procedure of the Court of Justice*, [2012] OJ, L 265/1 art 18.

and assisted by a Deputy Registrar.[63] The Registrar of the ECJ is the Secretary-General of the CJEU as an institution and is responsible for its global administration. The Deputy Registrar of the ECJ and the Registrar and Deputy Registrar of the General Court are responsible for the day-to-day functioning of their respective Courts and track the cases before the Courts. The Deputy Registrar of the ECJ has around fifty people presently working under him, who are from different Member States and fluent in their languages. On the other hand, the Registrar and Deputy Registrar of the General Court have a larger team of seventy people assisting them in their functions. The Registry staff undertakes a preliminary review of the application to ensure compliance with procedural rules, liaises with the relevant parties in the case, and proposes to the President of the Court whether a case should be dismissed. The decision-making is kept firmly within the mandate of the judges through procedural steps, which we will discuss in further detail below. Two other divisions work for the institution as a whole: the Directorate-General of Multilingualism, which provides language services to the CJEU; and the Research and Documentation Directorate, which undertakes the filtering function,[64] conducts comparative research on a question of law, and collates the jurisprudence across Member States and even other jurisdictions.

In contrast, référendaires are legal secretaries to the judges and Advocates General that form their cabinets. The judges and Advocates General of the ECJ presently have four référendaires each. In the General Court, each judge is assigned two référendaires, and each Chamber of five judges is assigned two additional référendaires. Each of these additional référendaires is shared between two judges in the Chamber, and the President of each Chamber has an additional référendaire to assist them with their functions. The respective judges and Advocates General have complete discretion in the selection of their référendaires, who are formally appointed by the general meeting of the Court.[65] This framework allows the judges strengthen their decision-making

63 Caroline Heeren, "The Court of Justice of the European Union" in Freya Baetens, ed, *Legitimacy of Unseen Actors in International Arbitration* (Cambridge: Cambridge University Press, 2019) 121 at 126.

64 This involves a review of the preliminary ruling applications and of some categories of appeals brought before the ECJ.

65 Daniel Sarmiento, "Référendaire: Court of Justice of the European Union" in Hélène Ruiz Fabri, ed, *Max Planck Encyclopedia of International Procedural Law*, (Oxford: Oxford University Press, 2018) at para 22. The official appointment is purely a formality, as the general meeting seems to have never rejected a référendaire. However, this does not imply that every single référendaire proposed by a Judge/Advocate General

function through individual assistants that are solely within their control, accountable to them, and appointed through a transparent selection process. Further, in terms of accountability, as in the case of WTO staff, the référendaires are also bound by a code of conduct, in addition to that generally applicable to the staff of the European Union.[66]

The balance between individual assistants for judges and an institutional office is reminiscent of the proposal made by the United States on improvement of the Appellate Body of the WTO in 2009.[67] They proposed, *inter alia*, that Appellate Body Members should be provided a law clerk in addition to the Appellate Body Secretariat staff. They stated that this would allow Appellate Body Members to be confident that they would have assistance in conducting the research and other work they consider important to their work and to elaborating their views.

d) Arbitration Institutions

We now turn to the practice of certain arbitration institutions that may provide guidance on improving the transparency in the functions undertaken by legal assistants. The majority of the arbitration institution rules provide that a tribunal secretary can only be appointed following consultation with[68] and consent of the parties.[69] For example, the 2015 Practice Note of the Singapore International Arbitration Centre (SIAC) provides that administrative secretaries may not be appointed without the consent of the parties; Article 15(5) of the Swiss Rules provides that the arbitral tribunal may, after consulting with the parties, appoint a secretary. Going further, the 2020 London Court

---

is accepted. The "rejection" will normally occur informally through the President/ Vice-President/President of Chamber warning the proposing Judge/Advocate General before the general meeting/plenary conference that the candidate they intend to propose may not be acceptable.

66 CJEU, *Décision du 17 février 2009 portant adoption des règles de bonne conduite des Référendaires* (entered into force 1 March 2009).

67 WTO, *Improvements for the Appellate Body: Proposal by the United States*, WTO Doc WT/DSB/W/398 (2009), online (pdf): docs.wto.org [perma.cc/L4MH-MRCN].

68 For example, the rules of the Hong Kong International Arbitration Centre (HKIAC), Singapore International Arbitration Centre (SIAC), Stockholm Chamber of Commerce (SCC), London Court of International Arbitration (LCIA), International Chamber of Commerce (ICC), Swiss Arbitration Centre (SAC), and ICSID.

69 HKIAC, *Guidelines on the Use of a Secretary to the Arbitral Tribunal* (2014), Guideline 2.1, online (pdf): hkiac.org [perma.cc/C9HL-E3FW]; SAC, *Guidelines for Arbitrators* (2021), art 16, online (pdf): swissarbitration.org [perma.cc/5BWD-9WLF].

of International Arbitration (LCIA) Arbitration Rules in their Article 14A set out a clear framework for the use of tribunal secretaries, expressly precluding any delegation of the decision-making function of the tribunal and stating that any tasks to be performed by the tribunal secretary must be expressly agreed to by the parties.[70] Such a requirement of consent by the parties for every aspect of the tasks performed by the tribunal secretary is also reflected in the Stockholm Chamber of Commerce (SCC) Arbitration Rules of 2023.[71] Further, under LCIA, the tribunal secretary is also subject to a continuing duty to disclose any circumstances that "are likely to give rise in the mind of any party to any justifiable doubts as to [their] impartiality or independence."[72]

In terms of accountability, in the PCA, ICSID, and the USMCA,[73] the legal assistants are bound by the same rules as the arbitrators, and their names are declared in the award/order. In the PCA and ICSID, individual assistants of the arbitrators are bound by the confidentiality of deliberations and proceedings[74] and must also sign the same declaration of independence and impartiality as the arbitrators.[75] In the USMCA, the assistants are bound by Article 9 of the Code of Conduct of USMCA, similar to staff members of the Secretariats (institutional office of USMCA).[76]

---

70   LCIA, *Arbitration Rules* (2020), arts 14.8, 14.10(i) and 14.11, online (pdf): lcia.org [perma.cc/5EA5-W872] [*LCIA Rules*].

71   SCC, *Arbitration Rules* (2023), art 24(2), online (pdf): sccarbitrationinstitute.se [perma.cc/3FUJ-7B9V].

72   *LCIA Rules*, above note 70, art 14.14.

73   Although the mechanism under Chapter 31 of the USMCA is not an arbitration institution, the process through which the disputes are resolved is arbitration and share practices with arbitration institutions under analysis. We are mindful of the differences between the other institutions in this category and the USMCA mechanism in this analysis.

74   ICSID, "Arbitration Rules" (2023) arts 34(1) and 66, online (pdf): icsid.worldbank.org [perma.cc/9XG3-BHZC].

75   ICSID, "Tribunal Assistants" (last visited 28 March 2025), online: icsid.worldbank.org [perma.cc/Z988-HKCJ].

76   USMCA, *Rules of Procedure for Chapter 31 (Dispute Settlement)*, art 5, online (pdf): ustr.gov [perma.cc/B9WK-NDLK], read with USMCA, *Code of Conduct*, art 9, online (pdf): can-mex-usa-sec.org [perma.cc/ZP4U-NQ5E].

2) Procedural Frameworks

a) The CJEU: Retention of Decision Making Through Face-to-Face Deliberations

In the CJEU, a very clear procedural framework emerges which ensures judges are firmly in charge of the decision-making, despite the référendaires undertaking all the drafting. The becomes evident first with respect to admissibility of cases: the Research and Documentation Directorate, as well as the Registry staff, undertake considerable work relating to admissibility of the cases before the CJEU. However, the decision-making is kept firmly within the purview of the adjudicators. For example, if the Registry staff finds that a case is manifestly inadmissible, they make a proposal to the President of the respective court with their recommendation. If the President agrees with their assessment, he assigns the case to a Judge Rapporteur. The Judge Rapporteur, after applying his independent judgement, makes a proposal for an order of dismissal to a Chamber of three judges. The procedure ensures that there are successive levels of decision-making solely within the purview of adjudicators.

The second layer of safeguards consists in the control exercised by the Judge Rapporteur over their individual assistants, i.e., référendaires. The Judge Rapporteur works with one of their référendaires in each case, who undertakes several functions, including drafting the preliminary report and the judgement. However, the Judge Rapporteur is firmly in control of the decision-making function despite not "holding the pen." There is evidence of this throughout the subsequent proceedings of both the ECJ and the General Court. For example, in cases where the opinion of an Advocate General is sought, the Judge Rapporteur is required to take a position with respect to the proposals in the opinion. In case of a difference of opinion, the President of the Chamber may conduct a "round table" with the other judges in the Chamber to understand their positions on the issues. This requires face-to-face interactions between the judges, where the legal assistants are not present to provide any additional assistance. It is only after such interactions that the Judge Rapporteur charges his référendaire with drafting a *projet de motifs* or a first draft of the judgment. In both the ECJ and the General Court, once the Judge Rapporteur finalizes the draft judgment (referred to as the *projet*), it is shared with the other judges in the Chamber. The other judges, with the assistance of their référendaires, send comments and notes on the *projet* to the Judge Rapporteur a few days before the deliberations.[77] Based on these inputs, the Judge Rapporteur instructs his référendaire to modify the *projet* into the *projet de motifs modifié,* and circulates the same to the other judges before the deliberation. Although there is considerable involvement of the référendaires at this drafting stage, the manner in which deliberations are conducted ensures that the judges are still in control of the decision-making function. The face-to-face deliberations conducted by the judges ensures that the judges themselves retain sufficient control over the final draft, and no other actor is able to exert unwarranted influence over the draft. As per the decisions taken during the deliberations, the Judge Rapporteur will instruct his/her référendaire to prepare a *projet d'arrêt,* incorporating all the final changes to the *projet de motifs modifié.* Therefore, the face-to-face interactions of the judges, in two stages, safeguards against claims that the legal assistants are encroaching on the decision-making functions despite drafting.

b) The ICJ: Balance in Functions Between the Registry and Individual Assistants

A similar robust process of drafting and deliberation exists in the ICJ. The first deliberation between the judges takes place immediately after the close of the oral procedure (it is referred to as the Article 3 Deliberation). The judges primarily discuss the List of Issues which is prepared by the Registry and approved by the President of the Court.[78] This document highlights the legal questions considered pertinent for the decision of the case and references to the sections of the pleadings and hearings where the parties raised an issue relating to one of the questions, known as the *précis.*[79] However, the judges are not just reliant on the List of Issues to guide them in their Article 3 Deliberations: the Associate Legal Officers of each judge prepare a memorandum for the hearing and revise it as per the oral proceedings, which will assist them in these deliberations. Subsequently, each judge prepares a Note in which they lay out their views on how the case should be decided. In this, they are

---

77 ECJ, *Rules of Procedure,* arts 32(1)–(2), online (pdf): eur-lex.europa.eu [perma. cc/9Q3M-GQUG].

78 Mamadou Hébié, "Des ombres furtives au Palais de la Paix?: Coup de projecteur sur les assistants juridiques des membres de la Cour internationale de Justice" in Jean-Marc Thouvenin & Jessica Joly Hébart, eds, *La Cour internationale de Justice à 75 ans* (Paris: Pedone, 2023) 73 at 77.

79 Higgins et al, *Oppenheim's International Law: United Nations* (Oxford: Oxford University Press, 2017) at para 29.169.

supported by their Associate Legal Officers and Judicial Fellows, who may for example do legal research on specific questions, draft memoranda for the Judge's attention or even draft part of the note. Once all the notes have been circulated, there is a second deliberation, known as the Article 5 Deliberation. Here, the case is discussed in more detail and each judge presents their Note. Once the majority view emerges and the general direction of the decision is decided,[80] the judges form a drafting committee out of the two members who in their estimation most cogently expressed the majority's views and the President. Therefore, there is a balance between the functions discharged by the institutional assistants and individual assistants of the judges during the deliberations.

The Drafting Committee meetings are attended by the judges, along with the two Associate Legal Officers of the judges, the Special Assistant to the President, the Registrar, and the Head of the Department of Legal Matters accompanied by two staff lawyers.[81] The Registrar actively participates in the discussion and may address any questions relating to jurisprudence, procedure, or the previous practice of the Court. The assistants and lawyers from the Registry intervene only exceptionally, with the permission of their respective judge/Registrar. It is common practice to divide the drafting of the judgment between the two judges, who undertake drafting their respective parts independently.[82] judges may rely on all of their individual assistants to support them; however, this is dependent on the individual judge. Assistants rarely, if ever, draft significant parts of the judgment. Instead, they are tasked with drafting shorter sections on specific topics. The Registry typically drafts the procedural history of the case, the main facts and the summary of arguments (referred to as the *qualités*), which is usually prepared and circulated to the Court before the first deliberation and then updated.[83] For the highly important orders for provisional measures, the first draft is produced by the Department of Legal Matters, reviewed by the Registrar, and then approved by the President before circulation to the judges, who will carefully study the drafts and make substantial amendments.[84] Even during the drafting stage,

---

80   Bruno Simma & Jan Ortgies, "Deliberation and Drafting: International Court of Justice (ICJ)" in Ruiz Fabri, above note 65 at para 52.

81   *Ibid* at para 61.

82   *Ibid* at para 62.

83   Antoine Ollivier & Cristina Hoss, "Registry: International Court of Justice (ICJ)" in Ruiz Fabri, above note 65 at para 20.

84   Hébié, above note 78 at 78.

there is a division between the tasks undertaken by the institutional assistants and the individual assistants of the judges, such that the decision-making function is still firmly within the control of the judges.

The draft is thereafter circulated to all judges for line-by-line written comments. The Drafting Committee revises the draft, which is submitted to the plenary for another deliberation, referred to as the "first reading." All the judges meet physically to debate the draft and finalize it. The following legal assistants attend the first reading: the Special Assistant to the President, the two Associate Legal Officers of the judges in the drafting committee, the Registrar and some lawyers from the Department of Legal Matters. However, only the Registrar participates at this stage.[85] The Registry incorporates any agreed changes and circulates a revised draft with the judges. The final draft is discussed at the "second reading," at the end of which the judges vote to produce the final judgment or advisory opinion.[86] At this final stage of deliberations, a similar procedural safeguard to that of the CJEU emerges, where the Drafting Committee and the remaining judges must justify their positions directly without inputs from their legal assistants.

Both the above institutions provide procedural steps during the proceedings of a case that strengthen the position of the adjudicator *vis-à-vis* the legal assistants, while also ensuring that they are benefitting from the assistance offered by such actors. While the longer timelines for completion of a case in the ICJ and CJEU allow for such robust mechanisms to be put in place, this should not discourage the WTO dispute settlement system from looking to such procedures. Some of the WTO reform proposals already provide guidance on changes that can facilitate these robust procedures: the first EU Proposal on Appellate Body Reform[87] proposes an amendment to the nine-day timeframe for Appellate Body reports provided in Article 17.5 of the DSU. It suggests allowing the parties to consent to a relaxation on the nine-day time frame.

---

85   Hébié, above note 78 at 87.

86   ICJ, "Resolution Concerning the Internal Judicial Practice of the Court" (last visited 2 June 2025) art 8(i), online: icj-cij.org [perma.cc/F8G4-9M5D].

87   WTO, *Communication from European Union, China, Canada, Norway, New Zealand, Switzerland, Australia, Republic of Korea, Iceland, Singapore and Mexico, to the General Council*, WTO Doc WT/GC/W/752 (2018), online (pdf): docs.wto.org [perma.cc/PM3S-4RBN].

E. Conclusion

THE AIM OF THIS CHAPTER has been to briefly point to the institutional structure and practice of other international adjudicatory bodies that can illuminate the role of legal assistants in these institutions. These comparative practices can also strengthen some of the proposals made in the Report by the Convenor of Informal DS Reform Discussions[88] relating to the scope of support provided by Secretariat staff.[89]

While we have refrained from going into the merits of the concerns raised about the role of the Secretariat in the WTO dispute settlement system, it would be a disservice to conclude this chapter without reiterating the importance of the role of legal assistants. A Secretariat that is hidden, unaccountable, and exercises undue influence over adjudicators in their decision-making function is unacceptable. However, we believe that is also not the reality of the WTO Secretariat as it stands today. There is ample evidence in the jurisprudence of the WTO dispute settlement system that the WTO Secretariat is very careful in exercising its functions. We borrow Valerie Hughes's example illustrating this point:[90] the panel reports in *US—Clove Cigarettes, US—Tuna II (Mexico),* and *US—COOL* were issued within weeks of each other and addressed similar issues under the *Technical Barriers to Trade (TBT) Agreement.* We agree with Valerie on the reason why these three reports failed to provide a uniform legal view on how the respective provisions of the TBT Agreement should be interpreted: because they reflected the views of the particular panel that decided the issue and not necessarily the views of the LAD teams who assisted them.

---

88   WTO, *Special Meeting of the General Council,* WTO Doc JOB/GC/385 (2024), online (pdf): docs.wto.org [perma.cc/R7GR-KQSW] [WTO, *Special Meeting of the General Council*]. See also Marco Tulio Molina Tejeda's contribution to this volume (Chapter 28).

89   WTO, *Special Meeting of the General Council* at Title VII.

90   Hughes, above note 10.

Reflections on the Appellate Body

CHAPTER 8

Building the Appellate Body: Lessons from the US Archives for Today's Dispute Settlement Crisis

Simon Lester

A. Introduction

IN A CAREER MARKED WITH great accomplishments, two positions that Valerie Hughes held stand out: Director of the World Trade Organization (WTO)'s Appellate Body Secretariat and Director of the WTO's Legal Affairs Division. She is the only person to have served in both positions, which play a crucial role in the WTO's dispute settlement system.

Prior to the establishment of the WTO, there were concerns that *General Agreement on Tariffs and Trade* (GATT) panels sometimes produced low-quality reports with inferior legal reasoning. To address this problem, during the Uruguay Round governments created the Appellate Body to provide second-tier review of the lower-tier panels. Under this new institutional structure, in the WTO system, the Legal Affairs Division (along with the Rules Division) took the lead in advising panels, and the Appellate Body Secretariat advised the Appellate Body. Based on her role as Director of each, Valerie has the unique experience of having been the lead adviser to both panels and the Appellate Body.

Unfortunately, this new system has recently run into serious trouble. While initially supportive of the Appellate Body, the United States later began a sustained critique of the institution, citing a number of its rulings and practices. This critique culminated with the United States blocking appointments to the Appellate Body, leaving the system only partially functional today.

The current US position on the Appellate Body is a marked change from its original one. My research in the US National Archives shows that the United States was one of the leaders in creating the Appellate Body. As part of this process, Office of the United States Trade Representative (USTR) officials were well aware of potential issues related to the role of the Appellate Body and discussed them with their colleagues and with other WTO Members. A series of internal messages documents these discussions in great detail and provides insights on some of the current debates on the role of appellate review in WTO dispute settlement.

B. The Problem: "Legally Unsound" Panel Reports

IN THE EARLIEST USTR MESSAGES about the issue of appellate review, the problem governments were addressing was made clear: Some GATT panel reports were thought to be "legally unsound." The first of the USTR messages that mentions the possibility of introducing an appeals process for GATT dispute settlement—from Jane Bradley to Dorothy Dwoskin, dated 20 July 1989—states: "Possibly: establishment of a mechanism to review panel findings upon request (in effect, an appeals process), to avoid the problem of legally unsound reports."[1]

A 5 April 1990 message from Bradley to Chris Parlin elaborates on the "problems encountered" with GATT panel reports. It notes that under GATT dispute settlement procedures, there is a process by which panels can review the factual portion of their reports, but there is no effective review for the legal reasoning in the report:

> If one of the parties believes the panel has made an error on the factual
> portion of the panel report, that error usually is corrected before the

---

1   Jane Bradley to Dorothy Dwoskin (20 July 1989) via DG Mail.

final report is issued. If a party believes there is an error of law, however, that party's only recourse under current procedure is to argue before the full GATT Council that the report is fatally flawed and should not be adopted. Most members of the Council will not have studied carefully the issues examined by the panel, nor researched the legal questions at issue. Thus, a sufficient review of the panel's reasoning is unlikely to occur in such a forum.[2]

Bradley's point was that review of panel reports by the GATT Council was insufficient to address the problem of low-quality legal reasoning in panel reports. Something else was needed.

C. Solutions: Two Kinds of Review

AMONG THE SOLUTIONS PROPOSED TO address the problem of low-quality panel reports were two forms of review. The focus of this chapter is appellate review, but there was also a proposal for "interim" review, under which the parties could provide comments to the panel on the legal reasoning in its report, and the panel could revise its report based on those comments. The idea for this interim review came from Canada, which made the proposal based on a similar procedure in the *Canada-United States Free Trade Agreement*.

The interim review and appellate review processes were seen by USTR officials as complementary. A message from Bradley to Parlin on 7 December 1989 notes that interim review could make appellate review less necessary: "Require that panels issue an interim report (including findings and conclusions) to the parties for comment, in advance of issuing a final report, to help reduce the potential for the parties to request [appellate] review."[3]

USTR tried to formally link interim review and appellate review, by conditioning the right to appeal on having made an interim review request. A 19 September 1990 message from Parlin to Bradley sets out some draft text that spells out the connection that USTR envisioned for tying an appellate review request to an interim review request: "A party to a dispute that has raised objections to the reasoning and legal basis of the panel's findings or conclusions pursuant to the interim review procedures . . . may seek review by the

---

2   Jane Bradley to Chris Parlin (5 April 1990) via DG Mail [5 April 1990 Communication 2].
3   Jane Bradley to Chris Parlin (7 December 1989) via DG Mail [7 December 1989 Communication].

Appellate Review Body."[4] Ultimately, the US proposal was rejected, and while interim review was incorporated into WTO dispute settlement, the Dispute Settlement Understanding (DSU) does not require an interim review request in order to appeal a panel report.

D. Key Issues in the Establishment of Appellate Review

IN CRAFTING AN APPELLATE REVIEW mechanism, there were a number of foundational issues that were discussed by USTR officials and the GATT contracting parties. They are set out below in the following categories:

- Structure of the Appellate Body: Who are the appellate "panelists," and who is the appellate secretariat?
- Scope of appellate review: How often would it be used, and what issues will be heard on appeal?
- Reversals of panel rulings: Will there be remand/completing the analysis?

1) Structure of the Appellate Body: Who Are the Appellate "Panelists," and Who is the Appellate Secretariat?

a) The Appellate Body Members

SOME OF THE KEY QUESTIONS in establishing an appellate review mechanism were; who would conduct the appellate review and what form of institution would appellate review involve? In a message from Bradley to Parlin on 7 December 1989, it is stated that the United States "seeks other delegations' views" about certain options that should be explored, including the following thoughts on the structure of the appellate review body as a "standing tribunal" or a "roster" to draw from:

> Consider whether to establish a standing tribunal for such review, or a roster of panelists (comprised of individuals who have served on several panels, whose opinions have proven sound), from which the Director General would select an appellate panel on a case-by-case basis[5]

---

4   Chris Parlin to Jane Bradley (19 September 1990) via DG Mail [19 September 1990 Communication].

5   7 December Communication, above note 3.

This issue gets at the nature of the institution that would be created, which is one of the points that has recently raised concerns for the United States. The United States now worries that the creation of a permanent institutional body led to the expansion of power by the Appellate Body, manifesting itself in procedural and substantive decisions that have been bad for the trading system.[6]

At the 5 April 1990 meeting of the Uruguay Round dispute settlement negotiating group, a Secretariat note explains that the European Communities (EC) representative said that "members of an Appellate Body should be distinguished people with professional experience in trade policy, that the authority of an Appellate Body would have to be hard to question."[7] It also states that "[t]he United States was looking at both a standing appeal body, as suggested by the European Communities, and a roster of appellate panelists."[8] A message from Bradley to Parlin on that same day then provides a text submitted by the EC, including the following on composition of the appeals body:

> The composition and operation of this appeals body should be authoritative. It should, therefore, be made up a small number of eminent figures known for their in-depth knowledge of trade policy issues and their professional experience of legal and economic problems. They should be appointed for a sufficient length of time by the GATT Council on proposals for the Director General or contracting parties.[9]

A message from Parlin to Bradley on 23 May 1990 provides details on a Quad discussion of these issues, with two options noted:

1. Lacarte Proposal:
   - Standing body of 3 eminent panelists
   - 7 alternates who serve sequentially (order drawn by lot)
   - All 10 panelists receive panel documents
   - All panelists serve for 2–3 years and their selection is negotiated

---

6   See USTR, *Report on the Appellate Body of the World Trade Organization* (Washington, DC: Office of the United States Trade Representative, 2020), online (pdf): ustr.gov [perma.cc/JHU7-JJB9] [*USTR Appellate Body Report*].

7   GATT, *Note by the Secretariat*, GATT Doc MTN.GNG/NG13/19 (1990) at para 7, online (pdf): docs.wto.org [perma.cc/5AX5-9YBG].

8   *Ibid* at para 8.

9   Jane Bradley to Chris Parlin (5 April 1990) via DG Mail [5 April 1990 Communication 1].

2. Alternative Proposal:
   - Standing body of 3-5 panelists designated by [contracting parties][10]

A 30 May 1990 message from Bradley to Suzanne Troje then notes the following on composition of the Appellate Body and the appointment of the appellate panelists:

> The composition of the Appellate Body would be decided by a consensus of the contracting parties, not by appointment by the Director General. Further consideration should be given to the EC's proposal for a standing body of 3 or 5 permanent panelists, and to a procedure suggested by Ambassador Lacarte, Chairman of the Dispute Settlement Negotiating Group. Under the Lacarte proposal, a standing body of 3 appellate panelists would be selected to serve two-year terms, along with 6 or 7 alternates (in an order drawn by lot) who would serve sequentially if one of the 3 panelists could not serve.[11]

And a 19 September 1990 message from Parlin to Bradley sets out draft text related to appellate review:

Appellate Mechanism
Establishment of Appellate Review Body

1. The CONTRACTING PARTIES shall establish a standing Appellate Review Body to review panel reports. The Body shall be established for an initial period of three years. At the end of that period, the Appellate Review Body may be extended by the Contracting Parties for such period as they may decide. The Body shall consist of three Members, one of whom shall be chosen by lot to be Chairman, and four Alternates. The Members constitute the Appellate Review Body for each dispute sent to appeal. In the event a Member is unable to take part in the review of a particular dispute, that Member shall be replaced by an Alternate chosen by lot.

2. Members and Alternates shall be appointed by the Director General in consultation with interested contracting parties. Members and Alternates shall be unaffiliated with any government and possess demonstrated expertise in GATT law and experience in GATT

---

10 Chris Parlin to Jane Bradley (23 May 1990) via DG Mail [23 May 1990 Communication].
11 Jane Bradley to Suzanne Troje (30 May 1990) via DG Mail [30 May 1990 Communication].

panel procedures. They shall possess the highest degree of personal integrity and objectivity and shall not take any instructions from any Government. Members and Alternates shall serve terms of three years.[12]

The foundations of the controversy now confronting the dispute settlement system can be seen here, with the role of the GATT Contracting Parties versus the role of the Director General in appointments having a real impact. With the power to appoint ultimately given to the Dispute Settlement Body, the consensus requirement has allowed one Member, the United States, to block the appointments process and stop the Appellate Body from operating. If the Director General had been given the power to make appointments in the absence of consensus (as is the case with the appointment of panelists), the situation today could have been very different.

A 5 May 1991 message from Bradley to Parlin further discusses the expertise of those who might serve on the Appellate Body, as well as its composition:

Again, we envision only one Appellate Body for all cases, all with general GATT law expertise. We have skirted the issue of composition up til now, and you might try to draw out others' views. I do see a problem if you are going to try to be sure there is diverse expertise on the Appellate Body, because I'm afraid your Appellate Body would look like this: one veterinarian, one patent examiner, one telecommunications standards techie, two traditional GATTologists, one Customs specialist, and one dumping margin expert (is there such a thing?)! I don't jest when I say I think the Appellate Body should be entirely composed of former appellate judges, or at least all lawyers, but that's not a popular proposal.[13]

Ultimately, questions related to the expertise and the diversity of Appellate Body appointments did not prove too daunting to handle. The first group of Appellate Body Members had a mix of backgrounds and regions represented, and that continued on in future iterations. The objections from the United States came, instead, from concerns about the behaviour and substantive positions taken by the Appellate Body, which formed the basis of a critique of the institution itself.

---

12   19 September 1990 Communication, above note 4.
13   Jane Bradley to Chris Parlin (5 May 1991) via DG Mail.

b) The Appellate Body Secretariat

WITH REGARD TO STAFF ASSISTANCE to the Appellate Body, there was a brief discussion of this point in the USTR messages. A 5 April 1990 message from Bradley to Parlin provides a text submitted by the EC that states: "The body would be assisted by a small team independent from the GATT Secretariat."[14] And a message from Parlin to Bradley on 23 May 1990 notes the "Secretariat Role" and states: "Provide appeal panelists with secretary, research assistant and fax machine."[15] A 30 May 1990 message from Bradley to Troje then notes that: The Appellate Body would be served by an independent Secretary who would "perform administrative functions such as setting up panel meetings, notifying parties, collecting and distributing written submissions, etc. Further consideration should be given to whether the Appellate Body (or individual appellate panelists) should also have a research assistant for legal questions."[16]

In practice, the Secretariat role turned out to be more substantial, and this became one of the concerns about the Appellate Body. Some of the reform proposals put forward by Jennifer Hillman, a former Appellate Body Member, involve reducing the role of the Secretariat by putting limits on the time that people can serve in that role.[17]

2) Scope of Appellate Review: How Often Would It Be Used, and What Issues Will Be Heard on Appeal?

Turning to the scope of appellate review, there were several issues raised in the USTR discussions that relate to general thinking about the frequency of appeals as well as limits on what issues will be heard on appeal.

A major concern expressed by a number of governments during the Uruguay Round discussions was that an appeals process could be abused for the purpose of delay. Two messages on 3 October 1989 between Nena Scott and Bradley discussed an informal meeting on GATT dispute settlement hosted by Canada with the Quad countries that took place on 27 September, the day before a formal Dispute Settlement Negotiating Group meeting. One message notes the problem of appeals being used as a way to delay the implementation

---

14   5 April 1990 Communication 1, above note 9.
15   23 May 1990 Communication, above note 10.
16   30 May 1990 Communication, above note 11.
17   Jennifer Hillman, "A Reset of the World Trade Organization's Appellate Body" (January 2020), online: cfr.org [perma.cc/X7CU-ZMHS].

of adverse findings: "[T]here was general agreement that any general right to appeal would result in virtually every panel report being reviewed, since countries would find it too difficult politically to implement panel findings without first exhausting all procedural avenues."[18] Along the same lines, in a GATT Secretariat note on the Negotiating Group on Dispute Settlement's meeting of 28 September, one government "cautioned against a standing appeal procedure, noting that the availability of such a procedure would result in virtually every case being appealed."[19]

These concerns reflect a different perspective than what is often heard today, which is that Uruguay Round negotiators expected appeals to happen only rarely.[20] In practice, the concerns expressed about the appeal process being overused proved to prophetic, as the actual appeal rate during the life of the Appellate Body was around 69 percent.[21] In contrast to how things turned out, it is clear that at the time of the negotiations, many governments wanted the number of appeals to be limited. Canada set out its position in a communication on 28 June 1990, stating the following with regard to the kinds of issues that should be reviewed on appeal:

> In rare cases, where a party to a dispute considered, despite the review by the panel, that a report was so fundamentally flawed that it should not be accepted, the GATT dispute settlement system should provide for a means of correcting errors. The addition of an appellate mechanism would serve that purpose. The intent would not be to have appellate review become a quasi-automatic step in the dispute settlement process. Rather, in those cases where a party to a dispute considered that the panel had made a fundamental error in interpretation of rights and obligations, that party could ask for appellate review.[22]

---

18   Nena Scott to Jane Bradley (3 October 1989) via DG Mail.

19   GATT, *Note by the Secretariat*, GATT Doc MTN.GNG/NG13/16 (1989) at para 21, online (pdf): docs.wto.org [perma.cc/N3UF-L5CK].

20   See, e.g., Debra P Steger, "The Founding of the Appellate Body" in Gabrielle Marceau, ed, *A History of Law and Lawyers in the GATT/WTO* (Cambridge: Cambridge University Press, 2015) 447.

21   WorldTradeLaw.net, "Proportion of Circulated Panel Reports That Have Been Appealed" (last visited 25 March 2025), online (pdf): worldtradelaw.net [perma.cc/C9QH-CMXU].

22   GATT, *Communication from Canada*, GATT Doc MTN.GNG/NG13/W/41 (1990) at 4, online (pdf): docs.wto.org [perma.cc/J8HE-MAR5].

But as noted, there were strong concerns that the actual practice could be very different. To address the concerns about overuse of the appeals process, USTR officials put forward a number of suggestions. In a message from Bradley to Parlin on 7 December 1989, USTR mentioned "a mechanism for a time-limited review (perhaps in 30 days)."[23] Such a short period would presumably constrain the appeals body's ability to carry out a detailed review and thus might discourage appeals. The eventual DSU language extended this review period to sixty days, and ninety on an exceptional basis, with the ninety days turning out to be the default period in practice. Over time, however, the Appellate Body began extending the period considerably beyond ninety days,[24] and this is one of the issues over which the United States expressed concern.[25]

The same USTR message also mentions "procedures that would discourage losing parties from routinely using the review process" and said there should be a consideration of "whether appeal should be automatic or whether there should be a screening process."[26] And in a follow-up message from Bradley to Parlin on 5 April 1990, Bradley says that a number of approaches to such review "can be envisioned" here, noting "[t]he right to review could be either automatic or granted by the Council."[27] If there were a standing review panel, she noted, "it could determine whether and what issues to review."[28]

A 5 April 1990 message from Bradley to Parlin entitled "EC Paper" then provides a text submitted by the EC, including the following language on appellate review suggesting that the appeals body would have discretion as to whether to hear the appeal:

> If one of the parties to the dispute felt that the legal considerations which led the panel to conclude that a violation of undertakings had taken place were erroneous or incomplete, it would have the option of taking its case to an appeals body, which would accept or reject the appeal depending on its assessment of its validity.[29]

---

23 7 December 1989 Communication, above note 3.

24 WorldTradeLaw.net, "Timing of Appeal, Circulation and Adoption of Appellate Body Reports" (last visited 25 March 2025), online (pdf): worldtradelaw.net [perma.cc/4RHJ-NQJV].

25 *USTR Appellate Body Report*, above note 6 at 29–32.

26 7 December 1989 Communication, above note 3.

27 5 April 1990 Communication 2, above note 2.

28 *Ibid.*

29 5 April 1990 Communication 1, above note 9.

And a message from Parlin to Bradley on 23 May 1990 then provides more details on the Quad discussions on this point. The message is entitled "Quad DS Options Paper" and describes a number of "Options That Were Discussed at Quad Meeting" on "Issues Related to an Appeals Process."[30] The first such issue was "Limiting Grounds for Appeal," with one possible limit set out in the form of discretion by the Appellate Body itself on what issues to hear: "Parties to the dispute pose questions on the legal findings of the panel report; the appeal body can decide which if any of these questions to address."[31] A 30 May 1990 message from Bradley to Troje then notes the following "[s]cenario being considered," which also involves discretion on the part of the Appellate Body as to whether to hear the appeal:

> In every dispute, any party to the dispute would be able to request an appellate review of the legal findings in a panel report, by framing specific questions to be presented to an Appellate Body. The Appellate Body would have discretion as to the scope of its review, including the ability to indicate that questions presented by the parties were frivolous.[32]

Along the same lines, there was the following statement by the EC on 19 July 1990 "The appeal body (but not the Council) would have the right to reject the request for an appeal if it judged that no issue of substance was being raised"[33]; and a 20 September 1990 message from Parlin reviews the 12–13 September meeting of the Dispute Settlement negotiating group, and notes that "[t]he EC argued that an appellate panel should have the right to reject a request for appeal."[34]

These suggestions continued deep into the negotiations. A message from Parlin to Bradley on 23 January 1991 contains a document entitled "Text on Dispute Settlement, 22 November 1990, Understanding on the Interpretation and Application of Articles XXII and XXIII 1 2."[35] A provision in this text describes in some detail the factors the Appellate Body may consider when deciding whether to accept an appeal.

---

30   23 May 1990 Communication, above note 10.

31   *Ibid.*

32   30 May 1990 Communication, above note 11.

33   GATT, *Statement by the Spokesman of the European Community*, GATT Doc MTN. GNG/NG13/W/44 (1990) at para 5, online (pdf): docs.wto.org [perma.cc/5BFA-JN7B] [emphasis in original] [*EC Statement*].

34   Chris Parlin (Message to Self) (20 September 1990) via DG Mail.

35   Chris Parlin to Jane Bradley (23 January 1991) via DG Mail.

In determining whether to accept an appeal, the Appellate Body may take into account, inter alia, such considerations as whether:

1. the panel report raises new issues of law which have not yet been considered and decided by the Appellate Body;

2. the issue is decided in a manner different from that of previous decisions;

3. the panel proceedings ignore procedural rights and obligations of the parties, in particular basic principles of due process of law as provided for in rules on GATT dispute settlement; or

4. the panel report is not consistent with the terms of reference. If the panel's findings in the final report have substantially changed, this limitation shall not apply.[36]

In addition to discretion about whether to accept an appeal, there was also consideration of allowing the Appellate Body to affirm an appeal without a hearing or detailed reasoning. A 2 July 1990 message from Parlin to Bradley and Dwoskin summarizes the views of the other three Quad members at a 25–26 June meeting, and notes that one issue was: "whether the appeals body could summarily affirm a panel report without a hearing."[37] On this issue, the EC view seemed to be that detailed reasoning would still be required in these circumstances: "All [delegates] agreed the appeals body could summarily affirm the panel, with [EU negotiator Bruno] Adinolfi saying that it would have to provide a full explanation of its reasons for so doing."[38]

Ultimately, issues related to Appellate Body discretion over which appeal issues to hear were a path not taken. In practice, the Appellate Body has not limited itself in any significant way. Arguably, the text of the DSU would allow the Appellate Body to affirm WTO panel findings and reasoning without further comment.[39] But the Appellate Body has not taken this approach, choosing to redo panel reasoning to a significant extent even where it agrees with the panel's ultimate conclusion. The Appellate Body's apparent view that it had to weigh in so extensively on appealed issues may have contributed to the later US concerns about judicial overreach.

---

36 *Ibid.*

37 Chris Parlin to Jane Bradley and Dorothy Dwoskin (2 July 1990) via DG Mail [2 July 1990 Communication].

38 *Ibid.*

39 Simon Lester, "WTO Dispute Settlement Misunderstandings: How to Bridge the Gap Between the United States and the Rest of the World" (19 April 2020), online (blog): ielp.worldtradelaw.net [perma.cc/YXT8-VNDA].

In the dispute settlement reform discussions currently underway, there has been no consideration of a "screening process," either through a US Supreme Court-style writ of *certiorari* or some lesser mechanism. But suggestions along these lines might be worth adding to the mix.[40]

Another issue related to the scope of appellate review is the Appellate Body's consideration of factual issues. This issue came up in the USTR discussions, with the 2 July 1990 message from Parlin to Bradley and Dwoskin noting: "All agreed that appeal should be limited to legal issues and interpretations (i.e., excluding facts and the recommendation)."[41]

However, a statement by the EC on 19 July 1990 noted that:

> It would be understood that appeals would be limited to legal issues and questions of interpretation arising out of panel reports. A written submission on the issues would be required. ...[42,43]

The EC seemed to be opening the door to appeals of factual issues here. And as it turned out, issues related to appeals of the facts have been another controversial point for the United States in recent years, as it has expressed concern that the Appellate Body is examining factual issues in ways not anticipated by the DSU drafters.[44]

3) Reversals of Panel Rulings: Will There Be Remand/Completing the Analysis?

If the Appellate Body were to reverse a panel's finding or legal reasoning, that would raise a question about what to do next. In this regard, the possibility of remanding the dispute back to the panel for further consideration was discussed. A message from Bradley to a number of USTR officials on 19 June 1991, entitled "Report on DS Quad," sets out a summary of the discussion of appellate review, including the tasking of follow-up papers, from the

---

40 Simon Lester, "Should a WTO Appeals Body Be Able to Uphold an Appealed Issue Without Any Reasoning?" (28 January 2024), online (blog): ielp.worldtradelaw.net [perma.cc/2XWB-TZS6]; Alan O Sykes, "The Utility of Appellate Review and its Optimal Structure" (2024) 27:3 *Journal of International Economics* 424.

41 2 July 1990 Communication, above note 37.

42 There might be one exception to this rule, where a Panel—despite the review process in para. 4—has maintained in its report a factual account which one party considers to be inaccurate and misleading

43 *EC Statement*, above note 33 at para 5, fn 1.

44 *USTR Appellate Body Report*, above note 6 at 37–40.

Meeting of Quad Dispute Settlement Negotiators in Washington, DC, 18–19 June 1991. It explains that the United States noted "several areas in which the Brussels text required modification, or at least rethinking," including this point on remand: "[S]houldn't H.2(d) specifically permit the Appellate Body to remand issues to the panel (the [United States] will prepare a paper on this prior to the next meeting)."[45] It later notes that the United States will propose "[p]ossible language on remand by [the] Appellate Body" in a paper to be circulated prior to 11 July.[46]

An 11 October 1991 message from Parlin to Bradley contains a number of "Suggested Modifications to Brussels Dispute Settlement Text," including a provision on remand:

> Appellate Body Remand to Panel
>   Modify para H.2.(d) of the Brussels text to read:
>   "The Appellate Body may uphold, modify or reverse the legal findings and conclusions of the panel, or remand the matter to the panel for further findings not inconsistent with the legal conclusions of the Appellate Body. Where the Appellate Body remands a matter, the panel shall issue a new report to the parties within [x] days. If one of the parties wishes to appeal the decision of the panel upon remand, the Appellate Body shall review only the new issues raised upon remand, and shall issue its report within [30] days."[47]

Ultimately, no such language was included in the DSU, and remand is not part of WTO dispute settlement.

> In the absence of remand, the Appellate Body came up with a workaround that it referred to as "completing the legal analysis." In a situation where it reversed the panel's reasoning, if it had sufficient facts before it, the Appellate Body would apply its reasoning to the facts of the case in order to determine whether a violation exists.[48] In a 20 May 1991 message, USTR official Ken Freiberg wrote to Bradley raising a number of questions about how appellate review would work in specific situations and in doing so anticipated the issue of completion of the legal analysis:

---

45   Jane Bradley to Robert Cassidy and Peg MacKnight (19 June 1991) via DG Mail.
46   *Ibid.*
47   Chris Parlin to Jane Bradley (11 October 1991) via DG Mail.
48   The Appellate Body first used this approach in *Canada—Certain Measures Concerning Periodicals (Complaint by the United States)* (1997), WTO Doc WT/DS31/AB/R at 23–24 (Appellate Body Report), online (pdf): docs.wto.org [perma.cc/24JM-2G45].

As I understand it, the Appellate Body ("AB") will be limited to reviewing questions of law and legal interpretations developed by the panel. If the AB doesn't agree with the panel's interpretation, the AB's only choices are to reverse or modify the panel's conclusions. I take this to mean that the AB must change the outcome if it finds an error of law.

I can imagine situations, however, in which the AB decides that the panel has applied the wrong legal test but the AB is not really in a good position to decide what the outcome would be if the correct test had been employed.

For example, suppose a party alleged a violation of Article III and the other party defended on the grounds that 1) there was no Art III violation and 2) anyway an Art XX exception applied. Suppose further that the panel agreed with the defending party that there was no Art III violation. Presumably, the panel would not necessarily go on to discuss the Art XX defense since any comments on that issue would be pure dictum. If the AB rules that the panel was wrong on the Art III issue, is it then required to go ahead and make a panel-like decision on whether the defending party qualified for an Art XX exception? What would happen in a case in which the party had not raised the Art XX before the panel or where the AB finds that the factual record is insufficient to decide whether the exception applied? Suppose the panel and the parties simply forgot about one key element to be applied in deciding whether there was a violation and so there was no factual record at all?

In such a case (and others) wouldn't it be necessary for the AB to remand the matter to the panel for further proceedings consistent with the AB's ruling? In other words, won't further factfinding and/or application of the facts to the law be necessary in some cases? Or do you intend to limit the legal issues that can be raised before the AB to those fully briefed (both factually and legally) below? If so, won't this lead to results unintended under the GATT?

If the AB simply must decide the case no matter what—and there is no possibility of remand—I suspect that panels will start to produce lots of dicta, since they will want to present their views on every contingency in the event the AB reverses them on one point or another. Another possibility is that parties (and the AB) will start to stretch the rule that only "legal" issues may be decided at the AB level.[49]

---

49   Ken Freiberg to Jane Bradley (20 May 1991) via DG Mail.

Freiberg's last two points have proven to be prescient. Panels have sometimes addressed issues beyond what was strictly necessary to resolve the dispute, in part due to concerns about Appellate Body reversals.[50] This has contributed to panel proceedings taking longer than they otherwise would have, and the timeframes for these proceedings have greatly exceeded what is set out in the DSU.[51] And on the point about appeals going beyond legal issues, as noted above, that has happened and has been raised by the United States as a concern.

C. Conclusions

GIVEN THE CURRENT CRISIS IN WTO dispute settlement, creative solutions are needed. It is possible that ideas from the original discussions could help with this. In addition to the points noted above, a 20 September 1990 message from Parlin reviewing the 12–13 September meeting of the dispute settlement negotiating group sets out an interesting avenue not ultimately taken in terms of the role of appellate review:

> There was an inconclusive discussion of what would constitute reversible error: Morocco stated that any legal error constitutes ground for reversal, while Canada, Switzerland and Chile suggested that the legal error must be fundamental or "manifest" to warrant a reversal.[52]

Perhaps a more deferential standard for determining that a panel has committed reversible error would keep the Appellate Body from intruding so often and so deeply into sensitive domestic political issues and generating resentment. Of course, panels might still do so, but they present less of an institutional target than the Appellate Body does: If governments are unhappy with a particular panel decision, they can simply decide not to appoint those panelists to future panels.

Along the same lines, perhaps giving the Appellate Body discretion over which appeals to hear, as discussed above, would have a similar effect. If the

---

50 See, e.g., *Indonesia—Importation of Horticultural Products, Animals and Animal Products (Complaint by New Zealand)* (2016), WTO Doc WT/DS477/R, WT/DS478/R (Panel Report), online (pdf): docs.wto.org [perma.cc/KA4H-2M9R].

51 WorldTradeLaw.net, "Timing of Establishment, Composition, Issuance and Circulation of WTO Panel Reports" (last visited 25 March 2025), online (pdf): worldtradelaw. net [perma.cc/3JMM-CEBE].

52 2 July 1990 Communication, above note 37.

Appellate Body used that discretion to affirm panel rulings except in cases of egregious error, there would be less of a concern with the institution exerting too much power.

The original drafters anticipated a lot of the potential problems that arose with regard to a WTO appeals process. It is now up to the next generation to resolve the current disagreements and create a path forward that can get WTO dispute settlement working again. A look back at the original discussions may help guide them.

CHAPTER 9

Valerie Hughes—The Light behind the Bushel of the Appellate Body of the WTO

A. V. Ganesan

A. Introduction

WALKING DOWN THE MEMORY LANE after nearly two decades, I wish to recall the immense, but inadequately recognized, contribution of Valerie Hughes in laying the foundation of the dispute settlement system in the formative years of the Appellate Body of the World Trade Organization. My association with Valerie Hughes almost coincided with my own appointment as a Member of the Appellate Body in June 2000 and her appointment as the Director of the Secretariat of the Appellate Body a few months later, and it lasted for over half of my eight-year tenure with the Appellate Body.

The Uruguay Round agreements, establishing the World Trade Organization (WTO) as an institution, marked a watershed in international economic and trade relationships due to the range of the areas and issues covered by the agreements, for example, agriculture, textiles, intellectual property rights, services, investment, trade remedy rules, and the dispute settlement mechanism. Given that coverage and given the lackadaisical dispute settlement record of the *General Agreement on Tariffs and Trade* (GATT), the developed countries, with the United States in the lead, were naturally keen to establish an effective and credible dispute resolution mechanism for the enforcement of the obligations incorporated in the new agreements. Although apprehensive and hesitant, the developing countries (and perhaps developed countries like Japan and South Korea also to some extent) were willing to subscribe to such a legal and binding dispute resolution mechanism if it would be the sole basis for determining an alleged violation of the agreements by any Member country. Their hope and expectation were that it might put an end to the unilateral action being taken by the United States under its domestic law, such as Section 301, and that the new mechanism alone would rule upon any violation of the obligations under the *Marrakesh Agreement Establishing the World Trade Organization* (WTO Agreement). A highly legalistic and elaborate system of rules was thus put in place, including an Appellate Body, for a binding and timely resolution of disputes. The new mechanism was a complete departure from the casual diplomacy and conciliation-oriented approach of the GATT 1947 for dispute resolution.

The Appellate Body was indeed a novel and suspect creature when it came into being in 1996 and had to prove itself as an unbiased, competent, and reliable organ for resolution of trade disputes in accordance with the provisions of the Dispute Settlement Understanding (DSU), especially Article 3.2. The DSU had provided the architecture, but the Appellate Body had to establish the structure brick by brick and earn the confidence of not only the WTO Members but also the wider trade, legal, and academic community.

B. Major Contributions of Valerie Hughes to the Evolution of WTO Law

VALERIE HUGHES ASSUMED THE LEADERSHIP of Appellate Body Secretariat at this critical juncture. Before Valerie Hughes came on the scene, the Appellate Body had held in *US—Gasoline* and *Japan—Alcoholic Beverages II* that the WTO treaty should not be read in "clinical isolation from public international law," that the fundamental rules of treaty interpretation are codified most authoritatively and succinctly in Articles 31 and 32 of the *Vienna Convention on the Law of Treaties* (VCLT), and that these two articles of the VCLT have attained the status of "customary rules of interpretation of public international law" as envisaged by Article 3.2 of the DSU. Valerie Hughes carried forward this approach and assisted the Appellate Body in a cogent, consistent, and logical usage of these two articles of the VCLT, especially Article 31. She was, however, wary and skeptical about the usage of Article 32 in the circumstances of the hazy negotiating history of the WTO Agreements.

Valerie Hughes clearly advocated a "textual approach" for the interpretation of the provisions of the covered agreements, mainly for the following reasons. The words of the treaty say, in their ordinary meaning, what the negotiators of the treaty agreed to. Going beyond the words ran the risk of adding to or diminishing the rights and obligations envisaged under the agreements, which is forbidden explicitly by Article 3.2 of the DSU. Valerie Hughes regularly attended the meetings of the Dispute Settlement Body when it discussed the Appellate Body reports and gave feedback to the Appellate Body Members on the concerns expressed by the WTO Members. The most common criticism from the losing party (and its supporting third parties) was that the Appellate Body had overreached and had added obligations not accepted or intended by the negotiators. The winning party (or its supporting third parties) seldom rebutted this allegation, as it may say the same thing when it loses a case.

Valerie had the knowledge and the foresight to see that the WTO Agreements were consciously woven into a "single undertaking," implying that all the agreements were integrated in a single coherent package. WTO Members, big or small, had given concessions under one or more agreements in order that they gain advantages in one or more other agreements. A textual approach would more likely ensure that this carefully crafted balance of give and take across the board is not unwittingly unravelled.

As a part of the approach to avoiding the criticism that the Appellate Body has written into the agreements new obligations not envisaged by the negotiators, Valerie Hughes was keen that the Appellate Body should say only what needed to be said minimally to resolve the dispute at hand and nothing more extravagantly. She was of the view that expansive statements of law or principles, or *obiter dicta*, not necessary or relevant to rule on the dispute, should be eschewed as they may set off unforeseen consequences in a subsequent dispute. She felt that the Appellate Body should avoid as far as possible the need to explain their earlier statements and distinguish them in a subsequent case. Ruling only on what needed to be ruled upon, and nothing more, would be a safeguard against this possibility. In this cautionary approach, she had a strident supporter in Julio Lacarte, the doyen of GATT and WTO law.

Valerie was certainly not in favour of the philosophy of "judges creating or advancing the law" in the circumstances of the WTO treaty and the mandate given to the Appellate Body. She cautioned against the inclination of some Members of the Appellate Body to push the boundaries of the provisions of the agreements, albeit ever so slightly, to support the current thinking on economic, environmental, or other issues. She felt that any such attempt would further aggravate the criticism that the Appellate Body was overstepping its mandate and was expanding the obligations undertaken by the Member countries.

C. Other Contributions of Valerie Hughes to the Efficient Functioning of the Appellate Body and its Secretariat

1) Issues Paper Preparation

The Secretariat of the Appellate Body prepares an Issues Paper in every case to assist the Members of the Appellate Body in their discussions. Basically, it sets out the facts of the case, the gist of the submissions of the parties and third parties, the relevant previous reports of the Appellate Body, and the substantive issues that arise for consideration. The Issues Paper does not, however, offer any opinion or advice on those issues. Valerie Hughes paid great attention to the preparation of the Issues Paper as it was important for a proper discussion in the Exchange of Views among Appellate Body Members. She took great pains in the preparation of the Paper and guided the Secretariat staff in understanding and highlighting all the issues raised in the dispute by the parties and third parties.

2) Exchange of Views

The Exchange of Views is a very important mechanism devised by the Appellate Body Members for a meaningful discussion of each and every case that comes before the Appellate Body. It takes place after the division hearing a case has completed its oral hearing. All the seven Members of the Appellate Body take part in the Exchange of Views. It ensures that the views of all the Members of the Appellate Body are brought to bear upon each and every case. Not only all the written submissions of the parties, but also the Issues Paper and the transcript of the oral hearing are made available to each Member of the Appellate Body.

Valerie Hughes invariably made a valuable contribution in the discussion of both the legal and factual issues arising in a case. She was particularly at her forte in the examination of the legal issues, including the proper application of Articles 31 and 32 of the VCLT and in ensuring that all the legal issues raised by the parties are addressed without fail and that, moreover, a consistency was maintained with previous rulings of the Appellate Body. Given her legal acumen and her objectivity in addressing the issues involved, her views invariably carried great respect with the Appellate Body Members.

3) Scrutiny and Issue of the Final Report of the Appellate Body

Valerie Hughes played a crucial role in a thorough scrutiny of the final report of the Appellate Body and in ensuring that the report was issued as per the law within the prescribed time limit. Although it was the responsibility of the Division hearing a case to formulate and issue a report, Valerie Hughes used to pay meticulous attention to its proper drafting, especially from the legal angle and to ensure that it addressed all the issues involved and was internally cogent and consistent.

4) Management of the Appellate Body Secretariat

Valerie Hughes assumed charge of the Appellate Body Secretariat at a critical time and had to contend with several issues, not only in guiding the Secretariat staff in understanding the legal issues, but also in raising their morale and in their working as a cooperative team. She honed their drafting skills and infused confidence in their abilities, with the result that she could leave a well-knit unit at the time of her departure. Her legacy was carried forward by her successor Werner Zdouc, who worked with her closely in those years. The assistance provided by the Appellate Body Secretariat is vital to the functioning of the Appellate Body and the credit for building up an efficient and reliable Secretariat in the formative years of the Appellate Body must go in a large measure to Valerie Hughes.

5) Some Personal Reflections

The Members of the Appellate Body, including me, had a high regard for the legal knowledge, competence, and objectivity of Valerie Hughes. Her views and opinions were therefore listened to seriously even when the Appellate Body chose, on rare occasions, to differ from them. On a personal plane, I had a warm and friendly relationship with her that is subsisting until today, benefitted as I was by both her legal skills and large-hearted nature. She knew that I was not an international legal expert, as others in the Appellate Body were, and that my strength lay in my knowledge and understanding of the way the WTO Agreements worked at the national levels. She therefore thought that I could be a good sounding board for establishing the facts of the dispute to which the WTO law was to be applied. This was perhaps because in most cases, the interpretation and application of the WTO law did not pose much of a problem, as there were enough precedents and previous rulings for guidance, but the facts to which the law was to be applied were unique to each case and were often in dispute.

In a lighter vein, I wish to add that she used to check with me whether the footnotes in the submissions of the parties and the draft Appellate Body report were correct and in order. Footnotes were galore in those days in WTO reports and the Members of the WTO used to joke that the Appellate Body had made the Concise Oxford Dictionary and footnotes as a part of the covered agreements and that more was stated or concealed in the footnotes rather than in the main body of the Appellate Body reports. I had a penchant for looking at the footnotes not only for their accuracy but also for their stating something that ought to have been stated, or not stated, in the main body of the report. For Valerie Hughes, I was the footnote Member of the Appellate Body for more reasons than one!

In an even lighter vein, I recall the BMW Roadster car in which Valerie used to come to her WTO office. Valerie is of a tiny build and she and her car were nicely made for each other. I used to joke with her that she could carry the car in her bag into her office without much of a problem instead of trying to park and locate it in the WTO premises.

I last met Valerie in Geneva in 2015 when I was in the WTO as the Chairman of a dispute settlement panel (if I may reveal, on the persuasion of Valerie) and also to attend a WTO seminar on the negotiating history of the *Agreement on Trade-Related Aspects of Intellectual Property Rights* (TRIPS Agreement). It is not easy for me to forget the days we spent together at the Appellate Body and her enormous contribution to the building up of the WTO dispute settlement system as it was envisaged by the DSU.

6) Present Status of the WTO Dispute Settlement System

Alas, the dispute settlement system as established in those halcyon days is in tatters now. Many say that it has become a victim of its own success. Mike Moore, the then Director General of the WTO, called it the jewel in the crown of the WTO. In my eight years (2000–08) at the Appellate Body, nearly sixty-five disputes were settled by the Appellate Body within the time limit of ninety days. The rulings were by and large accepted by the trade, legal, and academic community as fair, impartial, and in accordance with the provisions of the WTO Agreements. Legalization of the obligations to be observed and judicialization of the dispute resolution mechanism found favour in international economic relations in those days. That gave birth to the WTO Agreements and the dispute resolution mechanism. But the pendulum has swung the other way now with almost all nations now wanting to reassert their national sovereignty in their trade and economic policies. The contours of international trade have also been changing dramatically with the growth in digital commerce and developments in the technological field. A time will come soon to reveal that the Uruguay Round agreements of the WTO have become outdated. Both the issues to be addressed in international trade and the skills of the judges to address them in the event of a dispute will be of a different nature. In such a situation, the resurrection of the Appellate Body of the olden days is extremely unlikely. But whatever be the new kind of dispute resolution mechanism that may be put in place, it would need experts of the calibre and commitment of Valerie Hughes.

WTO Dispute Settlement and Developing Countries

Some Developing Countries Are More Equal Than Others: The Enduring Challenge of Making Trade Dispute Settlement Work for All

Mateo Diego-Fernández Andrade[*]

Only a few people know that Valerie Hughes spent her childhood years in Mexico City.

A. A Tribute to Valerie

I FIRST MET VALERIE HUGHES in 1997 at an Asia-Pacific Economic Cooperation (APEC) meeting in Bangkok, Thailand. Even though I had heard her name many times before, I did not know what to expect from her. By then she was already a legend. Valerie does not know that yet, but that meeting

---

[*] Founding partner at Agon, member of the MPIA, and the roster of panelists of *Canada-United States-Mexico Agreement* (CUSMA) Chapter 31. The author wishes to thank Messrs. Angel López, Roberto Zapata, Eduardo Díaz, and Carlos Vejar for their comments to this chapter. All errors are entirely attributable to me.

changed my life. This is when I learned that I wanted to do international trade disputes, which is what, twenty-seven years later, I still do.

Coming from a developing country to the international arena can be challenging. I first arrived in Geneva as a Mexican delegate one year after this APEC meeting and got the impression—rightly so—that everyone was better prepared than me. I noticed everyone spoke a secret language full of acronyms, shared memories of negotiating rounds that took place when I was still at school, and talked with great familiarity about people whose names I had only read in the news or academic papers.

As time went by, I started to learn the acronyms, met some of these larger-than-life figures and acquired experience as a negotiator. It was just then that I became aware of how lucky I was. I belonged to a mid-sized delegation that was reasonably active in disputes, most of them as a third party. This allowed me to witness from relative safety how cases were argued; to meet people like Julio Lacarte, Georges Abi-Saab or Giorgio Sacerdoti in action; and to start earning flight hours. This gave me an edge over smaller delegations, whose delegates divided their time between the World Trade Organization (WTO), UN Trade and Development (UNCTAD), Human Rights Council, World Health Organization (WHO), World Intellectual Property Organization (WIPO) and many, many other meetings. It also gave me an advantage over delegations with focused trade interests, like sugar, or cotton. Me, one day I would attend a hearing of a dispute over anti-dumping duties, the next day I would be hearing arguments about Article XX exceptions, and the week after I would learn about grandfathering clauses.

This is where I found Valerie again, as she went to Geneva to take the position of Director of the Appellate Body Secretariat. Our time together there cemented our friendship, which has endured her return to Ottawa, my return to Mexico City, her going back to Geneva as Head of the Legal Affairs Division, our respective exits from the government, and lastly, our designations as members of the Multi-Party Interim Appeal Arbitration Arrangement (MPIA) pool of arbitrators.

Throughout the years, Valerie has always been the same intelligent, down-to-earth, Canadian woman with a great sense of humour, who not only knows what she is talking about but who can easily anticipate everyone's next move and direct any discussion toward consensus. I have always strived to absorb all the knowledge I can from our interactions, and my admiration for her is immense, both intellectually and personally. Did I mention how funny she is?

This chapter is intended to serve as a tribute to her enormous contributions to the multilateral trading system and international trade in general.

B. What Is a Developing Country?

DURING MY TIME IN GENEVA, I always fought to make the point that Mexico was a developing country, and no one could strip that status away from us. The concept was clear: there are three types of countries: developed, developing, and Least Developed Countries (or LDCs). However, the boundaries between these categories were not as clear.

LDCs are defined by the UN's Economic and Social Council (ECOSOC), based on criteria such as Gross National Income (GNI), human assets index, and economic and environmental vulnerability.[1] There are currently forty-four countries with this condition, most of them in Africa.[2]

Developing countries, on the other hand, are self-designated. For example, all countries in the Latin American region claim to be developing countries and enjoy the benefits granted by the plethora of special and differential treatment (SDT) clauses contained in various agreements.[3] However, one would ask: why is a country like Brazil or Mexico treated the same way as El Salvador or Suriname? No one can deny that all these countries face challenges of an economic, social, and environmental nature, among others. However, it is difficult to reconcile the idea of treating equally a country like Mexico, an Organisation for Economic Co-operation and Development (OECD) Member, with a Gross Domestic Product (GDP) of USD 1.79 trillion[4] and active participation in the automotive and aerospace industries,[5] and, for example,

---

1   United Nations Department of Economic and Social Affairs, "LDC Identification Criteria & Indicators," online: un.org [perma.cc/3K84-D9NV].

2   United Nations Trade & Development, "What are the least developed countries?" (7 November 2023), online: unctad.org [perma.cc/3ZHS-GLQC].

3   SDT can consist of larger time frames to implement their obligations under the agreements, special consideration in implementing policy measures, either active or passive (for example, safeguard measures cannot be applied to developing countries in certain circumstances, or they have greater policy space to implement agricultural subsidies). Furthermore, developing countries benefit from technical assistance from the WTO Secretariat.

4   World Bank Group, "GDP (current US$)—Mexico" (last visited 13 June 2025), online: worldbank.org [perma.cc/K6WX-JMRX].

5   Central Intelligence Agency—The World Factbook, "Mexico" (12 February 2025), online: cia.gov [perma.cc/34ZB-WF7Q].

El Salvador, with a GDP of USD 34.02 billion,[6] with an economy that relies greatly on primary products. Two countries separated by 500 kilometres that share profound cultural heritages have completely different sets of cards to play in the trade and economic arena. So, why should they be treated equally?

. The question becomes more relevant when you learn that countries like Israel, Korea, Malaysia, and China are also considered developing countries. Is Cyprus really better off than Korea? Is the Romanian economy more solid than that of Israel?

Trying to answer these questions may result in my banning from visiting any of these countries. Therefore, I will refrain from doing so. What I will observe, however, is that this question lies at the centre of many discussions in trade and economic fora. The 2030 Agenda contains substantive goals linked to the development dimension, in the understanding that development is closely linked with economic growth, social well-being, and environmental sustainability.[7] At the WTO, the beginning of the century welcomed the Doha Development Agenda, which sought to make SDT provisions more effective. For example, it addressed the concerns of small and vulnerable economies by creating working groups on trade, debt, and transfer of technology and by establishing a Framework Agreement on SDT.[8] Later, at the Hong Kong Ministerial, the initiative on Aid for Trade appeared. This initiative does not apply equally to all developing countries.[9]

The OECD goes a step further in distinguishing between developing countries by recognizing categories such as "landlocked developing countries," countries "in fragile contexts," and "small island developing States."[10] To the OECD, a country like Mexico is considered a developing country,[11] but it is treated differently than others. It is not unusual for people there to refer to countries like Mexico as "emerging economies" (which I always interpreted

---

6   World Bank Group, above note 5.

7   WTO, "The WTO's Contribution to Achieving the SDGs" (last visited 4 June 2025), online: wto.org [perma.cc/RHL4-WUNQ].

8   WTO, "Ministerial declaration" (20 November 2001), online: wto.org [perma.cc/CN7Z-HTE8].

9   WTO, "Aid for Trade" (last visited 4 June 2025), online: wto.org [perma.cc/YCA4-5FE9].

10   OECD, "Countries and Territories Most in Need" (6 March 2024), online: oecd.org [perma.cc/Z4XE-K5Q5].

11   Gov UK, "Countries Defined as Developing by the OECD" (26 April 2021), online: gov.uk [perma.cc/9PR5-BE8M].

as "middle-class countries"). One might argue that being in the OECD itself differentiates Mexico from other countries.

In any case, it is clear that there are vast differences between developing countries. Therefore, having SDT provisions that apply on a "one-size-fits-all" basis ignores the reality and is simply not fair. Some of these provisions may be necessary for some countries, while others only consider them as "nice to have."

C. Developing Countries in Dispute Settlement

IN ORDER TO REAP THE full benefits of trade concessions, some trade agreements have established mechanisms to settle controversies arising from the interpretation or application of the agreement. These provisions can constitute insurance that what has been negotiated will be respected. It does not always need to be exercised. The sole existence of the mechanism is an important deterrent for "innovative" ideas that run counter the obligations, but also helps to ensure that investors and exporters can plan their businesses in a more structured way. Developing countries may not be the largest users of dispute settlement, but being able to trigger this mechanism allows them to level their relative disadvantage in terms of political leverage towards others.

The WTO's webpage[12] shows the levels of activity by country. While it comes as no surprise to see that the United States[13] and the European Union[14] are by far the biggest users of the system, some countries from the developing world, like China, India, Brazil, Mexico, and Korea, can certainly hold their own.[15]

---

12 WTO, "Disputes by Member," online: wto.org [perma.cc/FYR3-QMJ9].

13 124 cases as complainant, 164 as respondent, and 183 as a third party.

14 114 cases as complainant, ninety-eight as respondent, and 221 as third party.

15 In the Latin American region alone, there are countries with high activity levels, like Argentina (twenty-three cases as complainant, twenty-two as respondent, and seventy-two as third party); Brazil (thirty-four as complainant, seventeen as respondent, and 177 as third party); Chile (ten as complainant, thirteen as respondent and forty-eight as third party); Colombia (five as complainant, seven as respondent and seventy-two as third party); Guatemala (ten as complainant, two as respondent, and fifty-nine as a third party), or Mexico (twenty-five as complainant, fifteen as respondent, 114 as a third party). In Asia, China has thirty cases as complainant, fifty-three as respondent, and 198 as a third party; India has twenty-four as complainant, thirty-two as respondent, and 186 as a third party; Indonesia fifteen as complainant, fifteen as respondent, and fifty-two as a third party; Korea has been a complainant twenty-one times, respondent nineteen times, and third party 147 times; Taiwan has been a complainant on seven cases and a third party in 142 cases; while Thailand has participated fourteen times as a complainant, four as respondent, and 109 as a third party.

There are several factors that explain a country's participation in dispute settlement, the most obvious being the level of participation in international trade. A country with greater participation will be more likely to be involved in trade disputes, or one which is the leader in some products. Take, for example, Venezuela, whose energy sector has been the main driver for the country's participation in dispute settlement.[16]

Other factors may include countries with highly protected sectors: think of all the disputes involving the steel industry, for example.[17] Also, think of all the disputes dealing with the agricultural sector[18] or textiles.[19] Subsidized sectors are also prone to be the subject of disputes.[20]

The WTO and many other agreements allow only governments to participate in disputes concerning the interpretation and implementation of their texts.[21] This is when the imbalances become evident. Governments that

---

16 WTO disputes involving Venezuela as a complainant are DS2 *US—Gasoline*, DS574 *United States—Measures Relating to Trade in Goods and Services* and DS575 *Colombia—Measures Concerning the Distribution of Liquid Fuels*.

17 WTO, "Index of Disputes Issues," online: wto.org [perma.cc/UFN6-L829].

18 By mid-2025, almost one-quarter of all disputes at the WTO dealt with anti-dumping measures—many of which involved the steel sector—while almost another quarter with the *Agreements on Agriculture and SPS*.

19 See WTO Dispute Settlement cases, DS24 *US—Underwear*, DS29 *Turkey—Restrictions on Imports of Textile and Clothing Products*, DS32 *US—Wool Coats*, DS33 *US—Wool Shirts and Blouses*, DS34 *Turkey—Textiles*, DS47 *Turkey—Restrictions on Imports of Textile and Clothing Products*, DS56 *Argentina—Textiles and Apparel*, DS57 *Australia—Textile, Clothing and Footwear Import Credit Scheme*, DS77 *Argentia—Textiles and Clothing*, DS85 *United States—Measures Affecting Textiles and Apparel Products*, DS106 *Australia—Automotive Leather I*, DS123 *Argentina—Safeguard Measures on Imports of Footwear*, DS126 *Australia Automotive Leather II*, DS140 *European Communities—Anti-Dumping Investigations Regarding Unbleached Cotton Fabrics from India*, DS141 *EC—Bed Linen*, DS151 *Unites States—Measures Affecting Textiles and Apparel Products (II)*, DS181 *Colombia—Safeguard Measure of Imports of Plain Polyester Filaments from Thailand*, DS190 *Argentina—Cotton*, DS192 *US—Cotton Yarn*, DS229 *Brazil—Anti-Dumping Duties on Jute Bags from India*, DS243 *US—Textiles Rules of Origin*, DS267 *US—Upland Cotton*, DS288 *South Africa—Definitive Anti-Dumping Measures on Blanketing from Turkey*, DS305 *Egypt—Measures Affecting Imports of Textile and Apparel Products*, DS461 *Colombia—Textiles*, and DS489 *China—Demonstration Bases*.

20 WTO, "Disputes by Agreement," online: wto.org [perma.cc/B5GF-DN6L]. To date, 138 disputes have included one claim from the *Agreement on Subsidies and Countervailing Measures* (SCM Agreement).

21 Take, for example, CUSMA. This agreement allows for investors of one country to present challenges against a government in certain cases where their investments are substantially affected. There are also provisions where private companies can

are active in dispute settlement will build expertise which, in turn, will allow them to continue participating effectively in disputes. On the other hand, countries that are not very active in international trade will not have the need to participate in disputes and, therefore, their lawyers will not be able to acquire this capacity, at least to the same extent as others.

D. STD Is Not Enough to Integrate Developing Countries into the Dispute Settlement World

IN GENERAL, THE SDT PROVISIONS in the Dispute Settlement Understanding are the following:

1. Good offices: Article 3.12;
2. Longer timeframes: Article 12.10;
3. Possibility of appointing one panelist from a developing country Member: Article 8.10;
4. "Special consideration": Articles 4.10, 12.11, 21.2, 21.7, 21.8; and
5. Secretariat assistance: Article 27.2.

In practice, the provisions regarding longer timeframes provide the only substantive advantage. Any WTO Member welcomes more time to prepare their submissions, especially if they are the respondent.

Other provisions are nice to have, like the possibility of appointing a developing country national as a panelist. However, this makes very little difference—if any—when a dispute is underway. As a delegate from a Spanish-speaking country, I preferred to secure a Spanish speaker rather than a developing country national to serve on a panel. Coincidentally, most Spanish speakers come from developing countries.

The Secretariat's help can be useful in discussing avenues and strategies, but it is limited to specific consultations and is no substitute for full representation during a panel procedure.

The provision on good offices is residual from the *General Agreement on Tariffs and Trade* (GATT) days. I was unable to find a single register of this mechanism ever being used.

---

request a binational panel to settle a dispute involving anti-dumping duties. However, the general chapter dealing with disputes in all chapters is reserved for government-to-government involvement.

The provisions on special consideration are in general goodwill clauses with little to no relevance.

In light of this, there are not many factors in favour of developing countries that offset their lack of expertise in disputes. There is no substitute for having experienced counsels who know the law, including the precedents and decisions of the relevant bodies, people who are capable of convincing experts in the field of their positions are essential for developing country participation. This is why countries who can afford it have devoted important resources to obtaining outside help or to prepare their officials. Dispute settlement is a substantive forum and leaves no ground for political statements.

E. What Has Worked

WITH THIS IN MIND, SOME of the inherent disadvantages of developing country government participation in trade disputes can be overcome or, at least, minimized. Some examples of this are as follows.

1) Private Sector Involvement

In disputes that are worth hundreds of millions of dollars, it is only logical that the private sector will want to work shoulder-to-shoulder with their governments to secure the best outcome possible. This will usually require the participation of outside experts to assist governments. In those cases, the government's and company's or association's interests are aligned and therefore, there are incentives for companies to pay to participate, albeit indirectly.

Some cases are only possible with the support of the private sector: the "banana disputes"[22] may not have been possible had it not been for the involvement of outside counsels paid by large companies with clear interests at stake. The *Dominican Republic—Import and Sale of Cigarettes* case between Honduras and the Dominican Republic was also argued by proficient outside

---

22   A series of disputes dealing with the European measures for the importation, sale and distribution of bananas: DS16 *EC—Regime for the Importation, Sale and Distribution of Bananas*, DS27 *EC—Bananas III*, DS105 *EC—Regime for the Importation, Sale and Distribution of Bananas*, DS152 *US—Section 301 Trade Act*, DS158 *EC—Regime for the Importation, Sale and Distribution of Bananas*, DS165 *US—Certain EC Products*, DS361 *EC—Regime for the Importation of Bananas (Colombia)*, and DS364 *EC—Regime for the Importation of Bananas (Panama)*.

counsel on both sides of the table. Private money was again a factor to make this possible.

Governments that face many disputes at the same time, like Mexico, retain outside counsel regularly. Many of these have worked for the Government for years;[23] others are paid by companies or associations with a stake in a particular case.[24]

2) The ACWL

The Advisory Center on WTO Law (ACWL) is an intergovernmental organization created in 2001, with the purpose of allowing developing countries and LDCs to more effectively participate in negotiations and disputes at the WTO.[25] Their staff is as prepared as any law firm and have the added value that they are in constant contact with delegations and WTO officials. This makes them particularly well-versed in the details of the development of the law. Besides, most of its lawyers are experienced former government officials or come from reputed law firms. The ACWL is effectively a disruptive factor to the hegemony of big governments and major law firms.

The Center provides full legal assistance to countries at all stages of the proceedings. To date, it has participated in more than seventy disputes directly and some others through external legal counsel. Countries like Thailand, Türkiye, Pakistan, Indonesia, and Guatemala have greatly benefited from their services.

While the ACWL services are not free of charge, their rates are well below those of international law firms. This makes it more accessible to governments with limited budgets. Besides, the Center has several free activities directed at members of developing country delegations, which allows them to have a grasp of how disputes are solved in the real world.

---

23   See Tereposky & Derose LLP—Experience and Expertise that Transcends Boarders, "Investor-State Dispute Settlement" (last visited 4 June 2025), online: tradeisds.com [perma.cc/EU7E-GLLG].

24   See Sidley, "Sanitary and Phytosanitary Measures / Technical Barriers to Trade" (last visited 4 June 2025), online: sidley.com [perma.cc/K3PF-B6G5].

25   ACWL, "The ACWL's Mission" (last visited 4 June 2025), online: acwl.ch [perma.cc/WL32-89P3].

3) Policy Decisions

Lastly, there are developing countries that make a conscious effort to create expertise in their governments by participating in disputes. Take, for example, Guatemala, a country of 18 million inhabitants, the eighty-fourth largest exporter of goods and ninety-sixth of services in the organization has a remarkably active participation, far greater than their neighbours Belize (four cases as a third party); El Salvador (one case as complainant and twenty-three as a third party), or Nicaragua (one case as complainant, two as respondent, eighteen as a third party).

While Guatemala is an important user of the ACWL, its participation as a third party (fifty-nine cases) can be explained by the decision to create "national champions" in the field.[26] Other clear examples are Brazil, China, India, Korea, Mexico, Taiwan, Thailand, and Türkiye, all of which have been third parties in more than 100 cases.[27]

It is common for the WTO Secretariat to teach courses to developing country officials as part of their capacity-building activities. These efforts include full-fledged trade policy courses or more focalized on specific areas like Sanitary and Phytosanitary Measures (SPS), trade remedies, or dispute settlement. There are also plenty of materials on the WTO website to learn from and e-courses. This is an important tool for officials to get acquainted with the system, and it can be as detailed as needed.

The problem with these policy decisions is that—absent a solid career path for dispute settlement experts, which is common in many developing countries—knowledge will probably be wasted or underused.

F. FTAs and the WTO

FREE TRADE AGREEMENTS (FTAS) CAN be strange animals. There are treaties with unilateral concessions from developed countries to some developing countries with which they have a special historical or cultural relationship or with which there are policy objectives. Examples of these are the concessions

---

26 In fact, it was a Guatemalan diplomat, Marco Tulio Molina Tejeda, who chaired the informal discussions for a reform of the dispute settlement mechanism until early 2024.

27 See WTO, above note 13. Other notable examples are Argentina (sixty-eight cases), Chile (forty-eight cases), Colombia (sixty-nine cases), Ecuador (thirty-eight cases), Honduras (thirty-six cases), Indonesia (forty-nine cases), Saudi Arabia (fifty-four cases), and Singapore (seventy-two cases).

granted by the EU to some of its former colonies (the African, Caribbean and Pacific Group of States [ACP] countries)[28] or the US-Africa Partnership, which includes not only trade concessions but also assistance packages for African countries with little to no concessions from the African partners.

There are other agreements where countries are treated on an equal, or semi-equal basis, for example, the *Canada-United States-Mexico Agreement* (CUSMA). It consists of two developed countries and one developing country participating on almost equal footing. There are no SDT provisions *per se*, but during the negotiation of the original *North American Free Trade Agreement* (NAFTA) (the predecessor of CUSMA), Mexico enjoyed long liberalization schedules for many products and was able to negotiate exceptions in the services and investment chapters. However, when it comes to procedural rules, neither Chapter XX of NAFTA (State-to-State dispute settlement), nor Chapter 31 (its CUSMA equivalent) provide any special consideration to Mexico based on its developing country status.

Other agreements, like the *Comprehensive and Progressive Agreement for Trans-Pacific Partnership* (CPTPP), devote full chapters to Cooperation and Capacity Building (Chapter 21) or Development (Chapter 23) but reserve no exceptions for developing countries in dispute settlement.[29]

Perhaps one of the main differences between the WTO and free trade agreements is that the WTO, being a multilateral setting, requires standardized rules and standardized exceptions in the form of SDT. FTAs do not need to do so. They are tailor-made for the countries that participate in it. At the same time, they are the result of a negotiation between countries with relative degrees of political muscle, who will push for their agendas as much as they can. Without large coalitions to offset them, countries negotiating FTAs are left to their own devices.

Nevertheless, the fact that developing countries are able to participate on an equal footing in disputes under FTAs is an indication that SDT provisions for dispute settlement are redundant.

---

28   European Commission, "Economic Partnership Agreements (EPAs)" (last visited 4 June 2025), online: trade.ec [perma.cc/LE3L-H6QP].

29   New Zealand Foreign Affairs & Trade, "Comprehensive and Progressive Agreement for Trans-Pacific Partnership Texts," online: mfat.govt.nz [perma.cc/885X-FYJG].

G. Concluding Remarks

SDT PROVISIONS MAY MAKE SENSE in substantive agreements, for example, when they involve larger periods of tariff liberalization, flexibilities to grant agricultural subsidies, or exceptions to allow them not to suffer safeguards from other countries. Other than this and a few other exceptions, many SDT provisions are either empty promises or political rhetoric. This old negotiator would argue that this fact should permeate developing countries' negotiating positions much more than it has until now.

In the case of dispute settlement, procedural SDT provisions make sense only to the extent that larger timeframes are used by government officials arguing a case. If outside counsels are assisting the governments, they are on equal footing with the most advanced governments. Therefore, allowing them extra time is nice to have but not essential to a country's defence.

Furthermore, developing countries come in all shapes and sizes. Standard SDT provisions are not equally beneficial to all of them and represent a negotiating cost that may be better placed somewhere else. Instead, the greatest benefit that developing countries should aim for is to have competent lawyers at their disposal when needed. This may take the form of career officials if their institutions are solid enough or professional advice via law firms or a dedicated ACWL.

There are many international firms that would be ready to provide their services at heavily discounted prices for the possibility of having the bragging rights of having assisted sovereign governments in their defences.

To realize this admittedly abstract opportunity, perhaps it would make sense for the WTO—Members and Secretariat alike—to discuss the usefulness of having a body, or a recruiting mechanism, that would allow developing countries to participate in international disputes without breaking the piggy bank.

CHAPTER 11

China's Experience in WTO Dispute Settlement: Lessons for Developing Countries

Henry Gao and Wenhua Ji

A. Introduction

CHINA ACCEDED TO THE WORLD Trade Organization (WTO) on 11 December 2001. According to WTO data,[1] as of 1 April 2024, China had participated as a disputing party in seventy-three WTO disputes: as a complainant in twenty-four disputes and respondent in forty-nine disputes. China has also actively participated as a third party in a total of 195 disputes. The United States is the main target of China's litigation, accounting for eighteen of China's twenty-four complaints, while the European Union accounts for five. Similarly, the United States initiated the largest number of disputes against China with twenty-three, followed by the European Union with eleven.[2] See Figure 1.

---

1   See WTO, "Disputes by member" (last visited 17 March 2025), online: wto.org [perma. cc/6FD3-GYNH].

2   See WTO, "Map of Disputes between WTO Members" (last visited 17 March 2025), online: wto.org [perma.cc/9UQ9-72XC].

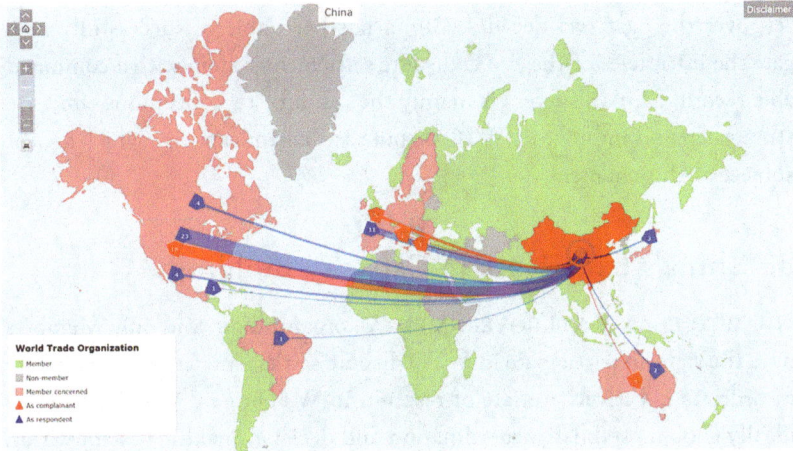

FIGURE 1. MAP OF WTO DISPUTES INVOLVING CHINA AS COMPLAINANT OR RESPONDENT.

SOURCE: WTO, 2024.

Overall, China has been one of the most active participants in WTO dispute settlement over the last two decades. It has largely maintained a balanced profile, with slightly fewer cases as complainant than respondent because complaints were often jointly brought against China by different complainants. Despite the large number of cases, China has become more and more capable of using the WTO dispute settlement system. Moreover, despite the recent paralysis of the Appellate Body, China has reaffirmed its confidence in the WTO dispute settlement system by bringing new cases.[3] As a developing country that only acceded to the WTO six years after the organization's establishment, China faced many obstacles when it comes to participation in the WTO dispute settlement system: it had very limited experience in international litigation, and it also faced a language barrier as its own language is not one of the three working languages of the WTO.[4]

---

3   For instance, China requested consultation with the United States regarding certain subsidy measures adopted by the United States that are contingent upon the use of domestic over imported goods or that otherwise discriminate against goods of Chinese origin on 26 March 2024. See WTO, "China Initiates Dispute Regarding US Tax Credits for Electric Vehicles, Renewable Energy" (28 March 2024), online: wto.org [perma.cc/MD8H-R3QE].

4   In assessing the performance of a Member's participation in WTO dispute settlement, factors other than trade volume and economic size should also be considered. These include the technical complexity of WTO dispute settlement procedures, the slowness of capacity building and accumulation of experience, and administrate and legal traditions.

Yet, over the past two decades, China has been able to successfully navigate the intricacies of the WTO dispute settlement system with a commendable record. China's success is mainly the result of its continuous efforts to strengthen and improve its WTO dispute settlement capacity, which are the subject of this chapter.

B. China's Experience in Capacity Building

THE WTO IS AN INTERGOVERNMENTAL organization, and only Members have the right to participate in WTO dispute settlement activities. Therefore, in order to effectively initiate or respond to WTO cases, a WTO Member ideally should establish a coordination and decision-making system within its government, invest adequate human and financial resources, and make appropriate institutional arrangements. However, developing countries generally face more challenges than developed countries in bringing cases to the WTO, partly due to their relative lack of legal expertise, financial resources, and non-legal constraints resulting from power imbalances. When China joined the WTO in 2001, it also had to deal with these issues, even though it was a leading developing country in terms of trade size and had less political status disparity with its major trading partners. It appears that China did not adopt a wait-and-see strategy in this regard, as many senior officials and trade experts not only foresaw legal challenges against China in the near future but also felt that it was politically in China's best interest to quickly seize the ability to use the dispute settlement system to protect its trade interests.[5] This understanding and foresight led the Chinese government to take a very proactive approach to addressing its legal capacity constraints, with the active participation of various stakeholders. In this process, China's central

---

5   For instance, Minister Shi Guangsheng of the Ministry of Foreign Trade and Economic Cooperation (MOFTEC) pointed out at National Conference on Foreign Trade and Economic Cooperation Legal Works in March 2002 that "as a new member of the WTO, our country should consciously apply the rules, fully understand and grasp the rights conferred on us by the WTO, strengthen the work of multilateral and bilateral consultations, and, in particular, make full use of the dispute settlement mechanism of the WTO in order to fight resolutely against new trade protectionism and to effectively safeguard the interests of our country." See "Shi Guangsheng, Minister of Foreign Trade and Economic Cooperation: The Most Important Thing is to Understand and Use the WTO rules" (30 February 2002), online (pdf): news.sina.cn [perma. cc/WWW8-MFR7] [translated by author].

government plays a leading role, with wide support from different sectors in the society.

1) Institutional and Personnel Arrangements within Governments

At the central government level, China's Ministry of Commerce (MOFCOM) is responsible for WTO matters. More specifically, its Department of WTO Affairs handles all WTO issues except WTO dispute settlement. This is the result of careful internal deliberations. In early 2002, shortly after China's accession to the WTO, the Ministry of Foreign Trade and Economic Cooperation (the predecessor of MOFCOM), after many internal debates, decided to assign WTO dispute cases to its Department of Treaty and Law (DTL) rather than to the newly established WTO Department, and such arrangement was formally confirmed after MOFCOM was established in 2003.[6] This institutional arrangement was important and demonstrated that China was fully aware of the legalistic nature of the WTO dispute settlement system and was therefore making specialized professional preparations for future participation. As a result, a WTO Law Division was established in the DTL to deal with WTO legal issues, including dispute settlement, with about four government officials who had some knowledge of WTO dispute settlement but no practical experience. They had to learn by doing in the course of their work. In China's Mission to the WTO in Geneva, dispute settlement issues were assigned to a diplomat with a legal background, although there was no position dedicated to dispute settlement.

Another challenge facing many developing countries in WTO dispute settlement is the lack of coordination between the trade ministry and other line agencies which have jurisdictions on the issues involved in the disputes. Therefore, after the establishment of the WTO Law Division in the DTL, MOFCOM worked hard to successfully obtain the support and approval of

---

6   The main functions of the Department of Treaty and Law include, among others, "(v) responsible for initiating, responding to and appealing trade disputes involving China in the WTO, as well as China's participation as a third party in the WTO dispute settlement procedures; and participate in external consultations on trade disputes involving China prior to recourse to the WTO dispute settlement system." See Circular of the Ministry of Commerce on the Issuance of the Main Functions and Internal Divisions of the Departments (Offices, Bureaus) of the Ministry of Commerce, Ban Fa [2003] No 7, 26 June 2003.

the State Council to establish an inter-ministerial coordination mechanism on WTO disputes. This inter-ministerial working mechanism is internal, coordinated by MOFCOM and responsible not only for formulating policy recommendations for consideration and decision by the State Council but also for formulating government positions and important legal interpretations on many technical issues when necessary. Given the political impact of WTO cases on bilateral trade relations, it is necessary and appropriate for the State Council to make recommendations on many issues of political and strategic importance, especially when China is a disputing party in WTO cases. Another important value of this mechanism is that it enables many other Chinese government agencies to understand the importance of complying with WTO rules and obligations and to cultivate their own internal legal teams to help them do so.

These efforts appear to have yielded positive results, improving the Chinese government's ability to use the WTO dispute settlement system, in particular to respond to and resolve cases against China more quickly and effectively. Against this background, it is no coincidence that China's participation in third-party proceedings, an important way of learning from the actual dispute settlement process, has become more active since 2003. This was a deliberate move by MOFCOM to protect its broad trade and systemic interests and to familiarize itself with WTO dispute settlement procedures and techniques. It is also worth noting that many Chinese government officials in charge of WTO dispute settlement matters have not confined themselves to administrative work but have invested heavily in self-learning and research on WTO dispute settlement issues.[7] Relevant ministries and agencies of the State Council have become more familiar with WTO rules and dispute settlement techniques and tactics. This has gradually improved the ability of both these individuals and the Chinese government as a whole to use the WTO to resolve disputes.

Meanwhile, China's growing experience has led it to adjust and improve its internal mechanisms accordingly. As China's WTO dispute settlement

---

7   For example, an English book on WTO dispute settlement rules written by DTL staff was published in 2005. See Yang Guohua, Bryan Mercurio, & Li Yongjie, eds, *WTO Dispute Settlement Understanding: A Detailed Interpretation*, (The Hague: Kluwer Law International, 2005). Yang Guohua and Li Yongjie were directors of the WTO Law Division of the DTL at the time of publication of this book. Dr. Yang Guohua is a professor of law at Tsinghua University, and Li Yongjie is Director General of the DTL at the time of this writing in April 2024.

activities increased since 2008, with more cases on both the complainant and respondent sides, the Chinese government decided to allocate more administrative resources to dispute settlement. Around mid-2009, a second WTO law division in the DTL with about five legal officers was added by MOFCOM. At the same time, the legal capacity of the Chinese Mission to the WTO was strengthened. At the end of 2009, an independent and specialized legal division was established in China's WTO Mission in Geneva, and MOFCOM dispatched a senior government legal expert from Beijing to lead this Geneva-based legal team, which is seen as "a sign of the importance Beijing places on using the world trade body to shape the international rules of commerce and to defend and advance Chinese commercial interests in trade-related legal disputes."[8] The number of staff focusing on dispute settlement issues at China's Mission in Geneva has increased accordingly, from no dedicated staff at the beginning, to one quasi-dedicated legal affairs officer around 2010, to about two dedicated staff since 2016. Of course, all these legal teams, whether based in Beijing or Geneva, are responsible not only for dispute settlement activities but also for a wide range of WTO compliance issues and other matters (e.g., regional trade agreement dispute settlement, etc.). All these institutional and staffing arrangements have remained relatively stable so far, providing MOFCOM and the Chinese Mission with relatively ample administrative resources to engage in both offensive and defensive WTO litigation.

2) Government's Use of External Legal Services

WTO dispute settlement proceedings typically involve complex procedural and substantive issues, strict time limits, and a high degree of oral and written debate and exchange. For these reasons, very few WTO Members can fully rely on their own in-house governmental capacity to handle both the factual and legal aspects of WTO disputes. For a variety of reasons,[9] the Chinese government's current in-house legal teams are not yet able to fully

---

8   Inside US–China Trade, "China Upgrades WTO Mission's Legal Capacity on Disputes, IPR, Rules," 23 December 2009.

9   The total number of staff in the two WTO legal affairs divisions of the DTL is relatively small (only around eight people). They are responsible not only for WTO dispute settlement cases but also for many other administrative and legal matters and do not have extensive experience in legal drafting and fact-finding compared with commercial lawyers.

meet the need to independently initiate and litigate WTO cases. Following the example of many other WTO Members,[10] there is a need for China to seek external legal assistance.

In this regard, China has adopted from the outset a "two-tier/three-party" working model in cases where China is a disputing party. The Chinese government's legal team led by DTL will take the lead, direct, and supervise all aspects of the work but will receive legal technical assistance from both foreign and Chinese lawyers. This model, which was tried for the first time in the *US—Steel Safeguards* case and further refined in subsequent cases, should be seen as appropriate for China's current situation: first, it allows the government to fully participate, control, and lead, and maintains the government's flexibility and maneuverability, which is politically and legally crucial; second, it can ensure the high quality of legal documents and oral responses on important issues, while providing a platform to promote the growth of both in-house legal officers and local commercial legal talent. In contrast, China's initial strategy in third-party cases was to use only local lawyers to provide legal assistance. This has had several positive effects: on the one hand, it has gradually attracted and trained a small group of local lawyers to set up WTO legal practices; on the other hand, it has provided them with a relatively stable business in which to survive and grow. Although Chinese lawyers as a whole are not as experienced as their counterparts in the United States or the European Union, the emergence and gradual expansion of domestic WTO legal teams is an encouraging signal and a demonstration of the effectiveness of the government's efforts. One change that has occurred since around 2014 is that as China's indigenous legal teams have developed, the Chinese government has gradually begun to only use local lawyers for support and services in some relatively less sophisticated cases, while the government legal team continues to play a leading role. This has further enhanced the legal capacity of local Chinese lawyers and also resulted in cost savings. It is fair to say that because of the expansion of in-house government legal teams and

---

10   It is a common practice for WTO Member governments to engage private legal services in WTO disputes, not only because many WTO Members do not have a permanent and efficient in-house legal team to carry out this work, but also because even if some WTO Members do have an in-house legal team, it is important that this team is well-versed in the issues that can arise in WTO disputes. Even if some WTO Members have in-house legal teams, it is almost impossible for such teams to be well-versed in all the issues that may arise in a WTO dispute.

the availability of outside private lawyers,[11] China has a greater capacity to both actively engage in more WTO disputes and effectively maintain high legal quality, which undoubtedly exerts a kind of pressure on other WTO Members.

There is another very important factor that is closely related to the use of commercial legal services: funding. In order for the government to hire high quality external lawyers, there needs to be adequate and stable financial support within the government. In this regard, thanks to the arduous but successful internal coordination work of the relevant MOFCOM leaders, the Ministry of Finance finally agreed to set up a special fund to strongly support China's participation in WTO disputes, including the use of commercial legal services. In some years when China's participation in WTO cases was high, the annual expenditure in this regard could reach several million dollars per year.

---

11   It should also be noted that the cultivation and development of China's local WTO commercial legal service team is also in a process of change. There are some Chinese lawyers who have been persistently engaged in WTO-related legal work, some lawyers who have abandoned this field and turned to other fields, and some new lawyers who are joining WTO-related legal work. With the change in management style, since 2013, the MOFCOM has established a pool of local law firms and a pool of foreign law firms through a bidding process, and only the law firms included in the pool have the opportunity to bid and provide services when there is a real need to hire lawyers for the preparation and litigation of a specific WTO case. The pool of law firms is updated and put out to tender every three years. For example, the 2021 list of bid winners of domestic law firms includes: Beijing Jincheng Tongda Law Firm, Beijing King & Wood Law Firm, Beijing Zhonglun Law Firm, Shanghai Jintiancheng (Beijing) Law Firm, Beijing Junzejun Law firm, Beijing Tuiyin Law Firm, Beijing Zhuowei Law Firm, Beijing Global Law Firm, Beijing Gao Wen Law Firm, Beijing Lantai Law Firm, Taihe Tai (Beijing) Law Firm, Beijing Dacheng Law Firm, and Shanghai Haihua Yongtai Law Firm. The 2021 list of bid winners of foreign law firms includes: Sidley Austin LLP, Akin Gump Strauss Hauer & Feld LLP, Steptoe & Johnson LLP, Morris Manning & Martin LLP, Moulis Legal Pty Limited Perkins Coie LLP, Mayer Brown LLP, VVGB Advocaten-Avocats (Edwin Vermulst BVBA), Dentons Europe LLP, and Bennett Jones LLP. See Ministry of Commerce's Candidate List of Law Firms-Sub-List for WTO and RTA Dispute Resolution Domestic Law Firms Bid Winning Announcement; Ministry of Commerce's Candidate List of Law Firms-Sub-List for WTO and RTA Dispute Resolution Foreign Law Firms Bid Winning Announcement.

3) Government Support for Academic and Social Institutions

The government's active participation in the WTO dispute settlement system will face many difficulties in the long run without strong support from academic and social institutions. Based on this understanding, in the years following China's accession to the WTO, relevant Chinese government departments have invested considerable resources to promote capacity building at the societal level, for example, by organizing international and regional seminars and training courses, raising awareness among industry, establishing specialized institutions and promoting research, conducting secondment programs for junior university professors of international economic law to work in the DTL for around one year, and holding issue-specific seminars on WTO cases with academia and practitioners, etc.

These initiatives have also produced some encouraging results. Academic research on WTO law and dispute settlement has flourished, and some English books on WTO dispute settlement have been translated into Chinese. China now has two "WTO Chair Programme" universities, one awarded in 2010 and the other in 2022.[12] Many local think tanks on WTO issues have been established with the support of local governments,[13] and some of them are functioning well. The MOFCOM also actively supports the WTO Moot Court in China. In fact, the "China WTO Moot Court Competition" was initiated by the DTL of MOFCOM together with Southwest University of Political Science and Law of China, China University of Political Science and Law, and the WTO Law Research Institute of China Law Society in 2012. This competition is held every year and has now been held thirteen times. It aims to promote the mastery and application of WTO rules by university students and to promote the training and selection of future WTO negotiation and dispute settlement talents through the simulation of the panel procedure of the WTO dispute settlement system.

---

12   See WTO, "WTO to Establish Chairs at 14 Developing Country Universities" (26 January 2010), online: wto.org [perma.cc/XSC2-VT3V]; WTO, "DDG Zhang Welcomes Launch of New Phase of WTO Chairs Programme" (9 December 2021), online: wto.org [perma.cc/TV3C-2NA2].

13   See Gong Baihua, "Shanghai's WTO Affairs Consultation Center: Working Together to Take Advantage of WTO Membership" in Peter Gallagher, Patrick Low, & Andrew L Stoler, eds, *Managing the Challenges of WTO Participation: 45 Case Studies* (Cambridge: Cambridge University Press, 2005) 167.

4) Government's Interactions with Domestic Industries

A prerequisite for the government to consider initiating WTO proceedings is that it is at least aware of the existence and details of foreign trade barriers or measures. In practice, however, it is domestic industry rather than the government that is at the frontier of international trade and investment activities. So, there is a clear gap. Quite a number of WTO Members have adopted special rules to reduce this information gap and take the necessary measures. The best known of these is probably Section 301 of the US *Trade Act of 1974*.[14]

Evidence shows that the Chinese government understands the importance of government-industry interaction and has sought to assist its industries by establishing a routine process for collecting, processing, and prioritizing information on trade barriers from domestic industries shortly after its WTO accession. In July 2002, the MOFCOM published a non-binding document named *Guidance for Collecting Trade and Investment Barrier Information*, which listed many kinds of trade and investment barriers ranging from technical barriers to trade (TBT) measures to service investment restrictions. Two months later, in September 2002, the MOFCOM promulgated a legal document, the *Interim Rules on Foreign Trade Barrier Investigation*, formally mandating and regulating the investigation of trade barriers in foreign markets. On 6 April 2004, the Standing Committee of the National People's Congress (NPC) approved amendments to the Chinese Foreign Trade Law, Section 7 of which was explicitly titled *Foreign Trade Barrier Investigation*. In 2005, MOFCOM issued an updated *Rules on Foreign Trade Barrier Investigation* (FTBI Rules).

It should be noted that despite the existence of these rules and instruments against foreign trade barriers, actual recourse to the investigation of foreign trade barriers by Chinese enterprises or industry associations has not been very frequent, and only three investigations have been formally carried out by MOFCOM to date.[15] One reason is the lack of the lobbying culture

---

14   *Trade Act of 1974*, 19 USC § 2411, s 301.

15   On 22 April 2004, MOFCOM launched a trade barrier investigation into Japan's regulatory measures on nori imports. On 25 November 2011, MOFCOM initiated a trade barrier investigation into some of the US support policies and subsidies for the renewable energy industry. See MOFCOM Announcement on the Final Findings of the Investigation on Trade Barriers to Certain Supportive Policies and Subsidies for the US Renewable Energy Industry.

in China and the absence of Western-style industry associations.[16] At the same time, it is worth noting that the petition mechanism provided by the FTBI Rules is not the only way to address foreign trade barriers in China, let alone to initiate WTO proceedings. In practice, there are several other formal and informal channels through which domestic industries can report foreign trade barriers—directly through local governments, various trade associations or chambers of commerce, to the heads of MOFCOM or higher-level government agencies,[17] and requests for bilateral government consultations, use of the WTO dispute settlement mechanism, or direct retaliation. Sometimes informal channels prove to be more effective and efficient, which in turn limits the potential use of the formal petition mechanism. This may explain why, despite the low use of FTBI Rules, there has been no shortage of WTO cases initiated by China and supported by its domestic industry over the past twenty years.

C. Can Other Developing Countries Replicate the Success of China?

DESPITE ITS RELATIVELY LATE ACCESSION to the WTO, China has been able to quickly build up its capacity in WTO dispute settlement and has become one of the most active and sophisticated players. Yet, it seems that it has not been easy for other developing countries to replicate the success of China. First of all, not many developing countries are frequent participants in the WTO dispute settlement system. Second, even among those developing countries with active participation in the dispute settlement system, i.e., India, Brazil, Argentina, and Mexico, most do not have a strong in-house legal team or a big group of local lawyers who are capable of handling WTO disputes on their own. Instead, they often resort to foreign lawyers to handle

---

On 12 April 2023, MOFCOM conducts a trade barrier investigation on Taiwan's trade restrictive measures against the mainland. See Announcement of the Ministry of Commerce on the Final Findings of the Trade Barrier Investigation on Taiwan's Trade Restrictive Measures Against Mainland China.

16   See Henry Gao, "Taking Justice into Your Own Hand: The TBI Mechanism in China" (2010) 44:3 *Journal of World Trade* 633.

17   Some of these are institutionalized in the Quadrilateral Coordination' system, which pools together the resources of the Ministry of Commerce, local government, and relevant industry associations to help affected individual firms fight foreign trade barriers. See Henry Gao, "Public-Private Partnership: The Chinese Dilemma" (2014) 48:5 *Journal of World Trade* 983.

their WTO disputes. This begs the question: how could other developing countries replicate the success story of China?

As demonstrated by China's experience we outlined in this chapter, the main element of China's success formula is the strong support of the government, which took deliberate efforts to nurture WTO expertise both within the government and beyond. This has been the consistent policy of the Chinese government for the past twenty plus years. Yet, this might not be possible in other developing countries, as due to election cycles, it is not uncommon to see radical shifts in government policy when it comes to international trade, including WTO dispute settlement. Thus, it would be unrealistic for these countries to have a consistent strategy of participation in WTO dispute settlement, let alone building up the capacity consciously over a few decades.

On the other hand, one could legitimately ask the question: do most other developing countries need to develop the types of expertise on WTO dispute settlement like China? The answer, surprisingly, is probably no. To start with, many developing countries do not participate in WTO dispute settlement frequently because most of their trade is not covered by the WTO regime but by various preference regimes such as the Generalized System of Preferences, the *African Growth and Opportunity Act*, and the *Cotonou Agreement*. As these agreements are not part of the "covered agreements," it certainly does not make sense for the developing countries that are exporting under them to actively pursue WTO disputes. Second, as most developing countries do not have as stable a supply of WTO cases either as complainants or respondents as China, it does not make sense for their law firms to develop capacities in WTO dispute settlement, which are expensive to develop and equally expensive to maintain. This is also the case in China, as more than a dozen firms wanted to specialize in WTO disputes upon China's WTO accession but currently, only less than a handful law firms in China have actual WTO dispute settlement practices. Developing and maintaining WTO practices requires financial support from both the government (such as through special funds as discussed earlier) and the law firms (with the other practices of the firm subsidizing the WTO practice), but without many WTO cases, neither of such support is sustainable. Instead, for most developing countries, a better alternative is resorting to the legal representation provided by the Advisory Centre on WTO Law (ACWL), which provides a highly competent WTO practice for developing countries at a highly subsidized rate. Thus, China's experience might remain as the exception rather than the rule for developing countries in WTO dispute settlement.

D. Concluding Remarks

IN THE OVER TWENTY YEARS since its accession to the WTO in December 2001, China has gradually and steadily improved its participation in the WTO dispute settlement mechanism and has become a major player. In terms of institutional and capacity building, after years of efforts, the Chinese government has built a stable government legal team and has a relatively strong capacity to initiate and respond to WTO dispute settlement cases, based on effective cooperation with international and domestic lawyers. At the same time, China's efforts to cultivate the capacity of social institutions and local commercial legal services have also made great progress. All this shows that, with the right support and resources, developing countries can still successfully navigate the WTO legal system.

Of course, China also faces some challenges in maintaining and improving its WTO legal capacity, such as the constant turnover of government legal talent, the gap in overall staff strength compared to its major litigation rivals, and the relatively limited business opportunities for local WTO legal teams. Should significant improvements be made in these areas, the efficiency and effectiveness of China's use of the WTO dispute settlement system and other international trade-related legal fora could be further enhanced.

At the same time, it is worth noting that China's successful experience in building up its WTO dispute settlement capacity might remain an exception among developing countries and might not provide a viable model for other developing countries, as few countries can match the volume and breadth of the trade networks of China and thus have different needs that might be better met by third-party institutions such as the ACWL rather than having to develop their own in-house and home grown legal capacity.

Specific Topics in WTO Dispute Settlement

CHAPTER 12

The Past, Present, and Future of Energy Disputes in the WTO

Iain Sandford[*]

A. A Brief Tribute to Valerie Hughes

VALERIE HUGHES HAS MADE A singular contribution to the World Trade Organization (WTO) dispute settlement system. I have seen first-hand her stewardship of the WTO's substantive rules, procedures, and institutions,

---

[*] All views expressed are personal to the author and are not attributable to any client or organization to which I am or have been affiliated. All errors are solely my responsibility. Thanks: I wish to thank the editor plus Donald McRae, Jennifer Hillman, James Flett and Jenya Grigorova for comments on an initial draft of this chapter. Disclosures: I have assisted WTO Members to litigate disputes throughout my career, including in the following cases referenced in this chapter: DS248, 249, 251, 252, 253, 254, 258, 259 US—Steel Safeguard, DS431, 432, 433 China—Rare Earths, DS473 EU—Biodiesel (Argentina), DS412 Canada—Renewable Energy / DS426 Canada Feed-In Tariff Program, and DS567 Saudi Arabia—IP Rights. I have nevertheless tried to offer an objective account of the cases and their significance for understanding the past, present, and future of energy disputes in the WTO. I did not use AI for research or in the initial drafting of this chapter. I used AI to critically evaluate my initial draft and to suggest copy edits—a handful of which are reflected in the final version.

as well as her fostering of the human resources of the dispute settlement ecosystem—including me and several other contributors to this collection.

The word "reckoning" in the title of this collection recognizes that the WTO dispute settlement system faces fundamental challenges, with the most obvious being the inability of Members to appoint individuals to the Appellate Body. The unipolar global order of the post-Cold War era has passed and with it, for now, the global appeal of liberal ideas, rule-of-law-based international relations, and the (historically unusual) enthusiasm of great powers for compulsory and binding adjudication of disputes. Yet, the WTO dispute settlement system hangs on, with some WTO Members having found alternative means to ensure that compulsory and binding adjudication remains alive through non-appeal pacts and "appeal arbitration" procedures. Members still initiate disputes. And Valerie continues to contribute—lately as a member of the pool of appeal arbitrators under the Multi-Party Interim Appeal Arbitration Arrangement (MPIA).

The selection of the "Past, Present and Future of Energy Disputes in the WTO" as the topic for this chapter is my attempt to pay tribute to Valerie in two ways. First, in my experience, one of Valerie's defining characteristics as a lawyer and leader has been a practical and no-nonsense approach to problems. I cannot think of a topic that is more practical or in need of no-nonsense approaches than energy policy. So, the subject matter seems apposite. Second, energy policy—including the energy transition—is an issue at the centre of contemporary discussions about world order. Despite the challenges that the WTO dispute settlement system faces, I am convinced that it will continue to function as a forum for addressing trade-related aspects of these important issues. The fact that the WTO dispute settlement system remains capable of contributing to the resolution of pressing issues in international relations is itself a tribute to the careerlong stewardship of people like Valerie.

B. Introduction

DISPUTES INVOLVING, OR PARTICULARLY RELEVANT for, trade in energy products (labelled "energy disputes" in this chapter) have been a recurring feature of WTO dispute settlement. Few resources are as important to national economies and international relations as energy. Accordingly, energy disputes are interesting not only in themselves but also because they present a meaningful subset of disputes through which to consider underlying issues, preoccupations, and trends in the multilateral trading system.

The high-level analysis in this chapter looks at energy disputes across four decades, divided into three time periods, loosely labelled the "past," "present," and "future."[1] Section C provides necessary background, describing relevant policy areas, rules and exceptions, as well as the function of the WTO dispute settlement system. The chapter then discusses a selection of energy disputes over time. In Sections D (the past) and E (the present), the chapter highlights how disputes about regulatory measures struck a balance between the scope for environmental protection and trade disciplines, and how a broader range of energy disputes followed the accession of large energy-consuming or energy-producing countries. Section F identifies disputes that are likely to arise in the foreseeable future, notably disputes about trade-related environmental measures, industrial policy, and asserted security interests. Section G concludes by summarizing the WTO dispute settlement system's experience with energy disputes and highlighting the system's continued utility.

C. Background: Four Policy Areas, Five Basic Principles, and Three Key Functions Relevant for Understanding WTO Energy Disputes

ALTHOUGH ENERGY IS A SPACE in which goods and services are closely intertwined, virtually all of the energy disputes addressed in this chapter arise in connection with WTO rules concerning trade in goods.[2] As noted in the introduction, the category of "energy disputes" is defined broadly in this chapter, encompassing not only disputes about trade in energy products themselves but also disputes relevant for energy trade, for example disputes concerning the permissible scope of environmental regulation of energy

---

1   A more accurate—but less snappy—title for the chapter might have mentioned the distant past (the 1990s), the more recent past (between then and now), some contemporary developments, as well as likely controversies going forward.

2   Energy is traded internationally as flows of electricity (often considered a good—as evidenced by code 2716 in the harmonized system) or through products with high energy content, such as petroleum products (goods). Also relevant are goods that can be used to generate, transmit, distribute, or store energy, as well as the raw materials and intermediate goods from which they are made. Although numerous services are intertwined with energy and energy products, as well as energy-related intellectual property (IP), issues concerning energy-related services or IP have not been a major feature of WTO disputes. One exception is the dispute in DS476 *EU—Energy Package*, in which Russia raised several claims under the *General Agreement on Trade in Services* ("GATS") (for discussion, see Section E, below in this chapter).

products, or about trade in the mineral resources essential for the energy transition. This approach expands the pool of disputes available for analysis by including cases that are both directly[3] and indirectly[4] on point.

With notional exceptions,[5] WTO disputes focus on *governmental measures* that pursue economic or other policy objectives. WTO rules recognize that Members regulate, tax, or otherwise engage with their economies in numerous ways. Rules and disciplines set forth in the treaties annexed to the *Marrakesh Agreement Establishing the World Trade Organization* (WTO Agreement) require governmental measures affecting trade to take specific forms, such as ordinary customs duties on imports of goods (tariffs) or non-discriminatory internal taxation or regulation, which facilitate trade liberalization over time.

At the same time, the trade rules acknowledge that economic and trade policies are not the only responsibilities of government and allow space for Members to pursue non-trade objectives.[6] The balance between discipline on

---

3   As of March 2024, I count thirteen disputes pertaining *directly* to energy products or energy trade: DS2 *US—Gasoline* (Panel and Appellate Body), DS412 *Canada—Renewable Energy* / DS426 *Canada Feed-In Tariff Program* (Panels and Appellate Body), DS456 *India—Solar Cells and Solar Modules* (Panel and Appellate Body), DS473 *EU—Biodiesel (Argentina)* (Panel and Appellate Body), DS476 *EU—Energy Package*, DS480 *EU—Biodiesel (Indonesia)* (Panel), DS510 *US—Renewable Energy* (Panel), DS562 *US—Solar Safeguard* (Panel) and DS600 *EU—Palm Oil Biofuels (Malaysia)*. A dozen or so further disputes directly related to energy trade have not resulted in a published panel report; most of these appear to have been settled or abandoned by the complainant at an early stage in the proceedings.

4   This chapter deals with a number of disputes as *indirectly* related to energy trade. The cases include: DS58 *US—Shrimp* (Panel and Appellate Body), DS431, 432, 433 *China—Rare Earths* (Panel and Appellate Body); DS394, 395, 398 *China—Raw Materials* (Panel and Appellate Body).

5   In theory, a Member could bring a dispute about a "situation" (see Article XXIII:1(c) of the *General Agreement on Tariffs and Trade* 1994 (GATT 1994), Article 26.2 of the *Understanding on Rules and Procedures Governing the Settlement of Disputes* (DSU) and Article 64 of the *Agreement on Trade-Related Aspects of Intellectual Property Rights* (TRIPS Agreement). There is also potential for WTO rules to discipline actions by non-State actors, including in areas relevant for energy trade such as subsidies and technical regulation, as Jan Bohanes and I explain in Jan Bohanes & Iain Sandford, "The Untapped Potential of WTO Rules to Discipline Private Trade-Restrictive Conduct" (2008) Society of International Economic Law, Working Paper No 56/08, online (pdf): papers.ssrn.com [perma.cc/M3JR-PUKH].

6   This point is reflected in the Preamble's recognition of the importance of economic development of developing countries as well as Member's objective of "seeking . . . to protect and preserve the environment," as well as the substantive exceptions to the basic WTO rules discussed further in this Section.

the way in which Members pursue trade objectives, on the one hand, and the "policy space" allowed for non-trade objectives, on the other, has been a feature of many of the disputes relevant for trade in energy products reviewed later in the chapter.

1) Relevant Policy Areas

Given that trade rules and exceptions regulate WTO Members' pursuit of various trade and non-trade policy objectives, it is useful for purposes of this chapter to identify four broad policy areas relevant in connection with trade in energy products.

First, *energy policy*. Energy policy concerns a given government's approach to the sourcing and development of energy resources, as well as the production, distribution, and use of energy, including the energy mix and related considerations such as greenhouse gas emissions. Energy policy typically impacts trade—and thereby falls within the scope of matters regulated in the WTO Agreement—through implementation of fiscal measures such as taxes, incentives (including access to resources, grants, or similar measures, as well as tax exemptions and credits), and regulatory actions.

Second, a WTO Member's *broader economic policy* agenda. This includes trade policy and industrial policy. As with energy policy, governments may pursue broader economic policy objectives through fiscal or regulatory measures, or subsidies—and thereby affect trade. Political considerations often mean that governments seek to favour domestic producers, while trade rules require non-discrimination. This political-economic-legal triangle sometimes leads to obfuscation around the true objectives of a measure, leading to disputes alleging that measures are "disguised restrictions" on trade.

Third, *environmental protection* is also relevant in the energy context because the production, transportation and use of energy products often come with environmental costs or risks. Given that environmental issues frequently arise upstream to consumption of energy, environmental regulation often targets production processes associated with energy products, as well as issues arising from the products themselves.

Fourth, governments increasingly view trade, including trade relating to energy and energy products, through a prism of *security policy*, which they are defining in new ways.[7] Security measures can take various forms, but they usually involve additional controls on trade in products—for instance, prohibitions on imports or exports, subject to case-by-case licensing. Assertions of "security interests" are beginning to affect trade in energy products, as discussed later in this chapter.

All the trade disputes addressed in this chapter arise out of the interplay of these policy areas. While the WTO rules and exceptions provide a scheme for balancing the different objectives, specific disputes are important because they draw the line of equilibrium in particular instances.

2) Basic Principles Reflected in Relevant Trade Rules and Exceptions

Energy disputes emerge where one Member's measure affects a relevant market and impinges on the interests of another. Five basic principles describe the general scheme of relevant WTO rules and exceptions applicable to trade in goods and applied in the disputes addressed later in this chapter.

First, subject to exceptions, WTO rules permit trade restrictions only if they take certain forms, particularly tariffs and export taxes. Article XI:1 of the GATT 1994 prohibits restrictions on importation or exportation of products, other than taxes, duties, and other fiscal charges. Article II:1 allows Members to commit to certain levels of such taxes, duties, or charges on traded products by inscribing concessions in their GATT Schedules. In principle, Schedules can include commitments relating to import tariffs as well as concessions relating to export taxes and duties, although this latter category of concession is unusual.[8]

---

7   See, e.g., Peter Navarro "Why Economic Security is National Security" (10 December 2018), online: trumpwhitehouse.archives.gov [perma.cc/SA2C-PDA3] or, for a Biden administration view, "Remarks by National Security Advisor Jake Sullivan on Renewing American Economic Leadership at the Brookings Institution" (27 April 2023), online: bidenwhitehouse.archives.gov [perma.cc/G26F-GSD2] .

8   Note that the Schedules of newly acceded resource-rich Members including China, Russia, and Saudi Arabia all include concessions on export taxes. As discussed below in respect of the DS431, 432, 433 *China—Rare Earths* and DS394, 395, 398 *China— Raw Materials* disputes, China's inability to use export duties to control export of important mineral resources appears to have contributed to its use of export quotas found by panels and the Appellate Body to be inconsistent with Article XI:1 of the GATT 1994.

Second, subject to exceptions, government measures must be non-discriminatory. Article I:1 of the GATT 1994 lays down a general most-favoured-nation (MFN) obligation, covering a wide variety of measures affecting imported or exported products. With respect to internal fiscal and regulatory measures that apply to both imported and domestic products, the provisions of GATT Article III require equally favourable treatment of both. Additional non-discrimination provisions appear throughout the WTO covered agreements.

Third, WTO rules permit product subsidies, subject to disciplines. Part II of the *Agreement on Subsidies and Countervailing Measures* (SCM Agreement) prohibits subsidies contingent upon export performance (export subsidies) or upon use of domestic over imported goods (import substitution subsidies).[9] The rules permit other subsidies,[10] provided they do not cause "adverse effects" to the interests of another Member. If they have such effects, they are subject to the disciplines in Part III of the SCM Agreement.[11]

Fourth, WTO rules permit contingent trade remedies (such as anti-dumping, anti-subsidy, and safeguard measures), subject to disciplines. Members can deviate from their non-discrimination obligations and may impose trade barriers on foreign products, at levels and in forms not otherwise permitted, when they take such action to remedy injury to one of their domestic industries resulting from significantly increased imports (safeguards),[12] international price discrimination (anti-dumping),[13] or subsidies (countervailing measures).[14]

Fifth, subject to disciplines, WTO rules permit regulation for non-economic reasons (such as the environment), even if it violates other rules. Members can deviate from their WTO obligations to pursue legitimate non-trade

---

9   See also Article XVI of the GATT 1994.

10 The *Fisheries Subsidies Agreement*, concluded in 2022 but not in force at the time of writing, will prohibit subsidies for Illegal, Unregulated or Unreported fishing, fishing overfished stocks, and for fishing in unregulated areas of the high seas. Such subsidies could, in principle, include energy-related subsidies, such as fuel subsidies. However, because the agreement is not yet in force, it is not considered further in this chapter.

11 Subsidized products may also be subject to countervailing measures where certain conditions are met, as discussed immediately below.

12 See Article XIX of the GATT 1994 and the *Agreement on Safeguards* ("Safeguards Agreement").

13 See Article VI of the GATT 1994 and the *Agreement on the Implementation of Article VI of the GATT 1994* (or "Anti-Dumping Agreement").

14 See Article VI of the GATT 1994 and Part V of the SCM Agreement.

concerns. To this end, exceptions allow governments to take measures to protect security interests[15] or to pursue certain other objectives (including conserving natural resources, protecting public morals or human, animal or plant life or health, or to secure acquisition or distribution of products in short supply). Measures that fall within these latter exceptions, found in the subparagraphs of Article XX of the GATT 1994, are subject to the so-called "chapeau," which requires that they "not be applied in a manner constituting arbitrary or unjustifiable discrimination between countries where the same conditions prevail or a disguised restriction on trade."[16]

The WTO rules that embody these principles comprise the key parts of the applicable substantive law relevant for the energy disputes discussed in this chapter.

3) The Function of Dispute Settlement in the WTO Community

Finally, by way of background for a discussion of energy disputes in the WTO, it is useful to describe key functions of dispute settlement in the WTO system. According to the DSU, the dispute settlement system serves at least three important roles.

---

15   In the case of trade in goods, the key exception is set forth in Article XXI of the GATT 1994. Equivalent exceptions are provided for trade in services and trade-related aspects of intellectual property rights.

16   WTO adjudicators have effectively read these same exceptions into the non-discrimination provisions in Article 2.1 of the TBT Agreement, which is discussed briefly below in connection with the DS600 *EU—Palm Oil Biofuels (Malaysia)* and DS593 *EU—Palm Oil Biofuels (Indonesia)* disputes. The panels in those disputes felt that the issues to be examined under Article 2.1 and the relevant GATT provisions were so coterminous that it dealt with the latter issues largely through cross references to its analysis of the former (see, most notably, *European Union and certain Member States—Certain Measures Concerning Palm Oil and Oil Palm Crop-Based Biofuels (Complaint by Malaysia)* (2024), WTO Doc WT/DS600/R at para 7.1097 (Panel Report), online (pdf): docs.wto.org [perma.cc/H8XL-Y3AR] [*EU—Palm Oil Biofuels (Malaysia)*] and WTO, *European Union—Palm Oil Biofuels (Complaint by Indonesia)* (2025), WTO Doc WT/DS593/R at para 7.1105 (Panel Report), online (pdf): docs.wto. org [perma.cc/4EQF-46GX] [*EU—Palm Oil Biofuels (Indonesia)*]where the respective panels (which were comprised of the same individuals and issued reports in much the same form) concluded that its "assessment under the 'legitimate regulatory distinction' step of the analysis in Article 2.1 thus applies *mutatis mutandis* to the *chapeau* of Article XX").

a) Settling Disputes and Providing an Outlet for Tension Between Members

Article 3.7 of the DSU states that the "aim of the dispute settlement mechanism is to secure a positive solution to a dispute." Article 3.3 states that the "prompt settlement" of disputes "is essential to the effective functioning of the WTO."

b) Security, Predictability and Preserving the Agreed Balance of Rights and Obligations

Article 3.2 of the DSU affirms that the dispute settlement system "is a central element in providing security and predictability" to the WTO system and "serves to preserve the rights and obligations of Members under the covered agreements." Dispute settlement is a key accountability mechanism preventing State interventions contrary to the agreed substantive rules.

c) Clarifying the Rules Consistent with International Law Rules of Treaty Interpretation

Article 3.2 also recognizes that the dispute settlement system serves "to clarify the existing provisions of [the covered] agreements in accordance with the customary rules of interpretation of public international law."[17] By interpreting the rules in particular cases, adjudicators[18] set Members' expectations about how they will apply to other measures.

WTO panels and the Appellate Body have emphasized all these roles, and WTO Members are now debating their relative priority as they undertake discussions about systemic reform. These discussions have underscored the importance of settling individual disputes (rather than resolving disputes predictably through consistent application of principles),[19] and the United

---

17   In practice, this is accepted to refer to Articles 31 and 32 of the *Vienna Convention on the Law of Treaties*.

18   In this chapter, the term "adjudicator" is meant as a generic reference to WTO panels, the Appellate Body, arbitrators and the individuals from which these bodies are composed.

19   See, e.g., WTO, *Special Meeting of the General Council*, WTO Doc JOB/GC/385 (2024), online (pdf): docs.wto.org [perma.cc/BA86-UPQG], which includes a report from facilitator Marco Tulio Molina Tejeda highlighting no fewer than six times that Members are resolved to "focus on what is necessary to resolve the dispute."

States has taken issue with the Appellate Body's judicial policy of seeking consistency in its reasoning, especially in connection with trade remedies.[20]

Discussions on dispute settlement reform take place against the backdrop of Members' inability to agree on appointments to the Appellate Body, which has resulted in the Appellate Body no longer functioning. The right of appeal in Articles 16 and 17 of the DSU, together with a non-functioning Appellate Body means that a party can frustrate binding resolution of a dispute by appealing panel reports "into the void." In effect, this means that the WTO currently operates an "opt in" system for binding dispute settlement in which disputing Members must take positive steps to *accept* binding resolution by agreeing not to appeal or by referring appeals to an alternative mechanism.[21] Unless disputing Members accept binding resolution, the process stops with issuance of a panel report.[22]

Having set out background useful for understanding energy disputes in the WTO framework, the chapter can now explore examples of energy disputes across the history of the WTO.

D. The Past: Disputes Relevant to Trade in Energy Products Between 1995 and the Early 2000s

THIS SECTION DEALS WITH ENERGY disputes in the early years of the WTO, specifically the period between 1995, when the WTO Agreement entered into

---

20   See, e.g., United States Trade Representative, *Report on the Appellate Body of the World Trade Organization*, (Washington, DC: Office of the United States Trade Representative, 2020) and in particular Sections II.E. and III, online (pdf): ustr.gov [perma. cc/JHU7-JJB9] .

21   At the date of writing, seventy-nine of the WTO's 164 Members (counting the European Union as twenty-seven) had agreed to use an alternative system of appeal under the MPIA. The MPIA develops the idea of using a special arbitration procedure under Article 25 of the DSU to substitute for appeals under Article 17. The idea of using "appeal arbitration" under Article 25 as a stop-gap measure in the absence of a functioning Appellate Body was first mooted in Scott Andersen et al, "Using Arbitration under Article 25 of the DSU to Ensure the Availability of appeals" (2017) Centre for Trade and Economic Integration, Working Paper 2017-17, online (pdf): repository. graduateinstitute.ch [perma.cc/UNG5-9B7Y].

22   Panel reports contain findings on issues of fact, law, and the application of the covered agreements to the matter at hand—and can, therefore, contribute to dispute resolution as a sort of non-binding conciliation procedure. In this respect, unadopted WTO panel reports resemble the conciliation commission reports contemplated by Article 7 of Annex V to the *United Nations Convention on the Law of the Sea*.

force, and the early 2000s, when the changing context led to new kinds of energy disputes. Later sections deal with subsequent periods.

1) The Context

A relatively cohesive atmosphere prevailed among WTO Members in the institution's early years. Key Members shared basic values relevant to the trading system. That is unsurprising, given that the original WTO Membership had just concluded the ambitious Uruguay Round of Multilateral Trade Negotiations, agreeing to establish the WTO with a binding and compulsory dispute settlement system. The geopolitical context was post-Cold War and unipolar. Although the Uruguay Round did not open all markets or even resolve all existing disagreements,[23] the philosophy reflected in the agreements was one of greater market orientation and with ambitions for progressive liberalization over time.[24]

The GATT system that preceded the WTO had always provided scope for environmental exceptions. Such issues were garnering greater attention in the early WTO period, with States having recently concluded an ambitious suite of multilateral environmental treaties at the Rio Earth Summit in 1992.[25] This was true especially for the energy sector, with the 1990s seeing reform of regional markets, innovation and a focus on environmental concerns.[26]

---

23   An interesting feature in the history of WTO dispute settlement is that 1997 was the year in which the greatest number of individual consultation requests were filed (fifty-one), followed by 1998 (forty-one) and 1996 (thirty-nine): see WTO, "Dispute Settlement Activity - Some Figures" (last visited 4 June 2025), online: wto.org [perma. cc/JE72-ESFX].

24   See, e.g., the *Agreement on Agriculture* (which begins by recalling the objective of establishing a market-oriented agricultural trading system), the *Agreement on Textiles and Clothing* (establishing a transitional arrangement to end sectoral arrangements for garment trade), and the GATS (which establishes a "multilateral framework of principles and rules for trade in services with a view to … progressive liberalization").

25   Indeed, the relationship between environment and trade was an early focus for WTO Members, with Ministers referring to the Rio Declaration and directing the WTO General Council to establish a Committee on Trade and Environment at its very first meeting: see Ministerial Decision on Trade and Environment.

26   Regional market reforms in the energy sector coincided with the adoption in 1994 of the Energy Charter Treaty, which includes provisions on environmental aspects. For discussion, see, e.g., Qinglin Zhang, "Analysis of the Impact on Sustainable Development by Investment Regulations in the Energy Charter" (2015) 8:6 *Journal of World Energy Law and Business* 542; Ole Kristian Fauchald, "International Investment Law and Environmental Protection" (2006) 17:1 *Yearbook of International Environmental*

2) Energy Disputes

As noted above in Section C.2, as a rule, WTO rules on trade in goods address treatment of *products* and regulate measures that affect the relative conditions of competition between products of different origins. Disputes directly relevant to energy trade were rare in the early days of the WTO. However, a pair of disputes concerning environmental regulation addressed two critical issues regarding a Member's ability to restrict product trade to pursue environmental objectives. These cases—*US—Gasoline* and *US—Shrimp*—elucidated principles that remain relevant for energy disputes today.[27]

US—Gasoline was a dispute concerning environmental regulation of fuel. The measure at issue regulated the *product characteristics* of competing gasoline products by imposing standards for cleaner fuels. It affected fuel sales in the United States but treated domestic and imported products differently. The Appellate Body made clear that regulation of gasoline to make it cleaner was permissible under the defence in Article XX(g) of the GATT 1994,[28] even if it had a detrimental impact on imports. However, it explained that the specific regulatory criteria must operate in a manner that does not unjustifiably favour domestic products.[29]

The *US—Shrimp* dispute arose because the United States restricted imports of shrimp from the complainants (India, Malaysia, Pakistan, and Thailand) harvested without devices to protect sea turtles. While not directly concerning energy, the interaction between trade policy and environmental policy sheds light on the balance in the WTO rules between the two—an issue highly relevant for energy trade.

The basic facts of the *US—Shrimp* dispute differed from *US—Gasoline* in two important ways. *First*, the US restriction barred imports not because of the product characteristics of the imported product but instead because of the *process or production method* used to harvest them. *Second*, the relevant

---

Law 3; Rolf Wagenbaur and Richard Wainwright, "European Community Energy and Environment Policy" (1996) 16:1 *Yearbook of European Law* 59; Clare Shine, "Environmental Protection Under the Energy Charter Treaty," in Thomas W. Wälde, ed, *The Energy Charter Treaty: An East-West Gateway for Investment and Trade* (Alphen aan den Rijn: Kluwer Law International, 1996) 520.

27   See also Mateo Ferrero's contribution to this volume (Chapter 13).

28   *United States—Standards for Reformulated and Conventional Gasoline (Complaint by Venezuela)* (1996), WTO Doc WT/DS2/AB/R at 12-20 (Appellate Body Report), online (pdf): docs.wto.org [perma.cc/Z7C8-8PYY] [*US—Gasoline*].

29   *Ibid* at 20–27.

activity occurred outside of US territory, raising questions about the ability of Members to regulate environmental impacts occurring in areas under the jurisdiction of others.

On the first question, the Panel and Appellate Body differed. The Panel held that the measure fell outside the chapeau to Article XX of the GATT 1994 because the United States conditioned market access on the exporting Member adopting certain conservation policies.[30] By contrast, the Appellate Body did not take issue with the United States' right to condition market access on the use of specific production methods.[31]

On the second question, the Appellate Body neatly avoided having to deal with extraterritorial regulation by noting that turtles were migratory, including into US waters, thereby creating a territorial nexus with the United States sufficient to justify exercise of US regulatory powers.[32]

Nevertheless, the Appellate Body (like the panel) still concluded that the measure arbitrarily and unjustifiably discriminated, notably because of the United States' failure to engage in international cooperation to address its transborder regulatory objective.[33]

---

30 *United States—Import Prohibition of Certain Shrimp and Shrimp Products (Complaint by India et al)* (1998), WTO Doc WT/DS58/R at paras 7.44–7.45 (Panel Report), online (pdf): docs.wto.org [perma.cc/LH3X-P3UC] [*US—Shrimp*] .

31 *United States—Import Prohibition of Certain Shrimp and Shrimp Products (Complaint by India et al)* (1998), WTO Doc WT/DS58/AB/R at paras 163–65 (Appellate Body Report), online (pdf): docs.wto.org [perma.cc/Z2HL-EAHE].

32 The Appellate Body thus declined to enter into a discission raised in previous trade/environment disputes about an "implied jurisdictional limitation" that would prevent Members from regulating matters entirely beyond their territory: see *ibid* at para 133. This remains a live issue today—the recent panels in DS600 *EU—Palm Oil Biofuels (Malaysia)* and DS593 *EU—Palm Oil Biofuels (Indonesia)* ventured into this space, finding that the EU's right to regulate was explained by a sufficient nexus between the climate system and the EU territory. The panels also highlighted other factors that they indicated could justify extra-territorial regulation: see *EU—Palm Oil Biofuels (Malaysia)*, above note 17 at para 7.315; see also *EU—Palm Oil Biofuels (Indonesia)*, above note 17 at para 7.327.

33 The United States was able to remedy these deficiencies in its measure: in compliance proceedings under Article 21.5 of the DSU, the Appellate Body found that an amended measure *complied* with US obligations because it related to conservation of exhaustible natural resources and now met the requirements of the Article XX chapeau because the United States had made genuine efforts to negotiate an international agreement to achieve levels of turtle protection that would be "comparable in effectiveness" to the US measure: see *United States—Import Prohibitions of Certain Shrimp and Shrimp Products (Article 21.5) (Complaint by Malaysia)* (2001), WTO Doc WT/

Together *US—Gasoline* and *US—Shrimp* established a new balance between trade discipline, on the one hand, and the regulatory space that Members enjoy to pursue environmental regulation, on the other. As such, the cases have enduring resonance. Members can regulate both product characteristics (such as the composition of fuels) and production methods (for example, energy production leading to distinct levels of pollution), even where such regulation negatively affects imported products.

E. The Present: Disputes Relevant to Trade in Energy Products Since the Early 2000s

1) The Context

The cohesive atmosphere of the early WTO began to break down around the time of the failed 1999 Ministerial Conference in Seattle[34] and continued to erode as the composition of the WTO changed with important accessions, such as China in 2001.[35] Other major energy-consuming, energy-producing, or resource-rich Members such as Russia and Saudi Arabia subsequently joined the WTO. Over time, the diverging priorities of different WTO Members has eroded the degree to which common values and interests support a shared vision of the WTO's role. North/South and East/West fractures have emerged, including in response to growing concerns in some regions about energy security and diversification of the energy mix.

At the same time, the focus of the international community on climate change has sharpened, with WTO Members, virtually all of which are parties

---

DS58/AB/RW at para 144 (Appellate Body Report), online (pdf): docs.wto.org [perma. cc/DXD4-8VH7] [*US—Shrimp (Article 21.5—Malaysia)*].

34 Dubbed in popular culture "the Battle in Seattle." The most well-remembered group of protestors in Seattle donned turtle suits to protest against the WTO's elevating of trade over environmental concerns. The choice of costume was ironic given that the US loss in *US—Shrimp* (also known as the "Shrimp-Turtle" dispute) was on narrow and easily fixed grounds, representing an important shift in WTO culture towards giving Members policy space to adopt *bona fide* environmental measures.

35 Members agreed on China's accession at the Doha Ministerial Conference, which also saw the launch of the "Doha Development Agenda" or "DDA." While the title of the DDA promised a focus on development, it failed to deliver outcomes. This has contributed to developing country disillusionment with the WTO system.

to the *Paris Agreement*,[36] transitioning away from fossil fuels and towards sustainable energy sources (the energy transition) at different paces.

2) Energy Disputes

Against that backdrop, two broad sets of energy disputes have emerged. The first relates to the use by resource-rich countries (particularly developing countries) of measures to promote domestic value-add and the use of natural resources to promote development. The second relates to the energy transition and includes both incentives for take-up of renewable energy as well as trade measures that affect conditions of competition between imports and domestic renewable energy products.

a) Pricing Natural Resources to Encourage Domestic Value-Add

With the accession of countries like China, Saudi Arabia, and Russia, there has been a greater focus on the use of export restrictions (and similar measures) on raw materials and energy products. Export restrictions are an economic policy instrument that stimulates domestic use of raw materials. Export restraints separate domestic and export markets, effectively increasing domestic supply and driving down domestic prices (with the opposite effects on international supply and prices). As such, they stimulate domestic use of, or value-add to, raw materials, provide economic support to domestic users, and thereby stimulate investment.

As noted above, Article XI:1 of the GATT 1994 prohibits restrictions on exports, other than export taxes. In acceding to the WTO, China[37] and Russia[38] respectively made commitments limiting their freedom to impose export duties, including on certain energy products and materials necessary for renewable energy equipment and batteries. Coupled with the GATT's general prohibition on quantitative export restraints, these "WTO-plus" commitments appear intended to significantly restrict the legal use of policy measures restraining exportation of raw materials.

36　Only States are party to the Paris Agreement, whereas WTO membership is open to separate customs territories as well.

37　See, in particular, Article 11.3 of China's Accession Protocol, which commits to eliminating export taxes not listed in an Annex.

38　See, in particular, para 638 of Russia's Working Party Report (made binding under Article 2 of its Accession Protocol), which commits Russia to implementing scheduled concessions on export duties.

Two disputes concerning China's post-accession maintenance of export taxes and quantitative export restrictions tested these commitments and, in particular, whether they could be justified under GATT exceptions.[39] When challenged in *China—Raw Materials* (2009-12)[40] and *China—Rare Earths* (2012-14),[41] China sought to defend its measures principally through Article XX(b) and (g) of the GATT 1994.[42] The respective panels and the Appellate Body, however, rejected China's environmental defences. For China's export *duties*, they held that a GATT defence, such as Article XX, could not be invoked to defend a violation of China's Accession Protocol in the absence of explicit language applying Article XX to accession commitments.[43] For China's *quantitative* export restraints, the respective adjudicators found that the violations of Article XI:1 could not be justified under Article XX on the facts, in particular because the measures at issue did not properly fall within a subparagraph of that provision.[44]

---

39   Unlike many other disputes addressed in this chapter, these disputes are therefore less about the intersection of competing policy areas and more about the applicability of specific WTO disciplines.

40   The European Union, the United States, and Mexico challenged export duties and quotas on certain bauxite, coke, fluorspar, magnesium, silicon carbide, silicon metal, yellow phosphorus, and zinc.

41   The European Union, the United States, and Japan challenged export duties and quotas on rare-earth elements as well as tungsten and molybdenum.

42   For one product in the *Raw Materials* dispute (refractory grade bauxite), China also raised a defence under Article XI:2(a) of the GATT 1994, arguing that the restrictions were "temporarily applied" to prevent or relieve a "critical shortage" of the product in China. The Appellate Body upheld findings by the panel rejecting this defence: see *China—Measures Related to the Exportation of Various Raw Materials (Complaint by the United States, the European Union and Mexico)* (2012), WTO Docs WT/DS394/AB/R, WT/DS395/AB/R, WT/DS398/AB/R at para 334 (Appellate Body Reports), online (pdf): docs.wto.org [perma.cc/2LAZ-RBMH] [*China—Raw Materials Appellate Body Reports*].

43   *Ibid* at paras 278–307; *China—Measures Related to the Exportation of Rare Earths, Tungsten, and Molybdenum (Complaint by the United States, the European Union and Japan)* (2014), WTO Docs WT/DS431/R, WT/DS432/R, WT/DS433/R at paras 7.63–7.117 (Panel Reports), online (pdf): docs.wto.org [perma.cc/53TU-CFA7] [*China—Rare Earths*].

44   *China—Measures Related to the Exportation of Rare Earths, Tungsten, and Molybdenum (Complaint by the United States, the European Union and Japan)* (2014), WTO Docs WT/DS431/AB/R, WT/DS432/AB/R, WT/DS433/AB/R at para 6.2(c) (Appellate Body Reports), online (pdf): docs.wto.org [perma.cc/26BR-NN9B]; *China—Measures Related to the Exportation of Various Raw Materials (Complaint by the United States, the European Union and Mexico)* (2011), WTO Docs WT/DS394/R, WT/DS395/R, WT/

Leaving to one side the factual issues concerning the quantitative restraints, the legal finding that Article XX did not apply to the export duty commitments in China's Accession Protocol surprised many.[45] Nevertheless, based on the text of China's commitments, and in particular the absence of a textual "hook" to bring Article XX into the analysis, the adjudicators prioritized trade considerations (the international supply of raw materials) and declined to find policy space for China to pursue non-trade objectives—including in regard to energy resources and minerals critical for the energy transition.

The domestic price impacts of export restraints on products such as natural gas or feedstocks for biofuels have also been central to a series of disputes concerning trade remedies on downstream products. These cases are also revealing of how WTO rules discipline State action—in this case, the remedies that are available against perceived distortions in markets (including energy markets) upstream to the production of goods.

Several countries, including the European Union, Ukraine, and Australia, have adopted a practice under their anti-dumping legislation of offsetting the market price advantage conferred by measures such as export restraints on inputs to exported manufactured goods. They do so through adjustments to costs when "constructing" the "normal value" of exported products from producers' costs of production.

In principle, "dumping" is international price discrimination by producers/exporters; in other words, selling a product in an export market at a price less than the normal value of those goods.[46] Normal value is, in principle, the home market sales price of an equivalent product.[47] However,

---

DS398/R at paras 8.17(c)—8.17(d) (Panel Reports), online (pdf): docs.wto.org [perma. cc/J8AT-RCNG].

45 It certainly surprised China: at the DSB meeting when the reports were adopted, China stated that "Members had the right to promote 'fundamental societal interests' besides trade liberalization" and that "resort to exceptions was important to allow Members to balance trade commitments with the right to pursue non-trade interests, such as the protection of human health and the conservation of exhaustible natural resources." It stated that "China had not, in acceding to the WTO, given up its right to promote these interests when regulating trade in goods." See WTO, *Minutes of Meeting*, WTO Doc WT/DSB/M/312 (2012) at 26, online (pdf): docs.wto.org [perma. cc/3BWP-BYXD].

46 See Article VI:1 of the GATT 1994. Under Article VI:1 and the *Anti-Dumping Agreement*, dumping may be remedied when it causes material injury to the domestic industry producing like goods.

47 Article 2.1 of the *Anti-Dumping Agreement*.

authorities may construct normal value from costs to produce the product in certain circumstances.[48] Under the EU/Ukrainian/Australian practice, the investigating authority can replace a producer's own costs in favour of another—higher—cost, when the authority finds the producer's costs to be distorted by governmental market interventions, such as export restraints or similar measures.

Complainants in disputes have called into question the legality of this practice, arguing that it reinvents anti-dumping as a tool to deal with foreign government market interventions, whereas the drafters had limited anti-dumping remedies to price discrimination by exporters.

Adjudicators have, for the most part, agreed with complainants. For instance, the Panel and Appellate Body in *EU—Biodiesel (Argentina)* found the European Union's cost adjustment practice wanting. In the underlying investigation, the EU authority had determined that an export tax on soybeans and soybean oil (feedstock for biodiesel) drove down the domestic price of those products, compared to the export price, by the amount of the tax. On this basis, they rejected domestic biodiesel manufacturer's costs of soybean oil and substituted the export price. The Appellate Body found that this was impermissible, holding that a producer's own costs must be used, provided they have "a genuine relationship with the production and sale of the specific product under investigation,"[49] or—in the words of the Panel— they should be the "costs actually incurred, and not . . . some hypothetical costs . . . which the investigating authority considers more 'reasonable' than the costs actually incurred."[50]

The Panel in a parallel case concerning biodiesel from Indonesia adopted a similar approach,[51] as did the Panel in a subsequent case concerning ammo-

---

48   Article 2.2 of the *Anti-Dumping Agreement* allows construction of normal value from the costs of production in the country of origin when there are no or insufficient sales of the like product in the domestic market or because of a particular market situation. Article 2.2.1.1 deals with use of producers' recorded costs for purposes of Article 2.2.

49   *European Union—Anti-Dumping Measures on Biodiesel from Argentina (Complaint by Argentina)* (2016), WTO Doc WT/DS473/AB/R at para 6.56 (Appellate Body Report), online (pdf): docs.wto.org [perma.cc/VY63-NSWT] [*EU—Biodiesel (Argentina)*].

50   *European Union—Anti-Dumping Measures on Biodiesel from Argentina (Complaint by Argentina)* (2016), WTO Doc WT/DS473/R at para 7.242 (Panel Report), online (pdf): docs.wto.org [perma.cc/6972-LQ8T] .

51   See *European Union—Anti-Dumping Measures on Biodiesel from Indonesia (Complaint by Indonesia)* (2018), WTO Doc WT/DS480/R at para 8.1(a) (Panel Report), online (pdf): docs.wto.org [perma.cc/359V-RWCK] [*EU—Biodiesel (Indonesia)*].

nium nitrate from Russia in which Ukraine's investigating authority substituted Russian prices for exported natural gas for Russian producer's actual natural gas costs.[52]

Again, as in the export restraints cases, when faced with issues limited to economic policy, adjudicators have adhered closely to the text of the WTO Agreement, constraining Members' attempts to carve out greater room to manoeuvre.

b) Disputes Arising out of the Energy Transition

Adjudicators have allowed wider policy space, however, in disputes arising in connection with measures broadly related to the energy transition. Unlike disputes limited to solely economic policy issues, such disputes call for balancing of economic and non-economic concerns. As such—in much the same way as the WTO's early regulatory cases—these disputes are revealing as to how adjudicators approach the interface between trade policy, industrial policy, and environmental protection.

Two groups of cases disputes deserve mention.

The *first* group of cases involve the trade impacts of the conditions of access to schemes that promote use of renewable energy. In each case, the respondent Members imposed domestic content requirements as a condition for certain advantages to renewable energy infrastructure (or its owners/developers), such as the right to supply electricity to government schemes.[53]

---

52 Ukraine's authority had determined that the Russian State regulated the domestic price of gas, holding it lower than export prices. The Panel and Appellate Body both determined that the authority was not entitled to adjust producers' gas costs, merely because of the government's pricing regulation: *Ukraine—Anti-Dumping Measure on Ammonium Nitrate (Complaint by the Russian Federation)* (2019), WTO Doc WT/DS493/AB/R at para 6.108 (Appellate Body Report), online (pdf): docs.wto.org [perma.cc/4E8H-2WAJ]; Subsequent cost adjustment disputes (dealing with both energy and non-energy products) have largely followed the same line of reasoning—see, most recently, *Australia—Anti-Dumping and Countervailing Duty Measures on Certain Products from China (Complaint by China)* (2024), WTO Doc WT/DS603/R at paras 7.79, 7.309 (Panel Report), online (pdf): docs.wto.org [perma.cc/YF9H-YSAJ] [*Australia—AD/CVD (China)*] .

53 Commentators have raised the question why only renewable energy subsidies, and not fossil fuel subsidies, have been challenged in WTO disputes. As discussed in the following paragraphs, the challenged renewable energy subsidies have all been found to involve discriminatory elements. Fossil fuel subsidies, by contrast usually take the form of consumer subsidies with origin neutral eligibility criteria and hence take a form more compatible with WTO disciplines. For a useful discussion, see Henok Birhanu Asmelash, "Energy Subsidies and WTO Dispute Settlement: Why Only

In *Canada—Renewable Energy/Canada—Feed in Tariff Program*, the European Union and Japan challenged domestic content requirements for receiving guaranteed feed-in tariffs. The complainants challenged the measures under both the SCM Agreement (alleging prohibited domestic content subsidies) and the GATT 1994 (alleging regulatory discrimination, contrary to Article III). The SCM claims were left unresolved.[54] On the GATT claims, the Appellate Body concluded that the measures were discriminatory, contrary to Article III:4.[55]

In *EU—Energy Package*, the Panel rejected claims by Russia concerning several European pro-competitive measures aimed at promoting efficient supply and distribution of energy resources. It nevertheless identified two narrow areas in which the European Union (or certain Member States) imposed discriminatory regulatory conditions against Russian gas and gas suppliers, contrary to GATT and GATS discrimination provisions.[56]

Renewable Energy Subsidies Are Challenged" (2015) 18:2 *Journal of International Economic Law* 261.

54   After reversing on appeals of certain panel findings concerning the *SCM Agreement*, the Appellate Body found it was unable to complete the analysis of the claims: see *Canada—Certain Measures Affecting the Renewable Energy Generation Sector (Complaint by Japan)* (2013) / *Canada—Measures Relating to the Feed-in Tariff Program (Complaint by the European Union)* (2013), WTO Docs WT/DS412/AB/R, WT/DS426/AB/R at para 6.1(a) (Appellate Body Reports), online (pdf): docs.wto.org [perma.cc/F6VJ-V6GU] [*Canada—Renewable Energy/Canada—Feed in Tariff Program*].

55   *Ibid* at para 5.79. The Appellate Body addressed whether the carve out for government procurement measures in Article III:8(a) applied and, reversing the panel, found that it did not, because—on the facts—the government did not procure the generation equipment subject to discrimination. *India—Solar Cells and Modules* involved similar facts and claims. The adjudicators upheld the United States' claim under GATT Article III:4 (*India—Certain Measures Relating to Solar Cells and Solar Modules (Complaint by the United States)* (2016), WTO Doc WT/DS456/AB/R at para 5.40 (Appellate Body Report), online (pdf): docs.wto.org [perma.cc/B6SP-RNPD] [*India—Solar Cells and Modules*]). In addition to unsuccessfully invoking Article III:8(a), India also raised defences under Articles XX(j) and XX(d) of the GATT 1994, relating, respectively, to materials in short supply and to measures necessary to secure compliance with GATT-consistent laws and regulations. On appeal, the Appellate Body found that solar modules were not, in fact, in "short supply" and that India had failed to identify relevant "laws or regulations." It accordingly rejected these additional defences (*India—Solar Cells and Modules* at paras 6.4, 6.6).

56   *European Union and its Member States—Certain Measures Relating to the Energy Sector (Complaint by the Russian Federation)* (2018), WTO Doc WT/DS476/R at paras 8.2.f.ii, g.1 (Panel Report), online (pdf): docs.wto.org [perma.cc/244Q-5JHW] [*EU—Energy Package*]. Subsequent to the release of the Panel report, Russia appealed into the void; the dispute remains pending before the non-functioning Appellate Body.

The common threads in these cases appear to be that (1) Members often seek to tilt the competitive playing field in favour of local suppliers when providing renewable energy-related incentives, and (2) WTO adjudicators consistently rule against discriminatory conduct. In other words, the environmental policy backdrop to the measures at issue did not lead adjudicators to create space for the Members concerned to pursue *economic* (industrial policy) objectives, even though adjudicators recognized space to pursue *environmental* aims and even *"energy security."*[57]

The *second* group of cases concerns the use of trade remedies to protect domestic energy industry from foreign competition. Notable in this group is the dispute in *US—Solar Safeguard*, which proceeded after the Appellate Body had ceased to function in December 2019. In contrast to the trade remedy cases reviewed above where adjudicators have taken remarkably consistent approaches, the *US—Solar Safeguard* Panel represents a departure from previous jurisprudence.

In particular, the *US—Solar Safeguard* Panel relaxed the requirements for a Member to successfully defend a safeguard measure compared to earlier Appellate Body jurisprudence. It did so by applying a more deferential standard of review for the US investigating authority's findings on two conditions for the imposition of safeguard measures,[58] namely the existence of "unforeseen developments" and the demonstration of a causal link between increased imports and injury to the domestic industry. The Panel's standard of review required the complainant to substantiate flaws in the authority's reasoning.[59] This contrasts with the standard adopted by the Appellate

---

57 The EU raised a "public order" defense under Article XIV(a) of the GATS in respect of one of the findings of violation in the DS476 *EU—Energy Package* dispute. Specifically, the EU argued that "security of energy supply is 'one of the most basic necessities of modern society'" (*Ibid* at para 7.1145). The panel accepted that a measure necessary to protect "energy security" could fall into subparagraph (a) of Article XIV (*Ibid* at para 7.1240). However, it rejected the EU defense because it discriminated in the sense of the Article XIV chapeau (whose text parallels that of GATT Article XX, discussed earlier in this chapter) (*Ibid* at para 7.1253).

58 Adjudicators have, in the past, found that the obligations of Article XIX of the GATT 1994 and the Safeguards Agreement apply cumulatively, meaning that an authority must address the existence of "unforeseen developments" under Article XIX as well as the conditions set forth in Article 2 of the Safeguards Agreement, namely increased imports resulting in serious injury to a domestic industry producing goods like the imported products.

59 See, as one example, *United States—Safeguard Measure on Imports of Crystalline Silicon Photovoltaic Products (Compliant by China)* (2021), WTO Doc WT/DS562/R at

Body in safeguard disputes, which required panels to "critically examine" the authority's explanation, including whether the authority took account of alternative explanations for the facts.[60] Based on the Panel's standard of review, the United States defeated all claims—the first occasion on which a Member has been able to successfully defend a global safeguard measure in a WTO dispute.[61]

The more deferential standard applied by the *US—Solar Safeguard* Panel provides wider scope for Members to apply trade remedies in respect of energy—and indeed other—products.[62] Members may therefore have a freer hand to favour domestic industry in the energy transition than earlier jurisprudence would indicate.

---

para 7.25 (Panel Report), online (pdf): docs.wto.org [perma.cc/63XZ-N8UY] [*US—Solar Safeguard*] (stating that China had not demonstrated that it was inappropriate for the US authority to find "unforeseen developments" rather than examining the US authority's explanation).

60   See, e.g., *United States—Safeguard Measures on Imports of Fresh, Chilled or Frozen Lamb Meat from New Zealand and Australia (Complaint by Australia and New Zealand)* (2001), WTO Docs WT/DS177/AB/R, WT/DS178/AB/R at para 166 (Appellate Body Report), online (pdf): docs.wto.org [perma.cc/8YV7-BKKR] [*US—Lamb*];The standard extends generally throughout the Safeguards Agreement: *United States—Definitive Safeguard Measures on Imports of Certain Steel Products (Complaint by the European Communities)* (2003), WTO Doc WT/DS248/AB/R, WT/DS249/AB/R, WT/DS251/AB/R, WT/DS252/AB/R, WT/DS253/AB/R, WT/DS254/AB/R, WT/DS258/AB/R, WT/DS259/AB/R at para 276 (Appellate Body Report), online (pdf): docs.wto.org [perma.cc/C3E4-WP8R][*US—Steel Safeguard*].

61   In DS399 *US—Tyres (China)*, the United States successfully defended a special safeguard measure taken under the relaxed China-specific provisions of China's Accession Protocol. Under China's Accession Protocol, safeguard measures were permitted, during a transitional period, whenever imports increased over a fixed threshold level. This "brightline" test differs importantly from the standards for global safeguards, in particular doing away with requirements for "unforeseen developments" and injury caused by increased imports.

62   Interestingly, the MPIA arbitrator in *Colombia—Frozen Fries*, adopted an approach similar to that of the *US—Solar Safeguard* Panel, above note 56, relaxing the "reasoned and adequate explanation" standard in reviewing the interpretation and application of the *Anti-Dumping Agreement*. See, e.g., *Colombia—Anti-Dumping Duties on Frozen Fries From Belgium, Germany and the Netherlands (Complaint by the European Union)* (2022), WTO Doc WT/DS591/ARB25 at para 4.1.a (Award of the Arbitrators), online (pdf): docs.wto.org [perma.cc/B64H-XKCC] [*Colombia—Frozen Fries*] in which the arbitrator considered "whether the Panel erred … by requiring an explanation," concluding it did on the basis that the panel's approach "represent[ed], in our view, an overly stringent application of the legal standard" under Article 5 of the *Anti-Dumping Agreement*.

F. The Future of Energy Disputes in the WTO

THE WINDS OF CHANGING INTERNATIONAL relations will continue to buffet the WTO and its dispute settlement system. Recent years have seen a combination of assertive trade-related environment measures, policies of re-industrialization and aggressive industrial policy implemented in the name of the energy transition, plus an increasingly complex geopolitical situation. These factors will continue to result in new measures and new disputes, calling on adjudicators again to interpret and apply rules and exceptions to draw the line of equilibrium in particular matters between competing energy, economic, environmental, and security policies.

1) The Context

Current policy settings in the three largest WTO Members help frame the context for future disputes. Starting with the European Union, measures taken in support of energy self-sufficiency and under the "Green Deal" increasingly impinge on trade, including trade in energy products. Examples include extension of the EU emissions trading system (ETS) to sectors that previously benefited from free permits. The European Union now couples this with a "Carbon Border Adjustment Mechanism" designed to prevent production of emissions-intensive products (including hydrogen, an energy product) from "leaking" out of the European Union and into other countries, particularly countries with lower emissions standards. Various EU Members States have adopted incentives for uptake of low-polluting vehicles, such as electric vehicles (EVs). Other examples include measures under EU Renewable Energy Directives to stimulate changes in favour of renewable energy, including in the transportation sector. This has lately resulted in panel reports concerning the eligibility of palm oil-based biofuels to EU renewable energy targets.[63]

The European Union is not alone in spurring the energy transition with assertive government measures. Under the Biden administration, the United States adopted the *Inflation Reduction Act* (IRA), which supports uptake of renewable energy and EVs through hundreds of billions of dollars in tax advantages and other subsidies. The IRA transparently seeks to promote US

---

63 *EU—Palm Oil Biofuels (Malaysia)*, above note 17 and *EU—Palm Oil Biofuels (Indonesia)*, above note 17. These reports are discussed further below in this Section.

re-industrialization, and frequently conditions subsidies on domestic content requirements. At the time of writing, China had just launched a WTO challenge to IRA subsidies.[64]

For its part, China has recently imposed export controls on certain minerals that are critical in the supply chains of products such as batteries.[65] China has referred to control over such trade as being a matter of "national security," mimicking US policy *vis-à-vis* China in relation to other products and explicitly placing trade in products related to the energy transition into the realm of geopolitics.

2) Energy Disputes

What kinds of energy disputes are likely to arise in this context? There are three obvious sets.

First, EU Green Deal measures are likely to come under scrutiny. The European Union has coupled its increasingly ambitious strategies to reduce domestic greenhouse gas emissions with measures imposed at the border aimed at maintaining the competitiveness of EU producers *vis-à-vis* imports. This, in turn, leads to concern—particularly for developing countries—that the European Union is "exporting" its environmental requirements, limiting agreed market access, and failing to cooperate internationally.

The *EU-Palm Oil Biofuels (Malaysia)* and *EU-Palm Oil Biofuels (Indonesia)* panel reports—recent at the time of writing—suggest that WTO panels will continue to review sympathetically measures that appear motivated by environmental concerns. The *Palm Oil* disputes centered on how EU renewable energy targets dealt with the possibility that indirect land use change (ILUC) resulting from farmers growing feedstock for biofuels might—counterproductively—increase carbon emissions. The majorities[66] of the respective *Palm Oil* panels rejected the complainants' assertions that the challenged measures' exclusion of imported palm-based biofuels from renewable energy

---

64 See Request for Consultations by China, *United States—Certain Tax Credits Under the Inflation Reduction Act (Complaint by China)* (2024), WTO Docs WT/DS623/1, G/L/1526 G/TRIMS/D/47, G/SCM/D137/1 (Request for Consultations by China), online (pdf): docs.wto.org [perma.cc/2FK6-B7J8].

65 See, e.g., Bloomberg, "Chinese Exports of Battery Material Graphite Plunge on Controls" (22 January 2024).

66 The panels in the two *Palm Oil* disputes were comprised of the same individuals, and the reports address the issues common to both disputes in much the same ways.

targets reflected a protectionist objective by favouring domestic oilseed producers.[67] On this basis, the panels rejected the complainants' claim that the measure was an "unnecessary" technical regulation.[68] Although the panels found aspects of discrimination in aspects of the way the measure was applied,[69] leading to findings of violation under Articles I:1 and III:4 of the GATT 1994 and Article 2.1 of the *Agreement on Technical Barriers to Trade* (TBT Agreement),[70] the majorities did not question the European Union's ability to define novel eligibility criteria that effectively targeted imported palm oil feedstock for special and detrimental treatment.[71] In contrast to the Appellate Body's approach to the chapeau to GATT Article XX in *US—Shrimp*,

---

67   One panelist dissented, stating that "[i]n my view, Malaysia has provided sufficient evidence to meet its burden of demonstrating that the objective of the measure includes an element of protectionism," and on that basis led them to the view that the challenged measures "(a) do[] not have an exclusively 'legitimate objective', and is therefore fundamentally inconsistent with Article 2.2 of the TBT Agreement; (b) results in a detrimental impact on palm oil-based-biofuel that does not stem 'exclusively from a legitimate regulatory distinction,' and is therefore fundamentally inconsistent with Article 2.1 of the TBT Agreement; and (c) is applied in a manner that constitutes 'arbitrary or unjustifiable discrimination' and a 'disguised restriction on trade' within the meaning of the chapeau of Article XX of the GATT 1994." *EU—Palm Oil Biofuels (Malaysia)*, above note 17 at paras 7.1443 and 7.1459. See also *EU—Palm Oil Biofuels (Indonesia)*, above note 17 at para 7.1447: "In my view Indonesia has provided sufficient evidence to meet its burden of demonstrating that the objective of the measure includes an element of protectionism; and this conclusion is reinforced by the evidence showing there is an element of arbitrariness in singling out palm oil-based biofuel for the high ILUC-risk cap and phase-out when other types of oils, notably soybean, appear to pose the same alleged risk."

68   *EU—Palm Oil Biofuels (Malaysia)*, above note 17 at paras 7.191–7.397; *Ibid* at paras 7.191–7.417.

69   Specifically, the European Union's failure to conduct a timely review of data, an additionality criterion, plus the design of a ten-year time limit: see *EU—Palm Oil Biofuels (Malaysia)*, above note 17 at para 7.635 (addressing Article 2.1 of the TBT Agreement), para 7.1097 (applying *mutatis mutandis* the same considerations to find "arbitrary or unjustifiable discrimination" under the chapeau to Article XX of the GATT 1994); see also *ibid* at para 7.659 and para 7.1105 on the same points.

70   Article 2.1 of the TBT Agreement requires Members to accord non-discriminatory treatment in connection with technical regulations.

71   See notably the Panel's novel analysis creating a category of "a priori legitimacy" for a regulatory distinction based on low risk of indirect land use change (concluding at *EU—Palm Oil Biofuels (Malaysia)*, above note 17 at para 7.545 and *EU—Palm Oil Biofuels (Indonesia)*, above note 17 at para 7.561) and its subsequent approach to a number of substantive factors when undertaking an analysis of the "application of the regulatory distinction," concluding at *EU—Palm Oil Biofuels (Malaysia)*, above note 17 at para 7.635 *EU—Palm Oil Biofuels (Indonesia)*, above note 17 at para 7.659.)

the *Palm Oil* panels afforded greater scope for the European Union to unilaterally define the problem of ILUC in other countries, without first requiring attempts at international cooperation with those countries. The result in *Palm Oil* disputes suggests that complainants will need to work hard to demonstrate discriminatory or protectionist dimensions if they wish to succeed in challenging other EU Green Deal measures relevant for energy trade.

Second, the United States' approach of subsidizing the development by US industry of low emission technologies, including EVs—notable under the Biden administration—is likely to garner attention. This is especially true where there is discrimination in eligibility criteria for subsidies, or the measures otherwise lead to significant market distortions. At the time of writing, China had just initiated a dispute in relation to IRA subsidies. China's request for establishment of a panel takes issue with aspects of the US scheme that, among others, make subsidies contingent on use of critical minerals or ferrous metals produced in selected third countries or the United States, allegedly discriminating against imports from China.[72] In this way, past disputes about discriminatory subsidies for energy products appear to be prelude for future disputes about the same thing. Notably, China's willingness to bring disputes against the United States suggests that —China sees value in having a WTO panel point out what it perceives as WTO-inconsistencies, underscoring the continued utility of the system, even in a case where a binding decision is unlikely.[73]

---

72 See *United States—Certain Tax Credits Under the Inflation Reduction Act (Complaint by China)* (2024), WTO Doc WT/DS623/3 (Request for the Establishment of a Panel by China), online (pdf): docs.wto.org [perma.cc/SGD5-V8QF]. Notably, around the same time, the European Union requested consultations with Chinese Taipei in respect of allegedly discriminatory local content requirements in connection with offshore wind investments: see *Chinese Taipei—Measures Relating to Investments in Offshore Wind Installations (Complaint by the European Union)* (2024), WTO Doc WT/DS625/1 (Request for Consultations by the European Union), online (pdf): docs.wto.org [perma. cc/XG3L-URPQ].

73 At the time of writing, the United States had appealed into the void each of the three most recent disputes brought against it by China (and Hong Kong, China): *United States—Origin Marking Requirement (Complaint by Hong Kong)* (2023), WTO Doc WT/DS597/9 (Notification of Appeal by the United States), online (pdf): docs.wto. org [perma.cc/X3SP-TE25]; *United States—Certain Measures on Steel and Aluminium (Complaint by China)* (2023) WTO Doc WT/DS544/14 (Notification of Appeal by the United States), online (pdf): docs.wto.org [perma.cc/JC45-89B7]; *United States—Tariff Measures on Certain Goods from China (Complaint by China)* (2020) WTO Doc WT/DS543/10 (Notification of Appeal by the United States), online (pdf): docs.wto.org [perma.cc/FB3Q-HQC6].

Third, a key issue will be how disputes involving stated "national security" considerations play out. As noted, China has asserted national security as a justification for controlling exports of certain products relevant to the energy transition. China's approach comes as other Members, led by the United States, restrain exports of other critical products to China on asserted national security grounds. And indeed, the selection of preferred sources for critical minerals and ferrous metals in connection with US IRA subsidies also bears a relation to geopolitical considerations.

Although the security defenses of multilateral trade rules remained untested in disputes for seventy years,[74] a string of cases since 2017 have shown that panels will not treat these defenses as immune from scrutiny in dispute settlement. Indeed, respondents have failed to justify WTO-inconsistent measures with national security defenses in several disputes.[75]

Notably, China is party to the MPIA, meaning that compulsory and binding dispute settlement is available for other WTO Members wishing to challenge Chinese measures. Nevertheless, labelling a measure as relating to national security remains tantamount to a declaration by the Member

---

74   The nearest thing to a dispute settlement panel touching on the security exceptions of the pre-WTO GATT system is found in 1986 GATT Panel report in *United States—Trade Measures Affecting Nicaragua (Complaint by Nicaragua)* (1986), GATT Doc L/6053, online (pdf): docs.wto.org [perma.cc/NWB4-J4NE] *[US—Trade Measures Affecting Nicaragua]*. However, the GATT Contracting Parties established this Panel with special terms of reference precluding it from considering the merits of the US security defense and instead limiting itself to determining the existence and amount of trade harm (nullification or impairment) arising: see GATT, *Minutes of Meeting*, GATT Doc C/M/192 (1985), online (pdf): docs.wto.org [perma.cc/G44T-END7].

75   See *Saudi Arabia—Measures Concerning the Protection of Intellectual Property Rights (Complaint by Qatar)* (2020), WTO Doc WT/DS567/R at para 7.293 (Panel Report), online (pdf): docs.wto.org [perma.cc/2KMS-U8UU] (rejecting a defense under Article 73 of the TRIPS Agreement on the grounds of an insufficient connection between stated security interests and a WTO-inconsistent measure), and *United States—Certain Measures on Steel and Aluminum Products (Complaint by China)* (2022), WTO Doc WT/DS544/R at para 7.149 (Panel Report), online (pdf): docs.wto.org [perma.cc/E3XL-GC9R]; *United States—Certain Measures on Steel and Aluminum Products (Complaint by Norway)* (2022), WTO Doc WT/DS552/R at para 7.137 (Panel Report), online (pdf): docs.wto.org [perma.cc/LX25-GLXN]; *United States—Certain Measures on Steel and Aluminum Products (Complaint by Switzerland)* (2022), WTO Doc WT/DS556/R at para 7.167 (Panel Report), online (pdf): docs.wto.org [perma.cc/MX2L-8U89]; and *United States—Origin Marking Requirement (Complaint by Hong Kong)* (2022), WTO Doc WT/DS597/R at para 7.360 (Panel Report), online (pdf): docs.wto.org [perma.cc/P574-QY7R] (all rejecting defenses under Article XXI(b)(iii) of the GATT 1994 in the absence of a war or emergency in international relations).

concerned that it will not change an underlying policy regardless of how a WTO panel rules. In addition, recent US policy tied restoration of a fully functioning dispute settlement system to resolution of its concern that WTO adjudicators must not address the merits of national security defences, reportedly stating that "WTO dispute settlement cannot be a forum for debating and deciding on the essential security interests of members."[76] It may be that the Membership will find other approaches to disputes in which security interests are asserted.

G. Conclusion

THIS CHAPTER HAS SHOWN HOW the issues in play in energy disputes in the WTO have broadened over time, reflecting shifting attitudes with respect to the role of government in energy trade. Early cases concerning regulatory requirements were followed by cases raising wider concerns, including security of supply for raw materials and the remedies that Members might take when faced with enhanced foreign competitiveness, driven at least in part, by policy measures in exporting countries.

As Members give increasing priority to the energy transition—supporting it in ways that stimulate both supply of sustainable energy and demand for it—disputes concerning renewable energy have proliferated. The future will, no doubt, see more cases about assertive trade-related environmental measures, aggressive industrial policy measures aimed at capturing investment and employment in sectors relevant for the energy transition, as well as difficult issues arising out of the world's evolving geopolitical situation.

Over time, the WTO's dispute settlement system has shown itself to be capable of delivering reports on the various iterations of energy disputes discussed in this chapter, many of which have contributed to the successful resolution of the underlying issues. Indeed, this has been true even after

---

76 Borderlex, "WTO: United States Tables Its 'Objectives' for Dispute Settlement Reform" (5 July 2023), online: borderlex.net [perma.cc/6RDW-48L2] . Reportedly, the United States favours some form of codification of the approach adopted in the GATT *US—Trade Measures Affecting Nicaragua* dispute (see above note 68), whereby a panel would address nullification or impairment and not the merits of a security defence. Such an approach could helpfully de-politicize disputes in which a Member asserts security interests. However, panels (and complainants) could still face difficulties pinpointing the precise "benefits" nullified or impaired by measures taken in the name of security interests, as the experience in the *US—Trade Measures Affecting Nicaragua* case shows.

the Appellate Body ceased operating in December 2019. It has done so in a manner characterized by highly reasoned analysis and through a process that seldom—if ever—has been questioned as lacking impartiality. Where disputes call on adjudicators to address the balance between legitimate and other policy objectives, adjudicators have generally found the answer in the text of the covered agreements—finding flexibility within exceptions like GATT Article XX but declining to re-invent established concepts, like dumping. That said, the absence of an Appellate Body has allowed greater diversity in decision-making, leaving the future direction of travel in certain areas (notably trade remedies) less clear.

In any event, WTO Members will continue to litigate energy disputes in Geneva. For the foreseeable future, they will do so without a functioning Appellate Body, meaning that the DSB will adopt and enforce some decisions while others will remain non-binding, requiring complainants to be creative in using unadopted panel findings to secure a positive resolution. Either way, however, the WTO dispute settlement system remains a valuable tool available for the peaceful resolution of international disputes. Its continued relevance means that adjudicators must continue to adhere to the standards of analytical rigour and objectivity that Valerie Hughes has championed during her career in the WTO system.

CHAPTER 13

WTO Disputes on Trade and Environment: Contributions of the Multilateral Trading System to Effective Environmental Protection Policies

Mateo Ferrero[*]

THE TRIPLE PLANETARY CRISIS CAUSED by climate change, pollution, and biodiversity loss is increasingly leading governments around the world to adopt a wide range of measures to protect the environment. Many of these measures intersect with international trade, as they may introduce import or export bans, environmental charges on greenhouse gas emissions, or technical specifications for products or production processes, among others. World Trade Organization (WTO) covered agreements offer ample policy space to Members to pursue legitimate policy objectives, including the protection of the environment and the fight against climate change. However, how much policy space is effectively awarded to Members to pursue environmental

[*] Counsellor at the Trade and Environment Division of the WTO Secretariat. The views expressed in this article are the author's own and are without prejudice to the positions of WTO Members and to their rights and obligations under the WTO. The author wishes to express his profound gratitude to Valerie Hughes for the privilege of working with her and for the enduring lessons drawn from her integrity, professionalism, and generous mentorship.

objectives? And, in order to comply with WTO disciplines, are there any considerations that policymakers should keep in mind when adopting these types of measures? This chapter explores the main lessons that can be drawn from almost thirty years of WTO jurisprudence in the area of trade and environment, as these may provide useful guidance for future measures adopted to protect the environment and address the climate crisis.

A. Introduction

IN THE WORLD OF INTERNATIONAL governance, trade policies and environmental policies have different legal and institutional histories. Some argue that environmental and trade policies are set with little regard to their reciprocal implications, and their respective decisionmakers have few opportunities to meet in international fora. All this may give the impression that these two legal regimes belong to different planets.[1]

At the same time, the WTO has been able to efficiently manage this apparent tension and overcome potential divergences between the two sets of policies. This may be, in part, thanks to the fact that WTO disciplines recognize that Members may adopt measures having a trade impact in pursuance of environmental objectives. For example, the preamble to the *Marrakesh Agreement Establishing the World Trade Organization* (WTO Agreement) explicitly recognizes the objective of sustainable development and the need to protect and preserve the environment. However, how much policy space is effectively awarded to Members to pursue environmental objectives? And are there any considerations that policymakers should keep in mind when adopting this type of measures in order to comply with WTO disciplines and requirements?

Against this backdrop, this chapter seeks to examine two related issues on the basis of key WTO disputes addressing trade and environment policies. First, it explores the extent to which the WTO covered agreements as interpreted by WTO adjudicators offer policy space to Members to adopt measures seeking to protect the environment. Second, it analyzes whether, in providing this policy space, WTO adjudicators have also provided guidance with respect to procedural and substantive considerations that WTO

---

1 Jean-Marie Paugam, "Trade, Sustainability and Climate: What is at Stake 30 Years After WTO's Creation?" (10 January 2025), online (blog): wto.org [perma.cc/ F7T7-77XJ].

Members may wish to take into account in designing, adopting, and implementing trade measures with an underlying environmental objective.

This chapter does not seek to cover exhaustively *all* WTO disputes addressing trade and environment issues. Nor does it intend to examine in detail all the substantive aspects of the legal standards under WTO disciplines applicable to measures pursuing environmental objectives. Instead, the aim is to focus on key findings by WTO adjudicators that shed light on the extent of the policy space awarded to Members by the WTO legal framework, as well as on a selection of procedural and substantive considerations that WTO Members may wish to take into account when adopting trade measures that pursue environmental objectives. The overarching objective is to explore the main contributions that the WTO dispute settlement system has made towards shaping an international legal regime that, in addition to safeguarding the main disciplines of the multilateral trading system, also supports the adoption of effective environmental protection policies by WTO Members.

B. What Has Been the Policy Space Recognized by WTO Adjudicators When Reviewing Measures Aiming to Protect the Environment?

IN SEVERAL DISPUTES, WTO ADJUDICATORS have found that Members benefit from significant policy space, or flexibility, to adopt trade measures that seek to protect or preserve the environment. This section examines the main findings by WTO adjudicators in the following disputes: *US—Gasoline*, *US—Shrimp*, and *Brazil—Retreaded Tyres*.

The very first WTO dispute decided by the WTO Appellate Body, *US—Gasoline*, pertained to a measure with an underlying environmental objective. As elaborated below, the Appellate Body recognized important flexibilities that strike a careful balance between WTO obligations and the policy space awarded by the general exceptions under Article XX of the *General Agreement on Tariffs and Trade* (GATT) 1994.

The *US—Gasoline* dispute related to the implementation by the United States of its domestic legislation known as the *Clean Air Act* of 1990 and, more specifically, to the regulation enacted by the United States' Environmental Protection Agency pursuant to that Act, to control toxic and other pollution caused by the combustion of gasoline manufactured in or imported into the United States. This regulation was commonly referred to as the "Gasoline

Rule," and it imposed detailed baseline establishment rules applicable to domestic refiners and to imported gasoline. The Panel in that dispute found that the baseline establishment rules of the Gasoline Rule were inconsistent with Article III:4 of the GATT 1994 and that they were not justified under Article XX(g) because they did not constitute a measure "relating to the conservation of exhaustible natural resources" within the meaning of Article XX(g).[2] The United States appealed the panel findings under Article XX(g).

Two arguments were made by the complainants in this dispute that, if accepted, could have limited the policy space accorded to Members to pursue environmental protection measures. First, Venezuela and Brazil argued that clean air does not qualify as an "exhaustible natural resource" within the meaning of Article XX(g). Second, Venezuela argued that a measure can only be "relating to" or "primarily aimed at" conservation if the measure was both: (i) primarily intended to achieve a conservation goal; and (ii) had a positive conservation effect (i.e., that the measure must be shown to be "effective").[3]

The Appellate Body disagreed with both lines of argumentation. First, with respect to the classification of "clean air" as an "exhaustible natural resource," the Appellate Body seemed to agree with the panel's conclusions that clean air was a "natural resource" that could be "depleted" and thus that a policy to reduce the depletion of clean air was a policy to conserve an exhaustible natural resource within the meaning of Article XX(g).[4]

Second, on the basis of the following reasoning, the Appellate Body rejected the notion that, in order to be covered by the exception under Article XX(g), a Member would need to demonstrate that its measure has had a "positive conservation effect":

> We do not believe, finally, that the clause "if made effective in conjunction with restrictions on domestic production or consumption" was intended to establish an empirical "effects test" for the availability of the Article XX(g) exception. In the first place, the problem of determining causation, well-known in both domestic and international law, is always a difficult one. In the second place, in the field of conservation of exhaustible natural resources, a substantial period of time, perhaps years, may have to

---

2   *United States—Standards for Reformulated and Conventional Gasoline (Complaint by Venezuela)* (1996), WTO Doc WT/DS2/AB/R at 9 (Appellate Body Report), online (pdf): docs.wto.org [perma.cc/XEB3-72GH] [*US—Gasoline*].

3   *Ibid* at 10.

4   *Ibid* at 14.

elapse before the effects attributable to implementation of a given measure may be observable. The legal characterization of such a measure is not reasonably made contingent upon occurrence of subsequent events. We are not, however, suggesting that consideration of the predictable effects of a measure is never relevant. In a particular case, should it become clear that realistically, a specific measure cannot in any possible situation have any positive effect on conservation goals, it would very probably be because that measure was not designed as a conservation regulation to begin with. In other words, it would not have been "primarily aimed at" conservation of natural resources at all. [5]

In my view, the above reasoning by the panel and the Appellate Body goes in the direction of providing policy space to Members for the adoption of environmental protection measures. Indeed, both adjudicators rejected a "narrow" reading of the terms "exhaustible natural resource" for purposes of successfully establishing a defence under Article XX(g). In addition, the Appellate Body rejected the notion that justifying a measure under Article XX(g) requires establishing that the measure at issue has had a "positive conservation effect," a requirement that would have made it more onerous for Members seeking to defend measures pursuing environmental objectives under Article XX.

In *US—Shrimp*, the Appellate Body was again confronted with a trade measure pursuing an environmental objective. In this case, the measure at issue (Section 609) sought to protect sea turtles from shrimp harvesting activities. In essence, it required shrimp trawl vessels to use approved Turtle Excluder Devices (TEDs) in all areas where there was a likelihood that shrimp trawling would interact with sea turtles, with certain limited exceptions. The measure imposed an import ban on shrimp harvested with commercial fishing technology which may adversely affect sea turtles. The ban, however, was not applicable to harvesting nations that were certified.[6] In this dispute, the Appellate Body also had the opportunity to address important arguments having a bearing on Members' policy space for pursuing environmental protection measures.

---

5   *Ibid* at 21.
6   *United States—Import Prohibition of Certain Shrimp and Shrimp Products (Complaint by Malaysia et al)* (1998), WTO Doc WT/DS58/AB/R at paras 2–3 (Appellate Body Report), online (pdf): docs.wto.org [perma.cc/836S-MKLQ] [*US—Shrimp*].

First, the Panel found that the measure at issue fell within that class of measures excluded from the scope of Article XX of the GATT 1994 because Section 609 conditioned access to the domestic shrimp market of the United States on the adoption by exporting countries of certain conservation policies prescribed by the United States. In other words, the panel was of the view that measures conditioning market access in order to pursue conservation or environmental objectives were outside the scope of the general exceptions of the GATT 1994. The Appellate Body disagreed in no uncertain terms with this interpretation of Article XX. It considered that the Panel's standard "finds no basis either in the text of the chapeau or in that of either of the two specific exceptions claimed by the United States."[7] In rejecting the panel's findings, the Appellate Body reasoned:

> [C]onditioning access to a Member's domestic market on whether exporting Members comply with, or adopt, a policy or policies unilaterally prescribed by the importing Member may, to some degree, be a common aspect of measures falling within the scope of one or another of the exceptions (a) to (j) of Article XX. Paragraphs (a) to (j) comprise measures that are recognized as exceptions to substantive obligations established in the GATT 1994, because the domestic policies embodied in such measures have been recognized as important and legitimate in character.[8]

The above reasoning supports the view that measures pursuing any of the legitimate objectives covered by Article XX, including those related to environmental protection, may be justified by the general exceptions even in situations in which the measure is trade-restrictive (e.g., when market access is denied), as long as the conditions in this provision are fulfilled.

The second issue bearing on the policy space awarded to Members to pursue environmental protection policies concerned the interpretation of the terms "exhaustible natural resources" under Article XX(g). The complainants in that dispute contended that a "reasonable interpretation" of the term "exhaustible" is that the term refers to "finite resources such as minerals, rather than biological or renewable resources." One complainant added that sea turtles, being living creatures, could only be considered under Article XX(b),

---

7   *Ibid* at para 121.

8   *Ibid.*

since Article XX(g) was meant for "nonliving exhaustible natural resources."[9] The Appellate Body disagreed with these arguments and instead found:

> Article XX(g) is not limited to the conservation of "mineral" or "non-living" natural resources. The complainants' principal argument is rooted in the notion that "living" natural resources are "renewable" and therefore cannot be "exhaustible" natural resources. We do not believe that "exhaustible" natural resources and "renewable" natural resources are mutually exclusive. One lesson that modern biological sciences teach us is that living species, though in principle, capable of reproduction and, in that sense, "renewable," are in certain circumstances indeed susceptible of depletion, exhaustion and extinction, frequently because of human activities. Living resources are just as "finite" as petroleum, iron ore and other non-living resources.[10]

Noting that the Preamble of the WTO Agreement explicitly acknowledges the objective of sustainable development, the Appellate Body stated that the words of Article XX(g), "exhaustible natural resources," must be read by a treaty interpreter in the light of contemporary concerns of the community of nations about the protection and conservation of the environment. Thus, the generic term "natural resources" in Article XX(g) is not "static" in its content or reference but is rather "by definition, evolutionary." The Appellate Body elaborated that modern international conventions and declarations, such as the United Nations Convention on the Law of the Sea and the Convention on Biological Diversity, make frequent references to natural resources as embracing both living and non-living resources. On this basis, the Appellate Body concluded that measures to conserve exhaustible natural resources, whether living or non-living, may fall within Article XX(g).[11]

Brazil—Retreaded Tyres is another case in which the Appellate Body made important findings having a bearing on Members' policy space in the area of environmental protection measures. This dispute concerned the consistency with the GATT 1994 of a prohibition on the importation of retreaded tyres that had been adopted by Brazil.[12] Through the import ban, Brazil pursued

---

9   *Ibid* at para 127.
10   *Ibid* at para 128.
11   *Ibid* at paras 129–31.
12   See *Brazil—Measures Affecting Imports of Retreaded Tyres (Complaint by the European Union)* (2007), WTO Doc WT/DS332/AB/R at 1, fn 2 (Appellate Body Report), online (pdf): docs.wto.org [perma.cc/VJK2-8EGB] [*Brazil—Retreaded Tyres*] (defining

the objective of reducing exposure to the risks to human, animal, and plant life health arising from the accumulation of waste tyres. Brazil claimed that such policy fell within the range of policies covered by paragraph (b) of Article XX of the GATT 1994. Brazil's chosen level of protection was the "reduction of the risks of waste tyre accumulation to the maximum extent possible."[13]

In examining the claims on appeal, the Appellate Body noted the parties' agreement that, "it is within the authority of a WTO Member to set the public health or environmental objectives it seeks to achieve, as well as the level of protection that it wants to obtain, through the measure or the policy it chooses to adopt."[14]

The Appellate Body examined the methodology used by the panel in analyzing the contribution of the import ban to the achievement of its objective. For the Appellate Body, such a contribution exists when there is a genuine relationship of ends and means between the objective pursued and the measure at issue.[15] The Appellate Body made two important findings in that dispute in relation to an adjudicator's assessment of the contribution of the measure to the objective pursued, both of which have the effect of providing policy space to Members to pursue legitimate policy objectives.

First, the complaining Member argued that the Panel was under an obligation to quantify the contribution of the import ban to the reduction in the number of waste tyres and to determine the number of waste tyres that would be reduced as a result of the import ban.[16] The Appellate Body disagreed with this argument, emphasizing that an analysis of the contribution of a measure to the realization of the objective pursued by it can be done *either* in quantitative or in qualitative terms. In terms of the policy space accorded to WTO Members, the Appellate Body's conclusion is significant because agreeing that the contribution of the measure to the objective could *only be established* through *quantitative* methods could have severely limited the ability of Members to justify measures pursuing environmental objectives under the general exceptions of the GATT 1994.

---

retreaded tires as used tires that are reconditioned for further use by stripping the worn tread from the skeleton, or casing, and replacing it with new material in the form of a new tread).

13   *Ibid* at para 134.

14   *Ibid* at para 140 [footnotes omitted].

15   *Ibid* at para 146.

16   *Ibid* at para 147.

Second, the Appellate Body recognized that certain complex public health or environmental problems may be tackled only with a comprehensive policy comprising a multiplicity of interacting measures. In the short-term, it may prove difficult to isolate the contribution to public health or environmental objectives of one specific measure from those attributable to the other measures that are part of the same comprehensive policy. The Appellate Body further observed that the results obtained from certain actions—for instance, measures adopted in order to attenuate global warming and climate change or certain preventive actions to reduce the incidence of diseases that may manifest themselves only after a certain period of time—can only be evaluated with the benefit of time.[17] These statements by the Appellate Body are particularly important as they recognize that it may be possible to justify a measure under Article XX even if its contribution to the fulfillment of the legitimate policy objective is not apparent in the short term and even if it needs to be understood as part of a broader policy package.

The Appellate Body made another finding in *Brazil—Retreaded Tyres* that is important for the policy space awarded to *developing countries* seeking to adopt environmental protection measures. In determining whether a measure can be deemed to be "necessary" under Article XX(b) a frequently used conceptual step is to examine whether there are any reasonably available alternative measures that are less trade restrictive than the measure at issue. The Appellate Body recognized that "the capacity of a country to implement remedial measures that would be particularly costly, or would require advanced technologies, may be relevant to the assessment of whether such measures or practices are reasonably available alternatives to a preventive measure, such as the Import Ban, which does not involve 'prohibitive costs or substantial technical difficulties.'"[18] This finding gives flexibility to developing countries as it recognizes that they may not be expected to pursue environmental objectives through measures that are particularly costly or that would require advanced technologies, even if the chosen measure may be more trade restrictive.

---

17   *Ibid* at para 151.
18   *Ibid* at para 171.

C. What Checks Have WTO Adjudicators Recognized When Reviewing Measures Aiming to Protect the Environment?

A NUMBER OF WTO DISPUTES have also provided guidance with respect to some procedural and substantive considerations that WTO Members may wish to take into account in designing, adopting and implementing trade measures with an underlying environmental objective. In this section three types of considerations will be examined: (i) the importance of international cooperation; (ii) the importance of providing key due process guarantees; and (iii) the importance of ensuring that the measure seeks to achieve its environmental objective in a coherent and even-handed way. These considerations can be understood to establish certain procedural and substantive checks that should help ensure that a proper balance is struck between the pursuance of legitimate objectives (such as the protection of the environment) and key disciplines of the multilateral trading system. This section examines the main findings by WTO adjudicators in the following disputes: *US—Gasoline*, *US—Shrimp*, *Brazil—Retreaded Tyres*, and *US—Tuna II (Mexico)*.

1) The Importance of International Cooperation

In *US—Gasoline*, the Appellate Body emphasized in its examination of the chapeau of Article XX the importance of international cooperation among WTO Members, including in situations where a measure pursues an environmental objective. In that dispute, the United States indicated that imported gasoline was relegated to the more exacting statutory baseline requirement because of the difficulties of verification and enforcement associated with imported gasoline. In other words, for the United States' verification and enforcement of the Gasoline Rule's requirements for imported gasoline were "much easier when the statutory baseline is used." The Panel acknowledged that there could well be anticipated difficulties concerning verification and subsequent enforcement of rules applicable to imported gasoline. At the same time, these difficulties were seen by the panel as "insufficient to justify the denial to foreign refiners of individual baselines permitted to domestic refiners."[19] The Appellate Body agreed with this panel finding and noted the existence of established techniques for checking, verification, assessment,

---

19   *US—Gasoline*, above note 3 at 26.

and enforcement of data relating to imported goods, techniques which in many contexts are accepted as adequate to permit international trade. For the Appellate Body, "[t]he United States must have been aware that for these established techniques and procedures to work, cooperative arrangements with both foreign refiners and the foreign governments concerned would have been necessary and appropriate."[20] Moreover, the Appellate Body noted that the United States had not pursued the possibility of entering into cooperative arrangements with the governments of the complainants so as to mitigate the administrative problems pleaded by the United States. In the Appellate Body's view, it was not possible to meet the requirements of the chapeau of Article XX where the responding Member had omitted to explore adequately means of mitigating the stated administrative problems through international cooperation with the governments of the complainants. The Appellate Body also considered that the spirit of international cooperation enshrined in Article XX's chapeau would have required the United States to consider the costs for foreign refiners that would result from the imposition of statutory baselines, a factor that had been taken into account in relation to domestic refiners.[21]

In *US—Shrimp*, the Appellate Body again made important findings in the context of the chapeau of Article XX related to the importance of international cooperation. The examination of whether Section 609 had been applied in a manner constituting "unjustifiable discrimination between countries where the same conditions prevail" within the meaning of the chapeau led the Appellate Body to emphasize two different aspects of international cooperation that should be taken into account when adopting measures to protect environmental objectives: (i) the need to take into account different conditions in the territories of other Members compared to those of the Member adopting the measure; and (ii) the importance of seeking bilateral or multilateral avenues for cooperation on environmental matters among Members.

First, the Appellate Body noted that the measure at issue *required* other WTO Members to adopt a regulatory program that was not merely *comparable*, but rather *essentially the same*, as the one applied to the United States shrimp trawl vessels. In other words, the effect of the application of Section 609 was to establish a "rigid and unbending standard" by which United States

20   *Ibid* at 27.
21   *Ibid* at 28.

officials determined whether or not countries would be certified, thus grant-ing or refusing other countries the right to export shrimp to the United States. Other specific policies and measures that an exporting country may have adopted for the protection and conservation of sea turtles were, in practice, not taken into account. In the Appellate Body's view, "it is not acceptable, in international trade relations, for one WTO Member to use an economic embargo to *require* other Members to adopt essentially the same compre-hensive regulatory program, to achieve a certain policy goal, as that in force within that Member's territory, *without* taking into consideration different conditions which may occur in the territories of those other Members."[22] The main relevance of this finding is that the chapeau of Article XX calls for active consideration of whether there are different conditions in the terri-tories of other Members compared to those of the Member adopting the measure, which would call for introducing flexibilities or other mechanisms to calibrate the measure to the conditions of other WTO Members.

Second, the Appellate Body considered that another aspect of the appli-cation of Section 609 that had a bearing on the analysis under the chap-eau was the failure of the United States to engage relevant WTO Members exporting shrimp to the United States in serious, across-the-board negotia-tions with the objective of concluding bilateral or multilateral agreements for the protection and conservation of sea turtles, before enforcing the import prohibition against the shrimp exports of those other Members.[23] In support of this view, the Appellate Body referred to, among others, a report of the WTO's Committee on Trade and Environment indicating that "multilateral solutions based on international cooperation and consensus as the best and most effective way for governments to tackle environmental problems of a transboundary or global nature."[24]

In the compliance proceedings in that dispute (*US—Shrimp—Article 21.5 (Malaysia)*), the Appellate Body had the opportunity to elaborate on the nature and the extent of the duty of the United States to pursue international cooperation in the protection and conservation of sea turtles. Malaysia argued that demonstrating serious, good faith *efforts to negotiate* an international agreement for the protection and conservation of sea turtles is not sufficient

---

22   *US—Shrimp*, above note 7 at para 164.

23   *Ibid* at para 166.

24   *Ibid* at para 168 (quoting WTO, *Report (1996) of the Committee on Trade and Environ-ment*, WTO Doc WT/CTE/1 (1996) at para 171, online (pdf): docs.wto.org [perma. cc/4ZKH-5DCY]).

to meet the requirements of the chapeau of Article XX. Instead, the chapeau required the *conclusion* of such an international agreement.[25] The Appellate Body disagreed with this argument. For the Appellate Body, "[r]equiring that a multilateral agreement be *concluded* by the United States in order to avoid 'arbitrary or unjustifiable discrimination' in applying its measure would mean that any country party to the negotiations with the United States, whether a WTO Member or not, would have, in effect, a veto over whether the United States could fulfill its WTO obligations. Such a requirement would not be reasonable."[26] Instead, the United States would be expected to make good faith efforts to reach international agreements that are comparable from one forum of negotiation to the other. The Appellate Body added: "[I]t is one thing to *prefer* a multilateral approach in the application of a measure that is provisionally justified under one of the subparagraphs of Article XX of the GATT 1994; it is another to require the *conclusion* of a multilateral agreement as a condition of avoiding 'arbitrary or unjustifiable discrimination' under the chapeau of Article XX."[27] The Appellate Body found no such requirement.

2) The Importance of Due Process

In *US—Shrimp*, the Appellate Body made findings in the context of the *chapeau* of Article XX related to the importance of providing certain due process guarantees to trading partners and their economic operators. In assessing whether there was "arbitrary discrimination" under the *chapeau*, one of the salient aspects of the measure at issue (Section 609) was the requirement to apply for certification by the United States that the applicant country met the substantive requirements of Section 609. The Appellate Body considered certain aspects of the certification processes to be "problematic"[28] because there was no "transparent, predictable certification process."[29] The Appellate Body pointed to a number of issues, including: (1) the certification processes under Section 609 consisted principally of administrative *ex parte* inquiry or verification by staff of the Office of Marine Conservation in the Department

---

25 *United States—Import Prohibition of Certain Shrimp and Shrimp Products (Article 21.5) (Complaint by Malaysia)* (2001), WTO Doc WT/DS58/AB/RW at para 116 (Appellate Body Report), online (pdf): docs.wto.org [perma.cc/DXD4-8VH7].

26 *Ibid* at para 123 [emphasis in original].

27 *Ibid* at para 124 [emphasis in original].

28 *US—Shrimp*, above note 7 at para 178.

29 *Ibid* at para 180.

of State with staff of the United States National Marine Fisheries Service, (2) there was no formal opportunity for an applicant country to be heard, or to respond to any arguments that may be made against it, in the course of the certification process before a decision to grant or to deny certification is made, (3) no formal written, reasoned decision whether of acceptance or rejection, was rendered on applications, (4) countries whose applications were denied did not receive notice of such denial or of the reasons for the denial, and (5) no procedure for review of, or appeal from, a denial of an application was provided.[30] For these reasons, the Appellate Body considered that:

> [t]he certification processes followed by the United States . . . appear[ed] to be singularly informal and casual, and to be conducted in a manner such that these processes could result in the negation of rights of Members. There appear[ed] to be no way that exporting Members c[ould] be certain whether the terms of Section 609, in particular, the 1996 Guidelines, [we]re being applied in a fair and just manner by the appropriate governmental agencies of the United States.[31]

3) The Importance of Coherence and Even-Handedness

Through its jurisprudence, the Appellate Body has also established certain substantive checks to ensure that a proper balance is struck between the protection of the environment and key disciplines of the multilateral trading system. This section focuses on the Appellate Body's emphasis on ensuring that measures seeking to achieve environmental objectives do so in a coherent and even-handed way.

In *Brazil—Retreaded Tyres*, the measure at issue challenged by the complainant did not only encompass the import ban on retreaded tyres but also included an exemption from the import ban on imports of certain retreaded tyres from other countries of the Mercado Común del Sur (MERCOSUR), which was referred to in the dispute as the "MERCOSUR exemption."[32] On appeal, the European Union contended that the Panel had erred in finding that the MERCOSUR exemption had not resulted in the import ban being

---

30   *Ibid.*

31   *Ibid* at para 181.

32   *Brazil—Retreaded Tyres*, above note 13 at para 122.

applied in a manner that is inconsistent with the chapeau of Article XX.[33] In particular, the European Union argued that the MERCOSUR exemption did not further but undermined the stated objective of the measure. For this reason, the European Union contended, it had to be regarded as "unreasonable, contradictory, and thus arbitrary."[34]

In examining this claim, the Appellate Body stated that there is arbitrary or unjustifiable discrimination when a measure provisionally justified under a paragraph of Article XX is applied in a discriminatory manner "between countries where the same conditions prevail" and "when the reasons given for this discrimination bear no rational connection to the objective falling within the purview of a paragraph of Article XX, or would go against that objective."[35] The Appellate Body added that the assessment of whether discrimination is arbitrary or unjustifiable should be made in the light of the objective of the measure.[36]

In applying these considerations to the case at hand, the Appellate Body noted that the discrimination between MERCOSUR countries and other WTO Members in the application of the import ban was introduced as a consequence of a ruling by a MERCOSUR tribunal. However, in the Appellate Body's view, the ruling issued by the MERCOSUR arbitral tribunal was not an acceptable rationale for the discrimination because it bore no relationship to the legitimate objective pursued by the import ban under Article XX(b) and even went against that objective. For these reasons, the Appellate Body concluded that the MERCOSUR exemption had resulted in the import ban being applied in a manner that constituted arbitrary or unjustifiable discrimination.[37]

This decision is significant because, by taking issue with the MERCOSUR exemption, the Appellate Body sought to ensure that measures seeking to achieve environmental objectives do so in a coherent and even-handed way. There may have been a reason for the MERCOSUR exemption (i.e., the fact that it was a response to a ruling from the MERCOSUR tribunal). However,

---

33   *Ibid* at para 216 (the panel in that dispute had concluded that the operation of the MERCOSUR exemption had not resulted in the import ban being applied in a manner that would constitute "arbitrary or unjustifiable discrimination," within the meaning of the chapeau of Article XX).

34   *Ibid* at para 220.

35   *Ibid* at para 227.

36   *Ibid*.

37   *Ibid* at para 228.

for the Appellate Body, this introduced an "incoherence" in the operation of the measure in light of the objective being pursued. In other words, the fact that imports of retreaded tyres from MERCOSUR countries were allowed into Brazil (while imports from all other WTO Members were *not*) was considered by the Appellate Body as going *against* the environmental objective behind the import ban. In the Appellate Body's view, this lack of coherence between the operation of the measure and the objective pursued meant that the measure did not comply with the requirements of the *chapeau* of Article XX.

In *US—Tuna II (Mexico)*, the Appellate Body also made important findings in relation to the need to strike a balance between the pursuance of legitimate environmental objectives and key disciplines of the multilateral trading system, in particular the non-discrimination obligation. In that dispute, Mexico brought a challenge against certain legal instruments of the United States establishing the conditions for the use of a "dolphin-safe" label on tuna products. The measure at issue (i.e., the US "dolphin-safe" labelling provisions) set out the requirements for when tuna products sold in the United States may be labelled as "dolphin-safe." More specifically, they conditioned eligibility for a "dolphin-safe" label upon certain documentary evidence that varied depending on the area where the tuna contained in the tuna product was harvested and the type of vessel and fishing method by which it was harvested. In particular, tuna caught by "setting on"[38] dolphins were not eligible for a "dolphin-safe" label in the United States, regardless of whether this fishing method was used inside or outside the Eastern Tropical Pacific Ocean (the ETP[39]). The measure at issue also prohibited any reference to dolphins, porpoises, or marine mammals on the label of a tuna product if

---

38   *United States—Measures Concerning the Importation, Marketing and Sale of Tuna and Tuna Products (Complaint by Mexico)* (2012), WTO Doc WT/DS381/AB/R at 69, fn 355 (Appellate Body Report), online (pdf): docs.wto.org [perma.cc/AW9J-EEYL] [*US—Tuna II*] (the fishing technique of "setting on" dolphins takes advantage of the fact that tuna tend to swim beneath schools of dolphins in the Eastern Tropical Pacific Ocean. The fishing method involves chasing and encircling the dolphins with a purse seine net in order to catch the tuna swimming beneath the dolphins).

39   *Ibid* at 69, fn 356 (the ETP, as defined under US law, extends westward from the west coast of the Americas to include most of the tropical Pacific east of the Hawaiian Islands and includes high seas areas as well as the exclusive economic zones and territorial seas of Chile, Colombia, Costa Rica, Ecuador, El Salvador, France [due to the French overseas possession, Clipperton Island], Guatemala, Honduras, Mexico, Nicaragua, Panama, Peru, and the United States).

the tuna contained in the product did not comply with the labelling conditions spelled out in the measure at issue. However, the measure did not make the use of a "dolphin-safe" label obligatory for the importation or sale of tuna products in the United States.[40]

The panel in that dispute found that the measure at issue constituted a technical regulation and was therefore to be examined under the *Agreement on Technical Barriers to Trade* (TBT Agreement). The Appellate Body agreed with this panel finding.[41]

In examining whether the measure at issue was inconsistent with the non-discrimination obligations (most-favoured-nation and national treatment) under Article 2.1 of the TBT Agreement, the Appellate Body found that the lack of access to the "dolphin-safe" label of tuna products containing tuna caught by setting on dolphins had a detrimental impact on the competitive opportunities of Mexican tuna products in the US market.[42]

The Appellate Body turned next to the issue of whether that detrimental impact reflected discrimination that was inconsistent with Article 2.1. The United States argued that, to the extent that there were any differences in criteria that must be satisfied in order to substantiate "dolphin-safe" claims, they were "calibrated" to the risk that dolphins may be killed or seriously injured when tuna was caught.[43] For the Appellate Body, the question before it was whether the United States had demonstrated that this difference in labelling conditions was a legitimate regulatory distinction and hence whether the detrimental impact of the measure stemmed exclusively from such a distinction rather than reflecting discrimination.[44]

In examining this matter, the Appellate Body noted the Panel's uncontested findings that the fishing method of setting on dolphins caused observed and unobserved adverse effects on dolphins, and that these adverse effects were fully addressed in the measure at issue, since the measure denied access to the label to products containing tuna caught by setting on

---

40 *Ibid* at para 172.

41 *Ibid* at para 199 (the Appellate Body noted that the measure at issue set out a single and legally mandated definition of a "dolphin-safe" tuna product and disallowed the use of other labels on tuna products that did not satisfy this definition. In doing so, the US measure prescribed in a broad and exhaustive manner the conditions that apply for making any assertion on a tuna product as to its "dolphin-safety," regardless of the manner in which that statement was made).

42 *Ibid* at para 235.

43 *Ibid* at para 282.

44 *Ibid* at para 284.

dolphins. The measure at issue thus addressed the adverse effects on dolphins resulting from the use of the fishing method that Mexico's fleet predominantly employed by disqualifying all tuna products containing tuna harvested with that method from access to the "dolphin-safe" label.[45]

At the same time, the Appellate Body emphasized the panel's finding that there were "clear indications that the use of certain tuna fishing techniques other than setting on dolphins may also cause harm to dolphins." The Appellate Body also underscored the panel's disagreement with the United States' assertion that the risks to dolphins from other fishing techniques were insignificant and did not under some circumstances rise to the same level as the risks from setting on dolphins.[46]

In light of these facts regarding the existence of risks to dolphins outside the ETP, the Appellate Body found problematic that, where "tuna is caught outside the ETP, it would be eligible for the US official label, even if dolphins have in fact been caught or seriously injured during the trip, since there [wa]s, under the US measures as currently applied, no requirement for a certificate to the effect that no dolphins have been killed or seriously injured outside the ETP."[47] The Appellate Body underscored that the US measure fully addressed the adverse effects on dolphins resulting from setting on dolphins inside the ETP, whereas it did "not address mortality (observed or unobserved) arising from fishing methods other than setting on dolphins outside the ETP."[48]

In these circumstances, the Appellate Body was not persuaded that the United States had demonstrated that the measure was even-handed in the relevant respects, even accepting that the fishing technique of setting on dolphins is particularly harmful to dolphins.[49] The Appellate Body thus concluded that the United States had not demonstrated that the difference in labelling conditions for tuna products containing tuna caught by setting on dolphins in the ETP, on the one hand, and for tuna products containing tuna caught by other fishing methods outside the ETP, on the other hand, was "calibrated" to the risks to dolphins arising from different fishing methods in different areas of the ocean. It followed from this that the United States had not demonstrated that the detrimental impact of the US measure on

---

45   *Ibid* at para 287.
46   *Ibid* at paras 288–89.
47   *Ibid* at para 289.
48   *Ibid* at para 297.
49   *Ibid*.

Mexican tuna products stemmed exclusively from a legitimate regulatory distinction.[50]

In order to address the findings of inconsistency with its WTO obligations, the United States modified the measure at issue in a number of respects at different moments in time. The main modification to the US tuna measure was the incorporation of additional requirements applicable to tuna caught outside the ETP by fishing methods other than setting on dolphins. The findings by the original panel and Appellate Body were subject to two further rounds of compliance litigation under Article 21.5 of the DSU in order to determine whether the revised US tuna measure complied with WTO disciplines.[51] Ultimately, the Appellate Body concluded that the revisions introduced by the United States to the measure at issue meant that the 2016 tuna measure, as a whole, was calibrated to the risks to dolphins arising from the use of different fishing methods in different areas of the ocean.[52]

The tuna dispute between Mexico and the United States is significant for two main reasons. First, by taking issue with the fact that the US tuna measure was not calibrated to the risks to dolphins posed by different fishing techniques in different areas of the ocean, WTO adjudicators underscored the importance of designing and implementing measures pursuing environmental objectives in a coherent and even-handed way. Second, in light of the main findings by WTO adjudicators, the United States was aware that one possible way of bringing the measure into compliance with WTO obligations would be to calibrate it better to the risks to dolphins posed by different fishing techniques in different areas of the oceans. The United States decided to modify the measure to bring it into compliance with WTO obligations by increasing the requirements applicable to tuna caught outside the ETP and through fishing techniques other than setting on dolphins. In my view, this example illustrates how the process of reviewing national measures through WTO dispute settlement has not only helped to bring inconsistent measures

50   *Ibid.*

51   *United States—Measures Concerning the Importation, Marketing and Sale of Tuna and Tuna Products (Article 21.5—Mexico) (Complaint by Mexico)* (2015), WTO Doc WT/DS381/AB/RW (Appellate Body Report), online (pdf): docs.wto.org [perma.cc/2PJX-D9TE]; *United States—Measures Concerning the Importation, Marketing and Sale of Tuna and Tuna Products (Article 21.5—US / Article 21.5—Mexico II) (Complaint by Mexico)* (2015), WTO Doc WT/DS381/USA, WT/DS381/RW2 (Appellate Body Report), online (pdf): docs.wto.org [perma.cc/2N79-TZBS] [*US—Tuna II, Article 21.5 – US/Mexico II*].

52   *US—Tuna II, Article 21.5—US/Mexico II, ibid* at para 7.10.

into compliance with WTO disciplines but has also resulted in more effective outcomes from an environmental protection perspective.

D. Concluding Remarks

AT THE TIME OF WRITING, the WTO dispute settlement system finds itself at its most critical juncture in its almost thirty years of existence, as a result of the current *impasse* with the Appellate Body and the possibility of filing appeals to panel reports "into the void," which significantly weakens the proper functioning of the WTO dispute settlement system as a whole.

While this chapter's main aim is to examine the main contributions of WTO adjudicators on issues at the intersection of trade and environment, my hope would be that the above analysis also sheds light on how WTO adjudicators, and in particular the Appellate Body, made important contributions over the years to a more coherent understanding of how the international trade and environmental regimes should co-exist and even work in a mutually supportive manner.

In a nutshell, WTO adjudicators have found that Members benefit from significant policy space, or flexibility, to adopt trade measures that seek to protect or preserve the environment. For example, it was recognized that measures to preserve "exhaustible natural resources" may cover living creatures in addition to non-living resources. Similarly, it was also accepted that certain complex environmental problems may be tackled only with a comprehensive policy comprising a multiplicity of interacting measures whose results can only be evaluated with the benefit of time. At the same time, this policy space enshrined in the WTO legal framework also needs to be balanced against some procedural and substantive considerations that WTO Members may wish to take into account in designing, adopting, and implementing trade measures with an underlying environmental objective. This chapter focuses on three types of considerations identified by WTO adjudicators: (1) the importance of international cooperation, (2) the importance of providing key due process guarantees, and (3) the importance of ensuring that the measure seeks to achieve its environmental objective in a coherent and even-handed way.

The triple planetary crisis caused by climate change, pollution, and biodiversity loss is increasingly leading governments around the world to adopt a wide range of measures to protect the environment, which often intersect with international trade. The above guidance from WTO adjudicators may prove useful to Members aiming to adopt trade measures that pursue an environmental objective. My hope would be that this guidance also underscores the urgent need to reestablish a fully functioning WTO dispute settlement system that would then be able to address the new challenges arising at the intersection of the trade and environment international legal regimes.

CHAPTER 14

Where Angels Fear to Tread: the General Standard of Review in WTO Law

James Flett[*]

A. Introduction

MUCH HAS BEEN WRITTEN ABOUT the so-called "crisis" at the World Trade Organization (WTO), particularly with respect to dispute settlement, and many proposals for so-called "reform" have been made. Much of this material is, in my view, off-the-mark. As any serious student of problem-solving, whether theoretical, academic, or practical, should confirm, the most important part of the process is identifying the problem in the first place. As long as this has not been done, attempts at remedial action are very likely to be ineffective and quite possibly make the situation worse.

The United States' obstruction of Appellate Body appointments primarily results from cyclical dysfunction in US domestic politics (the election of Trump), with Biden lacking sufficient political margin to rectify the situation. Trump would never have joined a WTO with mandatory and binding dispute settlement and would never have agreed to China joining. Unable in practice to withdraw, he decided to do the next best thing, that is, to sabotage the dispute settlement system. To justify this, the United States fabricated

---

* European Commission, Legal Service. Any opinions expressed are personal and mine alone.

various accusations of so-called judicial "activism" by the Appellate Body. Blended into this narrative was the proposition that the system could not apprehend Chinese state capitalism, which is irrational, because if China is an issue, we should be using all means at our disposal to contain it. The third related strand was criticism by vested interests of certain outcomes in trade remedies litigation, such as zeroing, public bodies, double counting, and so forth. Trump would have done this in any event. The substantive content of twenty-five years of WTO adjudications would not have made one jot of difference. There is nothing that could have been done differently to avoid this outcome.

That said, in every crisis there is opportunity. From an academic perspective, one must look past the disingenuous and hypocritical affirmations of the Trump administration and its apologists and ask whether or not we can envisage anything different in an eventually revived WTO dispute settlement system. In my view, there is one central and critical issue, which is: what is a panel's "standard of review"? Should a panel (and by extension the Appellate Body), in light of the customary rules of interpretation of public international law (The *Vienna Convention on the Law of Treaties*, Articles 31–33), identify the interpretation *and application* of WTO law that *best fits* a particular case and consider this to be the *only lawful* outcome (this more or less corresponds to what has been done)? Or should a panel (and by extension the Appellate Body) rather afford some "*deference*" to the measure at issue and the defending WTO Member, whatever that might mean? This latter notion rather corresponds to what is contained in Article 17.6 of the *Anti-Dumping Agreement*, which refers to the concepts of: the "proper" "establishment" of the "facts," an "unbiased and objective" "evaluation" of the facts, and "permissible interpretation."

This chapter explores the proposition that, in WTO law, the general standard of review of panels, and by extension the Appellate Body, when it comes to applying the law to the facts, admits of multiple lawful outcomes. Section B discusses the general vocabulary of WTO dispute settlement: law, fact, evidence, application of the law to the facts, meaning of municipal law, interpretation. Sections C and D discuss respectively Article 17.6 of the *Anti-Dumping Agreement* and Article 11 of the Dispute Settlement Understanding (DSU); and Section E their concurrent application. Section F explores these issues through the lens of WTO regulatory law and the concept of regulatory space. Section G addresses certain institutional issues. The conclusion is that this less intense standard of review will be a central and critical part of any revived WTO dispute settlement mechanism.

B. The Vocabulary of WTO Adjudication

AS A THRESHOLD MATTER, TO ensure clarity, it is important to be as precise as one reasonably can about the terms one uses to discuss WTO adjudication, that is, the basic vocabulary or building blocks of WTO litigation, what we mean by those terms and what limitations may be associated with those terms, particularly the terms: law, fact, evidence, application of the law to the facts, meaning of municipal law, interpretation. Seasoned WTO lawyers will already be very familiar with such issues, but it may be that, in what follows, they find something new to them.

The "*law*" consists of the terms of the treaty as they are actually written, with no paraphrasing and nothing added or taken away. One needs to distinguish between the *directly operative legal terms* on the one hand and the context on the other hand, even if this is not always easy to do. The directly operative legal terms are those that circumscribe the *obligation* at issue, generally consisting of the term "*shall*" or its equivalent and the other treaty terms that are directly connected to it, grammatically or otherwise. Most obligations are expressed in the negative ("shall not") reflecting an implicit assumption that the context is one which Members are not obliged to act, but should they choose to do so they must respect certain limits. For example, if a Member would decide to adopt a regulatory measure, it shall not discriminate between goods on grounds of origin. However, some obligations are expressed in the affirmative ("shall"), such as the obligation to establish an anti-dumping authority. Although the treaty speaks of "*rights*," the WTO Agreement does not actually grant "rights" as such, in the sense that there is no such thing as a WTO dispute brought by a Member seeking to protect a "right." For example, in principle, there is no such thing as an original WTO dispute brought by a Member seeking to protect its "right" to adopt a sanitary and phytosanitary (SPS) measure. Rather, the treaty contains certain provisions, typically referred to, for example, as "exceptions," which simply qualify or circumscribe an obligation and which are grammatically tied to the term "*may*" or its equivalent. Most rights are expressed in the affirmative ("may") although some are expressed in the negative ("may not"). Thus, WTO Members have "rights" in the sense of the converse of the "obligations" imposed. For example, an importing WTO Member is obliged not to discriminate between goods on grounds of origin unless justified for public health reasons; and an exporting Member accordingly has the "right" to export the good in question, without discrimination, unless justified for public health reasons. The interesting point to note for the purposes of this chapter is that "deference" *in the application of the law* relaxes obligations and extends rights, irrespective of whether they are expressed in negative or positive terms. The context is merely a tool for interpreting (and applying) the directly operative legal terms and not itself the subject of the interpretative exercise.

The "*facts*," in a typical case, consist of the actual terms used in the measure at issue, translated into one or more of the three official WTO languages, typically English (and there may be significant issues surrounding the problem of translation). Typically, this means that the "facts" and the "*evidence*" are co-extensive, with a document setting out the terms of the measure at issue being, at the same time, both the "facts" and the "evidence" of those facts. However, these are somewhat strange "facts," since they merely consist of words on a page, not events in time and space that either were the case or were not the case and which could in theory have been physically witnessed, experienced, and recorded in some way. Furthermore, in many cases, one has to look further. For example, in a regulatory case, such as an SPS case, there will be the SPS measure itself (the measure at issue), but that in turn will be based on a file of "facts," not all of which may be expressly set out in the SPS measure. The same is true of an anti-dumping case. Often, something is presented as a "fact" when in truth it amounts to a characterization of fact. For example, the statement that a unit of the good at issue was imported may appear to be a fact. But it could open up a discussion about what one means by "imported": does this refer to physical crossing of a frontier (and if so, which frontier). or does it refer to customs clearance? It is rare for a WTO adjudicator to be presented with a direct record of a "fact"; rather, WTO adjudicators tend to be presented with documents that constitute "evidence" and litigants argue that such "evidence" establishes one or more propositions characterized as "facts," especially when not contested. In sum, what constitutes the "facts" and "evidence" is not always as simple or straightforward as one might assume.

The law then has to be *applied* to the facts. By definition, this requires the adjudicator to explain the "basic rationale," that is, the reasons for the outcome of the case. A document that simply set out the law on the one hand, and the facts (or evidence) on the other hand, then announced the outcome, would not be a proper adjudication. The reasoning can be deductive, from the general to the specific, from the law to the facts; or inductive, from the specific to the general, from the facts to the law; or a mix. But it should in principle allow the losing the party to understand why it has lost, and, eventually, reaffirm its consent not only to the adjudication but also to the outcome. This (necessary) "bridge of reason," which connects the law and the facts, can be characterized, at the same time, as an implicit *interpretative* statement, a statement about how the law is to be *applied* to the facts, or even a proposition about what the municipal law *means*. It can be very difficult, if not impossible, to distinguish between these things (the exercise is some-times referred to as a mixed statement of law and fact). As a peg of a certain shape either fits a hole of a certain shape (or not), intuitively, it is a holistic proposition. The implication is that, if the same facts would arise in a future case, it would be decided in the same way (given the most-favoured-nation (MFN) principle that underpins the WTO). In this sense the process may be seen as clarifying the law. That part of the "bridge of reason" most prox-imate to the terms of the treaty may be seen as essentially interpretative in nature. On the other hand, the fact patterns of two cases are never actually identical in all respects, so cases can always be distinguished on their facts (even if artificially so). That part of the "bridge of reason" most proximate to the terms of the measure at issue may be seen as essentially clarifying the facts, insofar as it explains what the measure at issue means. However, it is illusory to characterize the "bridge of reason" in its entirety as either "inter-pretative" or "factual" or to posit a one-size-fits-all rule that will allow one to deconstruct it into these constituent parts. Rather, it is simply what it is, which is a holistic process of reasoning that explains how the law has been applied to the facts in this particular case.

The holistic nature of the bridge of reason (interpretation, application, meaning of municipal law) is an intellectual conundrum that generates con-siderable miscommunication and controversy because interlocutors are often over analytical, pejoratively selective, and simply speaking about different things, thus passing like ships in the night. For example, one tends to read and hear a great deal about "interpretation," in isolation, which perhaps reflects a certain (understandable) diplomatic superficiality or academic laz-iness. Everyone is drawn to that conversation because it is relatively easy to express an opinion: all one needs is the text of the treaty and Articles 31–33 of the *Vienna Convention on the Law of Treaties* (Vienna Convention). One does not need to trouble oneself with the tedious business of examining the (often voluminous) evidence and assimilating the facts. This is a serious error, which overlooks the fact that the DSU contains no procedure for a so-called advisory opinion, and that every DSU adjudication is actually not an interpretative process (in isolation) at all but rather an application of the law to the facts and evidence of a particular case, which, at most, might, in part, imply a clarification of the law but subject always to the fact patterns of future cases. One cannot have a sensible systemic discussion if one conceptualizes the objects of the enquiry (panel and Appellate Body reports) in terms (interpretation) that constitute merely one-third of what they are (that is, excluding application of the law to the facts and the meaning of municipal law). The paradigm example is the issue of so-called "precedent," which is grounded in conceptualizing reports only as "interpretation." Once it is understood that reports also concern application of the law to the facts and the meaning of municipal law, and that probably this is more than 90 percent of their content, much of that debate is seen to be of considerably less significance.

The real intellectual challenge in approaching WTO case law is never forgetting this tripartite but holistic nature of adjudication (interpretation, application of the law to the facts, meaning of municipal law). This may seem unsatisfactory to some who might wish for a more analytical approach. But the analytical approach is not, itself, the problem. Rather, it is forgetting, having conducted such an analysis, to be synthetic. There are plenty of other examples of this in the law. For example, Articles 31–33 of the Vienna Convention, and even Article 31(1) viewed in isolation (which refers to good faith, ordinary meaning, context, and object and purpose) might tempt the adjudicator into a separate analysis of each of those elements (and one may read reports like that). But at the end of the day, as the title of Article 31 confirms, it is a single rule of interpretation, that is, a holistic exercise, that requires the adjudicator to be synthetic, that is, to explain how the different elements are to be considered not just separately but together. Another good example is the (very important) concept of "causation," which is not a fact but a proposition about the relationship between two sets of facts (the mooted causal agent and the mooted outcome). Once again, one can be analytical, for example by using a "but for" test or examining volume and price separately, but in the end, one must be synthetic, as is the case for this same concept in other areas of the law. Those who forget, or choose to forget, the holistic nature of the process are usually false prophets. Like the private sector lawyer decontextualizing and piling up past cases in an effort to persuade the adjudicator that the "interpretative" point has already been decided, when in truth the particular fact pattern has never before been considered. Or the public sector lawyer trying to argue that the "meaning of municipal law" is a "fact" outside the scope of appellate review, when in truth it is part of a mixed question of law and fact.

I turn now to the concept of the *"meaning of municipal law,"* which has already been touched upon. As indicated above, this actually constitutes part of the bridge of reason or the mixed question of law and fact. It is, if you like, the mirror image of the interpretative process: the concept of interpretation refers to that part of the bridge of reason proximate to the law and is directed towards elucidating the meaning of the law, whilst that part of the bridge of reason proximate to the facts (and evidence), or the measure at issue, may be seen as elucidating the meaning of municipal law. Those who advocate that the "meaning" of municipal law is a "fact" are committing an obvious intellectual error, usually driven by a teleological predisposition to limit the scope of judicial and especially appellate review. The statement is nonsense. The "meaning" of something cannot be a "fact." Facts are things that either were the case or were not the case in the past and are usually susceptible to generating evidence, which can be shared with others. "Meaning" refers to how we understand things, that is, what is going on in our heads. Others cannot experience or know this (and indeed sometimes we ourselves may not know fully why we understand the world the way we do). To be clear, if a municipal judge has handed down an adjudication clarifying what municipal law means, that judgment and its content are facts for a WTO adjudicator. But such adjudication may often be open to the possibility of appeal, so when a WTO adjudicator adopts such clarification of municipal law it makes it its own and takes the first step along the bridge of reason, constructed inductively, from the specific to the general, from the facts to the law.

Finally, I turn to the concept of *"interpretation."* I have intentionally left this to the end in an effort to counterbalance the strong tendency in WTO adjudication and political and academic discussion of it to begin with the question of interpretation. However, in many ways, it is the least important aspect of the process. In many ways, the most important element of the process is the facts (and evidence) because one cannot have a WTO case without a fact pattern, there being, by contrast, no procedure for so-called advisory opinions. As I have explained above, interpretation is actually an integral part of the bridge of reason. I do not think the interpretative rules are particularly controversial. The DSU directs us to the customary rules of interpretation of public international law, and almost everyone accepts that these are codified, at least in part, in Articles 31–33 of the Vienna Convention. They are, in my view, more or less complete. Sometimes one hears people arguing that prep—aratory work should carry greater weight and not be merely a supplementary means of interpretation. Often these are people involved in the negotiations, or negotiations more generally, and their opinions tend to reflect their own experiences and centre of interests. In truth, there is little preparatory work in WTO law (as opposed to submissions by Members). And in any event, it is almost always a two-edged sword, with one party arguing that the presence of particular terms in the preparatory work supports its position, whilst the other party argues that the omission of the very same terms from the final text of the treaty supports its position.

C. Standard of Review—Article 17.6 of the Anti-Dumping Agreement

HAVING DISCUSSED, AS A THRESHOLD matter, what I think most people would accept are the basic building blocks of WTO adjudication, I turn now to the question of what we mean by the term "standard of review." Intuitively, the term refers to the relative intensity of review, either by an adjudicator or an administrator or regulatory authority (in the municipal jurisdiction). That is, review may be relatively more intense or relatively less intense. Relatively more intense review would better correlate with the proposition that there is one solution to the problem, or one answer to the question, that is better than all the others and as the best, the only correct one. Relatively less intense review would better correlate with the proposition that there may be more than one solution to the problem or answer to the question and that a range of outcomes may therefore be acceptable, or permissible, from a legal point of view.

WTO law uses the term "standard of review" only once, with reference to Article 17.6 of the *Anti-Dumping Agreement*. We can, indeed should, therefore look to this provision to understand how WTO law conceptualizes what the term "standard of review" might mean, quite independently from the substantive content of the provision. A few points jump right off the page.

First, and most obviously, the provision distinguishes between the different elements, as outlined above: "the establishment of the facts" (this implicitly encompasses the evidential aspects), the "evaluation of the facts" (this corresponds to the application of the law to the facts), and the process of interpreting WTO law.

Second, as always, it is interesting to note what is missing (the dog that does not bark in the night): the statement of WTO law (as the treaty is actually written). It would seem that if a measure at issue is so foolish as to state applicable and relevant WTO law (as the treaty is actually written) incorrectly then the question of "standard of review" does not really arise. The measure is simply inconsistent with the balance of the Member's WTO obligations and rights, unless, perhaps, the defending Member can argue that the error is harmless, although this may be very difficult to do. If WTO law has been paraphrased, in a manner that implicitly involves an interpretation, then that matter would fall into the interpretative discussion.

Third, we read that the establishment of the facts (and by extension consideration of the evidence) must have been "proper." What does this term mean? It appears to contrast with the other terms used ("unbiased and objective"). It suggests procedural regularity, that is, in general terms, respect for the various facets of the concept of due process (particularly opportunity to submit information and comment). And probably more than that. If the collection of the evidence is "proper" in this procedural sense but the "establishment of the facts" directly contradicts the evidence, then it is doubtful that one could reasonably say that the "establishment of the facts" was proper. And yet the provision does not go so far as to require that the "establishment of the facts" is "unbiased and objective." One may reasonably suppose that this reflects the reality, explained above, that the distinction between facts and evidence is not always so clear, and that the process of considering the evidence in order to "establish the facts" often involves the exercise of judgment, such that it may be difficult to assert that there is only one "correct" "factual" conclusion that can be reached upon a consideration of the evidence.

Fourth, we read that the evaluation of the facts, that is, the application of the law to the facts, must be "unbiased and objective." These terms are rather similar, although the term "unbiased" is probably more focused on intentional and perhaps particularly flagrant behaviour. What does the term "objective" mean? Several other provisions of the DSU use this term. I do not think it can reasonably be taken to imply that the process of adjudication is machine-like and that adjudicators must be considered infallible. Any good adjudicator I have discussed this matter with has always acknowledged that, whilst one might strive towards some ideal of "objectivity," one cannot pretend that it is achievable. I think that the term "objective" means that the adjudicator should take into consideration only: the applicable and relevant law (as the treaty is actually written), the facts and evidence (eventually as the measure at issue is actually written), the agreed rules of interpretation, and the arguments of the parties (the court knows the law, but it cannot make the case for either party). And seek, in principle, to exclude all other exogenous considerations (such as the policy interests of a particular WTO Member).

Importantly, even critically, we need to ask the question whether the term "objective" implies that the standard of review is relatively more intense, that is, would correlate with the proposition that there is one solution to the problem, or one answer to the question, that is better than all the others, and as the best, the only correct one. The answer to that question is clearly no, since the last sentence of Article 17.6(i) contains the phrase "even though the panel might have reached a different conclusion." Of course, this provision implicitly assumes that any conclusion that the panel might reach would also have to be in accordance with the rules, including the rules on standard of review. Therefore, we can only conclude that there might be more than one way of *applying the law to the facts*, that is, a range of possibilities, and that this state of affairs is *not excluded* by the term "objective." We can confirm this conclusion with a simple thought experiment. If we recognize, as I think we must, the concept of variation in "standard of review," from relatively more intense to relatively less intense, is it not the case that we wish our adjudicator to strive for "objectivity" (in the sense outlined above) irrespective of where on the sliding scale we might find ourselves? That is, would we accept the proposition that an adjudicator exercising the least intense standard of review could be not objective, that is, subjective, by intentionally or consciously taking exogenous factors into account? The answer to that question is surely not.

Fifth, Article 17.6(ii) refers to "interpretation" and particularly the concept of "permissible interpretation." The order is certainly interesting: establishment of the facts, evaluation of the facts, and only then interpretation. This rather confirms the relative importance of these different elements, as outlined above. A great deal of the debate around Article 17.6 has jumped right into and focused on this concept of "permissible interpretation," rather overlooking that this is often the least important part of an adjudication, and that the more important part is the application of the law to the facts, which is dealt with in the preceding sub-paragraph, which rather indicates that the term "objective" is not inconsistent with a range of lawful outcomes.

Personally, I think that, also in the interpretative process, reasonable people can disagree, and it is difficult to say that there is always one "interpretation" that is the best and therefore the only correct one. That said, I do think there is such a thing as a "legal truth," which arises when the final adjudicator has spoken, which is almost procedural in nature, and in essence a necessary part of any legal system that has the ambition to provide security and predictability to its subjects. And in a multilateral organization such as the WTO, with MFN as the core rule, one does expect that the law will have the same meaning for everyone, including over time. However, my observation would be that, if one conceptualizes the bridge of reason as all about, or almost all about, interpretation, in isolation, this does tend to throw up the controversial issues of so-called precedent and, relatedly, the institutional rules that make new legislation very difficult. On the other hand, if one conceptualizes the bridge of reason as encompassing not only interpretation but also application of the law to the particular fact pattern of a given case, as well as the meaning of municipal law, then one moves away from those problems and to a significant extent. In other words, if one sees flexibility in the standard of review when it comes to *the application of the law to the facts*, much of the heat and controversy goes out of the debate surrounding "permissible interpretation." It is just not the concept that we need to be discussing. It is with this thought in mind that I turn to the question of standard of review in the DSU.

D. Standard of Review—Article 11 of the DSU

ONE THRESHOLD QUESTION WHEN ONE examines Article 11 of the DSU is whether or not it contains a standard of review at all or perhaps one that is incomplete. Unlike Article 17.6 of the *Anti-Dumping Agreement* that term is not actually used: Article 11 is titled "function of panels." It may seem shocking to suggest that there may be no standard of review clause in the DSU, or one that is incomplete, but this is perhaps not exceptional: there is also no properly written applicable law clause or any rules on burden of proof.

Interestingly, Article 11 refers to a panel's "assessment" of the matter and of the facts, that is, to the process by which the law is applied to the facts. This is confirmed by terms referring to the "conformity" with the covered agreements, of which "applicability" of the relevant agreement probably forms a part (for example, the "applicability" of the *Agreement on the Application of Sanitary and Phytosanitary Measures* (SPS Agreement) versus the *Agreement on Technical Barriers to Trade* (TBT Agreement)). Again, it is interesting to note what is not referred to: there is no reference to the establishment of the facts (merely their assessment).

Again, we see the term "objective" used in connection with the process by which the law is applied to the facts. But once again this raises the question: does this really tell us much, or indeed anything, about the standard of review? Does it imply that that the standard of review is relatively more intense, that is, one that would correlate with the proposition that there is one solution to the problem, or one answer to the question, that is better than all the others, and as the best, the only correct one? Does it exclude the possibility that there might be multiple outcomes all of which are lawful? I think the answer to that question must be no. I do not see why the same term ("objective") should have different meanings in the two provisions. I do not see how one can plausibly argue that the context of Article 17.6 means that the term "objective" used therein does not exclude multiple lawful outcomes, whilst the same term in Article 11 of the DSU does so.

E. Concurrent Application of Article 17.6 of the Anti-Dumping Agreement and Article 11 of the DSU

THE FOREGOING DISCUSSION RAISES THE question of the relationship between Article 17.6 of the *Anti-Dumping Agreement* and Article 11 of the DSU. The former is of course a special or additional rule that would prevail in the event of a conflict, to the extent of the conflict. But is there a conflict? In looking at these provisions, neither of which states there is a conflict, the presumption against conflicts applies, meaning that we must search for and prefer a harmonious reading, where one is reasonably available.

In answering this question, as indicated above, unlike most commentators, I am going to sidestep, at least for now, the question of "permissible interpretation," because, for the reasons indicated above, I am not persuaded that this is the crux of the problem.

Instead, I am going to focus on the process by which the law is applied to the facts. Both provisions require objectivity. There is surely no conflict there. And the *Anti-Dumping Agreement* makes it clear that the use of the term "objective" does not exclude the possibility of multiple lawful outcomes. I still do not see a conflict.

At this point it is perhaps interesting to consider the Decision on Review of Article 17.6 of the *Anti-Dumping Agreement*, which provides that the provision shall be reviewed after three years with a view to considering the question of "whether it is capable of general application." The decision leaves open how exactly that might be done. Unlike many other review clauses, it makes no reference, express or implied, to treaty change. Again, leaving aside the question of "permissible interpretation," is it possible that, on the basis of the DSU as it is written, one could reach the conclusion that, in the process of *applying the law to the facts*, one could admit of the possibility of multiple lawful outcomes? I think that may be so.

F. Standard of Review and Regulatory Space

AT THIS POINT I WOULD like to switch the discussion to WTO regulatory law. This is probably the most important aspect of WTO law (the litigation record is somewhat distorted by an excessive number of trade remedies cases, driven by commercial interests seeking to penetrate large markets, which use trade remedies to protect themselves). The basic proposition is that the concept of regulatory space at the very least implies a standard of review, when it comes to *applying the law to the facts*, that admits of multiple lawful outcomes.

I often say to students that, in my view, although not mentioned expressly, regulatory space is a central pillar of WTO law, along with MFN and national treatment. WTO law may encourage harmonization, but it does not impose it and rather accepts regulatory diversity as something that is a normal part of the system, as the concept of mutual recognition confirms. There is no proportionality rule in WTO law, only a necessity test. It is not for WTO adjudicators to weigh what they might think is the relative importance of a particular policy objective against the relative importance of what they might characterize as a "trade restriction." They only check that the measure has adopted the least trade restrictive approach and that there is no alternative reasonably available measure that would make at least the same contribution to the legitimate policy objective. And relatedly that the Member is being reasonably consistent when it comes to setting appropriate levels of protection and legislating accordingly. Importantly, when one examines the analytical tools available to a WTO adjudicator, I think one can only conclude that a number of them inherently involve significant uncertainty. And the point is, if one has such relatively blunt tools, can one have the pretension, *in the application of the law to the facts*, to be engaged in the process of identifying the best and only correct outcome? I doubt it.

Even before one gets to the issue of justification, significant uncertainty may arise. Leaving aside the SPS Agreement and the TBT Agreement, to catch a measure in the *General Agreement on Tariffs and Trade* recourse has often been had to the concept of so-called *de facto* discrimination. Although the concept is clearly present in national treatment fiscal law, and perhaps also regulatory law, it has been expanded to MFN. And we have been told that regulatory purpose is not relevant. We have also been told that actual trade effects are not determinative (because the adverse impact of a violating measure is to be presumed). So, we are supposed to look at design, architecture, and expected operation (that is, hypothesize about the future) to determine if there is a detrimental impact on competitors. There appears to be extreme reticence to look at the decisions firms have actually made or would like to make as a factor. This is not even to mention the considerable uncertainty associated with market definition issues. Today, the pendulum has swung so far that it is probably impossible to adopt a regulatory measure that does not *de facto* breach MFN (that is, impossible to design a measure that will impact all other WTO Members equally). A rule that says that all measures breach is no rule at all.

Once one gets into the necessity test, one is supposed to determine the expected trade restrictiveness of the measure (again, hypothesize). But we do not even have a clear explanation of what trade restrictiveness is supposed to mean. Is discrimination, *de jure* or *de facto*, by definition trade restrictive? Probably not. Do we look at volume or value or both? Do we only look at trade flows between complainant and defendant or others also?

Then, we are supposed to assess the hypothetical trade restrictiveness of the mooted alternative measure.

Then we are supposed to assess the hypothetical contribution of the actual measure and the hypothetical contribution of the mooted alternative to the legitimate policy objective, so that we can compare them. Often, it is not even clear what metric one can use to do that.

And all of this is supposed to accommodate the possible use of the concept of "precaution," according to which a Member can regulate to address an uncertain threat, provided it does so on the basis of the available information, seeks to obtain the necessary information for a more complete assessment, and reviews the measure within a reasonable period of time.

In sum, I would suggest that, in the field of WTO regulatory law, which is by far the most important part of international trade law, the concept of regulatory space, given the imprecise tools available, implies a standard of review that, when it comes to *applying the law to the facts*, whilst requiring objectivity, admits of more than one lawful outcome. In other words, one that aligns with Article 17.6(i) of the *Anti-Dumping Agreement*.

G. The Institutional Dimension

I TURN NOW TO CONSIDER the question from a more institutional perspective.

As is well known and documented, institutionally, the WTO is somewhat incomplete. The two most important issues are the lack of voting and the lack of an executive.

Although voting is provided for in the WTO treaties, the procedures are in practice not used. Consensus is the general rule. One of the reasons for this is that, unlike, for example, in the Council of the European Union, WTO Members have one vote each (leaving aside the provisions relating specifically to the European Union and its Member States). There is no weighting to take into account the relative size and importance of different Members. It is illusory to imagine that more powerful Members, like the United States and the European Union, would allow themselves to be outvoted by a coalition of developing countries, for example. There is little prospect of this issue being resolved at any time in the foreseeable future, since WTO Members will find it very difficult, if not impossible, at present, to agree on the criteria that would determine the relative voting rights. This chapter is not proposing a solution to that problem (although the problem does rather imply an increasing resort to plurilateralism).

Although, conceivably, the WTO secretariat might be thought of as an executive, it is not established in the same way that, for example, the European Commission is established, within the institutional structures of the European Union. This has a specific consequence when it comes to the standard of review. Within the EU jurisdiction, when the Commission, as an institution, appears before the European Court of Justice, it is in principle afforded a wide margin of discretion, especially on complex economic issues. There is a similar doctrine in the United States, the so-called Chevron doctrine, according to which the judiciary will not intervene when the executive's construction and application of a statue is reasonable. One can find similar doctrine in other Members with the classic tripartite structure of legislature, executive, and judiciary. And it makes sense. Usually, the executive is in some measure accountable to the legislature, at least eventually. And if the legislature disapproves of the way in which the executive has acted, it can change the law.

These observations help us to understand better the friction caused by a standard of review that posits, when it comes to applying the law to the facts, that there is one best conclusion, which is the only lawful outcome. I have witnessed many times the perplexity of lawyers for the US Department of Commerce who have successfully defended an anti-dumping measure before the US Court of International Trade, where they have asked for and received deference, when they appear before a panel and eventually the Appellate Body. They do not understand why what appears to them to be a more remote adjudicator subjects them to a more demanding standard of review. I have had similar comments from my own clients in other Commission departments. They do not understand why the standard of judicial review in the WTO appears to be more stringent than that in the European Court of Justice. One can see Article 17.6 of the *Anti-Dumping Agreement* as an attempt to transpose Chevron to the WTO context, either only for the *Anti-Dumping Agreement*, or even, perhaps, more generally. This is an attempt that, according to Appellate Body case law, has failed, on the grounds that a WTO adjudicator is engaged in a different type of law: multilateral, constitutional, treaty interpretation, focused on ensuring that the law means the same for all WTO Members. This conceptualizes the judicial task at the WTO as similar to the US Supreme Court, which takes cases to resolve divergent judgments in different US states, or the European Court of Justice when it receives a reference for a preliminary ruling on an interpretative issue and is concerned to ensure that an EU regulation, for example, has the same meaning throughout the European Union.

The question is, in light of the institutional realities described above, what approach to a panel's standard of review best fits the WTO? One often reads the commentary that the WTO is in difficulty because of a mismatch between the legislative branch and the judicial branch, followed by various proposals to address the legislative issues. But perhaps, rather than focusing mainly or even exclusively on the legislative situation, one should also examine the judicial side and particularly the question of standard of review. This is not to say that conceptualizing the standard of review as *akin* to Chevron, for all WTO law, would resolve the legislative issue. But it would surely contribute, or have contributed, to reducing the tension. With a more deferential standard of review, it is quite possible, or even likely, that a number of well-known cases that both the United States and the European Union have lost would have gone the other way.

I sometimes muse to myself that, if I would have been present at the first meeting of the Appellate Body and been given the chance to express a view on this issue, I might have suggested, with the benefit of hindsight, that the

WTO dispute settlement system was less a jewel in the crown (mandatory and binding third-party dispute settlement as the Holy Grail of international trade law) and more a poisoned chalice. Given the half-finished institutional structures of the WTO, and the changing world, it was always only going to be a question of time before the tensions that we see today between legislature and judiciary would surface. And the impossibility of the judiciary ever making up for the essentially insoluble legislative problems should surely have been apparent. Perhaps, sometimes, it is better not to rush in where angels fear to tread. Against that background, perhaps the one aim, above all others, and essentially at all costs, would have been *to endure for as long as possible*. And perhaps the key to achieving that would have been a lighter touch, that is, a less intense standard of review.

Of course, it is always going to be a problem when deference is given not to a particular entity within an institutional structure but rather to a subject of the law. Perhaps inevitably the subject of the law is always going to push for the flexibility that suits it in that particular case (one thinks, for example, of the United States pushing for out-of-country benchmarks in subsidies law). And that is always going to make it hard to maintain a constant line of jurisprudence. But in any event, a line of jurisprudence is never straight but zigzags like the teeth of a saw, with the varying fact patterns of different cases, so this is always going to be just a question of degree.

Relatedly, there would surely also be an issue about the appointment of panelists and the advice they receive from the WTO Secretariat, since it must be the case not only that they are not influenced by powerful Members, but that this is seen to be the case and believed. I personally consider that the WTO Directors-General could and should have taken their institutional, indeed constitutional, responsibility to appoint the right panelists much more seriously, particularly over spurious objections raised by one or another litigant. And perhaps, instead of dismantling the office arrangements used by the Appellate Body Secretariat, designed to insulate and ensure independence, such arrangements should have been extended also to persons advising panels.

H. Conclusion

TO CONCLUDE, AS INDICATED AT the outset of this chapter, I would submit that one can give very serious consideration indeed to the proposition that the general standard of review of panels, and by extension the Appellate Body, when it comes to *applying the law to the facts*, does not exclude multiple lawful outcomes. This does not mean that the adjudicators are doing anything other than striving to be objective, that is, taking into consideration only the law, the facts and evidence, the interpretative rules, and the arguments of the parties. In other words, there should be some degree of deference to Members. Whilst not perfect in all respects, I think that perhaps this would better fit the incomplete institutional structures of the WTO. I also think that this may feature as a central and critical feature of a revived WTO dispute settlement mechanism. It would not require any treaty changes nor, therefore, agreement among the Members: the adjudicators can do it on the basis of the existing treaty texts. There are already indications in the first full MPIA case (the *Columbia—Frozen Fries* case) that this may be the direction in which things are moving.

CHAPTER 15

Not So Member-driven After All: The GATT-Era Origins of the WTO's System of Remedies

Geraldo Vidigal

A. Introduction

THE PREVAILING UNDERSTANDING OF THE World Trade Organization (WTO) is that, more so than other international organizations, it is "member-driven."[1] As a book drafted by the WTO Secretariat explains, "the WTO is a member-driven, consensus-based organization"; it is "different from some other international organizations [in that] power is not delegated to a board of directors or the organization's head."[2] Instead, "the WTO is run by its member governments."[3] These elements are reflected in the WTO's constitutive agreement, which provides the two highest organs, both composed of all Members, with "exclusive authority to adopt interpretations" of WTO Agreements, while requiring them to follow, whenever possible "the practice of decision-making by consensus followed under GATT 1947."[4]

---

1   See, e.g., Manfred Elsig, "The World Trade Organization at Work: Performance in a Member-Driven Milieu" (2010) 5:3 *Review of International Organizations* 345 at 346.

2   WTO Secretariat, *Understanding the WTO*, 3rd ed (Geneva: World Trade Organization, 2005) 104.

3   *Ibid.*

4   *Marrakesh Agreement establishing the World Trade Organization*, 15 April 1994, 1867 UNTS 154 arts IX:2 and IX:1 (entered into force 1 January 1995).

The notion that the WTO is a Member-driven organization, and that this feature was inherited from the 1947 *General Agreement on Tariffs and Trade* (GATT 1947), is ingrained in thinking about the WTO. Indeed, one of the prevailing explanations for the demise of the Appellate Body is that the Appellate Body ignored this organizational principle. More than its substantive rulings—many were concerned with "judicial activism" and "judicial overreach" even before the Appellate Body was composed[5]—a significant portion of the grievance developed by the United States over the years concerned the Appellate Body's self-understanding and attitude to its role in dispute settlement procedures. The idea that the WTO Appellate Body was "a world trade court,"[6] eventually leading to two decades of "governance by judiciary,"[7] was perceived by many as a significant, if not determinative, reason for the mounting dissatisfaction in the US government with the Appellate Body's "rise to prominence."[8,9]

This chapter sets aside discussion of the recent past and potential futures of WTO dispute settlement.[10] Instead, it seeks to challenge the idea that the development of WTO dispute settlement itself was primarily "mem-

---

5   John H Jackson, "The Great 1994 Sovereignty Debate: United States Acceptance and Implementation of the Uruguay Round Results" (1997) 36 *Columbia Journal of Transnational Law* 157 at 182–83.

6   Claus-Dieter Ehlermann, "Six Years on the Bench of the 'World Trade Court': Some Personal Experiences as Member of the Appellate Body of the World Trade Organization" (2002) 36:4 *Journal of World Trade* 605; Hélène Ruiz Fabri, "La juridictionnalisation du règlement des litiges économiques entre États" (2003) 3 *Revue de l'arbitrage* 881.

7   Robert Howse, "The World Trade Organization 20 Years On: Global Governance by Judiciary" (2016) 27:1 *European Journal of International Law* 9.

8   Peter Van den Bossche, "From Afterthought to Centrepiece: the WTO Appellate Body and its Rise to Prominence in the World Trading System" in Giorgio Sacerdoti, Alan Yanovitch, & Jan Bohanes, eds, *The WTO at Ten: The Contribution of the Dispute Settlement System* (Cambridge: Cambridge University Press, 2006) 289.

9   See Joost Pauwelyn, "The WTO 20 Years On: 'Global Governance by Judiciary' or, Rather, Member-driven Settlement of (Some) Trade Disputes between (Some) WTO Members?" (2016) 27:4 *European Journal of International Law* 1119; Robert McDougall, "The Crisis in WTO Dispute Settlement: Fixing Birth Defects to Restore Balance" (2018) 52:6 *Journal of World Trade* 867.

10   See on this Geraldo Vidigal, "Re-Imagined Communities: The WTO Appellate Body and the Communitization of WTO Law" in Hélène Ruiz Fabri et al, eds, *International Judicial Legitimacy: New Voices and Approaches* (Baden-Baden: Nomos, 2020); Geraldo Vidigal, "Living Without the Appellate Body: Multilateral, Bilateral and Plurilateral Solutions to the WTO Dispute Settlement Crisis" (2019) 20:6 *Journal of World Investment & Trade* 862.

ber-driven." As I will argue, the key features of the WTO dispute settlement system as we know it were largely developed by the Secretariat of the GATT 1947, in the 1950s and 1960s, based on a handful of early dispute settlement reports. The system of remedies formulated then, with its approach often termed "prospective" or "forward-looking," decisively influenced the design of WTO dispute settlement and is now reproduced in virtually every trade agreement. In this system of remedies, dispute settlement does not offer retrospective reparation for injury but focuses on securing a change in conduct and a return to substantive compliance with agreed rules.[11]

B. From Suspension of Concessions to Retaliation in the GATT

THE CURRENT SYSTEM OF WTO remedies originates from the compliance control procedure under the GATT 1947. The GATT's single provision on dispute settlement, Article XXIII, provided that, following unsuccessful consultations between parties, disputes could be referred to the "Contracting Parties."[12] The Contracting Parties—an organ composed of representatives of all the parties to the GATT acting collectively—were empowered under Article XXIII:2 to "investigate any matter . . . referred to them," make "appropriate recommendations" and " give a ruling, as appropriate." In case of "serious enough" circumstances, they could "authorize a contracting party or parties to suspend the application" of GATT concessions and obligations towards the offender.[13] The authorization to suspend concessions was therefore asso-

---

11   See Geraldo Vidigal, "Re-Assessing WTO Remedies: The Prospective and the Retro-
      spective" (2013) 16:3 *Journal of International Economics* 505 and the literature cited
      therein.

12   *General Agreement on Tariffs and Trade*, 30 October 1947, 58 UNTS 187 art XXIII:2
      [*GATT 1947*] (disputes "may be referred to the CONTRACTING PARTIES. The CON-
      TRACTING PARTIES shall promptly investigate any matter so referred to them and
      shall make appropriate recommendations to the contracting parties which they con-
      sider to be concerned, or give a ruling on the matter, as appropriate . . . If the CON-
      TRACTING PARTIES consider that the circumstances are serious enough to justify
      such action, they may authorize a contracting party or parties to suspend the applica-
      tion to any other contracting party or parties of such concessions or other obligations
      under this Agreement as they determine to be appropriate in the circumstances." The
      GATT 1947 uses uppercase to refer to the Contracting Parties as an organ, acting
      collectively).

13   *Ibid.*

ciated not with the failure to comply with previous decisions but rather with particularly grievous circumstances.

While the GATT is silent regarding the purpose of suspensions of concessions, it is likely that this was not initially intended as a means of exerting pressure on the wrongdoer. Writing in 1949, Clair Wilcox, who chaired the negotiations leading to the GATT, noted that authorizing the reciprocal suspension of concessions was regarded by negotiators "as a method of restoring a balance of benefits and obligations" between the parties.[14] The underlying view was that trade agreements are instruments permitting reciprocal concessions in trade liberalization. Following this view, a violation—or rather, the "nullification or impairment" of negotiated trade benefits—would allow the other party to suspend equivalent concessions, permitting the parties to move on with the same balance of concessions. In other, words, authorized suspension of concessions was not seen as a "retaliation," in the sense of a sanction aiming at restoring compliance by a rule violator. Instead, it was envisaged as a permitted reciprocal downgrading of the level of trade benefits agreed between two parties.

At the same time, Wilcox himself predicted already in 1949 that this instrument would "operate in fact as a sanction and a penalty."[15] This would take place if the instrument of suspension of concessions was seen not as a mechanism for rebalancing the agreement—viewed as contract that can be violated "efficiently," provided an equivalent price is paid—but as a retaliation instrument, permitting harm to the interests of the violator. As discussed below, the instrument itself is indifferent to these functions; it is the way in which the parties use it that determines it perceived function.

C. The Early Years: Retaliation in GATT Practice

THE GATT 1947 DISPUTE SETTLEMENT mechanism enjoyed an early success in the late 1940s and early 1950s, with a number of Working Parties—which would later evolve into GATT panels—established by the Contracting Parties to assess trade irritants and propose solutions. This was also the only time the Contracting Parties authorized suspension of concessions under Article XXIII:2. In 1951, a dispute settlement report found that US restrictions on dairy imports were impairing GATT benefits of Netherlands and Denmark.

---

14   Clair Wilcox, *A Charter for World Trade* (London: MacMillan, 1949) 159.
15   *Ibid.*

This report stated that the circumstances of the violation were serious enough to justify suspension of concessions.[16] Rather than authorizing this response, however, the Working Party counselled the two claimants "to afford to the United States Government a reasonable period of time . . . to rectify the situation."[17] In deferring the authorization to suspend concessions, the Working Party already hinted at the treatment that would be given to reciprocal suspension of concessions: not as a sufficient remedy in and of itself (i.e., as a means of reparation for trade injury and rebalancing of the scales) but as a subsidiary possibility, available in case the offender failed to "rectify" its conduct.

In 1952, considering that the United States had not complied with the first report in *US—Dairy Products*, the Netherlands requested authorization to suspend concessions, restricting its imports of wheat flour from the United States in the following year to 57,000 tons. A follow-up Working Party was constituted to address the appropriateness of the request. The terms of reference, drafted by the Contracting Parties, indicated that this Working Party should assess the "equivalence of the measure proposed to the impairment" caused by the violation.[18] The 1952 Working Party found that the response proposed by the Netherlands was not unreasonable. Conducting an "independent review"[19] of the matter, it authorized the Netherlands to limit its imports of wheat flour from the United States in 1953 to 60,000 tons.[20]

Despite its success from a legal perspective, this early instance of GATT-authorized suspension of concessions did not lead to actual retaliation. In subsequent cases, the Contracting Parties never authorized retaliation

---

16   GATT, *United States Import Restrictions on Dairy Products—Resolution* GATT Doc CP/130 (1951) at 14, online (pdf): docs.wto.org [perma.cc/VJ9K-QRRE] [*US—Dairy Products*].

17   *Ibid* at para 1.

18   GATT, *Summary Record of the Tenth Meeting*, GATT Doc SR.7/10 (1952) at 9, online (pdf): docs.wto.org [perma.cc/74X6-FKL7].

19   GATT, *Working Party 8 on Netherlands Action under Article XXIII:2, Report to Contracting Parties*, GATT Doc L/61 (1952) at para 6, online (pdf): docs.wto.org [perma.cc/TF5C-PXVR].

20   *Ibid* at para 7. The report was adopted by the Contracting Parties with both parties to the dispute abstaining while declaring that they considered the report to be satisfactory. See GATT, *Summary Record of the Sixteenth Meeting* GATT Doc SR.7/16 (1952), online (pdf): docs.wto.org [perma.cc/5ETF-YPB3] (two other contracting parties, New Zealand and Czechoslovakia, questioned whether the Working Party should have second-guessed a proposal that it considered not to be unreasonable).

again, instead emphasizing the need for compliance.[21] The procedure none-theless was codified and developed through a mix of documents issued by the Secretariat, Working Party documents, and panel reports, later consolidated in decisions by the GATT Contracting Parties.

Thus, a 1955 Working Party rejected, in the context of a review of the GATT, a proposal favouring permanent rebalancing measures as a response to non-compliance, which would be established by the Contracting Parties and aimed at "the maintenance of a general level of reciprocal and mutually advantageous concessions." The Working Group esteemed that this proposal "would not accord with the intent and spirit" of Article XXIII, since it would amount to accepting "that the provision of appropriate compensation, on the one hand, and the removal of a measure inconsistent with the Agree-ment, on the other hand, are fully equivalent and satisfactory alternatives."[22] The Working Party stated, in this context, that the primary objective of the GATT Contracting Parties, following a finding of inconsistency, should be "to secure the withdrawal of the measures," offering as an alternative the possi-bility of temporary compensation for the damage suffered.[23]

In subsequent disputes, GATT dispute settlement Working Groups and panels continued to seek the removal of measures, while often propos-ing the negotiations and the provision of a reasonable period of time for respondents to adjust their domestic laws and measures to their GATT com-mitments, consolidating the prospective nature of remedies. Even panels that identified clear breaches of GATT provisions recommended negotiation and withdrawal of GATT-inconsistent measures.[24] In *France—Import Restrictions*, the Panel went beyond addressing the respondent with recommendations and recommended to the United States, the claimant, "that it refrain, for a

21   For the attempt to do so in *US—Superfund*, see below note 41.

22   GATT, *Report of Review Working Party IV on Organization and Functional Questions*, GATT Doc L/327/Rev 1 (1955) at para 62, online (pdf): docs.wto.org [perma.cc/ A9YU-LYCG].

23   *Ibid* at para 64.

24   *Italy—Discrimination Against Imported Agricultural Machinery (Complaint by the United Kingdom)* (1958), GATT Doc L/833, 7th Supp BISD (1958) 60 at para 25, online (pdf): docs.wto.org [perma.cc/7U25-N9NF]; *French Assistance to Exports of Wheat and Wheat Flour (Complaint by Australia)* (1958), GATT Doc L/924, 7th Supp BISD (1958) 46 at para 12, online (pdf): docs.wto.org [perma.cc/V7EJ-QNJ8].

reasonable period, from exercising its right . . . to propose suspension of the application of equivalent obligations or concessions."[25]

A further development and consolidation of the prospective approach to GATT remedies arose in the context of the 1962 dispute *Uruguayan Recourse to Article XXIII*. This Panel found a number of violations of the GATT by the various respondents against whom Uruguay brought the dispute. Rather than authorizing retaliation, the Panel established what it termed a "two-stage procedure." It recommended the removal of the GATT-inconsistent measures, followed by "the possibility of further action, in case of non-fulfilment." Failing compliance by the respondents within a reasonable period of time, Uruguay would "be entitled immediately to ask for the authorization of suspension of concessions or obligations."[26]

In follow-up proceedings, Uruguay did not request an authorization to retaliate, though. It focused instead on seeking findings of non-compliance with the previous rulings and recommendations for substantive compliance. A 1963 report, identifying persistent violations of GATT rules, recommended their withdrawal by the wrongdoers, highlighting that Uruguay was entitled to request the suspension of concessions.[27] A subsequent report restated this view, specifying that "the relevant recommendations [for compliance] would *ipso facto* have become inoperative with the disappearance of the restrictive measures."[28]

In short, GATT Article XXIII:2 enabled adjudicators to follow recommendations with an immediate determination of authorized retaliation under GATT, based on the seriousness of situations. However, Working Groups, Panels and the contracting parties largely adopted a prospective approach to remedies, favouring demands for substantive compliance. The Panels in *US—Dairy Products* and *France—Import Restrictions* withheld the requested authorization, instead awarding the offender a "reasonable period" to comply with its rulings. In *Uruguayan Recourse to Article XXIII*, the claimant itself preferred a declaration of non-compliance in respect of the challenged measures, over

---

25 *France—Import Restrictions (Complaint by the United States)* (1962), GATT Doc L/1921, -11th Supp BISD (1962) 94 at para 7, online (pdf): docs.wto.org [perma.cc/ ZZ4P-VY9Z] [*France—Import Restrictions*].

26 *Uruguay—Recourse to Article XXIII* (1962), GATT Doc L/1923, 11th Supp BISD (1962) 95 at paras 19–21, online (pdf): docs.wto.org [perma.cc/2H28-L3FZ].

27 *Uruguay—Recourse to Article XXIII* (1963), GATT Doc L/2074, 13th Supp BISD (1963) 35 at para 6, online (pdf): docs.wto.org [perma.cc/85M7-V65W].

28 *Uruguay—Recourse to Article XXIII* (1964), GATT Doc L/2278, 13th Supp BISD (1964) 45 at para 6, online (pdf): docs.wto.org [perma.cc/6SXG-J9ZY].

the Panel's offer that it request authorization to retaliate. Retaliation was therefore not seen, by parties or panels, as a means of "reparation" or "rebalancing of concessions" but as potential instruments to enforce rulings and obtain substantive compliance.

The two decades following *Uruguayan Recourse to Article XXIII* saw the rise of an "antilegalistic" sentiment at the GATT.[29] As Rajesh Babu put it, "[a]fter having processed 59 claims up to mid-1963, the GATT adjudication system simply vanished. No formal legal claim at all was filed from 1963 to 1969."[30] One important trade dispute at the time, the so-called *Chicken War*, was addressed through recourse to an *ad hoc* panel. This dispute, between the United States and the European Economic Communities (EEC), arose when the EEC's import regime for poultry replaced West Germany's lower duties on chicken in 1962. The *ad hoc* Panel was tasked with issuing an "advisory opinion" determining the value of lost exports for the United States as a result of West Germany's "unbindings concerning this product."[31]

The *Chicken War* Panel was perhaps the only one that led to a permanent "rebalancing" of trade concessions. The *ad hoc* Panel understood its mandate as arising from GATT Article XXIV:6, which requires "compensatory adjustment" for increased trade barriers following the formation of customs unions, rather than Article XXIII. The panel's determination of a dollar amount for US lost exports was followed by corresponding increases in US tariffs on light trucks, brandy, potato starch, and dextrin, all on a most-favoured-nation (MFN) basis rather than on the EU alone.[32] One commentator praised this "improvisation," noting that "the amount of the incidental injury [from the MFN increase] appears to be minor [since] third-country trade in the products selected is less than a million dollars, dispersed among several suppliers."[33] The fact that, sixty years later, the United States continues to apply its 25 percent "chicken" tariff on light trucks, shows the problematic potential of the idea of permanent authorized rebalancing.

---

29 Kenneth W Dam, *The GATT: Law and International Economic Organization* (Chicago: University of Chicago Press, 1970) 356.

30 Rajesh Babu, *Remedies under the WTO Legal System* (Leiden: Martinus Nijhoff, 2012) 25.

31 *Panel on Poultry (Complaint by the United States)* (1963), GATT Doc L/2088, online (pdf): docs.wto.org [perma.cc/M8GS-P9ZG].

32 Herman Walker, "The Chicken War" (1964) 58:3 *American Journal of International Law* 671 at 681.

33 *Ibid* at 681 and 683.

D. Legalized Dispute Settlement and Unilateral Retaliation

THE LULL OF REGULAR GATT adjudication in the 1960s did not prevent the procedure developed in the previous decade from being consolidated, through the Secretariat's work, as well as through discussions among the Contracting Parties. In 1965, a Note from the GATT Secretariat, directed at securing "compensation for less developed contracting parties for loss of trading opportunities" owing to the residual application of quotas, reaffirmed the two-phase structure set out by the Panel in *Uruguayan Recourse to Article XXIII*. The Note stated that "the normal course" of disputes involved one phase for adjudication and the other for determination of authorized retaliation.[34]

This structure was then picked up by the Contracting Parties when dispute settlement once again started operating, in the 1970s.[35] It was consolidated in the 1979 Tokyo Round Understanding on Dispute Settlement (TRUDS). TRUDS and its Annex, the "Agreed Description of the Customary Practice of the GATT in the Field of Dispute Settlement," codified and gave legal status to adjudicatory panels (which are not mentioned in the GATT) as well as to the compliance-oriented two-phase approach to remedies. Prior to TRUDS, therefore, this entire construction was based on the embryonic practice of the 1950s and early 1960s, codified by the GATT Secretariat.

TRUDS required GATT dispute settlement panels to make "an objective assessment of the facts of the case and the applicability of and conformity with the General Agreement" and issue "findings in a written form."[36] If the

---

34   GATT, *Note by the Secretariat*, GATT Doc COM.TD/5 (1965) at paras 8–10, online (pdf): docs.wto.org [perma.cc/7WSW-XWUG].

35   Babu, above note 30 at 26.

36   GATT, *Understanding Regarding Notification, Consultation, Dispute Settlement and Surveillance*, GATT Doc L/4907 (1980), arts 16–17, online (pdf): docs.wto.org [perma. cc/QL6N-83HF] [*TRUDS*]; See John H Jackson, "The Birth of the GATT-MTN System: A Constitutional Appraisal" (1980) 12:1 *Law & Policy in International Business* 21 at 42 (John Jackson notes that many panels had responded to the antilegalistic sentiment of the 1960s and 1970s by "tr[ying] to play the role of conciliators . . . assisting the negotiation in reference to the power positions of the disputing parties and not with reference to the interpretation or application of an agreed-upon rule"); See also *Jamaica—Margins of Preference (Complaint by the United States)* (1971), GATT Doc L/3485, 18th Supp BISD (1971) 183 at paras 15–17, online (pdf): docs.wto.org [perma.cc/436D-G5NN] (in one case involving Jamaican preferences, the Panel effectively recommended the adoption of a waiver to accommodate for temporary non-compliance).

panel found a violation, the party found in breach should resume compliance with its commitments. A negotiated arrangement, or an authorization to retaliate, could be available "as a temporary measure" if "immediate withdrawal of the [violating] measure is impracticable."[37] The "last resort" in this system or remedies was to authorize bilateral responses, in the form of Article XXIII:2 suspension of concessions or other obligations "on a discriminatory basis vis-à-vis the [wrongdoer]."[38]

Despite having the approval of the GATT Contracting Parties, the highly codified TRUDS rules governing dispute settlement were never used to their full extent—that is, they never led to authorized retaliation. In 1988, following US non-compliance with the panel report in *US—Superfund*,[39] the European Communities and Canada sought authorization to retaliate against the United States. The United States, however, opposed the request. Arguing that "legislation to achieve compliance with the Panel's recommendation was imminent," the United States representative stated that it was "inappropriate to consider retaliatory withdrawal of tariff concessions.[40] It then blocked Canada's proposal to establish "a small group, perhaps along the lines of a panel, to examine Canada's request."[41]

Even though no authorization to retaliate was ever granted after 1952, the instrument of retaliation itself was threatened and used. In *EEC—Oilseeds*, a 1990 Panel found that the EEC's measure undermined the "reasonable expectations" of the United States but suggested allowing the EEC a reasonable period of time to adjust.[42] Two years later, a follow-up panel found that benefits accruing to the United States continued to be impaired and

---

37 This adjustment, labelled "compensation," should not be confused with the homonymous remedy under general international law.

38 *TRUDS*, above note 36, Annex at para 4. This provision originated Article 3.7 of the *Dispute Settlement Understanding*. Subsequent clarifications were added in 1989. GATT, *Decision of 12 April 1989 on Improvements to the GATT Dispute Settlement Rules and Procedures*, GATT Dec L/6489, 36th session (1989) BISD 61.

39 *United States—Taxes on Petroleum and Certain Imported Substances (Complaint by the European Communities and Canada)* (1987), GATT Doc L/6175, 34th Supp BISD (1987) 136, online (pdf): docs.wto.org [perma.cc/UWB2-W767] [*US—Superfund*].

40 GATT, *Communication from the European Communities*, GATT Docs C/W/540, C/W/540/Add.1 (1988), online (pdf): docs.wto.org [perma.cc/M858-Q7SJ]; GATT, *Minutes of Meeting*, GATT Doc C/M/236 (1989) at 18, online (pdf): docs.wto.org [perma.cc/Y3DR-HBGS].

41 *Ibid* at 20.

42 *European Economic Community—Payments and Subsidies Paid to Processors and Producers of Oilseeds and Related Animal-Feed Proteins (Complaint by the United States)*

recommended that, unless the dispute were resolved expeditiously, "the CONTRACTING PARTIES should, if so requested by the United States, consider further action under Article XXIII:2 of the General Agreement."[43]

Rather than complying with the recommendation, the EEC blocked adoption of the latter panel report and sought to renegotiate its schedule of concessions.[44] The United States objected to the EEC's calculation of the injury and announced its intention to "restore the balance unilaterally upset by the Community" by imposing 200 percent *ad valorem* tariffs on EC imports of white wine, rapeseed oil and wheat gluten—a clearly retaliatory, rather than restorative, measure.[45] The process culminated in December 1993 with the signature of the Oilseeds Agreement, which set new rules for the products involved.[46]

Retaliation in *EEC—Oilseeds* was exceptional for its time, not because it was applied but because it was preceded by GATT adjudication. In the late years of the GATT 1947, contracting parties increasingly invoked an entitlement to resort to responses outside the GATT system. Pointing to the fundamental weakness of the GATT's otherwise quasi-judicial mechanism for dispute settlement—the need for consensus among the GATT Contracting Parties at each stage of the procedure—throughout the 1980s, the United States increasingly resorted to unilateral reactive measures. Employing US laws permitting its government to react to unfair trade practices, the United States imposed retaliation on alleged offenders based on its own assessment of breach. Jadish Bhagwati labelled this practice "aggressive unilateralism"

(1989), GATT Doc L/6627, 37th Supp BISD (1989) 86 at paras 148, 157, online (pdf): docs.wto.org [perma.cc/5BB3-594N].

43 *European Economic Community—Payments and Subsidies Paid to Processors and Producers of Oilseeds and Related Animal-Feed Proteins (Follow-Up on the Panel Report)* (1992), GATT Doc DS28/R - 39S/91 at para 92, online (pdf): docs.wto.org [perma.cc/QT3W-QHVE].

44 GATT, *Proposal by the European Economic Community*, GATT Doc DS28/2 (1992), online (pdf): docs.wto.org [perma.cc/4UVL-THAT].

45 GATT, *Request by the United States for Establishment of an Arbitral Body*, GATT Doc DS28/3 (1992), online (pdf): docs.wto.org [perma.cc/T7FD-MGRC]; GATT, *Communication from the United States*, GATT Doc DS28/4 (1992), online (pdf): docs.wto.org [perma.cc/FF84-NPF8].

46 Giovanni Anania, Colin A Carter, & Alex F. McCalla, "Agricultural Policy Changes, GATT Negotiations, and the U.S.-E.C. Agricultural Trade Conflict" in Giovanni Anania, Colin A Carter, & Alex F. McCalla, eds, *Agricultural Trade Conflicts and GATT: New Dimensions in U.S.-European Agricultural Trade Relations* (New York: Routledge, 1994) 1.

and considered it a threat to the world trading system.[47] This aggressive unilateralism, Robert Hudec recalls, was the "precipitating event" of the Uruguay Round negotiations that established the WTO.[48] Andrew Stoler, the main negotiator for the United States, concurs that a major objective of all other contracting parties at the Uruguay Round was to prevent US unilateralism.[49] In other words, the WTO's prospective system of remedies, including retaliation as a last resort, emerged not solely from the United States' desire to employ retaliation but also from a fifty-year practice in which the relationship between retaliation and adjudication was in dispute.

The increasing resort to unilateral retaliation by the United States in the 1980s resulted, paradoxically, in a highly legalized WTO Dispute Settlement Understanding (DSU). The DSU, at least while it functioned as planned, ensured that WTO Members could resort to adjudication and obtain a final dispute settlement report, ultimately allowing them to obtain an authorization to retaliate in case of non-compliance. On the other hand, it legally prohibited resort by WTO Members to unilaterally determined trade retaliation.

The function of suspension of concessions remained in dispute even after the DSU consolidated it into a post-adjudicative remedy, with many claiming that it offered the possibility of "efficient breach," allowing the harmed WTO Member to "take back" concessions it made in negotiations as a response to breaches.[50] It is true that the standard of suspending "substantially equivalent concessions"[51] is similar to that which appears in a number of other GATT provisions as a means of "rebalancing" the agreement to a wronged party.[52] In practice, however, neither under the GATT 1947 nor

---

47   See Jagdish Bhagwati & Hugh T Patrick, eds, *Aggressive Unilateralism: America's 301 Trade Policy and the World Trading System* (Ann Arbor: University of Michigan Press, 1990). But see Alan O Sykes, "Constructive Unilateral Threats in International Commercial Relations: The Limited Case for Section 301" (1992) 23 *Law & Policy in International Business* 263.

48   Robert E Hudec, "Broadening the Scope of Remedies in WTO Dispute Settlement" in Friedl Weiss & Jochem Wiers, eds, *Improving WTO Dispute Settlement Procedures* (London: Cameron May, 2000) 345 at 373–74.

49   Andrew L Stoler, "The WTO Dispute Settlement Process: Did the Negotiators Get What They Wanted?" (2004) 3:1 *World Trade Review* 99 at 103.

50   Eric Posner & Alan O Sykes, "Efficient Breach of International Law: Optimal Remedies, Legalized Noncompliance, and Related Issues" (2011) 110 *Michigan Law Review* 243.

51   *GATT 1947*, above note 12 arts XXVIII:3, XXVIII:4(d). See also *GATT 1947*, above note 12 arts XVIII:7(b), XVIII:21 and XIX:3(a).

52   *GATT 1947*, above note 12 art XXVIII (a state may respond to a withdrawal of concessions with a reciprocal withdrawal of "substantially equivalent concessions").

under the WTO have adjudicators or parties treated retaliation as a satisfactory substitute for compliance. Reciprocal suspension of concessions is used as a means of retaliating against, or sanctioning, the non-complying party, and pressuring it to comply with its commitments.[53]

E. Conclusion

SO-CALLED WTO RETALIATION—OR RATHER, THE authorization to suspend concessions in case of persistent non-compliance—has its roots in a long-standing practice under the GATT 1947. The GATT 1947 foresaw collective authorization to suspend concessions as a possible consequence of a particularly egregious nullification or impairment of GATT benefits. In the practice under the agreement, the contracting parties and adjudicators showed a clear preference for treating retaliation as a last resort, privileging the ability of panels to offer legal interpretation and specify compliance duties. Despite the lack of practical use, both the GATT Secretariat and various Working Groups and panels reinforced the idea that GATT retaliation remained a threat against wrongdoers. Even in 1970, after a decade in which GATT contracting parties rarely resorted to its dispute settlement system, Kenneth Dam found that suspension of concessions was "the heart of the GATT enforcement system."[54]

This design of the WTO system of remedies, now replicated in virtually every international trade agreement, was first constructed in practice. This system operates very differently both from the set of remedies usually associated with international adjudication, geared towards the award of reparation for injury, and from that which the GATT negotiators seemingly intended, geared at restoring the balance of concessions by permitting reciprocal withdrawal of benefits. This system did not emerge through legislative action by the GATT Contracting Parties, as one could expect in a "member-driven" institution. Instead, a decades-long dialogue, involving adjudicators in Working Parties and GATT panels, parties to disputes, and the drafting hand of the GATT Secretariat, resulted in an original system that privileges future compliance over redress for past injury.

---

53   See Gregory Shaffer & Daniel Ganin, "Extrapolating Purpose from Practice: Rebalancing or Inducing Compliance" in Chad P Bown & Joost Pauwelyn, eds, *The Law, Economics, and Politics of Trade Retaliation in WTO Dispute Settlement* (Cambridge: Cambridge University Press, 2009).

54   Kenneth W Dam, *The GATT: Law and International Economic Organization* (Chicago: Chicago University Press, 1970) at 364

Broader Reflections on WTO Dispute Settlement

CHAPTER 16

Thirty Years of Trade Concerns at the Goods Council: How Do They Relate to Disputes Under The DSU?[*]

Roy Santana and Adeet Dobhal[**,***]

---

[*]   Disclaimer: The opinions expressed are those of the authors. They do not represent
      the positions or opinions of the WTO or its Members and are without prejudice to
      Members' rights and obligations under the WTO. Any errors are attributable to the
      authors.

[**] This chapter draws, in part, from the authors' earlier work: Roy Santana & Adeet
      Dobhal, "Canary in a Coal Mine: How Trade Concerns at the Goods Council Reflect
      the Changing Landscape of Trade Frictions at the WTO" (2024) WTO Economic
      Research and Statistics Division, Working Paper No ERSD-2024-04. This chapter
      covers the disputes initiated up to 15 October 2024, and new disputes may have been
      initiated after the analysis was undertaken.

[***] The authors would like to thank Valerie Hughes, Suja Rishikesh Mavroidis, Professor
      Robert Wolfe, Manuel Henriques, Thomas Verbeet, and Victor Stolzenburg for their
      valuable comments and suggestions. We would also like to thank Nicolas Lamp and
      the team at the Queen's University Faculty of Law and the University of Toronto Press
      for their hard work and collaboration.

A. Introduction

DISCUSSIONS IN TECHNICAL AND HIGHER-LEVEL Committees and Councils form the bulk of the World Trade Organization (WTO)'s regular work. Depending on the body, these discussions can range from reviewing notifications and trade policies to deliberations on Members' draft measures concerning standards and the like—all of which contribute to multilateral trade governance. More recently, several WTO bodies have been increasingly discussing "trade concerns," where Members express concerns or complaints about measures introduced or to be introduced by other Members.

In the hierarchy of the WTO bodies, the Council for Trade in Goods (CTG or the Goods Council) is uniquely positioned between the technical committees on goods and the General Council (GC), the highest WTO body. As a result of this distinctive positioning, we previously argued that trade concerns at the CTG serve as a good proxy for analyzing the evolving nature of trade frictions at the WTO.[1] Accordingly, discussions on trade concerns in WTO bodies are pivotal for the governance of international trade and can be vital in resolving trade frictions among WTO Members, going beyond the conventional realms of diplomatic negotiation and legal adjudication.[2] Further, a review of discussions on trade concerns at the CTG can provide valuable insights into their indispensable function in enhancing policy transparency, facilitating constructive dialogue on trade measures, and offering a platform for Members to voice concerns over the trade practices of others. Notwithstanding these efforts, some trade concerns eventually become disputes under the Understanding on Rules and Procedures Governing the Settlement of Disputes (DSU).

The interaction between trade concerns and disputes is typically described as one of progressive escalation, where trade frictions begin as bilateral disagreements, which are then raised multilaterally in a technical body or Committee by the affected Member and then elevated to a more political body like the CTG or the General Council. These concerns can then become disputes under the DSU if no solution is found through discussions in those bodies. In our past paper, we discussed the relationship between the CTG and its subsidiary bodies, showing that Members have been relatively selective regarding issues they choose to elevate to the CTG and only rarely elevate issues to the General

---

1   Santana & Dobhal, above note ** at 14.
2   See generally, Robert Wolfe, "Reforming WTO Conflict Management: Why and How to Improve the Use of 'Specific Trade Concerns'" (2020) 23:4 *Journal of International Economics* 817 at 818.

Council. We also showed that, depending on scope and coverage, Members may simultaneously raise trade concerns for the same measure in different Committees; there are no rules prescribing which issues can be elevated from the subsidiary bodies to the higher-level bodies, as this is at a Member's discretion.[3]

Similarly, a Member is not required to follow a mandatory hierarchy or path through WTO bodies to bring disputes under the DSU, and the reasons and strategies for deciding when to elevate a trade concern to a dispute may vary across the Membership. They may be driven by internal considerations and perceptions of the respective roles of different bodies, the probability of resolution of the problem by raising a trade concern first in a WTO body, the desire for more visibility or increased pressure to resolve an issue, etc. This raises the question of the degree to which formal disputes under the DSU over the past thirty years were previously elevated through the ordinary bodies and the CTG.

Building on previous work and utilizing novel data, we aim to analyze the extent to which trade concerns have been raised at the CTG and some of its subsidiary bodies before being raised as disputes under the DSU. Our previous research has shown that the CTG usually has been the last body for multilateral discussions, at least in the area of goods, before Members pursued some of these trade concerns through the formal Dispute Settlement Mechanism. Indeed, based on new calculations, we found that approximately 23 percent of the 220 unique trade concerns raised at the CTG translated into eighty-three of the 629 disputes under the DSU as of 30 August 2024. We also found that the extent to which an issue is raised in the CTG differs considerably across the WTO agreements on goods and is the lowest for the *Anti-Dumping Agreement* and the *Agreement on Subsidies and Countervailing Measures*.

This contribution strives to provide insights based on information from almost three decades of work at the WTO and argues that linkages between trade concerns at the CTG and disputes under the DSU have, thus far, been relatively limited, particularly in disputes relating to subsidies and trade remedies.

B. Trade Concerns at the Council for Trade in Goods

WHILE THERE IS NO FORMAL definition of the term, and the scope and terminology vary across different WTO bodies, "trade concern processes" can broadly be described as specialized discussions conducted within the purview

---

3   Santana & Dobhal, above note ** at 14.

of a WTO body to call attention to or to allow a Member to express concerns over policy measures of other WTO Members. These discussions may take different forms and formats, and WTO bodies may have different mechanisms to track these trade concerns. Some bodies even have different names to refer to similar processes, such as specific trade concerns or STCs in Sanitary and Phytosanitary Measures (SPS), Technical Barriers to Trade (TBT) and Market Access Committees or the "questions and answers" process in the Committee on Agriculture.[4]

Discussions on trade concerns are becoming increasingly important across several WTO committees, including at the CTG, which devotes most of its meeting time to discussing them. As some commentators have observed, exchanges that take place in committees, including discussions on trade concerns raised by Members over each other's measures, are more often than not the first step in "diffus[ing] conflicts."[5] Others have described them as a "decentralized peer review of trade measures."[6] Given their role in improving transparency and facilitating discussions among Members, some have also suggested utilizing the "STC mechanism," in place in certain WTO bodies, to deal with contentious issues, like national security, to address trade frictions among WTO Members.[7] At its core, trade concerns are a "mechanism" that enhances transparency in trade policy measures, increases Members' accountability for their measures, and may further encourage the adoption of good regulatory practices.[8] However, it should be clarified that trade concerns

---

4   Wolfe, above note 2.

5   Kian C Possada, Emmanuelle Ganne, & Roberta Piermartini, "The Role of WTO Committees Through the Lens of Specific Trade Concerns Raised in the TBT Committee" (2022) 21:4 *World Trade Review* 411 at 412.

6   Fabian Bohnenberger, "What is the 'Regular Work'? Constructing and Contesting Everyday Committee Practices in the World Trade Organization" (2022) 29:6 *Review of International Political Economy* 2088 at 2097.

7   See, e.g., Bernard M Hoekman, Petros C Mavroidis, & Douglas R Nelson, "Geopolitical Competition, Globalisation and WTO Reform" (2023) 46:5 *World Economics Journal* 1163. Some others have suggested creating a dedicated forum, such as a Committee on National Security, at the WTO to discuss issues related to national security. See Simon Lester & Inu Manak, "A Proposal for a Committee on National Security at the WTO" (2020) 30:2 *Duke Journal of Comparative & International Law* 267.

8   Possada, Ganne, & Piermartini, above note 8 at 412. On accountability and the WTO, see Robert Wolfe, "An Anatomy of Accountability at the WTO" (2015) 6:1 *Global Policy* 13.

are not "formal disputes in the legal sense of the term" and that Members do not have to raise trade concerns in WTO bodies before initiating disputes.[9]

In the context of the CTG, the term "trade concerns" is generally used to describe trade frictions (i.e., the perceived WTO incompatibility of a draft/final measure), and since 2023, they have been discussed in a dedicated segment of CTG meetings. The scope of these concerns, in terms of substance and coverage, range from trade concerns on particular aspects of a measure to those pertaining to the measure itself or a series of measures taken by a Member. Trade concerns are included in the agenda of a formal CTG meeting when one or more WTO Member(s) (the so-called "raising Members") seek to express a concern or complaint over a measure that is already implemented or due to be implemented by another WTO Member (the so-called "responding Member").

1) General Trends at the Council for Trade in Goods

Since its inception in 1995, the CTG has served as a forum for Members to raise trade concerns. The number of issues and the way the discussions are organized have significantly changed over the past years. Overall, the CTG has discussed 220 trade concerns in eighty-six of the 149 formal meetings between 1995 and 2024 or 57.7 percent of all its meetings.

Between 1995–2010, only a few trade concerns were raised at each CTG meeting, but many of them were subsequently followed by requests for consultations under the DSU. There were also four years when no trade concerns were raised at this forum (i.e., 1999, 2000, 2008, and 2009). This started to change in 2010. A significant turning point was the CTG meeting of October 2013, when, for the first time, more than ten trade concerns were discussed in a single meeting by Members, followed by the inclusion of seven new trade concerns raised at the subsequent meeting of April 2014. Following a reduction in trade concerns in some of the meetings held in

---

9   Henrik Horn, Petros C Mavroidis, & Erik N Wijkström, "In the Shadow of the DSU: Addressing Specific Trade Concerns in the WTO SPS and TBT Committees" (2013) 47:4 *Journal of World Trade* 729.

2015, their number at the CTG has multiplied nine-fold from March 2015 to April 2022. See Figure 1.

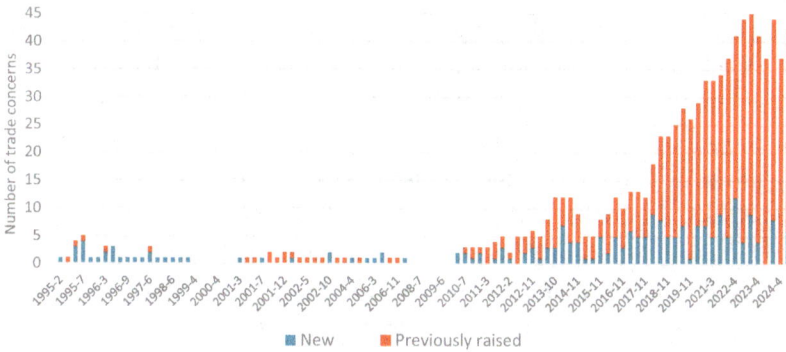

FIGURE 1. GOODS COUNCIL: NUMBER OF UNIQUE TRADE CONCERNS RAISED PER YEAR (1995–2024*)

SOURCE: SANTANA & DOBHAL BASED ON THE WTO TRADE CONCERNS DATABASE.
*DATA UNTIL OCTOBER 2024.

We have previously argued that trade concerns raised at the CTG are a good proxy for analyzing the trade frictions discussed at the WTO as a whole. This is because, first, the discussions in technical Committees are, by definition, narrower in scope (i.e., they focus on the implementation of one agreement and not all agreements on Goods like the CTG) or do not necessarily reflect trade frictions in all cases (but always reflect trade frictions when escalated to the CTG).[10] Second, the number of trade concerns raised at the General Council is not high, and these mainly refer to measures related to trade in goods.[11] A standalone analysis of STCs raised in these bodies can also be an equally useful indicator of similar trends or distinct micro-trends concerning specific issues. However, it is understood that further analysis of the discussions in the area of services and intellectual property would be necessary to have a complete picture. Nonetheless, it is worthwhile noting that most WTO disputes are in the goods area; disputes concerning services and intellectual property are relatively few.

2) Relationship with Other WTO Bodies

In the context of the trade concerns discussions at the CTG, Members often indicate whether the same or closely related concerns have been raised in

---

10   Santana & Dobhal, above note ** at 23–25.

11   *Ibid.*

other bodies. Based on information extracted directly from the minutes of the different bodies, Figure 2 shows that the overwhelming majority of the 220 trade concerns which have been raised by Members at the CTG until October 2024 correspond to issues also raised in one or more of the following five bodies: the Committee in Market Access (CMA), TBT Committee, Committee on Agriculture (CoA), SPS Committee, and the Committee on Import Licensing (CIL). It is also worth noting that, despite accounting for approximately half of the formal disputes over the past thirty years, trade remedies and subsidies disciplines (such as the Committee on Subsidies and Countervailing Measures (SCM), the Committee on Anti-Dumping Practices (ADP), and the Committee on Safeguards (SG)) form a small number of trade concerns raised in the CTG. Indeed, as discussed in more detail below, the latter group of issues appears to be the one where escalation is not so visible.[12] Further, the chart shows an increasing overlap with issues discussed at the Committee on Trade and Environment (CTE), which is not a CTG subsidiary body. Finally, only eight out of 220 trade concerns at the CTG have been raised subsequently at the General Council.

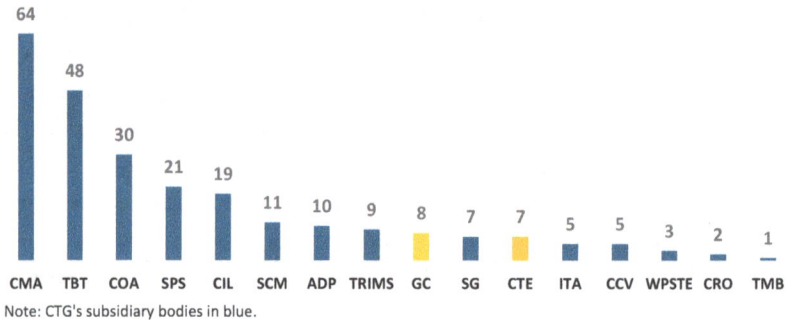

Note: CTG's subsidiary bodies in blue.

FIGURE 2. GOODS COUNCIL: NO. OF TRADE CONCERNS ALSO RAISED IN OTHER WTO BODIES (1995–2024*)

SOURCE: SANTANA & DOBHAL BASED ON THE WTO TRADE CONCERNS DATABASE AND ADDITIONAL INFORMATION EXTRACTED FROM THE CTG MINUTES. * DATA UNTIL OCTOBER 2024. THIS NUMBER REFERS TO THE UNIQUE NUMBER OF TRADE CONCERNS, SOME RAISED IN MORE THAN ONE BODY.

---

12   That said, some have noted that hundreds of questions were raised in the SCM Committee between 2008–13. See Gregory Shaffer, Robert Wolfe, & Vinhcent Le, "Can Informal Law Discipline Subsidies?" (2015) 18:4 *Journal of International Economics* 721. However, as we note above, these discussions form only a small portion of trade concerns raised or escalated to the CTG.

3) Types of Measures Discussed at the Goods Council

As Members express concern over measures imposed by other Members, they ordinarily provide considerable information about them. Based on information extracted from the minutes of the CTG meetings (between 1995 and October 2024), it is possible to identify the type or types of underlying measures addressed by the trade concerns being raised. Some 140 of the 220 unique trade concerns raised at the CTG have referred to an alleged lack of transparency in the application of the measure, representing the single most important issue raised. These concerns relate to the alleged failure to publish the measure, lack of notification, or failure to respond to questions raised by Members. Quantitative restrictions (QRs), typically in the form of import or export prohibitions or other kinds of restrictions (eighty-five unique trade concerns), are the second most important type of measure, which are followed by standards and technical regulations (seventy) in the TBT or SPS spheres, tariff-related issues (sixty), alleged violations of national treatment (forty-nine), trade remedies (forty-five), and alleged discrimination amongst Members (violations of the most-favoured-nation (MFN) clause) (forty-three). Given the enormous scope of issues that are regulated by the WTO agreements in the goods area, it should not come as a surprise that there is, in addition, a wide range of other issues (120) which have been raised as trade concerns under the CTG that do not fall under any of the main categories described above, including transit, tariff classification, implementation of minimum price schemes, mixing regulations, and even certain issues related to intellectual property. See Figure 3.

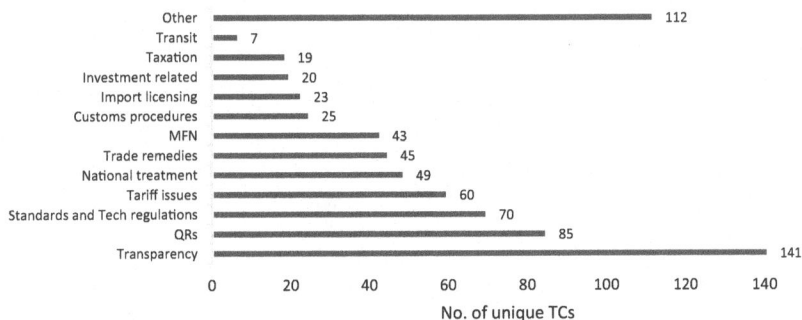

FIGURE 3. GOODS COUNCIL: MAIN TYPES OF ISSUES REFERRED TO IN TRADE CONCERNS DELIBERATIONS (1995–2024*)
SOURCE: SANTANA & DOBHAL BASED ON THE WTO TRADE CONCERNS DATABASE AND ADDITIONAL INFORMATION EXTRACTED FROM THE CTG MINUTES. * DATA UNTIL OCTOBER 2024.

4) Main WTO Provisions Cited in the Council for Trade in Goods' trade concerns

Members frequently cite one or more WTO provisions when they raise trade concerns at the CTG, which, in their opinion, are being violated by the challenged measure. In other instances, they refer to a violation of specific *General Agreement on Tariffs and Trade* (GATT 1994) and WTO principles, such as the most-favoured-nation and national treatment principles and despite no specific provision being cited, it is nevertheless possible to associate the concern with a particular provision.[13] Based on the information in the minutes of the CTG for the past thirty years, we have tried to estimate the number of trade concerns where specific WTO agreements and provisions have been mentioned.

With 141 unique trade concerns out of 220, equivalent to 64 percent of the concerns, the GATT 1994 is, by far, the most frequently cited agreement in the context of these deliberations at the CTG. It is followed by, in a distant second place, the *TBT Agreement* (forty-four unique trade concerns), with the *Agreement on Agriculture* (twenty-one), the *SPS Agreement* (twenty), and the *Agreement on Import Licensing Procedures* (eighteen). Interestingly, Members have also referenced the Protocols of Accession of acceding Members in the trade concerns discussions, although this number is not high (seven). Further, we note that Members have referenced the *General Agreement on Trade in Services* (GATS) and the *Agreement on*

---

13   For example, a Member stating that another Member is not fully respecting the MFN principle can be considered as a reference to Article I of the GATT 1994, or complaints about the undue introduction of quantitative restrictions could be considered a reference to Article XI.

Trade-Related Aspects of Intellectual Property Rights (TRIPs) in some of the trade concerns they have raised in the CTG for cross-cutting measures. See Figure 4.

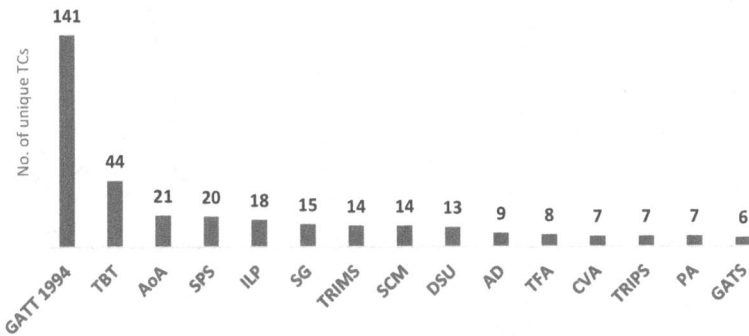

FIGURE 4. GOODS COUNCIL: MAIN WTO AGREEMENTS REFERRED TO IN TRADE CONCERNS DELIBERATIONS (1995−2024[*])

SOURCE: SANTANA & DOBHAL BASED ON THE WTO TRADE CONCERNS DATABASE AND ADDITIONAL INFORMATION EXTRACTED FROM THE CTG MINUTES. [*] DATA UNTIL OCTOBER 2024. THE AGREEMENT WAS REFERRED TO BY AT LEAST ONE MEMBER IN AT LEAST ONE MEETING IN RELATION TO A UNIQUE TRADE CONCERN.

Within the specific references at the CTG to the GATT 1994, the most frequently cited provision for the trade concerns was Article XI (sixty-three out of 220 unique trade concerns), which deals with the general elimination of quantitative restrictions, the majority of which relate to import restrictions. This being said, the number of export-related restrictions questioned at the CTG has been increasing over the past few years. This provision is followed by Article III (National Treatment), Article I (General Most-Favoured-Nation Treatment), and II (Schedule of concessions) of the GATT 1994, reinforcing the key role of these fundamental provisions in the General Agreement. See Figure 5.

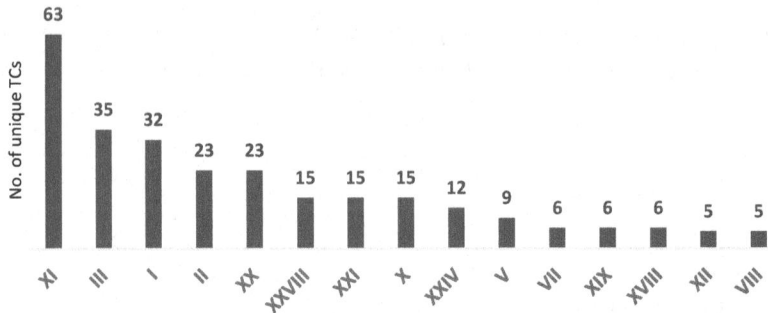

FIGURE 5. GOODS COUNCIL: MAIN GATT ARTICLES REFERRED TO IN
TRADE CONCERNS DELIBERATIONS (1995–2024*)

SOURCE: SANTANA & DOBHAL BASED ON THE WTO TRADE CONCERNS DATABASE AND ADDITIONAL INFORMATION EXTRACTED FROM THE CTG MINUTES. * DATA UNTIL OCTOBER 2024.

An analysis of the data as a time series reveals that the high concentration of references to Article XI is a relatively recent phenomenon. It intensified since 2019 and coincided with the Appellate Body impasse.[14] See Figure 6. Interestingly, and despite what the timeline may suggest, the underlying trade concerns that were discussed at the CTG during 2020–22 are not associated with the response to the COVID-19 pandemic. Instead, they relate to a plethora of issues and products and involve a wide range of Members. It is also worth noting that the references to Articles I and III have been relatively stable throughout the last three decades, while the references to Articles II and XXVIII (Modification of Schedules) are also concentrated mainly over the later part of the period in question (2019 onwards), coinciding with Brexit and the ensuing negotiations with the EU and the UK to establish their schedules.

---

14   The Appellate Body is unable to review appeals currently due to its ongoing vacancies. The term of the last sitting Appellate Body Member expired on 30 November 2020.

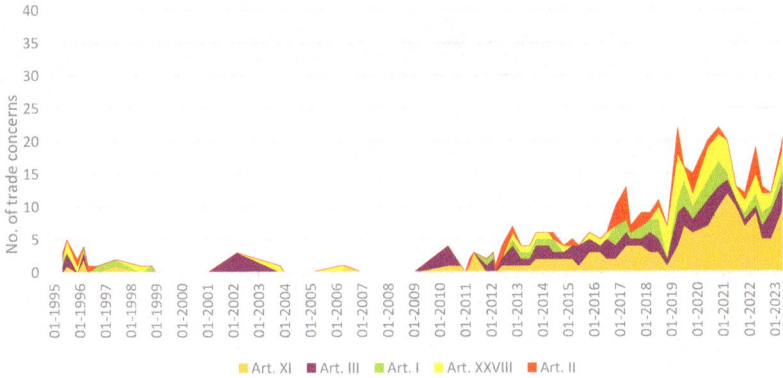

FIGURE 6. GOODS COUNCIL: EVOLUTION OF THE TOP FIVE GATT
1994 PROVISIONS REFERRED TO IN THE TRADE CONCERNS
DELIBERATIONS (1995–2024*)
SOURCE: SANTANA & DOBHAL BASED ON THE WTO TRADE CONCERNS DATABASE AND ADDITIONAL
INFORMATION EXTRACTED FROM THE CTG MINUTES. * DATA UNTIL OCTOBER 2024.

Taking a step forward in our analysis of the provisions of the GATT
1994, which have been referred to in the trade concerns discussions, we found
that Article XX (General Exceptions) and Article XXI (Security Exceptions)
saw an increase in their invocation during the more recent CTG meetings.
These exceptions were scarcely used before 2017, but since then, they have
been referred to more often in Members' interventions, reaching thirteen and
sixteen invocations for Article XX and XXI, respectively, in 2024.

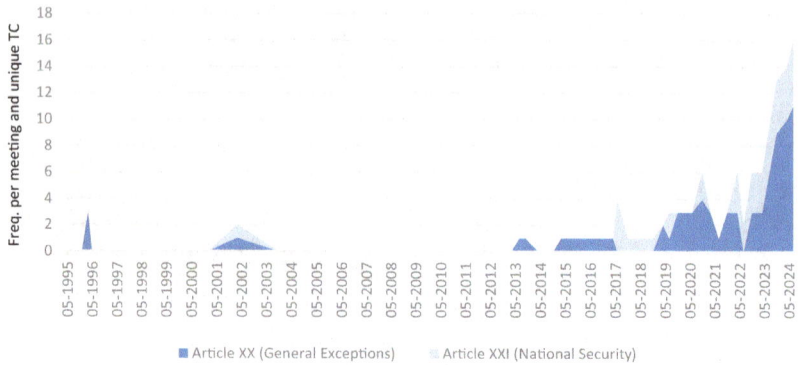

FIGURE 7. GOODS COUNCIL: EVOLUTION IN THE NUMBER OF
REFERENCES TO THE GENERAL AND NATIONAL SECURITY
EXCEPTIONS OF THE GATT 1994 IN THE TRADE CONCERNS
DELIBERATIONS (1995–2024*)

SOURCE: SANTANA & DOBHAL BASED ON THE WTO TRADE CONCERNS DATABASE AND
ADDITIONAL INFORMATION EXTRACTED FROM THE CTG MINUTES. * DATA UNTIL OCTOBER
2024.

5) Trade Concerns that Became Disputes under the Dispute Settlement Understanding

A final point we examine in this section is the extent to which trade concerns raised at the CTG have escalated to disputes under the DSU. Before presenting the results of our analysis, a few caveats are necessary. First, although tracking the evolution of some of these issues is relatively straightforward since the titles of most CTG trade concerns and the corresponding disputes are almost identical, there are several other instances where this is not the case. For example, the titles can differ, requiring a deeper comparison of whether the measure that was challenged in the dispute was the same measure that was discussed as a trade concern in the CTG. Second, the main parties involved in trade concerns and disputes are not always identical. For example, there have been several instances where a Member who did not raise the trade concern at the CTG but supported it as an "other interested Member" later became the complainant in a dispute.

In this chapter, we considered a dispute to have been escalated from a trade concern if it involved the same measure and was initiated within a reasonable period after the trade concern was last discussed at the CTG, even if the complainant had not directly sponsored or co-sponsored the concern at the CTG but had been an "other interested Member."

With all these caveats in mind, we found that, overall, fifty-two of the 220 unique trade concerns discussed in the CTG from 1995 until October 2024 have thus far resulted in eighty-three disputes being initiated under the DSU. In other words, almost a quarter of the CTG's trade concerns have resulted in disputes, and there is not a one-to-one relationship between them (i.e., some trade concerns resulted in more than one dispute and some disputes are related to more than one trade concern).

In our previous research, we observed a high correlation between the considerable increase in the number of trade concerns being raised at the CTG and the Appellate Body impasse but stressed that it was unclear whether there was causality between them. By undertaking a similar analysis of this relationship, we observe that the highest proportion of CTG trade concerns that became disputes were raised during the first two years of the WTO. During this period, more than half of trade concerns discussed turned into litigation. This decreased significantly during the stabilization phase between 1997 and the launch of the Doha Development Agenda by the end of 2001. Here, the number of trade concerns was not only much smaller, but the proportion that became disputes was also at its lowest point (i.e., only one out of ten trade concerns). The situation began to change considerably in 2010 and until 2018, when the number of trade concerns multiplied exponentially, and the proportion of trade concerns that became disputes also increased to 26.6 percent. Since 2019, a period that coincides with the Appellate Body impasse, the number of trade concerns has continued to grow considerably, while the proportion of trade concerns that resulted in litigation has decreased to 15.7 percent. See Table 1.

WTO phase	No. of trade concerns (1995–Oct. 2024)	AVG per year	No. that became a dispute (until 8 October 2024)	Share
Initial phase (1995–1996)	18	9.0	10	55.6%
Stabilization phase (1997–2001)	10	2.0	1	10.0%
Doha Development Agenda (2002–2009)	9	1.1	2	22.2%
Post-negotiations phase (2010–2018)	94	10.4	25	26.6%
Appellate Body impasse (2019–October 2024)	89	17.8	14	15.7%
Grand Total	**220**	**7.3**	**52**	**23.6%**

SOURCE: SANTANA & DOBHAL BASED ON THE WTO TRADE CONCERNS DATABASE AND ADDITIONAL INFORMATION EXTRACTED FROM THE CTG MINUTES. * DATA UNTIL OCTOBER 2024.
NOTE: THE NUMBER OF TRADE CONCERNS CORRESPONDS TO THOSE RAISED UNTIL THE JULY MEETING OF THE CTG, WHICH WERE THEN MATCHED WITH THE STATUS OF WTO DISPUTES UNDER THE DSU UNTIL 8 OCTOBER 2024. NEW DISPUTES MAY HAVE BEEN INITIATED SINCE THEN.

Multiple reasons could explain the decrease in this proportion, including that: 1) Members are less willing to litigate or 2) the incentives to litigate have not changed, but the concerns are too recent, so the disputes have not yet been filed.

Finally, a curious observation is that, despite the reduction in the proportion of trade concerns discussed in each CTG meeting that has led to litigation under the DSU over the past decade, their absolute number has remained relatively constant, oscillating between one and three new trade concerns raised in most of the CTG's meetings. See Figure 8.

Thirty Years of Trade Concerns at the Goods Council

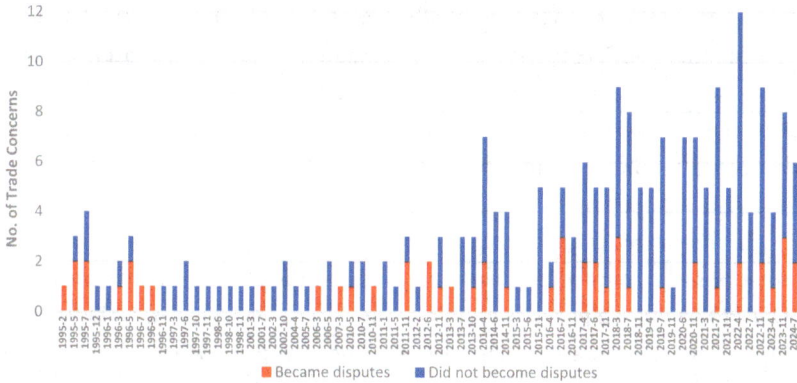

FIGURE 8. GOODS COUNCIL: NEW TRADE CONCERNS RAISED PER
COUNCIL MEETING AND WHETHER THEY BECAME DISPUTES
(1995–2024*)
SOURCE: SANTANA & DOBHAL BASED ON THE WTO TRADE CONCERNS DATABASE AND ADDITIONAL
INFORMATION EXTRACTED FROM THE CTG MINUTES. * DATA UNTIL OCTOBER 2024.

C. Relationship with the Disputes

THIS SECTION WILL EXPLORE WHETHER the disputes first raised at the
CTG behave differently from other disputes raised under the DSU, including
from the point of view of the procedural steps, the legal provisions cited, and
the main parties involved in these proceedings.

1) Evolution of the Disputes Under the DSU and Link to Trade Concerns

Before we discuss our findings on the trade concerns—disputes nexus, we
briefly outline the WTO dispute settlement process, which broadly comprises three main stages. The first formal stage is consultations between the
parties.[15] Given that the preferred objective of the DSU is to allow the dis-

---

15   *Marrakesh Agreement Establishing the World Trade Organization*, Annex 2, 15 April
     1994, 1869 UNTS 3 at 401, Understanding on Rules and Procedures Governing the
     Settlement of Disputes, art 4 (entered into force 1 January 1995).

puting Members to reach a mutually acceptable solution to their disputes in a manner consistent with the covered agreements,[16] consultations represent a key element that serves that objective. Consultations under the DSU also seem to resemble the discussions of trade concerns in WTO bodies in that consultations are conducted between the disputing parties, without the involvement of a panel.

If the parties cannot reach a mutually agreeable solution through consultations, the complaining party may request the Dispute Settlement Body (DSB) to establish a panel to adjudicate the dispute. Panel review is the second stage in the dispute settlement process. Once the panel is established, it is composed on an *ad-hoc* basis, typically of three individuals, who decide the dispute and issue a report. If no party appeals, the panel report is adopted by the DSB unless the DSB decides by consensus not to adopt the panel report.

According to the DSU, if a party notifies its decision to appeal, the Appellate Body is mandated to address the issues of law and legal interpretations developed by the panel that have been appealed by the parties.[17] The Appellate Body may uphold, modify or reverse the appealed panel findings. Where a panel report is appealed, it is considered for adoption by the DSB, together with the Appellate Body report, only after the completion of the appeal. The DSB adopts, and the parties unconditionally accept, the Appellate Body report and the panel report unless the DSB decides by consensus not to adopt them. The final stage is the implementation of the ruling, whereby the measures found to be inconsistent with the covered agreements need to be brought into conformity with such agreements within a reasonable period of time. Figure 8 provides an overview of the status of the procedural steps until October 2024, at which point 629 requests for consultations had been filed.

---

16   *Ibid*, art 3.7.
17   *Ibid*, arts 17.6 and 17.2.

DSU disputes overall 1995-10.2024		First raised at the CTG 1995 – 10.2024
629	Request for consultations	**83** (13.2% of total req. for cons)
372	Panel established	**64** (17.2% of total)
330	Panel composed	**52** (15.8%)
293	Panel report circulated	**44** (15.0%)
116 mutually agreed solutions 17 lapse of authority 26 withdrawals 3 Art. 25 arbitration awards notified	**194** Appealed **32** (16.5%) **166** AB Rep **19** (11.4%)	11 mutually agreed solutions 4 lapse of authority 4 withdrawals 1 Art. 25 arbitration awards notified

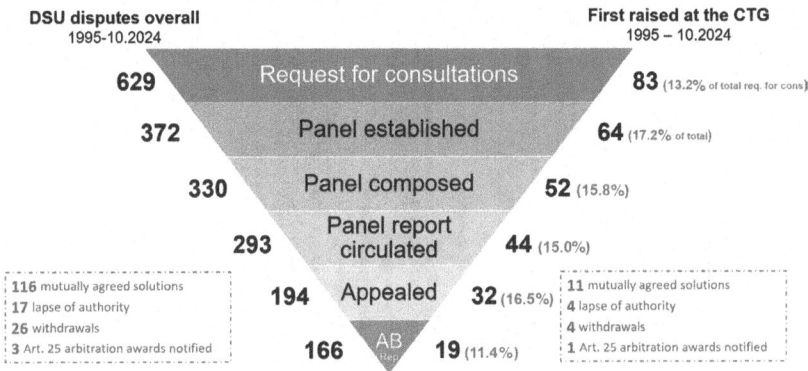

FIGURE 9. STATUS OF WTO DISPUTES UNDER THE WTO, BY PROCEDURAL STEP (1995–2024*)

SOURCE: SANTANA & DOBHAL BASED ON DATA EXTRACTED FROM THE WTO TRADE CONCERNS DATABASE AND THE WTO WEBSITE. * DATA UNTIL OCTOBER 2024.
NOTE: ONLY INCLUDES ORIGINAL PROCEEDINGS AND EXCLUDES THOSE RELATING TO COMPLIANCE, IN WHICH A MEMBER CHALLENGES A MEASURE TAKEN TO COMPLY WITH AN EARLIER DISPUTE SETTLEMENT RULING. THE STATISTICS FOR ALL STEPS ARE CALCULATED BASED ON THE DS NUMBER OF THE CASES, WHICH MAY OVERESTIMATE THE ACTUAL NUMBER FOR SOME OF THE STAGES.

While Figure 9 may suggest that the share of requests for consultations that were first raised as trade concerns at the CTG is relatively small, it is pertinent to recall that approximately half of these disputes relate to trade remedies and subsidy disciplines (meaning anti-dumping (AD), countervailing duties (CVDs), subsidies, and safeguards, which are, for the most part, not raised as trade concerns at the CTG. The shares would be twice as high if this aspect is considered. Moreover, the shares of requests for consultations that were first raised as trade concerns vary considerably across the types of issues and covered agreements, i.e., goods, services, or intellectual property.

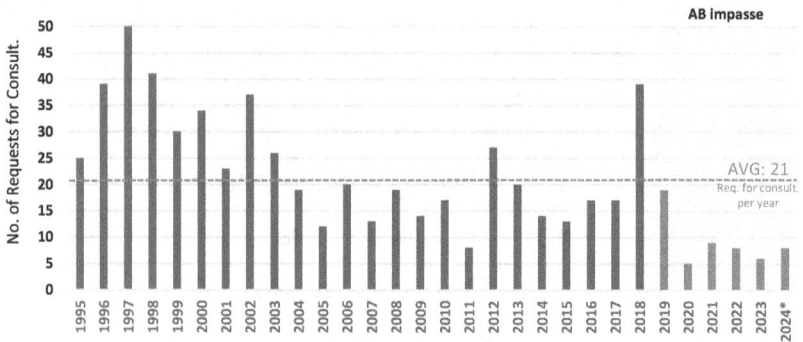

FIGURE 10. EVOLUTION IN THE NUMBER OF REQUESTS FOR
CONSULTATIONS UNDER THE DSU
(1995–2024*)

SOURCE: CALCULATIONS BY SANTANA & DOBHAL BASED ON THE WTO WEBSITE. * DATA UNTIL OCTOBER 2024.

Since 2019, the Appellate Body has ceased to operate due to the lack of consensus in the DSB to appoint new Members, leaving only the panel process active.[18] For this reason, if a panel report is appealed, its adoption by the DSB is delayed indefinitely, a situation referred to by some practitioners as an "appeal into the void." The uncertainty generated by the Appellate Body impasse may be one of the reasons behind the considerable decrease in the number of disputes filed under the DSU after 2019, where the number of requests for consultations has been consistently below the average of twenty-one per year established over almost three decades from 1995–2024 (see Figure 10). While it is true that the data suggest that there is an inverse correlation between, on the one hand, the Appellate Body impasse and the reduction in the number of disputes and, on the other hand, the increase in the number of trade concerns at the WTO (see Figure 1 above),

---

18 However, alternative appeal mechanisms, such as the DSU Article 25 process and the Multi-Party Interim Appeal Arbitration Arrangement (MPIA) are available but only among Members who have agreed to use them. Thus far, these mechanisms have been used only twice.

it should be stressed that there is not necessarily causation between them. Other reasons, such as an increased number of measures that affect multiple Members, or increased participation of Members that were not previously active in raising trade concerns, among others, may also explain this trend.[19]

2) Comparison of Procedural Steps

The primary aspect we test is whether disputes first raised as trade concerns in the CTG proceeded here differently from others *vis-à-vis* how far they went in the dispute settlement process and the procedural steps. In this regard, the first interesting observation is that a striking 76 percent of the eighty-three requests for consultations concerning issues that were first raised at the CTG led to the establishment of a panel, which is a significantly higher proportion than the 57 percent observed for the other disputes that were not (i.e., almost twenty percentage points). Although more research would be needed to clarify the reasons behind such a difference, one hypothesis could be that the measure at issue had already been sufficiently discussed through the Committee and CTG trade concern processes, so there was a lower chance that the additional discussions following a request for consultations would allow the parties to resolve the issue bilaterally.

The disputes first raised as trade concerns have led to cases that have a higher probability of continuing through the remaining procedural steps of a dispute, with the notable exception of the issuance of a report by the Appellate Body. In the same vein, the proportion of disputes in which the appeal is pending ("appealed into the void") is significantly higher for disputes initially raised as trade concerns in the CTG. We believe that these two aspects are closely linked and likely explained by their timing, i.e., there is a high concentration of disputes first raised as trade concerns in the CTG that were filed a few years before the Appellate Body impasse, which led to several panel reports being issued after the Appellate Body ceased to operate. This perhaps increased the probability that such disputes would be "appealed into the void" (thirteen out of the eighteen relevant disputes), without taking into account two compliance panel reports under Article 21.5 of the DSU. Figure 11 compares the share of the relevant groups of disputes.

---

19   Santana & Dobhal, above note ** at 15.

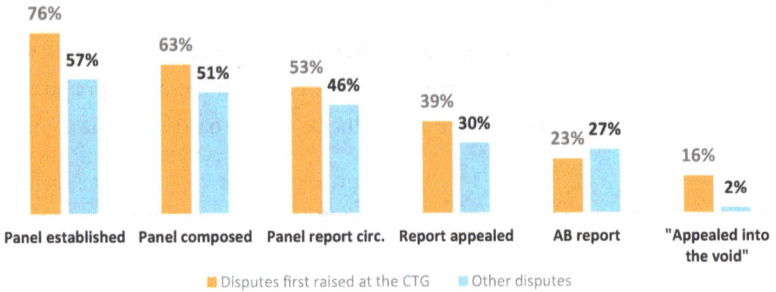

Disputes first raised at the CTG ■ Other disputes

FIGURE 11. COMPARISON OF THE EIGHTY-THREE DISPUTES THAT WERE
FIRST RAISED AS TRADE CONCERNS AT THE GOODS COUNCIL VS
THE OTHER 546 DISPUTES THAT WERE NOT (1995–2024*)
SOURCE: SANTANA & DOBHAL BASED ON DATA EXTRACTED FROM THE WTO TRADE CONCERNS
DATABASE AND THE WTO WEBSITE. * DATA UNTIL JULY 2024.

3) Comparison of WTO Provisions Cited

A second aspect that can be studied is the extent to which there are differences between disputes filed and trade concerns raised at the CTG in terms of the WTO agreements cited by Members as the legal basis for their claims.[20] Based on the data for the request for consultations between 1995 and October 2024, it is possible to assess an agreement's relative weight in proceedings in which more than one legal provision is cited. Figure 12 below shows that, as with the CTG's trade concerns, the GATT 1994 remains, by far, the primary source of legal claims. Indeed, up to 82 percent of the requests for consultations have included claims based on the GATT 1994, which is significantly higher than the 62 percent of the CTG's trade concerns. The difference is even more significant concerning the agreements on Anti-dumping, Subsidies and CVDs and, to a lesser extent, Safeguards, which have been significantly more important in the share of requests for consultations than the role they play in the CTG's trade concerns. This suggests that most of these issues are discussed in the relevant technical committees and then raised directly as disputes without being escalated to the CTG.[21] The reverse appears true for the TBT Agreement, which has played a disproportionately higher role as a basis for trade concerns in the Goods Council and a considerably lower

---

20   For a similar kind of analysis focused on disputes, see Bernard M Hoekman, Petros C Mavroidis, & Maarja Saluste "Informing WTO Reform: Dispute Settlement Performance, 1995–2020" (2021) 55:1 *Journal of World Trade* 1.

21   Shaffer, Wolfe, & Le, above note 12.

proportion has resulted in disputes. Horn et al have argued that this could be due to a "dispute prevention" function of the ordinary bodies, particularly the TBT Committee.[22] The role of the CTG in such dispute prevention functions remains unexplored and falls outside the scope of this chapter.

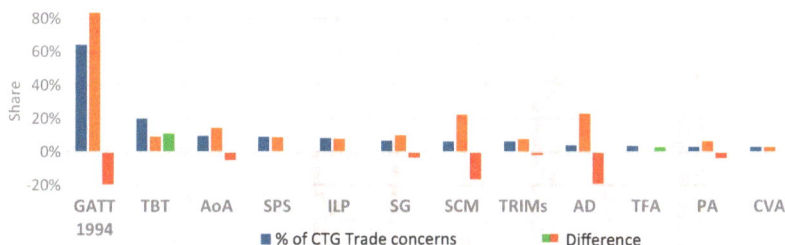

FIGURE 12. COMPARISON OF THE PROPORTION OF REFERENCES TO WTO AGREEMENTS CITED IN 220 TRADE CONCERNS AT THE GOODS COUNCIL VS 629 REQUESTS FOR CONSULTATIONS UNDER THE DSU (1995–2024*)

SOURCE: SANTANA & DOBHAL BASED ON DATA EXTRACTED FROM THE WTO TRADE CONCERNS DATABASE AND THE WTO WEBSITE. * DATA UNTIL JULY 2024.
NOTE: THE NUMBER OF CTG'S TRADE CONCERNS IS THE TOTAL NUMBER OF UNIQUE TRADE CONCERNS RAISED UNTIL JULY 2024. THE NUMBER OF REQUESTS FOR CONSULTATIONS IS AS OF 8 OCTOBER 2024.

There are also differences in the extent to which specific GATT 1994 provisions are cited in the CTG trade concerns and the disputes under the DSU. Generally, and with the notable exception of Articles XXIV (Customs Unions and Free Trade Areas) and XXVIII (Modification of Schedules), specific GATT 1994 provisions tend to be cited proportionally less in the context of the trade concerns at the CTG, while they represent a higher proportion of the disputes, in particular for those that were first raised at the CTG. For instance, while Article XI (Quantitative Restrictions) was mentioned in 63 of the 220 (28.6 percent) unique trade concerns raised in the Goods Council, it was cited in thirty-three of the eighty-three (39.8 percent) requests for consultations that were first raised at the CTG as trade concerns, and in 129 of the 546 (23.6 percent) other requests for consultations. The difference is particularly stark with respect to Article VI (AD and CVD), which, as

---

22   Horn, Mavroidis, & Wijkström, above note 9.

previously mentioned, is explained by the fact that most disputes relating to anti-dumping practices, subsidies, and CVDs are not raised as trade concerns in the Goods Council. Interestingly, safeguards and references to Article XIX (SG) of the GATT appear slightly different in this respect. See Figure 13.

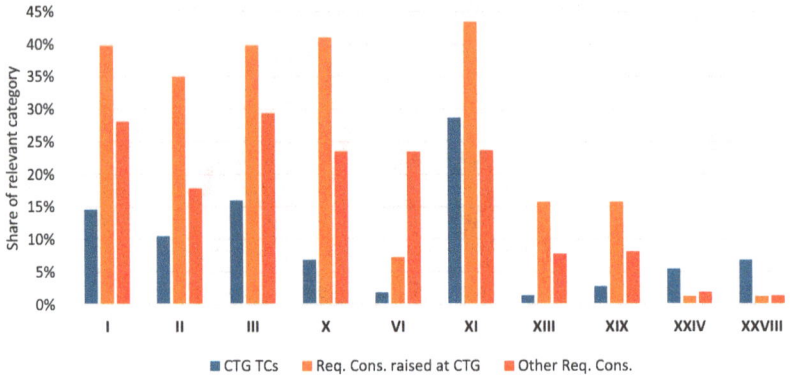

FIGURE 13. COMPARISON OF SELECTED GATT 1994 PROVISIONS CITED IN 220 TRADE CONCERNS AT THE GOODS COUNCIL VS 629 REQUESTS FOR CONSULTATIONS UNDER THE DSU (1995–2024*) SOURCE: SANTANA & DOBHAL BASED ON DATA EXTRACTED FROM THE WTO TRADE CONCERNS DATABASE AND THE WTO WEBSITE. * DATA UNTIL JULY 2024.

In Section 2.4 and Figure 6 above, we demonstrated that in the context of the trade concerns raised at the CTG, most references to Article XI of the GATT 1994 had taken place since 2019, coinciding with the Appellate Body impasse, which raises the question of whether there was a similar pattern with respect to the requests for consultations under the DSU. Contrary to expectations, the disproportionate increase in the context of the trade concerns procedures has not yet translated into requests for consultations involving this provision and, in fact, there appears to be a significant contraction. See Figure 14. However, given the lag between when trade concerns are raised and requests for consultations are submitted, these numbers might increase in the coming months or years, so it is probably too early to draw conclusions.

Thirty Years of Trade Concerns at the Goods Council

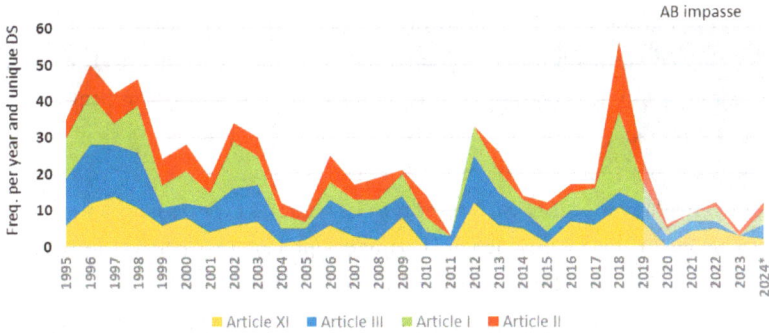

FIGURE 14. EVOLUTION OF MAIN GATT 1994 PROVISIONS CITED IN 629 REQUESTS FOR CONSULTATIONS UNDER THE DSU (1995–2024*)

SOURCE: SANTANA & DOBHAL CALCULATIONS BASED ON DATA EXTRACTED FROM THE WTO WEBSITE. * DATA UNTIL JULY 2024.

4) Comparison of Main Parties Involved

A final point we explore in this chapter is whether there are differences with respect to the parties implicated in the requests for consultations *vis-à-vis* those involved with trade concerns at the Goods Council. Raising a trade concern at the Goods Council is a significantly lower bar than filing a dispute under the DSU as the former requires only a request by a Member to include an item on the CTG agenda while the latter is a separate legal process. Our previous paper observed that, with some exceptions, the list of most active Members raising trade concerns coincided largely with the list of leading exporters and the list of Members responding to them with the list of leading importers.[23] The hypothesis we put forward as a possible explanation based on the economic interests was that the largest exporters had the highest interest in raising trade concerns, and the largest importers would typically be the target of the highest number of trade concerns.

a) Main Complainants

FIGURE 15 COMPARES THE OVERALL share of trade CTG trade concerns raised (blue dots) and the consultations requested under the DSU (orange dots) for the top twenty exporters in the world. Each Member appears twice,

---

23   Santana & Dobhal, above note ** at 16.

and both variables are aligned to the relevant share of exports (i.e., they are fully aligned vertically). If the share of exports fully correlated to the degree of participation in both types of procedures, Members would appear exactly over the line at a 45-degree angle in the chart. The further up that the dot is located from that line, the more the Member would be overrepresented in that particular procedure with respect to its share of exports in 2023, whereas positioning below it would mean it is underrepresented. Annex 1 provides the complete list of Members and the data used in this figure, which shows that there are marked differences in these shares *vis-à-vis* their participation in world exports, i.e., having both cases of over and under-representation. While useful to illustrate the point, it should be stressed that this methodology is based on the comparison of the Members' share of exports in a particular year (2023), with the cumulative share of trade concerns and requests for consultations over three decades (1995–2024). A proper comparison would have required calculating the average share of exports for the same period, so the 2023 exports are only proxy.

Leaving aside this issue, a first observation on these shares is that, for practically all the top exporters in 2023, the relative degree of participation in raising trade concerns at the CTG is higher than their degree of participation as complainants under DSU procedures. One notable exception to this trend is Brazil, which has proportionately participated in more requests for consultations (5.4 percent) than trade concerns at the CTG (4.5 percent). In addition, there is only a marginal difference in the degree of participation of Mexico, Viet Nam, the Kingdom of Saudi Arabia, and the UAE, with the last two having only minimal participation in both types of procedures.

Second, we observe a marked difference in the degree to which some of these top exporters in 2023 have participated more in the CTG trade concerns discussions than in the DSU proceedings, as measured by the difference between both indicators. Such difference tends to be relatively high for most developed country Members in the list of top exporters, and in particular for Japan (+10.5 percentage point difference), Australia (+7.8), Switzerland (+6.5), the European Union (+6.3), and the Russian Federation (+5.1), suggesting that these Members have been proportionately more active in CTG proceedings than in the disputes. Beyond these top exporters, several smaller exporters have also been considerably more active in raising trade concerns at the CTG than requesting consultations under the DSU, particularly Uruguay, Norway, Türkiye, New Zealand, and Thailand.

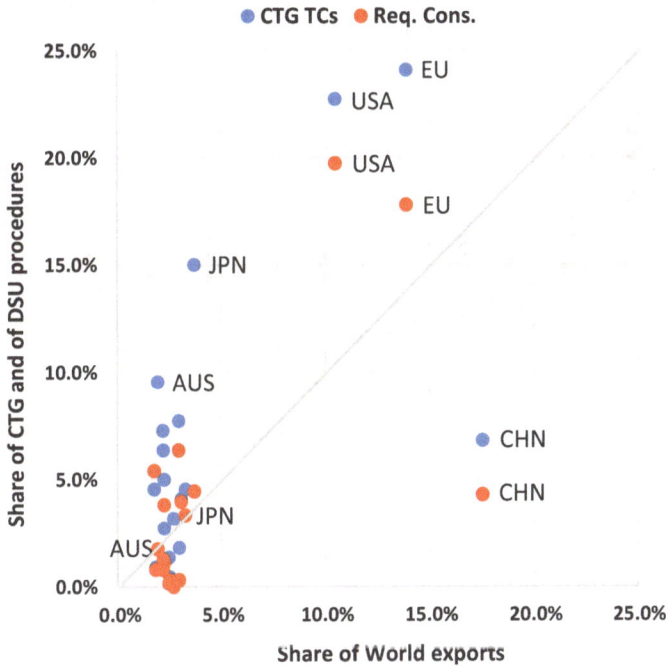

FIGURE 15. TOP TWENTY EXPORTERS: SHARE OF 2023 WORLD EXPORTS VS PARTICIPATION IN CTG TRADE CONCERNS AND DSU REQUESTS FOR CONSULTATIONS (1995–2024*)

SOURCE: SANTANA & DOBHAL CALCULATIONS BASED ON THE WTO TRADE CONCERNS DATABASE, WTO WEBSITE, AND THE WTO ANALYTICAL DATABASE. * DATA UNTIL JULY 2024. NOTE: THE CALCULATIONS EXCLUDE INTRA-EU TRADE.

A third and final observation has to do with the complainants in the eighty-three requests for consultations under the DSU that were first raised as trade concerns in the CTG and how they differ from the complainants in the remaining 546 requests for consultations, which may serve as a proxy of their preference of one over the other. In this regard, it is interesting to note that the proportion of those disputes is nearly identical for Argentina. However, four Members have relatively lower participation in these eighteen-three procedures (United States, European Union, Canada, and Brazil) than in the remaining 546 requests for consultations, suggesting that they tend to favour requesting consultations over escalating the issue as a trade concern in the CTG. Conversely, the remaining seven Members (Japan, China, Qatar,

Russian Federation, Australia, Indonesia, and New Zealand) have disproportionately higher participation in the eighteen-three requests for consultations that were previously raised at the CTG than in the other ones, suggesting that they have a preference for first trying to solve them at that level. See Figure 16.

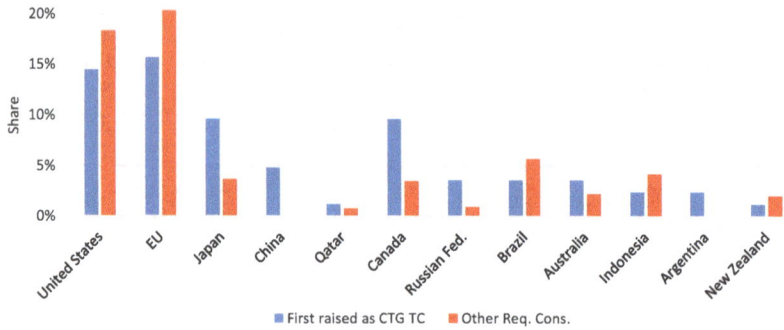

FIGURE 16. MAIN COMPLAINANTS IN THE EIGHTY-THREE REQUESTS FOR CONSULTATIONS FIRST RAISED AS CTG TRADE CONCERNS VS SHARE IN THE REMAINING 546 REQUESTS FOR CONSULTATIONS (1995–2024*)

SOURCE: SANTANA & DOBHAL CALCULATIONS BASED ON THE WTO TRADE CONCERNS DATABASE AND WTO WEBSITE. * DATA UNTIL JULY 2024.

b) Main Respondents

Figure 17 compares, for the top twenty importers in 2023, the overall share of trade CTG trade concerns that have been responded to (blue dots), as well as the requests for consultations where one or more of their measures has been challenged (orange dots) for the period 1995–2024. Like with the previous section, each Member appears twice in the chart, and both variables are aligned to the relevant share of world imports in 2023 (i.e., they are fully aligned vertically). If the share of imports fully correlated to the degree of participation in both types of procedures, Members would then appear exactly over the line at a 45-degree angle in the chart. The further up that the dot is located from that line, the more the Member would be overrepresented in that particular procedure with respect to their share of imports, whereas positioning below it would mean they are underrepresented. Annex 1 provides the complete list of Members, and the data used in this figure, which shows marked differences in these shares *vis-à-vis* their participation in world exports, i.e., having both cases of over and under-representation. As explained above, more proper comparison would have required calculating the average share of exports for the same period instead of using a single year, so the 2023 imports are only a proxy.

Unlike the case of the exporters, where participation in the CTG procedures was proportionally higher for practically all the exporters, we observe a more diverse situation with respect to the top importers. Four of these top importers have practically either not at all, or only very rarely, been challenged at the CTG or the DSU (Singapore, United Kingdom, UAE, and Viet Nam). However, seven of the top twenty importers show a proportionately lower share of participation in responding to CTG's trade concerns than in requests for consultations (Australia, Canada, European Union, India, Mexico, Türkiye, and United States), suggesting that when other Members decide to challenge measures by these Members, they tend to favour going directly to the DSU rather than raising trade concerns at the CTG, although to different degrees. The highest difference is for the United States as a respondent (−5.7 percentage points) and India (−5.1). The remaining nine top importers have responded proportionally to more trade concerns at the CTG than requests for consultations under the DSU (China; Hong Kong, China; Japan; Korea, Republic of; Malaysia; Russian Federation; Switzerland; Chinese Taipei; and Thailand) and, again to different degrees. The importers with the largest difference are the Russian Federation (+9.2 percentage points), Japan (+4.7) and China (+2.1). Unlike with the top exporters, here there is no clear pattern with respect to the developed country Members.

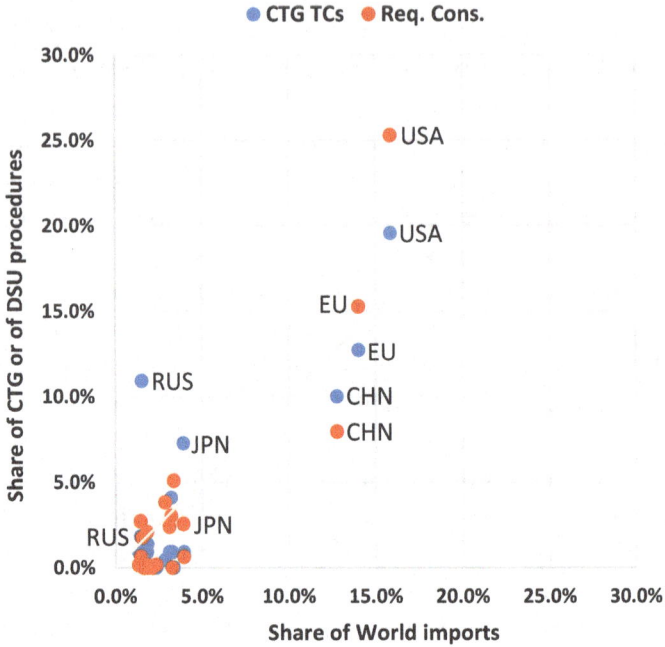

FIGURE 17. TOP TWENTY IMPORTERS: SHARE OF 2023 WORLD IMPORTS VS PARTICIPATION IN CTG TRADE CONCERNS AND DSU REQUESTS FOR CONSULTATIONS (1995–2024*)

SOURCE: SANTANA & DOBHAL CALCULATIONS BASED ON THE WTO TRADE CONCERNS DATABASE, WTO WEBSITE, AND THE WTO ANALYTICAL DATABASE. * DATA UNTIL JULY 2024. NOTE: THE CALCULATIONS EXCLUDE INTRA-EU TRADE.

A third and final observation concerns the respondents in the eighty-three requests for consultations under the DSU that were first raised as trade concerns in the CTG and how these differ from the respondents in the remaining 546 requests for consultations. In this regard, only three of the main respondents in these CTG procedures have proportionately lower participation in the eighteen-three DSU procedures (Brazil, European Union, and United States), and with a relatively small difference, suggesting a similar probability that complaining Members would first bring the issue to the CTG than raising it directly under the DSU. However, the difference for the remaining nine Members is relatively high and disproportionately in favour of the requests for consultations that were first raised as trade concerns in the CTG. This is particularly the case for disputes brought against Indonesia (+7 percentage points), Argentina (+4.3), Japan (+4), India (+3.9) and the Russian Federation (+3.5). This suggests that, when dealing with these Members, the other Members may have a preference for first raising the issue as a trade concern in the CTG before requesting consultations. See Figure 18.

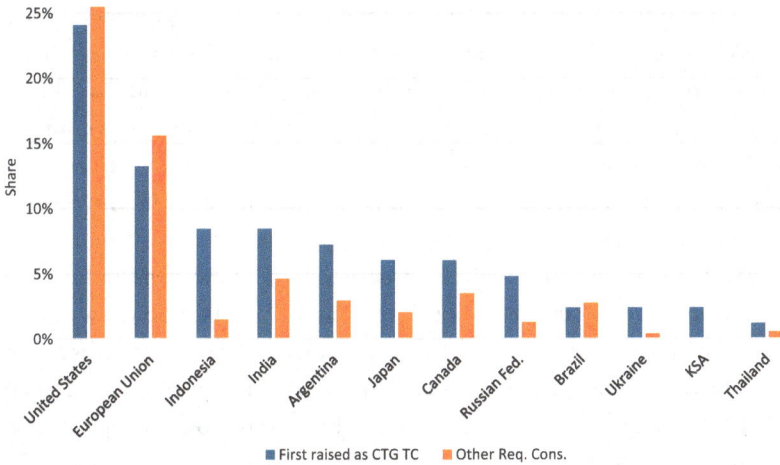

FIGURE 18. MAIN RESPONDENTS IN THE EIGHTY-THREE REQUESTS FOR CONSULTATIONS FIRST RAISED AS CTG TRADE CONCERNS VS SHARE IN THE OTHER 546 REQUESTS FOR CONSULTATIONS (1995–2024*)

SOURCE: SANTANA & DOBHAL CALCULATIONS BASED ON THE WTO TRADE CONCERNS DATABASE AND THE WTO WEBSITE. * DATA UNTIL JULY 2024.

D. Main Takeaways and Conclusions

OVER THE PAST THREE DECADES, trade concern discussions at the CTG played an increasingly important role in the way WTO Members engage with each other and discuss trade-related frictions. Building on previous work, this chapter advances our analysis and examines the substance of the trade concerns, including the types of issues discussed and the degree to which trade concerns raised at the CTG have progressively escalated into disputes. Our analysis of thirty years of data reveals several critical insights:

- General trends: Over the past three decades, 220 unique trade concerns have been raised at the CTG, with a marked increase post-2010 and a peak coinciding with the Appellate Body impasse. While the CTG's role has expanded over the past few years, and eighty-three requests for consultations have first been raised as trade concerns at the CTG, only 23 percent of these concerns have escalated to disputes under the DSU.
- Trade concerns—disputes nexus: We found that while there was some truth to the narrative of escalation (i.e., issues are first raised as trade concerns and then as disputes), this was not the case for a significant proportion of requests for consultations and, in particular, for those relating to trade remedies and subsidies disciplines. Our analysis found that almost a quarter of the trade concerns were eventually escalated to the formal dispute process. However, once the CTG trade concerns were raised as requests for consultations under the DSU, there was a significantly higher probability that the complainant(s) would request the establishment of a panel and continue through all subsequent procedural steps, rather than resolving the dispute before a ruling is issued. Drilling down, we noted that despite the reduction in the proportion of trade concerns discussed in each CTG meeting that have led to litigation in the past decade, their absolute number has remained relatively constant, oscillating between one and three of the new trade concerns raised in most of the CTG's meetings. Interestingly, our analysis also noted that while disputes pertaining to trade remedies formed almost half of all the disputes filed, their corresponding share in CTG trade concerns was small, and one area where escalation is visible to a lesser extent.
- Continued significance of the key GATT 1994 provisions: A key takeaway from our analysis is the continued importance of the fundamental GATT 1994 provisions in trade concerns discussions and disputes, as evidenced by disciplines on quantitative restrictions, national treatment, and most-favoured-nation principles being the most frequently cited legal provisions in the CTG trade concerns. Further, the fact that most trade concerns at the CTG dealt with transparency or aspects of transparency around the measures under discussion underscores the vital role that transparency plays in multilateral trade governance. Similarly, the

GATT 1994 is the most frequently cited agreement, both in CTG Trade concerns and requests for consultations under the DSU. While Article XI (quantitative restrictions), Article III (national treatment), and Article I (Most-Favoured-Nation) are the most frequently cited provisions in both types of proceedings, different trends can be observed in their evolution. For example, the increased relevance of Article XI in the context of CTG trade concerns has not yet translated into a similar increase in requests for consultations.

- Participation by Members: Major exporting Members have been more active in raising trade concerns at the CTG than in initiating disputes. We found that the top twenty exporters in the world participated more actively in trade concerns than in requests for consultations, suggesting that these Members participated proportionally more actively in the CTG deliberations than they did as complainants in disputes. Conversely, the results were not as conclusive for the top twenty importers, as there was no clear pattern on whether Members challenging their measures would first bring them to the CTG or raise them directly as requests for consultations under the DSU.

- A potential tool for dispute prevention: The findings suggest that WTO Members could enhance their use of the CTG as an effective platform for discussion, conflict prevention, and resolution, at least for some of these cases. By leveraging the transparency and dialogue facilitated through trade concern discussions, Members could reduce the need for formal litigation, particularly during periods of procedural impasses.

This chapter has tried to demonstrate how Members participate in trade concerns *vis-à-vis* disputes by analysing data covering close to thirty years. While we have speculated about potential reasons for the trends, the question of why and how Members interact, and approach disputes and trade concerns merit further research and analysis. Areas for future exploration could include:

- Dispute Outcomes: Analyzing whether trade concerns that escalate to disputes have more favourable outcomes for complainants than direct disputes.

- Members' Motivations and Strategies: Investigating the internal factors influencing Members' decisions to seek to resolve trade concerns within the CTG framework or escalate matters to formal dispute settlement under the DSU.

- Relationship to Regional Trade Agreements: It remains unclear whether the consultation and dispute resolution mechanisms established in the context of regional trade agreements have influenced (up or down) the number of trade concerns and requests for consultations raised at the WTO among the parties to those agreements.

The CTG's increasing role in addressing trade concerns highlights its importance as a platform for transparency, dialogue, and the potential prevention of formal disputes. While not all trade concerns escalate into disputes, the discussions in the CTG following the raising of trade concerns contribute to a more robust understanding of trade measures and foster a cooperative spirit among Members. The observed trends and patterns underscore the value of continuing to adapt and strengthen the CTG's processes to better serve the evolving needs of WTO Members.

Annex 1

Detailed Data Used For Figures 15 To 18

A. Top twenty exporters in 2023 and their share of trade concerns responded to at the CTG and share of requests for consultations under the DSU (1995–2024)

Top Twenty exporters 2023	Share of exports 2023 (%)	Share of trade concerns responded to at the CTG (%)	Share of Request for consultations under the DSU (%)	Difference (CTG-DSU)
China	17.54	6.8	4.3	2.5
European Union	13.90	24.1	17.8	6.3
United States	10.49	22.7	19.7	3.0
Japan	3.72	15.0	4.5	10.5
Korea, Rep.	3.28	4.5	3.3	1.2
Mexico	3.08	4.1	4.0	0.1
Hong Kong, China	2.98	1.8	0.3	1.5
Canada	2.95	7.7	6.4	1.4
UK	2.71	3.2	0.0	3.2
United Arab Emirates	2.52	0.5	0.3	0.1
Singapore	2.47	1.4	0.2	1.2
Chinese Taipei	2.24	2.7	1.1	1.6
India	2.24	5.0	3.8	1.2
Russian Fed.	2.20	6.4	1.3	5.1
Switzerland	2.18	7.3	0.8	6.5
Australia	1.93	9.5	1.7	7.8
Viet Nam	1.84	0.9	0.8	0.1
Brazil	1.76	4.5	5.4	−0.9
Saudi Arabia, Kingdom of	1.66	0.5	0.2	0.3
Malaysia	1.62	2.7	0.3	2.4

SOURCE: SANTANA & DOBHAL CALCULATIONS BASED ON THE WTO TRADE CONCERNS DATABASE, WTO WEBSITE, AND THE WTO ANALYTICAL DATABASE.
NOTE: TRADE DATA EXCLUDES INTRA-EU TRADE.

B. Top twenty importers in 2023 and their share of trade concerns raised at the CTG and share of requests for consultations under the DSU (1995–2024)

Top Twenty importers 2023	Share of imports 2023 (%)	Share of trade concerns raised at the CTG (%)	Share of Request for consulta-tions under the DSU (%)	Difference (CTG-DSU)
United States	15.9	19.5	25.3	-5.7
European Union	14.0	12.7	15.3	-2.5
China	12.8	10.0	7.9	2.1
United Kingdom	4.0	0.9	0.6	0.3
Japan	3.9	7.3	2.5	4.7
India	3.4	0.0	5.1	-5.1
Hong Kong, China	3.3	0.9	0.0	0.9
Korea, Republic of	3.2	4.1	3.0	1.1
Mexico	3.1	0.9	2.4	-1.5
Canada	2.9	0.5	3.8	-3.4
United Arab Emirates	2.3	0.0	0.2	-0.2
Singapore	2.1	0.0	0.0	0.0
Switzerland	1.8	1.4	0.0	1.4
Türkiye	1.8	0.9	2.1	-1.2
Chinese Taipei	1.8	1.4	0.2	1.2
Viet Nam	1.6	0.0	0.0	0.0
Russian Federation	1.5	10.9	1.7	9.2
Thailand	1.4	1.8	0.6	1.2
Australia	1.4	1.8	2.7	-0.9
Malaysia	1.3	0.9	0.2	0.8

SOURCE: SANTANA & DOBHAL CALCULATIONS BASED ON THE WTO TRADE CONCERNS DATABASE, WTO WEBSITE, AND THE WTO ANALYTICAL DATABASE.
NOTE: TRADE DATA EXCLUDES INTRA-EU TRADE.

CHAPTER 17

Women in WTO Dispute Settlement: The Role of Individuals as Catalysts for Gender Inclusion

Penelope Ridings

A. Introduction

THE WORLD OF INTERNATIONAL TRADE is often identified as a male-dominated arena. Studies have lamented the lack of engagement with women in international trade and sought to encourage a gender perspective in trade.[1] The need to mainstream gender issues in trade gained strength in recent years, notably after the Buenos Aires Declaration on Trade and Women's Economic Empowerment agreed in December 2017, adopted in the margins of the 11th Ministerial Conference of the World Trade Organization (WTO). Currently 127 WTO Members and observers have endorsed the Buenos Aires Declara-

---

1   World Bank & WTO, *Women and Trade: The Role of Trade in Promoting Gender Equality* (Washington, DC: World Bank & WTO, 2020); International Trade Centre, *Women in Trade: New Data and New Insights* (Geneva: International Trade Centre, 2024); International Trade Centre, *Unlocking Markets for Women to Trade* (Geneva: International Trade Centre, 2015); Organisation for Economic Co-operation and Development, *Trade and Gender: A Framework of Analysis* (Paris: Organisation for Economic Co-operation and Development, 2021); Organisation for Economic Co-operation and Development, "Women Led Firms in International Trade" in *SME and Entrepreneurship Outlook 2023* (Paris: Organisation for Economic Co-operation and Development, 2023).

tion which includes a commitment to work together in the WTO to remove barriers to women's economic empowerment and increase their participation in trade.[2] The Buenos Aires Declaration was followed in September 2020 by the establishment of the Informal Working Group (IWG) on Trade and Gender which aims to implement the Declaration.[3]

Recognition of the importance of women's economic empowerment in the WTO followed the adoption in 2015 by the United Nations (UN) of the 2030 Agenda for Sustainable Development and its seventeen Sustainable Development Goals, including Goal 5: "Achieve gender equality and empower all women and girls." At the organizational level, the UN Secretary-General António Guterres launched a United Nations Gender Parity Strategy in 2017 which had a target of reaching gender parity across the UN system by 2028.[4]

At the same time the WTO sought to play its part in women's empowerment in trade. In 2016 the WTO Director-General at the time, Roberto Azevêdo, became an International Gender Champion. He committed to promote gender equality in all aspects of the WTO work and to support WTO Members' efforts to place trade and gender more prominently in the organization.[5] In June 2017, he appointed the first WTO Trade and Gender Focal Point to lead this work in the WTO—Anoush der Boghossian. These efforts have further progressed under the stewardship of the first woman Director-General of the WTO, Dr Ngozi Okonjo-Iweala, appointed in February 2021.

Nevertheless decades prior to the current efforts to promote gender diversity, when men were dominant in the WTO, notable women were role models and played a part in seeking to promote gender diversity in the WTO, including in WTO dispute settlement. Among them were Valerie Hughes, Director of the WTO Appellate Body Division from 2001 to 2005 and Director of the Legal Affairs Division from 2010 to 2016, and to whom this book is dedicated. This chapter examines the place of women in WTO dispute settlement from

---

2   WTO, "Buenos Aires Declaration on Trade and Women's Economic Development" (last visited 26 March 2025), online: wto.org [perma.cc/5849-J2KS].

3   WTO, *Interim Report Following the Buenos Aires Joint Declaration on Trade and Women's Economic Empowerment*, WTO Doc WT/L/1095/Rev.1 (2020), online (pdf): docs.wto.org [perma.cc/4YXX-NNCK].

4   United Nations, "System-Wide Strategy on Gender Parity" (2017), online (pdf): un.org [perma.cc/3LHF-U9SV].

5   International Trade Centre, *Delivering on the Buenos Aires Declaration on Trade and Women's Economic Empowerment* (Geneva: International Trade Centre, 2020) at 51.

the establishment of the WTO to the present and their involvement in the various facets of the resolution of trade disputes.

The WTO *Understanding on the Rules and Procedures Governing the Settlement of Disputes*,[6] known as the Dispute Settlement Understanding (DSU) and concluded contemporaneously with the *Marrakesh Agreement Establishing the WTO* (WTO Agreement), established a two-tier system for dispute settlement, with a built-in automaticity designed to ensure that disputes were resolved through the application of trade rules.[7] The WTO Agreement, including the DSU, was once thought to be "gender neutral" in that there is no reference to terms such as "gender," "gender equality," or "men and women."[8] However, rather than "gender neutral" the WTO Agreement started off as "gender blind" in that there was no provision for representation of women or the interests of women.[9] This has been tempered somewhat as the WTO organization has become more "gender aware" and even "gender responsive."[10] There is much discussion in the WTO on the need to apply a "gender lens" in assessing trade policy, but to date a gender lens has not been applied to the WTO dispute settlement system.

This chapter seeks to remedy this by adopting a conceptual framework which involves an examination of the dominant structure of the legal institution, an assessment of the impact of the structure on women, including the extent to which women are represented in the institution, the impact of the lack of diversity on the legitimacy of the institution, and an identification of some possible solutions which might enable the institution to be transformed to a more gender-inclusive institution.[11] The conclusions of this chapter have

---

6   *Marrakesh Agreement Establishing the World Trade Organization*, Annex 2, 15 April 1994, 1869 UNTS 3 at 401, Understanding on Rules and Procedures Governing the Settlement of Disputes, art 3.7 (entered into force 1 January 1995) [*DSU*].

7   For a description of this WTO dispute settlement system see WTO, *A Handbook on the WTO Dispute Settlement* System, 2nd ed, (Cambridge: Cambridge University Press, 2017).

8   Anoush der Boghossian, "Gender-Responsive WTO: Making Trade Rules and Policies Work for Women" in Amrita Bahri, Dorotea López, & Jan Remy, eds, *Trade Policy and Gender Equality* (Cambridge: Cambridge University Press, 2023) 21 at 27 [Der Boghossian, "Gender-Responsive WTO"].

9   Judit Fabian, "Global Economic Governance and Women: Why Is the WTO a Difficult Case for Women's Representation?" in Bahri, López, & Remy, *ibid* at 69.

10   Der Boghossian, "Gender-Responsive WTO" above note 8.

11   This is based on that adopted by Cochav Elkayam-Levy, "A Path to Transformation: Asking 'The Woman Question' in International Law" (2021) 42:3 *Michigan Journal of International Law* 429.

wider application to judicial bodies than just those of the WTO dispute settlement system. In particular, they demonstrate the important role that the organization itself plays in promoting gender diversity and the role that individuals play as catalysts for enhancing gender inclusivity.

Following this Introduction, Section B introduces the WTO dispute settlement system and provides information on women in WTO dispute settlement and the role that the Secretariat plays in providing support to trade adjudication. While many women have served as counsel representing WTO Members before panels and the WTO Appellate Body, this chapter concentrates on women within the organization and within the dispute settlement system. It identifies the number and proportion of women who have been WTO panelists and Members of the Appellate Body and moves to increase women's participation in dispute settlement. Section C compares the WTO dispute settlement system with some other comparable judicial bodies. As the WTO dispute settlement system has fallen behind recent advances in gender parity in other similar institutions, Section C seeks to identify some of the reasons for the disparity. It goes on to suggest that the absence of women in the WTO system affects its legitimacy. Section D draws on this discussion to identify some potential responses to address the gender imbalance, including the contribution that WTO Members, the Secretariat and individuals in the Secretariat can make to organization-wide efforts to promote improved gender balance in WTO dispute settlement. Section E offers a few conclusions.

B. The Women in WTO Dispute Settlement

THE ROLE OF WOMEN IN WTO dispute settlement is an inherently multi-faceted one. Women serve as diplomats in the permanent missions to the WTO based in Geneva, as counsel and advocates in WTO dispute settlement cases before the WTO, as members of the Secretariat assisting with the composition of panels and assisting panels and other adjudicatory mechanisms, as panelists for WTO disputes, as Members of the Appellate Body, and as members of the pool of arbitrators under the Multi-Party Interim Appeal Arbitration Arrangement (MPIA). The question of gender balance can be addressed through looking at these various layers of involvement in the WTO dispute settlement system. This section looks at each of these and highlights the role of WTO Members and the WTO Secretariat in enhancing gender diversity in the WTO dispute settlement.

1) Women in WTO Member Delegations

There is little empirical evidence of the number of women active in the delegations of WTO Members, including as counsel and advocates in WTO dispute settlement. Debra Steger, the first women Director in the WTO Secretariat, has described the paucity of women negotiators during the Uruguay Round, with a few notable exceptions.[12] The dispute settlement negotiations were unique among negotiating groups in that a number of female negotiators played leading roles.[13] In general, however, the presence of women among WTO Member delegations was lacking in the first decades of the WTO, a situation which largely continues. This is exemplified by the number of delegates attending MC10 in Nairobi in 2015, 28.6 percent of whom were women.[14] Of the 168 heads of delegation participating in MC10, twenty-four (14.3 percent) were women. Statistics for attendance at MC11, MC12, and MC13 are not publicly available. However, of the 127 WTO Members that made statements at MC13 in 2022, twenty-seven (21.3 percent) were made by women heads of delegation.[15] It is estimated that a quarter of the Ambassadors to the WTO are women.[16] This shows that although there has been an increase in women leaders of trade delegations, the percentage of women in power is still relatively low.

This is in turn manifested in the positions held by women in senior positions in the Membership of the WTO. Of the General Council and the fourteen bodies that report to it, four (28.6 percent) were led by women in 2025.[17] Seven women serve as Chairpersons of bodies established under the Trade Negotiations Committee, the Council for Trade in Goods, the Council for Trade in Services, and of Committees of Plurilateral Agreements.[18] These

---

12   Debra Steger, "Gender Equality in the WTO: The Need for Women Leaders" (2018), online: cigionline.org [perma.cc/M5G7-4XR9].

13   *Ibid.* Two women were lead negotiators in the dispute settlement negotiations (American and Canadian) and several female negotiators from developed and developing countries.

14   WTO, *Women and the WTO: Gender Statistics (1995-2016)* at 21, online (pdf): wto.org [perma.cc/X5NQ-N4AJ] [WTO, *Women and the WTO*].

15   WTO, "13th WTO Ministerial Conferences: Statements by Members and Observers" (last visited 26 March 2025), online: wto.org [perma.cc/77YD-UWRM].

16   Mia Mikic, "Advances in Feminizing the WTO" in Bahri, López, & Remy, above note 8 at 62.

17   See WTO, "Current WTO Chairpersons" (2025), online: wto.org [perma.cc/35V9-NF5B] for Chairpersons of the General Council and reporting bodies.

18   *Ibid.*

figures seem to parallel past appointments to these bodies.[19] There have been five women Chairs of the Dispute Settlement Body (DSB) in its almost thirty year existence: Ms. Amina Chawahir Mohamed of Kenya (2004), Ms. Elin Østebø Johansen of Norway (2011), Ms. Sunanta Kangvalkulkij of Thailand (2018), Dr. Athaliah Lesiba Molokomme of Botswana (2022), and Ms. Clare Kelly of New Zealand (2025).[20] The position of Chair of the DSB is particularly important because the Chair of the DSB usually "graduates" to the position of Chair of the General Council.[21]

The appointment of three women to Chair of the DSB since 2018 may be indicative of the increased attention to gender issues since the Buenos Aires Ministerial in 2017. In April 2024 Ambassador Ursha Dwarka-Canabady of Mauritius (who has herself been a panelist resolving WTO disputes) was appointed to facilitate the negotiations for dispute settlement reform.[22] Work will continue to progress the negotiations among WTO Members on the basis of the latest draft text issued by the Chair of the Dispute Settlement Body on 16 February 2024.[23] The draft text is well advanced and negotiations are expected to concentrate on appeal and/or review, accessibility, and the technical work of drafting texts.[24]

While there is some available information on the number of women in leadership roles among WTO Members, there is a paucity of information on the number of women who appear as counsel and advocates before dispute settlement panels and the Appellate Body. Nevertheless, it is illustrative to consider the Indicative List of Governmental and Non-Governmental Panellists, which is maintained by the Secretariat in accordance with Article 8.4

---

19 WTO, *Women and the WTO*, above note 14 at 26–45.

20 *Ibid* at 24; WTO, *2018 Dispute Settlement Body Annual Report*, WTO Doc WT/DSB/76 (2018), online (pdf): docs.wto.org [perma.cc/6S3Q-3EPM]; WTO, *2022 Dispute Settlement Body Annual Report*, WTO Doc WT/DSB/84 (2022), online (pdf): docs.wto.org [perma.cc/NGY7-TAEU].

21 See WTO "Former Chairpersons of the General Council" (2025), online: wto.org [perma.cc/CR7F-NZ64].

22 WTO, "New Facilitator Details Next Steps for Dispute Settlement Reform Talks After Consultations" (14 May 2024), online: wto.org [perma.cc/X4VJ-5Z7A].

23 WTO, *Special Meeting of the General Council Report*, WTO Doc JOB/GC/385 (2024), online (pdf): docs.wto.org [perma.cc/BA86-UPQG] [WTO, *GC Special Meeting Report*] .

24 WTO, "General Council Chair Welcomes 'Significant Progress' in Dispute Settlement Reform Talks" (17 December 2024), online: wto.org [perma.cc/D8UL-3CZD]. Further discussion of the draft text, including its references to gender balance, is set out in Section D, below in this chapter.

of the DSU.[25] The Indicative List contains nominations from Members of persons who may be selected to be panelists for WTO disputes and includes persons who have been active in the WTO system and are knowledgeable of WTO rules. The January 2025 list comprises 77.6 percent men and 22.4 percent women. Of the seventy-five WTO Members which have nominated persons to the Indicative List, five Members have only women on their lists,[26] nine Members have achieved gender parity,[27] and four have a reasonable gender balance.[28] That leaves 76 percent of Members who have yet to achieve gender balance in their nominations to the Indicative List. This is likely to be reflective of the preponderance of men in WTO Member delegations, as trade policy officials and as counsel and advocates in dispute settlement proceedings.

The lack of women in WTO Member delegations and as counsel and advocates has downstream effects. Because women are less likely to be included on the Indicative Lists of WTO Members and are less known to those engaged in the selection of panelists, they are less likely to be selected as a panelist to hear WTO disputes. This raises the role of the WTO Secretariat in contributing to bringing about change, particularly with regard to the composition of WTO panels.

2) The WTO Secretariat

The WTO Secretariat is a relatively flat organization comprising a senior management of the Director-General and four Deputy Director-Generals, eighteen Directors and 639 staff of Grades 0 to 10.[29] At present, there is gender parity in the senior management team of the Director-General and four Deputy Director-Generals, although this was not the case prior to the appointment of the current Director-General. At the Divisional Director

---

25 For the latest list, see WTO, *Indicative List of Governmental and Non-Governmental Panelists*, WTO Doc WT/DSB/44/Rev.64 (2025), online (pdf): docs.wto.org [perma.cc/ K2DS-BVCD].

26 Cote d'Ivoire, Cuba, Dominican Republic, Kazakhstan, and Moldova.

27 Denmark, Hungary, Romania, Sweden, Ghana, Indonesia, Montenegro, the Separate Customs Territory of Taiwan, Penghu, Kinmen and Matsu, and Türkiye.

28 Australia, Brazil, Colombia, and Norway.

29 WTO, "Allocation of Staff by Division, as of 31 December 2022" (archived 24 August 2024), online: wto.org [perma.cc/42JW-F2YL].

level, 41.1 percent of the positions are held by women.[30] The proportion of women in professional positions has increased markedly since the WTO was first established. At the beginning of 1995, 12.7 percent of staff were professional women, compared to 28.4 percent professional men. By the end of 2022 the proportion of staff who were professional women had increased to 30 percent, while the proportion of staff who were professional men was 33.1 percent.[31] The commitment of the previous and current Director-Generals to gender parity appears to have had an impact on the organization. Before examining this with respect to WTO dispute settlement, it is useful to examine the context in which the Secretariat operates.

3) The Role of the Secretariat

The Secretariat within any intergovernmental organization is responsible for the administrative and executive support to the Members.[32] As international civil servants Secretariat staff must discharge their duties with the interests of the organization in mind and with integrity, impartiality, and independence. The WTO styles itself as a "member-driven organization." However, in the area of WTO dispute settlement, the role of the Secretariat in WTO dispute settlement is powerful, largely due to the legal and other support the Secretariat provides to panels which hear individual disputes and the legal support it used to provide to the Appellate Body when it existed.[33]

Panels are composed of three persons who are selected to serve in their individual capacities and not as governmental representatives or representatives of any organization.[34] Panel members must be well-qualified governmental or nongovernmental individuals, and may include those who have served on a panel, argued before a panel, represented a WTO Member, served as a senior trade policy official, or taught or published on international trade

---

30 WTO, "Annual Report 2023" (2023) at 191, online (pdf): wto.org [perma.cc/RJ47-DBVH]. The author calculates that six of the seventeen Divisional Director positions are held by women.

31 Ibid at 189.

32 For a description of the role of the Secretariat in the WTO in comparison with its sister organizations: the World Bank, the International Monetary Fund, and the OECD, see Alan W Wolff, "Constructing an Executive Branch" (2022) Peterson Institute for International Economics, Working Paper No 22-8.

33 Ibid at 11.

34 DSU, above note 6, art 8.9.

law.[35] The composition of panels seeks to ensure the independence of members and their diversity of background and experience.[36]

The Secretariat plays a crucial administrative role in the selection of panelists, which has been described elsewhere.[37] In brief, the parties to a dispute may agree between themselves on panel members, but almost invariably this process involves the WTO Secretariat.[38] The parties each convey to the Secretariat the background and experience they would prefer in panelists. The Secretariat usually has regard to the WTO Indicative List of Panellists and responds with a list of names of two potential chairs and four potential panelists, which are then considered by the parties. The potential candidates may be rejected or placed on a "possible" list. The process continues for some weeks as the parties seek to narrow their differences and agree on one or more panelists. Where the parties cannot agree, the Director-General of the WTO may be requested by either party to compose the panel.[39] After consulting with the parties on the selection criteria, and the Chair of the Dispute Settlement Body and the relevant Chair of the relevant Council or Committee, the parties are informed of the panel selection.

The role of the Director-General, with assistance from the relevant Secretariat staff from the Legal Affairs Division or the Rules Division, is

---

35   *DSU*, above note 6, art 8.1.

36   *DSU*, above note 6, art 8.2. Art 8.9 also provides that Members shall "not give them instructions nor seek to influence them as individuals with regard to matters before a panel."

37   See Reto Malacrida, "WTO Panel Composition: Searching Far and Wide for Administrators of World Trade Justice" in Gabrielle Marceau, ed, *A History of Law and Lawyers in the GATT/WTO: The Development of the Rule of Law in the Multilateral Trading System* (Cambridge: Cambridge University Press, 2015) 311; Valerie Hughes, "Adjudicating International Trade Cases in the World Trade Organization: Does Gender Make a Difference?" in Freya Baetens, ed, *Identity and Diversity on the International Bench: Who is the Judge?* (Oxford: Oxford University Press, 2020) 330 at 338 [Hughes, "Adjudicating International Trade Cases"]; Tania Parcero Herrera & María J Pereyra, "The Role and Assistance of the WTO Secretariat in WTO Dispute Settlement Proceedings" in Marco Tulio Molina Tejeda, ed, *Practical Aspects of WTO Litigation* (Alphen aan den Rijn: Wolters Kluwer, 2020) 63.

38   The Secretariat support that is provided for dispute settlement cases, including for the composition of panels, depends on the subject matter of the case, with the Rules Division providing support for trade remedy cases and the Legal Affairs Division provides support for any other WTO matter.

39   *DSU*, above note 6, art 8.7. The Director-General selects the panelists in consultation with the Chairperson of the Dispute Settlement Body and the Chairperson of one of the relevant WTO Councils or Committees.

important because approximately 70 percent of panels are composed by the Director-General. However, this bare statistic does not reveal the full story. It obscures the potential for the parties to agree on one or more panel members, which limits the role of the Director-General to the selection of the remaining panelist(s). It is noteworthy that the last few years has seen a reversal of the trend towards appointments by the Director-General. Of the six panels composed in 2022, half were composed with the agreement of the parties.[40] In 2023/2024, four of the five panels were selected by the parties.[41] This may suggest that in the absence of a functioning Appellate Body, parties are seeking to take greater control over the panel selection process.

The WTO Secretariat has been perceived as "unseen actors" in a system created by WTO Members in order to avoid the excesses of rogue adjudicators through reliance on *ad hoc* panelists drawn from the ranks of trade diplomats and assumed, therefore, to be more attune to the political interests of Members.[42] Joost Pauwelyn and Krzysztof Pelc have criticized the opaque role played by WTO staff in WTO panel and Appellate Body proceedings,

---

40 *China—Anti-Dumping and Countervailing Duty Measures on Wine from Australia (Complaint by Australia)* (2022), WTO Doc WT/DS602/4, online (pdf): docs.wto.org [perma.cc/8XGU-WYKH] [*China—AD/CVD on Wine*]; *Australia—Anti-Dumping and Countervailing Duty Measures on Certain Products from China (Complaint by China)* (2022), WTO Doc WT/DS603/3, online (pdf): docs.wto.org [perma.cc/H3DC-ACDS] [*Australia—AD/CVD on Certain products*]; *Russian Federation—Certain Measures Concerning Domestic and Foreign Products and Services (Complaint by the European Union)* (2022), WTO Doc WT/DS604/3, online (pdf): docs.wto.org [perma.cc/AYZ4-A97P]. This is in addition to the three arbitrations under Article 25.

41 *China—Enforcement of Intellectual Property Rights (Complaint by the European Union)* (2023), WTO Doc WT/DS611/6, online (pdf): docs.wto.org [perma.cc/PU2Y-WR6U] [*China—IPRs Enforcement*]; *European Union—Countervailing and Anti-Dumping Duties on Stainless Steel Cold-Rolled Flat Products from Indonesia (Complaint by Indonesia)* (2023), WTO Doc WT/DS616/3, online (pdf): docs.wto.org [perma.cc/XT6K-2ZXB]; *United States—Anti-Dumping Measure on Oil Country Tubular Goods from* Argentina *(Complaint by Argentina)* (2024), WTO Doc WT/DS617/4, online (pdf): docs.wto.org [perma.cc/7JDJ-XPYE]; *European Union—Countervailing Duties on Imports of Biodiesel from Indonesia (Complaint by Indonesia)* (2024), WTO Doc WT/DS618/3/Rev.1, online (pdf): docs.wto.org [perma.cc/A8RV-T3Z3].

42 Joost Pauwelyn & Krzysztof Pelc, "Who Guards the 'Guardians of the System'?: The Role of the Secretariat in WTO Dispute Settlement" (2022) 116:3 *American Journal of International Law* 534 [Pauwelyn & Pelc, "Who Guards the 'Guardians of the System'?"]; Joost Pauwelyn & Krzysztof Pelc, "WTO Rulings and the Veil of Anonymity" (2022) 33:2 *European Journal of International Law* 527; Jasper Wauters, "The Role of the WTO Secretariat in WTO Disputes – Silent Witness or Ghost Expert?" (2021) 12:3 *Global Policy* 83.

including the extent of staff influence over panel appointments.[43] There has been a robust defence of the Secretariat involvement which emphasized the role of the parties in setting the criteria for panel selection.[44] Nevertheless, in practice the Director-General has discretion as to the composition of the panel.[45]

In describing the process of panel composition, Reto Malacrida highlights the tendency for parties to be comfortable with a panel that includes a current or former government official, to require at least one panel member with previous panel experience, and to "customize" the composition of a panel with appropriate sectoral experience. He considers that this, combined with natural turnover and efforts by Directors-General to enlarge the pool of experienced panelists and Members supplying them, has resulted in a large and diverse body of panelists and ensures that panels remain in touch with the legitimate needs and concerns of WTO Members.[46] This, he argues, is "an emphatically democratic system" based on the diversity of backgrounds, specializations and experiences of the individuals selected.[47] It remains to be seen whether the panel system is "democratic" in terms of its gender diversity.

4) WTO Panels

The 2020 WTO Dispute Settlement Dataset compiled by the WTO Case Law Project provides a dataset of 306 individual panelists appointed between 1995 and 2020.[48] Disaggregating the dataset by gender shows that fifty-six individual women were panelists over the period, comprising 18.3 percent of the total. Some women have been appointed multiple times. For example, Claudia Orozco of Colombia has been appointed to sixteen panels, including three times as chair of the panel, and Enie Neri de Ross of Venezuela has been appointed to fourteen panels, twice as chair. However, the number of men who have been appointed to multiple panels is greater, to the extent that eleven men have been selected to serve on panels more than ten times.

43 Pauwelyn & Pelc, "Who Guards the 'Guardians of the System'?" above note 42.

44 Gabrielle Marceau & Akshaya Venkataraman, "Unmasking the Phantom of the Opera: Is there a Hidden Secretariat in the WTO Dispute Settlement System?" (2022) 116 *American Journal of International Law* 395 at 396.

45 Hughes, "Adjudicating International Trade Cases," above note 37 at 339.

46 Reto Malacrida, above note 37 at 311–33.

47 *Ibid.*

48 European University Institute, "Global Governance Program: WTO Dispute Settlement and Case Law Project" (2025), online: eui.eu [perma.cc/9L5M-F9AS].

The preference for appointing men to panels carries through in the analysis of the composition of individual panels. Until December 2024 there had been no all-female panels, while the majority of panels comprise only men.[49] The Director-General has composed panels of three women on one occasion, two women and one man on sixteen occasions, and ten times since 2017.[50] In comparison parties have agreed to a panel composition with two women only

---

49 WTO, *Women and the WTO*, above note 14 at 15.

50 *Turkey—Measures Concerning Electric Vehicles and Other Types of Vehicles from China (Complaint by China)* (2025), WTO Doc WT/DS629/3, online (pdf): docs.wto. org [perma.cc/TG87-Y4XH; *China—Measures Concerning Trade in Goods (Complaint by the European Union)* (2023), WTO Doc WT/DS610/9, online (pdf): docs.wto. org [perma.cc/N8A9-JKMR] [*China—Goods*]; *Panama—Measures Concerning the Importation of Certain Products from Costa Rica (Complaint by Costa Rica)* (2022), WTO Doc WT/DS599/5, online (pdf): docs.wto.org [perma.cc/6QX4-SSFN]; *China— Anti-Dumping and Countervailing Duty Measures on Barley from Australia (Complaint by Australia)* (2021), WTO Doc WT/DS598/6, online (pdf): docs.wto.org [perma. cc/969S-3V4T] [*China—AD/CVD on Barley*]; *Indonesia—Measures Relating to Raw Materials (Complaint by the European Union)* (2021), WTO Doc WT/DS592/4, online (pdf): docs.wto.org [perma.cc/9BAU-FQS4]; *Turkey—Certain Measures Concerning the Production, Importation and Marketing of Pharmaceutical Products (Complaint by the European Union)* (2020), WTO Doc WT/DS583/4, online (pdf): docs.wto.org [perma.cc/6CAY-CLBK] [*Turkey—Pharmaceutical Products (EU)*]; *Saudi Arabia— Measures Concerning the Protection of Intellectual Property Rights (Complaint by Qatar)* (2020), WTO Doc WT/DS567/4, online (pdf): docs.wto.org [perma.cc/A3KD-XE3W]; *United States—Countervailing Measures on Softwood Lumber from Canada (Complaint by Canada)* (2018), WTO Doc WT/DS553/3, online (pdf): docs.wto.org [perma.cc/D9FK-ZJEK]; *India—Certain Measures on Imports of Iron and Steel Products (Complaint by Japan)* (2017), WTO Doc WT/DS518/6, online (pdf): docs. wto.org [perma.cc/3GUK-VLPC]; *Ukraine—Anti-Dumping Measures on Ammonium Nitrate (Complaint by Russia)* (2017), WTO Doc WT/DS493/3, online (pdf): docs.wto. org [perma.cc/Y8JT-NYB5]. The single instance in which the Director-General has composed a panel of all women occurred in December 2024: *United States—Certain Tax Credits Under the Inflation Reduction Act (Complaint by China)* (2024), WTO Doc WT/DS623/4, online (pdf): docs.wto.org [perma.cc/P5JS-AYMU], which included Ms Athaliah Lesiba Molokomme, Ms Elaine Feldman and Ms Amina Mohamed.

three times: once in 2018,[51] once in 2020,[52] and once in 2022.[53] The enduring gender imbalance is striking in light of both Goal 5 of the Sustainable Development Goals and the 2017 Buenos Aires Joint Declaration on Trade and Women's Economic Empowerment. Where the objective is to maintain the diplomatic character of panels,[54] it is apparent that the male domination of WTO delegations has knock-on effects in the establishment of dispute settlement panels.

5) The Appellate Body

Article 17.3 of the DSU sets out the criteria for election to the Appellate Body which is to include persons who are "broadly representative of Membership in the WTO."[55] Selection of Members of the Appellate Body has been in the hands of WTO Members, who have expended considerable energy seeking information on the background to the applicants, including how they might rule in potential cases.[56] However, it appears that little thought was given to the need for "representativeness" to cover not only geographical representativeness but also representativeness from a gender perspective. Indeed, between 1995 and 2019 there were nine nominations of women out of over seventy nominees (three from the United States, two from China, and one each from Australia, Brazil, the Philippines, and Zimbabwe).[57] This comprises 13 percent of nominations. The total number of female Appellate Body

---

51 *United Arab Emirates—Measures Relating to Trade in Goods and Services, and Trade-Related Aspects of Intellectual Property Rights (Complaint by Qatar)* (2018), WTO Doc WT/DS526/3, online (pdf): docs.wto.org [perma.cc/YKH8-BG8C], which included Ms. Dell Higgie and Ms. Valerie Hughes.

52 *Colombia—Anti-Dumping Duties on Frozen Fries from Belgium, Germany and the Netherlands (Complaint by the European Union)* (2020), WTO Doc WT/DS591/4, online (pdf): docs.wto.org [perma.cc/3TVQ-NNQD] [*Colombia—Frozen Fries*], which included Ms. Leane Cornet Naidin and Ms. Margarita Trillo-Ramos.

53 *Australia—AD/CVD on Certain Products*, above note 40, which included Ms. Elaine Feldman (as Chair) and Ms. Silvia Lorena Hooker Ortega.

54 Pauwelyn & Pelc, "WTO Rulings and the Veil of Anonymity," above note 42 at 540.

55 For a description of the selection process for the Appellate Body see Hughes, "Adjudicating International Trade Cases," above note 37 at 343–45.

56 Manfred Elsig & Mark A Pollack, "Agents, Trustees, and International Courts: The Politics of Judicial Appointment at the World Trade Organization" (2014) 20:2 *European Journal of International Relations* 391.

57 Hughes, "Adjudicating International Trade Cases," above note 37 at fn 83.

Members has comprised five (18.5 percent) of the twenty-seven Appellate Body Members.[58]

Under the DSU, Appellate Body Members are to be appointed for a four-year term, which may be extended. There were no women Members of the Appellate Body from 1995 until 2003, when Merit Janow (United States) was appointed. She was replaced in 2007 by Jennifer Hillman (United States). For the period 2008 to 2011, there were three women on the Appellate Body, effectively ensuring a gender balance on the institution. However, Jennifer Hillman was not re-appointed, essentially due to the dissatisfaction on the part of the United States with the Appellate Body's rulings on trade remedy issues.[59] It has been suggested that both Janow and Hillman were not put forward for a second term because they were not considered sufficiently aggressive in defending the position of the United States.[60] An unfortunate consequence was that the Appellate Body lost any degree of gender balance.

6) The Multi-Party Interim Appeal Arbitration Arrangement (MPIA)

Due to the impasse over appointments to the Appellate Body, in April 2020 a group of WTO Members established the Multi-Party Interim Appeal Arbitration Arrangement (MPIA).[61] The participants in the MPIA now number twenty-nine, with the EU and its twenty-seven Member states counting as

---

58   The first women Appellate Body Member was Merit Janow (United States) who served from 2003 to 2007. Two women—Jennifer Hillman (United States) and Lilia Bautista (Philippines)—served from 2007 and were joined in 2008 by Yeujiao Zhang (China) until 2011. Zhang was reappointed from 2012 to 2016, when she was replaced by Hong Zhao (China), whose term expired on 30 November 2020. See WTO, "Appellate Body Members" (last visited 25 March 2025), online: wto.org [perma.cc/2YP7-7M4E].

59   For an account of this based on interviews with key players, see Paul Blustein, "China Inc. in the WTO Dock: Tales from a System under Fire" (2017) CIGI Papers, Working Paper No 158 at 11.

60   Pieter Jan Kuijper, "From the Board: The US Attack on the WTO Appellate Body" (2018) 45:1 Legal Issues of Economic Integration 1; Jeffrey L Dunoff & Mark A Pollack, "The Judicial Trilemma" (2017) 111:2 American Journal of International Law 225.

61   WTO, Multi-Party Interim Appeal Arbitration Arrangement Pursuant to Article 25 of the DSU, WTO Doc JOB/DSB/1/Add.12 (2020), online (pdf): docs.wto.org [perma.cc/D74Z-L9UJ] [MPIA]. See also Geneva Trade Platform, "Multi-Party Interim Appeal Arbitration Arrangement (MPIA)" (last visited 22 June 2025), online: wtoplurilaterals.info [perma.cc/JV8Q-HULE].

one.[62] The MPIA participants propose not to pursue appeals under Articles 16.4 and 17 of the DSU of panel reports in disputes among them and may instead resort to arbitration under Article 25 of the DSU as an interim appeal arbitration procedure as long as the Appellate Body is not able to hear appeals due to an insufficient number of Appellate Body Members.[63] The parties to eleven disputes have formally indicated that they will resolve any appeals through the MPIA.[64] Recourse to the MPIA has been used to resolve the (author's comment: there have now been two MPIA cases: the last one just this week. Rather than adding a lot of substance, we can the cut off date for the article as June 2025) dispute between the European Union and Colombia.[65] In another dispute between the European Union and Türkiye, the parties agreed to enter into an Article 25 appeal arbitration using some of the

---

62   The current participants are: Australia; Benin; Brazil; Canada; Chile; China; Colombia; Costa Rica; Ecuador; the European Union; Guatemala; Hong Kong, China; Iceland; Japan; Macao, China; Malaysia; New Zealand; Nicaragua; Norway; Macao, China; Mexico; Montenegro; Pakistan; Peru; the Philippines; Singapore; Switzerland; Ukraine; and Uruguay.

63   *MPIA*, above note 61 at paras 1–2.

64   Finalized MPIA Dispute: *Colombia—Frozen Fries*, above note 51. Ongoing Disputes: *China—Goods*, above note 50; *China—IPRs Enforcement (EU)*, above note 41. Finalized without MPIA Appeal, Withdrawn or Settled Disputes: *Canada—Measures Concerning Trade in Commercial Aircraft (Complaint by Brazil)* (2018), WTO Doc WT/DS522/10, online (pdf): docs.wto.org [perma.cc/59TS-6972]; *Costa Rica—Measures Concerning the Importation of Fresh Avocados from Mexico (Complaint by Mexico)* (2019), WTO Doc WT/DS524/3, online (pdf): docs.wto.org [perma.cc/9YMH-X75A]; *Canada—Measures Governing the Sale of Wine (Complaint by Australia)* (2019), WTO Doc WT/DS537/9, online (pdf): docs.wto.org [perma.cc/UUS6-SFLG]; *China—Measures Concerning the Importation of Canola Seed from Canada (Complaint by Canada)* (2021), WTO Doc WT/DS589/6, online (pdf): docs.wto.org [perma.cc/H4MB-U8AD]; *China—AD/CVD on Barley*, above note 50; *China—Anti-Dumping Measures on Stainless Steel Products from Japan (Complaint by Japan)* (2022), WTO Doc WT/DS601/3, online (pdf): docs.wto.org [perma.cc/J9VJ-JUV3]; *China—AD/CVD on Wine*, above note 40; *Australia—AD/CVD on Certain Products*, above note 40.

65   *Colombia—Frozen Fries*, above note 52. The European Union has requested WTO consultations with Colombia to address measures taken by Colombia to comply with an earlier WTO panel ruling and arbitration award regarding Colombia's anti-dumping duties on imports of frozen fries originating in Belgium, the Netherlands and Germany: see WTO, "European Union Initiates Compliance Proceedings Over Colombian Duties on Frozen Fries" (4 June 2024), online: wto.org [perma.cc/5A46-H9XE]. For a description of how the MPIA works authored by one of the arbitrators in this dispute, see Joost Pauwelyn, "The WTO's Multi-Party Interim Appeal Arbitration Arrangement (MPIA): What's New?" (2023) 22:5 *World Trade Review* 693.

MPIA rules.[66] Almost all of the remaining cases have been resolved through mutually acceptable solutions or decisions not to seek recourse to arbitration.

The MPIA provides for the selection of a pool of arbitrators to hear appeal arbitrations. The pool is to comprise persons who are unaffiliated with any government and are of recognized authority, with expertise in law, international trade, and the subject matter of the covered agreements. The composition of the pool of arbitrators "will ensure an appropriate overall balance."[67] It is unclear what is meant by "an appropriate overall balance." Followed a selection process that took place in July 2020, four (40 percent) out of the ten MPIA arbitrators appointed by the participants were women, including Valerie Hughes.[68] In June 2025 the MPIA pool of arbitrators was partially recomposed and as a result there are now two (20 percent) women members of the pool.[69]

The selection of arbitrators from the pool to head individual arbitrations follows the same principles and methods that apply to form a division of the Appellate Body.[70] In the first case under the MPIA, the three arbitrators randomly selected were men and in the second case, two women were randomly selected.[71]

C. WTO Dispute Settlement Compared

THE PREVIOUS SECTION HAS SHOWN that the proportion of women engaged in adjudicating WTO disputes hovers around 20 percent. The proportion is increasing, but gender balance is absent. This section briefly compares gender diversity in WTO dispute settlement with that of other judicial bodies. It then asks the question: why does the lack of gender diversity matter?

---

66 *Turkey—Pharmaceutical Products (EU)*, above note 50.

67 *MPIA*, above note 61 at para 4.

68 See the list of the initial composition of MPIA arbitrators contained in WTO, *Statement on a Mechanism for Developing, Documenting and Sharing Practices and Procedures in the Conduct of WTO Disputes*, WTO Doc JOB/DSB/1/Add.12/Suppl.5 (2020), online: docs.wto.org [perma.cc/HX4M-X2MT].

69 WTO, *Statement on a Mechanism for Developing, Documenting and Sharing Practices and Procedures in the Conduct of WTO Disputes*, WTO Doc JOB/DSB/1/Add.12/ Suppl.14 (2025), online: docs.wto.org [perma.cc/5FMT-BZNG].

70 *MPIA*, above note 6 at para 6.

71 A similar random selection was undertaken in *Turkey—Pharmaceutical Products (EU)*, above note 50 and produced three male arbitrators.

1) A Comparison with Other Judicial Institutions

Previous studies have shown the WTO in a slightly better light than some other dispute settlement mechanisms, notably the International Court of Justice (ICJ), the International Tribunal for the Law of the Sea (ITLOS) and *ad hoc* arbitration panels International Centre for Settlement of Investment Disputes (ICSID).[72] However, more recent statistics show that these other bodies have improved their gender diversity, whereas the WTO has remained static.

In 2024 there were four women judges on the fifteen-member bench of the ICJ comprising 26.6 percent, up from two (13.3 percent) in 2010.[73] In 2010 there were no women tribunal members on ITLOS, whereas currently there are six women (28.6 percent).[74] In 2009, only 9 percent of arbitrators in ICSID arbitrations were women.[75] By 2015, the number of women engaged as international arbitrators had increased to 17.6 percent.[76] More recently the proportion of female arbitrators has increased. Of the twenty most recently concluded cases under ICSID Rules where arbitrators were selected, there were sixteen women arbitrators (26.6 percent).[77] Of note was that four of these women were appointed by the Chair of the Administrative Council or the ICSID Secretary-General.[78]

72　See Nienke Grossman, "Shattering the Glass Ceiling in International Adjudication" (2016) 56:2 *Virginia Journal of International Law* 339; Nienke Grossman, "Achieving Sex-Representative International Court Benches" (2016) 110:1 *American Journal of International Law* 82; Susan D Franck et al, "The Diversity Challenge: Exploring the Invisible College of International Arbitration" (2015) 53 *Columbia Journal of Transnational Law* 429; Ruth Mackenzie et al, *Selecting International Judges: Principle, Process, and Politics* (Oxford: Oxford University Press, 2010).

73　See Nienke Grossman, "Sex on the Bench: Do Women Judges Matter to the Legitimacy of International Courts?" (2012) 12:2 *Chicago Journal of International Law* 647 at 648 [Grossman, "Sex on the Bench"]; ICJ, "Members of the Court" (last visited 6 June 2025), online: icj-cij.org [perma.cc/2XG2-T9MS].

74　ITLOS, "Members" (last visited 24 February 2025), online: itlos.org [perma.cc/N5P9-8R7B].

75　Grossman, "Sex on the Bench," above note 72 at 649.

76　Franck et al, above note 71 at 453.

77　ICSID, "Concluded Cases" (last visited 24 February 2025), online: icsid.worldbank.org [perma.cc/M82G-L82B].

78　*Buse v Panama* (2017) ICSID Case No ARB/17/12; *Enerflex US Holdings Inc and Exterran Energy Solutions, LP v United Mexican States* (2023) ICSID Case No ARB/23/22; *Freeport-McMoRan Inc v Republic of Peru* (2023) ICSID Case No ARB/20/8; *Gabriel Resources Ltd and Gabriel Resources (Jersey) v Romania* (2020) ICSID Case No

Over time the percentage of women in other judicial bodies has fluctuated, notably in the area of international criminal law and human rights. In 2010, for example, 58 percent of judges on the International Criminal Court (ICC) were women.[79] This fell to 39 percent in mid-2015.[80] However, currently there are eleven female judges on the ICC, comprising 61 percent of the Court.[81] Furthermore, the President of the Court is a women and the Presidency of the Court has a majority of women.[82] A similar fluctuation is found in other courts and tribunals.[83] These fluctuations have implications which will be addressed in the following Section.

In any study of gender diversity in judicial and other institutions, there is a danger that the analysis is reduced to "counting the women," rather than propelling change.[84] Transformational change requires looking behind the data at the possible explanations for the absence of women from WTO dispute settlement. The various reasons that have been articulated include the dominance of men in international trade circles and the proclivity for men to be familiar with and therefore to choose other men for positions.[85] The WTO is a Member-centric structure where men still dominate the delegations of WTO Members. Often to be appointed a panelist the person needs to be seen and to be known, for example as a Member of a WTO delegation or a counsel in a WTO dispute. Where delegations are led by men, there may be fewer opportunities for women to progress in dispute settlement.

WTO dispute settlement system also has certain characteristics that are a hangover from the diplomatic resolution of trade disputes under the

---

ARB/15/31, where the original female Chair appointed by the ICSID Secretary-General was replaced by a man.

79 Grossman, "Sex on the Bench," above note 72 at 654.

80 Grossman, "Shattering the Glass Ceiling" above note 71 at 15.

81 ICC, "Current Judges" (last visited 24 February 2025), online: icc-cpi.int [perma.cc/25BD-BQQX].

82 The Presidency consists of the President and the two Vice-Presidents. See ICC, "The Presidency" (last visited 24 February 2025), online: icj-cij.org [perma.cc/FYV8-FWTG].

83 Grossman, "Shattering the Glass Ceiling" above note 71.

84 Gina Heathcote & Paola Zichi, "Feminist methodologies" in Rossana Deplano & Nicholas Tsagourias, ed, *Research Methods in International Law* (Elgar Online, 2021) 458 at 463.

85 Hughes, "Adjudicating International Trade Cases," above note 37 at 342; Joost Pauwelyn, "The Rule of Law without the Rule of Lawyers? Why Investment Arbitrators are from Mars, Trade Panelists are from Venus" (2015) Graduate Institute of International and Development Studies, Working Paper at 26.

pre-WTO *General Agreement on Tariffs and Trade* (GATT). In the composition of WTO panels, WTO Members often prefer to select trade policy experts or specialists in particular areas covered by the WTO Agreements, rather than international trade lawyers or international lawyers in general. This too is reminiscent of the "diplomatic" approach to resolving trade disputes of the GATT era.

2) Why Does the Absence of Women Matter?

It is frequently suggested that the absence of women adjudicators affects the legitimacy of the institution and its decisions. Legitimacy can be assessed from a normative perspective, which asks whether the decisions are "justified" to the extent they are accepted, or from a social perspective, which considers the perception of those accepting the authority of the judicial body.[86] Legitimacy also has an internal dimension, which focuses on the organization itself and those Members and individuals active within it, and an external dimension which considers the perspective of those outside the organization, including the governments, parliaments, organizations, and people of the members of the organization.[87]

Legitimacy of an international organization matters. From an internal perspective, legitimacy influences the extent to which Members are prepared to put their energy towards ensuring that the organization remains a viable policy coordination mechanism and a mechanism for the development of new rules and norms, and it influences whether the organization can facilitate compliance with international rules.[88] The current impasse over the Appellate Body is indicative of a perceived lack of legitimacy of the WTO dispute settlement system on the part of the United States. From an external perspective, diversity ensures that the institution is more representative of

---

86 Daniel Bodansky, "The Legitimacy of International Governance: A Coming Challenge for International Environmental Law?" (1999) 93:3 *American Journal of International Law* 601.

87 Joseph H H Weiler, "The Rule of Lawyers and the Ethos of Diplomats Reflections on the Internal and External Legitimacy of WTO Dispute Settlement" (2001) 35:2 *Journal of World Trade* 191.

88 Jonas Tallberg & Michael Zürn, "The Legitimacy and Legitimation of International Organizations: Introduction and Framework" (2019) 14:4 *Review of International Organizations* 581 at 582.

multiple perspectives, represents different stakeholders, and is reflective of the constituencies which it serves.[89]

Joost Pauwelyn adopts a wider conception of legitimacy by looking not merely at the adjudicators themselves but more broadly from a systemic perspective at the institution as a whole. Although it is accepted that the decisions of an adjudicatory body will affect the legitimacy of the institution,[90] it is also the system as a whole, including the WTO Secretariat, and its representativeness and diversity, which serves to enhance the legitimacy of the institution.[91] This seems to be borne out a study by Cosette D Creamer and Zuzanna Godzimirska into representativeness in terms of gender, nationality, and legal tradition of WTO panelists and Appellate Body Members.[92] The study concluded that the identity of the adjudicators did not strongly matter in a meaningful way, and that a permanent institutional framework may be more important for legitimacy.[93] There may also be another reason for the unexpected results—the "hidden" hand of the WTO Secretariat in assisting panels and the Appellate Body.[94]

Valerie Hughes has asked the question "does gender make a difference" in the adjudication of international trade disputes.[95] In other words, do women bring a feminist perspective to trade adjudication in the sense that women adjudicators are more sensitive to the notion that trade policies have a differential effect on women and men? In some areas of international law, such as international criminal law, and international human rights law, female judges have contributed to the development of the law on gender-based crimes and played an instrumental role in ensuring there is sensitivity towards victims

---

89   Grossman, "Sex on the Bench," above note 72 at 670.

90   Cosette D Creamer & Zuzanna Godzimirska, "(De)Legitimation at the WTO Dispute Settlement Mechanism" (2016) 49:2 *Vanderbilt Journal of Transnational Law* 275.

91   Joost Pauwelyn, "Who Decides Matters: The Legitimacy Capital of WTO Adjudicators Versus ICSID Arbitrators" in Nienke Grossman et al, eds, *Legitimacy and International Courts* (Cambridge: Cambridge University Press, 2018) 224.

92   Cosette D Creamer & Zuzanna Godzimirska, "Diversity and Legitimacy of the World Trade Organization's Bench" in Freya Baetens, ed, *Identity and Diversity on the International Bench* (Oxford: Oxford University Press, 2020) 427. The study compared these characteristics with the degree of critical statements of the panel and Appellate Body reports between 1995 and 2016.

93   *Ibid* at 445.

94   See Pauwelyn & Pelc, "Who Guards the "Guardians of the System?" above note 42; Blustein, above note 59.

95   Hughes, "Adjudicating International Trade Cases," above note 37.

of sexual crimes.[96] In the sphere of international trade law, it appears that empirical evidence for a differential adjudicatory position is lacking.[97] However, irrespective of whether gender makes a difference to the outcome of a decision, the lack of legitimacy arises from a lack of representativeness. Conversely, gender representation strengthens legitimacy by reflecting the population subject to the authority.[98]

A final word needs to be said concerning the way in which gender diversity within the WTO dispute settlement sits uneasily with the work that is underway both internationally and within the organization itself on women's economic empowerment. In particular, the lack of gender representativeness implicates Article 8 of the 1979 Convention on the Elimination of Discrimination against Women (CEDAW) requiring States Parties to ensure that women, on equal terms as men, have the opportunity to participate in the work of international organizations.[99] To date little attention has been paid to this. However, the UN Committee on the Elimination of Discrimination against Women, one of the UN human rights treaty bodies, has prepared a draft of a future General Recommendation 40 on women's equal and inclusive participation in decision-making systems.[100] All organizations, including the WTO, should have regard to its recommendations. The Committee has stressed that "ensuring women's equal and inclusive representation requires dismantling the patriarchal structures at the root of women's exclusion from decision-making."[101]

---

96 Grossman, "Sex on the Bench," above note 72 at 658; Navi Pillay, "Foreword" in Freya Baetens, ed, *Identity and Diversity on the International Bench* (Oxford: Oxford University Press, 2020) vii.

97 Hughes, "Adjudicating International Trade Cases," above note 37 at 352.

98 Grossman, "Sex on the Bench," above 72 at 668.

99 *Convention on the Elimination of All Forms of Discrimination Against Women*, 18 December 1979, 1249 UNTS 13 (entered into force 3 September 1981).

100 GQUAL, "Expert Consultation: Perspectives on CEDAWs Future General Recommendation," (29 September 2023), online: gqualcampaign.org [perma.cc/BFY3-Z9ES]. See also Liesbeth Lijnzaad, "The *Smurfette* Principle: Reflections about Gender and the Nomination of Women to the International Bench" in Freya Baetens, ed, *Identity and Diversity on the International Bench* (Oxford: Oxford University Press, 2020) 29 at 38, who also suggests that a CEDAW General Recommendation on art 8 may contribute to enhanced gender balance on the international bench.

101 CEDAW Committee, "Draft General Recommendation 40: Equal and Inclusive Representation on Women in Decision-Making Systems" (2024), online (pdf): ohchr.org [perma.cc/X8ET-V49G].

D. The Path Forward

BOTH WTO MEMBERS AND THE Secretariat have a role to play in ensuring that the number of females and males involved in WTO dispute settlement are sufficient to enhance the legitimacy of the organization without compromising the quality of its outputs. When addressing a similar issue in other legal institutions, various options have been advocated to address gender diversity, ranging from the more ambitious establishment of quotas or thresholds,[102] to establishing general legal requirements,[103] and to making aspirational statements that encourage States to nominate and elect women Members.[104]

Similar practical proposals have been made to enhance gender representativeness in WTO dispute settlement. One such proposal is to amend Article 8.10 of the DSU to provide that a panel comprise at least one women panelist.[105] Other proposals are to require diversity in the selection of adjudicators[106] or to appoint more women panelists in WTO dispute settlement cases through appointments by the Director-General.[107]

There is recognition among WTO Members that these are sound objectives. The February 2024 draft text on reform of the WTO dispute settlement system includes a preambular paragraph which acknowledges "the importance of selecting highly qualified adjudicators while fostering diversity in the

---

102 As in the European Court of Human Rights, see *Guidelines of the Committee of Ministers on the Selection of Candidates for the Post of Judge at the European Court of Human Rights*, Resolution CM (2012) 40 final (29 March 2012). See also Stéphanie Hennette Vauchez, "More Women – But Which Women? The Rule and the Politics of Gender Balance at the European Court of Human Rights" (2015) 26:1 *European Journal of International Law* 195 at 200; Freya Baetens, ed, *Identity and Diversity on the International Bench* (Oxford: Oxford University Press, 2020) 14.

103 For example, in the selection of judges for the International Criminal Court, Art 8(a) of the Rome Statute provides: "The States Parties shall, in the selection of judges, take into account the need, within the membership of the Court, for: (i) The representation of the principal legal systems of the world; (ii) Equitable geographical representation; and (iii) A fair representation of female and male judges. In addition, at least one third of the Court's 18 judges are required to be from each sex."

104 Grossman, "Sex on the Bench," above note 72 at 84. By way of example, UN General Assembly Resolution 33/143 contributed to the improvement of both geographical and gender representation among the staff of the UN: *Personnel questions*, UNGA, 33rd Sess, UN Doc A/RES/33/143 (1978) GA Res 33/143.

105 Hughes, "Adjudicating International Trade Cases," above note 37 at 342.

106 Valerie Hughes, "Gender Chapters in Trade Agreements: Nice Rhetoric or Sound Policy?" (9 October 2019), online: cigionline.org [perma.cc/R472-7JQ8].

107 Steger, above note 12.

composition of panels, with a specific emphasis on achieving gender balance, geographical representativeness, and a diverse range of legal backgrounds."[108] According to the draft text, the proposed Indicative Lists would be considerably smaller and consist of up to three citizens on the list and one non-citizen and the draft provides that Members should promote gender balance and geographic representation in making nominations to the Indicative List.[109] To support the implementation of the reforms, statistical data, including on gender diversity in panels, would be collected.[110]

Whether or not the WTO dispute settlement reforms proceed ahead, WTO Members should be encouraged to select women panelists. They should place a premium on gender balance as one of the criteria for panel selection. Individual WTO Members can take the lead in placing women on their Indicative Lists and in insisting that at least one woman be appointed to panels.

However, it is not simply a matter of WTO Members selecting women panelists. There is a need for Members to ensure that their female delegates have the requisite exposure and the right balance of skills and experience to be a panelist. There are structural impediments which prevent women from being selected because they may not have followed a traditional career path in trade or law nor had the right kind of opportunities open to them. The identification of the pathways by which persons are selected for involvement in WTO dispute settlement and improving the access of women to these pathways will help to remove these structural impediments.[111] The challenge is to examine and expose the hidden social assumptions that prevent women from participating fully in the resolution of international trade disputes.

This is not all that needs to be done. The Secretariat of the organization has an important role to play in supporting gender diversity and implementing any reform proposals. It cannot hide behind the mantra of the WTO as a "Member-led organization." It is here that individuals can make a real difference. The role of the previous Director-General as an International Gender Champion and male ally in promoting the participation of women in trade, the decision of the current Director-General to appoint two women Deputies, and the progress that has been made in promoting gender diversity

---

108 WTO, *GC Special Meeting Report*, above note 23 at para 7.

109 *Ibid*, Section II at paras 2–3.

110 *Ibid*, Appendix I.

111 Lijnzaad, above note 99 at 42 (where this proposal is made in relation to international courts and tribunals).

within the Secretariat are examples of the influence that individuals can bring to an organization. The former Director of the Appellate Body Division, Debra Steger, proposed that a woman be appointed to the position in the Secretariat responsible for assisting the Director-General with the composition of panels.[112] Since 2016 a woman has been in this role, and despite the limitations imposed by the criteria parties seek in panelists, there have been more woman appointed to panels in the years since.

The presence of women in leadership roles within an organization, as Ambassadors, Chairs of Committees, Directors, panelists, Appellate Body Members, and members of the MPIA pool of arbitrators gives encouragement to other women aspiring to play a part in WTO dispute settlement. There is anecdotal evidence that senior women within the organization support and speak up for other women, including for the purposes of promotion. WTO Internships and professional development assignments provide opportunities to young women which might not otherwise have been available. Senior women in WTO dispute settlement often engage in active mentoring of young women, which is a practical rather than merely symbolic effect of their presence.[113]

It is also imperative to address the fluctuating nature of gender representativeness within WTO dispute settlement bodies. For example, at one time the Appellate Body comprised three women out of seven Members, but in a matter of years this was reduced to one. Both the Appellate Body Division and the Legal Division were led by women before being replaced by men. While not rejecting the necessity of merit-based appointments, there is a constant need to keep an eye on gender balance. Efforts to bring about gender parity may sometimes provoke a backlash and a perception that "enough women have been appointed."[114] Reform efforts therefore need to be undertaken with necessary sensitivity so that the long-term objective is achieved.

E. Conclusion

A SYSTEMIC APPROACH SHOULD BE adopted to address the lack of gender diversity in WTO dispute settlement. WTO Members have recognized the

---

112 Steger, above note 12.

113 Rosemary Hunter, "More than Just a Different Face? Judicial Diversity and Decision-making" (2015) 68:1 *Current Legal Problems* 119 at 123.

114 Sally Kenney, "Choosing Judges: A Bumpy Road to Women's Equality and a Long Way to Go" (2012) 2012:1499 *Michigan State Law Review* 1499 at 1509.

nexus between trade and gender and the need to remove barriers to women's economic empowerment and increase their participation in trade. However, the trade and gender focus has been on matters external to the organization. Attention needs to be turned inwards and on the organization itself and the way in which the Members and the organization can promote gender diversity. There is a need to "walk the talk." WTO Members and the organization cannot just pay lip-service to gender diversity but must face the reality that the WTO dispute settlement system is lagging behind other international dispute resolution systems. Efforts to improve gender diversity need to be enhanced and sustained over the longer term.

The conclusions of this chapter have wider application to judicial bodies than just those of the WTO dispute settlement system. They highlight ways in which organizations can promote women into the judicial settlement of international disputes and ensure improved gender diversity. They demonstrate the important role that the organization itself, both Members and Secretariat, plays in promoting gender diversity, the important role that male allies within the organization play, and the role of individuals within the organization as role models and mentors. This is where individual role models, such as Valerie Hughes, make a difference. Committed individuals are the catalyst for enhancing gender inclusivity.

CHAPTER 18

WTO Dispute Settlement 1.0 and the Intricate Cycle of Governance

Sivan Shlomo-Agon

A. Introduction

ALL GOVERNANCE INSTITUTIONS, INCLUDING INTERNATIONAL ones, operate through an intricate cycle between their legitimacy and effectiveness[1]—two institutional qualities that are often seen as the "genuine acid tests" for governance.[2] When functioning properly, the relationship between these qualities can create a positive feedback loop, where high levels of legitimacy increase the effectiveness of a governance institution, and the effective provision of goods and services enhances its legitimacy.[3] However, this cycle can easily become compromised, transforming into a downward spiral where diminishing legitimacy undermines effectiveness, and declining effectiveness further erodes legitimacy.[4] An institution's trajectory is thus defined, to a

---

1 Cord Schmelzle, "Evaluating Governance: Effectiveness and Legitimacy in Areas of Limited Statehood" (2011) Collaborative Research Center (SFB) 700, Working Paper No 26, online (pdf): sfb-governance.de [perma.cc/K9UR-DM55].

2 Karl Hogl et al, "Legitimacy and Effectiveness of Environmental Governance: Concepts and Perspectives" in Karl Hogl et al, eds, *Environmental Governance: The Challenge of Legitimacy and Effectiveness* (Cheltenham, UK: Edward Elgar, 2012) 1 at 9.

3 Cord Schmelzle & Eric Stollenwerk, "Virtuous or Vicious Circle? Governance Effectiveness and Legitimacy in Areas of Limited Statehood" (2018) 12:4 *Journal of Intervention & Statebuilding* 449.

4 *Ibid.*

significant extent, by its ability to navigate this delicate balance and cultivate an upward spiral between legitimacy and effectiveness.

The World Trade Organization (WTO) dispute settlement system (DSS) offers a compelling case study of this governance cycle in action. Legitimacy and effectiveness have long been recognized as representing key conceptual frameworks for evaluating international adjudicative institutions like the WTO DSS, as researchers have sought to analyze the authority and performance of these global governance structures.[5] Yet, while numerous studies have examined the DSS's legitimacy[6] and effectiveness[7] as separate analytical frameworks, existing research has rarely explored how these qualities interact within WTO judicial governance, potentially generating mutually reinforcing or, conversely, mutually undermining dynamics.[8] This interaction, however, seems to have grown particularly acute as the DSS has marked its thirtieth anniversary while embroiled in an existential crisis.[9] The continued blocking of Appellate Body appointments by the United States since December 2019

---

5 See, e.g., Nienke Grossman et al, eds, *Legitimacy and International Courts* (Cambridge: Cambridge University Press, 2018); Robert Howse et al, eds, *The Legitimacy of International Trade Courts and Tribunals* (Cambridge: Cambridge University Press, 2018); Yuval Shany, *Assessing the Effectiveness of International Courts* (Oxford: Oxford University Press, 2014) 145–50 [Shany, "Assessing Effectiveness"].

6 See, e.g., Joost Pauwelyn, "The Rule of Law Without the Rule of Lawyers? Why Investment Arbitrators Are from Mars, Trade Adjudicators from Venus" (2015) 109:4 *American Journal of International Law* 761 [Pauwelyn, "Rule of Law"]; Cosette D Creamer & Zuzanna Godzimiriska, "(De)Legitimation at the WTO Dispute Settlement Mechanism" (2016) 49:2 *Vanderbilt Journal of Transnational Law* 275; Yuku Fukunaga, "Civil Society and the Legitimacy of the WTO Dispute Settlement System" (2009) 34:1 *Brooklyn Journal of International Law* 85.

7 See, e.g., Arie Riech, "The Effectiveness of the WTO Dispute Settlement System: A Statistical Analysis" in Toshiyuki Kono, Mary Hiscock, & Arie Reich, eds, *Transnational Commercial and Consumer Law* (Singapore: Springer Nature, 2018) 1 at 3, 38; Giorgio Sacerdoti, "The WTO Dispute Settlement System: Consolidating Success and Confronting New Challenges" in Manfred Elsig, Bernard Hoekman, & Joost Pauwelyn, eds, *Assessing the World Trade Organization: Fit for Purpose?* (Cambridge: Cambridge University Press, 2017); William J Davey, "The WTO and Rules-Based Dispute Settlement: Historical Evolution, Operational Success, and Future Challenges" (2014) 17:3 *Journal of International Economic Law* 679 [Davey, "Rules-Based Dispute Settlement"].

8 On the interaction between legitimacy and effectiveness in the broader context of international judicial institutions, see Yuval Shany, "Stronger Together? Legitimacy and Effectiveness of International Courts as Mutually Reinforcing or Undermining Notions" in Grossman et al, above note 5 at 354 [Shany, "Stronger Together?"].

9 William J Davey, "WTO Dispute Settlement: Crown Jewel or Costume Jewelry?" (2022) 21:3 *World Trade Review* 291 at 292.

has not merely paralyzed the Appellate Body but has severely undermined the effectiveness and consequently the credibility of the whole WTO dispute settlement system,[10] disrupting the governance cycle that sustained the system for more than two decades.

This disruption illustrates the vulnerability of governance cycles in international institutions, demonstrating how a breakdown in one element can trigger a cascading effect throughout the entire system. What began as a challenge to the legitimacy of certain Appellate Body practices and outcomes by a critical constituency—the United States—has eventually evolved into a systemic effectiveness decline. This, in turn, has worked to further erode the integrity and credibility of the system among wider circles of WTO Members, ultimately creating a self-reinforcing cycle of institutional attrition that now threatens the relevance of the DSS and the entire WTO edifice in global trade governance.

This chapter examines the WTO DSS through the lens of this intricate governance cycle. It recounts how the system successfully maintained a mutually reinforcing cycle for most of its existence before recent developments transformed this dynamic into a negative feedback loop. By analyzing this evolution, the chapter provides an instructive framework for understanding the authority and operation of WTO DSS 1.0, its current existential crisis, and potential paths toward recovery and a reformed WTO DSS 2.0. To develop this analysis systematically, the chapter proceeds in Section B by defining legitimacy and effectiveness in international governance. Section C explores the relationship between these concepts, discussing how they may create either a synergetic governance cycle or a negative feedback loop. Section D examines how this relationship has evolved in WTO dispute settlement over three decades, resulting in the current crisis. Section E concludes with a future outlook.

---

10   Peter Van den Bossche, "Is There a Future for the WTO Appellate Body and WTO Dispute Settlement?" (2022) World Trade Institute, Working Paper 01/2022 at 3, online (pdf): wti.org [perma.cc/W5FG-CEPC] [Van den Bossche, "Future for the WTO"].

B. Defining Elusive Concepts

1) Legitimacy

LEGITIMACY REFERS TO THE JUSTIFICATION and acceptance of authority,[11] with a distinction typically drawn between two aspects: normative and sociological.[12] Normative legitimacy is an objective measure addressing whether an institution "has a right to rule" in that it meets certain standards—e.g., democratic pedigree, transparency, or expertise—that normatively justify its authority.[13] Sociological legitimacy concerns whether an institution's authority is actually accepted by relevant constituencies[14] and is thus a subjective quality defined by audiences' beliefs or perceptions of the institution.[15] For the WTO DSS, these constituencies include both "insiders," primarily WTO Member States, and "outsiders" such as economic operators, civil society, and the media.[16]

While conceptually distinct, these two aspects are interrelated.[17] Sociological legitimacy—i.e., the acceptability of an institution's authority—partly depends on how well it meets certain normative standards of justified authority like equality, transparency, and participation.[18] In turn, normative legitimacy "has an intrinsically social quality," as an institution could not be normatively legitimate if no one perceived it as such.[19] In any event, under both the normative and sociological approaches, legitimacy ultimately relates to authority—"a notion that pertains to the social force or power that

---

11   Daniel Bodansky, "Legitimacy in International Law and International Relations" in Jeffrey L Dunoff, & Mark A Pollack, eds, *Interdisciplinary Perspectives on International Law and International Relations: The State of the Art* (Cambridge: Cambridge University Press, 2013) 321 at 324 [Bodansky, "Legitimacy in International Law"].

12   Allen Buchanan, "The Legitimacy of International Law" in Samantha Besson & John Tasioulas, eds, *The Philosophy of International Law* (Oxford: Oxford University Press 2010) 79.

13   Bodansky, "Legitimacy in International Law," above note 11 at 327.

14   *Ibid.*

15   Ian Hurd, *After Anarchy: Legitimacy and Power in the United Nations Security Council* (Princeton: Princeton University Press, 2008) 7.

16   Joost Pauwelyn, "Who Decides Matters: The Legitimacy Capital of WTO Adjudicators Versus ICSID Arbitrators" in Grossman et al, above note 5 at 216, 218–19, 225 [Pauwelyn, "Who Decides Matters"].

17   Daniel Bodansky, "The Legitimacy of International Governance: A Coming Challenge for International Environmental Law?" (1999) 93:3 *American Journal of International Law* 596 at 601–2 [Bodansky, "Legitimacy of International Governance"].

18   Shany, "Stronger Together?" above note 8 at 355–56.

19   Bodansky, "Legitimacy in International Law," above note 11 at 327.

generates obedience or, where relevant, generates support and acceptance of public institutions."[20] Importantly, this support is distinct from constituency acceptance of specific decisions or policies the relevant institution renders.[21] The concept of legitimacy thus reflects "diffuse support,"[22] meaning that constituencies may disagree with particular decisions delivered by a governance institution such as an international court while still recognizing its authority, accepting that it possesses the right to render decisions that should be followed.[23]

For adjudicative institutions, this quality of legitimacy is crucial. It "provides courts authority," enabling them "to make decisions contrary to the perceived immediate interests of their constituents" and fostering acceptance and obedience to judicial decisions.[24] This is especially vital for international courts, which lack the strong law-enforcement mechanisms available at the domestic level—their legitimacy directly influences parties' disposition to cooperate with the court and ultimately determines their willingness to comply with its rulings.[25]

Like other institutions, the legitimacy capital of international courts may derive from the source of their authority (source-based legitimacy), the processes through which this authority is exerted (process-based legitimacy), and the outcomes these processes produce (outcome-based legitimacy).[26] For an international adjudicative institution like the DSS, source legitimacy stems primarily from sovereign states' consent to its jurisdiction.[27] Process legitimacy derives from the procedures the court employs in exercising its legal power, such as adhering to established rules for judicial appointments and maintaining fair and timely decision-making processes.[28] Outcome-based legitimacy (also called performance-based legitimacy) rests on the court's ability to produce outcomes that are deemed desirable, whereas its failure to

---

20 Shany, "Stronger Together?" above note 8 at 356.

21 *Ibid.*

22 Erik Voeten, "Public Opinion and the Legitimacy of International Courts" (2013) 14:2 *Theoretical Inquiries in Law* 411 at 415.

23 *Ibid* at 415.

24 James L Gibson & Gregory A Caldeira, "The Legitimacy of Transnational Legal Institutions: Compliance, Support, and the European Court of Justice" (1995) 39:2 *American Journal of Political Science* 459 at 460–61.

25 Pauwelyn, "Who Decides Matters," above note 16 at 217.

26 Shany, "Assessing Effectiveness," above note 5 at 145–50.

27 Pauwelyn, "Who Decides Matters," above note 16 at 218.

28 *Ibid.*

meet these outcomes can erode its legitimacy.[29] Thus, even when established by legitimate actors (such as states or international organizations) and following pre-agreed procedures, an international court risks losing legitimacy if it produces decisions whose impacts are considered inadequate by its constituencies, potentially leading to an erosion of its authority.

Source, process, and outcome legitimacy each influences an international court's legitimacy and may vary in strength over time and across constituencies.[30] Since these three categories form the building blocks of institutional legitimacy, "strength in one legitimacy aspect may compensate for weakness in another aspect."[31] The overall legitimacy of an international court may thus exceed or fall below the threshold needed for it to survive or for legitimacy to generate cooperation and induce compliance.[32]

B. Effectiveness

WHEREAS LEGITIMACY CONCERNS THE ACCEPTANCE and justification of governance institutions' authority, effectiveness evaluates their performance and impacts.[33] It assesses institutions against their *intended* effects.[34] On this view, governance institutions, including international courts, are means for achieving specific ends,[35] which they either set for themselves or which are assigned to them by stakeholders.[36] Their institutional effectiveness is thus measured by how well they achieve these desired outcomes.[37]

Based on this conceptualization, an international court is considered effective if it attains its goals—if it solves the social problems it was designed to address.[38] Within this evaluative framework, the desirability of the goals assigned to the court is not questioned. Effectiveness assessment is therefore primarily descriptive and analytical rather than normative, unlike legitimacy evaluation which encompasses both empirical and normative dimensions.[39]

---

29 Shany, "Assessing Effectiveness," above note 5 at 148–49.

30 Bodansky, "Legitimacy in International Law," above note 11 at 335.

31 Shany, "Stronger Together?" above note 8 at 359.

32 Pauwelyn, "Who Decides Matters," above note 16 at 219.

33 Schmelzle & Stollenwerk, above note 3 at 454.

34 *Ibid* at 455.

35 Shany, "Assessing Effectiveness," above note 5 at 13–30.

36 Schmelzle & Stollenwerk, above note 3 at 455.

37 *Ibid*.

38 *Ibid*.

39 Shany, "Stronger Together?" above note 5 at 14.

Nevertheless, effectiveness analysis too is grounded in normative propositions—that institutions should fulfill their mandates and meaningfully influence their social environments.[40]

In practice, effectiveness analysis denotes comparison of an institution's record of achievements (i.e., the outcomes it produces) against the goals (i.e., desired outcomes) set by relevant constituencies. Under this analytical approach, the key to evaluating DSS effectiveness lies in the examination of judicial outcomes—whether the outputs the system generates (e.g., judicial decisions) and their social effects are consistent with the goals set by its "mandate providers"—Member states and the international organization responsible for its establishment and operation.[41] For example, if one DSS goal is to support the operation of the WTO regime and its underlying objectives, among them, trade liberalization, an investigation of DSS effectiveness would consider the extent to which DSS rulings have induced changes in trade flows in disputed areas or generated revision of trade-restrictive practices. Similarly, if promoting dispute settlement is another goal, effectiveness assessment would examine the extent to which DSS proceedings have resulted in withdrawal of WTO-inconsistent measures or facilitated pre-ruling and post-litigation settlements.

Given its multiple goals, the DSS may, at a given point in time, exhibit varying degrees of effectiveness across different objectives. Like legitimacy, effectiveness is therefore relative and fluctuating.[42] The DSS may demonstrate partial effectiveness, showing impressive record in achieving certain institutional objectives and limited success in attaining others, while its overall level of effectiveness may change over time, depending on its performance in respect to its multiple objectives. Finally, constituencies' perceptions of DSS effectiveness may likewise vary according to how well it achieves the goals they prioritize.

C. The Intricate Cycle of Governance

DESPITE BEING ANALYTICALLY DISTINCT, LEGITIMACY and effectiveness are closely interconnected, making their interplay crucial in governance

---

40   *Ibid.*

41   Sivan Shlomo-Agon, *International Adjudication on Trial: The Effectiveness of the WTO Dispute Settlement System* (Oxford: Oxford University Press, 2019) 36–41.

42   Shany, "Assessing Effectiveness," above note 5 at 157.

settings. While potential trade-offs exist between these qualities, they are generally assumed to form a mutually reinforcing relationship, creating what scholars describe as a virtuous cycle of governance. In this dynamic, the more legitimate a governance institution is, the more effective it is, and the more effective it is, the more legitimate it becomes.[43] However, the inverse relationship can also occur, where diminished legitimacy and reduced effectiveness create a negative feedback loop—illegitimate governance leads to ineffective governance and vice versa.[44]

To understand these potential dynamics more deeply, consider first the pathway through which legitimacy may affect effectiveness. Legitimacy, as previously defined, is the quality that leads people, states, and other subjects to accept authority—independent of coercion, self-interest, or rational persuasion—because of a general sense that the authority is justified.[45] Legitimacy thus creates a sense of obligation that results in voluntary compliance and cooperation by the governed. These behavioural attitudes in turn lead to more effective governance by facilitating the achievement of intended institutional goals.[46] Consequently, legitimacy represents an "important basis of effectiveness, in addition to power and self-interest," and plays a significant role in the long-term success of governance institutions.[47]

This relationship between legitimacy and effectiveness is particularly pronounced in the judicial context: "Since courts typically have neither the power of the 'purse nor the sword,' this moral authority is essential to judicial effectiveness."[48] This especially true for international adjudicative institutions like the WTO DSS. Their effectiveness—i.e., their ability to achieve their goals—depends heavily on their legitimacy capital,[49] which allows them to gain acceptance of their jurisdiction, attract cases for judicial settlement, and secure adherence to their decisions.[50] It further enables them to establish authoritative legal interpretations, induce rule-compliance, and facilitate dispute resolution.[51]

---

43   Schmelzle, above note 1 at 5.

44   Shany, "Stronger Together?" above note 8 at 354.

45   Bodansky, "Legitimacy of International Governance," above note 17 at 600.

46   *Ibid*; Schmelzle & Stollenwerk, above note 3 at 460–61.

47   Bodansky, "Legitimacy of International Governance," above note 17 at 603.

48   Gibson & Caldeira, above note 24 at 460.

49   Shany, "Stronger Together?" above note 8 at 354.

50   Shany, "Assessing Effectiveness," above note 5 at 149.

51   *Ibid*.

That said, the pathway from legitimacy to effectiveness may not always produce a positive governance cycle. In some instances, there may be a trade-off between the demands of legitimacy and effectiveness. For instance, an international court's efforts to strengthen legitimacy through carefully reasoned judgments may compromise its goal of prompt dispute settlement. In other cases, diminished legitimacy can severely undermine the court's effectiveness by leading to reduced voluntary cooperation and support or even to active resistance against it.[52] Such incidents of illegitimacy may stem from a lack of democratic authorization, perceptions of flawed decision-making processes or mandate overreach, or failures to deliver intended outcomes. A lack of legitimacy not only prevents a virtuous cycle of governance from emerging but may trigger a vicious cycle, where illegitimacy and ineffectiveness reinforce each other in a downward spiral.[53]

These potential dynamics along the path from legitimacy to effectiveness nevertheless tell only half of the story. Let us now turn to consider the reverse pathway from effectiveness to legitimacy, as it is not only legitimacy that affects the performance of governance institutions; their effectiveness equally impacts their legitimacy. This connection is evident in the fact that effectiveness constitutes one powerful component of legitimacy for governance institutions, often referred to as outcome-based or performance-based legitimacy. This type of legitimacy arises from constituencies' experiences with an institution's performance, which align with the values and goals they expect it to promote.[54] The underlying idea is that reliable attainment of desired outcomes can secure the respective institution both cooperative attitudes and the right to be obeyed, even when compliance may not serve the immediate self-interest of constituencies.[55]

Importantly, while effectiveness is not a sufficient condition for legitimacy, it is a necessary one.[56] A certain level of effectiveness is essential to justify the existence of governance institutions, especially if they impose costs on their subjects.[57] Since international courts lack the kind of democratic legitimation possessed by domestic institutions, their legitimacy particularly depends on effective performance. Such performance may enhance both their

---

52   *Cf* Schmelzle & Stollenwerk, above note 3 at 458.
53   *Ibid.*
54   *Ibid.*
55   *Ibid.*
56   Schmelzle, above note 1 at 13.
57   Schmelzle & Stollenwerk, above note 3 at 455.

normative and sociological legitimacy: an international court that achieves its prescribed goals is more likely to be considered legitimate from a normative standpoint as well as to garner greater support for its operations among constituencies.[58]

That said, the pathway from effectiveness to legitimacy is not always straightforward, and some conditions would have to be met for it to yield a positive feedback loop.[59] Thus, effective performance will only increase legitimacy if an institution and its audiences share the same governance goals and values.[60] For an international court, for example, the effective provision of legal interpretations will only enhance judicial legitimacy if a significant portion of the relevant audiences values that very type of interpretation.[61] Moreover, in the case of politically contested goods and services like law interpretation, it may be harder to transform effectiveness into legitimacy gains,[62] whereas a chronic gap between the judicial outcomes generated by an international court and audience preferences could result in the sociological delegitimization of the court.[63]

Another challenge to establishing a positive feedback loop from effectiveness to legitimacy lies in the diversity of legitimacy audiences[64] and the subjective nature of sociological legitimacy.[65] Thus, while some members of an international court may view certain judicial practices of norm interpretation as aligned with their understanding of the law, these same practices may conflict with other members' beliefs. In such situations, an international court must often choose which audience's demands to prioritize to initiate a virtuous governance cycle. However, this prioritization can trigger a downward spiral of illegitimacy, resistance, and judicial ineffectiveness among other audiences.[66] This scenario demonstrates that the relationship between effectiveness and legitimacy is inherently complex, with no automatic path to a virtuous cycle, as such a cycle will take hold and endure only under specific

---

58   Shany, "Stronger Together?" above note 8 at 354, 366–67.
59   Schmelzle & Stollenwerk, above note 3 at 450.
60   *Ibid* at 460.
61   *Ibid.*
62   *Ibid.*
63   Shany, "Stronger Together?" above note 8 at 370.
64   Schmelzle & Stollenwerk, above note 3 at 463.
65   Shany, "Stronger Together?" above note 8 at 369.
66   Schmelzle & Stollenwerk, above note 3 at 463.

conditions.[67] Below we consider how the relationship between the two qualities has unfolded in the case of WTO DSS over the past three decades.

D. WTO DSS 1.0: Navigating the Legitimacy— Effectiveness Dynamic

THE WTO DSS BEGAN OPERATING on 1 January 1995, governed by the Dispute Settlement Understanding (DSU), which established its procedural framework and a set of institutional goals.[68] This set includes several ultimate ends: providing security and predictability to the multilateral trade system, preserving the balance of rights and obligations between WTO Members, sustaining the operation of the WTO and the realization of its goals, and conferring legitimacy upon the WTO and its rules. Alongside these general, open-ended objectives, the DSS was tasked with several more-strategic, intermediate goals, including inducing compliance with WTO law, securing the positive and prompt settlement of disputes, preventing unilateralism, leveling the playing field among WTO Members, and clarifying WTO law.[69]

Upon its establishment, the WTO DSS was also endowed with an initial legitimacy capital. This derived, first and foremost, from the DSS's creation by legitimate actors—sovereign states—who consented to its delegated powers through the DSU.[70] The wide acceptance of the DSS's compulsory jurisdiction by a high number of states further strengthened its source legitimacy capital,[71] as did the "halo effect" associated with the international efforts to establish a more rule-based multilateral trade system with a legalized DSS at its heart.[72] Finally, the appointment of seven distinguished generalist jurists as the first Appellate Body Members also contributed to the DSS's initial legitimacy capital by enhancing its image of justice and professionalism and

---

67   John D Ciorciari & Stephen D Krasner, "Contracting Out, Legitimacy, and State Building" (2018) 12:4 *Journal of Intervention & Statebuilding* 484 at 485.

68   *Marrakesh Agreement Establishing the World Trade Organization*, Annex 2, 15 April 1994, 1869 UNTS 3 at 401, Understanding on Rules and Procedures Governing the Settlement of Disputes (entered into force 1 January 1995).

69   See generally Shlomo-Agon, above note 41 at 62–88.

70   Shany, "Assessing Effectiveness," above note 5 at 145.

71   *Ibid* at 148.

72   *Ibid* at 146.

by drawing on the adjudicators' record to further justify and reinforce the DSS's authority.[73]

1) The WTO DSS 1995–2019: A System in Sync

When the WTO DSS opened its doors in January 1995, its initial legitimacy capital served as a useful asset in eliciting support for its operations and facilitating attainment of its goals. In particular, it enabled the DSS to attract cases, encourage compliance with its rulings, and foster collaborative behaviour among WTO Members. These factors, in turn, contributed to the DSS's effectiveness in achieving its goals and delivering desired outcomes, as empirical assessments at the close of the system's first decade demonstrated.[74]

Thus, during this formative period, the system generated prolific outputs. It exhibited an impressive usage record of 324 consultation requests, filed by both developed and developing countries and resulting in 109 panel reports and sixty-four Appellate Body reports. The DSS also achieved a positive compliance rate of over 80 percent with its rulings.[75] These judicial outputs, in turn, supported attainment of its fundamental objectives of compliance inducement and dispute settlement,[76] including in several difficult cases that the positive consensus requirement under the old *General Agreement on Tariffs and Trade* (GATT) DSS had previously prevented from adjudication.[77] While the DSS did not fully attain its goal of prompt dispute settlement due to panels' failure to meet statutory deadlines,[78] the lifespan of WTO cases was also "significantly shorter, on average, then their GATT counterparts."[79] The WTO DSS further proved effective in achieving the goal of fending off unilateralism

73 Claus-Dieter Ehlermann, "Six Years on the Bench of the 'World Trade Court': Some Personal Experiences as Member of the Appellate Body of the World Trade Organization" (2002) 36:4 *Journal of World Trade* 605 at 607–10.

74 William J Davey, "The WTO Dispute Settlement System: The First Ten Years" (2005) 8:1 *Journal of International Economic Law* 17 [Davey, "WTO: First Ten Years"]; Bruce Wilson, "Compliance by WTO Members with Adverse WTO Dispute Settlement Rulings: The Record to Date" (2007) 10:2 *Journal of International Economic Law* 397.

75 Davey, "WTO: First Ten Years," above note 74; Wilson, above note 74.

76 Davey, "WTO: First Ten Years," above note 74 at 45–49.

77 Bernhard Zangl, "Judicialization Matters! A Comparison of Dispute Settlement Under GATT and the WTO" (2008) 52:4 *International Studies Quarterly* 825.

78 Davey, "WTO: First Ten Years," above note 74 at 49–50.

79 Earl L Grinols & Roberto Perrelli, "The WTO Impact on International Trade Disputes: An Event History Analysis" (2006) 88:4 *Review of Economics & Statistics* 613 at 623.

in international trade relations.[80] Finally, increased participation rates of developing countries[81] and their positive record in terms of trade liberalization obtained through DSS rulings[82] helped promote a more level playing field in the multilateral trading system, though the limited legal capacity of developing countries and their challenges in employing WTO-authorized retaliation constrained their more meaningful use of the DSS.[83]

Overall, by the close of its first decade, the DSS produced a range of judicial outcomes consistent with its intermediate goals. This enabled the system to advance its overarching ultimate ends, such as providing security and predictability to the multilateral trade system and maintaining the balance of benefits between WTO Members, thereby consolidating perceptions of its effectiveness.

Similar assessments of DSS performance were made by the end of its second decade.[84] Although usage rates decreased somewhat, the DSS continued to present impressive judicial outputs: 164 consultation requests were filed by both developed and developing states, leading to eighty-nine panel reports and fifty-one Appellate Body reports,[85] with a compliance rate close to 90 percent.[86] These judicial outputs allowed the DSS to advance many organizational goals. The system performed well in resolving disputes between WTO Members,[87] and "excelled . . . in diffusing . . . trade spats"—such as the EU-US disputes over hormones or aircraft subsidies—that might otherwise have jeopardized broader economic, political, and security relations.[88] In such

---

80 Keisuke Iida, "Is WTO Dispute Settlement Effective?" (2004) 10:2 *Global Governance* 207 at 215–16.

81 *Ibid* at 217; Davey, "WTO: First Ten Years," above note 74 at 24.

82 Chad P Bown, "Developing Countries as Plaintiffs and Defendants in GATT/WTO Trade Disputes" (2004) 27:1 *World Economics* 59 at 66–68.

83 Andrew T Guzman & Beth A Simmons, "Power Plays and Capacity Constraints: The Selection of Defendants in World Trade Organization Disputes" (2005) 34:2 *Journal of Legal Studies* 557; Marc L Busch, Eric Reinhardt, & Gregory Shaffer, "Does Legal Capacity Matter? A Survey of WTO Members" (2009) 8:4 *World Trade Review* 559.

84 See Reich, above note 7.

85 Joost Pauwelyn, "The WTO 20 Years On: 'Global Governance by Judiciary' or, Rather, Member-driven Settlement of (Some) Trade Disputes between (Some) WTO Members?" (2016) 27:4 *European Journal of International Law* 1119 at 1121.

86 Manfred Elsig, Bernard Hoekman, & Joost Pauwelyn, "Thinking About the Performance of the World Trade Organization" in Manfred Elsig, Bernard Hoekman, & Joost Pauwelyn, above note 7 at 32; Davey, "Rules-Based Dispute Settlement," above note 7 at 689.

87 Reich, above note 7 at 22; Elsig, Hoekman, & Joost, above note 86 at 36.

88 Pauwelyn, "The WTO 20 Years On," above note 85 at 1123.

prolonged disputes, the DSS not only effectively contained the trade feuds within defined legal boundaries but also stimulated renegotiations towards mutually agreed solutions that re-established the parties' reciprocal balance of concessions.[89] Furthermore, during its second decade, the DSS continued to successfully constrain large players like the United States from resorting to unilateralism.[90] In so doing, the DSS not only enhanced the stability of the WTO regime but also helped to redress power asymmetries among its Members. Finally, the DSS produced a rich body of "sophisticated and well-respected jurisprudence,"[91] providing clarifications to numerous WTO rules and thereby promoting greater rule adherence and legal predictability in the multilateral trade system.

In light of these judicial outcomes, at its twentieth anniversary the WTO DSS "was celebrated as one of the organization's biggest achievements."[92] That said, the DSS never fully achieved all its organizational goals (arguably an inescapable outcome considering its varied—and sometimes contradictory—aims).[93] As Reich observed: alongside its achievements over the first two decades, the system remained "far from perfect," and numerous Members advocated for improvements to its effectiveness by tackling concerns such as the escalating duration of WTO proceedings that undermined attainment of the DSS's prompt dispute settlement objective[94] or the limitations embedded in DSS remedies that impeded timely enforcement of WTO rules.[95] These calls, however, did not overshadow the multiple judicial outcomes the DSS did produce, which aligned with many of its prescribed objectives. These outcomes solidified perceptions of DSS effectiveness among numerous WTO Members as well as beyond the WTO, with many international legal scholars and partitioners voicing admiration for its operation and accomplishments.[96]

The DSS's perceived effectiveness then worked to further bolster its legitimacy, creating a mutually reinforcing cycle that strengthened the system's

---

89 Shlomo-Agon, above note 41 at 259–61.

90 Elsig, Hoekman, & Joost, above note 86 at 19.

91 Pauwelyn, "Rule of Law," above note 6 at 763.

92 *Ibid* at 761.

93 Shlomo-Agon, above note 41 at 32–34.

94 Reich, above note 7 at 38–39; Davey, "Rules-Based Dispute Settlement," above note 7 at 692, 696–97.

95 Davey, "Rules-Based Dispute Settlement," above note 7 at 692, 698–700.

96 See, e.g., Robert Howse, "The World Trade Organization 20 Years On: Global Governance by Judiciary" (2016) 27:1 *European Journal of International Law* 9; Reich, above note 7.

resilience against legitimacy challenges from both within and outside the WTO. As Shany noted, "it may be harder for actors to challenge effective international courts than to challenge ineffective ones, as the perceived success of a court may facilitate greater support for it. This, in turn, shields successful courts, to some extent, from legitimacy challenges."[97]

This synergetic relationship between effectiveness and legitimacy in the DSS was highlighted by Robert Howse in his overview of the system's first twenty years.[98] Describing the DSS's effectiveness, Howse wrote: while the WTO's political-legislative arm struggled to function and deliver results—culminating in the collapse of the Doha Round negotiations after nearly two decades of political paralysis—the WTO's judicial branch was "in full evolution through this entire period, entertaining hundreds of claims and producing a vast jurisprudential *acquis*."[99] As a result, despite deep division among WTO Members about the future of the multilateral trading system and continuing critiques of economic globalization, "the WTO judicial system has been largely spared attacks on its legitimacy."[100]

Howse then went further to emphasize the "significant positive relation" between the DSS's perceived operational success and the high level of legitimacy it possessed, while pointing out that Member States' broad acceptance of the system's authority manifested not only in the "sheer number of disputes that the states parties . . . have been prepared to submit" to the DSS but also in the "relative lack of instances where Members have, upon losing a ruling, explicitly chosen not to implement it."[101] He added that while "losing parties and sometimes other WTO Members have criticized individual rulings," such "critiques have rarely challenged the overall authority or legitimacy of the WTO judicial mechanism."[102] A similar assessment was echoed by Pauwelyn, who observed that despite major powers like China, the European Union, and the United States frequently finding themselves on the losing side of WTO disputes, at the DSS's twentieth anniversary, "overall support for the system remain[ed] high. If anything, it has increased over time, with early criticism by civil society waning."[103]

---

97 Shany, "Assessing Effectiveness," above note 5 at 145.
98 Howse, above note 96 at 11.
99 *Ibid*.
100 *Ibid* at 10–11.
101 *Ibid* at 11.
102 *Ibid* at 11.
103 Pauwelyn, "Rule of Law," above note 6 at 761.

In accordance with the virtuous cycle argument, the DSS's consolidated authority and support operated in turn to further strengthen its effectiveness,[104] enabling it to consistently attract cases and, along the way, secure compliance with high-cost rulings,[105] even from powerful Members like the United States and China.[106] However, as previously indicated, neither the establishment nor the preservation of such a positive governance cycle is guaranteed. Since both legitimacy and effectiveness are evolving constructs, even a long-entrenched cycle can disintegrate under certain circumstances— as eventually transpired when the DSS approached its quarter-century milestone.

2) The WTO DSS Post-December 2019: A Governance Cycle Disrupted

Not long after the DSS turned twenty, it came to face a severe backlash from the United States under the first Trump administration—a backlash that eventually led to the Appellate Body's collapse in December 2019. While this crisis, driven by the claim that the Appellate Body "lacks sufficient legitimacy to perform its functions,"[107] reached its apex under Trump, it had been building for some time, with concerns raised by successive US administrations.[108] As Van den Bossche notes, particularly since 2010, the United States adopted an increasingly antagonistic stance toward the Appellate Body, vigorously criticizing its jurisprudence on safeguards, subsidies, countervailing duties, and anti-dumping measures, while undermining the independence and impartiality of WTO adjudicators by blocking the reappointment of Appellate Body Members in 2007, 2011, and 2016.[109]

---

104 Reich, above note 7 at 38.

105 *Cf* Shany, "Assessing Effectiveness," above note 5 at 156.

106 Weihuan Zhou, "The Impact of the WTO Dispute Settlement System on China: Effectiveness, Challenges and Broader Issues" in Henry Gao, Damian Raess, & Ka Zeng, eds, *China and the WTO: A Twenty-Year Assessment* (Cambridge: Cambridge University Press, 2023) 252 at 253, 259–62.

107 Frank Altemöller, "WTO Appellate Body Without Legitimacy?: The Criticism of the Dispute Settlement System and the Response of Member States" (2021) 16:4 *Global Trade & Customs Journal* 139 at 143.

108 Van den Bossche, "Future for the WTO," above note 10 at 8.

109 *Ibid* at 6.

For quite a while, though, the DSS's strong legitimacy among many other WTO Members offset its diminishing standing with the United States,[110] allowing it to maintain sufficient legitimacy to sustain its effectiveness. However, this legitimacy deterioration—particularly significant given the United States's key role in the WTO—became acute when the Trump administration elevated it to active resistance, blocking the process of re-appointment of Appellate Body Members each time a vacancy arose in 2017, 2018, and 2019.[111] Consequently, on 11 December 2019, the Appellate Body became inoperative, reverting the WTO DSS to a de facto panel-only system—a state that has persisted through the Biden administration and current Trump term.

The United States has challenged the DSS's legitimacy on both process and outcome grounds. It has criticized the Appellate Body for allegedly disregarding DSU procedural rules, particularly the ninety-day timeframe for appellate review.[112] Such deviations, according to the United States, have undermined its expectations for proper judicial process, damaging the DSS's perceived legitimacy. The United States has further challenged the Appellate Body's judicial outcomes, alleging persistent "judicial overreach."[113] Specifically, it has accused the Appellate Body of creating new legal obligations through erroneous interpretations of WTO provisions, issuing unnecessary advisory opinions, improperly reviewing panel factual findings despite its limited mandate under DSU Article 17.6, and treating past Appellate Body reports as binding precedents.[114]

Therefore, the United States has not merely objected to specific Appellate Body decisions but broadly criticized its case law development and interpretation methods for deviating from Members' intentions and infringing state sovereignty. The United States has argued that the Appellate Body, encouraged by some Members seeking to achieve through adjudication what the WTO's failed negotiating function could not provide, "attempted to fill in 'gaps' in th[e] agreements," creating "rights or obligations to which . . . WTO Members never agreed."[115] This created a chronic gap between DSS outcomes

---

110 *Cf* Pauwelyn, "Who Decides Matters," above note 16 at 219.

111 Van den Bossche, "Future for the WTO," above note 10 at 6.

112 USTR, *Report on the Appellate Body of the World Trade Organization* (Washington, DC: Office of the United States Trade Representative, 2020) at 26–32 [*USTR Appellate Body Report*].

113 *Ibid* at 1.

114 Van den Bossche, "Future for the WTO," above note 10 at 7.

115 *USTR Appellate Body Report*, above note 112 at 2–3.

and those deemed desirable by a key constituency, resulting in the system's "sociological delegitimization."[116] As a US representative stated: "when the Appellate Body overreached and abused the authority it had been given within the dispute settlement system, it undermined the legitimacy of the system and damaged the interests of all WTO Members who cared about having the agreements respected as they had been negotiated."[117]

The US challenge to the DSS's outcome legitimacy further illuminates the divergence that has emerged over time between Member states and the DSS, and among Member states themselves, regarding the exact judicial goals and tasks to be pursued. This is because the US-triggered crisis facing the DSS is essentially "an identity crisis, caused by conflicting visions" of the system and its objectives.[118] While the United States contends for a restrictive interpretation of DSS goals, such as clarifying WTO law, other Members, like the European Union, China, and India, exhibit a more flexible stance and disagree that the "AB systematically engaged in judicial activism or demonstrated consistent . . . disregard for procedural . . . rules."[119] In such a situation, as noted in Section C, where a key actor holds a divergent understanding of expected judicial outcomes, translating other actors' perceptions of judicial effectiveness into heightened legitimacy in the orchestration of a virtuous governance cycle becomes significantly more challenging. Hence, it was when the United States decided to resolutely act on its growing perception of DSS illegitimacy, that the virtuous governance cycle in WTO dispute settlement began to unravel, triggering instead a vicious cycle where declining legitimacy and effectiveness fed each other.

And so, the US blockage of Appellate Body appointments did not only paralyze the Appellate Body but impaired the functioning of the entire DSS, placing it in a position where it could no longer effectively fulfill its goals.[120]

---

116 *Cf* Shany, "Stronger Together?" above note 8 at 370.

117 WTO, *Minutes of Meeting*, WTO Doc WT/DSB/M/441 (2020) at 30, online (pdf): docs.wto.org [perma.cc/HEG5-J8Z2].

118 Georgie Juszczyk, "Legitimacy Crisis at the World Trade Organisation Appellate Body: Other Ways Than the MPIA?" (2021) 12 *European Yearbook of International Economic Law* 87 at 89.

119 Peter Van den Bossche, "Can the WTO Dispute Settlement System Be Revived?: Options for Addressing a Major Governance Failure of the World Trade Organization" in Ernst-Ulrich Petersmann & Armin Steinbach, eds, *Constitutionalism and Transnational Governance Failures* (Leiden: Brill, 2024) 308 at 316 [Van den Bossche, "Reviving WTO Dispute Settlement"].

120 Juszczyk, above note 118 at 90–91.

This is because as of 11 December 2019, any notice of appeal in the WTO has become an appeal into the void, leading losing parties to systematically appeal panel reports to prevent them from taking binding effect.[121] Of the thirty-nine panel reports issued between 11 December 2019, and 31 December 2024, merely eight were adopted by the DSB, while twenty reports were appealed into the void.[122] Consequently, "most disputes brought to the WTO in recent years have remained in a legal limbo,"[123] rendering the DSS incapable of effectively achieving its goals, including its basic dispute settlement and compliance inducement objectives.

The US-triggered paralysis of the Appellate Body has thus "severely undermined the effectiveness" of the DSS.[124] In turn, the DSS's diminished capacity to perform its functions and the increasing likelihood of unresolved disputes have quickly eroded the DSS's credibility among broader circles of WTO Members.[125] Evidence of this erosion appears in the sharp decline in disputes filed with the DSS after 2020.[126] This downward trend further diminishes prospects for judicial effectiveness, illustrating how, by the end of its third decade, effectiveness-decreasing and legitimacy-detracting factors have come to operate in the WTO DSS in a compounding negative feedback loop.

E. Toward WTO DSS 2.0: Reform and Renewal

THE TRAJECTORY OF THE WTO DSS over the past three decades illustrates the vulnerability of governance cycles in international institutions. What initially operated as a synergetic cycle, where legitimacy reinforced effectiveness and effectiveness, in turn, enhanced legitimacy, has unravelled into a negative feedback loop of institutional attrition. The paralysis of the Appellate Body and the resulting decline in the DSS's dispute resolution capacity have exposed the fragility of the WTO's judicial architecture, leaving the system at a crossroads. Yet rather than marking the demise of the DSS, this crisis

---

121 Van den Bossche, "Reviving WTO Dispute Settlement," above note 119 at 312.
122 See WorldTradeLaw.net, "WTO Panel Reports" (last visited 15 March 2025), online: worldtradelaw.net [perma.cc/YAL9-D6WY].
123 Van den Bossche, "Reviving WTO Dispute Settlement," above note 119 at 312.
124 Van den Bossche, "Future for the WTO," above note 10 at 4.
125 *Ibid.*
126 See WTO, "Dispute Settlement Activity – Some Figures" (last visited 15 March 2025), online: wto.org [perma.cc/FK2Z-BKU8] (In each of 2020, 2021, 2022, and 2023, only five, nine, eight, and six disputes were brought to the DSS, compared to seventeen, seventeen, thirty-eight, and twenty in each of 2016, 2017, 2018, and 2019).

presents an opportunity for reform—a chance to construct WTO DSS 2.0. In carrying out this endeavour, it is clear that any reform efforts must deliberately address both legitimacy and effectiveness as interconnected dimensions; reforms that enhance one while neglecting the other will inevitably fall short. The future of the system thus depends on restoring this dual foundation while adapting to the evolving realities of global trade governance.

A central challenge in reviving the DSS and reversing the current downward legitimacy-effectiveness spiral lies, as the above discussion suggests, in reconciling the diverging expectations of WTO Members. The paralysis of the Appellate Body was not merely a procedural failure but a reflection of deeper tensions regarding the goals, role, and authority of the DSS in the multilateral trade system—divergences that go to the heart of the DSS's effectiveness and legitimacy foundations. Some Members, particularly the United States, have come to advocate for a more restrained system, wary of judicial overreach. Others, including the European Union, China, and many developing countries, see a robust adjudicative system as essential for legal predictability and stability, as evidenced by the creation of interim solutions like the Multi-Party Interim Appeal Arbitration Arrangement (MPIA), which demonstrates their continued commitment to rules-based dispute resolution. A reformed DSS must navigate these competing visions, putting forth a mechanism that is authoritative yet flexible, rigorous yet politically sustainable.

This denotes that the path forward requires, first and foremost, an institutional recalibration within the WTO DSS—redesigning the system to address concerns over potential judicial overreach while maintaining its core function as an independent and binding dispute resolution system. This could include refining appellate review procedures, clarifying the limits of judicial interpretation, and establishing structured mechanisms that allow WTO Members to provide guidance on contentious legal issues. Recent efforts, in the framework of the Molina Process[127] and the now formalized DSS reform process,[128] signal a growing recognition that a holistic approach to reinstituting both legitimacy and effectiveness is needed—one that restores faith in the system without undermining its capacity to perform.

Still, rebuilding the governance cycle in WTO dispute settlement will require addressing broader structural factors that have exacerbated the current

---

127 WTO, *Special Meeting of the General Council*, WTO Doc JOB/GC/385 (2024), online (pdf): docs.wto.org [perma.cc/VFN3-59Y4].

128 WTO, *Dispute Settlement Reform Process*, WTO Doc JOB/GC/DSR/5 (2024), online (pdf): docs.wto.org [perma.cc/WMU4-WD96].

DSS crisis. Particularly, beyond reforms to the WTO's judicial function, revitalizing and strengthening the WTO's legislative arm is crucial to reestablishing the DSS's legitimacy and effectiveness. Although the DSS was never intended to compensate for a stalled negotiating arm, it has been increasingly pressured to clarify ambiguities in WTO law, a challenge that has grown over time due to legislative inaction in the multilateral trade system. In other words, the paralysis of the WTO's negotiating function has placed unsustainable pressure on its judicial branch, creating expectations that adjudication can compensate for the lack of new trade rules. This judicial-legislative imbalance has in turn contributed to legitimacy concerns, particularly regarding perceptions of judicial overreach, which have eventually impaired the DSS's ability to operate effectively. Hence, strengthening the WTO's legislative function to modernize trade rules is crucial. Without a more dynamic and responsive legislative process and a recalibrated judicial-legislative balance, existing tensions are likely to persist, further threatening the DSS's legitimacy and effectiveness. Complementing this legislative renewal, the creation of channels for constructive dialogue between the WTO's judicial and legislative branches—for example, through mechanisms that enable the latter to provide appropriate legislative fixes and clarifications when necessary—could promote a more sustainable balance of power within the WTO and help reinvigorate a positive governance cycle within the DSS.

Hence, true revitalization of the WTO DSS demands a comprehensive approach that addresses judicial processes, legislative functions, and the interface between them. The path toward WTO DSS 2.0 will undoubtedly be complex, requiring political will, institutional creativity, and sustained commitment from diverse stakeholders. Yet, the alternative—allowing the system to further deteriorate—risks undermining decades of progress in rules-based trade governance. By embracing this moment as an opportunity for meaningful transformation rather than merely managing decline, WTO Members can restore the legitimacy-effectiveness nexus that is essential for a dispute settlement system capable of navigating the increasingly complex landscape of twenty-first century trade relations.

CHAPTER 19

Reflections on WTO Dispute Settlement as an International Dispute Settlement Mechanism

Donald McRae

A. Introduction

IN THE EARLY 1980S, VALERIE Hughes and I were junior counsel for Canada involved in the preparation and presentation of Canada's pleadings in the Gulf of Maine Case before the International Court of Justice (ICJ).[1] In the following years we were co-counsel for Canada in two arbitrations between Canada and France: the Case Concerning Filleting in the Gulf of St. Lawrence[2] and the dispute over the maritime boundary between Canada and France over the islands of St. Pierre and Miquelon.[3] From these beginnings in dispute settlement relating to the law of the sea, Valerie moved on to dispute settlement in the economic area, disputes between Canada and

---

1   *Delimitation of the Maritime Boundary in the Gulf of Maine Area (Canada v United States)*, [1984] ICJ Rep 264 [*Gulf of Maine*].

2   United Nations, "Case Concerning Filleting in the Gulf of St. Lawrence Between Canada and France: Decision of 17 July 1986" (1990) 19 RIAA 296.

3   "Court of Arbitration for the Delimitation of Maritime Areas between Canada and France: Decision in Case Concerning Maritime Areas (St. Pierre and Miquelon)" (1992) 31:5 International Legal Materials 1145.

the United States relating to trade, and heading the Trade Law Bureau (JLT), the legal unit in the Canadian government responsible for trade and investment disputes. From there, she came to head the Secretariat for the World Trade Organization (WTO) Appellate Body and later she became the head of the WTO legal Secretariat, responsible for WTO dispute settlement at the panel level.

This career in dispute settlement, starting with the settlement of disputes by the ICJ and then through international arbitration and moving to WTO dispute settlement, evokes comparisons between dispute settlement in the WTO and dispute settlement in other domains of international law. All are forms of third-party dispute settlement, but while the models of third-party international dispute settlement extant today find their origins in the Hague Peace Conferences of the latter 1890s and the early 1900s, WTO dispute settlement had quite a different origin. This chapter will explore those differences and the implications that they have for the current state of WTO dispute settlement.

B. Origins of WTO Dispute Settlement

THE STORY OF THE EMERGENCE of WTO dispute settlement from the early days of the *General Agreement on Tariffs and Trade* (GATT) has been often told. Rulings were made initially by the chair of the Contracting Parties, then Working Parties were established and then a panel process that ultimately found its way into the WTO.[4] There are several important aspects of this progression of dispute settlement to be recalled.

GATT provided for consultations between parties to resolve differences between them (Article XXII) and reference to the Contracting Parties as a whole if disputes were unresolved (Article XXIII). The process that developed was all about resolving the dispute, through recommendations to the disputing parties or giving a ruling "as appropriate." The practice in appointing panel members was to choose from "government representatives based in Geneva."[5] Panel members were supported by GATT staff members, who put together "common-sense working procedures" for the operation of the panel and worked closely with the panel members. Christina Schroeder has pointed

---

4   Christina Schröder, "Early Dispute Settlement in the GATT" in Gabrielle Marceau, ed, *A History of Law and Lawyers in the GATT/WTO* (Cambridge: Cambridge University Press, 2015) 141.

5   *Ibid* at 146.

out that from the earliest dispute settlement proceedings, "panel members have not usually drafted their reports. The servicing staff has been expected to do that in accordance with instructions given by the panel."[6]

Thus, in the early days of the GATT, dispute settlement was not seen as something distinct from other aspects of the administration of GATT. Specific attention was given to dispute settlement with the creation of a Panel on Complaints whose name was later changed, revealingly, to a Panel on Conciliation.[7] Panels, whose function was to make recommendations to the GATT Council, saw it as important to give losing parties something, again evidencing a conciliation approach.

This was the GATT that Frieder Roessler joined in 1973 where, to his astonishment as a lawyer, he discovered that pragmatism, not legal principle, was the governing ethos.[8] The predominant approach in GATT and in international economic relations more generally was to manage issues, not to reach decisions on the basis of rules. The creation of an Office of Legal Affairs in 1981, which was later to become a Division of Legal Affairs, was in part a result of greater awareness of the role that law should be playing in the work of GATT but also it was in order to provide legal support to panels. This was a reaction to a number of panel reports in the 1980s that were regarded as legally unsound and were not adopted by the GATT Council. By this time, too, more defined procedures for dispute settlement had been developed for the panel process—the 1979 Understanding Regarding Notification, Consultation, Dispute Settlement, and Surveillance.

Thus, by the time of the Uruguay Round of Negotiations that led to the creation of the WTO, there was a well-established dispute settlement process in GATT. It consisted of panels appointed *ad hoc* for each dispute, composed largely from government representatives based in Geneva, that were serviced by GATT staff lawyers. In fact, GATT staff were often the principal source of legal skills because panels would not necessarily have members who were lawyers and certainly not lawyers whose primary skills were in dispute settlement. There had been some attempts to appoint judges to panels, with mixed

---

6   *Ibid* at 147.

7   *Ibid* at 145.

8   Frieder Roessler, "The Role of Law in International Trade Relations and The Establishment of The Legal Affairs Division of the GATT" in Gabrielle Marceau, ed, *A History of Law and Lawyers in the GATT/WTO* (Cambridge: Cambridge University Press, 2015) 161.

results,[9] and the occasional professor with expertise in international trade law. But they did not adapt easily to the GATT model of dispute settlement. Robert Hudec, who had been appointed to several GATT panels, once recounted to the author his battles with panel secretariats because he wanted to draft his own decisions rather than having the drafting done by GATT staff. Of course, being Hudec, he always won!

C. GATT Dispute Settlement and other Processes of International Dispute Settlement

HOW DOES THE ADJUDICATIVE PROCESS developed under GATT compare with other international adjudicative processes? The answer is that apart from both being forms of third-party dispute settlement, the GATT process was remarkably different from other adjudicative processes in origin, in form, and in objectives. In the 1980s, the active models of international adjudication were the ICJ and international arbitration. Both had their origins in the 1899 and 1907 Peace Conferences. The major difference between international arbitration and the ICJ was that the former involved *ad hoc* arbitral tribunals whose members were appointed by agreement of the parties, and the latter was a permanent court whose members, judges, were elected through a process in the United Nations. The Statute of the Permanent Court of Internal Justice, on which the ICJ Statute is substantially based, was drawn up in light of the existing provisions of the 1907 Convention for the Pacific Settlement of Disputes—the source for the Permanent Court of Arbitration—and also of rules established for arbitrations set up since the 1907 Agreement. Article 17 of 1907 Convention provided, "International arbitration has for its object the settlement of disputes between States by Judges of their own choice and on the basis of respect for law."[10] The ICJ Statute provides that

---

9   Ernst-Ulrich Petersmann, "The Establishment of a GATT Office of Legal Affairs and The Limits of "Public Reason" in the GATT/WTO Dispute Settlement System" in Gabrielle Marceau, ed, *A History of Law and Lawyers in the GATT/WTO* (Cambridge: Cambridge University Press, 2015) 192.

10   *International Convention for the Pacific Settlement of International Disputes*, 19 July 1899, Martens Nouveau Recueil des Traites (Ser 2d) 720, 32 Stat 1779, TS No 342, art 37 [*PCID Convention*].

the function of the Court is to decide disputes submitted to it "in accordance with international law."[11]

GATT dispute settlement was not based on the Hague Peace Conferences model of third party dispute settlement where disputes were to be resolved "on the basis of respect for law."[12] It grew organically from a provision in GATT, where disputes were not triggered by a breach of the law but from a belief that benefits expected to be received under the Agreement were being nullified or impaired or that the attainment of the objectives of the Agreement were being impeded. The cause of such a nullification or impairment could be a breach of an obligation under the Agreement, but it could also be something that did not amount to a breach. The focus, then, was on whether benefits had been impaired, not on whether there had been a breach of the agreement. The objective of dispute settlement was to achieve a "satisfactory adjustment of the matter."[13] If that could not be achieved through consultations between the parties, then the matter could go to the Contracting Parties, who would then make recommendations to the parties or "as appropriate" make rulings.

Giving the objectives of dispute settlement under GATT and the role that panels had, it is not surprising that the pool for selection of panelists was government representatives in Geneva. They are the people who would understand the trade issues in dispute and are best-positioned to find a satisfactory resolution of the matter. And when the function of the members of a panel was not primarily or at all legal interpretation, the legal role of a legal secretariat for a panel was enhanced. Frieder Roessler noted that he had attended virtually all panel meetings and had been able to ensure there was consistency between the panels in the way they interpreted the provisions of GATT. In Roessler's view, the role of the legal secretariat was to ensure a "consistent and uniform approach to legal matters."[14]

A consequence of the GATT approach to dispute settlement was that GATT dispute settlement was little known in the broader public international

---

11 *Statute of the International Court of Justice*, 26 June 1945, Can TS 1945 No 7, art 9 [*ICJ Statute*].

12 *PCID Convention*, above note 10.

13 *Marrakesh Agreement Establishing the World Trade Organization*, Annex 2, 15 April 1994, 1869 UNTS 3 at 401, Understanding on Rules and Procedures Governing the Settlement of Disputes, art 4.5 (entered into force 1 January 1995) [*DSU*].

14 Frieder Roessler, "The Role of Law in International Trade Relations and The Establishment of The Legal Affairs Division of the GATT" in Gabrielle Marceau, ed, *A History of Law and Lawyers in the GATT/WTO* (Cambridge: Cambridge University Press, 2015) 168.

law field. The work of John Jackson and Robert Hudec were clear exceptions, but standard texts on public international law simply made no mention of GATT dispute settlement.[15]

D. The Impact of the WTO

THE WTO AGREEMENTS BROUGHT QUITE fundamental changes to the international trading system. They broadened the range of disciplines to include, alongside trade rules, commitments on services and intellectual property. In the area of dispute settlement, the WTO brought into being a form of compulsory dispute settlement and introduced an appellate function into international trade.

The Understanding on Rules and Procedures Governing the Settlement of Disputes (DSU), the constitutional document for dispute settlement in the WTO, created a specific intergovernmental body for the management of WTO disputes, the Dispute Settlement Body (DSB), and streamlined the process for dispute settlement. Time limits for the various stages were included to ensure the efficiency of the proceedings. The process of dispute settlement was more fully articulated, and, in Article 3, some guiding principles for dispute settlement were set out.

A distinctive break from the past, partly linked to the creation of an Appellate Body, was a greater emphasis placed on legality in dispute settlement. In a provision that is frequently cited, DSU Article 3.2 provides:

> The dispute settlement system of the WTO is a central element in providing security and predictability to the multilateral trading system. The Members recognize that it serves to preserve the rights and obligations of Members under the covered agreements, and to clarify the existing provisions of those agreements in accordance with customary rules of interpretation of public international law.

The objective of dispute settlement was still to "secure a positive resolution of a dispute."[16] But such a resolution unless agreed to by the parties had to derive from recommendations or rulings of the DSB that were in

---

15 Donald M McRae, "The Contribution of International Trade Law to the Development of International Law" in *Recueil des cours de l'Académie de La Haye* (Leiden: Brill Academic Publishers, 1996) 99 at 111–19.

16 *DSU*, above note 13, art 3.7.

accordance with the rights and obligations under the covered agreements.[17] And even mutually acceptable solutions were preferably to be "consistent with the covered agreements."[18]

There are indications that the provisions of the DSU were influenced by dispute settlement provisions in international arbitration. DSU Article 8.4 provides that the secretariat is to maintain an "indicative list" of panelists who could be drawn on for disputes.[19] The qualifications of potential panelists are set out in DSU Article 8.1. Further, recourse to dispute settlement is not to be regarded as a contentious act.[20] A similar sentiment is found in the 1907 Convention establishing the Permanent Court of Arbitration (PCA).[21] But, in large part, the DSU was simply an extrapolation and further development of the GATT model.

1) WTO Panels

Notwithstanding the innovations in the DSU and the general modernization of dispute settlement, the process of dispute settlement at the panel level remained essentially unchanged. The focus in the appointment of panelists was again on government representatives.[22] As Joost Pauwelyn said:[23]

> Twenty years after the creation of the WTO, its panelists continue to be predominantly diplomats and ex-diplomats, often without law degrees and mostly with relatively little experience.

DSU Article 8.1 provided that panels were to be composed of:

> well-qualified governmental and/or non-governmental individuals, including persons who have served on or presented a case to a panel, served as a representative of a Member or of a contracting party to GATT

---

17 *Ibid*, art 3.4.

18 *Ibid*, art 3.7.

19 The PCA establishes a list of members of the Court who are available for selection as arbitrators in arbitrations administered by the PCA; *PCID* Convention, above note 10, art 44.

20 *DSU*, above note 13, art 3.10.

21 *Cf PCID Convention*, above note 10, art 3.

22 Of course, the expansion of the WTO agreements to cover services and intellectual property meant an extension in the range of expertise required of potential panelists.

23 Joost Pauwelyn, "The Rule of Law Without the Rule of Lawyers? Why Investment Arbitrators Are from Mars, Trade Adjudicators from Venus" (2015) 109:4 *American Journal of International Law* 763.

1947 or as a representative to the Council or Committee of any covered agreement or its predecessor agreement, or in the Secretariat, taught or published on international trade law or policy, or served as a senior trade policy official of a Member.

The legal component of these qualifications related to those who had taught or published on international trade law and potentially those who had presented a case to a WTO panel. This did result in a number of professors of international trade law being appointed to panels, but it did not change the primary focus of appointing government representatives to panels. However, with the new focus on legality in the WTO, government representatives increasingly included those with legal skills. Missions in Geneva would include individuals who were legally trained, and these individuals, as government representatives, would get appointed to panels.

The qualifications for panelists set out in the DSU stand in contrast with the qualifications for arbitrators in international arbitration systems and for judges on the ICJ. The 1907 Convention described the individuals to be appointed as members of the PCA to be those with "known competency in questions of international law."[24] The ICJ Statute is more explicit; members of the Court are to "possess the qualifications required in their respective countries for appointment to the highest judicial offices or are jurisconsults of recognized competence in international law."[25]

There was, however, also a turn to legality by governments in the way they approached WTO disputes. Increasingly, they established legal units focusing on trade disputes. While under GATT disputes were often argued before a panel by government trade policy experts, in the WTO governments would have their own lawyers presenting their case or would hire a private law firm of trade lawyers to make their legal arguments to the panel.

Yet, while the way in which governments formulated their disputes and presented them before panels became more legalistic and adversarial under the WTO, the process before panels did not change significantly. Panels would receive written submissions from the parties, there would be two oral hearings, and the panel would then reach its decision and make its recommendations to the DSB.

In practice under the WTO, the basic ethos of panels had not changed. They were composed of individuals, largely government representatives, with

---

24 *PCID Convention*, above note 10, art 44.
25 *ICJ Statute*, above note 11, art 2.

expertise on trade matters or in specific aspects of trade depending on the subject and often with some expertise on trade law.[26] Reto Malacrida has said that usually one member of each panel would be legally qualified.[27] The WTO secretariat provided administrative support and legal expertise in the WTO agreements as well as subject matter expertise. This applied whether the panel was organized by the Legal Affairs Division or by the Rules Division.

And the practice of the division of function between the panel and the secretariat remained as it was from the early days in dispute settlement under GATT. The panel members would make decisions and indicate how the report of the panel was to be drafted but drafting was generally in the hands of the secretariat. While individual panel members may insist on playing a role in drafting, the general practice was that drafting was a secretariat function.

Nor could it have been otherwise. Panel members were selected generally on the basis of their expertise on trade issues. They were not selected because of their expertise in resolving legal issues or in dispute settlement generally. It is true that having participated on a panel is a qualification for a further appointment, but that does not mean that the individual concerned had had experience in drafting a panel report.

The situation in WTO panels may be compared with international arbitration and the ICJ. In international arbitration, whether investor-state arbitration or state-to-state arbitration, the arbitrators are legally trained often with experience as counsel or as judges at the domestic level. They decide on the issues and then draft their own awards. This can be done collectively by all of the arbitrators (generally three or five) or by one arbitrator and then critiqued and finally adopted by all. In the ICJ decisions are made collectively by the judges and then a sub-committee of two judges is responsible, together with the President and the Registry, for drafting the judgment.

Of course, it is not possible to determine whether, under either international arbitration or the ICJ, the work of an individual arbitrator or judge is in fact the work of an assistant or of a junior lawyer. And the secretariats

---

26 In one WTO panel on which I served, the chair, an experienced trade diplomat, explained the composition of our panel as follows: one member, not a lawyer, was appointed because of expertise in safeguards administration, one member (me) was appointed because of expertise in trade law, and the third (him) was appointed because he understood the politics of the situation!

27 Reto Malacrida, "WTO Panel Composition: Searching Far and Wide for Administrators of World Trade Justice" in Gabrielle Marceau, ed, *A History of Law and Lawyers in the GATT/WTO* (Cambridge: Cambridge University Press, 2015) 322.

in both the International Centre for Settlement of Investment Disputes and the PCA will take on a greater or lesser role at the request of a tribunal. But the practice of assigning the drafting to a secretariat is simply not the practice in these bodies. In this regard, the WTO panel process is quite unique.

2) Appellate Body

The inclusion of an appellate process within the WTO brought the potential for quite fundamental change to dispute settlement in international trade. Although controversial in its negotiation, the creation of an Appellate Body epitomized the trend towards legality in the WTO. Appellate review was to be a legal review; appeals from the panel reports were to be "limited to issues of law covered in the panel report and legal interpretations developed by the panel."[28]

Expertise in law was a criterion for appointment to the Appellate Body although it went alongside expertise in "international trade and the subject matter of the covered agreements generally."[29] The working procedures adopted by the Appellate Body result in a process not dissimilar from the panel process, although unlike panels, the Appellate Body has only one oral hearing in each case.

From the outset the Appellate Body was very conscious of its role as the custodian of the WTO agreements. As former Appellate Body Member Georges Abi-Saab has said, "throughout its decade of existence, the Appellate Body's approach to interpretation has been a constant affirmation by the Appellate Body of itself as a judicial organ."[30] This may not have been evident from the outside given the organ's designation as a "body" not a "court" and the fact that its outcome was a report and not a binding decision. Indeed, in the early days of the Appellate Body, former ICJ President, Judge Guillaume wrote that although the Appellate Body was like a judicial institution, "considerations of law will perhaps not be the only factor it will have to take into account."[31]

---

28   *DSU*, above note 13, art 17.6.
29   *DSU*, above note 13, art 17.3.
30   Georges Abi-Saab et al, "The Appellate Body and Treaty Interpretation" in Giorgio Sacerdoti et al, eds, *The WTO at Ten: The Contribution of the Dispute Settlement System* (Cambridge: Cambridge University Press, 2006) 453.
31   Gilbert Guillaume, "The Future of International Judicial Institutions" (1995) 44 *Institute of International and Comparative Law* 860.

Notwithstanding that what the Appellate Body produces is a report to the DSB and not something styled as an award or judgment, the reality is that as a result of the reverse consensus rule in the DSB, Appellate Body rulings are binding and the prediction of Judge Guillaume that the Appellate Body will take considerations other than legal consideration will govern its decision-making has not been borne out.

In fact, apart from its unique function of acting as an appellate authority, the Appellate Body in design resembles much more closely other international courts or tribunals than do WTO panels. The WTO Appellate Body as structured was essentially an international court, whereas WTO panels are quite dissimilar from other forms of international arbitration. And the original Members of the Appellate Body saw their function clearly as that of a court.

Subsequent Members of the Appellate Body no doubt believed that they were a court. Yet a number of considerations suggest that it was not able to function like a court and increasingly did not do so. Indeed, arguably as time went on, the Appellate Body became less like a court and more like a WTO panel.

First, Membership on the Appellate Body was more focused on trade expertise[32] than on demonstrated expertise in law and certainly did not (with some exceptions) reflect the kind of qualifications required for the ICJ, the Law of the Sea Tribunal, or other international courts where the capacity to resolve disputes in accordance with law is the principal focus.[33] Responsibility for the composition of the Appellate Body was with WTO Members and the fact they did not consistently appoint persons whose primary expertise was legal or those with experience in resolving disputes indicated that the Members themselves did not see the functions of Appellate Body Members as substantially different from those of panel members.

Second, while at the beginning the Appellate Body made significant efforts to ensure that the WTO agreements were interpreted consistently, on the basis of the customary rules of interpretation of customary international law as embodied in the *Vienna Convention on the Law of Treaties* (Vienna

---

32   Joost Pauwelyn & Krzysztof Pelc, "Who Guards the 'Guardians of the System'? The Role of the Secretariat in WTO Dispute Settlement" (2022) 116:3 *American Journal of International Law* 534.

33   Statute of the International Tribunal for the Law of the Sea, Article 2(1): "persons enjoying the highest reputation for fairness and integrity and of recognized competence in the field of the law of the sea."

Convention), over time its approach rigidified. Although there is no basis in the DSU for the application of a doctrine of precedent, the Appellate Body insisted on panels applying the law it had articulated in its interpretation of the agreements, creating *de facto* a precedential regime. Alongside this, the Appellate Body became reluctant to change its own position even though that position had been based on a doctrinaire approach to the interpretation of a treaty provision and had been criticized.

Both aspects of rigidity are illustrated by the zeroing saga. Panels that disagreed with the Appellate Body's approach to the interpretation of Article 17.6 of the *Anti-Dumping Agreement* were simply overturned.[34] Yet the fact that panels, the entities with primary expertise on trade issues, were continuing to express their disagreement with the Appellate Body might have been a strong hint to the Appellate Body that its approach should be reconsidered. This was particularly so since the Appellate Body's reasoning in the zeroing cases was fundamentally flawed. But the Appellate Body was not prepared to change its view.

The crux of the zeroing problem was that although the second sentence of Article 17.6.ii contemplates the possibility of there being two permissible meanings of a provision of the Agreement, the Appellate Body focused on the requirement in the first sentence of Article 17.6.ii which provides that provisions are to be interpreted in accordance with the customary rules of interpretation of public international law. Applying the relevant rules of interpretation, the Appellate Body would reach a conclusion about the meaning of a provision and then conclude that since a meaning had been established there was no possibility of two "permissible" meanings. Thus, as long as the Appellate Body saw its role as finding a single meaning, there could never be two permissible meanings of a provision, and thus the second sentence of Article 17.6.ii was essentially otiose.

Perhaps in response to the criticism of its approach, in 2009 the Appellate Body provided some clarification. In *US—Continued Zeroing*,[35] it said that the second sentence in Article 17.6.ii "allows for the possibility that the application of the rules in the Vienna Convention may give rise to an interpreta-

---

34 See *United States—Final Anti-Dumping Measures on Stainless Steel from Mexico (Complaint by Mexico)* (2008), WTO Doc WT/DS344/AB/R (Appellate Body Report), online (pdf): docs.wto.org [perma.cc/S3CR-3V54].

35 *United States—Continued Existence and Application of Zeroing Methodology (Complaint by European Union)* (2009), WTO Doc WT/DS350/AB/R (Appellate Body Report), online (pdf): docs.wto.org [perma.cc/874A-3JU3].

tive range and if it does, an interpretation within that range is permissible." This suggested that the Appellate Body was foreseeing the possibility of the existence of two permissible interpretations. But any such expectation was quickly shut down when the Appellate Body went on to say that since it had found that zeroing was inconsistent with Article 9.3 of the Agreement, it could not find a permissible interpretation that was inconsistent with Article 9.3. In other words, the Appellate Body interprets the first sentence of Article 17.6.ii as a direction to find a single meaning of a provision of the treaty, and this overrides the second sentence requirement to uphold the measure if there are two permissible interpretations.

The justification of the Appellate Body that the second sentence had to be read in light of the first sentence ignores the equally plausible approach that the first sentence has to be read in light of the second sentence. In other words, the search for meaning under the customary rules of interpretation of public international laws (first sentence) read in light of the second sentence was a search to determine whether there were two permissible interpretations, not a search for a single meaning. But, as the Appellate Body made clear in *US—Continuing Zeroing*, a search for a single meaning was precisely what it was doing. Again, notwithstanding the Appellate Body's talk of an "interpretative range," the second sentence of Article 17.6.ii was still rendered otiose.[36]

What this shows is an Appellate Body speaking the language of treaty interpretation but utilizing it in a way that renders a particular provision of the treaty without any effect. The fact that this provision reflected an important compromise in the negotiation of the Uruguay Round agreements regarding a measure of deference to be accorded to national authorities concerned with anti-dumping measures has been essentially ignored. It gives the impression less of an impartial decision-maker applying treaty provisions and more of a body concerned to achieve a preferred outcome in the administration of national anti-dumping regimes.

Third, while at the outset of its existence the Members of the Appellate Body acted as judges in a court and the Secretariat was given no role in deliberations or in the writing of decisions, over time the situation changed, and the Appellate Body Secretariat assumed a greater role. By 2022, in their

---

36 This analysis is more fully articulated in, Donald McRae, "Treaty Interpretation by the WTO Appellate Body: The Conundrum of Article 17(6) of the WTO Antidumping Agreement" in Enzo Cannizzaro, ed, *The Law of Treaties Beyond the Vienna Convention* (Oxford: Oxford University Press, 2011) 164.

seminal article on the role of the WTO Secretariat, Pauwelyn and Pelc[37] treated the Secretariat that administered WTO panels and the Appellate Body Secretariat as identical in their role and function. This meant that the Appellate Body Secretariat was playing a major role in writing issues papers, participating in deliberations, and drafting decisions.

By this time, the role of the Appellate Body Secretariat had come in for criticism not only from those outside the system but also within the Appellate Body as well.[38] Indeed, it seems that the Members of the Appellate Body were divided on the role of the Secretariat, some were publicly critical, even to the point of calling for resignation of its Director,[39] while others were publicly supportive.[40] By now, it appeared that the Appellate Body as a collegial adjudicative organ had lost its way.

The increased role of the Appellate Body Secretariat can be linked to the factors mentioned above. An Appellate Body whose Membership is less focused on the capacity for legal decision-making is more likely to place a heavier reliance on a secretariat with legal expertise and institutional memory. Indeed, the rationale for a legal secretariat in the GATT days was precisely to provide the legal knowledge and expertise that panel members might lack. In other words, the way in which the WTO Members went about making appointments to the Appellate Body was a contributing factor to increasing the role of the Appellate Body Secretariat.

As Pauwelyn and Pelc have pointed out, a Secretariat that is ultimately accountable to the WTO and not to the panel members or to the Members of the Appellate Body, is likely to be concerned about institutional credibility and favour consistency in panel and Appellate Body decisions and thus precedent.[41] Indeed, the intransigence of the Appellate Body in the zeroing cases may well reflect greater Secretariat influence at the Appellate Body level and a lack of sufficient legal expertise among the Members of the Appellate Body to go in a different direction. The interpretative fallacy in the zeroing cases

---

37   Pauwelyn & Pelc, above note 32.

38   Paul Blustein, "China Inc. in the WTO dock, Tales from a System under Fire" (2017) Centre of International Governance Innovation Paper No 158, online (pdf): cigionline. org [perma.cc/4L8H-BBET].

39   Hannah Monicken, "Appellate Body's Future Could Depend on Whether its Director Keeps his Job" (6 December 2019), online: insidetrade.com [perma.cc/4L7F-S8QG].

40   See Peter Van den Bossche, Address (delivered before the Dispute Settlement Body, 28 May 2019), online: [perma.cc/P4RP-PJT2].

41   Pauwelyn & Pelc, above note 32 at 559.

should not have got past adjudicators with expertise in treaty interpretation.[42] But it did enhance the institutional value of consistency.

E. The Distinctive Roles of Panels and the Appellate Body in WTO Dispute Settlement

AFTER THEIR REVIEW OF THE role played by the Secretariat in both panel and Appellate Body decisions, Pauwelyn and Pelc conclude that WTO dispute settlement rather than being a judicial process is more like domestic processes of "administrative review."[43] While it is true that this is what the panel process is and what the Appellate Body had become, it is not clear that this is what was originally intended when the Uruguay Round agreements continued the existing GATT panel process and created a new organ, the Appellate Body.

The negotiators could have replaced GATT panels with an arbitral process where decisions would be made by independent arbitrators appointed because of their independence and expertise in the law of international trade. But they did not do that. They retained a system where panels were constituted by individuals with expertise on trade issues who could make decisions designed to solve trade disputes between WTO Members. And the pool from which panel members would be selected was government officials with experience in trade. Panels had the support of a legal Secretariat that could provide expertise on the interpretation of the agreements and provide institutional memory. As time went on, the Secretariat also brought considerable subject matter expertise to panel deliberations.

This was a perfectly legitimate form of dispute settlement, which continued giving panels the primary role of settling disputes. For GATT "insiders" it was a process with which they were quite familiar. To those coming to GATT dispute settlement for the first time, the process did seem novel, particularly the role of the Secretariat. But in fact, the secretariat was responsive to each panel. It would go as far as the panel would let it. If that meant playing

---

42 In the first MPIA decision, the Article 25 arbitrators rejected the focus of the Appellate Body on the first sentence of Article 317.6.ii and said that the first sentence must be read in the light of both Article 17.6.i and the second sentence of Article 17.6.ii: *Colombia—Anti-Dumping Duties on Frozen Fries from Belgium, Germany and the Netherlands (Complaint by European Union)* (2022) WTO Doc WT/DS591/15 (Report of the Arbitrators) at para 4.12, online (pdf) : docs.wto.org [perma.cc/53FU-LKTJ].

43 Pauwelyn & Pelc, above note 32 at 562.

an active if not predominant role in deliberations, it would do that. However, if the panel wanted to take more control, then it could do so. And panels have continued functioning in that role effectively throughout the WTO.

The panel process can, therefore, be characterized as in the nature of an administrative process more than as an independent arbitral process.[44] The fact that this process was not changed in the Uruguay Round agreements can partly be attributed to the fact that it was understood by the negotiators and it worked but also to the fact that the Uruguay Round had established an Appellate Body. The jurisdiction of the Appellate Body was "limited to issues of law covered in the panel report and legal interpretations developed by the panel." In light of this, there was no need to restructure the panel system so that panel members would all be legally qualified with experience in dispute resolution—an independent arbitral process.

However, the Appellate Body did not become in fact the independent judicial organ that Georges Abi Saab said that the early Members were consistently trying to be. In part, this was a consequence of the system. They were not full-time judges with a considerable tenure, like judges on the ICJ who are appointed for nine years. They were part-time Members with four-year renewable terms. Nor did the WTO Members always appoint persons with the background and expertise that would enable them to be independent arbiters on legal issues in international trade. In these circumstances, it was probably inevitable that the Appellate Body Secretariat would assume a greater role. It became more like the WTO Secretariat that was administering panels. Yet WTO panels had a broader role than the Appellate Body. They were finders of fact and not just making definitive conclusions on issues of law and legal interpretation.

Moreover, as time went on the Members of the Appellate Body clearly did not have a unified view of their role as a judicial organ. They acquiesced in the secretariat increasing their role and becoming more actively involved in decision-making. Yet clearly the Appellate Body was divided on this as some Members spoke publicly against the powers being asserted by the Secretariat.

When the Appellate Body Secretariat plays the same role as panel secretariats, the WTO dispute settlement becomes, as Pauwelyn and Pelc have

---

44 Daniel Bethlehem et al, "The International Trading System—Looking to 2100" in Daniel Bethlehem et al, eds, *The Oxford Handbook of International Trade Law*, 2nd ed (Oxford: Oxford University Press, 2022) 1069.

identified, a form of administrative review. Decisions of panels, heavily influenced by the WTO Secretariat, are being reviewed by a body which is dominated by another branch of the WTO Secretariat. At this point, the necessity for a separate Appellate Body beyond the panel level becomes questionable.

F. Conclusions

WTO DISPUTE SETTLEMENT IS A unique form of international dispute settlement and cannot be readily equated with other dispute settlement forms either in its origin or in the way in which it functions. This is primarily because of the particular nature of the WTO panel process which gives a decision-making role to *ad hoc* panelists with expertise on trade issues but with no necessary legal qualifications or expertise or experience in dispute settlement. This has resulted in the legal secretariat that supports the panel having a central role in panel decision-making. Depending on how much control is exercised by the panel members, the role of the secretariat can extend to being the effective decision-maker in a particular case.

This notwithstanding, WTO panels have functioned effectively throughout the existence of the WTO, and although there has been criticism of the role of the secretariat and some proposals for reform, it is difficult to see how the role of the secretariat can be changed without changing the composition of panels from government trade officials to independent arbitrators. Nor is it clear that this would be a good thing. The credibility and legitimacy of WTO dispute settlement is in part precisely because panels are composed in large part by government trade officials. To change the panel process into an independent arbitral process and reduce the role of the secretariat to a purely administrative one might make the WTO process look more like other international arbitral bodies, but it is not clear what the WTO system would gain.

The Appellate Body is different. The original intent was a body removed from the panel process that could guard against "rogue panels" and reach decisions on issues of law and legal interpretation. The was the mandate of a judicial organ, which is what its early Members tried to make it. And judicial organs by their very nature are independent, impartial, and not dominated by a secretariat. The Appellate Body had the potential for becoming like other international courts and tribunals. But somehow the Appellate Body lost its direction and ended functioning more like a WTO panel than a judicial organ.

The challenge for WTO reform is to decide what kind of Appellate Body is needed. If the original idea of something in the nature of a judicial organ is still appropriate, then the criteria for appointment and term of office of Appellate Body Members has to be adjusted and the role of the Secretariat changed. This requires commitment by the WTO Members to change and a clearer understanding by those appointed as Appellate Body Members of their judicial role. To re-establish an Appellate Body that is no different from the Appellate Body that existed at its demise—simply another version of a panel—would in the end be a somewhat pointless exercise.

CHAPTER 20

Panel and Appellate Body Report Adoption at Any Cost: Is Perfect the Enemy of Good?

Christopher Cochlin, Mallory Felix, and
Alexander Hobbs

A. Introduction

REVERSE CONSENSUS ADOPTION OF DISPUTE settlement reports, which is a
key feature of the Dispute Settlement Understanding ("DSU") of the World
Trade Organization ("WTO"), has been identified, together with the establishment of a standing Appellate Body for appellate review of panel findings,
as a component of the rules-based multilateral system of trade that developed
after World War II. However, on 11 December 2019, after twenty-five years
in operation and 146 appeals heard, the Appellate Body ceased functioning
and the state of WTO dispute settlement was thrown into disarray. While
serious efforts have since been made to preserve the relevance of the settlement
of trade disputes through the WTO's Dispute Settlement Body ("DSB"), the
demise of the Appellate Body can be seen as a real tragedy for both the legitimacy and the future legacy of dispute settlement under the WTO. Whether
the Appellate Body will ever resume its functions, either as currently set out
in the DSU or otherwise, is at best an open question. Much has been written
from Geneva and elsewhere about how this came to be. Much has also been

written in critique of the Appellate Body's performance as well as in defense of the Appellate Body as an adjudicative institution. More recently, a new Multi-Party Interim Appeal Arbitration Arrangement ("MPIA") has been agreed to and is currently in operation for those Members who are voluntary participants.

Against this backdrop, this chapter explores the extent to which reverse-consensus adoption of dispute settlement reports contributed to the current situation. We posit that the Appellate Body likely would still be functioning today but for the reverse-consensus adoption of reports. We further conclude that a serious reassessment—with the benefit of hindsight—of the *General Agreement on Tariffs and Trade* ("GATT") practice of consensus adoption of reports is warranted, and that WTO Members should consider whether a return to that GATT practice (with necessary modifications) could revive WTO dispute settlement and ensure its long-term viability going forward.

Our argument proceeds as follows. In Section B, we identify the key drivers of the negotiated agreement on the reverse-consensus provisions of Articles 16.4 and 17.14 of the DSU. Section C evaluates whether and how any of the objectives behind these provisions were met in the twenty-five years in which the Appellate Body operated. Section D then explores how the absence of these two key DSU provisions might have shaped differently the circumstances and factors that led to the demise of the Appellate Body. Key considerations in this respect include an assessment of: (1) the extent to which the DSU already contemplates, albeit implicitly, that "binding" dispute settlement ultimately (and invariably) requires voluntary WTO Member conduct to achieve compliance; (2) with the benefit of hindsight, the extent to which WTO Members' expectations for binding dispute settlement outcomes and compliance therewith were more aspirational than they were realistic; and (3) whether reverse-consensus adoption of panel and Appellate Body reports has or has not, at bottom, meaningfully advanced the pursuit of certainty and predictability provided by trade rules differently than did the pre-1995 dispute settlement system under the GATT.

B. Key Drivers of ReverseConsensus Adoption of Dispute Settlement Reports under the DSU

1) GATT Dispute Settlement—Key Shortcomings Identified

THE EVENTS LEADING UP TO the Uruguay Round of GATT negotiations are important background for understanding the genesis of the reverseconsensus

provisions of the DSU.[1] The period between the Tokyo Round (1978) negotiations and the ministerial meeting in Punta del Este that launched the
Uruguay Round (1986) was marked by diminishing confidence in the effectiveness and credibility of dispute settlement under the GATT.[2] Before the
time of the Uruguay Round negotiations, the most recent and comprehensive review of dispute settlement provisions had occurred during the Tokyo
Round of negotiations. This review led to incremental contributions to the
GATT's existing dispute settlement process through the adoption of the
1979 "Understanding Regarding Notification, Consultation, Dispute Settlement and Surveillance,"[3] which brought several institutional improvements
to panel procedures, to customary practices, and to transparency in dispute
settlement.[4] Despite these improvements, dispute settlement conduct by certain contracting parties appears to have emerged in the years that followed
that prevented the system from resolving disputes. The conduct in question
involved the "vetoing" of panel establishments and of the adoption of panel
reports under the consensus practice that prevailed at the time and that had
existed since the founding of the GATT.

In a submission to the Negotiating Group on Dispute Settlement on 6
April 1990, the United States identified itself as an early and strong proponent of both appellate review of panel reports as well as automatic adoption
of dispute settlement reports.[5] In its submission, the United States urged the
Group to focus on "two interrelated areas" for the remainder of the negotiations: (1) "procedures to ensure high quality of panel reports," which included
consideration of "appellate review of panel reports" and (2) "procedures to
ensure that panel results are implemented," which included consideration of
new procedures for "adoption of panel reports."[6] The United States then went

---

1   Understanding on Rules and Procedures Governing the Settlement of Disputes, *Mar-
     rakesh Agreement Establishing the World Trade Organization*, Annex 2, 1869 UNTS 401,
     33 ILM 1226 (1994) [DSU].

2   *General Agreement on Tariffs and Trade*, 30 October 1947, 61 Stat A-11, 55 UNTS 194
     [GATT].

3   *General Agreement on Tariffs and Trade*, Understanding Regarding Notification, Con-
     sultation, Dispute Settlement and Surveillance, Basic Instruments and Selected
     Documents, (26th Supp 1980).

4   Andrew Stoler, "The WTO Dispute Settlement Process: Did the Negotiators Get What
     They Wanted?" (2004) 3:1 *World Trade Review* 100.

5   GATT, *Communication from the United States*, GATT Doc MTN.GNG/NG13/W/40
     (1990), online (pdf): docs.wto.org [perma.cc/7SV8-BAH8]. See also Simon Lester's
     contribution to this volume (Chapter 8).

6   *Ibid* at 2.

on to summarize succinctly the key issues at stake from its perspective at that time. After outlining the practice for panel report adoption, the United States described the "problems encountered" in this respect as follows:

> The ability of a losing party to block adoption of a panel report permanently, even when unsupported by other contracting parties, remains a serious impediment to the system.[7]

Having framed the issue as such, the United States lists the proposals made in the Group up to that point in the negotiations to address the problem as well as further "solutions to explore" from the US perspective. The proposals consisted of: (1) automatic adoption of panel reports by the General Council "if, after a specified period, no specific objections to adoption are raised" (which would eliminate the need for affirmative action to effect adoption of reports), (2) automatic adoption of panel reports "unless an appellate review is requested within a specified time" (which would focus the Council's deliberations to addressing implementation time frames alone), (3) adoption of specific panel interpretations annually as part of Council decisions "to clarify any legal obligations that might flow from the adoption of panel findings," and, finally (4) retention of the existing practice of consensus-based adoption of reports "but with an additional procedure to break a stalemate if a losing defendant is the only party blocking that consensus."[8]

As a means of adding emphasis, the United States followed up immediately after this listing with the following statement: "This is the single most difficult issue facing this Negotiating Group."[9] The United States was not alone in its concern relating to panel report adoption, however. For example, in a submission made to the Group only a few months later in follow up to the US submission, Canada framed the panel report adoption issue as follows:

> As the GATT dispute settlement system now operates, governments have been able unilaterally to block adoption of a report which finds against them and then delay implementation indefinitely. It is in the interest of an effective system that a panel report be responded to quickly. At the same time governments have legitimate concerns about changing

---

7   *Ibid* at 7.
8   *Ibid* at 7–8.
9   *Ibid* at 8.

domestic measures as a result of a GATT ruling. Any panel decision must be a reasonable interpretation of the rules.[10]

Canada's proposal for a solution to this issue was an echo of the US proposal of automatic adoption of the panel report "unless one of the parties to the dispute formally notifies the Council of its intention to appeal the report to the Appellate Body."[11] Canada went on to propose that there would be "no formal requirement for Council to adopt a panel report" and further that, if no appeal was made, "the report would be considered accepted and therefore final."[12]

The concerns driving these proposals appear to have crystalized in several high-profile trade disputes that saw panel report adoption blocked.[13] Interestingly, notwithstanding the perception that existed at the time that the system may have become ineffective, dispute settlement under GATT was—by the numbers—overwhelmingly effective in resolving disputes. Empirical studies have found that the GATT dispute settlement procedures resolved 88 percent of the valid or likely valid complaints submitted between 1948 and 1989, as measured by full or partial compliance.[14] And during the period of heightened concern relating to "blocking" conduct (*i.e.*, between the period 1980–89), compliance with dispute settlement outcomes under the GATT stood at 81 percent.[15] Despite evidence supporting an objective view as to the tremendous general success of dispute settlement under the 1979 Understanding, the marked decline in instances of compliance with dispute settlement outcomes is certainly also observable beginning in the 1980s.

Notably, during this period of decline in compliance with (and adoption of) panel reports, a disproportionate number of disputes related to trade in agricultural products. Between the end of the Tokyo Round and the Punta del Este ministerial meeting, twelve of the thirty-six complaints brought to

---

10   GATT, *Communication from Canada*, GATT Doc MTN.GNG/NG13/W/41 (1990) at 3, online (pdf): docs.wto.org [perma.cc/R37W-CBVG].

11   *Ibid.*

12   *Ibid.*

13   Robert Read, "Trade Dispute Settlement Mechanisms: The WTO Dispute Settlement Understanding in the Wake of the GATT" (2005) Lancaster University Management School, Working Paper 2005/012, online (pdf): eprints.lancs.ac.uk [perma.cc/CK79-3YYN].

14   Robert E Hudec, Daniel L M Kennedy, & Mark Sgarbossa "A Statistical Profile of GATT Dispute Settlement Cases: 1948 - 1989" (1993) 2:1 *Minnesota Journal of International Law* 1 [Statistical Profile].

15   *Ibid.*

dispute settlement involved agricultural trade.[16] Of those twelve cases, only three produced an outcome that met the expectations of the complaining party.[17] Many of these disputes concerned the European Economic Community ("EEC") and its Common Agricultural Policy and often pitted the United States against the EEC.[18] Very clearly, both the nature of the disputes and the stakes had increased in terms of importance and political sensitivity during this time.

In recognition of these pervasive issues, the Punta del Este Declaration outlined at a high level the shared objectives of the negotiations on dispute settlement as follows:

> In order to ensure prompt and effective resolution of disputes to the benefit of all contracting parties, negotiations shall aim to improve and strengthen the rules and procedures of the dispute settlement process, while recognizing the contribution that would be made by more effective and enforceable GATT rules and disciplines. Negotiations shall include the development of adequate arrangements for overseeing and monitoring of the procedures that would facilitate compliance with adopted recommendations.[19]

These concerns evolved and were taken up by the Negotiating Group on Dispute Settlement during the WTO Uruguay Round negotiations. Interestingly, in its submission to the Group on 6 April 1990, the United States made clear in a footnote at the very outset of the submission that the issue was not one of large numbers of reports being blocked on adoption but rather an issue relating to the underlying disputes themselves and seemingly the parties at issue:

> The defending party has blocked adoption of a panel report for several years (with no ultimate Council or Committee action) in only six cases. The EC blocked adoption of reports on pasta, citrus, and canned fruit; Canada blocked reports on gold coins and manufactured beef; and the United States blocked adoption of a report on wine.[20]

---

16   Stoler, above note 4 at 100.

17   *Ibid.*

18   *Ibid*; Statistical Profile, above note 14.

19   GATT, *Draft Ministerial Declaration on the Uruguay Round*, GATT Doc MIN(86)/W/19 (1986) at 14, online (pdf): docs.wto.org [perma.cc/9RBA-DKM7].

20   GATT, Communication from the United States, GATT Doc MTN.GNG/NG13/W/40 (1990) at 2, fn 1, online (pdf): docs.wto.org [perma.cc/PX87-HXMA].

And, at the same time, attention had also turned to stakeholder communities seeking better enforcement of intellectual property rights due to a failure on the part of World Intellectual Property Organization (WIPO) to effectively address the issues.[21] The United States was the primary driver of this effort at the Punta del Este ministerial meeting, putting negotiations on intellectual property on the agenda for the Uruguay Round.[22]

By the time the Uruguay Round negotiations were launched, the United States' frustrations with the lack of progress in settling agricultural trade disputes and intellectual property issues under the GATT were well known.[23] The United States Trade Representative at the time had increasingly threatened unilateral trade action under Section 301 of the *Trade Act of 1974*, leading to a concurrent objective by other contracting parties in the Uruguay Round negotiations to prevent any such unilateral US trade action.[24] There appears to have been broad agreement among the GATT's contracting parties, therefore, that dispute settlement was in need of significant improvement.

In an irony that has been lost on no one who has followed the demise of the Appellate Body, it was thus the United States that sought the automatic establishment of panels and the automatic adoption of panel reports. This led to proposals to ensure automaticity through negative consensus adoption of dispute settlement reports, which would prevent losing parties from "blocking" panel reports and ensure that the DSB would authorize retaliation in cases of non-compliance.

As Stoler reports, this US objective was primarily driven by the US agricultural exporting stakeholders who had fared so poorly in GATT dispute settlement outcomes throughout the 1980s and by US stakeholders seeking better enforcement of intellectual property rights.[25] The premise underlying the US negotiating objective appears to have been twofold in this respect: (1) there was a belief that the United States would primarily be on the winning side of disputes; and (2) there was a belief that rights and obligations would be correctly and reasonably interpreted by panels to resolve disputes.[26] In particular, the United States seemed to believe that the odds were low

---

21 Stoler, above note 4 at 102.
22 "Ministerial Declaration on the Uruguay Round," GATT Press Release, GATT Secretariat, Geneva, No 1396, 25 September 1986.
23 Stoler, above note 4 at 102–3.
24 *Ibid.*
25 Stoler, above note 4 at 100–3.
26 Stoler, above note 4 at 113.

that truly problematic treaty interpretations would be arrived at through dispute settlement, such as the findings of the panel *Spain—Measures Concerning Domestic Sale of Soyabean Oil*.[27] Further, if interpretations did arise, the United States believed that a new appellate level of review mechanism (what became the Appellate Body) would correct any such interpretations (rather than be the source of them), with new additional provisions (in the form of Articles 3.2 and 19.2 of the DSU) further ensuring that the dispute settlement system would not add to or diminish the rights and obligations agreed to in the treaty text.[28]

On the other side of the negotiating table, it seems apparent that the EC ultimately agreed to the judicialization of dispute settlement inherent in the adoption of reverse-consensus provisions in the DSU as a means to secure agreement outlawing US unilateral trade action under Section 301 of the *Trade Act of 1974*.[29] This objective is reported as having been shared by all major players during negotiations but with the EC having had particular interest in such an outcome due to the disproportionate number of agricultural disputes it faced.[30]

2) From the GATT 1979 Understanding to the WTO DSU—Uruguay Round Outcomes

As can be seen from the text of the DSU itself, a number of provisions bring automaticity to the dispute settlement process. In terms of panel establishment, Article 6.1 makes clear that a panel is established at the request of the complaining party at the latest by the second DSB meeting at which a request is made "unless at that meeting the DSB decides by consensus not to establish a panel." Additionally, Article 16.4 provides for the adoption of a panel report at the DSB within sixty days after the date of its circulation "unless a party to the dispute formally notifies the DSB of its decision to appeal or the DSB decides by consensus not to adopt the report." Finally, Article 17.14

---

27 *Spain—Measures Concerning Domestic Sale of Soyabean Oil (Complaint by the United States)* (1981), GATT Doc L/5142, online (pdf): docs.wto.org [perma.cc/AAA7-V7RJ]. The US brought this dispute but, due to the Panel's poor legal reasoning, argued against the adoption of the Panel Report for fear that its adoption into GATT jurisprudence would create "bad" GATT law.

28 Stoler, above note 4 at 113.

29 *Ibid.*

30 *Ibid.*

of the DSU provides, in respect of an Appellate Body report, that it is to be adopted by the DSB "unless the DSB decides by consensus not to adopt the Appellate Body report within 30 days following its circulation."

C. How Reverse Consensus Contributed to the Downfall of the Appellate Body

UNDER THE GATT DISPUTE SETTLEMENT system, the contracting parties maintained direct political oversight of dispute settlement panels through their ability to effectively veto any report issued by any panel. By adopting a reverse-consensus system as a result of the Uruguay Round of negotiations, those same contracting parties (now acting as WTO Members) collectively seemed prepared—perhaps naively—to accept that political oversight of dispute settlement in the WTO was no longer required, nor even desired in light of certain abuses that could be made of an effective veto over the establishment of dispute settlement proceedings and over the adoption of reports. In fact, through the adoption of a reverse consensus system, WTO Members arguably had removed political oversight of adjudicated outcomes under the DSB entirely.[31]

As described below, it would appear that the adoption of the reverse-consensus system necessarily redirected any political criticism, which historically had been levied at the disputing parties as between themselves, towards the legitimacy of dispute settlement outcomes and the adjudicators themselves. Indeed, in the absence of a veto over the adoption of dispute settlement reports, one of the only remaining political options for a Member to exercise regarding politically unacceptable panel or Appellate Body report outcomes was to impugn the legitimacy of the adjudicator and the DSB itself.

Paradoxically for the United States in particular, as the proponent of the new reverse consensus approach, these new provisions of the DSU did anything but "ensure that such mechanisms provide for more effective and expeditious resolution of disputes" within the meaning of Section 1101(a) the *1988 Trade Act*. Section 1101(a) outlined the US negotiating objectives for dispute settlement.[32] Instead, the operation of the reverse-consensus system

---

31 Robert McDougall, "Crisis in the WTO: Restoring the WTO Dispute Settlement Function" (2018) CIGI Papers, Working Paper No 194 at 6.

32 *Omnibus Trade and Competitiveness Act of 1988*, 102 USC § 1107 [*Omnibus Trade and Competitiveness Act*].

became a major factor contributing to the collapse of WTO dispute settlement and to the demise of the Appellate Body.

1) Reverse Consensus Shifted Criticism to the DSB

Under the GATT dispute settlement system, consensus-based adoption of panel reports and the consequent extensive direct political oversight of dispute settlement outcomes resulted in the contracting parties focusing disagreements as to outcomes at each other's conduct. Among the earliest examples is *Article XXI - United States Exports Restrictions*, decided in 1949, where Czechoslovakia's request to find certain US export restrictions in violation of US obligations was rejected. It is clear that the adjudicative process itself was not the target of criticism, with no party questioning the legitimacy or strength of the GATT dispute settlement system at that time.[33] Instead, Czechoslovakia levelled its concern at the parties to the GATT at that time:

> It could not consider that the CONTRACTING PARTIES had made a legally valid decision or correct interpretation of the General Agreement. In consequence, his Government would regard itself free to take any steps necessary to protect its national interests.[34]

While this early system of dispute settlement evolved to become a panel process, with panel reports being issued to the disputing parties and the broader collective of contracting parties, the target of political criticism relating to dispute settlement outcomes remained the contracting parties themselves rather than the panels struck to hear disputes. For instance, in *United States—Restrictions on the Importation of Sugar and Sugar-containing Products Applied under the 1955 Waiver and under the Headnote to the Schedule of Tariff Concessions*, the discussion on whether to adopt the panel report centered around related negotiations rather than the findings of the panel. In the discussions, both the United States and Canada criticized the EC decision to veto adoption of the panel report. In reply to this criticism, the EC spoke to the impact that the adoption of the report would have on its relationship with other parties and the negotiation of further trade concessions. In fact, rather than impugning the dispute settlement process itself, the EC expressly acknowledged its

---

33 GATT, *Summary Record of the Twenty-Second Meeting*, GATT Doc GATT/CP.3/SR.22 (1949) online (pdf): docs.wto.org [perma.cc/DV9T-EP85].

34 *Ibid.*

obligation to strengthen dispute settlement under the GATT.[35] A summary reporting of the EC's position (as expressed by the EC ambassador) on why it could not allow the adoption of the panel report puts it this way:

> In doing so he was not escaping from his stated moral obligation to strengthen the dispute settlement system, but simply allowing the negotiations to assume their full and significant potential, without prejudging on their outcome nor privileging one partner, in this case the United States, to the detriment of others.[36]

In contrast to the above, the reverse-consensus approach under the DSU inexorably led to Member criticism of the dispute settlement system itself. Indeed, according to a database of statements made at the DSB compiled by Terry Stewart, between 1997 and 2017, at least twenty Members have levied criticism pertaining to the legitimacy of at least sixty-two dispute settlement reports.[37] In addition to the United States, other WTO Members who have questioned the legitimacy of findings adopted by the DSB—or of the DSB itself—include the EC (now the European Union), Canada, Japan, Brazil, India, Mexico, Argentina, and Australia among many others. Together, these states were heretofore responsible for the vast majority of Member activity under the WTO's dispute settlement system.[38]

And Member criticism towards the dispute settlement system began almost immediately after the shift to reverse-consensus adoption of reports. By 1997, just two years after the establishment of the WTO, Member criticism began already to identify panels and the Appellate Body, claiming that these adjudicating bodies were reading into the agreements terms that Members had not agreed to. For instance, regarding *US—Wool Shirts and Blouses*, Costa Rica stated as follows:

> The observations of the panel and the Appellate Body had diverged from past practice and had modified the balance of rights and obligations which they claimed to be seeking to protect.[39]

---

35 GATT, *Minutes of Meeting*, GATT Doc C/M/241 (1990), online (pdf): docs.wto.org [perma.cc/Z5UL-6AKD].

36 *Ibid.*

37 Terence P Stewart, "The Broken Multilateral Trade Dispute System" (2018) Asia Society Policy Institute [*Broken Multilateral Trade Dispute System*].

38 *Ibid*; WTO, "Disputes by Member" (last visited 30 April 2024), online: wto.org [perma. cc/742U-NMBC].

39 *Ibid* at 6.

Similarly, in response to panel findings in *Mexico—Measures Affecting Telecommunications Services*, Mexico stated as follows:

> In finding that the limitations at issue had no such effect, the Panel imposed on Mexico obligations that Mexico had not undertaken during the negotiations . . . It must be worrying for other Members that any panel should interpret in a Member's Schedule commitments that had not been offered.[40]

This criticism grew to encompass the very functioning of the DSB system. The United States illustrates this well in the context of its statements relating to the findings and rulings in *US—Zeroing (EC)*:

> In conclusion, we would note the observation on the Appellate Body Report from a supporter of the outcome in the dispute: 'This ruling is an important development in the WTO jurisprudence. In a sense, the AB made a huge contribution to free trade, which could not be made by negotiation alone.' It is troubling that even supporters of the outcome in this dispute thus perceive that it did not result from the negotiated text of the agreement, nor could it be expected to result from subsequent negotiation among the Members. The perception that the dispute settlement system is operating so as to add to or diminish rights and obligations actually agreed to by Members, notwithstanding DSU Articles 3.2 and 19.2, is highly corrosive to the credibility that the dispute settlement system has accumulated over the past 11 years.[41]

Notably, while the United States today certainly is viewed as the principal architect of the demise of the Appellate Body, and therefore of WTO dispute settlement as envisaged under the DSU, the above-noted statements critiquing the legitimacy of the system under the DSU show that the United States was not alone in its concerns and that appellate review brought with it new—and ultimately fatal—problems that could not have been foreseen by the proponents who sought an "increase in the quality" of reports and findings as outlined above.

---

40   *Ibid* at i.

41   *Ibid* at 3, citing *United States—Laws, Regulations and Methodology for Calculating Dumping Margins (Zeroing) (Complaint by the European Communities)* (2006), WTO Doc WT/DS294/16 at 29 (Communication from the United States), online (pdf): docs. wto.org [perma.cc/6L2R-YSNA].

2) Lack of Oversight as a Key Concern

There is a clear record confirming that the current predicament is traceable to issues identified by the United States as far back as 2000 concerning the Appellate Body. The issues were aired systematically by the United States beginning at WTO DSB meetings in 2016[42] and were most recently summarized in a scathing critique written in 2020 under then-United States Trade Representative, Ambassador Robert Lighthizer.[43]

Included in these historic critiques noted by the United States was a claim that the Members understood that they were only to resort to using the Appellate Body in the case that a panel had made an egregious error within that panel's report.[44] In fact, according to Ambassador Lighthizer, this was a predicate element to Members' agreement to the reverse consensus system in the first place.[45] However, as further posited by the United States, Members' unwillingness to come together to prevent the adoption of such reports also enabled the Appellate Body to expand the scope of issues that it would review on appeal beyond that which was originally contemplated in the DSU.[46] As a practical matter, in order for Members to prevent the passage of these reports, as Ambassador Lighthizer suggested they should,[47] every WTO Member would have had to agree on the non-adoption of any given panel or Appellate Body report as a result of the reverse-consensus approach adopted in the DSU; a highly unlikely outcome to say the least considering that at least one Member would directly benefit from the adoption of the report.

These and other positions outlined by the United States were reflected in the United States' refusal to appoint new Members of the Appellate Body after it blocked the re-appointment of Mr. Chang in 2016. Then, in November of 2018, Australia, Canada, China, Iceland, India, South Korea, Mexico, New Zealand, Norway, Singapore, and Switzerland published a proposal on Appellate Body reform. While these WTO Members stated that the reason

---

42   See for instance WTO Dispute Settlement Body, *Statement by the United States at the Meeting of the WTO Dispute Settlement Body* (23 May 2016), online (pdf): wto.org [perma.cc/Q6CV-RFXQ].

43   USTR, *Report on the Appellate Body of the World Trade Organization*, (Washington, DC: Office of the United States Trade Representative, 2020), online (pdf): ustr.gov [perma. cc/JHU7-JJB9].

44   *Ibid* at 120.

45   *Ibid* at 120.

46   *Ibid* at 120.

47   *Ibid* at 120.

for their proposed reforms was to break the deadlock over the appointment of Appellate Body Members (i.e., their reforms were in *response* to the United States' historic criticism), the suggested reforms were consistent with or directly reflected criticisms that multiple WTO Members had made over the prior twenty years, including:

- Putting in place new rules for outgoing Appellate Body Members which make clear which proceedings they may continue to adjudicate on expiry of their term;
- Ensuring that appeal proceedings are finished on time in line with the 90-day timeframe set out in the DSU, unless the parties in the dispute agree otherwise;
- Clarifying that the legal issues that are subject to appeal by the Appellate Body do not include the meaning of domestic legislation;
- Indicating that the Appellate Body should only address issues necessary to resolve the dispute;
- Introducing annual meetings between WTO Members and the Appellate Body to discuss in an open way systemic issues or trends in jurisprudence.[48]

Notably, this list of proposed reforms did not include any mechanism for additional political oversight. Unsurprisingly, therefore, the United States rejected the proposals as not going far enough to address core concerns that it had with the Appellate Body. In the words of the United States:

> Rather than seeking to make revisions to the text of the Dispute Settlement Understanding to permit what is now prohibited, the United States believes it is necessary for Members to engage in a deeper discussion of the concerns raised, to consider why the Appellate Body has felt free to depart from what WTO Members agreed to, and to discuss how best to ensure that the system adheres to WTO rules as written.[49]

Importantly here, and as seen through the statements of other WTO Members noted above, the reverse-consensus approach under the DSU unwittingly allowed the Appellate Body scope for judicial action that quickly made

---

48   European Commission, Press Release, "WTO reform: EU Proposes Way Forward on the Functioning of the Appellate Body" (26 November 2018), online: europa.eu [perma.cc/GYX5-72P8] [*WTO Reform*].

49   US Mission to International Organizations in Geneva, "Statements by the United States at the February 25, 2019, DSB Meeting" (25 February 2019), online (pdf): geneva.usmission.gov [perma.cc/W4JF-Z4TN].

apparent the consequence of eliminating consensus-based adoption under the GATT: direct political oversight of dispute settlement outcomes was lost. Indeed, the reverse-consensus approach under the DSU was a necessary precondition to the adoption of Appellate Body reports that the United States and other Members considered legally and/or politically unacceptable.

3) Member's Current Attempts to Remedy the Appellate Body Crisis Raise Questions as to the Utility of Reverse Consensus Adoption of Reports

With the demise of the Appellate Body, several WTO Members turned to adopt the Multi-Party Interim Appeal Arbitration Arrangement ("MPIA"). Under the MPIA, participating Members have agreed to bring all appeals of panel reports to arbitration in accordance with Article 25 of the DSU as a type of alternative appeal process.[50] The decision of Members on whether to use the MPIA system rather than to appeal panel decisions "into the void" raises important questions for the future of the WTO dispute settlement system and the future utility and legitimacy of a reverse consensus approach to dispute settlement report adoption.

First, despite many Members claiming that the United States has acted unilaterally to dismantle the Appellate Body against their wishes, several WTO Members have used a non-functioning Appellate Body as a *de facto* "veto" tool for political oversight going forward. Rather than engaging DSU Article 25 dispute settlement either on an *ad hoc* basis or under the MPIA, these Members have opted to essentially block panel reports, as needed, much like the practice was under the GATT dispute settlement system. In fact, at the time of writing, there had already been twenty disputes where a Member has appealed a panel report "into the void."[51] Members who have done so include India, Russia, the United States, Brazil, South Korea, Pakistan, and Indonesia. All of these Members have previously noted their displeasure with, or have directly impugned, the WTO DSB system in their prior statements.[52] In other words, this practice in itself marks a return to direct

---

50 WTO, *MPIA Pursuant to Article 25 of the DSU*, WTO Doc JOB/DSB/1/Add.12 (2020), online (pdf): worldtradelaw.net [perma.cc/AD3L-HSBE].

51 Peter Ungphakorn, "Technical Note: Appeals 'Into the Void' in WTO Dispute Settlement" (19 September 2023), online (blog): tradebetablog.wordpress.com [perma. cc/9LSM-A2KE].

52 *Ibid*, see Section 2(i).

political oversight and consensus-based adoption of panel reports at least on a *de facto* basis.

Second, at the time of writing, there had been two reports issued under Article 25 of the DSU. One dispute was pursuant to the provisions of the MPIA, and the other used procedures very similar to those outlined in the MPIA: (1) *Colombia—Anti-Dumping Duties on Frozen Fries from Belgium, Germany and the Netherlands* and (2) *Turkey—Certain Measures concerning the Production, Importation and Marketing of Pharmaceutical Products*. The difference in content between these two DSU Article 25 reports and what had become a "typical" panel or Appellate Body report is striking to even the most casual observer: these DSU Article 25 reports are far more focused and concise, with page lengths measuring thirty-nine pages and fifty pages, respectively.[53] It is doubtful that the separate MPIA process would have been devised if not for demise of the Appellate Body. It will be interesting, therefore, to observe how MPIA reports continue to develop and evolve going forward and how the MPIA members view their role.

D. An Appellate Body with Consensus-Based Adoption of Reports?

AS CAN BE SEEN FROM the above review of the drivers of the reverse-consensus approach under the DSU and of what came of over twenty-five years of reverse-consensus adoption of panel and Appellate Body reports, it may be argued that the inflexibility inherent in the reverse-consensus approach was a fundamental factor contributing to the demise of the Appellate Body.

To be clear, this is not to say that the position of the United States on Appellate Body Member appointments was not the most obvious and proximate cause. Very clearly the United States effected a desired outcome here, and very clearly also the United States does not contend otherwise. The collective failure by the WTO Membership to meaningfully discuss and address fundamental issues of political oversight and legitimacy concerning dispute

---

53 Arbitration under Article 25 of the DSU, *Turkey—Certain Measures Concerning the Production, Importations and Marketing of Pharmaceutical Products (Complaint by the European Union)* (2022), WTO Doc WT/DS583/ARB25 (Article 25 Arbitration Award), online (pdf): docs.wto.org [perma.cc/4794-MTB3]; Arbitration under Article 25 of the DSU, *Colombia—Anti-Dumping Duties on Frozen Fries from Belgium, Germany and the Netherlands (Complaint by European Union)* (2022), WTO Doc WT/DS591/ARB25 (Article 25 Arbitration Award), online (pdf): docs.wto.org [perma.cc/XJ4F-CW6B].

settlement outcomes that were identified by the United States, as the Member with both the largest economy and therefore, arguably, the most at stake in a properly functioning system, was instead to ignore the immediate practical reality in favour of legal, diplomatic, political, and/or academic finger-pointing and hand wringing. None of the debate concerning the non-functioning of the Appellate Body to date, nor the adoption of the MPIA, points to any potential path back towards broadly backed multilateral dispute settlement at the WTO.[54]

It should come as no surprise that the adoption of the reverse-consensus rule in Articles 16.4 and 17.14 of the DSU runs counter to the legitimization of the panel and Appellate Body reports and their outcomes. As John Jackson has explained in the context of the decision-making practice of the WTO Membership outside of the DSU: "The [consensus] rule forces the membership to achieve as wide an acceptance of new measures as possible, thus lending political legitimacy to measures that are finally adopted."[55] At least one major WTO Member—the United States—no longer sees political legitimacy in the reports of an Appellate Body whose findings were rendered unchallengeable and irremediable due to the near-total paralysis of parallel ongoing negotiating activity since the launch of the Doha Round. This, at a minimum, can now be readily acknowledged. As noted above, however, the United States has not been alone in recognizing the lack of political legitimacy underlying problematic panel and Appellate Body reports.

What does come as a surprise, however, is how such a fundamental exception to the otherwise long-standing (*de facto*) general rule of consensus-based decision-making across the WTO was ultimately agreed to.

Surprising, in particular, and with the benefit of hindsight, is how easily Articles 16.4 and 17.14 of the DSU overrode any concerns regarding the serious implications for political legitimacy of DSB outcomes. The threat of US unilateral trade action under Section 301 appeared to have been so serious as to prevail over a core tenet of GATT practice that had existed since 1947. Also a surprise, given how and why the demise of the Appellate Body was brought about, is that the United States had been the original lead proponent of reverse-consensus adoption of reports under the DSU. In this respect, Andrew Stoler has remarked as follows more than a decade ago

---

54 On the most recent dispute settlement reform discussions, see Marco Tulio Molina Tejeda's contribution to this volume (Chapter 28).

55 W Guan, "Consensus Yet Not Consented: A Critique of the WTO Decision-Making by Consensus" (2014) 17:1 *Journal of International Economic Law* 77 at fn 80.

already: "'Automaticity' was probably the single most important objective of the US team in the original DSU negotiations. United States negotiators got what they wanted, but they don't want it any longer."[56]

As can be seen from the review in Section C, above, for the United States, the underlying rationale and motivation appear fundamentally rooted in concerns relating to the legitimacy of the substantive outcomes of Appellate Body reports.[57]

The question arises, therefore, as to whether the same outcome would have occurred if instead panel and Appellate Body reports were adopted by the DSB by consensus. In the view of the authors, the answer is a clear "no." What possible motivation would the United States have had to effect the full *de facto* decommissioning of the Appellate Body if the adoption of problematic reports could simply have been legitimately vetoed? As noted above, non-adoption of panel reports before 1995 under the GATT dispute settlement system was relatively limited and only occurred by and large in the most politically sensitive of cases regarding measures that ultimately were the subject of negotiations in any event. In addition, how might the conduct of the Appellate Body Members and staff have been impacted by the prospect of non-adoption of reports? Consider, by way of illustration, the two reports issued to date under the MPIA and similar procedures. These reports, as discussed, show a seemingly remarkable change in direction away from all-encompassing and comprehensive reviews of claims with extraordinarily lengthy and complex reasoning (often also questionable in terms of substantive treaty interpretation and analysis) characterized by focused adherence to past findings. The two reports indicate a move towards findings that are more concise in nature and limited in scope to addressing only those issues needed to resolve a dispute. And it is no coincidence that this seemingly new approach to appellate level reports is being taken only in the aftermath of the Appellate Body's demise.

To the authors, it is hard to imagine any Code of Conduct or other initiative relating to decision-making or dispute settlement procedures that

---

56 Andrew Stoler, "Addressing 21st Century 'WTO-plus' Issues in the Multilateral Trading System" in Ricardo Meléndez-Ortiz, Christophe Bellmann, & Miguel Rodriguez Mendoza, eds, *The Future and the WTO: Confronting the Challenges. A Collection of Short Essays* (Geneva: ICTSD, 2012) at 115.

57 See also USTR, *Report on the Appellate Body of the World Trade Organization*, (Washington, DC: Office of the United States Trade Representative, 2020), online (pdf): ustr. gov [perma.cc/JHU7-JJB9] at B. 2.

would or could guarantee such an approach. Panelists and other appellate level adjudicators must remain free from any outside influence to decide a matter in the way they deem appropriate. The quality of the decision rendered should speak for itself, and the adoption of reports with the highest quality of reasoning would be expected to become the trend going forward, even with consensus-based adoption of reports or other procedures such as automaticity of rulings in the case of the MPIA. In all cases, the reports would stand on their own analytical quality even if, in some instances, practical political circumstances relating to the nature of the underlying challenge that was brought did not allow for the adoption of such a high-quality report.

Moreover, one can consider the benefits of consensus adoption of dispute settlement reports that were abandoned in the move to reverse consensus under the DSU. Specifically, the new reality in which the WTO dispute settlement system finds itself today makes clear that there were benefits to the GATT dispute settlement system of consensus-based adoption of panel reports, including: (1) unadopted reports still serve an important role in clarifying rules by providing interpretations and findings (factual or otherwise) that could inform potential immediate attempts that WTO Members could make to resolve a dispute through ongoing consultations or any later bilateral or broader-reaching negotiations on new rules; (2) well-reasoned and persuasive findings, even where panelists or Appellate Body Members expect that a report may not get adopted due to underlying political sensitivities relating to the subject matter of the dispute itself, will remain persuasive in other contexts (Member discussion and debate at the DSB; consideration by future negotiating groups; driver of potential future Member policy changes regarding the measures at issue) resulting in a strong incentive for panelists and Appellate Body Members to provide the best possible findings and the highest quality reasoning in their reports; and (3) WTO Members would become more disciplined and circumspect in what they choose to challenge, since they would no longer operate under any expectation (delusion?) that an adopted panel or Appellate Body report would resolve trade disputes of increasing political sensitivity in areas where negotiations otherwise failed to produce an agreed solution.

On the first two benefits noted above, it would appear self-evident that for any report to have any value at all, even in unadopted form, it would need to be well-reasoned and persuasive such that the conclusions arrived at were beyond (or nearly beyond) any real reproach. Under a consensus-based adoption of reports, the authors submit that adjudicators would have a natural incentive to ensure adoption of their report by issuing the most carefully crafted and best-reasoned findings possible that would not, at the same time, overstep the scope of issues needed to be addressed to resolve the dispute or venture into policy-driven outcomes (inadvertently or otherwise). However, it is difficult to see such incentives existing under a reverse-consensus system where adjudicators know that they provide, *de facto*, the last word on any matter in dispute when there is little-to-no prospect of any "legislative" activity by the Membership through further negotiating rounds.[58]

On the third benefit to consensus-based adoption of reports noted above, it is arguable that all major users of WTO dispute settlement themselves, including the United States, have contributed to the downfall of the Appellate Body by bringing more and increasingly politically sensitive measures to dispute settlement. By all appearances, Article 3.7 of the DSU has gone by the wayside; this provision, which calls for the exercise of restraint by Members in the type of issues they choose to bring to dispute settlement, seemingly was of little relevance and of no practical application under the reserve-consensus approach of Articles 16.4 and 17.14.

In this context, it is interesting to consider whether a return to consensus-based adoption of dispute settlement reports could contribute to an effort to get multilateral trade negotiations at the WTO back on track rather than seeing such negotiating efforts further splintering into a growing multiplicity of bilateral and regional agreements. Afterall, some issues of universal concern and reach are simply better addressed in a multilateral forum. These include climate change-related rules and other truly "horizontal" issues that impact many if not all countries in one way or another. It is far too easy to overplay the potential influence that the return to consensus-based dispute could have on the prospects of future multilateral trade negotiations. However, one thing seems certain: without a "fix" to the loss of political legitimacy underlying the DSB, the prospects of such future negotiations appear to be *nil*. Not even joint proposals advanced by Chile and the United States itself on dispute settlement reform more than twenty years ago at the time of writing would appear to address the current state of affairs.[59]

---

58   See Nicolas Lamp, "Arrested Norm Development: The Failure of Legislative-Judicial Dialogue in the WTO" *Leiden Journal of International Law* (forthcoming).

59   WTO, *Contribution by Chile and the United States*, WTO Doc TN/DS/W/28 (2002), online (pdf): docs.wto.org [perma.cc/8CUT-X87U]; WTO, *Textual Contribution by Chile and the United States*, WTO Doc TN/DS/W/52 (2003), online (pdf): docs.wto.org [perma.cc/LQG4-R5N7].

It seems certainly plausible that consensus-based adoption of reports could form part of a path toward the rebuilding of political legitimacy underpinning WTO dispute settlement, particularly if such a proposal were coupled with new rules that would condition the exercise of any veto by a losing Member. By way of example, a losing Member could be required to set out in detail why and how that Member sees that a panel or the Appellate Body had overstepped its authority and thereby contribute to ongoing consideration and discussion of panel and Appellate Body judicial action to the benefit of all, both WTO Members and adjudicating bodies alike. The detailed reasons given by a losing Member vetoing adoption of a report would not only inform future negotiations on the issue in dispute, they would also inform future adjudicators why any given report may or may not have been adopted. At the same time, high-quality unadopted panel and Appellate Body reports would continue to help shape future negotiations and dispute settlement discussions.

With such new rules in place, any growth in the number of unadopted reports could also help catalyze the need for further negotiating rounds and new substantive rules. While no doubt, there could be frustration with a perceived lack of compliance with already-negotiated rules, the political legitimacy of the dispute settlement system would remain intact with the prospect of more disciplined and well-reasoned reports being issued, all of which deserving of adoption irrespective of whether or not they ultimately are adopted. And there would no longer be any basis for Members to think that they could litigate an outcome that they failed to secure through negotiation. In this way, consensus adoption of reports also would serve to discipline Members on the types of disputes they bring and the motives for bringing them. Finally, the very prospect of reciprocity on report adoption arguably would discipline Member decisions on whether to veto adoption. If a Member seeks compliance on a range of issues they have sought to resolve through dispute settlement proceedings, it will be in that Member's own interest to allow the adoption of reports and to bring its own measures into compliance with its obligations as interpreted and applied in those reports. As noted further above, to the extent that the United States sought resolution of agricultural export disputes against the EU under the GATT dispute settlement system and the EU sought to avoid compliance through the blocking of report adoption, the EU could then not expect the United States to adopt reports in disputes where the EU was successful. Invariably, the dynamic returns one to negotiating outcomes, just as was the case in the Uruguay Round outcomes on agricultural goods.

With all of the above having been said, there are clear downsides to consensus-based adoption of dispute settlement reports. Obviously, these include Members' potential lack of willingness to engage a dispute settlement system that allows the respondent party to simply veto a DSB report that it finds unacceptable or the adoption of reports that seek only to placate both parties to a dispute rather than to substantially adjudicate that dispute. However, with the benefit of hindsight, we now know that reverse-consensus adoption of dispute settlement reports is a clear contributor to the failure of the system as a whole and has led to a fulsome airing of criticism that put the political legitimacy of multilateral dispute settlement at the WTO in question. In this context, it would seem incontrovertible that consensus-based adoption of reports would be—on balance—a better outcome where the WTO dispute settlement system with appeals to the Appellate Body continued at the very least to function. And this is not to say that all automaticity provisions in the DSU agreed to during the Uruguay Round impugn the political legitimacy of the dispute settlement outcomes at the WTO. The system certainly has benefitted from automaticity on key procedural steps, such as most importantly the establishment of a panel under Article 6.1 and the right to appeal under Articles 16.4 and 17.4 of the DSU.

Fundamentally, the question becomes one of understanding the extent to which the perfecting of the GATT dispute settlement system through reverse-consensus rules adopted in the DSU became the true enemy of a system that—when benchmarked to the current status quo—might already have been "good enough."

Part II:

Renewal—New Directions in Trade Dispute Settlement

The Turn to FTA Dispute Settlement

CHAPTER 21

The Qualified Success of State-to-State Dispute Settlement under USMCA To Date

J. Anthony VanDuzer

A. Introduction

STATE-TO-STATE DISPUTE SETTLEMENT UNDER THE *North American Free Trade Agreement* (NAFTA)[1] was a notable failure. There were only three panel reports between 1 January 1994 when NAFTA came into force and 30 June 2020 when it was replaced by the *United States-Canada-Mexico Agreement* (USMCA).[2] The last panel report was made public in 2001. Despite

---

1   *North American Free Trade Agreement*, 17 December 1992, Can TS 1994 No 2 (Canada, Mexico, and US) [*NAFTA*].

2   *Protocol Replacing the North American Free Trade Agreement with the Agreement between Canada, the United States of America, and the United Mexican States*, 30 November 2018, Can TS 2020 No 5 [*Protocol Replacing NAFTA*]; *Canada-United States-Mexico Agreement as amended by Protocol of Amendment to the Agreement*

its apparent inutility, the United States sought to weaken state-to-state dispute settlement even more in the negotiations that led to USMCA. In the end, however, a more robust and transparent procedure was agreed to that addressed the fundamental problems with NAFTA.

USMCA state-to-state dispute settlement is already being actively used. As of July 2024, less than four years since the USMCA came into force, the parties have initiated five panel proceedings leading to four final panel reports. Unlike NAFTA, panel proceedings under the USMCA have been completed in a timely way. New features in the USMCA, like panels of three instead of five and non-governmental party submissions, have been frequently used. While panel reports have not always resolved the underlying problem giving rise to the dispute, the willingness of the parties, especially the United States, to resort to USMCA dispute settlement provides an encouraging signal regarding its perceived utility. This chapter takes stock of the USMCA dispute settlement system and the disputes to date with a view to explaining to what extent the panel process has been successful so far and some of the challenges it faces.[3]

B. A Brief History of North American State-to-State Dispute Settlement

THE *CANADA-UNITED STATES FREE TRADE Agreement* (CUSFTA) came into force in 1989, introducing a state-to-state process for the resolution of disputes regarding the interpretation and application of the agreement.[4] The process under CUSFTA Chapter 18 began with consultations regarding an actual or proposed measure of one party state that the other considered to affect the operation of the agreement. If a dispute could not be resolved through consultations, one party could request a determination by a panel of five experts appointed by the parties regarding whether the measure was

---

between Canada, the United States of America, and the United Mexican States, 10 December 2019, Can TS 2020 No 6 [*Protocol of Amendment*] [collectively *USMCA*].

3   This chapter does not address other dispute settlement procedures in the USMCA such as the facility specific rapid response mechanism for labour issues, investor-state dispute settlement, or the review of trade remedies determinations. Some of these procedures are addressed in other chapters in this volume.

4   *Canada-United States Free Trade Agreement*, 22 December 1987, Can TS 1989 No 3 (entered into force January 1, 1989) [*CUSFTA*].

or would be inconsistent CUSFTA obligations.[5] In the five years before the CUSFTA was superseded by NAFTA, the full panel process was used five times and worked remarkably quickly. All CUSFTA panels were appointed promptly and produced their reports within four to nine months of their establishment.[6]

In creating a state-to-state dispute settlement system for NAFTA, Chapter 18 was the model followed even though the CUSFTA process had been criticized[7] and the United States, which had lost three of five cases, was unhappy with it.[8] The parties' experience under NAFTA Chapter 20, however, was quite different. As noted, only three disputes resulted in panel reports over twenty-six years.[9]

The critical problem under NAFTA Chapter 20 was the appointment of panels. The appointment process under NAFTA provided that, where consultations failed to resolve the dispute within a certain period

---

5   *Ibid*, art 1807(2)–(5). Panels could also determine if a measure caused nullification or impairment as defined in art 2011 even where no violation of the treaty was alleged. Nullification or impairment can also be the basis for a complaint under the USMCA (see *USMCA* above, note 2, arts 31.2(c) and 31.7(2)).

6   Patrick FJ Macrory, "Chapters 19 and 20 of NAFTA: An Overview and Analysis of NAFTA Dispute Settlement" in Kevin C Kennedy, ed, *The First Decade of NAFTA: The Future of Free Trade in North America* (Ardsley, NY: Transnational, 2004) 473 at 487–92.

7   See, e.g., Joint Working Group on Dispute Settlement of the American Bar Association, Canadian Bar Association, & Barra Mexicana, cited in Sidney Picker Jr, "NAFTA Chapter Twenty—Reflections on Party-to-Party Dispute Resolution" (1997) 14:2 *Arizona Journal of International & Comparative Law* 465 at 475.

8   David Gantz, "Addressing Dispute Resolution Institutions in a NAFTA Renegotiation" (2018) Mexico Center, Baker Institute for Public Policy at 18, online (pdf): bakerinstitute.org [perma.cc/W4YP-4KAR].

9   *Re Cross-Border Trucking Services (Mexico v US)* (2001), USA-98-2008-01 (Ch 20 Panel), online (pdf): worldtradelaw.net [perma.cc/U69L-LU7J] [*Cross-Border Trucking*]. The other cases were *Re Tariffs Applied by Canada to Certain US-Origin Agricultural Products (US v Canada)* (1996), CDA-95-2008-01 (Ch 20 Panel), online (pdf): worldtradelaw.net [perma.cc/UF7S-4TBR] [*Agricultural Products from US*]; *Re US Safeguard Action Taken on Broom Corn Brooms from Mexico (Mexico v US)* (1998), USA-97-2008-01 (Ch 20 Panel), online (pdf): worldtradelaw.net [perma.cc/7UVB-YT29] [*Brooms from Mexico*]. A fourth case was commenced in 1998, *Cross-Border Bus Services* (USA-98-2008-02), though no panel decision was ever made public (see Rafael Leal-Arcas, "Comparative Analysis of NAFTA's Chapter 20 and the WTO's Dispute Settlement Understanding" (2011) 8:3 *Transnational Dispute Management* 1). Consultations and the other earlier stages of the dispute settlement process were used but there is no reliable estimate of how frequently this was done owing to the non-public nature of the process.

of time, a NAFTA party participating in the consultations could request the establishment of a five-person panel to hear the dispute.[10] Where there were only two disputing parties, they first had to try to agree on a panel chair. If there was no agreement on a chair within fifteen days of the panel request, a disputing party chosen by lot could choose the chair who could not be a citizen of either party. Each party then selected two panelists who were nationals of the other party state.[11] If no selection was made by a party within fifteen days, panelists who were nationals of the other party were to be selected by lot from members of a roster to be agreed to by the parties prior to NAFTA coming into force on 1 January 1994.[12]

Unfortunately, for most of the time that NAFTA was in place, the parties were unable to agree on a roster.[13] Without a roster, there was no way to give effect to the choosing by lot process where a party failed to appoint panelists. A party was entitled to exercise a pre-emptory challenge of any nominee by the other party because they were not on the roster.[14] In effect, the absence of a roster meant that panelists had to be agreed on by the parties. In the three cases under NAFTA where a panel was established, substantial delay in appointing panelists occurred partly as a consequence of pre-emptory challenges.[15] Panel selection in two of the NAFTA cases took six months while in the third it took sixteen and a half months. In at least one case, the failure by a party to choose panelists actually prevented a panel from being established. There had been a long ongoing dispute between Mexico and the United States regarding access to the US market for Mexican sugar. By refusing to appoint panelists, the United States frustrated Mexico's attempts to have a NAFTA panel adjudicate its claim that the United States was not in compliance with

---

10   *NAFTA*, above note 1, art 2008.

11   *Ibid*, art 2011(1)(c).

12   *Ibid*, art 2009(12).

13   J Anthony VanDuzer, "State-to-state Dispute Settlement under the USMCA: Better than NAFTA?" in Alfonso López de la Osa Escribano & James W Skelton Jr, eds, *Essays in Honor of Professor Stephen T Zamora: A Life Between Mexico and the United States* (Houston: Arte Público Press, 2022) 121 at 132–33.

14   *NAFTA*, above note 1, art 2011(3).

15   Debra Steger, "Dispute Settlement under the North American Free Trade Agreement" in Julio Lacarte & Jaime Granados, eds, *Intergovernmental Trade Dispute Settlement: Multi-Lateral and Regional Approaches* (London: Cameron May, 2004) 287, citing interviews with Canadian and US government officials.

its obligations.[16] Following this stalemate, the panel process was, effectively, abandoned by the parties.

C. State-to-State Dispute Settlement Procedure under the USMCA

EVEN THOUGH THE STATE-TO-STATE PROCESS under NAFTA had proved to be ineffective, in the negotiations for the new USMCA, the US government proposed to further weaken the role of authoritative panel adjudication.[17] The agreement initially agreed by the parties in November 2018 included a chapter on state-to-state dispute settlement that largely reproduced NAFTA Chapter 20 without addressing its failings.

The US House of Representatives threatened to stall or even deny approval of the November version of the treaty without a number of significant changes. On 10 December 2019, the USMCA parties agreed to a protocol of amendment that, among other things, enhanced the state-to-state dispute settlement process significantly.[18] Although the overall structure of NAFTA Chapter 20 was maintained in USMCA Chapter 31, the process was amended to make it virtually impossible for one state to block the formation of dispute settlement panels. The new rules provide that the failure of a party to designate panelists to the roster or to participate in the panel selection process does not prevent the establishment of a panel and the Rules of Procedure for Chapter 31 established by the Free Trade Commission address how to compose a panel in that situation.[19] The need to rely on these provisions, however,

---

16 For discussion on this topic, see *Cargill, Inc v United Mexican States* (2009), ARB(AF)/05/02 at paras 85–100 (International Centre for Settlement of Investment Disputes).

17 In its revised negotiating objectives released in November 2017, the USTR added the following goal: "Provide mechanisms for ensuring that the Parties retain control of disputes and can address situations when a panel has clearly erred in its assessment of the facts or the obligations that apply" (USTR, *Summary of Objectives for the NAFTA Renegotiation* (Washington, DC: USTR, 2017) at 17, online: ustr.gov [perma. cc/97AG-VFFQ]). See also Josh Wingrove & Eric Martin, "U.S. Proposes Gutting NAFTA Legal-Dispute Tribunals" *Bloomberg Markets* (14 October 2017).

18 *Protocol of Amendment*, above note 3. On the pressure from the US House of Representatives, see David A Gantz & Sergio Puig, "The Scorecard of the USMCA Protocol of Amendment" (23 December 2019), online (blog): ejiltalk.org [perma. cc/23QQ-KFQS].

19 USMCA, above note 2, art 31.8(1); USMCA, *Rules of Procedure for Chapter 31 (Dispute Settlement)* [*Chapter 31 Rules of Procedure*], art 17.

was substantially mitigated by the parties' agreement on a thirty-person roster of panelists before the USMCA came into force.

A variety of other changes were made to the dispute settlement process. For example, the parties can agree to have three instead of five panelists.[20] Some of the most significant changes, however, relate to transparency.

Under NAFTA Chapter 20, every aspect of the dispute settlement process and all documents were treated as confidential.[21] Limited openness was introduced in a subsequent exchange of letters.[22] Each party was permitted, though not obliged, to disclose their own pleadings and the submissions of other parties subject to the redaction of confidential information. Hearing transcripts could be made public by a party fifteen days after the final panel report was made public. In 2004, Canada, the United States, and Mexico agreed to having NAFTA Chapter 20 hearings open to the public. No such hearings were ever held because there were no new cases subsequent to that agreement. In practice, NAFTA panel reports were made public but otherwise NAFTA Chapter 20 proceedings were largely concluded behind closed doors.[23]

In contrast, while USMCA consultations are confidential, the treaty provides for transparency at every stage of the process.[24] Requests for consultations, the parties' submissions, any written versions of oral communications with the panel, and the panel's final report are to be made public as soon as possible, subject to the redaction of confidential information.[25] Any hearing must be open to the public unless the disputing parties agree otherwise. As well, the USMCA contemplates the possibility of non-governmental parties located in the territory of a disputing party with an interest in a dispute being able to seek the permission of the panel to file a written statement of

---

20   *Ibid*, art 31.9(1)(a).

21   *NAFTA*, above note 1, art 2012(1); NAFTA, *Model Rules of Procedure for Chapter Twenty*, r 35.

22   Supplementary Procedures to Rule 35 on the Availability of Information in exchange of letters dated 13 July 1995.

23   The United States made its submissions publicly available in *Cross-Border Trucking*, above note 9; see David Gantz, "Government to Government Dispute Resolution under NAFTA Chapter 20: A Commentary on the Process" (2000) 11:4 *American Review of International Arbitration* 481 at 508 [Gantz, "Government to Government Dispute Resolution"].

24   *USMCA*, above note 2, art 31.4(9).

25   Detailed requirements are set out for public disclosure of requests for consultations, written submissions, hearing transcripts, and final reports (*ibid*, art 31.11; *Chapter 31 Rules of Procedure*, above note 19, art 19).

their views regarding the dispute to assist the panel in evaluating the submissions and arguments of the disputing parties.[26] The party states are entitled to respond to any such submissions.

One other change in the USMCA is that the time period for the initial panel report has been extended from NAFTA's ninety days to a more reasonable 150 days.[27] The other timelines in the USMCA, however, are mostly unchanged. While some variation is permitted, the USMCA contemplates that from consultations to the presentation of the final panel report, the process will take almost eight months if all the time periods are met (approximately 240 days or almost eight months).[28]

The rules regarding what happens after a panel's report is completed are largely unchanged from NAFTA. If a panel finds a measure to be inconsistent with a party's obligations, the parties "shall endeavor to agree on a resolution of the dispute."[29] As an alternative to eliminating any non-conformity, the parties may resolve the dispute through the payment of mutually acceptable compensation or in some other way.[30] A preference for compliance embedded in NAFTA Chapter 20, however, has been removed.[31] Under NAFTA the resolution of a dispute following a panel decision "normally" should conform to the panel's conclusions and recommendations, including, "wherever possible," not implementing or removing any measure that the panel found not in compliance with NAFTA.[32] The USMCA also diminishes the role of the panel by providing that it is not to make any recommendation regarding the resolution of a party's non-compliance unless the parties jointly ask it to.[33] Under NAFTA Chapter 20, a panel could make any such recommendation it determined was appropriate.[34]

---

26 Detailed requirements are set out for the submission of written views by non-governmental entities (*USMCA*, above note 2, art 31.11; *Chapter 31 Rules of Procedure*, above note 19, art 20).

27 Once the initial panel report is provided to the parties, they have fifteen days to make comments and the final report should be presented within thirty days of the initial report (*USMCA*, above note 2, art 31.17).

28 *USMCA*, above note 2, arts 31.6(1), 31.9, and 31.17.

29 *Ibid*, art 31.18.

30 North American Free Trade Implementation Act, Statement of Administrative Action, reprinted in *North American Free Trade Agreements*, James R Holbein & Donald J. Musch, eds (Oceana, 1994) Booklet 8, 190, states that they are not binding (at 195).

31 *USMCA*, above note 2, art 31.18.

32 *NAFTA*, above note 1, art 2018(1).

33 *USMCA*, above note 2, art 31.13(1)(c).

34 *NAFTA*, above note 1, art 2016(2)(c).

Like NAFTA Chapter 20, if there has been no mutual agreement on a resolution of the dispute within forty-five days of a panel decision finding non-compliance, the complaining party can suspend trade benefits that are equivalent in effect to the non-conformity until the parties can agree on a resolution of the dispute.[35] A disputing party found not to be in compliance can ask for a review of any suspension of benefits that it thinks is "manifestly excessive" or a determination as to whether it has eliminated any non-conformity found by the panel.[36] The original panel is to be reconvened to consider these matters. If a panel determines retaliation to be manifestly excessive, the panel is to provide its views as to the level of benefits it considers to be of equivalent effect.

D. USMCA State-to-State Cases So Far

IT IS BEYOND THE SCOPE of this chapter to discuss the cases in detail, but a brief overview will illuminate how the USMCA process has worked in practice and permit some observations regarding why it has been attractive to Canada, Mexico, and the United States.[37]

1) Canada—Dairy I and Canada—Dairy II

In the first USMCA case, *Canada—Dairy TRQ Allocation Measures* (*Canada—Dairy I*), the United States successfully challenged Canada's practice of reserving almost all access to tariff rate quotas (TRQs) for fourteen dairy products to Canadian dairy processors (including further processors).[38] Under Canada's supply management system for dairy products, Canada severely restricts imports with very high tariffs. In the USMCA, Canada agreed to grant limited access to US dairy products with a TRQ, under which particular products up to a certain aggregate volume can enter Canada at a much lower

---

35 *USMCA*, above note 2, art 31.19(1). *NAFTA, ibid*, art 2019(1) is the same. As under the WTO, the sectors chosen for the suspension of benefits should be the same as those that have been affected by the measure that is inconsistent with the agreement or causing nullification and impairment unless that is not practicable.

36 *USMCA, ibid*, art 31.19(3). *NAFTA, ibid*, art 2018 is the same.

37 Basic details of the cases are set out in Appendix I.

38 *Re Dairy TRQ Allocation Measures* (*Canada v US*) (2021), CDA-USA-2021-31-01 (Ch 31 Panel), online (pdf): worldtradelaw.net [perma.cc/ZU9W-B34Q] [*Canada—Dairy I*]. Further processors are businesses that use the products of processors to make other products (*Canada—Dairy I, ibid* at para 44).

tariff rate.[39] Canada had allocated between 85 and 100 percent of the TRQs (depending on the product) to Canadian importers who are processors of dairy products. In practice, this meant that US exports to Canada were limited to lower-value dairy products used by processors, like industrial-sized blocks of cheese. The United States argued that restricting the TRQs available to other kinds of importers, like retailers and food service operators, was a breach of Canada's obligations. The United States requested consultations on 9 December 2020 and then a panel on 25 May 2021. In its 20 December 2021 decision, the panel agreed with the United States.[40]

In response to the panel decision, Canada posted proposed changes to its TRQ allocation scheme on 1 March 2022.[41] Essentially, the Canadian proposal was to allocate TRQs for dairy products to Canadian processors, further processors, and distributors on the basis of their market share. The US government and US dairy industry expressed their dissatisfaction with these proposals on several bases, including that they denied access to the TRQs for retailers, food service operators, and other types of importers.[42] Canada implemented its proposed changes on 16 May 2022.[43] The United States requested consultations regarding the new TRQ allocation scheme on 25 May 2022 and then a panel on 31 January 2023 (*Canada—Dairy II*).[44]

---

39 *USMCA*, above note 2, Appendix 2 ("Tariff Schedule of Canada – (Tariff Rate Quotas)") to Annex 2-B ("Tariff Commitments") of Chapter 2 ("National Treatment and Market Access for Goods") as well as under Annex 3-A ("Agricultural Trade Between Canada and the United States") of Chapter 3 ("Agriculture").

40 The panel found, among other things, that Canada had violated USMCA art 3.A.2.11(b) by failing to "ensure that," "unless otherwise agreed by the Parties," Canada "does not . . . limit access to an allocation to processors" (*Canada—Dairy I*, above note 38 at para 98). For a thorough analysis of this case see Ljiljana Biukovic, "The First Challenge to Canada's Supply Management System under CUSMA: Tweaking the Supply Management System One Dispute at a Time" (2022) 59 *Canada Yearbook of International Law* 341.

41 Global Affairs Canada, "Public Consultations: CUSMA Dairy Tariff Rate Quotas (TRQs) Panel Report Implementation – Proposed Allocation and Administration Policy Changes" (last modified 1 March 2022), online: international.gc.ca [perma.cc/2GJ2-U7ZU].

42 National Milk Producers Federation, "NMPF and USDEC Slam Canadian Proposal on USMCA Dairy Market Access (3 March 2022), online: nmpf.org [perma.cc/H9SU-5FWX].

43 The final notices to importers are available online (see Global Affairs Canada, "Notices to Importers Supply-Managed Tariff Rate Quotas (TRQs)" (last modified 6 September 2024), online: international.gc.ca [perma.cc/G23J-WEMW].

44 *Re Dairy TRQ Allocation Measures 2023 (Canada v US)* (2023), CDA-USA-2023-31-01 (Ch 31 Panel), online (pdf): worldtradelaw.net [perma.cc/5CSQ-8HB6] [*Canada—Dairy II*]; USTR, "Request for Consultations" (25 May 2022), online: ustr.gov [perma.

The United States challenged the market share basis used by Canada in its TRQs allocation regime, as well as Canada's application of different criteria to different types of eligible applicants for the allocation, among other things.[45] The main US concern was that the effect of the Canadian regime was to substantially limit the availability of TRQs to Canadian processors.[46] On 10 November 2023, the panel transmitted its decision to the parties. It concluded that Canada's scheme for allocating TRQs was consistent with its USMCA commitments. A separate opinion from one panelist, however, found that the Canadian regime was not consistent with its USMCA obligations because it systematically excluded participants in the dairy industry, other than processors, further processors, and distributors.[47]

Reactions to the panel decision from the US dairy industry and the United States Trade Representative (USTR), as well as many US politicians, have been uniformly negative.[48] Most critics have been concerned that the panel decision meant that the US industry was denied access to which it was entitled under the USMCA, rather than questioning the effectiveness of the USMCA commitments themselves.

2) US—Solar Panels

The second state-to-state case filed under the USMCA (after *Canada—Dairy I*) was a complaint by Canada that a US safeguard on Crystalline Silicon Photovoltaic Cells (*US—Solar Panels*) should not be applied to Canadian products.[49] Under USMCA Chapter 10, US safeguard actions can only be applied to Canadian (or Mexican) products if they account for a substantial share of total imports and contribute importantly to a serious injury or threat of serious

---

cc/YM6B-25WT]; International Dairy Foods Association, "IDFA Applauds U.S. Government's Renewed Call for Consultations with Canada on Dairy Tariff Rate Quotas, Urges USG to Remain Vigilant" (25 May 2022), online: idfa.org [perma.cc/HKT4-2WUR]. The US filed a second request for consultations expanding its complaint on 20 December 2022.

45 *Canada—Dairy II*, above note 44 at para 113.

46 *Ibid* at para 119.

47 *Ibid* at para 330. The panelist was not identified in accordance with the USMCA (art 31.13(8)).

48 USTR, "What Are They Saying: USMCA Dairy Ruling" (27 November 2023), online: ustr.gov [perma.cc/4A4N-8J4W].

49 *Re Crystalline Silicon Photovoltaic Cells Safeguard Measure (US v Canada)* (2022), USA-CDA-2021-31-01 (Ch 31 Panel), online: worldtradelaw.net [perma.cc/TW2V-328H] [*US—Solar Panels*].

injury to the US domestic industry.[50] The US International Trade Commission (USITC) had made a negative determination with respect to these two prerequisite conditions, but in January 2018, President Trump proclaimed that the safeguard measures would be imposed on Canada.[51] Canada complained about the safeguard under NAFTA Chapter 20 in 2018 but did not request a panel. Canada's request for consultations under the USMCA was filed on 22 December 2020 and on 21 June 2021, Canada requested a panel. The panel sent its final report to the parties on 1 February 2022. The panel agreed with Canada that the prerequisites for the application of the safeguard to Canada were not met.[52] The panel went on to recommend that the United States bring its safeguard measure into conformity with its USMCA obligations. This is the only case so far to make such a recommendation. As noted, the USMCA rules provide that recommendations are only to be made if the parties jointly request them. Canada requested the panel to make recommendations in its written submission, but there is no evidence on the record that the United States acceded to that request.[53]

This case appears to have been fully resolved. In July 2022, the USTR published a notice in the Federal Register announcing an agreement between Canada and the United States that "will ensure that imports of [solar panels] originating in Canada do not undermine the effectiveness of the safeguard action" but, at the same time, terminating the application of the solar panels safeguard to products from Canada retroactive to 1 February 2022.[54] On 5 August 2022, Canada and United States jointly notified the USMCA Secretariat that they had agreed on a resolution of this dispute.[55]

3) US—Automotive Rules of Origin

The fourth completed USMCA case, *United States—Automotive Rules of Origin* (*US—Auto Rules*) is by far the most economically significant. Mexico, joined by Canada, complained that US application of the USMCA rules of origin

---

50 *USMCA*, above note 2, art 10.2.1.
51 *US—Solar Panels*, above note 49 at para 15.
52 *Ibid* at para 137.
53 Canada's submission, 21 August 2021, at para 1.35; *US—Solar Panels*, *ibid* at para 148.
    USMCA, above note 2, art 31.13(1)(c).
54 *Suspension of the Safeguard Action on Imports of Certain Crystalline Photovoltaic Cells*, 87 Fed Reg 43369 (2022).
55 The notice is available on the Trade Agreement Secretariat website, online: trade.gov [perma.cc/UDZ9-USRN].

for passenger vehicles and light trucks was not consistent with its obligations.[56] Mexico made its request for consultations on 20 August 2021 and was joined by Canada on 26 August 2021. Mexico requested a panel on 6 January 2022 (joined by Canada on 13 January 2022). The USMCA sets a 75 percent threshold for regional (i.e., North American) value content (RVC) for vehicles to qualify for preferential treatment under the USMCA.[57] The US position was that in determining whether the RVC threshold was met for vehicles, it was entitled to count only the percentage content of core components of those vehicles that originated in North America.[58] Canada and Mexico argued that if core components themselves qualify as originating in the region under the appliable rules of origin, 100 precent of the value of those components should count toward the RVC without subtracting any incorporated foreign content.[59] The five-person panel transmitted its decision to the parties on 14 December 2022. It found that that the United States was not in compliance with its obligations.[60]

The United States disagreed with the ruling and has not changed its approach to the calculation of RVC. On 22 November 2023, the USTR announced its biennial review of trade in automotive goods under the USMCA.[61] The USTR invited comments concerning the operation of the USMCA with respect to automotive goods, including the implementation and enforcement of the USMCA rules of origin for automotive goods. On 1 July 2024, the USTR submitted it report to Congress reiterating its position that the US interpretation was consistent with the USMCA.[62] Consultations are ongoing and neither Mexico nor Canada have taken steps to retaliate though they are entitled to do so under the USMCA.[63]

---

56   *Re Automotive Rules of Origin (US v Mexico and Canada)* (2022), USA-MEX-CDA-2022-31-01 (Ch 31 Panel), online: worldtradelaw.net [perma.cc/B4TP-A27U] [*US—Auto Rules*].

57   *USMCA*, above note 2, art 4.5 and Annex 4-B.

58   The core components are the engine, transmission, body and chassis, axle, suspension system, steering system, and (where applicable) advanced battery.

59   *US—Auto Rules*, above note 56 at para 46. These provisions are referred to as "roll up provisions."

60   *Ibid* at paras 203–9.

61   *Request for Comments and Notice of Public Hearing*, 88 Fed Reg 81527 (2023).

62   USTR, *Report to Congress on the Operation of the United States-Mexico-Canada Agreement with Respect to Trade in Automotive Goods* (1 July 2024) at 14, online (pdf): ustr. gov [perma.cc/UH2U-UHEB] [*USTR Autos Report*].

63   As noted, where there has been no mutual agreement on a resolution of a USMCA dispute within forty-five days of the final panel report, the complaining party may

4) Mexico—Energy Sector

On 20 July 2022, Canada and the United States separately requested consultations with Mexico on certain Mexican measures related to electricity claimed to favour Mexico's state-owned Comisión Federal de Electricidad (CFE) negatively affecting Canadian and US companies operating in Mexico's electricity sector and investments in the sector.[64] The US request extends to measures claimed to favour Petróleos Mexicanos (PEMEX), the state oil and gas company, and harm US fuel exports to Mexico.[65] Consultations are ongoing. A recent Mexican court ruling struck down some of the provisions favouring CFE that are the subject of the requests for consultations.[66] The Mexican government has said it will seek to challenge this ruling.[67]

5) Mexico—Genetically Engineered Corn

The final state-to-state case brought under the USMCA so far is a US complaint about a 2023 Mexican decree banning the use of genetically modified (GM) corn for "nixtamalization" and flour production, as well as other measures governing the importation and sale of GM corn products other than for cultivation.[68] The United States requested consultations on 2 June 2023. Canada participated in the consultations as a third party. The United States requested a panel on 17 August 2023. Canada is participating as a third party in the panel process. Panel selection was completed on 19 October 2023. The complaint is primarily based on alleged violations of the sanitary

---

suspend trade concessions that are equivalent in effect to the non-conformity or nullification and impairment until the parties can agree on a resolution of the dispute (*USMCA*, above note 2, art 31.19(1)).

64 MEX-MEX-2022-31-01 [*Mexico—Energy*].

65 Both requests allege inconsistency with art 14.4 (national treatment of investors) among other USMCA provisions (Canada, Request for Consultations (July 2022), online: www.international.gc.ca [perma.cc/Z5NC-RVLB]; United States, Request for Consultations (July 2022), online (pdf): ustr.gov [perma.cc/DM89-9YUV]).

66 Second Chamber of the Supreme Court of Mexico, *Amparo en revisión 164/2023 (31 January 2024)*.

67 Agence France Presse, "Mexico President To Contest Ruling Against Energy Reforms" (1 February 2024), online: barrons.com [perma.cc/C8ZW-MG3M].

68 *Re Measures Concerning Genetically Engineered Corn (Mexico v US)* (2023), MEX-USA-2023-31-01 (Ch 31 Panel), online: worldtradelaw.net [perma.cc/B59P-X29L] [*Mexico—GE Corn*]; United States, Request for Panel (August 2023), online: ustr.gov [perma.cc/RYF7-ZZUJ]. Nixtamalization is a traditional process to prepare maize in which corn is soaked and cooked in an alkaline solution.

and phytosanitary measures obligations in USMCA Chapter 9. The disputing parties and Canada have made their submissions. Fourteen non-governmental parties sought leave to make submissions. Nine were granted leave and have filed their submissions. The hearing was held during the week of 25 June 2024.[69]

E. Assessment

THE PARTIES' RESORT TO USCMA state-to-state dispute settlement and willingness to work diligently within its rules to complete cases in a timely way represents a marked shift from the practice under NAFTA. Canada and Mexico, as the smaller parties in the North American relationship, have a strong interest in access to an authoritative decision by a panel as a lever to secure compliance by their larger common neighbour and have consistently advocated strong North American state-to-state dispute settlement. By contrast, the United States has not always been committed to the panel process. But the USTRs under both the first Trump and Biden administrations have expressed their interest in using the USMCA dispute settlement process to address concerns about non-compliance and emphasized the importance of the dispute settlement system.[70] The US approach to USMCA dispute settlement reflects a refreshing change. But what accounts for the renewed engagement of the parties, especially the United States, in North American dispute settlement?

Undoubtedly, the current problems with the World Trade Organization (WTO) dispute settlement process encourage Canada, Mexico, and the United States to resort to the USMCA process where possible, though it is noteworthy that the disputes so far, apart from *Mexico—GE Corn*, deal with USMCA obligations that have no analogue in the WTO agreements. Michael Solursh's chapter in this volume examines the relationship between WTO and USMCA dispute settlement in more detail and these issues will not be further addressed here.

The simplest reason for frequent resort to the USMCA system is that it is working more effectively than its predecessor. Fixing the problems with panel

---

69 USTR, "USTR Presents Oral Argument Before USMCA Biotech Corn Dispute Panel (1 July 2024), online: ustr.gov [perma.cc/43ZD-2LSM].

70 Alexander Panetta & Janyce McGregor, "New NAFTA takes effect next month. U.S. is already threatening legal challenges" (17 June 2020), online: cbc.ca [perma.cc/NH4L-7328].

selection that bedeviled the NAFTA process encourages all three countries to be confident that they can get their disputes before a panel when they want to. Their agreement on the roster before the USMCA came into force ensured that the panel selection process would work smoothly.[71]

Early success in obtaining high quality decisions on an expeditious basis and, for the United States, a win in *Canada—Dairy I*, may also be encouraging enthusiasm for the USMCA process. The USMCA provides that the findings, determinations, and recommendations of the panel shall not "add to or diminish the rights and obligations of the Parties under the [USMCA],"[72] reflecting long-standing US concerns regarding overreaching by the WTO Appellate Body.[73] Consistently, panel decisions have been relatively short and narrowly confined to resolving the necessary legal questions. Perhaps the best example of panels' disciplined approach is the *US—Auto Rules* decision which is just forty-one pages.[74]

While the tight USMCA timelines have not been fully met in all cases, panel selection and the rest of the panel process have been completed relatively smoothly and quickly. In *Canada—Dairy I*, *Canada—Dairy II*, and *US—Solar Panels* selection was completed in less than forty-six days. In *Mexico—GE Corn*, panel selection extended to sixty-four days. But even in *US—Auto Rules*, the only case in which the parties opted for five panelists, panel selection took only seventy-six days. Panel reports have been completed promptly too. The final reports in *Canada—Dairy I* and *US—Solar Panels* were submitted approximately seven months after the panel was requested. The panel process extended to more than nine months in *Canada—Dairy II*, but even in the high stakes *US—Auto Rules*, the panel completed its work in just over eleven months

Another factor contributing to use of the USMCA process could be the treaty's new transparency requirements and the procedure for non-governmental parties to participate. Greater transparency and the possibility of

---

71 But even a few off-roster appointments have not slowed down the process (e.g., Donald McRae and Jorge Miranda in *US—Automotive Rules of Origin*, above note 56).

72 *USMCA*, above note 2, art 31.13(2). This provision has no counterpart in NAFTA.

73 Simon Lester, Inu Manak, & Andrej Arpas, "Access to Trade Justice: Fixing NAFTA's Flawed State-to-State Dispute Settlement Process" (2018) 18:1 *World Trade Review* 63.

74 *Canada—Dairy I*, above note 38, is fifty-three pages, *Canada—Dairy II*, above note 43, is sixty-four pages, and *US—Solar Panels*, above note 49, is forty-two pages. By comparison the decision in, *Cross-Border Trucking*, above note 9, is eighty-four pages, though the other two NAFTA decisions are shorter (*Brooms from Mexico*, above note 9 (twenty-nine pages) and *Agricultural Products from US*, above note 9 (sixty pages)).

private party participation may encourage private interests affected by perceived non-compliance, as well as political actors, to pressure governments to pursue dispute settlement as a tool to further their interests.[75] Private parties have sought to take advantage of the new opportunity to participate in most USMCA disputes. In *Canada—Dairy I, Canada—Dairy II, US—Auto Rules*, and *Mexico—Energy*, non-governmental parties obtained leave to submit written views to the panel and made submissions.[76] It is noteworthy that panels have been able to complete their work in a timely way despite the additional procedural steps associated with these submissions.

If the USMCA Chapter 31 panel process is working well, perhaps the key question is whether it is contributing to the resolution of the concerns underlying disputes among the parties. If it does not, the parties' engagement with the process may tail off.

The *US—Solar Panels* case has been resolved, but the complaining parties concerns in the other cases that have gone to a panel have not.[77] The United States continues to be frustrated regarding the access for its dairy producers to Canada. Now that the *Canada—Dairy II* panel has upheld Canada's revised

---

75   *USMCA*, above note 2, art 31.11(a), (d), and (f); *Chapter 31 Rules of Procedure*, above note 19, art 19. The transparency requirements have been largely observed. Requests for consultation and for panels, third party participation, submissions questions comments, opening statements, exhibits, non-governmental party submissions, procedural orders and hearing transcript have all been made public in the cases to date (subject to redaction of confidential information). Of course, greater transparency might dampen state enthusiasm for the process in some cases. On the engagement of members of Congress on *Mexico—GE Corn*, above note 68, see USTR, "What They Are Saying: USTR Announces USMCA Technical Consultations with Mexico on Agricultural Biotechnology" (6 March 2023), online: ustr.gov [perma.cc/837Y-8QLL]. On the role of private sector parties in the dispute, see Logan Castellanos, "The GE Corn Dispute: U.S. Agriculture Challenges Mexican Culture" (11 January 2024), online (blog): ielp.worldtradelaw.net [perma.cc/LT3D-XMVF].

76   It is not clear whether these submissions have had any effect on panel decisions. The USMCA rules provide that panels are not required to address non-governmental party submissions in their decisions (*Chapter 31 Rules of Procedure, ibid*, art 20.9). So far, none has. One may wonder whether, ultimately, the non-governmental party submission process will prove to be useful in terms of contributing to the decisions made or the resolution of underlying disputes. The very similar process for non-disputing parties to participate in investor-state claims has generally been considered a failure. See, e.g., Nicolette Butler, "Non-Disputing Party Participation in ICSID Disputes: Faux Amici?" (2019) 66 *Netherlands International Law Review* 143.

77   As noted, this case was unusual in that the President decided that the safeguard should apply to Canadian products despite an International Trade Commission determination that the USMCA prerequisites for its application were not met.

regime, US concerns cannot be resolved through the panel process. The parties will have to reach a negotiated solution outside the Chapter 31 process.[78] By contrast, in *US—Auto Rules*, actions can be taken under Chapter 31 because the United States has not brought its regime into compliance with the panel decision and no other solution has been agreed to. Canada and Mexico can retaliate. So far, there is no evidence that they will do so and the dispute about automotive rules of origin continues. It is not clear what will be the outcome in the two cases against Mexico. In *Mexico—Energy*, consultations were requested more than a year and a half ago. Discussions seem to be stalled, and no panel has been requested. *Mexico—GE Corn* is ongoing. The panel's final report was originally scheduled for 4 July 2024 but will be late due to delays in prior stages of the case.

In evaluating the effectiveness of the USMCA dispute settlement in contributing to the resolution of disputes, it is essential to appreciate the limited role contemplated for panel adjudication in the treaty. David Gantz described panel decisions under NAFTA as only a "strong recommendation."[79] Where a violation of NAFTA was found, there was no unequivocal obligation on the party in violation to bring its regime into compliance. Solutions other than compliance, including compensation, were expressly permitted. The same is true under the USMCA. In fact, the USMCA modestly reduces the role of the role of panel decisions in encouraging compliance by eliminating NAFTA's stipulation that a resolution agreed to by the parties "normally" should conform to the panel's conclusions and recommendations, including, "wherever possible," not implementing or removing any measure that the panel found not in compliance.[80] The USMCA does not accord any priority to compliance over other ways of resolving disputes. Consistently, a USMCA panel is not to provide recommendations regarding how non-compliance should be resolved unless requested by both parties. Under NAFTA, a panel was entitled to provide recommendations unless the parties agreed otherwise.

---

78   The United States did expressly reserve its right to retaliate or seek a compliance panel in *Canada—Dairy I*, above note 38, when it requested consultations in *Canada—Dairy II*, above note 44. Footnote 3 of the US request says: "This request for consultations is without prejudice to U.S. rights under the USMCA relating to the prior USMCA dispute settlement proceeding or the Final Report of the Panel, dated December 20, 2021." These rights would appear to be effectively extinguished by the decision in *Canada—Dairy II*.

79   Gantz, "Government to Government Dispute Resolution," above note 23 at 487.

80   NAFTA, above note 1, art 2026(2).

Compliance with the agreement is essential to its success and the non-binding character of panel reports under NAFTA was lamented and criticized by some.[81] But the dispute settlement process in the USMCA, even more than its predecessor, was never intended to ensure compliance. Indeed, recent statements by USTR Catharine Tai confirm that the United States, at least, views panel decisions as just a part of a process toward a political solution to problems related to the agreement.[82] On this view, a panel decision regarding compliance or non-compliance simply changes the context for the discussion of what the parties will agree to by improving the winning party's negotiating leverage.

It is true that parties facing non-compliance with a panel decision can put pressure on the non-complying party by suspending benefits of equivalent effect forty-five days after the panel decision. But suspension of trade benefits is a clumsy and often ineffective tool to encourage compliance. It has not been used under the USMCA so far and was only used once under NAFTA.[83]

It is also true that, at least for some disputes, compliance with panel decisions will not be feasible. Reaching an agreed resolution can be a long and difficult process requiring governments to work with a variety of sometimes conflicting domestic political, commercial, and labour interests as well as the other state parties. In this sort of context, a politically acceptable resolution to a dispute may be different than compliance with the panel decision. *US—Auto Rules* provides an example of conflicting domestic interests. Most automakers favour the outcome found by the panel, whereas US labour unions support the US position.[84] As well, where the conditions that were

---

81 The failure of the NAFTA process to produce a binding decision was described as a "major flaw" by Canada's Standing Senate Committee on Foreign Affairs (Senate, *Uncertain Access: The Consequences of US Security and Trade Actions for Canadian Trade Policy (Volume 1)*, (June 2003) (Chair: Peter Stollery), online (pdf): parl.gc.ca [perma.cc/K56M-CS2V].

82 See Katharine Tai, Address (delivered at USMCA Forward 2024 Report Launch: A Conversation with USTR Katharine Tai, 6 March 2024), online: brookings.edu [perma. cc/9NBR-FC66] [Tai 2024 Comments].

83 In *Cross-Border Trucking*, above note 9, Mexico finally decided to retaliate eight years after the panel decision. Mexico imposed more than USD 2.4 billion in trade sanctions on US imports in 2009 (Diario Oficial (Mexico), 18 March 2009), cited in Leal-Arcas, 2011, above note 9 at 16.

84 Robert Howse, "Developments in USMCA Dispute Settlement" in Joshua P Melzer & Brahima S Coulibaly, eds, *USMCA Forward 2024: Gearing Up for a Successful Review*

the basis for the bargain represented in the treaty have changed by the time the parties are seeking to resolve their dispute, compliance with treaty terms becomes more difficult. Again, *US—Auto Rules* is an example. US concern to limit foreign—and especially Chinese—content in vehicles that qualify for preferences under the USMCA is stronger today than it was in 2018 when the USMCA was being negotiated, leading to a US desire for rules of origin that exclude all foreign content in automotive components. Finally, sometimes political factors unrelated to trade may affect a party's willingness to push for compliance or resort to dispute settlement in the first place. For example, it has been suggested that the United States did not want to pursue a panel in *Mexico—Energy* prior to the recent Mexican election.[85]

F. Conclusion

USMCA CHAPTER 31 HAS EFFECTIVELY addressed the problems with NAFTA Chapter 20 and all three USMCA parties have embraced state-to-state dispute settlement in the first few years of the treaty's operation. Their engagement has helped the panel process to function in an effective and timely way. At the same time, the relatively swift production of concise panel reports focused narrowly on the essential legal issues has encouraged states to use the process. The increased visibility of state-to-state dispute settlement arising from enhanced transparency rules and the rush of early cases encourage states to use the process to draw attention to perceived compliance problems. These features may also encourage private sector interests and their political allies to pay more attention to USMCA dispute settlement cases than under NAFTA and to advocate more frequently and forcefully for the use of the system to further their interests.[86]

Authoritative adjudication in the form of USMCA panel decisions shifts the context for party state disputes regarding the operation of the agreement by recognizing the existence of USMCA compliance or, where non-compliance is found, encouraging state action to comply. Good faith compliance with panel decisions is, of course, desirable in the interests of preserving

---

in 2026 (Washington, DC: Brookings, 2024) 75 at 80–81, online (pdf): brookings.edu [perma.cc/XZP7-FZD9].

85   Kenneth Smith Ramos, Address (delivered at USMCA: Are the Dispute Resolution Mechanisms Functioning as Intended?, 21 March 2023) online: wilsoncenter.org [perma.cc/DQ3V-3VGY].

86   *USTR Autos Report*, above note 62 at 14–15.

confidence in the reliability and predictability of treaty rules. Continuing non-compliance, even where agreed resolutions other than compliance have been reached, risks undermining both the value of the USMCA commitments and support for the dispute settlement system and its decisions about compliance.[87] The failure of the United States to change its regime to comply with the decision in *US—Automotive Rules of Origin*, for example, has caused frustration for automakers by creating uncertainty regarding how to organize their supply chains to obtain USMCA preferences and led to expressions of concern about the effectiveness of the dispute settlement process.[88]

The USMCA panel process, however, is not designed to guarantee treaty compliance. The impact of panel decisions on state behaviour will depend on the circumstances, including the economic significance of the dispute and its political context. The panel finding of non-compliance in *US—Solar Panels* seems to have provided the impetus for the United States to take action to resolve Canada's concerns by excluding Canadian exports from the solar panel safeguard. Undoubtedly, that resolution was encouraged by the limited trade effects of Canadian solar panel exports to the United States as found by the USITC. By contrast, the finding by two out of three panel members in *Canada—Dairy II* that Canada's revised TRQ regime complied with its obligations has done little to resolve US concerns that its exporters are not getting the access the Canadian dairy market that was bargained for. Even though Canada's market opening commitment was relatively limited, the United States is likely to continue to seek changes to Canada's TRQ regime because of the high political profile of the dispute in dairy producing states and one panelist's view supporting the US position. Finally, the finding of non-compliance in *US—Auto Rules* and continuing assertion by the United States that its approach to regional value content is permitted under the treaty underscores the limited effect of USMCA dispute settlement in relation to treaty rules that have significant economic and political implications and with respect to which policy priorities have shifted from those existing when the treaty was concluded.

---

87   Some have speculated that USMCA parties might seek to resolve one dispute by concessions in relation to other disputes (see, e.g., Simon Lester, International Economic Law and Policy Blog, 22 March 2023, available online (blog): ielp.worldtradelaw.net [perma.cc/V9NV-HRW4]). Political trade-offs across disputes will encourage skepticism regarding the value of the system for private sector interests and their political allies.

88   Howse, above note 84.

What happens with current and future disputes in the next couple of years will be key issues in the review of the USMCA that will take place in 2026. That assessment will not only be a matter of whether the panel process produced high quality decisions in a timely way but also the more complex and case specific issues related to whether the process is contributing to the resolution of the underlying disputes.[89]

89　*USMCA*, above note 2, art 34.7. USTR Katharine Tai recently confirmed that USMCA dispute settlement will be on the agenda (Tai 2024 Comments, above note 82).

Appendix I – USMCA State-to-State Cases as of 31 July 2024

Case	Complaining Party	Number of panellists	Outcome	Total length of proceedings (Consultations Request to Final report)	Length of panel process (Panel Request to Final Report)	Non-governmental parties participating
US—Dairy TRQ Allocation (2021)	US	3	Measure found inconsistent with Canada's obligations	377 days	210 days (Panel Selection 42 days)	1 of 1 granted leave to file a submission
US—Crystalline Silicon Photovoltaic Cells Safeguard (2021)	Canada (Mexico joined as a third party to the panel proceeding)	3 (2 off roster)	Measure found inconsistent with US's obligations	407 days	226 days (Panel Selection 45 days)	0
US—Automotive Rules of Origin (2022)	Mexico (Canada joined as complaining party)	5 (2 off roster)	Measure found inconsistent with US's obligations	482 days	343 days (Panel Selection 76 days)	2 of 2 granted leave to file a submission
Dairy TRQ Allocation (2023)	US (Mexico joined as a third party to the panel proceeding)	3	Measure found consistent with Canada's obligations (partial dissent by a panellist)	535 days	284 days (Panel Selection 42 days)	2 of 3 granted leave to file a submission
Mexico— Genetically Engineered Corn (2023)	US (Canada joined as third party to the consultations)	3	Ongoing	Request for consultations on 2 June 2023	Panel Request 17 August 2023 Panel selected 19 October 2023 (64 days)	9 of 14 granted leave to file a submission
Mexico— Energy Sector (2022)	Canada and US (separate complaints)	--	Ongoing	US and Canadian Requests for consultations on 20 July 2022	--	--

CHAPTER 22

Public Participation in FTA Disputes

Kathleen Claussen[*]

A. Introduction

FEW STATE-TO-STATE DISPUTES HAVE ARISEN under free trade agreements (FTAs), although the number has grown in recent years with the entry into force of new agreements, especially the *Canada-United States-Mexico Agreement* (CUSMA).[1] An expert in international disputes, especially trade disputes, Valerie Hughes has been involved as counsel or arbitrator in many of these disputes. Following her long and distinguished career in national and

---

[*]   Professor of Law, Georgetown University Law Center. Valerie has been a trusted mentor and friend to me since I have had the chance to get to know her in the last half-dozen years. I am deeply grateful to her for her generosity and thoughtfulness toward me. It is a privilege to participate in a project that honours her contributions to the field both in professional and personal respects. Thank you to Nicolas Lamp for undertaking such an important initiative. Thanks also to Daniel Kim for his excellent research assistance.

1   See, e.g., Kathleen Claussen, "The Future of Trade Agreement Dispute Settlement Provisions" in Kathleen Claussen, Manfred Elsig, & Rodrigo Polanco, eds, *The Concept Design of a 21st Century Preferential Trade Agreement* (Cambridge: Cambridge University Press, 2025) 565; Geraldo Vidigal, "Regional Trade Adjudication and the Rise of Sustainability Disputes: *Korea—Labor Commitments* and *Ukraine—Wood Export Bans*" (2022) 116:3 *American Journal of International Law* 567; Geraldo Vidigal, "Why Is There So Little Litigation under Free Trade Agreements? Retaliation and Adjudication in International Dispute Settlement" (2017) 20:4 *Journal of International Economics* 927.

international public service, she now acts as an arbitrator and appears on the roster of several FTA dispute settlement mechanisms, further contributing to the development of the field. This chapter takes up one of the many procedural aspects of these disputes that have evolved in the years since the earliest disputes through the present: the opportunities for public participation.

Since 2015, states have established nine dispute settlement panels under FTAs, and two fact-finding panels under a trade and labour mechanism built into the CUSMA.[2] This chapter reviews whether and how other actors are using these mechanisms to participate in dispute settlement. Its primary purpose is descriptive: taking stock of the numbers and demographics of these participants where known—again, limiting review to the last decade. Accordingly, the chapter begins by laying out data on who and what have provided governments with information in the context of FTA dispute settlement. It also comments on how governments have treated the communications they have received and how panels have treated the submissions provided to them. Second, the chapter evaluates the procedural mechanisms presently in place in modern trade agreements in light of the purposes they are intended to serve. It concludes by offering potential modifications to the present systems for trade treaty designers to contemplate.

To be sure, contemporary agreements regularly offer multiple entry points for collecting information from the public in service of disputes, in addition to informal or domestic mechanisms for the same. The agreements codify means for both groups and individuals to engage. Beyond those discussed here, there are also many other means through which members of the public can engage with their governments on topics related to trade. In sum,

---

2   As discussed further below, I do not consider here trade remedies review panels or investor-state dispute settlement panels for several reasons, although I note that Valerie notably has contributed to both types of proceedings and particularly the former where she presently sits as a panelist. As is clear from their fundamental nature, both include opportunities for participation by private parties. But trade remedies mechanisms under FTAs typically do not provide for outside participation apart from direct application by interested persons who have been affected by the trade remedy determination at the national level, for instance. By contrast, investor-state dispute settlement (ISDS) panels also often include opportunities for non-governmental entities (NGEs), but given their treatment by other scholars, I do not cover those here. I am also focused only on FTAs and therefore do not touch upon *amicus curiae* before the WTO or any of the international courts. Finally, the data here cover newly established panels; the Panel report was issued in a dispute between the United States and Guatemala after 2015, but that dispute began long before. The data collection for this chapter closed on 1 October 2024.

this short chapter is by no means comprehensive. Rather, it focuses on just a selection of these tools to evaluate their use and patterns in their application.

B. Data and Trends

PROGRESSIVE GOVERNMENTS AND COMMENTATORS HAVE heralded some of the latest generation trade agreements as advancing public participation opportunities in the resolution of these disputes. For example, the CUSMA expressly provides for non-governmental entity (NGE) participation in at least some types of disputes.[3] The *Comprehensive and Progressive Agreement for Trans-Pacific Partnership* (CPTPP) likewise offers NGEs the opportunity to submit written briefs in case of dispute.[4] These agreements also both provide mechanisms to allow members of the public to submit petitions or communications to alert the parties of potential violations of sustainability commitments such as through the North American Commission for Environmental Cooperation (CEC). This section begins by surveying the NGE avenues for participation, followed by the public complaint mechanisms.

As for whether members of the public are making use of these mechanisms to participate in dispute settlement or related mechanisms, the short answer is yes, some are trying. The longer answer is more complex for several reasons to which I will return. I will begin with the nine dispute settlement panels established under traditional FTA state-to-state provisions, which are (in English alphabetical order by respondent):

1) *Canada—Dairy TRQs* (CPTPP)
2) *Canada—Dairy TRQs I* (CUSMA)
3) *Canada—Dairy TRQs II* (CUSMA)
4) *Korea—Labor* (EU–Korea FTA)
5) *Mexico—Genetically Modified Corn* (CUSMA)
6) *Southern African Customs Union (SACU)—Chicken Safeguards* (EU–SADC EPA)
7) *Ukraine—Wood Export Ban* (EU–Ukraine Association Agreement)
8) *United States—Automotive Rules of Origin* (CUSMA)
9) *United States—Solar Safeguards* (CUSMA)

---

3   *Canada-United States-Mexico Agreement*, 10 December 2019, art 31.11, online: international.gc.ca [perma.cc/G9J2-NMFJ] [*CUSMA*].

4   *Comprehensive and Progressive Agreement for Trans-Pacific Partnership*, 8 March 2018, art 28.13, online: international.gc.ca [perma.cc/AE8Z-KBXP] [*CPTPP*].

As the above list reflects, in the last ten years, Canada and the United States have been the most active economies in dispute settlement panels under FTAs, and CUSMA is the agreement that has seen the most disputes.

CUSMA Chapter 31 requires that the parties establish Rules of Procedure that provide for panels to consider requests from NGEs located in the territory of a disputing party to provide written views regarding the dispute that may assist the panel in evaluating the submissions and arguments of the disputing parties.[5] Article 20 of the Chapter 31 Rules of Procedure elaborates on this provision. It states that a panel may consider applications made by NGEs to file written views. The application must fulfill eight separate requirements including that it must explain how the NGE's submission would assist the panel in the determination of "factual or legal issues related to the dispute by bringing a perspective, particular knowledge, or insight that is different from that of the participating Parties and why its views would be unlikely to repeat legal and factual arguments that a Party has made or is expected to make."[6]

In the very first dispute under the CUSMA, *Canada—Dairy TRQs I*, which concerned Canada's dairy tariff-rate quotas, one NGE filed a submission.[7] On 23 July 2021, per Article 20.3 of the Rules of Procedure for CUSMA Chapter 31, the International Cheese Council of Canada (ICCC) requested leave to submit written views in the dispute.[8] The Panel granted the ICCC such leave on 30 July 2021, although it noted that one issue the ICCC sought to address fell outside the Panel's mandate.[9] The ICCC submitted a ten-page argument, in which it maintained that Canada was in breach of the CUSMA in at least two respects.[10] The ICCC submission also described the consequences of Canada's approach on its members and suppliers.[11] Canada then filed comments related to the submission.[12]

---

5   *CUSMA*, above note 3, art 31.11.

6   *Rules of Procedure for Chapter 31 (Dispute Settlement) (CUSMA)*, art 20.2(c), online: can-mex-usa-sec.org [perma.cc/PF7C-J8BB].

7   *Re Dairy TRQ Allocation Measures 2021 (Canada v US)* (2021), CDA-USA-2021-31-010 (Ch 31 Panel), online (pdf): worldtradelaw.net [perma.cc/YZ8K-Y34Y] [*Canada— Dairy I*].

8   *Ibid* at para 9.

9   *Ibid* at para 10. The issue was "how Canada should allocate and administer its Tariff Rate Quotas (TRQs)."

10 ICCC Submission, 27 August 2021.

11 *Ibid*.

12 *Canada—Dairy I*, above note 7 at paras 12–13.

The second CUSMA dispute that featured NGE participation was the *United States—Automotive Rules of Origin*. This dispute involved a set of claims by Mexico and Canada against the United States concerning the United States' interpretation and application of the CUSMA rules of origin provisions relative to automobiles.[13] Two NGEs applied to participate and both were permitted to make a written submission: the Mexican Association of the Automotive Industry (AMIA) and Global Automakers of Canada (GAC).[14] Both NGEs argued that the US interpretation of the CUSMA was contrary to the text of the Agreement. Put differently, both NGEs supported the complaining parties, just as the one NGE had in the 2021 dairy dispute.

In the second dispute between the United States and Canada concerning Canada's dairy tariff-rate quotas, three NGEs applied to participate: the ICCC, the Retail Council of Canada, and Restaurants Canada.[15] The Panel permitted only two of the NGEs to submit written submissions; it rejected the request from Restaurants Canada on the basis that the request did not explain how its submission would assist the panel as required by the Rules of Procedure.[16] The other two NGEs made submissions and both offered perspectives in support of the United States' position.

Following these two disputes, one might conclude that NGEs are readily deployed by complaining parties to support their positions or that these NGEs were closely involved in the dispute from the earliest days, perhaps prompting the complaining parties to take action in the first place. It is more difficult to explain why no industry actors applied to participate from the respondent's side, though one could venture some hypotheses, and it may be that the reason is case-specific.

But this short trend was disrupted by the landscape of participants in the dispute between the United States and Mexico concerning genetically modified corn. This dispute is ongoing at the time of writing. Nevertheless, the Panel has already addressed applications by NGEs, which came quite early in the proceedings according to the timeline set out in the Rules. In

---

13 In the interest of transparency, I note that I was a member of this Panel.

14 *Re Automotive Rules of Origin (US v Mexico and Canada)* (2022), USA-MEX-CDA-2022-31-01 (Ch 31 Panel), online (pdf): worldtradelaw.net [perma.cc/B4TP-A27U] [*US—Auto Rules*].

15 *Re Dairy TRQ Allocation Measures 2023 (Canada v US)* (2023), CDA-USA-2023-31-010 (Ch 31 Panel), online (pdf): worldtradelaw.net [perma.cc/M5Y6-QNTM]. In the interest of transparency, I note that I was a member of this Panel.

16 *Ibid.*

contrast with the prior disputes, fourteen NGEs applied to participate, and the Panel permitted nine to submit written views. The Panel rejected the other five on two different grounds. In two instances, the Panel found that the NGE applicant did not "explain how [its] submission would assist the panel in the determination of the factual or legal issue related to the dispute by bringing a perspective, particular knowledge, or insight that is different from that of the participating Parties and why its views would be unlikely to repeat legal and factual arguments that a Party has made or is expected to make."[17] And three NGEs were rejected because they were Canadian entities and therefore not entities located on the territory of a disputing party.[18] Still more interesting is that, of the nine that filed written briefs, all but one supported the position of the responding party (Mexico), a significant contrast with the prior disputes.

Among the commercial panel experiences outside of CUSMA, most NGE filings are similar in nature to those in the early CUSMA disputes: NGEs tend to align with complaining parties. And like in the CUSMA disputes, panels do not readily cite these submissions in their findings. In the dairy-related dispute between New Zealand and Canada, four NGEs provided written views, pursuant to Article 28.13 of the CPTPP.[19] The Panel does not indicate how many NGEs originally sought leave to file such views, but it notes that it granted leave to all that applied. With respect to their views, all four NGEs supported New Zealand's complaining party position. As noted by one observer, each discussed "how [Canada's measure] impacts their ability to trade in New Zealand dairy products. Their contents are generally critical of Canada's administration of dairy tariff rate quotas (TRQs), with most having a commercial interest in increasing the access in Canada to New Zealand dairy products."[20]

---

17 *Re Measures Concerning Genetically Engineered Corn (Mexico v US)* (2024), MEX-USA-2023-31-01 (Ch 31 Panel), Revised Panel Decisions on the Applications for Leave to File Written Views at 2–3, online (pdf): iatp.org [perma.cc/8DP7-2G3B].

18 *Ibid* at 2–3.

19 *Canada—Dairy Tariff Rate Quota Allocation Measures* (2023), CDA-NZ-2022-28-01, at para 6, online (pdf): worldtradelaw.net [perma.cc/4BPH-NW8H].

20 Watson Farley & Williams LLP, "CPTPP Canada – Dairy Dispute: Early Lessons for Governments and Investors" (26 June 2023), online: wfw.com [perma.cc/RQ5M-AEW5].

Three *amici curiae* delivered submissions in the context of the EU–SACU dispute.[21] The three *amici* were: the Association of Meat Importers and Exporters (AMIE), the Association of Poultry Processors and Poultry Trade in the European Union, and the South African Poultry Association (SAPA). As their names may suggest, the former two *amici* argued in favour of the complainant, while SAPA sought to supplement the position of the respondent.[22] Notably, AMIE also sought permission to intervene at the hearing, but the disputing parties declined to consent to this request.[23]

Finally, in the *Ukraine—Wood Export Ban* dispute, one *amicus curiae* submission was received from the Ukrainian Association of the Club of Rome.[24] In addition, the Panel fielded a second request from a large manufacturer of layered wood floors and clarified that the company wished to make a submission as part of the hearing, which would be open to the public.[25] The panel report notes that neither party referred to the NGE submission in their respective submissions.[26] No additional information appears to be publicly available about this NGE intervention.[27]

Beyond traditional state-to-state dispute settlement, the CUSMA also provides two additional mechanisms for panel composition under its specialized labour and environment provisions. With respect to the environment, the CUSMA environment chapter sets out means through which the three parties must incorporate mechanisms for public engagement in their domestic law. It also requires each party to "provide for the receipt and consideration of written questions or comments from persons of that Party regarding its implementation" of the chapter.[28] Further, the CUSMA creates a mechanism through which "any person of a Party may file a submission asserting that a Party is failing to effectively enforce its environmental laws."[29] Those

---

21 *Southern African Customs Union—Safeguard Measure Imposed on Frozen Bone-In Chicken Cuts from the European Union* (2022) at para 22, online (pdf): worldtradelaw. net [perma.cc/RL2U-4SR8].

22 *Ibid* at paras 73–85. Unusually as compared to other FTA panel reports, the Panel provided summaries of the submissions of the *amici* in its final report.

23 *Ibid* at para 25.

24 *Restrictions Applied by Ukraine on Exports of Certain Wood Products to the European Union* (2020) at para 10, online (pdf): me.gov.ua [perma.cc/R4KL-MLST] [*Ukraine— Wood Products*].

25 *Ibid* at para 479.

26 *Ibid* at para 10.

27 The Panel's link to the submission is no longer in service as of the time of writing.

28 *CUSMA*, above note 3, art 24.5.

29 *Ibid*.

submissions are filed with the CEC Secretariat, a body created by a side agreement to the CUSMA called the *Agreement on Environmental Cooperation among the United States, Mexico, and Canada* (ECA). The CEC has a robust public submission process and a specialized team to review submissions from the public. It recently reported that it received 102 submissions from 1994 (since it dates to the *North American Free Trade Agreement* through the end of 2021.[30] It typically has received about four submissions per year, usually from NGEs and also sometimes from individuals.[31] Slightly more than half of the submissions have concerned allegations concerning Mexico.[32] Under the terms of the agreements, the submissions may prompt the creation of a factual record by the CEC staff, which can then trigger additional processes by and among the parties.

With respect to labour concerns, the CUSMA labour chapter also demands that the parties include public engagement in their domestic laws, and the chapter sets up a mechanism for receipt of public submissions concerning the chapter's content.[33] Further, in two annexes to Chapter 31 on Dispute Settlement, the parties created something called a Rapid Response Labor Mechanism (RRM). The RRM is the first of its kind in that it allows one of the parties to impose an economic sanction on a company where the party finds that workers at one of the company's facilities have been denied their right to bargain collectively.[34] NGEs regularly submit petitions and other information to the three governments to alert them to such denials. In an early survey of these petitions, my co-author and I noted that many of the NGEs that have submitted petitions among the more than two dozen in the four years since the Mechanism's entry into force have submitted more than one.[35] The body of petitions received by the governments is largely comprised of those from these repeat players.

Under certain circumstances that space does not allow me to elaborate here, the RRM provides that the parties may agree to have a panel determine

---

30 Commission for Environmental Cooperation, *Submissions on Enforcement Matters: What Have We Learned?* (Montreal: Commission for Environmental Cooperation, 2023).

31 *Ibid.*

32 *Ibid.*

33 *CUSMA*, above note 3, art 23.11.

34 See Kathleen Claussen & Chad P Bown, "Corporate Accountability by Treaty: The New North American Rapid Response Labor Mechanism" (2018) 118:1 *American Journal of International Law* 98.

35 *Ibid.*

whether such a denial of rights exists. This is a fact-finding exercise convened by, to date, the United States and Mexico. The first panel established under this Mechanism recently concluded its work.[36] The Panel invited written submissions from two labour unions involved in the unrest at the workplace as well as a written submission from the employer.[37] Note first that these submissions are distinct from those in the aforementioned commercial disputes because each of these actors is directly affected by or involved in the matter before the panel. In fact, they are the primary players in the matter the panel is tasked with deciding. The employer was also granted leave to submit additional information to the panel following its original submission. Some of the staff of the employer were invited to participate in the panel's verification process.[38] Finally, the Panel "authorize[d]" the employer and the unions to provide additional information following the panel hearing.[39] Of these three submissions, the employer and one of the unions largely aligned their views with Mexico, while the other union was largely aligned with the position of the United States.

Unexpectedly, the panel relied on one of the NGE submissions for an essential finding: that the facility met the treaty's requirements for the panel's review. The Panel found that the United States had failed to meet its burden on this point, but the NGE's representation was sufficient for the panel to reach the necessary conclusion to proceed.[40]

In the labour-related dispute between the European Union and Korea, the panel of experts similarly engaged extensively with multiple stakeholders, as did the parties. First, the Panel arranged to receive *amicus* submissions via email (given that the underlying rules did not so provide).[41] The Panel consequently received six briefs or submissions from institutions and

---

36 See Kathleen Claussen, "Factfinding Jurisdiction: A Review of the Determination from the First USMCA Rapid Response Labor Mechanism Panel" (2024) 51:3 *Legal Issues of Economic Integration* 289.

37 *Re Measures Concerning Labor Rights at the San Martín Mine (US v Mexico)* (2024), MEX-USA-2023-31A-01 (Ch 31 Panel), online (pdf): worldtradelaw.net [perma.cc/ Q5DJ-Q9VD]. In addition, the Panel declined an application from the United States Chamber of Commerce to submit written views because its application came after the deadline indicated in the Rules.

38 *Ibid.*

39 *Ibid.*

40 *Ibid.*

41 *European Union v Republic of Korea (Measures on Trade Union and Labour Relations Adjustment Act)* (2021) at para 11, online: europa.eu [perma.cc/3MQK-FNPD].

twenty-two briefs, submissions, petitions, and email comments from individuals. From what is known, most if not all of these appear to support the European Union's position. In some instances, the European Union relied on these submissions in its own submissions. This approach is a variation on the United States' approach to its labour dispute in Guatemala several years earlier. Second, the Panel made note in its report about some of the new and relevant information provided by the submissions such as the "on the ground" difficulties facing workers, and examples demonstrating the seriousness of the situation.[42] Thus, much like in the CUSMA context, these labour-related fact-finding exercises engage much more closely with NGEs and other participants than do the commercial disputes.

C. Reflections

IT IS EARLY IN THE lifetime of these "present generation" trade agreements, even if some of them soon will be under review and under consideration for possible renewal. We have only a handful of disputes thus far, and only four years of experience under non-traditional FTA tools. Nevertheless, certain trends emerge from the data available to date.

First, panels generally do not appear to rely on NGE submissions for any of their legal interpretations or to aid in their understanding of critical issues in dispute. None of the CUSMA panel reports involving NGE participation spoke to the arguments made by the NGEs apart from noting their submissions. The exception to this trend is among labour panels, such as the first RRM panel that relied on a non-party for a finding that was essential to its jurisdiction, and to a lesser extent, the panel reviewing the Korean labour situation. That panels do not engage more readily with so-called *amici* may be unsurprising to some, because they have the impression that NGEs are "in the facts" and panels "apply the law." According to this view, the purpose of NGE submissions is for "industry buy-in" rather than for additional arguments or to influence the outcome of a particular dispute, but the language of most agreements leaves space for panels to rely more heavily on such submissions.

Second, the low uptake of NGE participation in disputes may be a result of the fact that when dispute settlement panels announce their solicitations

---

42   *Ibid* at para 160.

for NGE participation, those announcements are poorly publicized.[43] They are often only made known via the FTA secretariat website (at best, when there is such a website) and those postings may be limited to a small number of days, constraining the ability of even those closely following a dispute to prepare a submission.

Third, some of the public-facing mechanisms established by states under recent FTAs do not make their utilization statistics publicly available. That is, we do not have an accurate count of public communications to certain mechanisms. We can request that information from governments but where such a request is possible, some governments provide only general data about the number of engagements, and more textured details, such as information about who is contributing, are not available. Even in the context of traditional dispute settlement panels, the publicly available information is limited regarding which NGEs have sought to participate in the dispute settlement proceedings.

Finally, in the case of the labour disputes, we see many of the same actors returning to provide input to governments on multiple occasions.[44] These repeat players have developed a degree of expertise in using the mechanisms. Thus, while the numbers may appear robust in terms of participation of NGEs with respect to certain FTA mechanisms, a closer examination yields that only a small number of actors are participating repeatedly, and diversity is lacking.[45]

D. Concluding Thoughts

ASTRID WIIK, IN HER COMPREHENSIVE doctoral dissertation on the subject in 2018, surveyed the evolving views on the purpose of *amici curiae* in international courts and tribunals.[46] Noting that technology and other changes in the global governance landscape may have changed the purpose and function of these contributions, Wiik nevertheless concludes that *amici* still

---

43 *Ukraine—Wood Products*, above note 24 (noting that the parties gave sixteen days, for example).

44 The repeat player issue is most salient under FTA mechanisms that deal with singular topics such as labour and environment.

45 For example, in the context of the CUSMA Rapid Response Mechanism, the same labour groups contribute repeatedly. By contrast, generalist NGEs from the business community are not regularly submitting to traditional dispute settlement panels.

46 Astrid Wiik, *Amicus Curiae before International Courts and Tribunals* (Baden-Baden: Nomos, 2018).

have something to offer tribunals in their representation of diverse interests that may enhance the legitimacy of an otherwise beleaguered international dispute resolution process.

The experiences under FTAs over the last ten years suggest that NGE submissions have such little visibility and their submissions are so significantly circumscribed that their function may be even more limited than Wiik and other scholars have supposed.[47] While FTA parties have successfully lessened the administrative burden of receiving many of these submissions at least those that are part of the panel process, it appears that the exercise of NGE submission under the CUSMA and other FTAs is largely performative.

What does this mean for parties in their future design of agreements, assuming future agreements have mechanisms that lend themselves to public participation? If we accept that public participation is essential to democracy and a foundational tenet to any good governance system, then future economic governance arrangements ought to at least continue to contemplate a means for public engagement, but designers may wish to re-evaluate the means through which they provide for such participation. For one, they ought to give additional notice and time for NGEs to apply for leave.

But, as noted at the outset, public engagement can take many forms. A more radical re-evaluation of FTA design could re-imagine the place of NGEs in the dispute resolution exercise. Rather than rely on a written submission exercise, panels could consider a specialized hearing for NGE views. Likely, these sorts of arrangements would only be appropriate for certain types of disputes where many groups may be aggrieved or where written submissions may present a barrier to less organized groups that are not in a position to prepare them. The RRM model presents a lesser barrier to entry, but it then creates an administrative burden for the government actors tasked with reviewing hundreds of submissions each year. Getting that balance right may demand tailoring to the tool and experimentation—as trade agreement negotiators are very much used to in recent times.

---

47   See, e.g., Niccolò Ridi, "What Are Amicus Interventions For? Some Provocations on Non-Disputing Party Submissions in International Investment Arbitration" (2024) *Questions of International Law* 98; Anna Dolidze, "International Dispute Resolution as Polyphony? Amicus Curiae Interventions before International Courts and Tribunals" (2022) 54:1 *Georgetown Journal of International Law* 1; David Livshiz, "Public Participation in Disputes Under Regional Trade Agreements: How Much Is Too Much – the Case for a Limited Right of Intervention," Note (2005) 61:3 *NYU Annual Survey of American Law* 529.

CHAPTER 23

The Role of WTO Jurisprudence in FTA Dispute Settlement[*]

Michael Solursh

A. Overview

THE WORLD TRADE ORGANIZATION (WTO) dispute settlement system (DSS), and the body of jurisprudence that has flowed from it, is a remarkable achievement. The WTO DSS has played a central role in clarifying and enforcing WTO rights and obligations for its Members and has often been called the "crown jewel"[1] of the WTO system. Indeed, WTO Members have initiated 633 disputes at the WTO since it came into force in 1995, resulting in over 500 panel and Appellate Body reports and arbitral awards.[2] This has led to the development of a rich body of WTO jurisprudence covering key provisions under many of the WTO agreements.

---

[*]   This chapter is a tribute to Valerie Hughes for long-standing contribution to, and advancement of, WTO law as director and general counsel with the Canadian Trade Law Bureau and as the director of both the Legal Affairs Division and the Appellate Body Secretariat at the WTO.

1   William J Davey, "WTO Dispute Settlement: Crown Jewel or Costume Jewelry?" (2022) 21:3 *World Trade Review* 291. See also WTO, "WTO Disputes Reach 400 Mark" (6 November 2009), online: wto.org [perma.cc/B3PD-BHZS].

2   WTO, "Dispute Settlement Activity – Some Figures" (last visited 27 February 2025), online: wto.org [perma.cc/RN6E-JP2D] [WTO, "Dispute Settlement Activity"].

Unfortunately, the WTO Appellate Body has been non-operational since late 2019 because there is no longer a quorum to hear appeals due to the United States repeatedly blocking the appointment of Appellate Body Members. This situation has led to uncertainty among some WTO Members as to whether disputes can be resolved through the WTO DSS which, in turn, has led to a sharp decline in the number of disputes initiated at the WTO since late 2019. Unless the Appellate Body impasse is resolved, it is expected that WTO Members will increasingly look to resolve disputes under Free Trade Agreements (FTAs) rather than at the WTO.

With the expected increase in disputes under FTAs, this chapter will explore the reasons why WTO jurisprudence will naturally play an influential role in many of those disputes. First, Section B of this chapter will discuss three key factors that will likely lead to an increase in the number of disputes initiated under FTAs rather than through the traditional route of initiating them at the WTO. Second, Section C will discuss why WTO jurisprudence is likely to play an influential role in many of those FTA disputes, including a brief review of completed disputes under some FTAs to illustrate that point.

B. An Expected Increase in Disputes Under FTAs

WHEN A WTO MEMBER DECIDES to initiate a trade dispute with another WTO Member and they are both Parties to the same FTA, the complaining WTO Member will have to determine whether it is strategically advantageous to initiate that dispute at the WTO or under an FTA. This section explores the following three factors that will likely result in a WTO Member resorting to dispute settlement with increased frequency under an FTA rather than at the WTO: (1) the state of WTO dispute settlement, (2) the proliferation of FTAs, and (3) expedited timelines available under FTAs.

Each of these factors will be discussed in turn.

1) The State of WTO Dispute Settlement

A WTO Member will consider many factors in determining whether to initiate a trade dispute at the WTO or under an FTA, including the likelihood of success under either forum, the subject-matter of the dispute, and whether other WTO Members have expressed similar concerns with the alleged non-compliant measure. However, a key consideration since late 2019 for any WTO Member deciding where to initiate a dispute is whether the chosen forum will ultimately bring finality to the matter.

Without a functioning Appellate Body, many WTO Members may look to dispute settlement under an FTA if they risk not achieving a final resolution to the matter at the WTO. To address this concern and preserve the appellate process, WTO Members have established the Multi-Party Interim Appeal Arbitration Arrangement (MPIA) that allows for appeals of panel reports.[3] The MPIA process, while not ideal, is generally an effective alternative to the Appellate Body, replicating most key features under Dispute Settlement Understanding (DSU) Article 17 and includes a standing appellate roster. Further, MPIA signatories commit to following Articles 21 (Implementation) and 22 (Compensation and Suspension of Concessions) of the WTO Dispute Settlement Understanding.[4]

However, the problem with the MPIA is not its effectiveness but rather that only thirty (counting the European Union (EU) as one member) of 166 WTO Members are currently signatories to it.[5] While a fair number of signatories to the MPIA have historically been frequent users of the WTO DSS or represent significant-sized economies, such as Australia, Brazil, Canada, China, the EU, Japan, and New Zealand, many other frequent WTO DSS users or significant-sized economies are not, including the United States, India, many Southeast Asian countries, and all of Africa. The relatively small number of WTO Members that have signed on to the MPIA serves to undermine its use as a reliable option for the majority of the WTO Membership. This is evidenced by the fact that WTO Members have only averaged seven requests for consultations annually since the Appellate Body stopped functioning in 2020 compared to an average of twenty-four requests for consultations annually from 1996–2019.[6]

Overall, without a functioning Appellate Body and only thirty WTO Members currently using the MPIA, this will almost certainly lead to an increased use of dispute settlement under FTAs when that option is available for disputing Members.

---

3   WTO, *Statement on a Mechanism for Developing, Documenting and Sharing Practices and Procedures in the Conduct of WTO Disputes*, WTO Doc JOB/DSB/1/Add.12 (2020) at Annex 1, para 1, online (pdf): docs.wto.org [perma.cc/YUN4-P2V8].

4   *Ibid* at Annex 1, para 17, which provides "pursuant to Article 25.4 of the DSU, Articles 21 and 22 of the DSU shall apply mutatis mutandis to the arbitration award issued in this dispute."

5   See Geneva Trade Platform, "Multi-Party Interim Appeal Arbitration Arrangement (MPIA)" (last visited 30 July 2025), online: wtoplurilaterals.info [perma.cc/QM9L-A9DY].

6   WTO, "Dispute Settlement Activity," above note 2 (there were 568 requests for consultations at the WTO from 1996–2019, which averages out to twenty-four requests annually. In comparison, there have been twenty-eight requests for consultations from 2020–23, averaging out to only seven requests annually. There were nine requests for consultations in 2024 and two in 2025, as of 14 February).

2) The Proliferation of FTAs

A second factor that will likely lead to the increased use of dispute settlement under FTAs is their rapid proliferation since the WTO came into force in 1995. FTAs have increased in number from approximately six FTAs in force in 1995 to 373 FTAs in force in 2025.[7]

Further, many recent FTAs, often termed "mega-regionals," involve a significantly larger number of countries compared to traditional FTAs. This includes the *Comprehensive and Progressive Agreement for Trans-Pacific Partnership* (CPTPP), which has twelve member-states spanning five continents and came into force in 2018; the *Regional Comprehensive Economic Partnership* (RCEP), which has fifteen member-states spanning two continents and came into force in 2022; and the *African Continental Free Trade Agreement* (AfCFTA), which has fifty-four member-states, covering almost all of Africa and came into force in 2019.[8]

In addition, many recently concluded "next generation" FTAs, such as the *Canada-European Union Comprehensive Economic and Trade Agreement* (CETA), CPTPP and *Canada-United States-Mexico Agreement* (CUSMA), have more comprehensive coverage when compared to earlier FTAs and the WTO agreements. This includes not only more extensive coverage for areas already covered by the WTO agreements, such as trade in goods and service, intellectual property, and monopolies and state enterprises but also for new areas of trade, such as digital trade, regulatory cooperation, competition, and inclusive trade.

Despite the proliferation of FTAs, a WTO Member may still choose to initiate a dispute at the WTO for strategic reasons or simply because no FTA exists between the two disputing Members. For example, none of the United States, the EU, or China have an FTA in force with the other. Accordingly, dispute settlement at the WTO is still the only recourse currently available for disputes between the world's three biggest economies.

Nonetheless, as the number of WTO Members that are parties to multiple FTAs continues to grow, and the Appellate Body impasse persists, dispute settlement under FTAs will likely become an increasingly appealing and normalized option for countries. This has certainly been the case under CUSMA, which has had five disputes initiated under it since it came into force on 1 July 2020, and no disputes between Canada, the United States, or

---

7   WTO, "Regional Trade Agreements" (last visited 27 February 2025), online: wto.org [perma.cc/S9BP-NXLC].

8   In addition, it is becoming more common to see trading blocs (e.g., the Association of Southeast Asian Nations) negotiate on behalf of all its members as a bloc, which translates to each member of that bloc having the individual option to bring disputes at the WTO or under that bloc's FTA.

Mexico initiated at the WTO since that time. This can be contrasted with the situation from 1995 to 2020 when almost every dispute between Canada, the United States, and Mexico was handled through the WTO system and not under the former *North American Free Trade Agreement* (NAFTA) (CUSMA's predecessor) dispute settlement system.[9]

3) Expedited Timelines Under FTA Dispute Settlement

The third factor that will likely lead to WTO Members turning with increased frequency to dispute settlement under FTAs is that it typically offers expedited timelines to resolve disputes compared to WTO dispute settlement. As an initial point, FTAs usually provide for only panel level review of disputes, not appellate level review, whereas both levels of review exist under the WTO DSS. However, even if WTO appeals are not factored in, the prescribed timelines for the panel process alone—from the request for the establishment of a panel until a final panel report is issued—are faster under recent FTAs than under the WTO DSS as illustrated by the following chart.

Trade Agreement	WTO	CUSMA	CETA
Prescribed Timeline for a Panel Proceeding[10]	304 days[11]	245 days	195 days

Furthermore, the actual duration of a WTO panel proceeding has taken 647 days on average to be completed, which is significantly longer in practice than the 304 days it is supposed to take under the WTO timelines.[12] In comparison, as illustrated in the chart below, CUSMA panel proceedings have taken 311 days on average to complete which, while still above the prescribed CUSMA timeline of 245 days, is less than half the time WTO panel proceedings have actually taken to complete.

---

9   There were only three NAFTA Chapter 20 state-to-state disputes, with the last dispute occurring in 2001 (see *Re Cross-Border Trucking Services (Mexico v US)* (2001), USA-98-2008-01 (Ch 20 Panel), online (pdf): worldtradelaw.net [perma.cc/U69L-LU7J]).

10 This includes the prescribed WTO DSU timeframe for a panel proceeding counting from the request to establish a panel to the issuance of a panel's final report. It does not include periods of appeal, implementation, compliance, or suspension phases.

11 In practice, thirty days should be added to the WTO prescribed timeline since WTO procedure dictates that a panel is established on a Member's second request to establish a panel, which occurs one month after the first request.

12 This number was rounded up from 646.55 days, which was arrived at by assessing publicly available information on the length of WTO panel processes from 1995–2024 (WTO, "Dispute Settlement Activity," above note 2).

CUSMA Dispute	Canada—Dairy TRQ Allocation Measures I (CDA-2021-31-010)	Canada—Dairy TRQ Allocation Measures II (CDA-USA-2023-31-010)	United States—Crystalline Silicon Photovoltaic Cells Safeguard Measure (USA-CDA-2021-31-01)	United States—Automotive Parts and Vehicles—Rules of Origin (USA-MEX-CDA-2022-31-01)	Mexico—Measures Concerning Genetically Engineered Corn (MEX-USA-2023-31-01)
Prescribed Timeline for a Panel Proceeding[13]	245 days				
Actual Length of Panel Proceeding	210 days	284 days	226 days	343 days	492 days

13   This includes the prescribed CUSMA timeframe for a panel proceeding counting from the request to establish a panel to the issuance of a panel's final report. It does not include periods of implementation, compliance, suspension, or mediation phases.

A WTO Member deciding to bring a claim at the WTO or under an FTA will certainly consider the likely quicker timelines for a panel proceeding to be completed under an FTA than under the WTO DSS when determining where to initiate a dispute.

Overall, this section has highlighted three key considerations as to why a WTO Member, which typically would have opted for WTO dispute settlement in the past, will be likely to turn to FTA dispute settlement in the future. In particular, the proliferation of FTAs has made FTA dispute settlement an option available to an increasing number of WTO Members. This fact, combined with the ability of FTA dispute settlement to offer quicker resolution of disputes and bring finality to them, will increasingly make FTA dispute settlement an appealing option, particularly until the Appellate Body situation is resolved.

C. The Role of WTO Jurisprudence in FTA Dispute Settlement

HAVING SET OUT IN SECTION B why there is likely to be an increased use of dispute settlement under FTAs, this Section discusses the influential role that WTO jurisprudence is likely to play in resolving those disputes.

First, the relationship between FTAs and the WTO agreements will be discussed. Second, it will be examined how that relationship, when combined with the rules of interpretation a panel is required to apply in an FTA dispute, should naturally lead to panels and disputing Parties seeking guidance from WTO jurisprudence. Last, a brief review of disputes under some EU FTAs and the CUSMA will be used to highlight the extent to which WTO jurisprudence has been used in FTA disputes to date.

1) The Relationship Between FTAs and the WTO Agreements

FTAs are not created in isolation. The WTO itself has acknowledged that FTAs and the multilateral WTO framework must operate in a coherent and harmonious manner.[14] Typically, the core obligations and main subject matter covered under the WTO agreements are also contained in FTAs. This

---

14   WTO, *Nairobi Ministerial Declaration*, WTO Doc WT/MIN(15)/DEC (2015) at para 3, online (pdf): docs.wto.org [perma.cc/7DVG-KA8E] (the declaration provides that "[w]

includes, *inter alia*, provisions governing trade in goods, services, intellectual property, sanitary and phytosanitary measures, technical barriers to trade, procurement, and subsidies. Moreover, not only is there substantial overlap in subject-matter covered by FTAs and the WTO agreements, but it is typical for key provisions and definitions of the latter to be directly incorporated by reference into FTAs.[15] While there can still be many differences in the subject-matter covered under FTAs and the WTO agreements, the essence of obligations under both typically are directed toward the same overlapping purpose: to prevent discriminatory treatment and other barriers to trade.

In addition, the subject-matter of disputes initiated under FTAs and the WTO agreements is also likely to overlap. The following chart sets out the subject-matter of WTO disputes to date.

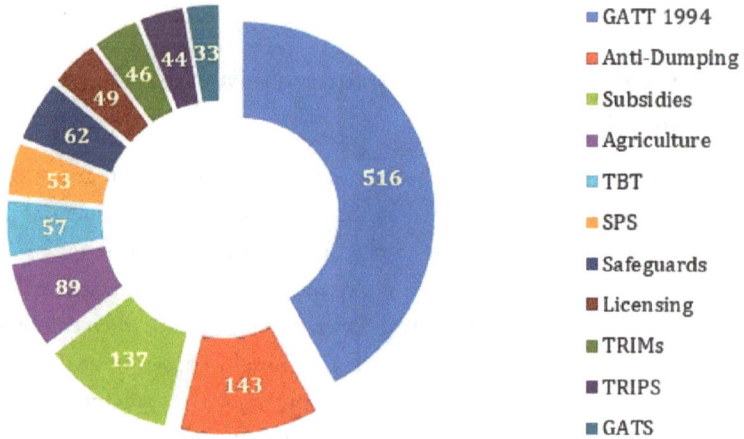

Legend:
- GATT 1994
- Anti-Dumping
- Subsidies
- Agriculture
- TBT
- SPS
- Safeguards
- Licensing
- TRIMs
- TRIPS
- GATS

Values shown: 516, 143, 137, 89, 57, 53, 62, 49, 46, 44, 33

AGREEMENTS RAISED IN WTO DISPUTES (1995-2024)
SOURCE: WTO, "DISPUTE SETTLEMENT ACTIVITY — SOME FIGURES" (LAST VISITED 27 FEBRUARY 2025), ONLINE: WTO.ORG [PERMA.CC/RN6E-JP2D].

---

e reaffirm the need to ensure that Regional Trade Agreements (RTAs) remain complementary to, not a substitute for, the multilateral trading system").

15   See, e.g., *Comprehensive Economic and Trade Agreement*, Canada and EU, 20 October 2016, arts 2.3 (National Treatment), 2.11 (Export-Import Restrictions), 7.1–7.8 (Subsidies and Countervailing Measures (SCM Agreement)), 4.2 (Technical Barriers to Trade (TBT) Agreement), 5.4 (Sanitary and Phytosanitary (SPS) Agreement), 20.32(4) (Trade-Related Aspects of Intellectual Property Rights (TRIPS) Agreement), and 28.3 (General Exceptions), online: international.gc.ca [perma.cc/6S5M-TXX7] [CETA]; *Comprehensive and Progressive Agreement for Trans-Pacific Partnership*, 8 March 2018, arts 2.3 (National Treatment), 2.10 (Export-Import Restrictions), 2.19 (Agriculture), 6.8 (SCM Agreement), 8.4 (TBT Agreement), 7.1–7.4 (SPS Agreement), and 29.1 (General Exceptions), online: international.gc.ca [perma.cc/AE8Z-KBXP] [CPTPP].

This chart illustrates that 89 percent of WTO disputes have involved trade in goods measures (*General Agreement on Tariffs and Trade* (GATT 1994), Agriculture, TBT, SPS), *General Agreement on Trade in Services* (GATS), and trade remedy matters (Anti-Dumping, Subsidies and Safeguards).[16] To date, the subject-matter of FTA disputes has generally involved similar content except for trade in services disputes. For example, under CUSMA, all five disputes initiated to date have involved trade in goods-related matters (market access, agriculture, safeguards, and SPS disputes).[17] The same is the case for disputes under the *EU-Ukraine Association Agreement* ("EU-Ukraine AA") and the *EU-South African Development Community Economic Partnership Agreement* ("EU-SADC EPA"), respectively. One would expect FTA and WTO dispute subject-matter to continue to overlap and expand to other areas of growing economic importance, such as trade in services, intellectual property, and digital trade.

2) The Interpretation Rules Applied in FTA Disputes and their Relevance to WTO Jurisprudence

The similar subject-matter covered under FTAs and the WTO Agreements will naturally result in both panels and disputing parties turning to relevant WTO jurisprudence for guidance in FTA disputes. However, this is particularly the case when that similar subject-matter is considered in light of the rules of interpretation that panels are required to apply in FTA disputes. First, some FTAs require a panel to consider relevant WTO jurisprudence to interpret FTA provisions. Second, almost all FTAs require a panel to interpret the FTA by applying the customary rules of interpretation under international law, namely Articles 31 and 32 of the *Vienna Convention on the Law of Treaties* ("Vienna Convention"). Each is discussed in turn.

a) FTAs that Require WTO Jurisprudence to be Considered

To differing degrees, many FTAs direct a panel to consider relevant WTO jurisprudence when relevant to a matter in dispute. Some apply this rule

---

16 WTO, "Dispute Settlement Activity," above note 2. It should be qualified that WTO disputes often involve multiple agreements being challenged in one dispute. Further, while subsidy and anti-dumping matters can fall under an FTA, typically FTAs direct such disputes to the WTO.

17 In addition, under NAFTA, the three Chapter 20 disputes involved a safeguards matter, agricultural goods, and a trade in services matter, respectively.

broadly, generally requiring a panel to consider interpretations in WTO panel and Appellate Body reports when relevant to any issue in dispute, while other FTAs apply it narrowly, only requiring a panel to consider such reports when WTO provisions are directly incorporated into an FTA.

Some EU FTAs take the broader approach. For example, Article 29.17 of CETA provides "[t]he arbitration panel shall also take into account relevant interpretations in reports of Panels and the Appellate Body adopted by the WTO Dispute Settlement Body."[18] Further, Article 15.21 of the EU-Vietnam FTA provides "[t]he arbitration panel shall also take into account relevant interpretations in reports of panels and of the Appellate Body adopted by the WTO Dispute Settlement Body under Annex 2 of the WTO Agreement."[19]

In comparison, other FTAs, such as the CPTPP, take a narrower approach by requiring a panel to consider adopted WTO panel and Appellate Body reports only when a WTO provision has been directly incorporated into an FTA.[20] Yet other FTAs, such as RCEP, take a middle ground approach that *require* a panel to consider relevant WTO panel and Appellate Body reports when a WTO provision is directly incorporated into an FTA but also acknowledge that a panel *may* still consider those reports even when a WTO provision is not directly incorporated.[21]

When an FTA includes the broader rule of interpretation, it is highly likely that such jurisprudence will be put forward by both Parties to a dispute and examined by the panel to assist in interpreting FTA provisions and other matters in dispute. However, even when an FTA contains the narrower approach or simply contains no rule whatsoever requiring WTO jurisprudence to be considered, it is still likely that an FTA panel will consider such jurisprudence when applying the interpretation rules under the Vienna Convention.

b) The Application of the Vienna Convention in an FTA Dispute

Even if an FTA does not include a rule requiring panels to consider relevant WTO jurisprudence, FTAs typically direct panels to apply Articles 31

---

18   *CETA*, above note 15, art 29.17.

19   *Free Trade Agreement between the European Union and the Socialist Republic of Viet Nam*, 30 June 2019, art 15.21, online (pdf): vntr.moit.gov.vn [perma.cc/HZE9-Z8Y4].

20   See *CPTPP*, above note 15, art 28.12(3); *Regional Comprehensive Economic Partnership*, 15 November 2020, art 19.4.2, online (pdf): asean.org [perma.cc/B34A-XYJU] [*RCEP*].

21   See *RCEP*, *ibid*, art 19.4(2).

and 32 of the Vienna Convention to interpret FTA provisions.[22] A proper application of the Vienna Convention should naturally make WTO jurisprudence relevant to the interpretation of FTA provisions, particularly when they are the same or similar to WTO provisions. Where exactly WTO jurisprudence should be considered under a Vienna Convention interpretation is up for debate.

Article 31 of the Vienna Convention provides in the relevant part:

1. A treaty shall be interpreted in good faith in accordance with the ordinary meaning to be given to the terms of the treaty in their context and in the light of its object and purpose, and...
2. There shall be taken into account, together with the context:
    (c) any relevant rules of international law applicable in the relations between the parties.

A reasonable argument could be made that jurisprudence interpreting WTO provisions constitutes relevant context to be considered under Article 31(1) when interpreting similar FTA provisions. Even if WTO jurisprudence is not properly characterized as "context" under Article 31(1), it would be reasonable to consider it under Article 31(3)(c) as "any relevant rules of international law applicable in the relations between the parties." While Article 31(3)(c) refers to "relevant rules," not "relevant jurisprudence," it is reasonable to expect that when an FTA panel considers relevant WTO provisions to assist in interpreting FTA provisions, it would necessarily also consider any "judicial" interpretations informing the meaning of those WTO provisions.[23] Alternatively, WTO jurisprudence could be considered under Article 38 of the Statute of International Court of Justice, which are certainly "relevant rules of international law." In particular, Article 38(1)(d) specifically applies to "judicial decisions" which should cover WTO jurisprudence as well. Last, WTO jurisprudence could likely be considered by an FTA panel as a supplementary means of interpretation under Article 32 of the Vienna Convention

---

22 See *CETA*, above note 15, art 29.17; *CPTPP*, above note 15, art 28.12(3); *Canada-United States-Mexico Agreement*, 10 December 2019, art 31.13(4), online: international.gc.ca [perma.cc/G9J2-NMFJ] [*CUSMA*]; *RCEP*, *ibid*, art 19.4(1).

23 An application of Vienna Convention Article 31(3)(c) that allows WTO jurisprudence related to a provision to be considered when comparing WTO and FTA provisions was implicitly the position of the EU and the Panel. See *Southern African Customs Union— Safeguard Measure Imposed on Frozen Bone-In Chicken Cuts from the European Union* (2022) at paras 218–19 and 231, online (pdf): worldtradelaw.net [perma.cc/RL2U-4SR8] [*SACU—Chicken Cuts*].

to confirm the meaning of an interpretation under Article 31 or when its application leads to an ambiguous or unreasonable interpretation.

While it can be debated how WTO jurisprudence should be best characterized under a proper application of Articles 31 or 32 of the Vienna Convention, undoubtedly it will be taken into consideration under those Articles in some manner if relevant to an issue in an FTA dispute. This fact was highlighted in *SACU—Safeguard Measures Imposed on Frozen Bone-In Chicken Cuts from the European Union* (*SACU—Chicken Cuts*), a dispute between the EU and the South African Customs Union under the EU-SADC EPA.

Unlike many EU FTAs, the EU-SADC EPA requires only that a panel interpret its provisions by applying the Vienna Convention rules but does not have a separate rule requiring a panel to consider WTO jurisprudence.[24] Despite the exclusion of a rule requiring relevant WTO jurisprudence to be considered, the EU argued that when "the WTO rules and agreements and the EPA's provisions contain language that is identical or closely resembling, it is logical and reasonable to interpret them in the same way, *as both this Panel, the WTO panels and the Appellate Body are bound by the same customary rules of interpretation of public international law*"[25] (emphasis added). The Panel agreed with the EU noting that in applying the Vienna Convention, while WTO law is not binding, "this leaves much room for the Arbitration Panel to discuss this case law in terms of persuasiveness and relevance to the issues at hand."[26]

The reliance on WTO jurisprudence under a Vienna Convention application becomes all the more likely when one considers that WTO panels and the Appellate Body are also mandated to apply the Vienna Convention under DSU Article 3.2.[27] Accordingly, an FTA panel will naturally turn to WTO jurisprudence when applying the Vienna Convention to assist in interpreting FTA provisions that are the same or similar to WTO provisions and which have already been interpreted by WTO panels or the Appellate Body that have applied *those very same rules* of interpretation.

---

24 *European Union—South African Development Community Economic Partnership Agreement*, 10 June 2016, art 304, online (pdf): europa.eu [perma.cc/E72G-HRAN].

25 *SACU—Chicken Cuts*, above note 23 at para 231.

26 *Ibid.*

27 *United States—Standards for Reformulated and Conventional Gasoline (Complaint by Venezuela)* (1996), WTO Doc WT/DS2/AB/R at 17 (Appellate Body Report), online: docs.wto.org [perma.cc/Z7C8-8PYY].

3) Examining the Use of WTO Jurisprudence in Disputes under EU FTAs and CUSMA

In the preceding subsections, I have advanced the position that due to the significant overlap between FTA and WTO provisions and the rules of interpretation commonly applied under FTAs, WTO jurisprudence will play an influential role in many FTA disputes. In this subsection, I briefly review disputes completed under some EU FTAs and the CUSMA[28] to gauge the extent to which, to date, they demonstrate that WTO jurisprudence is already playing an influential role in FTA disputes.

a) EU FTA Disputes

IN *SACU—CHICKEN CUTS* DISCUSSED IN subsection C. 2) b), above, the EU challenged an SADC safeguard measure imposed on frozen bone-in chicken cuts. While the main issues in dispute were with respect to bilateral safeguard provisions specific to the EU-SADC EPA, there was overlap between those provisions and the WTO *Agreement on Safeguards*. To assist in interpreting the relevant EU-SADC EPA safeguard provisions, as well as other secondary matters in dispute, the Panel turned frequently to WTO jurisprudence, citing twenty-three WTO panel or Appellate Body reports in its final report.[29]

A key reason for the Panel's extensive use of WTO jurisprudence was due to the overlap in subject matter and provisions between the EPA and relevant WTO Agreement. The Panel, highlighting this close relationship, noted:

> [T]rade agreements, such as the EPA, do not emerge from a vacuum; they do not seek to isolate their parties from the multilateral trade regime, but only to deepen and qualify their common relationship in light

---

28 Based on publicly available information, twenty-five state-to-state disputes have been initiated or completed under FTAs to date: five CUSMA disputes, three NAFTA disputes, one CPTPP dispute, four disputes under different EU FTAs, and twelve Mercosur disputes. This chapter focuses only on two EU FTA disputes because one has not yet been completed and the other, under the *EU-South Korea Free Trade Agreement*, pertains to labour, which is not covered under the WTO Agreements. In addition, only CUSMA, not NAFTA, disputes were reviewed in detail because the three NAFTA disputes were in the early years of WTO dispute settlement (yet still did reference available WTO jurisprudence and earlier GATT jurisprudence). The Mercosur panel reports were not reviewed because no English translations were available. Lastly, labour, investment, and procurement disputes were not considered.

29 See *SACU—Chicken Cuts*, above note 23 at 4–6 for the list of WTO jurisprudence cited by the panel.

of Article XXIV GATT. The language adopted by the EPA is key, and it is not a coincidence if it tracks or substantially follows that of the multilateral trade regime; when this is the case, the harmonious development and coherence of international (economic) law require the Arbitration Panel to give special care and consideration to the examples and findings of earlier decisions by international trade panels.[30]

Further, the Panel astutely noted that WTO jurisprudence was also relevant because the Parties in their pleadings "relied on (or criticised) WTO panel and AB reports . . . and *most of the reports and decisions cited by the Arbitration Panel in this Final Report stems from the discussions between the Parties*" (emphasis added).[31] This point is important to emphasize because panels adjudicating trade disputes, whether at the WTO or under an FTA, will naturally consider the arguments put forward in the written submissions of the disputing Parties. To the extent Parties advance arguments based on WTO jurisprudence, it is only natural that an FTA panel will have to also consider that jurisprudence in its assessment of the matter at hand.

In addition to *SACU—Chicken Cuts*, the panel in *Restrictions applied by Ukraine on exports of certain wood products to the European Union* (*Ukraine—Wood Products*) also turned to WTO jurisprudence to help interpret FTA provisions at issue.[32] In this dispute, the EU brought a claim under the *European Union-Ukraine Association Agreement* against an export ban imposed by the Ukraine on certain wood products and unprocessed timber from its territory.[33] The provisions at issue significantly overlapped with WTO provisions, even more so than in *SACU—EU Chicken Cuts*. This was in two respects. First, the EU claimed that the Ukrainian export ban on wood products and unprocessed timber was inconsistent with provisions under the EU-Ukraine AA, which both directly incorporated GATT Article XI (Import-Export Restrictions) but also contained its own customized provisions governing import and export restrictions. Second, Ukraine relied on GATT Article XX, which was

---

30   *Ibid* at para 233.

31   *Ibid* at para 229.

32   The *EU-Ukraine Association Agreement* contains two interpretation rules. First, it requires the Vienna Convention to be applied when interpreting the Agreement's provision. Second, it also requires WTO jurisprudence to be adopted when WTO provisions are directly incorporated into the Agreement.

33   *Restrictions Applied by Ukraine on Exports of Certain Wood Products to the European Union* (2020), online (pdf): me.gov.ua [perma.cc/R4KL-MLST] [*Ukraine—Wood Products*].

directly incorporated into the EU-Ukraine AA, to defend its measures if the Panel found a violation of the Agreement.

The EU and Ukraine both used WTO jurisprudence in their written submissions to support their arguments relating to matters at issue.[34] Given the extent to which the Parties raised WTO jurisprudence, the Panel cited thirty-five WTO panel and Appellate Body reports in its ruling, with respect to both the main provisions at issue that were similar to WTO provisions (i.e., GATT Articles XI and XX) but also to assist in resolving other procedural matters.[35] The Panel also referenced Article 320 of the EU-Ukraine AA in its rulings under GATT Article XI and XX that, when WTO provisions are identical to those under the FTA, required it to "adopt an interpretation which is consistent with any relevant interpretation established in rulings of the WTO Dispute Settlement Body."[36] *Ukraine—Wood Products*, similar to *SACU—Chicken Cuts*, is another example to illustrate that WTO jurisprudence will be turned to by both the disputing Parties and Panel when the subject-matter and provisions at issue in an FTA dispute are the same or similar to that under WTO agreements.

b) CUSMA Disputes

Turning to CUSMA, unlikely many EU FTAs, it does not contain an interpretation rule directing panels to consider relevant WTO jurisprudence. This is not surprising given it was negotiated by the first Trump Administration, which had openly taken issue with the WTO Appellate Body. Instead, the CUSMA only contains the more typical rule found in FTAs that panels apply the Vienna Convention to interpret the CUSMA.[37] Nonetheless, WTO jurisprudence has generally still been consistently referenced in CUSMA disputes, particularly where the provisions in dispute are similar to WTO provisions.

For example, in *Mexico—Measures Concerning Genetically Engineered Corn* (*Mexico—GMO Corn*), there was significant overlap between CUSMA provisions at issue and WTO provisions. The United States challenged two Mexican measures, one which prohibited the use of genetically modified corn grain for human consumption through flour processing (i.e., for dough

---

34   See, e.g., *ibid* at paras 98–103.

35   See *ibid* at 6–9 for a list of all the WTO disputes cited by the Panel throughout its report; see *ibid* at para 121 with respect to the Panel's use of WTO jurisprudence related to a procedural matter.

36   See *ibid* at paras 121, 203–5, 211, 217, and 327.

37   *CUSMA*, above note 22, art 31.13(4).

and tortilla) and the other which called for the gradual substitution and replacement of genetically modified corn for animal feed and industrial use for human consumption. The United States alleged that these two measures were inconsistent with the CUSMA SPS Chapter and CUSMA Article 2.11 (Import and Export Restrictions). Both the CUSMA SPS Chapter and Article 2.11 have significant overlap, and in many instances incorporate by reference, their counterpart WTO provisions under the SPS Agreement and GATT Article XI (Quantitative Restrictions), respectively. In addition, Mexico attempted to justify the alleged breach of its CUSMA obligations under CUSMA Article 32.1 (General Exceptions), which incorporates GATT Article XX.

Both Mexico and the United States frequently turned to WTO jurisprudence to support their positions with respect to the CUSMA SPS Chapter, CUSMA Article 2.11 and CUSMA Article 32.1, as well as other for other matters. Mexico referenced forty-six WTO panel and Appellate Body reports in its Initial Written Submission and fifty-two such reports in its Rebuttal Submission while the United States raised fourteen WTO panel and Appellate Body reports in its Initial Written Submission and twenty-seven such reports in its Rebuttal Submission.[38] The Panel issued its report in December 2025 finding that that Mexico's measure were inconsistent with the CUSMA.[39] In its final report, the Panel extensively referenced the WTO jurisprudence argued throughout the Parties' submissions, demonstrating that such jurisprudence was frequently part of its deliberations.

Secondly, in *United States—Crystalline Silicon Photovoltaic Cells Safeguard Measure* (*US—Solar Safeguards*), Canada challenged the United States' failure to exclude Canadian CSP Cells from a global safeguard action on those products as inconsistent with CUSMA requirements. Under the CUSMA, a safeguard action must be imposed in a manner consistent with Article XIX of the GATT 1994 and the WTO *Agreement on Safeguards*, but then products from the other CUSMA Parties can be excluded from that safeguard measure if certain CUSMA requirements are satisfied. While the specific provisions at issue were unique to CUSMA and there was not nearly as much overlap with WTO provisions as was the case in *Mexico—GMO Corn*, still, both the

---

38 See Table of Cases in Mexico's Initial and Rebuttal Written Submissions; See Table of Exhibits in United States First and Second Written Submissions.

39 *Re Mexico—Measures Concerning Genetically Modified Corn (Mexico v US)* (2023), MEX-USA-2023-31-01 (Ch 31 Panel), online: worldtradelaw.net [perma.cc/ B59P-X29L].

United States and Canada used WTO jurisprudence to support their legal arguments when the CUSMA provisions at issue were the same or similar to WTO provisions. This was both with respect to whether a safeguard measure was properly imposed in accordance with WTO obligations and if the CUSMA requirements to exclude certain countries from that safeguard measure were satisfied.[40] Canada cited two WTO panel and Appellate Body reports in its Initial Written Submission and eleven such reports in its Rebuttal Submission while the United States cited three WTO panel and Appellate Body reports in its Initial Written Submission and eight such reports in its Rebuttal Submission.[41]

While the Panel and Parties in *US—Solar Safeguards* did not cite WTO jurisprudence in its final report to the same degree as the *Mexico—GMO Corn* Panel, the dispute still demonstrates that Parties will raise such jurisprudence when the provisions at issue are the same or similar to WTO provisions, which should then require the Panel to consider its relevance in its deliberations. This is particularly so as the CUSMA Article 31.13(6) requires that "the panel shall base its report on . . . the submissions and arguments of the disputing Parties."[42]

In comparison, when there is not a strong substantive overlap between WTO and FTA provisions in dispute, Parties and the panel have still typically turned to WTO jurisprudence when relevant to a matter but naturally its use will be more limited. For example, there have been three CUSMA disputes where the provisions at issue are unique to CUSMA with little to no substantive overlap with WTO provisions. In *Canada—Dairy TRQ Allocation Measures I* and *Canada—Dairy TRQ Allocation Measures II* (Dairy Disputes), the United States challenged Canada's dairy quota allocation under CUSMA provisions that had no similar WTO provisions. Similarly, in *United States—Automotive Rules of Origin*, Canada challenged the United States auto rule of origin requirements under CUSMA that had no similar WTO provision. In all three disputes, while there was no substantive overlap between the FTA

---

40 See, e.g., *United States—Crystalline Silicon Photovoltaic Cells Safeguard Measure* (Initial Written Submission by Canada) at paras 71, 72, and 77 (including footnotes), online (pdf): international.gc.ca [perma.cc/JZ6K-QPPY]; *United States—Crystalline Silicon Photovoltaic Cells Safeguard Measure* (Rebuttal Submission of the United States) at paras 64 and 77 (including footnotes), online (pdf): ustr.gov [perma.cc/6D7F-K6DV].

41 See List of Exhibits in Canada's Initial and Rebuttal Written Submissions; See Table of Exhibits in United States First and Second Written Submissions.

42 *CUSMA*, above note 22, art 31.13(6).

provisions at issue and WTO provisions, WTO jurisprudence was still used in limited fashion when relevant to ancillary issues raised by the Parties, such as treaty interpretation, quota administration, and procedural matters.[43]

Overall, a review of disputes under some EU FTAs and the CUSMA indicates that Parties will raise, and panels will examine, WTO jurisprudence when relevant to an issue in dispute under an FTA. This is particularly the case when the FTA provisions at issue are the same or similar to WTO provisions but also for ancillary matters in dispute.

D. Conclusion

WTO JURISPRUDENCE OFFERS A RICH and comprehensive body of law to support Parties and panels in FTA disputes, often involving subject-matter and provisions that significantly overlap with those under FTAs. Furthermore, WTO jurisprudence offers FTA Parties and panels consistent and uniform interpretations to rely on that have often already accounted for WTO panel errors, particularly as FTA dispute settlement typically does not have an appellate level of review.

Much has been written about the need to resolve the Appellate Body impasse in light of the integral role dispute settlement plays in the WTO system. However, with the proliferation of FTAs, the need to resolve the impasse and foster the continued growth of WTO jurisprudence becomes even more pressing when one considers the important and influential role such jurisprudence will increasingly play in resolving disputes under FTAs as well.

---

43 For example, in the Dairy Disputes, both the United States and Canada relied on WTO jurisprudence to support the proper application of treaty interpretation principles, including Articles 31 and 32 of the Vienna Convention and how the principle of fairness should be applied in administering quota allocations. Further, in *United States— Automotive Rules of Origin*, while WTO jurisprudence played a more limited role in the Parties submissions, it was still used to support Party positions with respect to treaty interpretation, the GATT test for NVNI claims, and the legal effect of statements made by government officials.

CHAPTER 24

Beyond the Shores of Lake Geneva: Does the WTO Secretariat Have a Role to Play in PTA Dispute Settlement?

Scott Falls

A. Introduction

IN THE SPRING OF 2018, I had the pleasure of participating in the inaugural Queen's University/OttawaU Joint TradeLab Clinic, under Valerie's supervision. Normally, Canadian law school students in their final semester look to ride out the remainder of the academic year in as easy a fashion as possible. I, on the other hand, was still licking my wounds from a painful early exit in the previous year's John H Jackson Moot Court Competition (still, at that time, called the "ELSA") and eager to redeem myself with Valerie, who also happened to be our moot coach and therefore a key witness to my crash and burn.

It seems that Valerie was still sufficiently fond of me at the time to assign me to what was undoubtedly the most interesting project: assisting the Canadian Trade Law Bureau in assessing whether it was feasible to outsource the administration of disputes under Canadian preferential trade agreements (PTAs) to an external institution. The more our team examined this question, the more we began to understand the importance of quality secretariat services for the efficient and effective resolution of international trade disputes and the problems that can arise where parties and panelists lack such support.

Given the vast majority of PTA dispute settlement mechanisms (DSMs) do not establish a secretariat and provide limited (if any) details on the provision of secretariat support[1], PTA panels may face challenges in efficiently carrying out their mandates. But would assigning the secretariat functions to an external institution solve this problem, and if so, which institution would be best placed to take up this role?

As the former director of the Legal Affairs Division and Appellate Body Secretariat, it should be no surprise that Valerie was particularly intrigued by the prospect of the World Trade Organization (WTO) Secretariat playing a role in administering PTA disputes. Indeed, given its experience, expertise, and capabilities in administering state-to-state trade disputes, the WTO Secretariat appears on its face to be the most appropriate institution for providing secretariat support in PTA disputes. Yet the conclusion of our TradeLab Report was that it was "highly unlikely" that WTO Members would agree to the WTO Secretariat providing such services "in the short term," and we advised that "Canada and other members should undertake ongoing efforts to negotiate this type of arrangement in the future."[2]

Since our report was issued in May 2018, several notable developments—in particular the demise of the Appellate Body and proliferation of PTA disputes—have made it worthwhile to revisit the question of whether the WTO Secretariat could play a role in administering PTA disputes. This *festschrift* does not intend to exhaustively examine the issue but rather takes a high-level look at the challenges that arise in dispute settlement administration under PTAs and the feasibility of outsourcing this responsibility to the WTO Secretariat.[3]

---

1   The term "secretariat support" as used in this chapter captures all services that may be provided by individuals working with, for, or under the supervision of panelists. It therefore includes administrative and logistical services, as well as substantive legal work if such work is undertaken.

2   Brendan Robertson, Scott Falls, & Alycia Novacefski, *Secretariat Support for Ad Hoc Panels Under Canada's Free Trade Agreements: Challenges and Options* (Geneva: TradeLab, 2018) at 81, online (pdf): tradelab.org [perma.cc/D4T6-LZ6A].

3   For a recent in-depth analysis of the potential role of the WTO in WTA disputes, see generally, Cornelia Furculiță, *The WTO and the New Generation EU FTA Dispute Settlement Mechanisms* (Cham, CH: Springer, 2021) 341–62.

B. Secretariat Support in PTA Dispute Settlement

IN THE SAME WAY THAT judges of many domestic legal systems rely on the assistance of clerks and secretaries to carry out their mandates, arbitrators, judges, and other adjudicators at the international level are often supported by individuals carrying out an array of different tasks. These "unseen actors,"[4] as they are sometimes called, are in many ways integral to the efficient and effective resolution of international disputes. Secretaries and secretariat staff may be part of a permanent body or appointed on an *ad hoc* basis once a dispute has arisen. Their responsibilities can range from providing logistical and administrative support to more substantive legal functions. Ultimately, the roles of secretariats and nature of secretariat support vary significantly across international courts and tribunals because they are often tailored to the specific needs of the adjudicators they support.

This variation between different types of secretariats and levels of secretariat support is clearly illustrated in the institutional and dispute settlement provisions of the roughly 275 PTAs that provide for some form of *ad hoc* dispute settlement.[5] Only a small minority of PTAs envision the establishment of a permanent secretariat. One notable PTA establishing a secretariat and which has seen a number of active cases in recent years is the *Canada-United States-Mexico Agreement* (CUSMA). Like its predecessor agreement, the *North American Free Trade Agreement* (NAFTA), the secretariat under the CUSMA is divided into "national sections" and supervised by a Free Trade Commission composed of cabinet-level representatives of the CUSMA parties or their designees.[6] Each CUSMA party is responsible for setting up a permanent office for its own national section, ensuring its operational functionality, covering its costs, and appointing a secretary to oversee the section's administration and management.[7] In the event of a dispute, the CUSMA Secretariat is tasked with providing administrative assistance to panels and committees.[8] In addition, the national section of the respondent party is also responsible for ensuring that panelists were remunerated and reimbursed for their

---

4 See generally Freya Baetens, ed, *Legitimacy of Unseen Actors in International Adjudication* (Cambridge, UK: Cambridge University Press, 2019).

5 WTO, "Regional Trade Agreement Database" (last visited 30 March 2025), online: wto. org [perma.cc/LHF7-MQHR].

6 *Canada-United States Mexico Agreement*, 10 December 2019 art 30.6, online: international.gc.ca [perma.cc/G9J2-NMFJ] [*CUSMA*].

7 *Ibid*, art 30.6(2).

8 *Ibid*, art 30.6(3).

expenses. Each national section is made up of between three and six professional staff dedicated to supporting CUSMA panels.

The CUSMA's institutional design is, however, the exception; the vast majority of PTA DSMs do not provide for a permanent secretariat. The administration of disputes under such DSMs is thus conducted on an *ad hoc* basis. Some PTA DSMs require the treaty parties to designate a "responsible office" that, in the event a dispute is brought against that party, is tasked with administering the dispute. Under the Model Rules of Procedure of the *United States–Korea Free Trade Agreement* (KORUS), for example, the responsible office of the respondent party is tasked with providing administrative support to and being a point of contact for the panel, arranging for the remuneration of panelists and assistants, providing the panel with copies of documents relevant for the dispute, coordinating the logistics for hearings, and retaining a complete record of the proceedings.[9] Other PTA DSMs do not mandate the establishment of a "responsible office" or set out the specific administrative tasks assigned to the respondent party but nevertheless provide that the respondent party is responsible for the administration of the dispute.[10]

Many PTA DSMs are, however, silent on how disputes are to be administered and who is responsible for this assignment. In such cases, the responsibility of administering disputes may fall to the panelists, who in practice might appoint an *ad hoc* assistant or secretary to support the panel in carrying out its functions.[11] Where a PTA sets out specific rules of procedure for dispute settlement, those rules may expressly provide for the possibility of appointing an assistant and might also define or limit the assistant's role. For example, the rules of procedure of several PTAs expressly prohibit panels from delegating the drafting of any decisions or reports to an assistant.[12] In theory, such restrictions would not prohibit an assistant from providing legal support to the panel by preparing working papers, conducting legal research,

---

9   *United States-Korea Free Trade Agreement*, 30 June 2007, Model Rules of Procedure, Rule 88 [*KORUS*].

10 See, e.g., *European Union-Ukraine Associate Agreement*, 21 March 2014, Annex XXIV, para 2.

11 As discussed below further, even in cases under FTA DSMs that establish a secretariat, panels have typically appointed an *ad hoc* assistant to provide further support.

12 See, e.g., *China-Korea Free Trade Agreement*, 1 June 2015, Annex 20-A, Rule 16; *United Kingdom-New Zealand Free Trade Agreement*, 28 February 2022, Annex 31a, Rule 15; *Canada-Korea Free Trade Agreement*, 11 March 2014, Annex 21-C, Rule 16; *European Union-Ukraine Association Agreement*, above note 9, Annex XXIV, Rule 13.

and drafting memoranda, provided that the actual drafting of the decisions is done by the panel itself.

C. Deficiencies in PTA Secretariat Support

SECRETARIAT SUPPORT UNDER PTAS CAN generally be lumped into three categories. First, there are those PTAs that envision the establishment of a secretariat. Second, there are those that designate an office or party that is responsible for dispute administration without establishing a secretariat. Finally, there are those PTAs that are largely or totally silent on how disputes are to be administered. Each type has its advantages and disadvantages.

The first category of PTAs has the potential to streamline the dispute settlement process by delegating certain functions to an established, professional body. The disputing parties and panelists are relieved of the burden of having to serve as registrar, organize hearings, and deal with the financial aspects of proceedings, as these functions are typically handled by the secretariat.[13] Services are more likely to be higher quality as well where secretariats are staffed by a permanent team with experience in administering complex inter-state disputes. Being able to rely on a permanent secretariat frees up the panelists to focus on the legal elements of the case and leave the logistical and administrative tasks to others, which may avoid undue delays in the proceedings or increased costs as panelists do not have to busy themselves with organizational work.

That said, since staffing, resourcing, and maintaining a permanent secretariat inevitably entails costs, this structure is only feasible where the treaty parties expect that disputes will frequently (or at least occasionally) be brought under the PTA DSM. Given that only a handful of PTA DSMs have been utilized, for most States, it would make little sense to establish a distinct secretariat for each of their PTAs. Moreover, while PTA secretariats may be well placed to provide administrative and logistical support, unlike the WTO Secretariat, they do not typically offer legal support to panelists. Indeed, panelists in disputes under the CUSMA have routinely appointed *ad hoc* assistants to provide legal support in addition to relying on the responsible national section.[14] Even then, while *ad hoc* assistants may be highly qualified

---

13   See CUSMA Secretariat, "Canadian Section Mandate" (last visited 30 March 2025), online: can-mex-usa-sec.org [perma.cc/8DDR-HJLH].

14   See, e.g., *Re Measures Concerning Genetically Modified Corn (Mexico v US)* (2023), MEX-USA-2023-31-01 (Ch 31 Panel) at para 11, online: worldtradelaw.net [perma.

trade academics and practitioners, they still cannot be expected to have the same institutional knowledge and resources as the WTO Secretariat.[15]

For those PTAs that do not provide for a secretariat, there are evident cost savings from not having to establish and maintain a permanent body to administer disputes. However, the absence of a permanent secretariat increases the risk that the support received by the panelists and parties will be of low quality and this could have an effect on the efficiency and effectiveness of the proceedings.

For instance, in *Guatemala—Obligations under Article 16.2.1(a)* under the *Dominican Republic-Central America Free Trade Agreement* (CAFTA-DR), the panel chair cited the lack of resources of the responsible office—the Guatemalan Ministry of Economy—and low remuneration of the panelists and assistants as a significant constraint on the Panel's ability to conduct the proceedings efficiently. In a cover letter submitted to the parties with the Panel's final report, the panel chair noted that throughout the proceedings the Panel "had communicated to the Responsible Office and to the Disputing Parties themselves their concerns about being compensated for their services in a timely fashion."[16] In particular, despite the panelists having "diligently recorded their time and expenses and periodically sent requests for payment to the Responsible Office," the Panel chair explained that the panelists had "consistently encountered long, unexplained delays in receiving payment."[17] Moreover, the low remuneration of the panelists and assistants, capped pursuant to a 2012 decision adopted by the CAFTA-DR Free Trade Commission (FTC) (the "Decision on Remuneration"), had consistently been raised by the Panel throughout the proceedings.[18] Indeed, the low remuneration cap had a direct effect on the Panel's work, as "the Panel was not disposed to work on

---

cc/B59P-X29L]; *Re Dairy TRQ Allocation Measures 2023 (Canada v US)* (2023), CDA-USA-2023-31-010 (Ch 31 Panel) at para 12, online (pdf): worldtradelaw.net [perma. cc/M5Y6-QNTM].

15   At the time Valerie was Director of the Legal Affairs Division, that division alone staffed twenty-one dispute settlement lawyers tasked with assisting panels. Valerie Hughes, "The Role of the Legal Adviser in the World Trade Organization" in Andraž Zidar & Jean-Pierre Gauci, eds, *The Role of Legal Advisers in International Law* (Leiden: Brill, 2016) 237.

16   Letter from the Chair of the Panel, *In the Matter of Guatemala – Issues Relating to the Obligations Under Article 16.2.1(a) of the CAFTA-DR*, 1 [Guatemala Chair Letter].

17   *Ibid* at 2.

18   *Ibid*; CAFTA-DR, Decision of the Free Trade Commission to Establish the Remuneration of Panelists, Assistants, and Experts, and the Payment of Expenses in Dispute Settlement Proceedings Under Chapter 20 (Dispute Settlement), May 2012.

a translation of its Final Report into Spanish under the conditions."[19] The quality of logistical and administrative support provided by the responsible office, including translation services, varied greatly and was generally of low quality, however given the Decision on Remuneration capped the pay for assistants at 15 dollars per hour (or USD 3,750 dollars for the totality of the case), the Panel was unable to hire qualified translators.[20]

In other PTA disputes where the panel was not supported by a secretariat, similar logistical and administrative challenges have arisen. In *Korea—Compliance with Obligations under Chapter 13*, the panel of experts faced numerous procedural challenges that delayed the issuing of the final report which, according to two of the experts, at least in some part "seems to have been the result of the absence of adequate infrastructure and resources."[21] Reflecting on their experience, the two experts insisted that the "logistical obstacles" faced by the Panel "underscores the importance of contemplating the establishment of a standing administrative entity for a future FTA comprising a variety of different dispute settlement mechanisms."[22]

Similarly, in *Ukraine—Wood Exports Ban*, the Panel faced substantial delays largely attributable to the logistical challenges resulting from the COVID-19 pandemic, which resulted in a "prolonged period of travel restrictions" and led to the panel deciding to hold virtual hearings.[23] In its final report, the Panel noted that the virtual hearings entailed "considerable technical challenges" and made it practically impossible to open the hearings to the public.[24]

These cases illustrate the importance of quality secretariat support and the real impact that failure to receive such support can have on the efficiency of the proceedings and, quite possibly, the quality of the final report. With these challenges in mind, we turn to the question of whether outsourcing secretariat support under PTAs to the WTO Secretariat might offer a feasible solution.

---

19   *Ibid,* Guatemala Chair Letter at 2.
20   Robertson, Falls, & Novacefski, above note 1 at 15.
21   Laurence Boisson de Chazournes & Jaemin Lee, "The European Union–Korea Free Trade Agreement Sustainable Development Proceeding: Reflections on a Ground-Breaking Dispute" (2022) 23 *Journal of World Investment & Trade* 329 at 345.
22   *Ibid* at 344–45.
23   *Restrictions Applied by Ukraine on Exports of Certain Wood Products to the European Union* (2020), at para 16, online (pdf): me.gov.ua [perma.cc/R4KL-MLST].
24   *Ibid* at para 17.

D. The (Potential) Role of The WTO Secretariat in FTA Dispute Settlement

WHEN IT COMES TO ADMINISTERING international trade disputes, the WTO Secretariat is undoubtedly the most experienced institution. Panels are assisted by a team of lawyers, including those with specific expertise in the subject matter of the dispute, as well as technical experts.[25] Secretariat staff are then involved in every stage of the panel process, undertaking numerous functions which include preparing the timetable and working procedures for the case, drafting an "Issues Paper" "summarizing the arguments, identifying and explaining the relevant legal principles, setting out different approaches to the dispute that the panel could take," assisting with preparing questions to put to the parties, taking notes during hearings, conducting legal research, and supporting the panel in drafting all or parts of the panel report.[26] On the administrative side, the WTO Secretariat acts as registry and takes care of a host of important logistical and organizational tasks, ranging from dealing with payments and expenses, to handling travel arrangements, to providing the necessary translation services, facilities, and technical support for hearings.[27]

Given the comprehensive professional support that PTA panelists could benefit from by relying on the services of the WTO Secretariat, the prospect of outsourcing PTA dispute settlement administration to the WTO Secretariat appears in theory to be an attractive one. Many of the deficiencies in the administration of PTA proceedings outlined above could be resolved, as PTA panelists would benefit from the expertise of the Secretariat's lawyers and technical staff and could rely on the capable support of clerical staff for assistance with the logistical, administrative, and financial aspects of the proceedings.

However, while there are potential benefits to be gained from affording the WTO Secretariat a role in PTA dispute settlement, there would be several barriers to putting this idea into practice.

---

25   Daniel Ari Baker & Gabrielle Marceau, "The World Trade Organization" in Freya Baetens, ed, *Legitimacy of Unseen Actors in International Adjudication* (Cambridge: Cambridge University Press, 2019) 70 at 83.

26   *Ibid* at 83–84.

27   Furculiță, above note 2 at 350–54.

1) Legal Impediments

There are several legal impediments that could arguably prevent the WTO Secretariat from assuming any role in the administration of PTA disputes. First, it is not clear that the WTO Secretariat would have the authority under the WTO agreements to act in this capacity. Article 27 of the Dispute Settlement Understanding (DSU)—which sets out the WTO Secretariat's responsibilities in dispute settlement proceedings—does not expressly prohibit the WTO Secretariat from supporting panels in disputes outside of the WTO;[28] however, Article 1 of the DSU provides that the rules and procedures set out therein "shall apply to disputes brought pursuant to the consultation and dispute settlement provisions" of the WTO agreements.[29] The context of the DSU, and the WTO agreements more broadly, thus support the limitation of the WTO Secretariat's mandate to assisting only those panels established pursuant to the WTO agreements.

Moreover, outsourcing the administration of PTA disputes to the WTO Secretariat could conflict with Article VI.4 of the *Marrakesh Agreement Establishing the WTO*, which states that "[i]n the discharge of their duties, the Director-General and the staff of the Secretariat shall not seek or accept instructions from any government or any other authority external to the WTO."[30] The substance of Article VI.4, which underscores the importance of the independence and impartiality of the WTO Secretariat, is also incorporated into and expanded upon in the Staff Regulations and Staff Rules of the WTO.[31] Extending the role of the Secretariat to include the administration of PTA disputes could run afoul of these provisions, as it would require the Secretariat to take instructions from panels convened under the auspices of

28 *Marrakesh Agreement Establishing the World Trade Organization*, Annex 2, 15 April 1994, 1869 UNTS 3 at 401, Understanding on Rules and Procedures Governing the Settlement of Disputes, art 27.1 (entered into force 1 January 1995) [*DSU*] (providing that "[t]he Secretariat shall have the responsibility of assisting panels, especially on the legal, historical and procedural aspects of the matters dealt with, and of providing secretarial and technical support."

29 *Ibid*, art 1.

30 *Marrakesh Agreement Establishing the World Trade Organization*, art VI.6, 15 April 1994, 1869 UNTS 3 [*Marrakesh Agreement*].

31 See WTO, *Conditions of Service Applicable to the Staff of the WTO Secretariat*, WTO Doc WT/L/282 (1998), Annex B to Annex 2, online (pdf): docs.wto.org [perma.cc/A8SU-SZ5D] [WTO, *Staff Conditions*] (e.g., Regulation 1.4 of the Staff Regulations and point 4 of the Standards of Conduct).

a PTA DSM and it might also involve responding to requests from governments engaged in PTA disputes.

The same problem may also arise in the more specific context of remuneration. Many PTAs require the disputing parties to pay the costs associated with dispute settlement proceedings, including the remuneration of the arbitrators and assistants.[32] Likewise, under PTAs that establish a secretariat, the operational costs of the secretariat including the remuneration of its staff are typically borne by the parties to the PTA. By contrast, the salaries of the WTO Secretariat staff are paid directly from the WTO's budget. Further, the Staff Regulations and Staff Rules of the WTO expressly prohibit Secretariat staff from "accept[ing] remuneration from any government or other authority external to the WTO with respect to their service with the WTO either prior to, during or after such service."[33] As such, if Secretariat staff were asked in their official capacity to perform work that would be remunerated not through the regular WTO budget but by the States party to a PTA dispute, this could run contrary to their obligations under the Staff Regulations and Staff Rules.

In addition to being potentially incompatible with the WTO agreements and other rules and standards applicable to WTO staff members, contracting out the administration of PTA disputes to the WTO Secretariat could be incompatible with the terms of PTAs themselves. This could be the case for those PTAs that already establish a secretariat and provide specific procedures for how that body is to administer the dispute and limitations on the roles and functions of the PTA's secretariat. It may also be the case that the code of conduct provided for under a PTA DSM would constrain the types of activities the WTO Secretariat may regularly perform in WTO proceedings. For instance, WTO Secretariat lawyers may be prevented from assisting with the drafting of panel reports if the PTA's code of conduct expressly provides that the panelists themselves are exclusively responsible for this task.

Despite these potential limitations, it should be noted that WTO Members have at times contemplated and agreed to new arrangements with respect to the role of the WTO Secretariat in dispute settlement, with the most notable recent example being the Multi-Party Interim Appeal Arbitration Arrangement (MPIA). While the MPIA envisages that the arbitrators

---

32 See, e.g., CUSMA Rules of Procedure for Chapter 31, Article 12.1; *United States-Japan Economic Partnership Agreement*, 7 October 2019, Article 21.29; *Comprehensive and Economic Trade Agreement* (CETA), 30 October 2016, Annex 29-A, Article 2.

33 WTO, *Staff Conditions*, above note 30 at Annex 2, Annex B, para 31.

adjudicating appeals under that agreement will be assisted by a "support structure" that is "entirely separate from the WTO Secretariat staff and its divisions supporting the panels," it also anticipates that the MPIA Members will "request the WTO Director General to ensure the availability" of such a support structure.[34] In practice, this arrangement has involved the secondment of WTO Secretariat staff to MPIA arbitrators for the duration of the dispute settlement process, with these staff members being "answerable, regarding the substance of their work, only to appeal arbitrators."[35] One might thus envision a similar arrangement where WTO Secretariat staff could be seconded to PTA panels to provide professional support.

However, there are key differences between the MPIA and PTA dispute settlement mechanisms that make the involvement of WTO Secretariat staff in the former likely more acceptable. Unlike PTA dispute settlement, the MPIA is firmly rooted in the WTO system. Procedurally it finds its legal basis in Article 25 of the DSU, which allows WTO Members to engage in "[e]xpeditious arbitration within the WTO as an alternative means of dispute settlement."[36] Within this framework, MPIA Members have agreed to use Article 25 arbitration as an appellate mechanism for disputes involving alleged violations of the WTO agreements. Thus, as Joost Pauwelyn explains, the MPIA is merely "a form of arbitration implemented within a regular WTO dispute," and therefore "nested within the multilateral WTO and explicitly foreseen and allowed under DSU Article 25."[37] The same is not true for PTA dispute settlement, which operates independently from the WTO system. This distinction is significant both politically and financially and will be addressed in the next subsection.

2) Practical Challenges

Aside from the potential legal impediments, there are further practical challenges that would make outsourcing PTA dispute settlement to the WTO Secretariat difficult.

---

34 WTO, *Multi-Party Interim Appeal Arbitration Arrangement Pursuant to Article 25 of the DSU*, WTO Doc WT/JOB/DSB/1/Add.12 (2020) art 7, online (pdf): docs.wto.org [perma.cc/Z72W-ZMFR] [*MPIA*].

35 *Ibid*; Joost Pauwelyn, "The WTO's Multi-Party Interim Appeal Arbitration Arrangement (MPIA): What's New?" (2023) 22:5 *World Trade Review* 693 at 697–98.

36 *DSU*, above note 27, art 25.1.

37 Pauwelyn, above note 34 at 694.

First, there is the question of who would pay for the administration of PTA disputes. The costs of administering PTA disputes are typically borne by the disputing parties under the agreement, whereas in WTO dispute settlement, the costs are covered by the WTO's budget, which itself is funded through contributions by the Members. It seems unlikely that WTO Members would be willing to allocate resources to WTO Secretariat for the administration of PTA disputes, especially since such disputes do not involve the interpretation of agreements to which all WTO Members are a party nor afford WTO Members the same procedural rights as disputes brought under the WTO agreements.[38] Even in the context of the MPIA, the allocation of the WTO's resources has proved controversial among some Members.[39] In its opposition to the MPIA, the United States has argued that "[i]f Members desire a separate support staff for their dispute resolutions, those Members (and not the WTO Membership as a whole) should finance it."[40] It would not be unreasonable to expect a similar attitude to be taken towards the use of the Secretariat's staff and resources for disputes that fall outside of the WTO framework.

Second, the very prospect of using the WTO's resources and expertise for non-WTO disputes might face resistance from certain WTO Members. Members might object on the basis that it would overburden the Secretariat and divert resources away from WTO dispute settlement, or they could object in principle to the notion of the WTO Secretariat wading in on the interpretation of the PTA provisions of Member States.[41] While opposition to the MPIA has not prevented its successful establishment and use, if any of the legal impediments noted above required an authoritative interpretation of or amendment to the *Marrakesh Agreement* or DSU, significant buy-in from the WTO Membership would be required.[42]

Finally, a further problem could arise from a situation where the WTO Secretariat assists a panel with the resolution of a dispute under a PTA and

---

38 For instance, any third-party Member with a substantial interest in a WTO dispute have a right to intervene under Article 10 of the DSU, whereas the right to intervene in PTA disputes is generally limited to the parties to the PTA.

39 Letter from US Ambassador Dennis C Shea to the WTO Director-General Roberto Azevêdo (5 June 2020), online (pdf): currentthoughtsontrade.com [perma. cc/3D2N-DBZM].

40 *Ibid.*

41 See Robertson, Falls, & Novacefski, above note 1 at 37; Furculiță, above note 2 at 348.

42 Marrakesh Agreement, above note 29, arts IX.2, X.1. See also Robertson, Falls, & Novacefski, *ibid* at 37–38.

then is faced with essentially the same dispute brought under the WTO agreements by the same parties and involving similarly or identically worded legal provisions. While decision-making ultimately rests with the panelists and the Issue Paper prepared by the WTO Secretariat is in no way binding on the panel, there could be a perception that the Secretariat would advise the WTO panel to reach a similar conclusion as that reached by the PTA panel.[43] The WTO would have an interest in avoiding this possibility entirely and may serve as sufficient justification for declining to provide any form of legal support to panels in PTA disputes.

E. Conclusion

SEVERAL YEARS HAVE PASSED SINCE our TradeLab team first batted around the idea with Valerie of using the WTO Secretariat to administer PTA disputes, and despite having more evidence of the deficiencies in PTA secretariat support, the legal and practical barriers make what is an intriguing prospect an improbable one. Nevertheless, there may be other solutions to improving PTA secretariat support that do not involve the WTO Secretariat. As Kathleen Claussen has rightly observed, the Permanent Court of Arbitration (PCA) has extensive experience in administering complex inter-state disputes and could upon the request of PTA parties provide secretariat support.[44] In 2024, the PCA registered its first inter-state trade case under the *EU-UK Trade Cooperation Agreement* and the panel and disputing parties relied on substantial secretariat support from the PCA throughout the course of the proceedings.[45] While the PCA does not possess the same technical and legal expertise in international trade as the WTO Secretariat, it may nevertheless provide

---

43   Baker & Marceau, above note 24 at 83.

44   Kathleen Claussen, "Old & New Dispute Secretariats" in Symposium on Joost Pauwelyn & Krzysztof Pelc, "Who Guards the 'Guardian of the System'?: The Role of the Secretariat in Dispute Settlement" (2022) 116 *American Journal of International Law* 400 at 401 and 404. See also Scott Falls, "Outsourcing FTA Dispute Settlement Administration to Third-Party International Arbitral Institutions: Opportunities and the Role of the Permanent Court of Arbitration" (2020) 19:1 *Law & Practice of International Courts and Tribunals* 49.

45   *The European Union v the United Kingdom of Great Britain and Northern Ireland* (2024), PCA (Permanent Court of Arbitration) (Arbitrators: Dr Penelope Jane Ridings et al) [*UK-Sandeel*].

high quality administrative support to panelists while relieving PTA parties from the burden of establishing and maintaining a separate secretariat.[46]

Ultimately, the challenges of PTA dispute administration will require greater consideration as States increasingly make use of these DSMs. While recourse to the WTO Secretariat remains unlikely, States should be cognizant of the limitations set out in the structures of their existing PTAs and look for ways to resolve potential barriers to efficient and effective dispute administration before a dispute arises.

---

46 Notably, two PCA senior legal counsel also served as assistants to panelists in the *UK-Sandeel* dispute: *ibid.*

The Turn to Arbitration and
Dispute Settlement Reform

CHAPTER 25

From the *Alabama* to *Airbus*: A Note on the Evolution of International Arbitration in Geneva

Niall Meagher*

JUST OVER 150 YEARS AGO, a group of diplomats and jurists met in Geneva to decide claims made by the United States against the United Kingdom regarding damages caused by the CSS *Alabama* and other British-built vessels that served on the Confederate side during the US Civil War. The *Alabama*

* The author is Executive Director of the Advisory Centre on WTO Law (ACWL) in Geneva. All opinions and errors in this chapter are the individual responsibility of the author and should not be attributed to either the ACWL or its Members. I would like to thank the editor for the invitation to contribute to this volume in tribute to Valerie Hughes, for whom I have long had the utmost personal and professional respect. I would like to express sincere thanks also to David Palmeter, who showed me the *Alabama* room on my first visit to Geneva to work on a WTO dispute settlement proceeding with him and with whom I first discussed the historical parallels. Finally, I would like to thank Ms. Rukiya Ibrahim, a participant in the ACWL's Secondment Programme for Government Lawyers 2024–2025, for excellent research assistance with aspects of this chapter.

Claims arbitration is considered to be a crucial step towards the peaceful, law-based resolution of international disputes. More recently, the World Trade Organization (WTO)'s dispute settlement system has resolved hundreds of disputes in Geneva and, until the recent blockage of its appellate level, was often described as the jewel of the crown of the WTO. This note examines the similarities and differences across 150 years of history between the *Alabama Claims* case and the recent troubles in the WTO dispute settlement system. It examines how issues such as sovereignty, the jurisdiction of the tribunal, the selection of arbitrators, and even the length of submissions can be recurring issues affecting the effectiveness of international arbitration.

A. Introduction

A LITTLE OVER 150 YEARS ago, on 14 September 1872, a group of distinguished lawyers and diplomats gathered in a room in the Hotel de Ville in Geneva's Old Town to hear the decision of the arbitral Tribunal in the case of the *Alabama Claims* between the United Kingdom and the United States. The case arose out of the agreement between the two countries in the *Treaty of Washington* in 1871 to submit the United States' claims against the United Kingdom for losses caused to US shipping interests during the US Civil War by thirteen ships to third-party arbitration. These ships, including the CSS *Alabama*, were built in the United Kingdom for military purposes in violation of the United Kingdom's neutrality obligations and subsequently used by the Confederacy to attack Union ships. The Tribunal awarded damages of USD 15.5 million to the United States for these losses.[1]

The award was seen as a breakthrough in international law, where two governments agreed to binding arbitration to resolve long-standing diplomatic/legal differences between them. Notwithstanding some difficulties along the way, the process was a success. Faced with an adverse ruling, the United Kingdom did not hesitate to pay the award to the United States, even though there was no system of enforcement available to the United States in the event of non-compliance. While the *Alabama Claims* did not immediately lead to a pandemic of international arbitration of diplomatic disputes, the case is seen as the first step on a path that led to the International Court of Justice. To commemorate the event, the room in which the Tribunal met is

---

1 Tom Bingham, "The *Alabama Claims* Arbitration" (2005) 54:1 *International and Comparative Law Quarterly* 1 at 1.

now known as the *Alabama* room. Together with the First Geneva Convention on the treatment of those wounded in war and prisoners of war, signed in the same room in 1864, the *Alabama Claims* case also played an important role in establishing Geneva as a leading centre of international law and diplomacy.[2]

A century and a half later, in September 2022, delegates of the 164 Members of the WTO gathered for the usual monthly meeting of the WTO's Dispute Settlement Body (DSB), which supervises the WTO's dispute settlement system, in the WTO's headquarters, the Centre William Rappard, on the shores of the lake in Geneva. The mood was not as celebratory as the mood in the Hotel de Ville in September 1872, when the Geneva authorities marked the occasion with an artillery salute. Instead, the delegates in the WTO's lakeshore headquarters were sombre as they discussed the breakdown in the WTO's dispute settlement system.[3] For over twenty-five years, the WTO dispute settlement system had successfully addressed hundreds of complex trade disputes, including the long-running disputes (to which the title of this chapter refers, for purely alliterative reasons) between the United States and the European Union over their respective subsidies to the aircraft manufacturers Boeing and Airbus. Long seen as the WTO's "jewel in the crown," however, the dispute settlement system had been unable to function completely for several years.

Like the *Alabama Claims* case in its time, the WTO dispute settlement system was an innovation in international law when it came into effect in 1995. Unlike the predecessor *General Agreement on Tariffs and Trade* (GATT) system, under the WTO dispute settlement system, a losing defending Member could no longer block the "adoption" of a report containing adverse findings against it. For the first time also, governments that were party to a binding international arbitration enjoyed an automatic right of appeal to a standing, upper-tier Appellate Body that was mandated to address all issues of

---

2 At the time, Geneva was the largest city in Switzerland, with a population of approximately 100,000. This also played a role in its selection as host for the *Alabama* arbitration. In describing his time in Geneva, a junior member of the US legal team, Frank Warren Hackett, referred to Talleyrand's response to the question "is it not dull in Geneva?"—"Yes, especially when they amuse themselves"—but nevertheless said he liked Geneva and had "none other than exceedingly pleasing memories of the town and its people." See Frank Warren Hackett, *Reminiscences of the Geneva Tribunal of Arbitration, 1872: The Alabama Claims* (Boston: Houghton Mifflin, 1911) 208–9.

3 The discussions also took place in the shadow of the Russian invasion of Ukraine seven months previously, which was also condemned by some delegations during the meeting.

law raised on appeal. The WTO's two-tier system of dispute settlement was unique and, for the first twenty years or so of its operation, generally considered to be a success, albeit by no means perfect.

Nevertheless, over the years, the United States had developed significant concerns that the Appellate Body was exceeding its mandate on both substantive and procedural matters. In particular, the United States considered that the Appellate Body was exceeding its mandate to interpret WTO law only to the extent necessary to resolve disputes between Members and, instead, was creating new obligations by reaching interpretations that went beyond both the text of the agreements and the exigencies of the case before it. On procedural matters, the United States' objections included that the Appellate Body was acting inconsistently with its mandate by taking more than ninety days to issue its reports.[4]

After expressing those concerns by conventional means through statements in the DSB and elsewhere, the United States eventually took more direct action by blocking the initiation of the process to replace outgoing Appellate Body members at the end of their terms. The inability to replace members meant that by December 2019, the Appellate Body no longer had a minimum quorum of three members to hear each dispute and, therefore, could not function. Since then, the WTO dispute settlement system has continued to operate, although with a much-reduced caseload (the pandemic also affected this). As a matter of law, however, Members that lose at the initial "panel" stage of the process retain the right to *initiate* appeals, recognizing that those appeals may never resolved. This ability to "appeal into the void" means, in effect, that losing Members can block the process from reaching the stage at which they would be required to take action to implement any adverse findings.

Thus, at the September 2022 meeting of the DSB, a group of 127 WTO Members made a proposal to re-start the process of selecting Appellate Body members, thereby unblocking the process but to no avail.[5] The United States stated that its long-standing concerns with WTO dispute settlement

---

4   *Marrakesh Agreement Establishing the World Trade Organization*, Annex 2, 15 April 1994, 1869 UNTS 3 at 401, Understanding on Rules and Procedures Governing the Settlement of Disputes, art 17.5 (entered into force 1 January 1995) [*DSU*]. Article 17.5 of the *DSU* provides that the Appellate Body shall issue its decisions within a maximum of ninety days, without exception.

5   WTO, *Minutes of Meeting*, WTO Doc WT/DSB/M/470 (2022) at 6–13, online (pdf): docs.wto.org [perma.cc/8F2E-FJDD].

remained unaddressed and while it supported WTO dispute settlement reform and was working to achieve durable, lasting reform, it could not support the proposal until its concerns were addressed.[6] This *status quo* continues. Members propose reactivating the process, but the United States will not consent. In addition, efforts to negotiate a resolution to the problem have produced many proposals but no outcome. First, in 2023, an informal process facilitated by Sr. Marco Tulio Molina Tejeda, then the Deputy Permanent Representative of Guatemala to the WTO, generated a series of proposals.[7] Subsequently, at its 13th Ministerial Conference in Abu Dhabi in March 2024, the WTO adopted a deadline of December 2024 to restart a fully-functional dispute settlement system. A further series of negotiations, this time facilitated by Mauritius' Ambassador to the WTO, H.E. Madame Usha Dwarka-Canabady, produced further proposals.[8] Again, no agreement was reached. At the time of writing, no resolution appears imminent.

Much has changed in international law since the *Alabama Claims* arbitration. Moreover, the WTO dispute settlement system is a broad-based multilateral system with mandatory jurisdiction over matters within the scope of the WTO agreements, rather than a bilateral agreement to submit a discrete problem to arbitration. Nevertheless, reading accounts of the *Alabama Claims* case against the backdrop of the problems in WTO dispute settlement and the ongoing efforts to resolve those problems, one is struck by how many of the same problems encountered in the *Alabama Claims* case recur in very similar forms in the present and can be identified among the issues facing the WTO dispute settlement system. This chapter discusses some of these recurring issues, examining both their importance in the *Alabama Claims* case and their continuing relevance in the WTO dispute settlement system. These issues are: (1) the extent to which states are willing to concede sovereignty to third party arbitrators, (2) concerns over whether these third-party arbitrators remain within their mandate, (3) how to select the third-party arbitrators, and, finally, (4) the complexity of the proceedings.

---

6   *Ibid* at 6.
7   See WTO, *Special Meeting of the General Council*, WTO Doc JOB/GC/385 (2024), online (pdf): docs.wto.org [perma.cc/M2Q5-GWPZ] [WTO, *Molina Process*].
8   See WTO, *Statement by H.E. Mr. Petter Ølberg*, WTO Doc JOB/GC/DSR/5 (2024), online (pdf): docs.wto.org [perma.cc/PD6X-PGWY].

B. Sovereignty

AS NOTED, THE *ALABAMA CLAIMS* arbitration was seen as something of a breakthrough in international law and relations. In the words of Professor Brierly, "[a]rbitration was a fairly frequent method of settling international disputes in medieval times, but with the rise of the modern state system it fell into disuse until its revival in the nineteenth century, largely through the example of Great Britain and the United States in submitting the *Alabama Claims* to arbitration in 1871."[9] The decision to submit the case to arbitration was difficult on both sides (although, as discussed below, this decision is always more difficult for the defending party, which must accept the risk of having to accept an adverse ruling with compliance consequences).

In the words of the Sutherland Report on the WTO in 2005, "acceptance of almost any treaty involves a transfer of a certain amount of decision-making authority away from states, and towards international cooperation. Generally, this is exactly why 'sovereign nations' agree to such treaties. They realize that the benefits of cooperative action that a treaty enhances are greater than the circumstances that exist otherwise."[10]

In the *Alabama Claims* case, the parties clearly decided that the benefits of cooperative action outweighed the risks of ceding a little piece of their sovereignty for this purpose. Both were anxious to put the issue behind them, in the context of other frictions in their bilateral relationship. The United States was keen to get monetary compensation, in part because of pressure from domestic stakeholders to be compensated for their losses in the Civil War. As discussed below, the United Kingdom was also keen to move on from the dispute but was unwilling to admit responsibility unilaterally. The case was decided by arbitration, rather than by force (the United States was making threats against Canada, in part due to recent Fenian activity in Canada), therefore, because the relationship between the United States and Britain was "still rocky enough to be disturbed by major disagreements, yet close enough to make war seem irrational."[11]

---

9   James Leslie Brierly, *The Law of Nations: An Introduction to the International Law of Peace*, 6th ed (Oxford: Oxford University Press, 1963) at 348.

10 Peter Sutherland et al, *The Future of the WTO: Addressing Institutional Challenges in the New Millennium* (Geneva: World Trade Organization, 2004) at para 111, online (pdf): wto.org [perma.cc/ZQ9A-UFYB] [*Sutherland Report*].

11 Mark Mazower, *Governing the World: The History of an Idea* (New York: Penguin Books, 2013) 96 (quoting a slogan of the time: "Always Arbitrate before you Fight").

In this context, the United Kingdom's decision, as the defendant, to accept binding arbitration, is striking. In 1865, Earl Russell, who had been Foreign Secretary during the American Civil War, rejected an American offer of arbitration because "Her Majesty's government are the sole guardians of their own honour" and "cannot admit that they may have acted with bad faith in maintaining the neutrality they professed. The law officers of the crown must be held to be better interpreters of a British statute than any foreign government can be presumed to be."[12] Ultimately, however, the United Kingdom proved willing to enter into the *Treaty of Washington* and to submit the matter to binding arbitration.

Thus, the United Kingdom was not willing to accept that it had acted improperly, especially when it was accused of acting in bad faith (by breaching its neutrality obligations by not exercising due diligence to ensure that ships such as the *Alabama*, built in the United Kingdom, were not actually to be used for military purposes by a belligerent in the American Civil War).[13] Rather than admitting itself that it was wrong, however, the United Kingdom was willing to abide by a ruling on the American claims by a third-party adjudicator that, in effect, meant the same thing. In essence, the United Kingdom preferred to contract out the decision that it was responsible for the damage caused by the *Alabama* and the other ships.

Similar concerns apply in the WTO dispute settlement system. As noted, in the GATT system, a defending party could initially decline even to participate in a dispute. This right was removed over time, but even up to the end of the GATT era, the losing party could block the "adoption" of the report, meaning, in effect, that it would not have to be bound by an adverse result.

One of the goals of the negotiators in the Uruguay Round that led to the creation of the WTO and its dispute settlement system was to have a more binding system. For example, among the principal negotiating objectives of the United States were "to provide for more effective and expeditious dispute settlement mechanisms and procedures" and "to ensure that such mechanisms . . . provide for more effective and expeditious resolution of disputes and

---

12 See Richard Brent, "The Alabama Claims Tribunal: The British Perspective" (2022) 44:1 *International History Review* 21 at 22.

13 This position also finds echoes in WTO dispute settlement, where panels are notably reluctant to make findings on claims that a defending Member has failed to act in "good faith."

enable better enforcement of United States rights."[14] The reference to enabling better enforcement of US rights implies that the United States was thinking from the perspective of a complainant rather than as a potential defendant. However, as both a leading exporter and importer, the United States is always likely to have both offensive and defensive interests. Thus, binding dispute settlement can work both ways. In the words of one senior member of the US Senate at the time: "[T]he catch is this: If we want tough rules and a fast and effective dispute settlement system when we are plaintiffs in a case, we also have to live with the same rules when we are the defendants."[15]

The US Administration was quick to emphasize that accepting the WTO dispute settlement system did not entail a surrender of sovereignty. In its Statement of Administrative Action accompanying the proposed legislation to enact the Uruguay Round Agreements, the Administration stated that: "It is important to note that the new WTO dispute settlement system does not give panels any power to order the United States or other countries to change their laws. If a panel finds that a country has not lived up to its commitments, all a panel may do is recommend that the country begin observing its obligations. It is then up to the disputing countries to decide how they will settle their differences."[16] Nevertheless, given the different domestic interests involved and the sensitivity of the United States's defensive interests, the United States' approval of the creation of the WTO was "a striking political achievement considering the growing suspicion of multilateral institutions on Capitol Hill in those years."[17]

Over the years, the United States' view of the balance between its offensive and defensive interests—and the extent to which the WTO dispute settlement system was protecting even its offensive interests (notably in disputes concerning China) has clearly changed. In one of its earliest cases, the Appellate Body stated that "the WTO Agreement is a treaty—the international equivalent of a contract. It is self-evident that in an exercise of their sovereignty, and in pursuit of their own respective national interests, the Members of the WTO have made a bargain. In exchange for the benefits

---

14   See David Palmeter, *The WTO as a Legal System: Essays on International Trade Law and Policy* (London: Cameron May, 2003) 327.

15   *Ibid* at 327, fn 70, citing US Cong Rec, vol 138, 2, at 1725 (6 February 1992) (Rep Lloyd Bentsen). Bentsen was the then-Chairman of the US Senate Finance Committee.

16   US, Bill HR 5110, *Uruguay Round Agreements Act*, 103rd Cong, 1994, Statement of Administrative Action at 339 (enacted).

17   Mazower, above note 11 at 360.

they expect to derive as Members of the WTO, they have agreed to exercise their sovereignty according to the commitments they have made in the WTO Agreement."[18] As the Sutherland Report concluded: "Ultimately what counts is whether the balance between some loss of 'policy space' at the national level and the advantages of cooperation and the rule of law at the multilateral level is positive or negative."[19] For the time being at least, it appears that the United States considers that, from its point of view, this balance is negative.

C. Scope of the Proceedings and Jurisdiction of the Arbitrators

HAVING MADE THE DIFFICULT DECISION to surrender some of their sovereignty by agreeing to third-party adjudication, governments have a particular interest in ensuring that the adjudicators do not overstep their mandate. Governments that are willing to submit their international disputes to binding third-party adjudication want to make sure that the scope of the adjudication is carefully delineated and that they are not confronted with outcomes that go beyond the parameters of their agreement. Thus, Montague Bernard, a junior member of the British legal team in Geneva, wrote afterwards of the *Treaty of Washington* that "the agreement between the two nations did not invest the Tribunal with power to legislate for them, still less for the world at large; but empowered it only to settle a particular dispute, which related entirely to the past."[20] In our times, one of the United States' complaints about the WTO Appellate Body is that it has exceeded its mandate by creating new obligations rather than simply interpreting the provisions of the relevant WTO agreements.

Indeed, the *Alabama Claims* case was almost derailed by this problem when an issue arose concerning the scope of the *Treaty of Washington* and, hence, the proceedings themselves. Initially, the United States sought damages for both the direct losses caused by the *Alabama* and the other vessels and what were termed the resulting "indirect" losses. The direct losses covered the costs of the vessels and cargoes that were sunken by the *Alabama* and the other Confederate vessels. The "indirect" losses included secondary matters

---

18   *Japan—Taxes on Alcoholic Beverages (Complaint by the European Communities)* (1996), WTO Doc WT/DS8/AB/R, page 15 (Appellate Body Report), online (pdf): docs.wto.org [perma.cc/Z2CH-C5DA].

19   *Sutherland Report*, above note 10 at para 143.

20   See Brent, above note 12 at 22.

such as the cost of marine insurance and economic losses arising from a reduction in trade by American vessels, as well as the broader cost in terms of losses in economic growth. These "indirect" losses were estimated by the American side as $110 million (compared to approximately $15 million in direct losses). These claims had been controversial prior to the agreement in the *Treaty of Washington* to submit the *Alabama* claims to arbitration. Not for the first or last time in international law, the parties to the Treaty came away with different understandings as to the precise scope of their agreement. The United Kingdom thought that these claims had been excluded under the Treaty and were surprised to see them put forward in the United States' initial arguments to the Tribunal.

The issue was treated seriously on both sides. According to Frank Warren Hackett, a junior member of the United States' legal team, "[d]uring the entire season that had been occupied with the preparation of the [case], and even down to the hour of departure from Paris to Geneva, there prevailed the direst apprehensions of a rupture of the Treaty. That might have meant war."[21] The lead counsel on the British side, Sir Roundell Palmer, objected to the inclusion of the indirect claims, stating "nobody here would have been willing to go to arbitration upon such claims as these, advanced upon such grounds, if [the American claims] could have been seen beforehand . . . I look upon the [American] Case as an attempt to evade and enlarge the limits within which the subject-matter of the reference to the Arbitrators was intended to be confined by the Treaty of Washington, and to found enormous and intolerable claims upon the enlargement of those limits."[22]

The American point of view was that Article I of the *Treaty of Washington* did not exclude the indirect claims. It stated, *inter alia*, that "in order to remove and adjust all complaints and claims on the part of the United States, and to provide for the speedy settlement of such claims which are not admitted [accepted] by Her Britannic Majesty's Government, the High Contracting Parties agree that all the said claims, growing out of acts committed by the aforesaid vessels, and generically known as the 'Alabama Claims' shall be referred to a Tribunal of Arbitration." Thus, the United States' position was that all claims indeed meant *all* claims.

The British negotiators of the Treaty, however, considered that the reference to claims "growing out of the acts committed" by the *Alabama* and the

---

21 Hackett, above note 2 at 156.
22 *Ibid* at 167.

other vessels. According to the British side, "this limitation was not obtained without much difficulty . . . [we] pointed out to the Americans . . . that they ought to be content with a provision that would entitle them to bring forward claims founded on direct losses . . . without going further." Nevertheless, the British negotiators seemed to acknowledge that their point of view was not necessarily clear: "Of course, it is possible that [the Americans] may put forward claims of greater extent, as for instance, claims on account of pursuing and capturing the vessels; but there is nothing in the article to give direct colour to such claims, and our Counsel will, of course, be instructed to argue that they are inadmissible, if they should be presented."[23]

In Frank Warren Hackett's words, this difference of opinion "is an interesting example of how widely two opposing parties may differ as to the meaning of an agreement which they have taken great pains to reduce to writing, conceived to be as plain as possible."[24] Of course, this is also one of the major sticking points in the WTO dispute settlement system. For example, as many readers will be aware, one of the major controversies in WTO dispute settlement has concerned the so-called practice of "zeroing" in anti-dumping investigations. The United States came away from the negotiations of the WTO *Anti-Dumping Agreement* with the understanding that the practice was consistent with the Agreement, whereas other parties and, ultimately, the WTO Appellate Body disagreed.

In the *Alabama Claims* case, the jurisdictional issue was ultimately resolved by negotiations between the two parties. It appears that neither wanted the process to fail completely: "Attempts were made to come together and save the Treaty. The Legations at London and at Washington were kept busy at all hours of the day and night. The interchange of notes and telegrams was incessant."[25] Efforts were made to amend the *Treaty of Washington*, but during the debate in the US Senate (which would have to approve any amendment), the proposed amendment was itself amended in a manner unacceptable to the United Kingdom.

The issue was still not resolved by the time of the first meeting of the Tribunal with the parties in Geneva on 15 June 1872. The United Kingdom, noting that the issue of the indirect claims had not yet been resolved, asked the Tribunal to adjourn pending the negotiation of a supplemental treaty on

---

23   *Ibid* at 181–82.
24   *Ibid* at 180.
25   *Ibid* at 201.

the indirect claims. It seems to have been generally understood that had the Tribunal adjourned, it would never have re-convened. Instead, the United States asked to have a break over the weekend to get instructions from capital. During the weekend, the parties and the Tribunal reached agreement that the Tribunal would issue a ruling indicating that the indirect claims did not constitute a basis in international law for an award of compensation, without taking a position as to whether those claims were in fact provided for in the *Treaty of Washington* and therefore within the jurisdiction of the Tribunal. On that basis, the United States then announced that it would not further pursue the indirect claims. Thus, the parties were able to find a practical solution to the problem of what the Treaty actually said or meant. In the perhaps overly optimistic words of Frank Warren Hackett, "the Treaty of Washington had been preserved intact and the principle of Arbitration between nations now seemed destined to bring to mankind its blessings for the years to come."[26]

In the WTO, Article 3.2 of the Dispute Settlement Understanding (DSU) attempts to ensure that the dispute settlement system will not impose new obligations on the Members. It provides that the dispute settlement system "serves to preserve the rights and obligations of Members under the covered agreements and to clarify the existing provisions of those agreements in accordance with customary rules of interpretation of public international law. Recommendations and rulings of the [Dispute Settlement Body] cannot add to or diminish the rights and obligations provided in the covered agreements."

As early as 2005, the Sutherland Report noted the difficulties regarding the issue of whether the WTO dispute settlement system was exceeding its mandate merely to "clarify" the rights and obligations in the WTO agreements by "gap-filling" when, like the *Treaty of Washington* on the issue of the indirect claims, it found that a provision of the agreements was not entirely clear:

> Another criticism is that gap-filling is not an appropriate role for the dispute settlement system. This view itself is open to criticism since every juridical institution has at least some measure of gap-filling responsibility as part of its efforts to resolve ambiguity. On the other hand, it can also reasonably be argued that WTO obligations should generally be the product of negotiations between Members, not juridical proceedings.[27]

---

26   *Ibid* at 263.
27   *Sutherland Report*, above note 10 at para 247.

The Sutherland Report noted what has since become one of the key issues underlying the United States' complaints about the WTO dispute settlement process—the WTO's "legislative" or negotiating function has not worked as well as hoped (or, arguably, as well as the dispute settlement function). WTO Members have successfully negotiated only two new agreements since the Uruguay Round (the *Trade Facilitation Agreement* and the incomplete *Agreement on Fisheries Subsidies*). Moreover, the provisions in the *Marrakesh Agreement Establishing the WTO* (WTO Agreement) on authoritative interpretations (Article IX) and amendments (Article X) have not proven to be effective, leaving Members with no effective means to "legislate away" decisions of the dispute settlement system that are considered to overstep the mandate of the system. In 2005, the Sutherland Report was optimistic that this could be corrected: "the Doha Round, it is to be profoundly hoped, will eventually correct the imbalance between law-making and any tendency towards creative law enforcement through the dispute settlement system."[28]

As most readers will be aware, however, the Doha Round failed to achieve this. The ongoing difficulties in the WTO's "legislative" or negotiating function remain an important barrier to the restoration of a fully effective dispute settlement system. For this reason, Mr. Molina's process examined potential mechanisms to enable Members to review and, where appropriate, suggest authoritative interpretations or other avenues that would have the effect of "overturning" decisions of panels or an appellate instance that would be considered to be "incorrect."[29] A similar idea was found in the Sutherland Report, which suggested that an impartial, special expert group could review reports for the DSB.[30]

D. Selection of Arbitrators

THE *TREATY OF WASHINGTON* PROVIDED that the *Alabama Claims* case would be decided by a five-member Tribunal. Each of the parties had the right to nominate one arbitrator. The remaining three arbitrators would be nominated by the President of the Swiss Confederation, the King of Italy, and the Emperor of Brazil. Having an arbitrator from each party meant that "each nation through its Arbitrator was enabled to have someone present who could

---

28   *Ibid.*

29   See WTO, *Molina Process*, above note 7 at 33 and 38.

30   *Sutherland Report*, above note 10 at para 251.

explain from personal knowledge such points of difficulty as might arise from a lack of familiarity with the language and with the political history of the two opposing countries."[31] The United States nominated Charles Francis Adams, son and grandson of Presidents, and, more importantly, the United States' Minister (ambassador) in London during the American Civil War. As such, he had been involved in efforts to identify ships, like the *Alabama*, that had been commissioned by the Confederacy and to prevent them from leaving British waters. This appointment "proved to be a very wise one," even though Adams did not speak French, which became the *lingua franca* of the Tribunal.[32] The United Kingdom nominated the Lord Chief Justice, Sir Alexander Cockburn, who had "a head like a bullet, and the eye of an eagle."[33] Cockburn was considered a less successful appointment, as "he brought to his (admittedly very difficult appointment) the qualities of an ill-tempered partisan advocate and not the even-tempered objectivity of a judicial arbitrator."[34] There appears to have been no expectation that the American and British arbitrators would be neutral or impartial. Both Adams and Cockburn had extensive *ex parte* communications with their "national" legal teams. Cockburn shared a hotel with the British delegation.[35]

The three remaining arbitrators all had legal or diplomatic backgrounds. The Italian nominee was Count Sclopis, a lawyer, who served as Chairman of the Tribunal; the Brazilian nominee was the Baron d'Itajuba, a professor and diplomat; and, finally, the Swiss nominee was Mr. Staempfli, a former President of the Swiss Confederation.[36] These three were not held in universally high esteem, especially by the British delegation: Cockburn described Staempfli as "ignorant as a horse and obstinate as a mule," while a member of the British delegation described Sclopis as "a pasty faced, burly, fat, pompous, obstinate old man" with "inflated notions of self-importance." The Brazilian, Baron d'Itajuba, fared somewhat better: "a sensible man, but no jurist." All in all, the Tribunal was "an extraordinary miscellaneous assemblage" who were "little likely to observe the well-known rules of Arbitrations."[37] In these circumstances, who would want to be an international arbitrator?

---

31 Hackett, above note 2 at 218.
32 Bingham, above note 1 at 16.
33 Hackett, above note 2 at 214.
34 Bingham, above note 1 at 17.
35 Brent, above note 12 at 27.
36 Bingham, above note 1 at 17.
37 Brent, above note 12 at 29.

In the WTO, Article 8.1 of the DSU provides that the members of a (three-person) WTO panel shall be "well-qualified governmental and/or non-governmental individuals" that have served on or presented a case to a panel, served as a representative of a government to the WTO, worked in the WTO Secretariat, taught or published on international trade law or policy, or served as a senior trade official in a Member government. Article 8.2 provides that "panel members should be selected with a view to ensuring independence of the Members, a sufficiently diverse background, and a wide spectrum of experience." Unlike in the *Alabama Claims* case, under Article 8.3, they may not be citizens of a party to the dispute, unless the parties otherwise agree.

The Secretariat maintains an indicative list of potential panelists, which is intended to be a source of names to propose to the parties in the process of composing a panel.[38] In practice, however, this list has become somewhat obsolete, and the Secretariat maintains an informal list of individuals that have served before or that have expressed interest in doing so. When the workload of the dispute settlement system was at its busiest, there were approximately twenty to twenty-five new panels per year. This rapidly depleted the pool of candidates. It should be noted also that WTO panelists are not very well compensated. They receive a per diem compensation of approximately $900 per day for working on a case—a relative pittance compared to what seasoned arbitrators can earn in investor-state or commercial arbitrations. In these circumstances, it has not been easy to build a cadre of experienced and knowledgeable panelists that are willing and able to devote what might be many months or even years to some extremely complex cases.

Almost since the inception of the WTO system, therefore, there have been calls for a more professionalized roster of panelists. In 2005, the Sutherland Report noted that "a combination of roster and ad hoc appointments might serve the institution very well and ease somewhat the particular problems that have been witnessed in a few of the panel selection procedures." But selecting this roster would in itself be problematic: "there exists considerable worry that the usual diplomatic and political processes might not produce the best calibre individuals the tasks require. Thus, thought is needed about

---

38 Briefly, under Article 8 of the DSU, the Secretariat proposes lists of candidates to serve on the panel to the parties. If the parties agree on the proposed candidates, the panel is "composed." If the parties cannot reach agreement, they may ask the Director-General of the WTO to compose the panel (normally the complainant would make this request, as the defendant would not be in a hurry to have the process move forward).

a possible small apolitical body of experts who would examine nominations and produce a list of nominees who meet carefully set out criteria. This body could then work with the DSB in finalizing the roster."[39]

To date, these proposals have not led to any changes in the panel selection/composition process. This may be because of fears that a more professional roster would lead to excessive "institutionalization" of the process, making it more, rather than less, legalistic.

Nevertheless, concerns about the quality and availability of panelists have meant that this has been one of the most discussed topics in Mr. Molina's reform process.[40] However, there does not seem to be any appetite to return to an *Alabama Claims*-type approach where each party would nominate its own arbitrator, with one or more neutral arbitrators to be selected by other means.

E. Complexity—Size of Submissions

ONE OF THE BIG CONCERNS in the WTO dispute settlement has been the increased complexity of the cases. This arises in part from the nature of the cases—disputes such as the *Boeing/Airbus* cases, the disputes involving Australia's plain packing requirements on cigarettes, and many disputes about sanitary/phytosanitary measures involve very complex factual issues, which require the submission of extensive evidence, including expert witness statements. A further problem in WTO disputes is the number of claims brought by complaining Members. Many would argue that over-lawyering is an important part of the problem. In any event, WTO cases have become increasingly complex. As just one example, in the *Airbus* case to which I refer in the title of this chapter, the original panel's report was almost 1200 pages long.[41]

For better or worse, complaints about the prolixity of lawyers are nothing new. In the *Alabama Claims* arbitration, the parties' submissions were drafted

---

39   *Sutherland Report*, above note 10 at para 257.
40   See WTO, *Molina Process*, above note 7 at 20.
41   *European Communities and Certain Member States—Measures Affecting Trade in Large Civil Aircraft (Complaint by the United States)* (2010), WTO Doc WT/DS316/R (Panel Report), online (pdf): docs.wto.org [perma.cc/7TZP-Z8XX]. There is some anecdotal evidence to suggest that since the inception of the Appellate Body crisis, panels have made a diligent effort to shorten their reports, although in my view, it is perhaps too soon to decide whether this is a real trend or is affected by issues such as the nature or complexity of the cases.

in longhand or typed and then printed on printing presses. Both parties' first submissions were "substantial" documents. The United States' submission was 480 pages, including seven volumes of supporting documents. It was largely prepared in Paris, where the American delegation stayed for a few months before the actual proceedings in Geneva. Similarly, the British submission was "168 closely printed foolscap pages, with four volumes of supporting correspondence."[42] This is an impressive amount of work in the pre-word processing/personal computer era! It presented challenges that we do not face today: as they were concerned that French printers in Paris might make too many errors printing in English, the Americans brought English printers to Paris to do the typesetting. Apparently, this was "regarded by the French printers with perfect good-nature."[43] Similarly, the United Kingdom's counter-case (rebuttal submission) ran to over 1,100 pages, including supporting materials, although the American counter-case was "shorter."[44] Nevertheless, the final decision of the Tribunal was much shorter—approximately fifteen pages. Perhaps not surprisingly, the "massive" dissent of the British Arbitrator, Sir Alexander Cockburn, was much longer—"254 closely printed foolscap pages."[45]

The WTO dispute settlement system has attempted to grapple with this problem. In 2015, the Appellate Body noted a significant increase in the length of submissions to it and circulated a proposal to introduce page or word limits on these submissions. Notwithstanding concerns about the increasing legalization and complexity of the process, the proposal received little support.[46] Several WTO Members considered that page limits would be an infringement of Members' due process rights, while others raised more practical concerns. Accordingly, the Appellate Body decided not to impose limits. Nevertheless, the concern persisted. Under the Multi-Party Interim Appeal Arbitration Arrangement (MPIA), a plurilateral interim arrangement to replicate the WTO appeals process within the framework of an arbitration under Article 25 of the DSU, the arbitrators may impose word limits on the

---

42 Bingham, above note 1 at 19.

43 Hackett, above note 2 at 128.

44 *Ibid.*

45 Bingham, above note 1 at 23, fn 133.

46 See WTO, *2016 Appellate Body Annual Report*, WTO Doc WT/AB/27 (2017) at 100–1, online (pdf): docs.wto.org [perma.cc/GPK5-NVMA].

parties' submissions.[47] Mr. Molina's reform process also attempted to address this issue.[48]

Lawyers that have worked previously with page limits—perhaps in domestic courts—tend to be more receptive to the idea than others. The old joke about a lawyer writing a twenty-page memo for a client because he did not have time to write a five-page memo also comes to mind. Nevertheless, as Jan Bohanes discusses elsewhere in this volume and as indeed the Appellate Body learned when it canvassed the issue in 2015, sovereign states may see page limits as an intrusion on their due process rights. Also, page limits are more impractical in a tribunal of first instance that may have to address complex factual issues than at an appellate stage, which normally would not involve *de novo* review of the facts.

F. Conclusion

THE *ALABAMA CLAIMS* CASE CONCLUDED more or less to the satisfaction of all—the United States received its compensation and the feeling in the United Kingdom was generally that the issue had been resolved with honour (although the fact of having "lost" the case was unpalatable to some). The CSS *Alabama* itself had already met its demise towards the end of the American Civil War. In June 1864, it was tracked down and cornered by the Union warship, the USS *Kearsage*, in the waters off the French port of Cherbourg. On 19 June, a large audience, including the painter Édouard Manet, came out to watch from the cliffs of Cherbourg as the *Kearsage* engaged and sank the *Alabama* in battle. The vast majority of the 170 aboard were rescued by French ships and the *Kearsage* itself. [49]

As noted in the introduction, the *Alabama Claims* case lives on in the *Alabama* room in Geneva's Hotel de Ville. In the law, it spawned an enthusiasm for international arbitration that ultimately led to the Permanent Court of Justice and, perhaps, very indirectly to the GATT and WTO dispute settlement systems.

---

47 See *Colombia—Anti-Dumping Duties on Frozen Fries from Belgium, Germany and the Netherlands (Complaint by the European Union)* (2022), WTO Doc WT/DS591/ARB25/Add.1, Annex 2 (Addendum to Arbitral Award), online (pdf): docs.wto.org [perma.cc/C53C-877M].

48 WTO, *Molina Process*, above note 7 at 25.

49 Bingham, above note 1 at 7.

Notwithstanding the current travails of the WTO system, it remains a valuable mechanism for many of the WTO's 166 Members, especially those without the political or economic clout to resolve their trade differences by other means. As this chapter attempted to illustrate, many of the current problems in the system are reflections of constant challenges in international arbitration. The old French maxim that the more things change, the more they stay the same, certainly applies in this field. As explained above, therefore, the *Alabama Claims* case continues to be both an interesting chapter in the history of international arbitration and an important reminder of the difficulties in shaping and managing an effective system of international arbitration. It is to be hoped that the lessons to be learned will contribute to future successes of WTO dispute settlement.

CHAPTER 26

Arbitration in WTO Dispute Settlement: The Magic Toolbox of the System

Müslüm Yilmaz*

A. Introduction

THE UNDERSTANDING ON RULES AND Procedures Governing the Settlement of Disputes (DSU), in Annex II to the *Agreement Establishing the World Trade Organization* (WTO), embodies a mechanism for the settlement of disputes between WTO Members. The regular process starts with consultations among disputing Members, and proceeds, as appropriate, to the panel and appeal phases, and ends with the implementation phase. This mechanism provides for arbitration, when necessary, at two stages of the process, as laid down in Articles 21.3(c) and 22.6. The DSU further provides for "expeditious arbitration" as an alternative dispute resolution method, as explained in Article 25.

---

*   Counsellor, Senior Dispute Settlement Lawyer, WTO Legal Affairs Division. The views expressed are those of the author. They do not represent the positions or opinions of the WTO, its Secretariat, or of WTO Members. They are also without prejudice to Members' rights and obligations under the WTO. Any errors are attributable to the author. The author thanks Jorge Castro, Graham Cook, and Jenya Grigorova for helpful comments on earlier drafts, as well as Julian Eduardo Becerra and Cheryl Dine for their research assistance.

This chapter briefly explains the two provisions of the DSU providing for arbitration as part of the default dispute settlement process (Section B).[1] It then focuses on Article 25 arbitration and discusses this provision's use so far and its potential future use (Section C). With regard to Article 25 arbitration, the chapter does not go into the details of the Multi-Party Interim Appeal Arbitration Arrangement (MPIA) proposed by the European Union (EU) and signed by a number of other WTO Members, since this is the subject of another contribution to this volume.[2] Section D concludes.

Several papers have been published on the issue of arbitration under the DSU, including an early one by our dear colleague Valerie Hughes. To avoid repetition, this chapter does not provide extensive explanations about the DSU provisions governing arbitration and focuses, instead, on the trends in the use of arbitration by WTO Members.

B. Arbitration as Part of the Default Dispute Settlement Process

THE DSU PROVIDES FOR ARBITRATION at two stages of the default dispute settlement process. The first is for the determination of the reasonable period of time (RPT) for the respondent to bring its measure, found to be WTO-inconsistent, into compliance with the relevant provisions of the WTO Agreement (Art 21.3(c)), whenever the respondent finds it impracticable to comply immediately. The second is for the determination of the level of suspension of concessions or other obligations by the complainant in cases where the respondent fails to comply with the recommendations and rulings of the Dispute Settlement Body (DSB) (Art 22.6). Resorting to arbitration under either of these two provisions does not require the parties' agreement. If the circumstance necessitating arbitration arises, and the relevant party so requests (the

---

1   This chapter explains arbitration as provided for in the DSU. Other WTO agreements also provide for arbitration in different contexts, namely, Articles XXI:3(a) and XXII:3 of the *General Agreement on Trade in Services*; Article XIX:7 of the *Agreement on Government Procurement*; and Article 8.5 of the *Agreement on Subsidies and Countervailing Measures* (SCM Agreement) (expired on 31 December 1999). Article 44 of the *Investment Facilitation for Development Agreement* encourages its parties to consider resorting to Article 25 arbitration to facilitate the solution of their disputes. For the provisions of the SCM Agreement that modify the standard for the determinations to be made by DSU Article 22.6 arbitrators in the case of prohibited and actionable subsidies, see below note 7.

2   See Jan Bohanes's contribution to this volume (Chapter 27).

complaining party in the case of Article 21.3(c) and the responding party in the case of Article 22.6) the matter will be referred to arbitration. This section briefly explains these two types of arbitration and then discusses why the drafters preferred to call them "arbitration."

1) Arbitration to Determine the Reasonable Period of Time for Implementation—DSU Article 21.3(c)

Under the DSU, once the DSB makes recommendations and rulings when a challenged measure is found to be WTO-inconsistent, the general rule is "prompt compliance" with such recommendations and rulings (Art 21.1). If immediate compliance is impracticable, the respondent will be given an RPT to comply with those recommendations and rulings (Art 21.2). Article 21 provides for three methods for the determination of the RPT: a time period proposed by the respondent and approved by the DSB; if not, one mutually agreed by the two parties; and if not, one determined through binding arbitration. Article 21.3(c) explains two features of this arbitration. First, it is binding. Second, there is a guideline with regard to the arbitrated matter: the RPT should not exceed fifteen months from the adoption of the panel or Appellate Body (AB) report. However, a shorter or longer period may be determined if circumstances justify it.

The arbitrator acting pursuant to this provision may be composed of one or more individuals. So far, all such arbitrators were composed of one individual. If the disputing parties cannot agree on an arbitrator within ten days after referring the matter to arbitration, the Director-General of the WTO makes the appointment (fn 12 to the DSU). In the vast majority of these proceedings the arbitrator has been a current or former Member of the AB.[3] In the period from 1995 to December 2024, thirty-three arbitrations were conducted under Article 21.3(c).[4]

---

3   Our counting shows that of the fifteen individuals who served as arbitrators pursuant to Article 21.3(c), thirteen were then current or former AB members.

4   WTO, "Analytical Index Annex 2: Dispute Settlement Understanding - Information Tables" (last modified December 2024) at 52–55, online (pdf): wto.org [perma.cc/R3RL-DWU6].

2) Arbitration to Determine the Level of Suspension of Concessions or Other Obligations—DSU Article 22.6

The second point at which the DSU provides for the possibility of binding arbitration as part of the default dispute settlement process is where the respondent fails to comply with the DSB's recommendations and rulings indicated in the relevant panel and/or AB report. Where the respondent fails to comply with the DSB's recommendations and rulings, the parties may agree on compensation as a temporary measure (Art 22.2). If they fail to do so, the complainant may seek the DSB's authorization to suspend the application of concessions or other obligations under the covered agreements *vis-à-vis* the respondent until the situation is resolved. Upon the complainant's request for such authorization, the respondent may object to the level of the proposed suspension or allege that the complainant did not follow the principles and procedures set out in Article 22.3 laying down the process to be followed in making such a request. Upon such an objection, the matter is automatically referred to arbitration by the DSB.[5] Here too, the arbitrator may be composed of one or more individuals (fn 15 to the DSU).

In the period from 1995 to December 2024, eighteen arbitrations were conducted under Article 22.6.[6] In all of them, the arbitrator was composed of three individuals. To the extent possible, the individuals serving as members of the arbitrator were the panelists who served in the same dispute. The task of this arbitrator is explained in Article 22.7: the arbitrator has to determine whether the level of the proposed suspension is equivalent to the level of nullification or impairment resulting from non-compliance with the DSB's recommendations and rulings or, if relevant, whether the proposed suspension is allowed under the respective agreement.[7] If there is such a claim, the

---

5   Decisions by the Arbitrator, see *United States—Certain Country of Origin Labelling (COOL) Requirements (Complaint by Canada and Mexico)* (2015), WTO Decs WT/DS384/ARB, WT/DS386/ARB at paras 2.14–2.15 (Decisions by the Arbitrator), online (pdf): docs.wto.org [perma.cc/7AEX-LB9N].

6   WTO, above note 4 at 58 and 60.

7   Article 4.11 of the SCM Agreement stipulates that, in disputes involving prohibited subsidies, the standard for Article 22.6 arbitrators should be whether the countermeasures are "appropriate." Article 7.10 of that Agreement states that, in disputes involving actionable subsidies, the standard will be whether the countermeasures are "commensurate with the degree and nature of the adverse effects determined to exist."

arbitrator may also determine whether the principles and procedures with regard to resorting to suspension have been complied with.

Arbitration under Article 22.6 plays a crucial role in that it generally determines the magnitude of the response that a complainant can give to the respondent in case of non-compliance with the DSB's recommendations and rulings. As such, it assists in restoring the balance of concessions between the parties prior to the respondent's violation of its WTO obligations.[8]

3) Rationale for Providing for Arbitration as Part of the Default Dispute Settlement Process

Generally speaking, arbitration is an alternative dispute resolution method that can have advantages over litigation and may therefore be preferred by disputing parties. In today's world, it plays a significant role in domestic as well as international commercial disputes between companies. It is also used in inter-state and investor-state disputes. The advantages of arbitration over litigation include party autonomy over the process both procedurally and in terms of applicable law as well as easy enforcement without significant court involvement.[9]

Arbitration under Articles 21.3(c) and 22.6 seems to differ from arbitration in the traditional sense. Arbitration under Articles 21.3(c) and 22.6 operates as part of the default dispute settlement process and therefore is not truly distinct from that process.[10] Some experts have characterized these two types of arbitration as *sui generis* for the reason that they do not correspond to the classical criteria that define arbitration.[11]

It is not clear why the drafters of the DSU preferred the term "arbitration" for these two instances in the default dispute settlement process. In this regard, it is important to note that the determination of the RPT and the level of suspensions are not the only two complications that may arise in

8   Brendan P McGivern, "Seeking Compliance with WTO Rulings: Theory, Practice and Alternatives" (2002) 36:1 *International Law* 141 at 141 and 144.

9   For instance, the UN Convention on the Recognition and Enforcement of Foreign Arbitral Awards (1958) lays down, in its Article V, limited grounds for the refusal of recognition and enforcement of an arbitral award.

10   David Jacyk, "The Integration of Article 25 Arbitration in WTO Dispute Settlement: The Past, Present and Future" (2008) 15 *Australian International Law Journal* 235 at 250, online (pdf): classic.austlii.edu.au [perma.cc/6R46-TV3N].

11   Laurence Boisson de Chazournes, "L'Arbitrage à l'OMC" (2003) 3 *Revue de l'arbitrage* 949 at 949 and 961, online (pdf): archive-ouverte.unige.ch [perma.cc/46F9-L8CP].

the implementation of the DSB's recommendations and rulings. Arguably, the most critical issue that may arise in the implementation phase of the default dispute settlement process is determining whether the respondent has complied with the DSB's recommendations and rulings set out in the relevant panel/AB reports. Article 21.5 of the DSU subjects this determination to a panel, and possibly appeal, proceeding. The negotiating history of the DSU does not clarify why the drafters subjected the determination of compliance with the DSB's recommendations and rulings to panel and appeal proceedings but the determination of the RPT and the level of suspensions to a process that they called "arbitration." A plausible explanation could be their desire to keep the decisions about these two issues outside the scope of appeal and thereby save time. Article 21.3(c) and Article 22.7 stipulate that arbitration for the determination of the RPT and the level of suspension, respectively, is binding. In other words, the decisions made by arbitrators in these two proceedings are not appealable. Indeed, Article 17.1 of the DSU stipulates that "[t]he Appellate Body shall hear appeals from panel cases." This provision could be viewed as suggesting that while panel reports issued in Article 21.5 proceedings are appealable, arbitrators' decisions made under Articles 21.3(c) and 22.6 are not.[12] The reason may be that the drafters did not want the determination of RPT and the level of suspension of concessions or other obligations to take too much time.

These characteristics of arbitration under Articles 21.3(c) and 22.6 demonstrate that these two proceedings do not have much in common with arbitration in the general sense, except in name.

C. Arbitration as an Alternative Dispute Resolution Method—DSU Article 25

1) The Legal Provision

Article 25 of the DSU allows WTO Members to use "expeditious arbitration" as an alternative to the default dispute settlement process. Article 25.1 states

---

12   There are, however, different views on this issue. For instance, Flett calls Article 22.6 arbitrators "arbitration panels" and argues that their decisions can be appealed pursuant to Article 17.1 of the DSU. See James Flett, "How can the Extent and Speed of Compliance of WTO Members with DSU Rulings be Improved?" in Simon J Evenett & Alejandro Jara, eds, *Building on Bali A Work Programme for the WTO* (London: Centre for Economic Policy Research, 2013) at 95, online (pdf): cepr.org [perma. cc/4GSY-Y256].

that such arbitration "can facilitate the solution of certain disputes that concern issues that are clearly defined by both parties." Article 25 arbitration is subject to the mutual agreement of the parties. The parties are free to draft their arbitration agreement, which they then have to notify to all Members (Article 25.2). Third party participation is subject to the agreement of the parties. The arbitration award is binding. In other words, such awards are not appealable. They must be notified to the DSB and the relevant Council or Committee. However, they are not adopted by the DSB (Article 25.3).

It is important to note that Article 25.1 refers to "certain disputes" as the object of the arbitration, as opposed to, for example, "certain issues" arising in the context of a dispute. Therefore, it could be argued that Article 25 arbitration was envisaged as an alternative dispute settlement method for certain types of disputes and not as an alternative avenue of resolving issues that arise in particular phases of a dispute following the issuance of a panel report. Put differently, Article 25 arbitration seems to have been designed as a method alternative to the panel part of the default dispute settlement process. For this reason, it has been noted that, unlike arbitration under Articles 21.3(c) and 22.6, Article 25 arbitration more closely resembles arbitration as an alternative dispute resolution method.[13] However, as explained in the following section, the use of Article 25 arbitration so far has focused either on issues that arose in the context of an ongoing panel proceeding or, in a more pronounced way, on appeals from panel reports.

Once the arbitration award is made, its implementation is subject *mutatis mutandis* to Articles 21 and 22 of the DSU. Thus, the implementation phase for an Article 25 arbitration award is governed by the same rules that govern the default dispute settlement process.

2) The Use of Article 25 Arbitration

WTO Members have not shown significant interest in using Article 25 arbitration until recently. This method was used for the first time in 2001 in *US—Section 110(5) Copyright Act*. The context in which arbitration was used in this dispute was peculiar. The parties resorted to Article 25 arbitration for the calculation of the amount of nullification or impairment of benefits of the European Communities because of the WTO-inconsistency of the challenged measure. It is important to note, however, that this arbitration was

---

13   Jacyk, above note 10 at 253.

not conducted *in lieu* of an Article 22.6 arbitration, the principal function of which is to make such a calculation. In fact, at the time this arbitration was conducted, the RPT provided to the United States had not expired and therefore the possibility of an Article 22.6 arbitration had not even arisen. The Arbitrator itself noted that this Article 25 arbitration "should not be applied so as to circumvent the provisions of Article 22.6 of the DSU."[14] The Arbitrator explained the purpose of resorting to Article 25 arbitration in this case "as a means of reaching a mutually acceptable compensation."[15]

Noting that this was the first resort to Article 25 arbitration, the Arbitrator made some observations concerning its jurisdiction. It noted, for instance, the potential argument that Article 25 arbitration is an alternative to a panel procedure and cannot therefore be used for the purpose of determining the level of nullification or impairment.[16] However, the Arbitrator noted that neither Article 25 nor any other provision of the DSU precludes this possibility. Further, it interpreted the phrase "the solution of certain disputes that concern issues that are clearly defined by the parties" in Article 25.1 as indicating that Article 25 arbitration is a method "to which members may have recourse whenever necessary within the WTO framework."[17] The Arbitrator also considered this approach to be compatible with the object and purpose of the DSU, particularly that of ensuring prompt settlement of a dispute, set out in Article 3.3.[18] The Arbitrator further stated that "[t]he possibility for the parties to a dispute to seek arbitration in relation to the negotiation of compensation operates to increase the effectiveness of that option under Article 22.2."[19] In this regard, the Arbitrator also noted that compensation "is always to be preferred to countermeasures of any sort, since it enhances trade instead of restricting or diverting it."[20] On this basis, the Arbitrator concluded that it had jurisdiction to conduct this arbitration under Article 25 "pending further interpretation by the Members."[21]

---

14   See *United States—Section 110(5) of the US Copyright Act (Complaint by the European Communities)* (2001), WTO Doc WT/DS160/ARB25/1 at fn 22 (Article 25 Arbitration Award), online (pdf): docs.wto.org [perma.cc/2J6B-KDST] [*US—Section 110(5) Copyright Act*].

15   *Ibid* at para 2.4.

16   *Ibid* at para 2.3.

17   *Ibid* at para 2.4.

18   *Ibid* at para 2.5.

19   *Ibid* at para 2.6.

20   *Ibid*.

21   *Ibid* at para 2.7.

This first Article 25 arbitration is important in that it underlines the significant amount of flexibility that WTO Members have in terms of choosing what "disputes" and "issues" are susceptible to arbitration under Article 25, and what reasons they may have for using this method of dispute settlement. In *US—Section 110(5) Copyright Act*, Article 25 arbitration was used for the purpose of determining the level of nullification or impairment before the expiry of the RPT given to the respondent, in order to assist the parties in negotiating a mutually acceptable compensation.[22] It is curious to note that the Arbitrator used the term "WTO framework," rather than, for instance, "WTO dispute settlement framework," in describing the breadth of the scope of Article 25 arbitration.

From 2001 to 2020 there was no further use of Article 25 arbitration. In the meantime, due to the lack of consensus in the DSB to select new Members to fill the vacancies in the AB, the number of AB Members dropped to zero in December 2020, and the AB became dysfunctional. WTO Members have since engaged in discussions on reforming the WTO dispute settlement system. While these discussions continue, several Members have turned to Article 25 arbitration for interim solutions regarding appeal. This shift has brought Article 25 arbitration into the spotlight at the WTO.

In 2020, the parties agreed on procedures for Article 25 arbitration for appeal purposes in three ongoing disputes. In *Costa Rica—Avocados (Mexico)*, neither party appealed the panel report, and therefore there was no resort to Article 25 arbitration pursuant to the agreed procedures.[23] In *Canada—Commercial Aircraft*, the complainant withdrew its complaint and requested the Panel to indefinitely suspend its work pursuant to Article 12.12 of the DSU.[24] In *Colombia—Frozen Fries (Article 25)*, the parties resorted to Article 25 arbitration for appeal purposes based on agreed procedures.

---

22 In this regard, it is also interesting to note the Arbitrator's statement that, unlike the level of suspension of concessions or other obligations, "the legal consequences of an overestimation in the case of compensation under Article 22.2 of the DSU are less, since it is not specified that the compensation to be offered should be equivalent to the level of nullification or impairment." *Ibid* at n 84.

23 The panel report in this dispute was adopted by the DSB on 31 May 2022. *Costa Rica—Measures Concerning the Importation of Fresh Avocados from Mexico (Complaint by Mexico)* (2022), WTO Doc WT/DS524/R (Panel Report), online (pdf): docs.wto.org [perma.cc/D35X-HR67].

24 *Canada—Measures Concerning Trade in Commercial Aircraft (Complaint by Brazil)* (2021), WTO Doc WT/DS522/23 (2021), (Withdrawal of Complaint) online (pdf): wto.org [perma.cc/XW93-HUF7].

In January 2021, China and Australia notified their agreed procedures for resorting to Article 25 arbitration for appeal purposes in *China—AD/CVD on Wine (Australia)*.[25] The parties subsequently reached a mutually agreed solution, and arbitration was not used.[26] In August 2021, China and Australia notified to the DSB the agreed procedures for Article 25 arbitration for appeal purposes in *China—AD/CVD on Barley (Australia)*.[27] The parties then found a mutually agreed solution to the dispute.[28] In September 2021, Canada and China notified to the DSB their agreed procedures for Article 25 arbitration for appeal purposes in *China—Canola Seed (Canada)*.[29] Canada then requested the Panel to suspend its work. After one year, the Panel's authority lapsed as per Article 12.12 of the DSU.[30]

In addition to these individual initiatives a group of members proposed the MPIA, an interim solution to the appeal problem, based on Article 25 arbitration, to be used in disputes among them.[31] So far, twenty-seven Members have endorsed this arrangement. The first MPIA arbitration was conducted in 2022 in *Colombia—Frozen Fries (Article 25)*.[32]

---

25 *China—Anti-Dumping and Countervailing Duty Measures on Wine from Australia (Complaint by Australia)* (2024), WT/DS602/3 (Panel Report), online (pdf): docs.wto. org [perma.cc/8B8W-VKHC].

26 *China—Anti-Dumping and Countervailing Duty Measures on Wine from Australia (Complaint by Australia)* (2024), WTO Doc WT/DS602/8 (Notification of Mutual Solution), online (pdf): docs.wto.org [perma.cc/2AF6-VDCE].

27 *China—Anti-Dumping and Countervailing Duty Measures on Barley from Australia (Complaint by Australia)* (2021), WTO Doc WT/DS598/5 (DSU Article 25 Agreed Procedures for Arbitration), online (pdf): docs.wto.org [perma.cc/7PJR-3P8Z].

28 *China—Anti-Dumping and Countervailing Duty Measures on Barley from Australia (Complaint by Australia)* (2023), WTO Doc WT/DS598/R (Panel Report), online (pdf): docs.wto.org [perma.cc/22W6-JCVS].

29 *China—Measures Concerning the Importation of Canola Seed from Canada (Complaint by Canada)* (2021), WTO Doc WT/DS589/5 (DSU Article 25 Agreed Procedures for Arbitration), online (pdf): docs.wto.org [perma.cc/XG8Y-DC5L].

30 *China—Measures Concerning the Importation of Canola Seed from Canada (Complaint by Canada)* (2023), WTO Doc WT/DS589/9 (Panel Report Lapse), online (pdf): docs. wto.org [perma.cc/AX6T-AK8B].

31 WTO, *Multi-Party Interim Appeal Arbitration Arrangement Pursuant to Article 25 of the DSU*, WTO Doc JOB/DSB/1/Add.12 (2020), online (pdf): docs.wto.org [perma.cc/ L2SP-VMM8].

32 See *Colombia—Anti-Dumping Duties on Frozen Fries from Belgium, Germany and the Netherlands (Complaint by the European Union)* (2022), WTO Doc WT/DS591/ARB25 (Article 25 Arbitration Award), online (pdf): docs.wto.org [perma.cc/XJ4F-CW6B]. In this dispute, Colombia and the European Union notified their agreed procedures for arbitration on 13 July 2020. On 20 April 2021, they submitted the revised version of

Prior to the completion of the first MPIA appeal arbitration, Article 25 arbitration was also used in 2022 in *Turkey—Pharmaceutical Products (EU)* for appeal purposes. The parties resorted to *ad hoc* appeal arbitration based on procedures that reflected, almost verbatim, MPIA procedures. Legally speaking, however, this was not an MPIA appeal proceeding.[33] In light of this experience, other Members who are not MPIA participants could also consider resorting to Article 25 arbitration for appeal purposes on an *ad hoc* basis, based largely on the MPIA procedures.

In January 2022, the United States and the European Union agreed to resort to Article 25 arbitration in two disputes that they had brought against one another, namely, *EU—Additional Duties (US)*[34] and *US—Steel and Aluminium Products (EU)*.[35] In both arbitrations, the arbitrators selected were members of the panels in the ongoing panel proceedings.[36] Both cases had previously been suspended pursuant to Article 12.12 of the DSU. Under this provision, if suspension lasts for more than twelve months, the authority for the establishment of the panel lapses. In order to avoid this situation, that is, in order to have the cases suspended for longer than twelve months, the parties decided to terminate the panel proceedings and switch to arbitration for the resolution of the disputes.[37] They also agreed that arbitration in both

these procedures in order to give effect to the MPIA that had in the meantime been proposed by the European Union at WTO, *Revision to the DSU Article 25 Agreed Procedures for Arbitration*, WTO Doc WT/DS591/3/Rev.1 (2021) at para 8, online (pdf): docs.wto.org [perma.cc/QDM7-QNGP].

33 See *Turkey—Certain Measures Concerning the Production, Importation and Marketing of Pharmaceutical Products (Complaint by the European Union)* (2022), WTO Doc WT/DS583/ARB25 (Article 25 Arbitration Award), online (pdf): docs.wto.org [perma.cc/4794-MTB3].

34 *European Union—Additional Duties on Certain Products from the United States (Complaint by the United States)* (2022), WTO Doc WT/DS559/7 (DSU Article 25 Recourse), online (pdf): docs.wto.org [perma.cc/9ZJ4-6LR9][*EU—Additional Duties (US)*].

35 *United States—Certain Measures on Steel and Aluminium Products (Complaint by the European Union)* (2022), WTO Doc WT/DS548/19 (DSU Article 25 Recourse), online (pdfo: docs.wto.org [perma.cc/H89M-QZTP].

36 *European Union—Additional Duties on Certain Products from the United States (Complaint by the United States)*(2022), WTO Doc WT/DS559/10 (DSU Article 25 Recourse), online (pdf): docs.wto.org [perma.cc/J8AP-YTD7]; *United States—Certain Measures on Steel and Aluminium Products (Complaint by the European Union)* (2022), WTO Doc WT/DS548/22 (DSU Article 25 Recourse), online (pdf): docs.wto.org [perma.cc/549M-D6D2].

37 In this regard, the agreed procedures provide: "The phrase 'for a period not to exceed 12 months' in Article 12.12 of the DSU shall not apply to these arbitration proceedings." See *EU—Additional Duties (US)*, above note 34 at para 6.

cases would, upon composition of the arbitrator, be immediately and indefinitely suspended.[38] This represents a situation in which the disputing parties used Article 25 arbitration to overcome a difficulty emanating from Article 12.12 of the DSU, and gained the flexibility to have their cases suspended without limit.

On 25 March 2022, the European Union and Türkiye notified the DSB of their agreed procedures for resorting to Article 25 arbitration for appeal purposes in *EU—Safeguard Measures on Steel (Turkey)*.[39] However, neither party resorted to arbitration under these procedures, and the panel report was adopted by the DSB.[40]

These developments point to significantly increased interest on the part of WTO Members in Article 25 arbitration. Even though in the majority of the cases described above the parties ultimately did not resort to arbitration, they agreed on arbitration procedures *ex ante* in case there would be a need to use them later in the proceedings. The varied manner in which arbitration was intended to be used in these cases underlines the significant amount of flexibility provided by Article 25. Particularly important in this regard is the use of Article 25 arbitration to create the MPIA. Here, Article 25 arbitration was used not to resolve a particular dispute or a particular issue arising in an ongoing dispute but to create an institutional framework to handle appeals for an undefined period of time in an undefined number of disputes among WTO Members that endorse this framework.

3) Is Article 25 Arbitration Underused?

As indicated by the Panel in *US—Section 110(5) Copyright Act*, it could be argued that Article 25 arbitration was meant to be an alternative method to panel proceedings. From this perspective, Article 25 arbitration has been underused because no such arbitration has taken place so far. However, since 2020, there have been twelve cases[41] in which the parties agreed to use Arti-

---

38   See WTO, above note 36.

39   WTO, *European Union—Safeguard Measures on Certain Steel Products (Complaint by Turkey)* (2022), WTO Doc WT/DS595/10 (DSU Article 25 Agreed Procedures for Arbitration), online (pdf): docs.wto.org [perma.cc/37LA-89S2].

40   WTO, *European Union—Safeguard Measures on Certain Steel Products (Complaint by Turkey)* (2022), WTO Doc WT/DS595/R (Panel Report), online (pdf): docs.wto.org [perma.cc/CQW5-QB6W].

41   WTO, above note 4 at 79 & 80.

cle 25 arbitration for appeal purposes in their ongoing disputes. Even though only two of these resulted in actual arbitration being conducted, the numbers clearly show that Members are aware of the significant amount of flexibility that Article 25 provides in terms of the issues for which arbitration can be used. In what follows, the chapter discusses, first, the possible reasons for WTO Members' reluctance to use Article 25 arbitration as an alternative method to panel proceedings and, second, whether that might change in future.

a) Why WTO Members Appear to be Reluctant to Use Article 25 Arbitration as an Alternative to Panel Proceedings?

This section first explains the advantages of Article 25 arbitration that have been identified in the literature and examines why this method has never been used as an alternative to panel proceedings despite such advantages. It then identifies other reasons that might explain this situation.

i. Advantages of Article 25 Identified in the Literature

SEVERAL FACTORS HAVE BEEN PUT forward by commentators as potential advantages of Article 25 arbitration over the default dispute settlement process. The first is that arbitration awards are not appealable. In this regard, it has been argued that the fact that Article 25 arbitration awards are not appealable "would reinforce the notion of the negotiated resolution and potentially reduce the energy expended on legal manoeuvring."[42] This, however, does not seem to have encouraged the use of Article 25 arbitration. On the contrary, experience shows that many WTO Members appear to value the existence of an appeal mechanism. The rate of appeal of panel reports in the 1995 to 2020 period was sixty-three percent[43]. The negotiations and other exchanges of views among Members following the appeal problem have demonstrated support by a significant group of Members for the restoration of the two-tier WTO dispute settlement process.[44] The fact that since 2020 there have been twelve cases in which the parties agreed on procedures under Article 25 for appeal purposes also seems to reinforce this view. In this regard,

---

42   Jacyk, above note 10 at 244.

43   For calculation based on data see WTO, "Statistical Reports on Dispute Settlement" (last visited 19 June 2025), online: wto.org [perma.cc/AAW2-6H6H].

44   See WTO, *Indonesia—Safeguard on Certain Iron or Steel Products (Complaint by Viet Nam)* (2019), WTO Doc WT/DSB/496 (Minutes) at para 3.2 for minutes of the December 2024 meeting.

it is also useful to note Valerie Hughes' view that the absence of appeal might actually be an impediment to the use of Article 25 arbitration.[45]

Another advantage of Article 25 arbitration relates to the fact that this method is to be used in disputes involving "issues that are clearly defined by both parties," as indicated in the first paragraph of this provision. This phrase has generally been interpreted to mean that Article 25 arbitration would be an appropriate dispute resolution method in disputes that do not involve complex issues. For instance, a discussion paper presented by the United States during the Uruguay Round negotiations, proposing arbitration as an alternative dispute resolution method, stated that a disadvantage of subjecting all disputes to the same default dispute settlement process was that "issues that should be relatively simply and easily settled are taking too long and becoming too political because of procedures and practices designed for harder cases."[46] The European Economic Community, for its part, pointed out that "the categories of disputes that could be handled by this alternative procedure should be factual and not involve questions of interpretation or of conformity with the *General Agreement*. The outcome of this process could not constitute a legal precedent."[47] Similarly, the Korean delegation stated that arbitration "might facilitate resolution of certain disputes basically of a factual nature" while also acknowledging that "it would not be very easy to pre-determine what sort of disputes shall be subjected to a binding arbitration."[48]

As noted by Korea at the time, it is not easy to categorize WTO disputes into complicated versus uncomplicated ones or into ones that are of a factual versus legal nature. That said, there have been some disputes that presented less contentious issues than an average dispute. For example, in *US—Shrimp (Ecuador)*, the United States as respondent did not contest Ecuador's claim of violation of the *Anti-Dumping Agreement*. Specifically, the United States

---

45   Valerie Hughes, "Arbitration Within the WTO" in Federico Ortino & Ernst-Ulrich Petersmann, *The WTO Dispute Settlement System 1995–2003* (Kluwer Law International, 2004) 85. Note, however, that this view was expressed many years before Article 25 was seen as a possible mechanism to appeal dispute settlement panels' legal findings.

46   GATT, *Improved Dispute Settlement: Elements for Consideration*, GATT Doc MTN. GNG/NG13/W/6 (1987) at 2, online (pdf): wto.org [perma.cc/S35T-73VM].

47   GATT, *Communication from the European Economic Community*, GATT Doc MTN. GNG/NG13/W/12 (1987) at 3, online (pdf): wto.org [perma.cc/58BW-EWXY].

48   GATT, *Communication from Korea*, GATT Doc MTN.GNG/NG13/W/19 (1987) at 3, online (pdf): docs.wto.org [perma.cc/6JGP-AE2E].

acknowledged that Ecuador's description of the challenged measure was correct, and that a similar measure had been found to be inconsistent with the *Anti-Dumping Agreement* in a previous dispute brought against the United States.[49] Noting that the parties had not reached a mutually agreed solution despite their common understanding of the challenged measure as well as its consistency with the *Anti-Dumping Agreement*, the Panel considered that it was required under Article 11 of the DSU to conduct an objective assessment of the case.[50] Both parties and some of the third parties also agreed with the Panel's approach.[51] The Panel proceeded to its assessment of the case and concluded that the challenged measure was in violation of the *Anti-Dumping Agreement*, as argued by the complainant and conceded by the respondent.[52]

In this dispute, the complainant filed its request for consultations on 17 November 2005, the panel report was circulated on 30 January 2007 and adopted by the DSB on 20 February 2007. Thus, it took the parties fifteen months to obtain an official solution to the dispute through the default dispute settlement process. Presumably, resolving such a dispute through Article 25 arbitration would have taken less time. There is no official record of whether the parties considered resorting to Article 25 arbitration to resolve this dispute. Ultimately, the parties went through the motions under the default dispute settlement process, to reach an outcome that the respondent did not challenge at the outset of the proceedings.

It has also been argued that Article 25 arbitration could be used to deal with disputes of a political nature.[53] In this context, it has been proposed to integrate arbitration into the DSU through "dispute diversion" whereby "politically charged" cases would first have to be submitted to arbitration, before proceeding to the default dispute settlement process. Under this view, it has been argued that the lack of appeal would allow the disputing parties to engage in negotiations. Such diversion would also lessen domestic criticism for governments in cases where they lose the case.[54] However, as the proponent of this idea also recognizes, the selection of politically charged

---

49   WTO, *United States—Anti-Dumping Measure on Shrimp from Ecuador (Complaint by Ecuador)* (2007), WTO Doc WT/DS335/R (Panel Report) at para 4.2, online (pdf): docs.wto.org [perma.cc/P8SH-H8J6].

50   *Ibid* at para 7.3.

51   *Ibid* at paras 7.4 and 7.6.

52   *Ibid* at para 7.43.

53   Jacyk, above note 10 at 256–57.

54   *Ibid* at 257–58.

cases would in itself prove difficult in the WTO context. In fact, it could be argued that many of WTO disputes are politically charged at least from the perspective of one of the parties. As for the view that losing through arbitration may generate less domestic reaction towards governments, the exact opposite could also be argued. In some countries, the stakeholders may be more sensitive if their government agrees to resort to an informal dispute resolution method such as arbitration, rather than the more formal, treaty-based, WTO default dispute settlement process.[55]

In support of this view, the same author states, with regard to arbitration under Articles 21.3(c) and 22.6 that "[i]n both cases, a process that at least resembles an arbitration process, and for which there is no appeal, has already been used to resolve political issues."[56] This, in his view, demonstrates the potential for the use of Article 25 arbitration among WTO Members.[57] In particular, this author notes that the determination of the RPT through Article 21.3(c) arbitration often takes into account political factors affecting the implementation process, such as scrutinizing the respondent's legislative or regulatory processes. On this basis, he argues that Article 25 arbitration could also be used by WTO Members to resolve disputes that are of a political nature.[58] This view does not seem convincing. It should be noted that the reason why such issues are taken into account in Article 21.3(c) arbitration is to give them due weight in determining an RPT, which has been interpreted to mean "the shortest period possible within the legal system of the Member to implement the recommendations and rulings of the DSB."[59] This fact, alone, hardly justifies the view that Article 21.3(c) arbitration deals with political issues.

It has also been stated that, unlike the default dispute settlement process, Article 25 arbitration could encourage the disputing parties to negotiate a

---

55 In support of this view, see Jan Bohanes & Hunter Nottage, "Arbitration as an Alternative to Litigation in the WTO: Observations in the Light of the 2005 Banana Tariff Arbitrations" in Y Taniguchi et al, eds, *The WTO in the Twenty-first Century Dispute Settlement, Negotiations and Regionalism in Asia* (Cambridge: Cambridge University Press, 2007) at 239 & 240.

56 Jacyk, above note 10 at 250.

57 *Ibid.*

58 *Ibid* at 251–52.

59 WTO, *European Communities—Measures Concerning Meat and Meat Products (Hormones) (Complaint by Canada)* (1998), WTO Doc WT/DS48/13 (Article 21.3(c) Arbitration Award) at para 26, online (pdf): docs.wto.org [perma.cc/3W3R-S4X8].

mutually agreeable solution.[60] In this regard, it would be fair to argue that the default dispute settlement process has proved relatively flexible and productive in giving the disputing parties the opportunity to find a mutually agreeable solution. There have been a number of cases in which the disputing parties reached a mutually agreed solution during the panel proceedings and asked the panel not to make findings in their dispute.[61] In some cases, this happened after the panel's issuance of its interim or even final panel report to the parties[62], which suggests that the findings in the panel's report encouraged the parties to find a mutually agreed solution.

Finally, it is pertinent to note that not only did WTO Members not make much use of Article 25 arbitration as an alternative to panel proceedings despite its potential advantages, but they did also not change this stance during periods in which the default dispute settlement process was strained due to heavy workload, which caused significant delays in servicing panels. Since 1995, there have been periods in which the number of new disputes went up significantly. For instance, from 1995 to 1997, the number of consultations requests doubled, and the number of panels established tripled. From 2017 to 2018, consultations requests more than doubled whereas panel establishments almost tripled.[63] Such increases naturally constrained the WTO Secretariat's ability to assist new panels in a timely fashion. This, in turn, led to queues in new panels waiting to be serviced. Members did not resort to Article 25 arbitration in these periods in order to avoid long delays in the resolution of their disputes.

---

60   Jacyk, above note 10 at 240.

61   WTO, above note 4 at 60–61.

62   For instance, see WTO, above note 28 at paras 3.5 & 3.6, 4.1 and 4.4; WTO, *United States—Final Anti-Dumping Measures on Stainless Steel from Mexico (Complaint by Mexico)* (2013), WTO Doc WT/DS344/RW (Article 21.5 Panel Report) at paras 1.7 and 1.10, online (pdf): docs.wto.org [perma.cc/9VTD-58VU].

63   The number of consultation requests in 1995, 1996, and 1997 were twenty-five, thirty-nine and fifty, respectively whereas in 2017 and 2018 they were seventeen and thirty-eight, respectively. In terms of the numbers of panels established, the figures in 1995, 1996, and 1997 were five, eleven, and fifteen, where those in 2017 and 2018 were ten and twenty-eight, respectively. See WTO, "Dispute Settlement Activity—some figures" (last visited 19 June 2025) online: wto.org [perma.cc/U7FH-XKSV].

ii. Other Factors That Might Explain the Underuse of Article 25 Arbitration as an Alternative to Panel Proceedings

What other factors could explain the underuse of Article 25 arbitration as an alternative to panel proceedings? It is difficult to point to one or more particular factors as being the reason(s) explaining this phenomenon. Several factors, together, may be considered to have led to this result.

First, most, if not all, WTO disputes contain issues that are highly contested between the disputing parties. Arguably, parties that have divergent views on the underlying issues in their dispute tend to be less inclined to jointly agree to resort to arbitration instead of the default dispute settlement process.

Second, respondents in disputes rarely seek to complete the dispute in an expedited manner. However, complainants also rarely propose an expedited timetable. More expeditious timetables, including shorter periods for parties to draft written submissions and prepare for panel hearings, may impose a significant burden on parties. It is difficult to point to any case in which the parties to a dispute proposed the default timetable provided in Appendix 3 to the DSU, which is shorter than the timetables adopted by most panels. For this reason, it might be that the "expeditious" nature of the arbitration foreseen in Article 25 has not been particularly attractive for WTO Members.

Third, it is not clear what is meant by "clearly defined" issues within the meaning of Article 25.[64] In this regard, factual issues might be distinguished from legal issues. Where parties agree on facts, it might not be difficult for an arbitrator to agree with the parties and then proceed to the legal aspects of the case. However, can the same be said for legal issues? Under the default dispute settlement process, parties' agreement on legal issues would perhaps have much less, if any, significance to a panel. Pursuant to Article 11 of the DSU, each panel must, as part of its functions, make an objective assessment of the applicability of the relevant covered agreements and an objective assessment of the conformity of the challenged measures with those agreements. *Indonesia—Iron or Steel Products* is a case in point in this regard. In this dispute, the respondent and the complainants agreed on the legal characterization of the challenged measure. They jointly considered it to be a safeguard measure. The Panel, however, declined to endorse this view, made its own assessment

---

64 Bashar H Malkawi, "Arbitration and the World Trade Organization—The Forgotten Provisions of Article 25 of the Dispute Settlement Understanding" (2007) 24:2 *Journal of International Arbitration* 173 at 184.

pursuant to Article 11 of the DSU, and came to the opposite conclusion.[65] The AB approved the Panel's approach.[66] What would an arbitrator have done if this case had been referred to Article 25 arbitration? It is important to note that Article 25.4 refers only to Articles 21 and 22 of the DSU as provisions that apply *mutatis mutandis* to arbitration awards under Article 25. Article 11, requiring panels to conduct an objective assessment of the matter, does not necessarily apply to such arbitration. It is unclear what the implication of this would be in such a case.

Fourth, the extent to which the default dispute settlement process has adapted itself to the changing circumstances and needs of the Members over time might also have lessened the need to resort to Article 25 arbitration. Of particular importance in this regard are the panels' flexibility in drawing up additional procedures for the protection of particular types of confidential information, opening meetings with the parties and third parties to public viewing, imposing limits on the length of the parties' and third parties' submissions, and in some cases holding only one substantive meeting with the parties. The flexibility shown by the default dispute settlement process might also have rendered Article 25 arbitration less attractive in the eyes of the Members.

b) What is the Future for Article 25 Arbitration as an Alternative to Panel Proceedings?

Does the fact that Article 25 arbitration has not been used as an alternative to panel proceedings constitute a problem for the WTO? It is not easy to give a clear answer to this question. There is no evidence indicating that more frequent use of Article 25 arbitration would have yielded better results in the functioning of WTO dispute settlement than has been observed. Is the level of the use of Article 25 arbitration as an alternative to panel proceedings likely to change in the future? Obviously, this depends on many factors, including, importantly, whether the ongoing discussions among Members will lead to a solution to the appeal/review issue. The outcome of

---

65   WTO, *Indonesia—Safeguard on Certain Iron or Steel Products (Complaint by Viet Nam)* (2017), WTO Doc WT/DS490/R (Panel Report) at para 7.10, online (pdf): docs.wto.org [perma.cc/MU2M-YJWC].

66   WTO, *Indonesia—Safeguard on Certain Iron or Steel Products (Complaint by Viet Nam)* (2018), WTO Doc WT/DS490/AB/R (Appellate Body Report) at para 5.68, online (pdf): docs.wto.org [perma.cc/BM7E-ZNVC].

these discussions may also affect the number of disputes filed by Members. If the developments in this regard lead to a significant increase in dispute settlement activity, Article 25 might draw renewed attention as an alternative to panel proceedings.

D. Conclusion

THE DSU PROVIDES FOR ARBITRATION in two contexts. First, Articles 21.3(c) and 22.6 provide for binding arbitration at two stages during the default dispute settlement process. These two proceedings, however, do not share much with the concept of arbitration as an alternative dispute resolution method. First, they are binding; the disputing parties cannot choose not to resort to these two types of arbitration if the circumstances in the process so require. Second, the mandate of the arbitrator in both processes is pre-determined by the DSU. Third, they do not replace the default dispute settlement process but rather complement it.

Second, Article 25 of the DSU allows WTO Members to resort to "expeditious arbitration" to resolve disputes entailing issues that are clearly defined by the parties. This method was used for the first time in 2001 in *US—Section 110(5) Copyright Act*. The parties resorted to Article 25 arbitration to calculate the amount of nullification or impairment caused by the challenged measure, prior to the expiry of the RPT as a means to reach a mutually agreed compensation. After a long period of no use, from 2020, WTO Members turned their attention to Article 25 arbitration to find interim solutions to the appeal problem. This led not only to individual uses of Article 25 arbitration for appeal purposes but also to the creation of the MPIA as an institutionalized framework for appeals among a subset of Members.

However, there has been no use of Article 25 arbitration as an alternative to panel proceedings. In this respect, Article 25 remains unused despite its possible advantages over the default dispute settlement process. Whether its use in this context will increase in the future depends on the circumstances, including, importantly, on whether WTO Members will find a solution to the appeal/review issue and whether the number of panel cases will increase. The use of Article 25 arbitration for appeal purposes since 2020 demonstrates, however, that this method may continue to be a tool available to WTO Members to overcome unexpected difficulties arising in the operation of the default dispute settlement process.

The Multi-Party Interim Appeal Arbitration Arrangement and the MPIA Drafters' Attempt to Improve on the Traditional Appellate Review Process

Jan Bohanes*

I HAD THE PRIVILEGE TO work with Valerie Hughes as a junior lawyer between 2002 and 2006 when she was the Director of the Appellate Body Secretariat. From today's vantage point, this period seems like the halcyon days of World Trade Organization (WTO) dispute settlement. It was a time when a description of the current state of the WTO dispute settlement system—with the Appellate Body nothing but an empty shell existing only on the pages of the Dispute Settlement Understanding (DSU) and the effective withdrawal of the United States from international trade law and multilateral trade governance—would sound to most stakeholders like some unthinkable dystopia.

Valerie, with her unique mix of intellectual rigour, vast knowledge of international and trade law, experience, pragmatism, and—as many have observed—a quick wit on par with a professional entertainer, was not only an excellent helmswoman for the Appellate Body Secretariat. She was also

* I am grateful to Lothar Ehring, Niall Meagher, and Werner Zdouc for comments on an earlier version of this draft. Any and all mistakes and inaccuracies are entirely mine.

a formative supervisor for a young lawyer like myself discovering the realities of government-to-government dispute settlement. Valerie's contribution to the work of the Appellate Body also lives on in the Multi-Party Interim Appeal Arbitration Arrangement (MPIA), which is also the subject of my contribution to this volume.

The MPIA is intended to replace temporarily the standard appeal procedure under Article 17 of the DSU until the—increasingly illusive—point in the future when the Appellate Body is reactivated. The MPIA has two essential characteristics.

First, the MPIA procedure is intended to emulate the Appellate Body procedure. It is based "on the substantive and procedural aspects of Appellate Review pursuant to Article 17 of the DSU, in order to keep its core features, including independence and impartiality."[1] The twenty-seven MPIA Members[2] thus effectively confirm their satisfaction with the design and operation of the Appellate Body over its twenty active years. They also express commitment to reviving the Appellate Body and to resuming Appellate Body Member appointments "as a matter of priority."[3] This expression of trust is a tribute to the quality of work of the institution, including under Valerie's leadership of the Appellate Body Secretariat. Valerie's contribution is also amply confirmed by the fact that she has been appointed as one of the ten MPIA arbitrators.

Second, although they confirmed their commitment to the Appellate Body as we know it, the MPIA drafters also sought to "enhanc[e] the procedural efficiency of appeal proceedings."[4] To do so, the MPIA Members introduced certain adjustments to the original Appellate Body procedure.[5] Some of these adjustments reflect the United States' criticism of the Appellate Body. In addition to allegedly improving the procedure, these adjustments

---

1   WTO, *Multi-Party Interim Appeal Arbitration Arrangement Pursuant to Article 25 of the DSU*, WTO Doc WT/JOB/DSB/1/Add.12 (2020) at para 3, online (pdf): docs.wto.org [perma.cc/Z72W-ZMFR] [*MPIA*].

2   Including the EU Member States in this count brings the total to fifty-four, which is approximately one-third of the total WTO membership.

3   *MPIA*, above note 1 at Preamble.

4   *Ibid* at para 3.

5   *Ibid* ("The appeal arbitration procedure will be based on the substantive and procedural aspects of Appellate Review pursuant to Article 17 of the DSU, in order to keep its core features, including independence and impartiality, while enhancing the procedural efficiency of appeal proceedings").

also function as a signal to the United States, seeking to entice it to "return" into the fold of a binding two-tier dispute settlement system.

In my contribution to this volume, I first summarize the basic functioning of the MPIA. Second, I provide a few reflections on the drafters' effort to improve appellate review. My comments also include impressions from the first MPIA procedure in which I participated as a member of the Advisory Centre on World Trade Organization Law legal team that assisted the Government of Colombia in the dispute *Colombia—Frozen Fries*. Due to space constraints, I do not address the substance of the arbitral award in that dispute.

A. Legal Basis of the MPIA

THE MPIA IS BASED ON Article 25 of the DSU, which envisages party-driven "arbitration" as an alternative to standard dispute settlement procedures. The purpose of Article 25 is to enable disputing parties to "customize" any procedures envisaged under the DSU to fit their case-specific needs. Prior to being used for the MPIA, Article 25 had been invoked in the *United States—Section 110(5) of the US Copyright Act (Irish Music)* dispute, as an alternative to the standard DSU Article 22 procedure to calculate suspension of concessions. As another example, the February 2024 dispute settlement reform text proposes detailed procedural rules under Article 25 to create alternative to standard panel proceedings.[6]

The MPIA system as a whole is set out in multiple legal documents. The foundational text is a "statement" / "communication" from the participating Members to the WTO Membership, which contains the MPIA "arrangement" itself, effectively an umbrella agreement between all the participating Members.[7] This umbrella agreement lays down the core elements of the MPIA, in particular its scope of application, the pool of arbitrators, the selection of three arbitrators for any given appeal as well as their administrative and legal support and the modalities of accession of new Members to the MPIA. This agreement also contains the above-mentioned programmatic principle that the MPIA shall be "based on the substantive and procedural aspects of Appellate Review pursuant to Article 17 of the DSU" and that it shall "keep

---

6   See WTO, *Special Meeting of the General Council*, WTO Doc JOB/GC/385 (2024) at 17ff, online (pdf): docs.wto.org [perma.cc/UF2F-4CGP] [WTO, *Special Meeting*].

7   WTO, *Multi-Party Interim Appeal Arbitration Arrangement Pursuant to Article 25 of the DSU*, WTO Doc JOB/DSB/1/Add.12 (2020), online (pdf): docs.wto.org [perma.cc/XA3V-9BJU].

[the Appellate Body's] core features, including independence and impartiality, while enhancing the procedural efficiency of appeal proceedings."[8]

The second document is Annex I to the MPIA, which contains the so-called "Agreed Procedures for Arbitration." It is a template that contains the details of the arbitration appeal procedure. MPIA signatories enter into these "Agreed Procedures" in particular panel proceedings against another MPIA signatory, by notifying this document jointly to the panel. This is necessary to make the MPIA applicable in an individual panel proceeding. The parties are entitled to adjust the template for purposes of their dispute. The third MPIA document is Annex II to the MPIA umbrella agreement, which contains the rules for composing the pool of arbitrators. Finally, fourth, as envisaged by the Agreed Procedures, each MPIA arbitral panel will issue a set of additional working procedures. These working procedures set out further details of the specific appeal procedures, such as deadlines, word limits for written submissions, the rules governing the oral hearing, and rules for filing documents. Based on the requirements of each appeal arbitration, the Arbitrators may issue additional documents to supplement the additional working procedures.[9]

B. Institutional Features of the MPIA

THE INSTITUTIONAL DESIGN OF THE MPIA mimics the Appellate Body. The umbrella agreement and Annex II envisage a pool of ten arbitrators, with divisions of three deciding any given appeal, which is of course analogous to an Appellate Body Division of three Appellate Body Members. The number

---

8   *MPIA*, above note 1 at para 3.

9   *Colombia—Frozen Fries from Belgium, Germany and the Netherlands (Complaint by the European Union)* (2022), WTO Doc WT/DS591/ARB25 at paras 1.11–1.12 (Arbitral Award), online (pdf): docs.wto.org [perma.cc/E5YA-H33P] [*Colombia—Frozen Fries* (Arbitral Award)]. In addition to the above-mentioned additional working procedures, the Arbitrators issued (1) a "Pre-Arbitration Letter," in order to ensure that the word limit applicable to the appellant's and appellee's submissions was known to the appellant when preparing the appellant's submission to be filed on Day 0 of the arbitration appeal; and (2) Additional Procedures for BCI Protection and Partial Public Viewing of the Hearing). See WTO, *Addendum to Award of the Arbitrators, Colombia—Frozen Fries*, WTO Doc WT/DS591/ARB25/Add.1 (2022), Annex A-2 at 12–17, Annex A-3 at 18–20, online (pdf): docs.wto.org [perma.cc/VD6Z-CH8B] [*Colombia—Frozen Fries* (Addendum)].

of ten arbitrators is of course higher than the seven Appellate Body Members envisaged in the DSU.

These ten arbitrators are nominated by the MPIA Members, reviewed by a "pre-selection committee" composed of the WTO Director-General and the Chairpersons of various WTO bodies[10] and subsequently appointed by consensus by the MPIA Members. In practice, MPIA Members will very likely propose their own nationals or nationals of other MPIA Members. The composition of the pool shall "ensure an appropriate overall balance" and will be periodically "re-compose[d]." Since the current MPIA Members are only a subset of the overall WTO Membership, the MPIA arbitration pool is unlikely going to be "broadly representative" of the WTO Membership, as required by the DSU for the Appellate Body. The current pool of arbitrators includes individuals from the EU, Brazil, Canada, Chile, China, Colombia, Mexico, Singapore, Switzerland, and New Zealand, all of whom are nationals of MPIA Members.

As in the former Appellate Body, MPIA arbitrators are not barred from adjudicating a dispute involving their country of citizenship. However, unlike in the Appellate Body, an arbitrator who is a national of one of the parties *may* be excluded from a dispute, at the request of a party to the dispute.[11] The sole explicit exclusionary rule is that two nationals of the same WTO Member shall not serve on the same case.

C. The MPIA Procedure

THE MPIA PROCEDURE REPLACES THE Appellate Body procedure and thus begins after panel procedures have effectively concluded. MPIA participants are explicitly prohibited from filing "appeals into the void."[12] Thus, if the MPIA procedure is not triggered, the panel report is adopted. Once the MPIA procedure has been concluded, the MPIA arbitral award—together with the panel report—enter into effect upon distribution of the award, without Dispute Settlement Body (DSB) adoption. Any implementation obligations for the responding party can be enforced via the "standard" procedures under Articles 21 and 22 of the DSU, which apply by virtue of Article 25.4 of the DSU.

---

10   The pre-selection process does not apply if the nominated person is a former Appellate Body Member (MPIA, above note 1, Annex 2, at para 1, fn 2).

11   *MPIA*, above note 1 at para 6, fn 2.

12   *Ibid* at para 2.

The detailed functioning of the procedure is as follows: Following circulation of the final panel report *to the parties* and up to ten days before the circulation of that report to the *rest of the membership (and the public)*, the appellant may request the panel to suspend its work.[13] This suspension request is made pursuant to Article 12.12 of the DSU, a provision routinely used by parties to suspend panel procedures to seek negotiated solutions. In the MPIA context, the suspension request is deemed to have been made by both parties.[14] The appellant may subsequently initiate the appeal within twenty days by filing a Notice of Appeal as well as an appellant's submission. At this point in time, the Appellate Body's Working Procedures for Appellate Review are triggered, *mutatis mutandis*.[15] The appellee will thus file a rebuttal to the appellant's brief and may also file an "other appellant's" submission, which the original appellant may also rebut. Third parties may file written submissions.[16] The deadlines applicable for these submissions are those in the Working Procedures for Appellate Review. Following an oral hearing (or at any other time), the three arbitrators may consult other MPIA arbitrators, in a procedure equivalent to the former Appellate Body's "exchange of views." The award is to be issued no later than ninety days after the Notice of Appeal has been filed.

The MPIA procedure is of course not mandatory. If no party moves to appeal the panel report, the MPIA mechanism will not be triggered and the panel report will be circulated to the entire membership and to the public, and either party may put up the panel report for adoption. The MPIA procedure may also be abandoned after it has been initiated: If the panel process was suspended in anticipation of an appeal (as described above) but the prospective appellant subsequently decides to discontinue the appeal, the suspension of the panel process will be lifted, and the panel process resumes. The panel report is then circulated to the membership as well as the public and can be put up for adoption by the DSB.

The way in which the panel report becomes binding depends on whether an MPIA appeal has been triggered. If no appeal is triggered, the panel report

---

13   This request is deemed by the umbrella agreement to be a joint request of both parties under Article 12.12 of the DSU.

14   The purpose of this clause is to enable the respondent to trigger the MPIA appeal procedure, given that Article 12.12 permits only the complainant to request suspension.

15   *MPIA*, above note 1, Annex 1 at paras 5, 7, 11, and 16. Rule 25 of the Working Procedures for Appellate Review applies *mutatis mutandis* already to the transmission of the panel record to the arbitrators under para 4(ii).

16   Third parties are not required to be MPIA signatories in order to participate as third parties or third participants in an MPIA appeal.

is adopted by the DSB in standard fashion, pursuant to Article 16.4 of the DSU.[17] In the event of an MPIA appeal, the panel report becomes binding as an attachment to the arbitral award, as modified by the arbitral award.[18] However, the arbitral award does not actually physically contain the panel report as an appendix. Rather, the panel report is made public as an attachment to the Notice of Appeal at the outset of the MPIA appeal.

The arbitral award becomes binding upon its issuance, without adoption by the DSB.[19] Subsequently, the standard WTO compliance procedures pursuant to Articles 21 and 22 of the DSU apply. Thus, the respondent may benefit from a reasonable period of time (RPT) for compliance. Following implementation and expiry of the RPT, the dispute is resolved or, alternatively, Article 21.5 and/or Article 22 procedures may be initiated.[20] At that point, the MPIA may again be triggered to appeal the report of the Article 21.5 panel. Article 21.5 of the DSU does not explicitly refer to the possibility of appeal,[21] but panel reports under Article 21.5 have been routinely appealed. The MPIA text explicitly envisages appeals against Article 21.5 panel reports.[22]

D. The Effort of MPIA Drafters to Improve the Appellate Review Procedure

THIS SECTION DESCRIBES AND REFLECTS on some of the ways in which the MPIA drafters have sought to improve the original appellate review procedure.

1) Strict Respect for the Ninety-Day Deadline, Unless the Parties Agree on an Extension

Paragraph 14 of the Agreed Procedures permits an extension of the ninety-day deadline—which is of course set out in Article 17.5—but only by the parties' agreement, upon proposal of the arbitrators. Paragraph 14 thus

---

17 *MPIA*, above note 1 at para 8.

18 *Ibid*, Annex 1 at para 9.

19 Like all panel reports and previously Appellate Body reports, the MPIA award must be translated into the WTO's three official languages.

20 The MPIA does not seek to address or change the well-established practice of concluding sequencing agreements to clarify the relationship between Articles 21.5 and 22.6 proceedings.

21 However, the phrase "these dispute settlement procedures" in Article 21.5 of the DSU can plausibly be read as including appeal procedures under Article 17 of the DSU.

22 *MPIA*, above note 1, Annex 1, fn 1.

explicitly denies arbitrators the "unilateral" authority to exceed the ninety-day deadline without the parties' authorization.

This emphasis on party control over the ninety-day deadline reflects a central point of criticism by the United States of the Appellate Body, for not only for repeatedly exceeding the ninety-day deadline but also for changing its practice relating to seeking the parties' approval: Prior to 2011, the Appellate Body had always secured the parties' confirmation, via so-called "deeming letters,"[23] for circulating its report beyond the ninety days. However, in 2011, this practice changed, and the Appellate Body began issuing "late" Appellate Body reports without securing "deeming letters" or the DSB's authorization.[24]

The MPIA parties' effort to ensure respect for the ninety-day deadline, including as a signal to the United States, and to claim exclusive authority to extend this deadline, is understandable and in line with the current trends in WTO dispute settlement reform. The December 2024 dispute settlement progress report repeatedly underscores the importance of the ninety-day deadline[25] and also lists the reasons why the Appellate Body exceeded the ninety-day deadline.[26] The February 2024 dispute settlement reform text also emphasizes deadlines for panel proceedings.[27]

Speedy proceedings and observance of treaty-mandated deadlines are crucial for the legitimacy and effectiveness of the dispute settlement process. Of course, reasons for lengthy dispute settlement proceeding in excess of these deadlines are many, and the many constraints under which both

---

23 The content of these deeming letters was the parties' confirmation that an Appellate Body report issued beyond the ninety-day deadline would be "deemed" a report issued within the ninety-day deadline. See, e.g., *United States—Subsidies on Upland Cotton (Complaint by Brazil)* (2005), WTO Doc WT/DS267/AB/R at para 8 (Appellate Body Report), online (pdf): docs.wto.org [perma.cc/6N4E-WPEW].

24 See, e.g., WTO, *Minutes of Meeting*, WTO Doc WT/DSB/M/414 (2018) at para 5.1ff, online (pdf): docs.wto.org [perma.cc/KG8Y-9EKT] (the DSB decision would extend the time period for adoption or appeal of panel reports, such that the Appellate Body would be placed in a position where it could complete the appeal in ninety days. See also WTO, *Joint Request by the European Union and China for a Decision by the DSB*, WTO Doc WT/DS397/6 (2011), online (pdf): docs.wto.org [perma.cc/V2AF-4JW6]; WTO, *Minutes of Meeting (25 January 2011)*, WTO Doc WT/DSB/M/291 (2011) at 15, online (pdf): docs.wto.org [perma.cc/5KZZ-R6B5].

25 See WTO, *Agenda Item 11: Dispute Settlement Reform Process*, WTO Doc JOB/GC/DSR/5 (2024) at 35–36, 49, online (pdf): docs.wto.org [perma.cc/8CKB-MQVJ] [WTO, *DS Reform Process*].

26 *Ibid* at 36–37.

27 WTO, *Special Meeting*, above note 6 at paras 12–21.

panelists and Appellate Body Members (and the Secretariat teams) have operated must be acknowledged objectively in order to ensure effective reform. In this context, however, it is neither helpful nor even-handed to single out the Appellate Body for alleged disregard of procedural deadlines, as the United States has done. Panel proceedings have historically exceeded their deadlines more frequently than the Appellate Body and by significantly greater margins. Based on the author's own analysis,[28] the Appellate Body exceeded the ninety-day deadline in 37 percent of appeals, some of which were released before to 2011 and were thus subject to the "deeming letters" signed by the parties. In contrast, since 1995, over 97 percent of original panel proceedings (that is, excluding Article 21.5 panels) exceeded the six-month deadline between panel composition and final report to the parties, and more than 95 percent exceeded the nine-month deadline between panel establishment and circulation of the final report. While the delay has sometimes been minor, in other instances the deadlines were exceeded by very significant margins, without any "deeming letters" or formal approval by the parties. It is true that the deadlines for panel proceedings are on their face couched in less binding language than at the appeal level.[29] But even this language indicates the expectations of drafters for conduct of panel proceedings, and panels have not been able to operate within these time constraints.

This is of course in no way not intended as criticism of the work of panels and the Secretariat staff; the DSU deadlines are tight and, in many disputes, as unrealistic as the ninety-day deadline at the appellate level. But the asymmetrical critique of, respectively, the Appellate Body and panels by some is striking, especially as many of the "late" Appellate Body reports occurred in large appeals and with an incomplete Appellate Body due to lack of appointments. Arguably, this double standard is not helpful in addressing a broader, systemic problem of which the Appellate Body was merely a symptom: the

28 Based on worldtradelaw.net statistics and my own calculations.

29 See, e.g., *Marrakesh Agreement Establishing the World Trade Organization*, Annex 2, 15 April 1994, 1869 UNTS 3 at 401, Understanding on Rules and Procedures Governing the Settlement of Disputes, art 12.8 (entered into force 1 January 1995) [DSU], providing that the period between panel composition and issuance of the report to the parties "shall, as a general rule, not exceed six months" and Article 12.9, which provides that "[i]n no case should the period from the establishment of the panel to the circulation of the report to the Members exceed nine months." At the same time, the February 2024 dispute settlement reform text signals Members' willingness to use fully binding language. See, e.g., WTO, *Special Meeting*, above note 6, Title II, Chapter IV at paras 12–14.

size of some WTO disputes that are simply impossible to resolve within the DSU deadlines and based on the existing DSU procedures, including oral hearings and a detailed published judgment (report). The main drivers of the duration of dispute settlement proceedings will thus more often than not be the parties themselves and their decisions about the size of disputes they wish to bring to the WTO.

2) Limiting Findings to What is Necessary for the Resolution of the Dispute

Another reform feature is the MPIA arbitrators' obligation under Article 10 of the Agreed Procedures to "address" only "those issues that are necessary for the resolution of the dispute." Article 10 also requires the arbitrators to "address only those issues that have been raised by the parties, without prejudice to their obligation to rule on jurisdictional issues."

Article 10 is in line with a broader trend in WTO dispute settlement reform discussions to ensure that panel and arbitral decisions focus on the essential elements of a dispute and that an adjudicative body not "make law," that is, interpret the law in the abstract outside of a real dispute.[30] The February 2024 dispute settlement reform text features a similar provision that requires panels to exercise judicial economy and also explicitly requires adjudicators to limit their reasoning to what is necessary "to support their findings and conclusions."[31] The February 2024 text even exhorts litigating parties to focus in their submissions to what is "necessary" to resolve a dispute.[32] Related issues have also been discussed in the ongoing DS reform negotiations, which seeks to limit the issues to be addressed by "appeal adjudicators" to those that would have a "material impact on implementation."[33] All these obligations fit into the broader picture of expediting dispute

---

30 *United States—Measures Affecting Imports of Woven Wool Shirts and Blouses from India (Complaint by India)* (1997), WTO Doc WT/DS33/AB/R at 17 (Appellate Body Report), online (pdf): docs.wto.org [perma.cc/XWB9-P8Z8].

31 See WTO, *Special Meeting*, above note 6, Title V, Chapter II at paras 1–2. In addition, the obligation to exercise judicial economy is also set out in the February 2024 DS reform text, in the model rules of procedure for arbitration pursuant to Article 25 of the DSU (WTO, *Special Meeting of the General Council*, WTO Doc JOB/GC/385 (2024), Appendix I, para 3, p 17).

32 WTO, *Special Meeting of the General Council*, WTO Doc JOB/GC/385 (2024), fn 37.

33 See WTO, *DS Reform Process*, above note 25.

settlement proceedings and, in the case of appeal procedures, ensuring compliance with the ninety-day deadlines.

Article 10 reflects an explicit prohibition of what is sometimes referred to as *obiter dicta*, as well as an obligation to exercise "judicial economy." The term *obiter dictum*—a remark made "in passing"—refers to a judicial statement or finding that do not constitute the reasoning (or *ratio decidendi*) in a judgment, for instance a statement on an issue that the court ultimately recognizes it need not resolve.[34] The term "judicial economy" for its part has typically been used in panel practice to refer to instances in which a panel leaves unaddressed *an entire claim of violation*, on the grounds that findings on other claims have rendered a resolution of that claim unnecessary. However, neither term is treaty language, and terminology in policy and academic discourse is sometimes inconsistent and overlaps. When the Appellate Body itself declined to address entire claims on appeal, on the grounds that doing so was not necessary to resolve the dispute, it has generally not used the term "judicial economy" to describe its approach, even though this is the analogue of panel practice with respect to entire claims of violation.[35]

The basic intention behind a strict prohibition on *obiter dicta* and a mandatory exercise of judicial economy is understandable. Article 10 conveys to MPIA arbitrators an important and easy-to-understand concern of the drafters. Effectively addressing this concern may have a salutary effect on the length and scope of appellate reports. However, because there is no definition in the MPIA of what is "necessary for the resolution of the dispute," details

---

34 LexisNexis, "Obiter dictum definition" (last visited 19 June 2025), online: lexisnexis. co.uk [perma.cc/HP7P-N95F]. See, e.g., *United States—Measures Affecting the Cross-Border Supply of Gambling and Betting Services (Complaint by Antigua and Barbuda)* (2005), WTO Doc WT/DS285/AB/R at para 131 (Appellate Body Report), online (pdf): docs.wto.org [perma.cc/CMR3-HZRX]. See also *United States—Final Dumping Determination on Softwood Lumber from Canada (Complaint by Canada)* (2006), WTO Doc WT/DS264/RW at E-32, para 63 (Panel Report), online (pdf): docs.wto.org [perma.cc/BJQ3-GGMV].

35 See WTO, *Australia—Certain Measures Concerning Trademarks, Geographical Indications and Other Plain Packaging Requirements Applicable to Tobacco Products and Packaging (Complaint by Honduras)* (2020), WTO Doc WT/DS435/AB/R at para 238 (Appellate Body Report), online (pdf): docs.wto.org [perma.cc/5DX5-DJJA] and WTO, *United States—Measures Concerning the Importation, Marketing and Sale of Tuna and Tuna Products (Complaint by Mexico)* (2018), WTO Docs WT/DS381/AB/RW/USA, WT/DS381/AB/RW2 at para 6.318 (Article 21.5 – US/Article 21.5 – Mexico II Appellate Body Reports), online (pdf): docs.wto.org [perma.cc/95CM-JDM7] [*Article 21.5 – US/Article 21.5 – Mexico II Appellate Body Reports*].

will ultimately emerge only over time. Existing panel practice,[36] as well as the on-going negotiations on appellate review,[37] indicate that "necessity" is often assessed in terms of whether a particular finding would shape, or have an impact, on the outcome of a dispute and on the responding Member's implementation obligations.[38]

With respect to *obiter dicta* and judicial economy, criticism of the Appellate Body's practice has arguably not always adequately taken into account that Article 17 appears to support findings that go beyond "necessity" as reflected in current reform discussions. Consider for instance Article 17.12 of the DSU that requires the Appellate Body to "address each of the issues raised," which arguably means that each issue raised must be *resolved on substance*, regardless of its impact on implementation or other "necessity" considerations. It is true that the Appellate Body over time came to read the term "address" not as issuing a substantive ruling but also as simply explaining why the resolution of the dispute as a whole did not require a ruling on that issue.[39] However, that was not the prevailing view in the early years of the institution and, indeed, several provisions in the covered agreements use the word "address" in the sense of requiring a discussion of substance.[40] (Even the *MPIA drafters themselves* used the word "address" in paragraph 10 of the

---

36   *European Union—Anti-Dumping Measures on Certain Footwear from China (Complaint by China)* (2011), WTO Doc WT/DS405/R at para 7.718 (Panel Report), online (pdf): docs.wto.org [perma.cc/H64L-BMNS]; *European Communities—Definitive Anti-Dumping Measures on Certain Iron or Steel Fasteners from China (Complaint by China)* (2010), WTO Doc WT/DS397/R at paras 7.116, 7.118 (Panel Report), online (pdf): docs.wto.org [perma.cc/JK89-6ZM8]; *Indonesia—Measures Concerning the Importation of Chicken Meat and Chicken Products (Complaint by Brazil)* (2017), WTO Doc WT/DS484/R at para 7.192 (Panel Report), online: docs.wto.org [perma. cc/8B4F-AERC].

37   See, e.g., WTO, *DS Reform Process*, above note 25 at 45.

38   Nevertheless, panel practice is often unpredictable and arguably does not pay sufficient attention to all implementation issues. For instance, when a measure is found to be inconsistent with a substantive WTO provision, panels routinely exercise judicial economy with respect to claims under Article X:3(a), concerning questions of administration. However, this is sometimes a short-sighted approach because the same implementation-related questions can arise with the new measure.

39   See *Australia—Certain Measures Concerning Trademarks, Geographical Indications and Other Plain Packaging Requirements Applicable to Tobacco Products and Packaging (Complaint by Honduras)* (2020), WTO Doc WT/DS435/AB/R, WT/DS441/AB/R at para 6.238, online (pdf): docs.wto.org [perma.cc/J53A-UPK7]; Article 21.5 – US/Article 21.5 – Mexico II Appellate Body Reports, above note 35 at para 6.318.

40   See for instance Article 26(2)(b) of the DSU, Articles XII(5)(d) and XVI:1 of the *General Agreement on Trade in Service* (GATS), Article 6 of the *Agreement on Trade-Related*

MPIA umbrella agreement to refer to a *substantive* ruling, by requiring MPIA arbitrators to "address" only necessary issues.) Another element in Article 17 of the DSU that arguably contemplates findings that may not be "necessary" by current standards is the phrase "legal interpretations developed by a panel" in Article 17.6 of the DSU. That phrase could be read as granting the Appellate Body the mandate to address panel interpretations that may not have a direct impact on the ultimate outcome of a claim/the dispute and/or on implementation and that, therefore, would not be "necessary" as used in today's reform discussions. Consider for instance the United States' accusation of the Appellate Body of alleged far-ranging *obiter dicta* in the *Argentina—Financial Services* case, when the Appellate Body reversed the panel's likeness finding[41] and went on to make findings on "treatment no less favourable," Article XIV of the GATS, and the prudential exception in the Annex on Financial Services. In the light of Articles 17.6 and 17.12, the United States' criticism of the Appellate Body, e.g., in *Argentina—Financial Services* is arguably incorrect, and the Appellate Body had at a minimum the discretion to make these findings.[42]

Paragraph 10 thus arguably represents a shift in WTO Members' judicial policy as compared to the original approach reflected in Article 17. That is of course perfectly legitimate and represents an evolution of the system in the light of the experiences gathered since 1995. However, as paragraph 10 of the MPIA Agreed Procedures will be operationalized in successive appeals, a degree of case-by-case flexibility would be useful when deciding which findings are "necessary." For instance, if a panel's finding of likeness under a national treatment provision is reversed, as in *Argentina—Financial Services*, it may indeed be unnecessary to address issues like less favourable treatment or Article XIV GATS defences, as was indeed argued by the United States.[43] However, this may be true only *in the immediate appeal at hand*. Should the complainant subsequently choose to return before a panel and litigate its case anew, and should the panel reiterate its likeness finding (even if based on a

---

Aspects of Intellectual Property Rights (TRIPS Agreement), Article 5 of the ATC, and paragraph 4 of the Understanding on the Balance of Payments provisions.

41   WTO, *Statement by the United States at the Meeting of the WTO Dispute Settlement Body* (23 May 2016), online (pdf): wto.org [perma.cc/P66V-3BJR] [WTO, *US Statement*].

42   One may also wonder whether it would have been appropriate for the Appellate Body to leave all claims on appeal of the original appellant Panama unaddressed, based on its decision concerning a cross-appeal by Argentina.

43   WTO, *US Statement*, above note 41.

revised legal standard), all "downstream" issues like less favourable treatment and Article XIV may become relevant again. In those circumstances, the silence of the original appellate tribunal on those issues may suddenly no longer appear as efficient, as another appeal may become necessary that may have otherwise been avoided. It would in my view not be improper for MPIA arbitrators to take into account the possibility of a scenario of this kind when deciding what is "necessary" to resolve the original appeal.

This ties into a broader point. An assertive view of what is (not) necessary to resolve the dispute could indeed lead to dispensing with large parts of an appeal, as the United States' criticism of the *Argentina—Financial Services* appellate decision suggests. But Members and arbitrators should not lose sight of one of the key functions of the dispute settlement system: the role of serving the political needs of its Members, especially the respondent, who must justify the dismantling of a protectionist measure to its affected domestic stakeholders. Not addressing claims and arguments on appeal that a respondent considers important enough to raise—even if for political reasons "only"—may affect the legitimacy of a ruling. Narrow judgments may be fine for the winning party because the winning party typically cares less about why it wins than the losing party cares why it lost. Thus, a core purpose of a ruling by an international body like the WTO is to explain to the losing party (and its commercial stakeholders) why they lost. Overly narrow rulings may not serve this purpose.

Similarly, adjudicators' concerns about avoiding *obiter dicta* should not have a chilling effect on broader contextual interpretations. For instance, when interpreting a treaty term under the *General Agreement on Traiffs and Trade* (GATT) 1994, arbitrators should not, out of fear of violating the *obiter dicta* prohibition, be deterred from considering the meaning of the same or similar term under another covered agreement, in order to analyze the wider context of the treaty term at issue.

As a final thought, even the strictest approach to avoiding *obiter dicta* and exercising judicial economy may not enable MPIA arbitrators to avoid exceeding the ninety-day deadline in cases as complex as, for instance, *EC and Certain Member States—Measures Affecting Trade in Large Civil Aircraft, US—Measures Affecting Trade in Large Civil Aircraft*, or *Australia—Plain Packaging*. The number and complexity of "necessary" issues in large dispute of this type will result in appeals that—even in the absence of Article 11 claims—will simply be impossible to resolve within ninety days if the parties wish to see those issues resolved through a traditional appeal procedure, which includes a briefing process, a hearing and detailed supporting reasoning published at the time of decision.

3) Enhancing the Efficiency of Proceedings Pursuant to Paragraphs 12 and 13 of the Agreed Procedures

The MPIA text also authorizes the arbitrators to adopt procedural and substantive measures to "streamline" the proceedings, with a view to complying with the ninety-day deadline.[44] These streamlining measures are "without prejudice to the procedural rights and obligations of the parties and due process."[45]

On the substantive side, paragraph 13 of the Agreed Procedures authorizes MPIA arbitrators to propose "an exclusion of claims based on ... Article 11 of the DSU." In *Colombia—Frozen Fries*, the Arbitrators issued a letter prior to the filing of submissions, "invit[ing the parties] to consider refraining from making claims based on the alleged lack of an objective assessment of the facts pursuant to Article 11 of the DSU."[46] This institutionalized disapproval of Article 11 appeals reflects another point of criticism of the United States, according to which the Appellate Body engaged excessively with factual panel findings. Of course, the Appellate Body addressed Article 11 claims not on a whim but because the parties made these claims. In any event, MPIA arbitrator proposals to drop claims are not binding, as the MPIA also proscribes any "prejudice to the procedural rights and obligations of the parties and due process."[47] Therefore, a party can insist on maintaining its Article 11 claim,[48] while the Arbitrators may always make use of judicial economy.

In the (non-MPIA) Article 25 arbitration appeal in *Turkey—Pharmaceutical Products (EU)*, under rules very similar to the MPIA legal framework, the Arbitrators did not seek to persuade Türkiye (Turkey) to drop an appeal under Article 11 but instead addressed and rejected it. This may be an indication that MPIA arbitrators will not make frequent use of their persuasion authority. But that does not detract from the effectiveness of the MPIA text on Article 11. The greatest practical impact of the Article 11-related provision probably lies primarily in its chilling effect on a party's intention to raise

---

44   *MPIA*, above note 1, Annex 1 at para 12.
45   *Ibid.*
46   *Colombia—Frozen Fries* (Addendum), above note 9 at 7.
47   *MPIA*, above note 1, Annex 1 at para 12.
48   *Ibid*, Annex 1 at 5, fn 6.

these claims in the first place. MPIA Members will likely pay attention to this stamp of disapproval of Article 11 claims and will consider carefully the claims they wish to bring. Thus, MPIA arbitrators should arguably respect a Member's ultimate choice, especially as they retain the authority to exercise judicial economy.

Turning to the *procedural* (organizational) streamlining tools, the MPIA text authorizes MPIA arbitrators to impose page limits.[49] In the proceedings in *Colombia—Frozen Fries*, a word limit was imposed. In the (non-MPIA) Article 25 arbitration appeal in *Turkey—Pharmaceutical Products (EU)*, under rules very similar to the MPIA legal framework, the arbitral panel also imposed a word limit.

The MPIA drafters chose to include in the MPIA text only a generic authorization to set page limits, without providing more detailed numerical guidance. Thus, each MPIA arbitral panel could theoretically tailor the word limit on a case-by-case basis. Nevertheless, the word limits in *Turkey—Pharmaceutical Products (EU)* and in the first MPIA appeal in *Colombia—Frozen Fries* were similar, imposing either an absolute word limit—which differed in the two cases—or 40 percent of the length of the panel report. This suggests that MPIA panels may follow an at least partially standardized approach. The fact that the pre-arbitration letter in *Colombia—Frozen Fries* that spelled out this word limit was issued by all the ten MPIA arbitrators also suggests an at least partially harmonized policy.

Word or page limits appear to be a tool for popular reform. The February 2024 DS reform text also sets out numerically precise word limits, based on a categorization of disputes into "standard," "complex" and "extra-ordinarily" complex[50] that would be interesting to observe in practice. GATT and WTO DS have historically operated without page limits, but domestic courts all over the world impose word or page limits on party submissions. These limits will in many situations undoubtedly have some salutary effect on the efficiency of proceedings. MPIA panels will not be confronted with unnecessarily long submissions. Moreover, word limits need not excessively limit appellants' choices because experienced legal counsel should have no difficulty arguing any claim effectively even under a word limit.

However, the positive effect of word limits comes with a few caveats. First, although experienced legal counsel can preserve persuasiveness of arguments

---

49 See *ibid*, Annex 1 at para 12.

50 See WTO, *Special Meeting*, above note 6 at 25.

even under word limits, due process concerns may arise when word limits are set too narrowly. Interestingly, when the Appellate Body in 2015 suggested introducing limits on the length of written submissions, four future MPIA members did not support the proposal, arguing that page limits were an infringement of WTO Members' due process rights and would be impracticable, given that the length of written submissions was determined largely by factors beyond the parties' control.[51] Similar concerns can arise in domestic legal systems: In 2021, when four Dutch appeal courts introduced page limits for legal briefs, these page limits were challenged by a group of lawyers, arguing that they inappropriately limited parties' right to be heard and to have judicial access.[52] The Dutch Supreme Court upheld the page limits, but at the same time found the matter sufficiently important so as to instruct the appeal courts to safeguard parties' right to be heard and to have judicial access, e.g., via flexibility with the word limits in the event of complex appeals.

In my view, the experience in the first MPIA appeal in *Colombia—Frozen Fries* suggests that these are not empty concerns. The MPIA arbitrators imposed a word limit, defined as the higher of 40 percent of the length of the panel report or 27,000 words.[53] At first glance, this limit seems sufficiently generous, and neither party to the appeal indicated that it perceived this as unduly limiting. However, these word limits were set *before* the scope of the appeal was known. For reasons unrelated to the word limit, Colombia chose to appeal only four out of eight panel findings of violation, which resulted in a relatively limited appeal. However, had Colombia chosen to appeal all of the eight findings of violation, I do not believe that this word limit would have permitted Colombia to present a sufficiently comprehensive and persuasive case on all eight points of appeal.

51 WTO, *Appellate Body Annual Report for 2016*, WTO Doc WT/AB/27 (2017), Annex 2, online (pdf): docs.wto.org [perma.cc/U7V7-HHW8].

52 Jan-Willem Meijer & Johan Valk, "Dutch Supreme Court: Courts of Appeal Free to Set and Enforce Page Limits" (27 June 2022), online: debrauw.com [perma.cc/QF59-BG5Z].

53 See *Turkey—Certain Measures Concerning the Production, Importation and Marketing of Pharmaceutical Products (Complaint by the European Union)* (2022), WTO Doc WT/DS583/12 (Arbitration Appeal), online (pdf): docs.wto.org [perma.cc/YLY7-LG2E]. Incidentally, a similar percentage-based approach was chosen by the Article 25 this arbitration appeal under rules very similar to the MPIA legal framework—40 percent or 40,000 words.

Word limits should under no circumstances be a tool to push parties towards appeals with fewer claims, although this has been (publicly) suggested and advocated by some. Using word limits in this way would be neither appropriate nor wise. First, at a textual level, as the MPIA text indicates, word or page limits are *procedural* streamlining measures, which means that they are tools intended to expedite the procedure—not to regulate the substance of the case. Nudging parties towards limiting or changing the substance of their case falls under the category of *substantive* streamlining measures, like dropping claims under Article 11 of the DSU.

Second, and more importantly, using word limits to limit the number of appeal claims denies to some extent the perfectly legitimate *political* objective of WTO dispute settlement. In a government-to-government dispute settlement system like the WTO, it is extremely important that a losing government can credibly claim before affected domestic stakeholders that the government exhausted all potential arguments and defended their interest to the best of its ability.[54] It is therefore crucial that a government has, and is seen to have, sufficient opportunity to argue one's case effectively. This applies with particular force in appeal proceedings in which only one written submission is possible. No interest group should be given the opportunity to argue that the WTO dispute settlement procedure in any way curtails a responding government's ability to defend itself. All these considerations apply with particular force at a time when the dispute settlement system as a whole, and international rule of law at large, is being put in doubt or even openly challenged by some.

These considerations demonstrate the need for sufficient flexibility when setting word or page limits. Streamlining measures should not affect the parties' due process rights.[55] This flexibility could come in the form of readily available extensions of the word or page limit, with sufficient deference to the parties' judgment. A possible alternative would be to set (average) word limits *per issue appealed*. This would result in a sliding scale of sorts, which could accommodate the streamlining objective without risking impairing the parties' legitimate choices as to the number of issues to be appealed.

---

54 WTO, *Special Meeting*, above note 6. This is all the more so in the light of the demands for ever-greater transparency, including the publication of summaries of submissions, as proposed in Title VIII, Chapter II, of the February 2024 informal dispute settlement reform text.

55 MPIA, above note 1, Annex 1 at para 12.

One final procedural tool deployed by the Arbitrators in *Colombia—Frozen Fries* was a so-called "pre-hearing conference" with the parties, to assist in the preparation of the oral hearing. This streamlining device is not explicitly mentioned in paragraph 12 of the MPIA Agreed Procedures. The objective of the pre-hearing conference was to "enhance procedural efficiency and facilitate meeting the nine-day time-period."[56] Specifically, the arbitrators stated that they would seek to "identify those issues that are necessary for the resolution of the dispute," as provided in paragraph 10 of the Agreed Procedures, or to "highlight the key issues raised by the parties in the appeal that need further discussion at the hearing."[57] As the arbitral award reveals, during this conference, one of the parties expressed the concern that the Arbitrators were seeking to explore issues that, according to that party, would more appropriately be explored at the hearing.[58]

This experience shows that the success of the Arbitrators' streamlining efforts will likely depend on how the litigating parties perceive them. If parties believe that their procedural rights are being encroached upon and that their litigation strategy is being improperly limited, streamlining efforts will cause more harm than good. This is especially so as, realistically, the streamlining efforts will in most instances not be the decisive factor for ensuring respect for the ninety-day deadline. As already noted, the most important practical consequence of these provisions will arguably be to induce litigating parties to exercise self-restraint in raising and/or arguing certain issues. Once parties have made their choices about their claims, MPIA arbitrators should probably limit their interference with these sovereign choices to exceptional cases only.

E. Conclusion

THIS FIRST RECOURSE TO THE MPIA was generally characterized as a success by WTO Members. During the DSB meeting following the circulation of the award, Colombia stated that the MPIA "had proven to be a viable and well-functioning interim mechanism," while the European Union stated that the MPIA had "safeguarded the possibility of exercising effectively the right to a binding, two-tier, independent and impartial adjudication in accordance

---

56 WTO, *Arbitral Award Addendum*, above note 46 at 9.
57 *Ibid.*
58 *Colombia—Frozen Fries* (Arbitral Award), above note 9 at paras 1.11–1.12.

with WTO rules" and "had confirmed that appeal proceedings in the WTO could be conducted swiftly and efficiently, while fully preserving the procedural rights of the parties."[59] Numerous other WTO Members also expressed satisfaction.

It remains to be seen how the efforts of the MPIA drafters to improve upon the original appellate review procedure fare in practice. Perhaps the rule of thumb for the introduction of new technologies is of relevance here: we might be overestimating the effect of these improvements in the short run but underestimate their impact in the long run. In any event, the greatest effect in terms of avoiding overly complex and voluminous proceedings may come less from the measures taken by the MPIA Arbitrators but instead from "upstream" changes in parties' autonomous decisions about how to litigate and what cases to bring to the WTO.

---

59   WTO, *Minutes of Meeting*, WTO Doc WT/DSB/M/475 (2023) at paras 2.3–2.9, online (pdf): docs.wto.org [perma.cc/NDU5-AM6J].

CHAPTER 28

The Dispute Settlement Reform Discussions—A New Approach

Marco Tulio Molina Tejeda

Creativity has the power to forge new paths and the most transformative changes often begin with a single idea.

A. Introduction

AROUND TWENTY YEARS AGO, IN my early days as a Guatemalan Delegate to the World Trade Organization (WTO), I heard Valerie Hugues speak at a conference. At that time, Valerie already had a spectacular career and was highly respected in our dispute settlement community. Valerie said, and I might be paraphrasing, *"Say what you mean and mean what you say."* I found those words compelling: they made an indelible impression and became the foundation of everything I do.

From that day onwards, my efforts centered on grasping the rationale and motivations behind each message, each idea, and each position underpinning our strategies, actions, and results. A brilliant idea or legal argument holds no value if it cannot be articulated clearly and understood by others. Of course, this is particularly critical in dispute settlement proceedings and complex international negotiations, where the precision and clarity of one's words are paramount. This realization became my guiding principle and foundation for my career. I have had the privilege to serve in various capacities, including government representative, negotiator, litigant, adjudicator, and, more recently, as the Informal Facilitator of the Dispute Settlement Reform Process.

In this role, I focused on unpacking the interests and concerns that were the basis of the ideas or positions presented by WTO Members.

This chapter has a dual purpose. First, it is intended to pay tribute to Valerie Hughes, for whom I have great admiration. Secondly, I will provide an anecdotal account of the Informal Dispute Settlement Reform Process and my experience as its Facilitator, a real-life testament to the importance of *saying what you mean and meaning what you say*. Of course, there is a caveat: this chapter is based on my personal notes and recollections. It is not intended to express any views on behalf of any delegate or Member, nor to pass judgment on their ideas or positions. I will not reveal any confidential information about the Informal Process nor make attributions.

I hope that after reading this chapter, the reader will appreciate the different ways in which negotiations at the WTO can take place and will gain a true perspective on the draft consolidated text that resulted from the Informal Dispute Settlement Reform Process.

B. Before the Start of the Informal Dispute Settlement Reform Process

THE LITERATURE IS ABUNDANT ON the reasons why Members embarked on the reform of the dispute settlement system and its objectives. To provide some context about the Informal Dispute Settlement Reform Process, I would like to recall the meeting of the General Council that took place on 15 October 2019, less than two months before the Appellate Body was paralyzed on 11 December 2019.

At that meeting, the Facilitator of the Informal Process on Matters related to the Functioning of the Appellate Body, H.E. Ambassador David Walker (New Zealand), reported on his consultations with Members, also known as the "Walker Process," and submitted a draft decision[1] addressing the concerns expressed by the United States on the operation of the Appellate Body and aiming to restore the functioning of the dispute settlement system. Ambassador Walker had been appointed by the then General Council Chair, H.E. Ambassador Dacio Castillo (Honduras), after consulting with WTO

---

1   WTO, *Statement in Support of the Process of Appointment of the Next Director-General of the World Trade Organization*, WTO Doc WT/GC/222 (2020), online (pdf): docsonline.wto.org [perma.cc/S7GL-2L96].

Members.[2] Most WTO Members had actively engaged in the Walker Process, with many submitting position papers with proposals for the reform of the Appellate Body between November 2018 and June 2019.[3]

At the 15 October 2019 General Council meeting, the United States stated that the draft decision proposed by Ambassador Walker was still far from reaching convergence, arguing that WTO Members had failed to address what it considered to be the most important question: "How have we come to this point?"[4]

Ambassador Walker continued his consultations with Members and submitted a revised version of his draft decision for adoption by the General Council. The Permanent Representative of the United States, however, did not support the adoption of the draft decision, expressing disappointment that he did not see convergence among Members on an understanding and

---

2   See WTO, *Minutes of the General Council*, WTO Doc WT/GC/M/176 (2019) at para 4.2, online (pdf): docsonline.wto.org [perma.cc/YRX6-DWYL].

3   See, for example, proposals submitted by the African Group, Australia, Brazil, Canada, China, European Union, Honduras, Iceland, India, Korea, Mexico, New Zealand, Norway, Paraguay, Singapore, Chinese Taipei, Thailand, and Switzerland, contained in WTO documents WTO, *Communication from the European Union, China, Canada, India, Norway, New Zealand, Switzerland, Australia, Republic of Korea, Iceland, Singapore, Mexico, Costa Rica and Montenegro to the General Council*, WTO Doc WT/GC/W/752 (2018), online (pdf): docsonline.wto.org [perma.cc/HHS7-4CYY], WTO, *Communication from the European Union, China and India To The Council,* WTO Doc WT/GC/W/753 (2018), online (pdf): docsonline.wto.org [perma.cc/4PSV-UDAJ], WTO, *Fostering A Discussion on the Function of the Appellate Body*, WTO Doc WT/GC/W/758 (2019), online (pdf): docsonline.wto.org [perma.cc/6Q35-4FK9], WTO, *Fostering A Discussion on the Functioning of the Appellate Body*, WTO Doc WT/GC/W/759 (2019), online (pdf): docsonline.wto.org [perma.cc/8CPF-34YM], WTO, *Fostering A Discussion on the Functioning of the Appellate Body Addressing the Issue of Alleged Judicial Activism by the Appellate Body,* WTO Doc WT/GC/W/760 (2019) online (pdf): docsonline.wto.org [perma.cc/Z7UH-PT4B], WTO, *Fostering the Discussion on the Functioning of the Appellate Body Addressing the Issue of Precedent,* WTO Doc WT/GC/W/761 (2019), online (pdf): docsonline.wto.org [perma.cc/QYU6-AVAP], WTO, *Guideline Development Discussion,* WTO Doc WT/GC/W/763 (2019), online (pdf): docsonline.wto.org [perma.cc/6R43-SMN6], WTO, *Guidelines for Work of Panels and the Appellate Body,* WTO Doc WT/GC/W/767 (2019), online (pdf): docsonline.wto.org [perma.cc/R7HF-K5PH], WTO, *Informal Process on Matters Related to the Functioning of the Appellate Body,* WTO Doc WT/GC/W/768 (2019), online (pdf): docsonline.wto.org [perma.cc/E7U4-SL4Q], and WTO, *Orden Del Día Propuesto,* WTO Doc WT/GC/W/766 (2019), online (pdf): docsonline.wto.org [perma.cc/J4FT-XCTY].

4   See US Mission Geneva, "Statements by the United States at the WTO General Council Metting" (15 October 2019), online: usmission.gov [perma.cc/98LE-LF77].

appreciation of the concerns raised.[5] Following the blockage of Ambassador Walker's draft decision, Members were unclear about the next steps. Many Members believed that Ambassador Walker had done an exceptional job in conducting the Informal Process and helping Members understand their positions regarding the operation of the Appellate Body. The draft decision appeared to contain all the necessary understandings and commitments that Members could collectively adopt to correct the operation of the Appellate Body. However, the United States disagreed, and Members essentially, after tabling several proposals, ran out of ideas on how to address the US concerns.

In March 2020, the COVID-19 pandemic led to a global lockdown. During 2020, conversations were limited to finding provisional solutions to a non-functional Appellate Body, like the Multi-Party Interim Appeal Arbitration Arrangement (MPIA).[6] There were no further discussions on how to address the paralysis of the Appellate Body, at least for the following two years.

Meanwhile, the 12th Ministerial Conference (MC12) which had been originally scheduled to take place in June 2020 in Nur-Sultan, Kazakhstan, was rescheduled to take place in Geneva, from 30 November to 3 December 2021.[7] At the time, Members were discussing a paragraph in the draft "MC12 Outcome Document" that would provide for a mandate to address the situation of the dispute settlement system. Just days before its start, the General Council decided to postpone MC12 indefinitely due to the outbreak of a new and highly transmissible strain of COVID-19.[8]

The MC12 finally took place from 12 to 17 June 2022 in Geneva.[9] Ministers adopted the MC12 Outcome Document, paragraph 4 of which reads: "[w]e acknowledge the challenges and concerns with respect to the dispute settlement system including those related to the Appellate Body, recognize the importance and urgency of addressing those challenges and concerns, and commit to conduct discussions with the view to having a fully

---

5   See WTO, *Minutes of Meeting*, WTO Doc WT/GC/M/181 (2020) at para 5.100, online (pdf): docsonline.wto.org [perma.cc/G3ME-LHYJ].

6   See WTO, *Statement on a Mechanism for Developing, Documenting and Sharing Practices and Procedures in the Conduct of WTO Disputes*, WTO Doc JOB/DSB/1/Add.12 (2020), online: docsonline.wto.org [perma.cc/R37P-K2CP].

7   See WTO, News Release, MC12, "Twelfth WTO Ministerial Conference" (12 June 2022), online: docsonline.wto.org [perma.cc/B8LP-GCLN].

8   *Ibid*.

9   *Ibid*.

and well-functioning dispute settlement system accessible to all Members by 2024."[10]

The essence of this paragraph had been agreed upon before the postponement of MC12 in December 2021. A few months later, in April 2022, the US delegation in Geneva initiated discussions with several WTO Members regarding the functioning of the dispute settlement system. Expectations were high, as many Members viewed these discussions as a renewed opportunity to better understand the concerns of the United States and to collectively explore solutions that could restore a fully operational dispute settlement system.

I participated in the initial meeting of dispute settlement experts convened by US delegates, who proposed starting discussions around the "interests" that Members had in the dispute settlement system. Initially, this term went mostly unnoticed. However, the US delegates emphasized the concept, providing examples and clarifying that the conversations should not be limited by the existing framework of the Dispute Settlement Understanding (DSU). This focus on "interests" led some delegates to suspect that it was a tactic to divert attention from the central issue of restoring the Appellate Body's functionality.

As the discussions progressed, the US delegation proposed creating a comprehensive list of primary interests that Members had in the dispute settlement system. They initiated with their list of interests to demonstrate their vision and expectations about the exercise. Although there was initial skepticism, other delegates, including myself representing Guatemala, fully engaged. Several delegates volunteered to make presentations of their interests, yielding a compilation of over 230 interests that proved to be extremely valuable.[11] Each presentation was met with rigorous questioning, which facilitated a deeper understanding of the various perspectives and interpretations Members held about the dispute settlement system. It also helped in identifying common interests among Members.

After compiling a list of over 230 interests, the US delegates proposed grouping them by topic. We had a thorough discussion about the proposed groupings to ensure a shared understanding. Once we agreed

---

10   WTO, *MC12 Outcome Document*, WTO Doc WT/MIN(22)/24 (2022), online (pdf): docsonline.wto.org [perma.cc/TR4F-2BSN].

11   WTO, *Special Meeting of the General Council*, WTO Doc JOB/GC/385 (2024) at para 1.13, online (pdf): docsonline.wto.org [perma.cc/RK6G-JUUG].

on the categorization, we moved to the next phase: identifying conceptual approaches that could address the different interests. The US delegates noted that some interests were closely aligned and that there could be multiple ways to address them. Other interests, they suggested, might be reconciled through innovative conceptual approaches. The goal was to identify as many approaches as possible and see which could address the majority of the identified interests. The hope was that, through mutual understanding, we could organically select approaches that reflected the consensus of all Members.

The second phase of discussions, which centered on identifying "conceptual approaches," was highly abstract, as delegates did not specify any particular issues they wanted to change or improve. Many of the conceptual approaches proposed to address specific interests closely resembled the existing content of the DSU. While delegates continued to engage constructively and with enthusiasm, the dynamic shifted notably when the discussion moved to the topic of the "appeal/review" mechanism. Among the conceptual approaches presented, one was identical to the Appellate Body as provided for in the DSU, while others did not look like either the Appellate Body or an appeal mechanism. This led to disappointment and renewed suspicion that the process might be a distraction or a strategy to diffuse responsibility for the paralysis of the Appellate Body. These concerns were compounded by the lack of clarity regarding the next steps in the US-led process and how this would ultimately align with the mandate set forth by Ministers at MC12.

C. Time for Action After MC12

THERE WERE MANY POSITIVE OUTCOMES from MC12, including a mandate on dispute settlement, which directed Members to "conduct conversations" aimed at achieving "a fully and well-functioning dispute settlement system accessible to all Members by 2024."[12] While the intent to engage in discussions and the primary objective were clear, the deadline, expressed as "by 2024," was ambiguous. Some Members interpreted this as requiring the conclusion of discussions before the start of 2024, others viewed the deadline as the end of 2024, and others believed any time within 2024 was permissible, with the dates of the 13th Ministerial Conference (MC13) in Abu Dhabi being a logical target for finalizing an outcome on dispute settlement.

---

12   WTO, *MC12 Outcome Document*, WTO Doc WT/MIN(22)/24 (2022), online (pdf): docsonline.wto.org [perma.cc/TR4F-2BSN].

Paragraph 4 of the MC12 Outcome Document also clarified that these discussions would address broader "challenges and concerns with respect to the dispute settlement system" not just the Appellate Body. However, at the time of negotiating the text in the document, Members had not yet clearly defined these challenges and concerns, leaving undefined the scope of what would later be termed as the Dispute Settlement Reform Process.

In the second half of 2022, after MC12, Members continued to participate in the US-led Informal Process but grew increasingly anxious for clarity on how to fulfill the MC12 mandate. Many delegates hoped for a swift resolution, ideally by the MC13, reflecting the urgency of the situation. Additionally, some Members, including those participating in the US-led Informal Process began voicing the need to start a more formal process regarding dispute settlement conversations.[13]

In response, Members initiated discussions on the next steps, but these quickly became mired in procedural debates. Some argued that the conversations should occur under the General Council, while others preferred the Dispute Settlement Body (DSB). There were differing views on whether the meetings should be chaired by one of the Chairpersons of these bodies or by a dedicated Facilitator. There were disagreements on the level of participation, with some advocating for both ambassadors and experts due to the political and technical nature of the subject, while others favoured limiting initial discussions to experts on dispute settlement to focus on finding substantive practical solutions.

In January 2023, to resolve these issues and considering that the United States had announced the imminent end of its informal process by 31 January, the General Council Chair, H.E. Ambassador Didier Chambovey (Switzerland), intensified consultations with Members. During these consultations, a consensus began to emerge around the idea of a dual-track process: a formal track under either the General Council or DSB Chairs and an informal track facilitated by a dispute settlement expert.

On 1 February 2023, after two weeks of consultations led by Ambassador Chambovey, I received a call from a delegate informing me that his Ambassador had proposed my name as the Facilitator for the Informal Process, a suggestion that had been well received by a majority of WTO Members. The following day, however, during an informal meeting of key Ambassadors,

---

13 See WTO, *Minutes of Meeting*, WTO Doc TN/C/M/43 (2022) at paras 4.67, 4.71, 4.96, 4.103, 4.112, and 4.115, online (pdf): docsonline.wto.org [perma.cc/AT8U-KERH].

one Ambassador objected to my formal designation by the General Council Chair as an Informal Facilitator, citing systemic reasons. The objecting Ambassador appeared to have proposed a selection process for choosing the Facilitator by consensus. The great majority of Ambassadors present at that meeting reportedly opposed this idea, citing past practice where the General Council or DSB Chairs typically had the prerogative of appointing facilitators after consulting Members. One recent example was the designation of Ambassador Walker by the General Council Chair as the Informal Facilitator in a previous process. There was also an interest in avoiding complex procedures, especially since no other candidates had been proposed nor considered.

After what was described to me as a "tense" and "convoluted" meeting, another Ambassador suggested that a formal designation might be unnecessary for an *Informal Process*. It was proposed that I could begin working and reporting on progress, with the understanding that formal negotiations would eventually be conducted under the auspices of either the General Council or the DSB. This compromise solution was met with no objections from those present, and it became the agreed path forward.

D. The Informal Dispute Settlement Reform Process was Born . . . Unofficially

THE INFORMAL DISPUTE SETTLEMENT REFORM Process had been launched or so I was told. There was no official record of the Ambassadors' meeting, no documentation of their agreed path forward, and no clarity on whether the decision would be acceptable to those who were not present. Moreover, I received no formal or written communication about it. The decision to proceed informally, without any formalities, certainly left both the process and myself in an awkward position.

First, I learned informally, through conversations in the corridors of the WTO, that there was an understanding among Members that I would facilitate the informal discussions. This understanding was conveyed to me by several Ambassadors, as well the General Council Chair. However, no specific mandate was ever provided to me.

Secondly, I was informed that the Guatemalan Ambassador had not participated in the meeting where my role had been discussed. Thus, I still needed his authorization to act as the Facilitator of the Informal Process, before accepting that role and start convening any meeting. Since he had already heard about this significant responsibility before I could approach him and despite the honour it meant for Guatemala and the Permanent Mission, our meeting was unfortunately very challenging. After a long conversation, he reluctantly agreed to the idea of me facilitating the Informal Dispute Settlement Reform Process, mainly because it was expected to remain low-profile, confidential, and limited to dispute settlement experts in Geneva only.

Thirdly, there was no clarity on when or how the formal process would start, nor on its format or structure. Given these uncertainties, there was little guidance on what was expected from the Informal Process or how it would contribute to the formal negotiations that were anticipated to start at a later, unspecified date.

Finally, I was informed that there was a tacit understanding that the Informal Dispute Settlement Reform Process would adhere to the modalities of the US-led discussions, with minimal changes to ensure a frank dialogue and a focus on delivering results. This meant the process was expected to operate without the involvement of the WTO Secretariat and would be conducted exclusively by Geneva-based delegates, in a confidential manner.

E. The Journey of a Thousand Miles Starts with the First Step

MANY THOUGHTS CROSSED MY MIND when I learned of the request from WTO Members to act as the Facilitator for the Informal Dispute Settlement Reform Process. On the one hand, I was deeply honoured to be entrusted with the monumental task of helping Members reconcile their diverse philosophical and conceptual views on how the System should operate. On the other hand, I was extremely concerned about how to approach a task that seemed almost impossible. As mentioned earlier, numerous challenging conditions were imposed on me and the Informal Process. Additionally, after nearly a year of deep and meaningful discussions on interests and conceptual approaches, it became increasingly clear that Members often held opposing views on the system's operation. Many of these views echoed those expressed in the negotiations on the Review of the DSU, which had not yielded results in the past twenty-five years. It was evident that I needed to adopt a different approach, one that most likely would diverge from the traditional WTO negotiating methods. It was a daunting prospect but necessary if we were to give the Informal Process a chance to make a meaningful impact in the negotiations.

I spent four days meticulously planning and outlining the objectives, schedule, and methodology for the Informal Process. The term "interests," used recently, resonated deeply with me, taking me back to the late 1990s when I began working at the Guatemalan Ministry of Economy. During that time, I served as the Guatemalan negotiator for dispute settlement chapters of free trade agreements. I participated in a course based on the Harvard methodology developed by Roger Fisher, William Ury, and Bruce Patton, authors of "Getting to Yes."[14] This training had a profound impact on my career, and I took the "interest-based approach" wherever I went next.

While WTO Members might have different perspectives and often disagree on methods, they do share common goals. Thus, the approach to focus on identifying interests is instrumental in building bridges between differing views. In my opinion, the interest-based approach served as the cornerstone for success in the Informal Dispute Settlement Reform Process and, most likely, could also be used in almost any negotiation with a wide variety of stakeholders.

I also believed that it was time to change gears and transition from a conversation that focused on "interests" and "conceptual approaches" to a more "solution-oriented" approach. We needed to find solutions to address specific interests and concerns, which Members had yet to fully articulate. If we were to deliver results on the MC12 mandate by MC13, efficiency was paramount.

After four days of planning, I began bilateral consultations with delegates. I personally sent invitations to all Permanent Missions to the WTO and asked them to identify the delegates responsible for dispute settlement reform. From 6 to 12 February 2023, I held over forty meetings with representatives from more than 130 Members including regional coordinators, essentially those who responded to my invitation. During these meetings, I outlined my plan and the methodology I intended to use to facilitate the conversations. I also sought to gauge support for the Informal Process, my role as Facilitator, and whether they would attend the first meeting, initially scheduled for 17 February 2023.

While some were skeptical about potential outcomes, all delegates expressed their support for me and the Informal Process and promised to

---

14   See Getting to YES - PON - Program on Negotiation at Harvard Law School.

participate constructively. They also provided valuable feedback, which I incorporated into the plan and methodology.

F. The Initial Plan

THE PLAN I PROPOSED WAS straightforward: the Informal Process would be governed by the principles of transparency *vis-à-vis* delegates from all WTO Members and inclusivity, following a bottom-up, solution-oriented, non-attributed, and focused approach. All decisions would be made in plenary sessions open to the participation of all WTO Members.

To ensure meaningful participation, I designed the process so that all participants would receive information simultaneously and have ample opportunity to express their views and ensure those views were considered. I used various tools, including online forms to build an updated distribution list, schedule meetings, and propose ideas. Meetings were scheduled to allow delegates to catch up on progress if they missed any sessions.

The cornerstone of the methodology was the interest-based approach, where initial proposals would be submitted and recorded in what we called the "red table," without any filtering or alteration. Subsequently, these proposals would be collectively discussed and refined and included in the "yellow table." The expectation was that through dialogue and mutual understanding, we would reach optimal solutions agreeable to all, which would then be recorded in a "green table" to serve as the basis for drafting text and initiating text-based negotiations.

In my invitation for Members to submit inputs for the "red table," I included the link to an online form that required a concise description of the topic, identification of the concern or improvement being sought, the proposed solution, any relevant observation, and the suggested means of implementation (e.g., DSB decision, DSU amendment, etc.). I explicitly requested not to propose any legal text but only ideas. Furthermore, this was the only occasion where the identity of the Member proposing the idea was required. After this stage, the entire process operated under the principle of non-attribution.

The rationale for attributing ideas in the red table was twofold: First, it aimed at establishing accountability, as these tables would define the scope of the negotiations; and second, attribution would enable delegates to identify and consult with the Members that had proposed specific ideas. After the red table, the intention was to proceed collectively, where non-attribution would be the norm, as Members were contributing with ideas and practical solutions.

Finally, I prepared a calendar of meetings through July 2023 and reserved meeting rooms well in advance. The sequence of meetings was organized to allow delegates time to consult with their capitals and other delegations between plenary sessions. On a more practical note, I ensured that the great majority of meetings took place in rooms E and C at the WTO building, hoping that the lake view would contribute to more productive discussions. Due to unavailability, very few meetings took place elsewhere.

With everything in place, we were ready to begin.

G. The "Official" Start of the Informal Dispute Settlement Reform Process

ON 17 FEBRUARY 2023, THE morning was sunny and crisp at seven degrees Celsius. I arrived early in Room E to ensure everything was in order—Power-Point facilities ready, microphones working and curtains open to see the beautiful *Lac Léman*.

Since this was an informal meeting, I decided not to use the traditional Members' nameplates. I intended to create a personal atmosphere. I knew almost all dispute settlement delegates by name from previous interactions.

As I greeted colleagues entering the room, I began to worry that we might not have enough seats for everyone. Room E can accommodate nighty-nine persons, and that day only a handful of chairs remained empty, reflecting the high level of interest delegations had in the Informal Dispute Settlement Reform Process.

After the customary ten-minute wait for late arrivals, I closed the door and took my place at the podium, a daunting experience, with everyone staring at me, waiting for the meeting to begin. I started with "Good morning, colleagues, welcome to this informal meeting." Those words would become the opening for every plenary session until the final one on 9 February 2024.

I spoke for about thirty minutes, outlining the calendar of meetings and the methodology we would follow while showing a PowerPoint presentation. Nothing was a surprise for the delegates in the room, as I had consulted with most of them during the previous week and discussed the calendar and methodology. My presentation included a refined plan, shaped by the valuable feedback and suggestions they had provided. Then, I opened the floor. Many raised questions, particularly the "what if?" type. I responded the best I could, though, in hindsight, none of us could foresee the outcome of our endeavour.

Notably, nobody questioned or objected to the methodology. Only one delegate, from the same delegation that had previously objected to my formal designation as Facilitator, pointed out that I was not officially a Facilitator but merely a Convenor of the conversations,[15] and that this process was not formally intended to fulfill the MC12 mandate. However, many others expressed their support for the process and their intention to participate actively and constructively.

H. The Real Work Begins

PLANNING IS ONE THING; EXECUTING the plan is entirely another. Within the established deadlines and using the online form, Members submitted over seventy proposals for discussion in the Informal Process, a significant number that defined the scope and breadth of our conversations. I promptly circulated the "red table" containing these proposals to all Members, enabling us to begin preparing for the first and second clusters of meetings.

At the outset of the process, I organized four clusters of three-day meetings, scheduled every three to four weeks, with a wrap-up session planned to take place before the summer break. These meetings were open-ended, inviting delegates from all WTO Members. I also convened small-group meetings to initiate conversations and better prepare for the larger discussions. These small-group meetings were organized in various configurations, depending on availability and the need to represent diverse views. To ensure transparency, I prepared reports from these meetings so that all delegates would have the information needed to effectively contribute to the plenary sessions.

At our first informal meeting on 17 February 2023, I stated that I would not assume any role that would supersede the collective decisions of Members. I explained that I would refrain from passing judgment on which interests, concerns, problems, challenges, or proposed solutions were acceptable.

---

15   In official WTO documents, the WTO Secretariat chose to use the term "Convenor," which refers to someone responsible for calling people together for meetings. However, my role, as detailed in this chapter, extended far beyond merely convening meetings. I facilitated discussions, guided conversations, and helped identify solutions by posing questions and proposing ideas for Members' consideration. For this reason, I prefer the term "facilitator," which more accurately reflects the work I undertook during the Informal Dispute Settlement Reform Process.

Instead, my role was to assist delegates by facilitating discussions and asking questions that would help them collectively navigate their differences and build bridges.

Rather than simply managing the floor, I posed questions in a way that encouraged delegates to share and identify ideas that addressed their interests and motivated them to work together in a cooperative spirit. The goal was to inspire creative solutions that could address all articulated interests and concerns. This approach differed significantly from the traditional role of Chairs and Facilitators at the WTO, who typically consult with Members and propose what they believe to be the best solution. In my case, the challenge was to guide delegates toward finding that solution themselves and allow them to take ownership of the outcome.

I. A Bumpy Ride...

WE WORKED DILIGENTLY, BUT THE process was not without its challenges, requiring constant adaptation.

As mentioned earlier, several conditions were imposed on me and the Informal Dispute Settlement Reform Process, including the requirement to forego the involvement of the WTO Secretariat in the conversations. This meant, at the beginning, that I had to handle not only substantive and procedural matters but also administrative tasks, such as reserving meeting rooms, sending communications to delegates, ensuring audiovisual equipment was available, taking notes, etc. While I managed to keep this "one-man show" running for a couple of months, it was humanly impossible to focus on substance and manage the logistics of the meetings at the same time.

I openly recognized the need for support. I consulted with Members and explained that I required at least one person from the WTO Secretariat to assist me. Taking into account the sensitivities around legal divisions and the need for utmost discretion, I am grateful to Santiago Wills and Antony Taubman, for finding and allowing Francisco Hernández Fernández, from the Intellectual Property Division, to provide invaluable assistance to the Informal Process on top of his usual responsibilities. This allowed me to focus more on the substance when facilitating the Informal Dispute Settlement Reform Process.

During my consultations, I also discussed with delegates the distinction between the "involvement" and "assistance" of the WTO Secretariat in the process. While I understood that some Members wanted to ensure the Secretariat would not advise me or the delegates on substantive matters, I believed that this did not preclude the Secretariat from providing specific assistance upon request. As the Informal Process moved forward, the support of the WTO Secretariat proved invaluable, particularly in providing specific information requested by delegates, translating documents, providing simultaneous interpretation and online participation to delegates, among other important tasks.

It would be remiss of me not to acknowledge the readiness of the WTO Secretariat to assist whenever needed. I am especially grateful to the Director-General, Dr Ngozi Okonjo-Iweala, for her trust and support. We met every two weeks and, when necessary, more frequently. I also received vital support from Deputy Director-General Angela Ellard, Clarisse Morgan, and Jorge Castro, who addressed questions by Members on the functioning of the dispute settlement system and the support provided to panels by the Rules and Legal Affairs Divisions; Bridget Chilala presented the technical assistance portfolio available to Members; and Santiago Wills and the staff of the Council & Trade Negotiations Committee Division prepared and coordinated meetings of the General Council and Senior Officials. I am deeply grateful to the teams of interpreters and translators and the Conference Office, whose contributions were instrumental to the smooth running of the Informal Process.

At the request by Members, Niall Meagher provided a detailed overview of the mission and offerings of the Advisory Centre on WTO Law, available for developing and least-developed country Members and Observers.

As we moved forward with the plan presented on 17 February, Members were engaging in productive conversations, and it became clear to me that more meetings would be necessary. Thus, I introduced the concept of "follow-up sessions," where after each cluster of plenary meetings, a delegate would coordinate further discussions to refine proposals before recording them in the "yellow table." These follow-up sessions were not intended to make decisions but rather to advance work on specific issues, which would then be submitted for consideration by the plenary.

Regarding transparency, some Members suggested that a report to the DSB should be made every two months to document the ongoing discussions. The concern was that, given the confidentiality of the Informal Process, external stakeholders might perceive that Members were not addressing the MC12 mandate on dispute settlement, which was not the case.

At the time, we had to address the question of how to report to the DSB given procedural technicalities that no one had considered when deciding to start the process without a formal designation of a Facilitator. On one hand, I could not make the statement on behalf of Guatemala, as I was acting as the informal Facilitator in my personal capacity and following standing WTO practice for chairpersons and facilitators. This distinction was crucial for both me and the Guatemalan Government, especially considering the geopolitical climate. Acting in my personal capacity allowed me to engage with delegates from all WTO Members, regardless of my Government's position on specific issues and in other fora. On the other hand, I could not request an agenda item for the DSB meeting as an individual, since I had no formal mandate or designation as a Facilitator. After extensive consultations, we concluded that the DSB Chair at the time, H.E. Ambassador Athaliah Lesiba Molokomme (Botswana), would introduce, on her own initiative, an agenda item for Members to report on any issues related to dispute settlement reform and then she would invite me to take the floor to provide a report, in my personal capacity, to the DSB for consideration and discussion.[16]

The first DSB meeting where I reported on the Informal Dispute Settlement Reform Process took place on 31 March 2023. Several Members praised the process and expressed their optimism about the progress of the discussions. However, others raised concerns about the intense work program and the overlap with other important meetings, which particularly affected smaller delegations.[17] After this crucial first report, the following reports took place organically with the same modality.

I subsequently provided reports to the DSB in May, July, October, and December 2023, as well as in January 2024.[18] At each of these meetings, two distinct groups emerged: those who praised the Informal Process and were satisfied with the "interest-based" and "solution-oriented" methodology and

---

16   WTO, *Minutes of Meeting*, WTO Doc WT/DSB/M/477 (2023) at para 3.1, online (pdf): docsonline.wto.org [perma.cc/YY7Q-YYCD].

17   *Ibid* at paras 3.3 to 3.36.

18   WTO, *Minutes of Meeting*, WTO Doc WT/DSB/M/479 (2023), online (pdf): docsonline.wto.org [perma.cc/GFG6-EWUJ], WTO, *Minutes of Meeting*, WTO Doc WT/DSB/M/482 (2023), online (pdf): docsonline.wto.org [perma.cc/4ZPB-UAPM], WTO, *Minutes of Meeting*, WTO Doc WT/DSB/M/484 (2023), online (pdf): docsonline.wto.org [perma.cc/T8UH-YLL5], WTO, *Minutes of Meeting*, WTO Doc WT/DSB/M/486 (2024), online (pdf): docsonline.wto.org [perma.cc/H9CK-Y98L], and WTO, *Minutes of Meeting*, WTO Doc WT/DSB/M/487 (2024), online (pdf): docsonline.wto.org [perma.cc/54RD-39BM].

those who sought to steer the process towards the traditional "position-based" approach used in other WTO negotiations. I also reported to the General Council in July and October 2023, as well as in February 2024, and to Senior Officials on 23 October 2023.[19]

The minutes of these meetings record the different views and arguments on the methodology or the Informal Process. Throughout 2023, I did everything in my power to reconcile diverging interests and visions, bearing in mind that all Members converged on the urgency to restore the dispute settlement system and that the great majority, including those complaining, was aiming at finalizing the negotiations by MC13.

As time passed, I adjusted the process to enable us to deliver an outcome by MC13 and, simultaneously, to facilitate the participation of small delegations. In consultation with Members, I introduced several changes, including the translation of documents, simultaneous interpretation, holding mostly plenary meetings, coordinating with other negotiating bodies to minimize overlaps, enabling online participation for Geneva-based delegates, organizing transparency meetings, offering on-demand briefings for Geneva and Capital-based delegates, and issuing written reports.

Interestingly, those who had initially opposed formalizing the Informal Process, including any report to the DSB, eventually shifted their stance and strongly advocated for formalization. The debate on formalization was intriguing, as Members had different interpretations of what "formalization" actually entailed. For some, formalization meant access to meetings via an online platform and the remote participation of Capital-based officials. For others, it meant using square brackets, colour coding, attribution of proposals, and other markers typical of traditional "position-based" negotiations. Some were uncertain about the specifics of formalization but supported the idea because likeminded Members believed that it would make the process more transparent and inclusive.

It is important to highlight that all those Members in favour of formalization participated actively and constructively in the Informal Process, ensuring that their views and interests were incorporated into the draft consolidated text that emerged from the discussions. It was also noteworthy that

---

19   WTO, *Minutes of Meeting*, WTO Doc WT/GC/M/205 (2023), online (pdf): docsonline. wto.org [perma.cc/N863-QENB], WTO, *Meeting of Minutes*, WTO Doc WT/GC/M/209 (2024), online (pdf): docsonline.wto.org [perma.cc/7RLR-36QX], and WTO, *Special Meeting of the General Council*, WTO Doc JOB/GC/385 (2024), online (pdf): docsonline. wto.org [perma.cc/W37Z-9CXQ].

delegates' participation was higher in the Informal Process than in the DSB meetings, which are, by their nature, formal.

J. A Defining Moment Before the Summer Break

BY MAY 2023, DELEGATES WERE deeply engaged in refining the concepts and ideas captured in the yellow table. Despite the significant progress, some ambassadors and capital-based officials grew increasingly anxious about the potential outcomes. As is common in WTO negotiations, the idea of an "early harvest" began to circulate, drawing parallels to the Fisheries negotiations where Members agreed on "Fish 1" at MC12, with the promise of finalizing "Fish 2" at MC13.

The notion of an early harvest disrupted the efforts and the planned trajectory of the Informal Dispute Settlement Reform Process. The initial expectation was that after refining the proposals in the yellow table, we would record the agreed-upon solutions in the green table, which would then serve as a basis for drafting legal texts.

However, resistance emerged from several delegations who were hesitant to agree on concepts that addressed their interests and concerns. Through bilateral consultations, I discovered that many were reluctant to move any elements to the green table, fearing that the table would be considered an "early harvest" that could exclude a solution for the appeal/review mechanism and other elements of their interest.

To address these concerns, I suggested that we continue working on the yellow table, refining the solutions as much as possible and incorporating any observations from delegates. The question remained: when and how should we proceed with the drafting exercise?

In a bilateral meeting, one delegate proposed to me a collective evaluation to determine which topics were sufficiently "mature" for drafting, rather than waiting until the end of the discussions to finalize everything for the green table. This was an excellent idea that I decided to test on 21 June in a plenary meeting held in Room CRI, one of the rare occasions where our "home" Room E was unavailable. At the outset of the meeting, I explained the need to start drafting legal texts after the summer break to implement the collective decisions we were working on. I reiterated the understanding that we would not yet work on the green table and emphasized the importance of collectively assessing which elements in the yellow table were ready for drafting.

As we reviewed the topics and subtopics in the yellow table, I provided a substantive summary of the status of each discussion and suggested which elements were mature enough for drafting. After the first suggestion, there was total silence in the room. Following the long-standing WTO practice that silence implies consent, I proceeded with the rest of the elements in the yellow table. Again, silence after each of my proposed evaluations. By the end of the meeting, we had a clearer understanding of which issues were mature and ready for drafting and which were close to that stage. Over the first three weeks in July, we focused all our efforts on closing as many pending issues as possible.

I consider the plenary meeting of 21 June as a defining moment in the Informal Dispute Settlement Reform Process, one that provided direction and created momentum. As a result, I reported to the DSB and the General Council meetings in July 2023 that delegates had reached an understanding on roughly 80 percent of the issues under consideration and that the drafting process would begin right after the summer break, alongside continued discussions to reach agreement on the remaining 20 percent.

K. Time to Start Drafting

IN EARLY SEPTEMBER 2023, WE resumed our conversations with two primary objectives: first, to finalize discussions on pending issues that still required solutions and second, to begin drafting the legal text for the elements that we had already agreed upon in June. We continued to use the interest-based and solution-oriented approach to find solutions for the pending 20 percent, steadily closing one by one.

As for the drafting exercise, I had openly stated at the outset that I would not draft the consolidated legal text. This marked a departure from long-standing WTO practice where Chairs and Facilitators typically assume this responsibility with the assistance of the Secretariat. My goal was to ensure that delegates took ownership of the text and that it accurately reflected the diverse perspectives of the membership. Given our non-attribution approach, drafting the different chapters carried significant responsibility, as drafters had to truthfully reflect the agreements reached and included in the yellow table.

I invited all Members to take part in the drafting process. Delegates were asked to indicate their desired level of participation: either as a drafter, contributor, or as a peer-reviewer. Additionally, those interested in drafting or contributing also had the opportunity to peer-review drafts prepared by others or request consultation on specific topics of interest."

After opening the drafting process, fifty-two delegates, encompassing nearly the entirety of the membership, as some represented regional groups, volunteered to participate. They worked in eleven drafting groups. Organizing a drafting process involving such a large and diverse group posed significant logistical challenges, but it proved immensely beneficial in fostering a truly inclusive and collaborative effort.

For more than two weeks in September 2023, hundreds of emails, supporting documents, and drafts were circulated among dispute settlement delegates. They took ownership and met frequently, in different configurations, to ensure that everyone's views were reflected in the initial draft. Their commitment to the process and the mandate was evident, with everyone working overtime to achieve our goals. I am proud and grateful to each of the fifty-two delegates, their dedication and professionalism were outstanding, and they played a pivotal role in the success of the drafting process. The result was a high-quality, well-advanced consolidated text.

By the time the zero draft was issued, three additional chapters had been added to the consolidated text. This draft was translated into French and Spanish. I also requested the assistance of the Secretariat for an editorial revision to ensure consistency across all chapters. Subsequently, the consolidated text underwent seven iterations, each diligently reviewed and refined by delegates. At some of the iterations, additional chapters were added and reviewed. The draft text was not the result of improvisation; it required long hours of meticulous work until we arrived at the seventh and final version of the consolidated draft text, before we made it public on 14 February 2024.[20] This draft text addressed almost the totality of the issues identified by Members, leaving only three issues pending: appeal/review mechanism, transitional provisions, and a final review for consistency.

L. The "Elephant in the Room"

WTO DELEGATES REGULARLY REFERRED TO the issue of the appeal/review mechanism as the "elephant in the room," recognizing it as one of the most

---

20   WTO, *Meeting of Minutes*, WTO Doc WT/GC/M/209 (2024) at para 1.174, online (pdf): docsonline.wto.org [perma.cc/7RLR-36QX].

sensitive and complex aspects of the Informal Dispute Settlement Reform Process. I constantly reminded delegates that this topic was, in principle, no different from others. By applying the same interest-based methodology and negotiating principles, we could find a practical solution to the question of appeal/review. However, it took several months to build the necessary trust among delegates to engage in meaningful conversations on this topic.

In the red, and later, in the yellow tables, two initial approaches to the appeal/review mechanism emerged. Both included access to an appeal/review mechanism, but one approach was nearly impossible to implement due to stringent conditions, such as requiring agreement between disputing parties. Delegates viewed these two approaches as fundamentally opposed: one aiming to preserve an appeal/review mechanism, and the other effectively eliminating it.

Before the summer break, I cautioned delegates that the discussion on appeal/review would be time-consuming and require significant creativity and energy. I suggested moving away from the binary choice between the existing options in the yellow table, which were either having an Appellate Body or not, and focusing on the underlying interests and concerns to identify common ground and explore new ideas that could bridge differences.

Several Members indicated that they were not ready to engage in discussions on appeal, preferring to take a strategic approach of waiting for progress on other issues before deciding if there was a realistic prospect of success for an appeal/review mechanism. I met with delegates, Ambassadors, and Senior Officials from these Members, urging them to engage in interest-based conversations sooner rather than later. I warned them of the risks of delaying the discussion until the end or close to MC13, as well as the potential mistake of resorting to position-based negotiations at the last minute, attempting to restore the Appellate Body in exchange for the remaining elements in the consolidated text.

It was only by late November 2023 that Members agreed to begin interest-based conversations on appeal. In my view, this was already too late, and subsequent events confirmed my concerns. We intensified discussions on appeal, exploring novel concepts aimed at reducing the number of appeals and limiting their scope to what was strictly necessary to resolve disputes.

Given the multidimensional nature of the negotiations, delegates needed time to reflect on ideas, conduct their research, and consult with domestic stakeholders before returning with feedback for further discussions. From the time we started these conversations until the end-of-year break, we had three weeks of intense consultations. We resumed in early January 2024, with another three weeks of discussions before starting preparations for MC13.

By early February, it became clear to me that we would not complete the conversation on appeal in time. While the conversations proved to be useful, we were still exploring and testing innovative ideas that would require time to mature. Therefore, I felt it was crucial to wrap up discussions on the consolidated draft text and prepare the necessary reports for the General Council and MC13, to continue the interest-based negotiations informally after MC13.

Furthermore, given the pressure from some Members to formalize the process as soon as possible, a compromise solution began to take shape in corridors: continue the Informal Process for another two to three months after MC13, with a deadline for formalizing the process later on. As mentioned earlier, "formalization" meant different things to different Members. In view of this potential compromise solution, it was important to wrap-up work and prepare for a post-MC13 conversation.

M. The Race Before MC13

WE CONTINUED TO MEET UNTIL 9 February 2024 and strived to refine the consolidated draft text as much as possible. Delegates knew that I had been requested to report to the General Council at its special meeting scheduled for 14 February. The expectation was for me to report on our progress and to make the seventh iteration of the consolidated draft text publicly available.

I recall that some Members were uncomfortable with the idea of making the text public at the General Council meeting but would not object to it; and others were interested in that publicity with a view to consolidating progress. At that point in time, it was clear that we would not finish the conversations under the Informal Process in time for MC13. Some Members continued to push for formalization, and rumors were circulating that the intention was to revert to position-based negotiations once the process was formalized. In this context, there was growing interest from numerous Members in having Ministers acknowledge the work done so far in the Informal Process. After all, the draft consolidated text was the result of collective conversations and the hard work of all WTO Members, including those advocating for formalization and a restart of the discussions.

There was also uncertainty about how to transition the work from the Informal Process into a formal setting. Ministers could not be expected to acknowledge the results if they did not have access to the text. As I had not been formally designated Facilitator, I could not directly forward anything to WTO Chairs, the Chair of the Trade Negotiations Committee, or Ministers. The DSB Chair could not send anything to Ministers, as he had not overseen the process. It was also clear that Ministers would not adopt the consolidated draft text, especially considering that Members had not agreed to an early harvest.

After several consultations and brainstorming sessions, we concluded that the best way to inform Ministers about the results of the Informal Process was to make a report to the General Council and attach the draft consolidated text to it. The resulting choreography included a report by the DSB Chair, who then invited me to report on the Informal Process. Both reports, along with the consolidated text, were circulated to all WTO Members in a JOB series document.[21] This would allow Ministers to refer to a WTO document at MC13, if necessary.

N. The Day the Text Was Revealed to the Public

THE SPECIAL MEETING OF THE General Council took place on 14 February 2024, an important date to remember. I had the honour to make my report to Heads of Delegations on the Informal Dispute Settlement Reform Process and reveal the draft consolidated text to the public. At that meeting, I was devoting my energy to consolidating the progress we had achieved and laying the groundwork to continue our conversations after MC13.[22]

I was also aware that some Members' were going to argue that the draft consolidated text did not reflect their positions and was therefore unacceptable to them. The reality is that the draft consolidated text does not reflect any single Member's position, rather, it is the product of reconciling the diverse interests and concerns articulated by Members, striving for the most optimal outcome through careful calibration.

The key question was not whether the text reflected specific positions, but whether it addressed the interests and concerns expressed by Members during the Informal Process. The rationale behind interest-based negotiations is that various goals can be achieved through different means, with any given position representing just one possible approach, not necessarily the only one.

---

21 WTO, *Meeting of Minutes*, WTO Doc JOB/GC/385 (2024), online (pdf): docsonline.wto. org [perma.cc/ W37Z-9CXQ].

22 See WTO, *Meeting of* Minutes, WTO Doc WT/GC/M/209 paras 1.168 and 1.169 (2024), online (pdf): docsonline.wto.org [perma.cc/7RLR-36QX].

Those Members who claimed that the text did not represent their position failed to demonstrate which of their articulated interests or concerns were not addressed, and they did not propose any alternative solutions that would maintain the delicate balance of interests among all Members.

For those outside the Informal Dispute Settlement Reform Process, the claim that the text did not consider Members' positions could seem more compelling than the fact that it addressed all interests and concerns, offering the best compromise solution available. Therefore, I felt it was necessary to clarify the nature of the interest-based approach and provide an example to contextualize the draft consolidated text. It was important, at least from my perspective, to counterbalance such narratives with facts.

Additionally, I needed to emphasize that the draft consolidated text was not something I had prepared on my own. It was, indeed, the result of collective efforts by Members, with delegates, representing the totality of the WTO Membership, actively contributing to its drafting and all changes being discussed in plenary sessions. My plan, therefore, was to inform WTO Members and all stakeholders, that against all expectations and in less than a year, we managed to produce a consolidated draft text covering almost all the issues identified by Members, presented in a way that optimally balanced their interests and concerns. I also had another ambition: to demonstrate that the interest-based approach could work in a complex, multilateral negotiation and, perhaps, replicate this methodology in other negotiations, revitalizing the WTO's negotiating function.

In this regard, I reported to the General Council that, since 17 February 2023, I had convened more than 350 meetings, including 110 plenary sessions open to all WTO Members, as well as numerous small-group and more than forty-five in-person and virtual meetings with Capital- and Geneva-based Officials, on top of spontaneous conversations. Additionally, numerous meetings took place among delegations to discuss specific topics. Over 145 Members, representing all regions, legal systems, and stages of development, had participated in the meetings. The seventh revision of the draft consolidated text, spanning more than fifty pages, reflected Members' collective understandings and expectations regarding the operation of the WTO dispute settlement system, and was organized into eleven titles; and while currently proposed as a Ministerial Decision, the final form would be decided by Members based on the document's substantive content.

Further, I illustrated the interest-based approach with an analogy, where two persons want to buy a pumpkin, and there is only one left in the shop. I explained that in a position-based negotiation, one person would end up taking the pumpkin home, and the other would return empty-handed. Another outcome of a position-based negotiation could be a sub-optimal compromise where both interested parties would split the pumpkin. In contrast, in an interest-based negotiation, by understanding their interests (for example, one person may be interested in using the pumpkin for decoration, while the other wants it for soup), they can agree to split the price of the pumpkin and then divide it according to their interests. The result is that both parties are satisfied, and the pumpkin is optimally used. This works. It is not only me saying it. Interest-based negotiations are highly recommended by top think tanks and universities, as one of the ways to achieve the best possible results.

O. The End of my Journey as the Facilitator of the Informal Process

I NEVER IMAGINED THAT THE General Council meeting of 14 February 2024 would mark my final report at the WTO.

After delivering my report to the General Council, I began receiving messages of congratulations and encouragement from Members, academics, and representatives of civil society and the private sector. I also received very positive feedback about the substantive content of the text and the process in general. The optimism was high, despite having missed the opportunity to adopt a package on Dispute Settlement Reform at MC13. Members realized that the culmination of the negotiations were within reach, and I was expected to continue participating in the post-MC13 conversations.

Furthermore, while we ran out of time and could not finalize the discussions before MC13, the draft consolidated text was already seen as a significant milestone. At the beginning of the process, no one expected this negotiation to succeed. Members feared that it would become another endless negotiation where they simply repeated their well-known and irreconcilable positions. One year later, we were very close to delivering a package of meaningful reforms to the dispute settlement system. Our collective achievement was remarkable and, in my view, a reason for celebration. We defied expectations and delivered a tangible result that few had anticipated.

Ironically, the success and attention garnered by the Informal Process and the draft consolidated text might have played a role in my dismissal from the Permanent Mission of Guatemala to the WTO. On 15 February 2024, one day after the special General Council meeting where the draft consolidated text was made public, the newly appointed Minister of Economy of Guatemala, Honourable Ms. Gabriela García Pacheco, signed my removal order. On 20 February, the Ambassador of Guatemala, H.E. Ambassador Eduardo Sperisen-Yurt, notified me of that order and instructed me to immediately vacate my office.

The Guatemalan Ministry of Economy has, so far, not provided any explanation, merely citing a vague need to "improve the administrative efficiency" of the Mission.[23] The news of my sudden dismissal spread fast through the WTO community and international media.[24]

I was not surprised about my removal as much as I was about the timing. I knew that it was coming as there had been a previous attempt to dismiss me shortly after the start of the Informal Process. At least, one of that I am aware of. In late February 2023, the Vice-Minister of Economy informed me that the Minister had received a letter from the Ambassador requesting my immediate dismissal for reasons not clearly stated. She assured me that the (then) government administration would not take any action against me. I cannot confirm whether my sudden dismissal by the new government was a continuation of that earlier attempt, but the coincidence is difficult to ignore.

Nevertheless, I am deeply grateful to the government of Guatemala for the opportunity to make tangible contributions to our country and successfully represent its trade interests in numerous significant negotiations and

23   See Guatemala, "Destituyen A Secretario General OMC De Guatemala" (22 February 2024) online: rrppguatenala.com [perma.cc/9WDX-6EWD].

24   See Farah Stockman, "Finally, Some Good News at the W.T.O." *The New York* (29 February 2024); Doug Palmer, "Guatemala Fires Key Official in Charge of WTO Eeform Talks" *POLITICO* (21 February 2024); Hannah Monicken, "Facilitator of WTO Dispute Settlement Reform Talks Abruptly Let Go" *Inside U.S Trade's World Trade* (21 February 2024) online: insidetrade.com [perma.cc/P8JA-AR8J]; Emma Farge, "WTO Hits Road Block Over Advancing Dispute Reform Talks" *SWI swissinfo.ch* (21 March 2024) online: swissinfo.ch [perma.cc/6UWU-FQ5V]; David Dodwell, "Inside Out | Trade Reforms Swept Under the Carpet as WTO Meeting Achieves Little" *South China Morning Post* (10 March 2024) online: scmp.com [perma.cc/NME3-M7SX]; Dr Ngozi Okonjo-Oweala, "MC13 Closing Speech" (delivered at the Thirteenth WTO Ministerial Conference, 1 March 2024) online: wto.org [perma.cc/4ZU8-JBNA].

disputes at the WTO, as well as at regional and bilateral levels, during my twenty years of service at the Permanent Mission. I have no regrets about my role as the informal Facilitator of the Dispute Settlement Reform Process, considering the honour it brought to Guatemala, the Permanent Mission, and myself in contributing to the Multilateral Trading System. My only disappointment is not having had the chance to complete what I confidently asserted from the first day of the Informal Process: that restoring a fully functional and accessible dispute settlement system by 2024 was indeed possible, and that the interest-based approach does work.

P. Final Reflections

WHILE DRAFTING THIS CHAPTER, I have had the opportunity to reflect on the Informal Dispute Settlement Reform Process and the lessons we learned.

The literature is full of commentary about the relevance of the WTO in the face of its various existential crises, such as the dysfunction of the dispute settlement system and the increasingly challenging negotiating pillar, where successful outcomes are often seen as "miracles."

In my view, the WTO is more relevant today than ever as the world grapples with significant global challenges and we all need to build a resilient system. The negotiating pillar is crucial for finding solutions to resolve issues that are increasingly multi-disciplinary and multi-dimensional. Successful negotiations should not be seen as miracles but as the natural result of cooperative conversations among interested parties. In these conversations, participants need to clearly articulate their objectives, interests, and concerns, and work collectively to find practical solutions.

Let me be clear: negotiations are not easy. There are often competing interests and opposing views. However, any potential agreement must be better than the *status quo*, where no one benefits.

Also, multilateral negotiations are processes undertaken and supported by human beings. While the institutional frameworks are essential, my experience shows that being genuinely interested in understanding interests and concerns goes a long way, further than digging in our heels defending a position.

The interest-based approach is a methodology designed to help negotiating parties understand their underlying interests and concerns that allow for creative and innovative solutions. It is not a magic solution or the solution to all negotiations. The goal is to reach an outcome that is optimal or realize when a negotiated agreement is not convenient for the parties involved.

Contrary to what some Members might believe, this approach does not weaken their position; rather, it enhances their participation, inclusivity, and leverage in any given negotiation. The objective is to collectively reconcile all interests and concerns through innovative approaches, as opposed to a position-based negotiation where parties compete rather than collaborate and those situated in a weaker position have less chance of being taken into consideration in any potential outcome. After all, in a position-based framework, the goal is often to undermine others' positions while defending one's own, leading to a painful exchange of concessions based on power dynamics.

Regarding the role of the Facilitator or Chairperson in negotiations, I have learned that a proactive approach can make all the difference. While some are wary of facilitators or chairpersons taking an active role due to the "Members-driven process" concept, I believe that those who are leading negotiations should do more than merely convene meetings, give the floor, and summarize discussions or propose negotiating legal texts. Facilitators or chairs have the opportunity to ask the right questions, engage the right Members, and stimulate open discussions to find solutions that accommodate all interests and concerns. This requires substantive knowledge of and practical experience on the subject matter.

Additionally, the role of negotiators is crucial. They must take a proactive stance, often advocating for optimal solutions with their stakeholders. Much of the success of the Informal Dispute Settlement Reform Process can be attributed to the invaluable contributions and active engagement of delegates experts in dispute settlement. These delegates put in countless extra hours and were, by far, the most effective interlocutors with capital officials and other stakeholders. I was fortunate to work with such admirable professionals. As I often emphasize, this was a truly collective effort, with its success entirely dependent on the active participation of every delegate expert in dispute settlement.

Moreover, and even though it might sound unorthodox to some, I am convinced that a text drafted by delegates themselves, rather than by a facilitator or chairperson, is the best approach to secure ownership and increase the chances of success. To achieve this, Members should begin drafting legal texts only after agreeing on the solutions, their terms, and conditions. This departs from the traditional approach at the WTO where proposed legal texts are tabled first with multiple brackets and attributions, color coding, and other markers typical of position-based negotiations, leading to the difficult task of reconciling them or the facilitator or chairperson aimed at drafting and presenting a balanced negotiating text. In this traditional scenario, the focus shifts to reconciling *drafts* rather than addressing the underlying *interests* and *concerns*, which are often neglected.

As I close, Valerie's wise words resonate in my mind: "say what you mean and mean what you say." If there is any hope for the WTO Members to steer the negotiating ship through turbulent waters and address current global challenges, we should all seriously consider alternative negotiating approaches, such as the interest-based model. I mean what I am saying. I am open to discussing further these views.

Part III:

Renewal—The Rulemaking Dimension

CHAPTER 29

An Immediate Role for the WTO in Fighting the Climate Crisis?

Jennifer Hillman[*]

A. A Modest Tribute to Valerie Hughes

VALERIE HUGHES RICHLY DESERVES TO be celebrated for all she has contributed to the development of trade law, to the international trade commun
ity—particularly its women—and to the World Trade Organization (WTO).
Her impact has been felt both during her tenure within the organization,
where she served as the Director of the Appellate Body Secretariat and the
Legal Affairs Division, and externally though her roles as a frequent speaker,
writer, teacher, colleague, and mentor to all those working to understand the
WTO and its contribution to our rules-based trading system.

This chapter—focused on what the WTO can do now in the fight against
climate change—is my small attempt to honour two of Valerie's most enduring messages to me and to the world. First is her positive can-do attitude,
which seeks to find solutions through practical approaches to problem-solving,
along with her understanding that timing is often everything and that certain

* The author is a Professor from Practice and the co-director of the Center on Inclusive
Trade and Development at the Georgetown University Law Center in Washington,
DC. From December 2007 through February 2012, she served as a member of the
WTO's Appellate Body. The author is grateful to Mario Osorio and Elizabeth Butscher
at Georgetown Law and to the participants at the Geneva book workshop for their
insightful comments on this Chapter.

issues require urgent action. I can think of no issue that is more urgent than the climate crisis or one that would better fit within Valerie's roll-up-your-sleeves-and-get-the-job-done approach. Second, Valerie always exuded an abiding faith in the work of the WTO Secretariat and in the professionalism and capability of those working around her. She taught and mentored so many to understand why doing first-rate work was so essential without ever becoming arrogant, either as individuals or in understanding the proper role and limits of the Secretariat. Hence, this chapter's focus on steps the WTO Secretariat can take to combat climate change falls squarely within that notion of unleashing the talent and creativity of those that make up the often-unheralded professionals that do the work to implement the mission of the WTO.

B. Introduction

FOR DECADES, THE WORLD WITNESSED explosive growth in the volume of international trade, driven by technological advances that have dramatically reduced transportation and communication costs, the development of far-flung supply chains, and the opening of new markets to trade and investment. Alongside that enormous expansion has been a parallel increase in the emission and accumulation of greenhouse gases (GHGs) that drive climate change and an increase in global and ocean temperatures, with 2023 becoming the hottest year on record and each month of 2024 surpassing the temperatures of the previous year. For many, these two trends have always been linked, with international trade's rise contributing significantly to climate change. As the former United States Special Presidential Envoy for Climate, John Podesta, put it: "Our current global trading system was built to promote open and competitive markets—which it has done well—but it wasn't built to curb emissions."[1] Recently, however, many in the international trade and climate change communities have begun examining the flip-side of that coin—the ability for trade and trade policy to help solve the climate crisis—as it has become clear that the world will not be able to achieve the speed and scale of decarbonization necessary unless climate mitigation and adaptation efforts are joined with trade policy.

Because climate change is a global phenomenon, addressing it effectively requires coordinated actions from all large emitters and by all those importing

---

1   John Podesta, Address (delivered at the Columbia Global Energy Summit, 16 April 2024) [unpublished] online: whitehouse.gov [perma.cc/98GQ-U939].

goods with significant embodied emissions. Historically, industrialized nations have been the largest contributors to GHGs, while developing and least-developed countries have played a much smaller role. Despite this, developing and least-developed countries are disproportionately affected by climate change and often lack the resources to invest in the technologies and infrastructure needed for adaptation and mitigation. Accordingly, any coordinated solutions require an equitable approach that ensures that developing countries are not only participants but also beneficiaries of global efforts to combat climate change.

To the extent that solutions involve trade policies, they need to be implemented in the context of the WTO and its rules-based system, lest climate-related trade policies result in trade conflicts. This gives the WTO, its Members, and its staff the opportunity to demonstrate the indispensable role that trade must play in climate change mitigation and adaptation and to shape the rules and policies that will allow that to happen with minimum trade friction. If the WTO can achieve this, its involvement in the efforts to fight against the climate crisis may lead to a revitalization of the organization, as the title of this book suggests. A WTO that is making a significant contribution to slowing GHG emissions while helping all countries adapt to extreme heat, drought, severe weather, food shortages, and climate migration is an institution worth investing in and restoring.

Additionally, while this chapter focuses on efforts at the WTO, the importance of coordination with other international organizations cannot be overstated. Collaboration with the World Customs Organization (WCO) concerning border adjustments and the potential of using tariff lines and nomenclature to differentiate the GHG intensity of traded goods; the Organisation for Economic Co-operation and Development (OECD) on ways to catalogue both green and harmful subsidies; and the World Bank and the International Monetary Fund with a view to providing developing countries with the necessary funding and resources to transition to sustainable practices is key to effectively combating climate change. The WTO already has a track record of working with these and other international organizations and is well-positioned to assist in such collaborative efforts.

C. WTO Engagement in the Climate Crises

THE RECOGNITION AMONG WTO MEMBERS and the WTO Secretariat of the need to engage in both the substance and the process of ensuring that trade and climate policies work in harmony can be seen on multiple fronts. In the fall of 2022, the WTO released its annual World Trade Report, which is always focused on an issue of great concern or on which the WTO wants to shine a spotlight. In 2022, the spotlight was on climate change. The report, *Climate Change and International Trade*,[2] underscored the economic underpinnings of the relationship between climate change and international trade. It conveyed four key messages: 1) that climate change is reshaping countries' economic and trade prospects and is a major threat to future growth and prosperity; 2) that while climate shocks will remain costly and disruptive, trade can help countries better prepare and respond, through access to technologies and critical goods and services; 3) that trade can reduce the cost of mitigation and speed up the low-carbon transition while creating green jobs; and 4) that international trade cooperation can make climate actions more effective and the low-carbon transition more just if trade frictions are minimized.

These messages stemmed from years of work at the intersection of trade and environmental policy, including at the WTO's Committee on Trade and the Environment (CTE). From its inception, the CTE has been focused on breathing life into the *Marrakesh Agreement Establishing the World Trade Organization* (WTO Agreement)'s Preamble which notes that trade is to be conducted with a view to "expanding the production of and trade in goods and services, while allowing for the optimal use of the world's resources in accordance with the objective of sustainable development, seeking both to protect and preserve the environment and to enhance the means for doing so in a manner consistent with their respective needs and concerns at different levels of economic development."[3] The CTE has often done so in conjunction with other environmental organizations, including by inviting participation from representatives of the United Nations Framework Convention on Climate Change (UNFCCC).

More recently, a more focused initiative was established in 2021: the Trade and Environmental Sustainability Structured Discussions (TESSD). This effort began with fifty countries organizing "structured discussions" among interested WTO Members and external stakeholders.[4] Since then, TESSD has met eighteen times in either informal working groups (on trade-related climate measures, environmental goods and services, circular economy, and

---

2   WTO, *World Trade Report 2022: Climate Change and International Trade* (Geneva: World Trade Organization, 2022), online (pdf): wto.org [perma.cc/XX48-5VJB].

3   WTO, *Marrakesh Agreement Establishing the World Trade Organization* (15 April 1994), preamble at para 1, online (pdf): wto.org [perma.cc/W2Q7-H4YV].

4   WTO, *Ministerial Statement on Trade and Environmental Sustainability*, WTO Doc WT/MIN(21)/6/Rev.2 (2021), online (pdf): docs.wto.org [perma.cc/M7AR-DAW4].

subsidies) or plenary sessions, with seventy-six WTO Members taking part in some or all sessions. At the 13th Ministerial Conference in February and March 2024, the TESSD participants issued an updated work plan and four documents outlining best practices in implementing trade-related climate measures, promoting renewable energy goods and services, supporting a circular economy, and designing subsidies that benefit the environment without unduly distorting trade.[5]

Parallel dialogues have been intensifying on a number of climate-related WTO fronts including the Fossil Fuel Subsidy Reform (FFSR) initiative that seeks to rationalize and phase out inefficient fossil fuel subsidies that encourage wasteful consumption and the Dialogue on Plastics Pollution and Environmentally Sustainable Plastics Trade, designed to explore ways the WTO can contribute to efforts to reduce plastics pollution, including through circular economy, and promote the transition to more environmentally sustainable trade in plastics. The world's trade ministers have similarly begun their own set of dialogues, with the creation in 2022 of the Coalition of Trade Ministers on Climate, led by the trade ministers from Ecuador, the European Union (EU), Kenya, and New Zealand.[6] The Coalition is focused on identifying ways to ensure the multilateral trading system contributes to the global response to climate change, including specific ways to promote trade and investment that foster the diffusion, development, accessibility,

---

5   WTO, *Member Practices in the Development of Trade-Related Climate Measures (TrCMs)*, WTO Doc WT/MIN(24)/11/Add.2 (2024), online (pdf): docs.wto.org [perma. cc/96UQ-4D6S]; WTO, *Analytical Summary on Environmental Goods and Services and Renewable Energy*, WTO Doc WT/MIN(24)/11/Add.3 (2024), online (pdf): docs.wto. org [perma.cc/3UGQ-6FGD]; WTO, *Mapping of Trade Aspects of Circular Economy Along the Product Lifecycle*, WTO Doc WT/MIN(24)/11/Add.4 (2024), online (pdf): docs.wto.org [perma.cc/8H6U-NMFA]; WTO, *Compilation of Experiences and Considerations Regarding Subsidy Design*, WTO Doc WT/MIN(24)/11/Add.5 (2024), online (pdf): docs.wto.org [perma.cc/3HBT-HAGT].

6   The Coalition of Trade Ministers on Climate includes the ministers from Angola; Antigua & Barbuda; Australia; Austria; Belgium; Barbados; Bulgaria; Cabo Verde; Cameroon; Canada; Colombia; Costa Rica; Croatia; Cyprus; Czechia; Denmark; Ecuador; Estonia; European Union; Fiji; Finland; France; The Gambia; Germany; Greece; Hungary; Iceland; Ireland; Italy; Japan; Kenya; Republic of Korea; Latvia; Lithuania; Luxembourg; Malta; Maldives; Kingdom of Morocco; Mozambique; Netherlands; New Zealand; Norway; Papua New Guinea; Philippines; Poland; Portugal; Romania; Rwanda; Saint Vincent and the Grenadines; Singapore; Slovakia; Slovenia; Spain; Sweden; Switzerland; Ukraine; United Kingdom; United States of America; Uruguay; Vanuatu; and Zambia. Coalition of Trade Ministers on Climate, "Members" (2024), online: tradeministersonclimate.org [perma.cc/DLD9-GFA7].

and uptake of goods, services, and technologies that support climate mitigation and adaptation in both developed and developing countries.

These initiatives have been supported, to varying degrees, by the WTO Secretariat's Environmental Database (EDB), which catalogues and makes available information on all environment-related notifications submitted by WTO Members as well as environmental measures and policies mentioned in the Trade Policy Reviews of WTO Members.[7] As of 1 June 2024, the database included 8,661 environment-related notifications and 12,274 Trade Policy Review entries.

The high level of WTO engagement in linking trade and the environment and the fight against the climate crisis was on full display at the meeting of the 28th Conference of Parties (COP28) of the UNFCCC. For the first time the meeting included a "Trade Day" during which WTO Director-General Ngozi Okonjo-Iweala led a number of meetings. Key among them was a global leaders meeting to promote "a just and ambitious global response to climate change" and the release of a WTO publication outlining specific trade policies—ranging from trade facilitation, government procurement, tariffs, to carbon taxes and more—that governments could include as part of their strategy for climate mitigation and adaption.[8]

D. Climate Actions Within the Current Rules (and Sometimes Beyond?)

AS ALL OF THIS ACTIVITY indicates, the WTO, its Members, and particularly its Director-General, recognize the crucial role that trade must play in fighting the climate crisis. Work is needed to address the concern that global trade is a major contributor to the climate problem, to ensure that measures taken by WTO Members do not create unnecessary trade frictions and to ensure that developing and least-developed countries are aided in the adoption of green technologies and not unduly burdened by compliance with trade-related climate measures. Indeed, the concern that trade is exacerbating the climate crisis is felt strongly enough in the United States that the Biden Administration created a White House Climate and Trade Task Force, driven in part by the

---

7   WTO, "Environmental Database" (2024), online: edb.wto.org [perma.cc/Y4FD-AB5P].
8   WTO, "WTO Secretariat at Climate Change COP28" (2023), online: wto.org [perma. cc/2PN4-RXBH]; WTO, *Trade Policy Tools for Climate Action* (Geneva: World Trade Organization, 2023), online: wto.org [perma.cc/7CSJ-VX9S].

fact that the emissions embodied inside tradeable goods account for about 25 percent of all global emissions. In announcing the establishing of this Task Force, United States Special Envoy for Climate John Podesta highlighted some of the key tensions between trade and climate policies:

> Right now, our existing trade policies and the international rules that govern them don't pay enough attention to the emissions embodied in tradeable goods.
>
> We don't have uniform standards or consistent, reliable data about embodied emissions.
>
> Global trading rules incentivize carbon leakage—when manufacturing-related emissions from a country with stronger climate policies shift to a country with weaker policies.
>
> There is no penalty for what I like to call carbon dumping—when high emissions in production are exported back into countries with stronger climate policies.[9]

Much of the work that the WTO has been doing in the climate arena is seeking to address those concerns. It is, therefore, no surprise that Podesta's vision for a "smart" twenty-first century climate and trade policy that "slashes pollution, creates a fair and level playing field, protects against carbon dumping, supports good manufacturing jobs and economic opportunity, and rewards every country that's doing the right thing,"[10] resonates with many WTO Members.

The good news for the WTO and for the climate is that much of the groundwork for progress has been laid, with possibilities for action in a number of categories. First are actions that Members can take unilaterally but ones which would work better if coordinated or done with WTO Secretariat support. Second are actions that the WTO Secretariat might take on its own but that would be more effective if adopted or expressly supported by WTO Members. Third are actions that could be taken under existing rules or mechanisms but only if something closer to consensus among Members could be achieved. And last are those actions that would likely require the negotiation of new rules or amendments to existing rules, which may take more time.

In the spirit of Valerie Hughes and her "let's just get the job done" attitude, this chapter sets forth a few actions that fall into each of these categories,

---

9   Podesta, above note 1.
10   *Ibid.*

understanding that this is far from a comprehensive list and that there is much more that can and must be done both within the trade realm and in the trade-related arenas of climate finance, technology transfers, human capital development, and labour if we are to arrive at that ideal "smart," twenty-first century approach to climate and trade policy.

1) Climate Actions Members Could Take Unilaterally but Better with Secretariat Support

a) Tariff Differentials Between Low- and High-GHG Embodied Goods

To effectively combat climate change, countries need to phase out goods with high GHG emissions by discouraging their importation through customs duties. While most developed countries cannot raise their tariffs on high GHG goods because they have bound their tariffs at the same level as their applied tariffs, most developing countries have higher bound tariff levels and lower applied tariffs—also known as "binding overhang" or "tariff water."[11] See Figure 1.

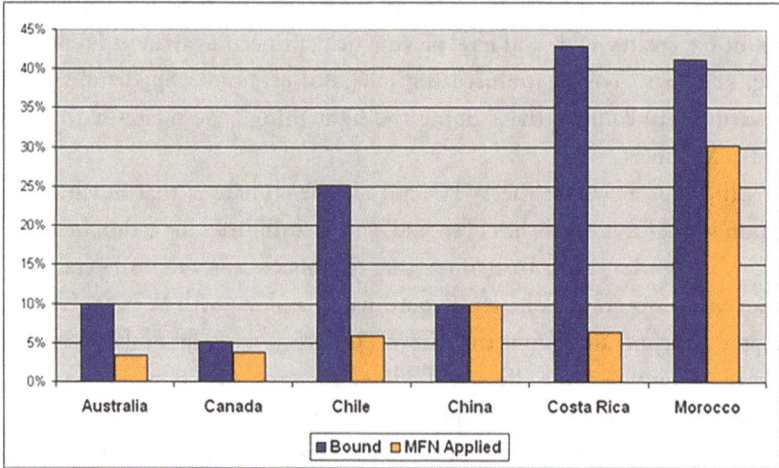

FIGURE 1. BOUND AND MFN APPLIED SIMPLE AVERAGE TARIFF FOR ALL PRODUCTS

SOURCE: WORLD BANK, "TYPES OF TARIFFS" (2010), ONLINE: WITS.WORLDBANK.ORG [PERMA.CC/ B5YP-PULS].

---

11   World Bank, "Types of Tariffs" (2010), online: wits.worldbank.org [perma.cc/ B5YP-PULS].

This provides an opportunity for these countries to create tariff differentials, imposing separate tariffs at higher applied rates for those goods with higher levels of embodied GHGs without exceeding bound rates. Such differentials could create strong incentives for exporting producers to lower their GHG levels while generating additional revenue in developing countries, revenue which could be used for climate mitigation or adaptation actions.

The beauty of this approach is that, if done through an objective tariff breakout within the discretion permitted to Members to determine their own tariff schedule, there should be no question of its WTO consistency, so long as countries choosing to raise their applied rates provided appropriate notice and transparency. The following example uses the default values established by the EU as part of its Carbon Border Adjustment Mechanism (CBAM) to distinguish high GHG cement that would be subject to a higher tariff. The use of objective, transparent criteria and the possibility of creating tiers of tariff levels correlated to GHG emissions would help address concerns that differential tariffs violate the WTO's most-favoured-nation rule that requires that "like" products from all WTO Members be subjected to the same tariff as products from other WTO Members. The use of such differential tariffs would be further aided by the adoption of a definitive interpretation regarding distinctions based on production processes (PPMs) discussed below. See Figure 2.

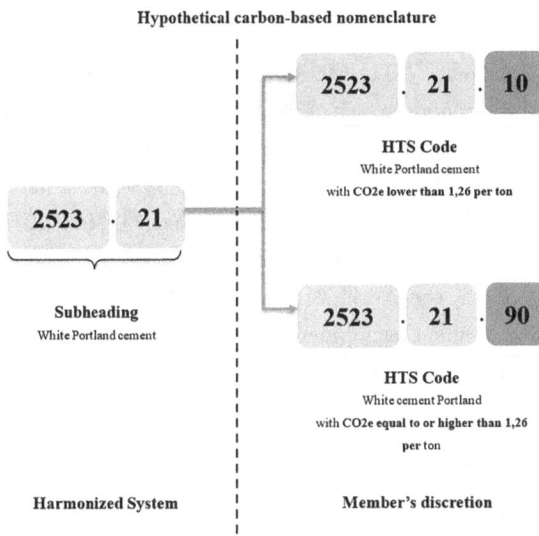

Hypothetical carbon-based nomenclature

2523 . 21 . 10

HTS Code
White Portland cement
with CO2e lower than 1,26 per ton

2523 . 21

Subheading
White Portland cement

2523 . 21 . 90

HTS Code
White cement Portland
with CO2e equal to or higher than 1,26
per ton

Harmonized System

Member's discretion

FIGURE CREATED BY ANA VIERIA SANCHES AT PART OF THE TRADE TOOLS FOR CLIMATE ACTION PROJECT AT THE CITD AND IS BASED ON THE HARMONIZED TARIFF SCHEDULE CLASSIFICATION FOR WHITE PORTLAND CEMENT AND THE EU'S DEFAULT VALUES FOR CEMENT IN ITS CBAM REGULATIONS

Coordinating this approach not only through the WTO, but also the WCO, can help develop common nomenclature for GHG-delineated goods, enhancing its effectiveness and ensuring consistency with international rules and existing practices. Coordination would also help ensure that enough countries adopted similar approaches to deter "export shuffling" whereby exporters send their high-GHG goods to markets without differential tariffs and their lower GHG goods to markets with differentiated tariffs. Adoption by a critical mass of importing countries would leave exporters of dirty goods with limited markets for their goods.

Coordination through the WTO might also help identify those places in which one of the major downsides of such an approach—the protection of high-GHG emitting domestic industries—is likely to occur. If a country has its own domestic industry producing similar goods to those potentially subject to increased tariffs, it will be important to understand whether those domestic goods are themselves relatively green, in which case the tariffs should, on balance, make a positive contribution to fighting climate change. But if the domestically-made goods are themselves "dirty," then the tariffs may prop up dirty domestic producers, even if they also allow for competition from "green" imports.

b) Common or Interoperable Methodologies for Measuring GHGs in Traded Goods

Another area in which WTO Members are free to go their own way is in establishing the methodology by which to measure the amount of GHGs embodied in a given good. While overall GHG emissions have been reported on a nationwide basis for decades under the Intergovernmental Panel on Climate Change (IPCC) guidelines for reporting to the UNFCCC,[12] and corporate-wide emissions are typically reported on the basis of the Greenhouse Gas Protocol developed by the World Resources Institute and the World Business Council for Sustainable Development,[13] there is no international standard for measuring the amount of GHGs in a single traded good.

---

12 IPCC, *2019 Refinement to the 2006 IPCC Guidelines for National Greenhouse Gas Inventories* (Geneva: Intergovernmental Panel on Climate Change, 2019), online: ipcc.ch [perma.cc/LN8Q-K5SL].

13 Greenhouse Gas Protocol, "About Us" (last visited 4 February 2025), online: ghg-protocol.org [perma.cc/NU9X-64J6].

Yet, with the growing number of trade-related climate measures being imposed, ranging from the EU's CBAM,[14] to numerous "Buy Green" government procurement policies, to corporate social responsibility disclosure requirements that include full supply chain tracing of GHG emissions, it is clear that producers, importers, and exporters are under increasing pressure to determine the amount of GHGs in the goods that they are trading. The absence of any international standards complicates trade and creates the potential for measures geared more toward the protection of domestic producers than toward the environment, while potentially creating substantial compliance burdens for developing country exporters.

While WTO Members are within their rights to determine their own methodologies, subject as always to the notice, transparency, and non-discrimination requirements of the *Technical Barriers to Trade (TBT) Agreement*, it would be far preferable if GHG accounting systems were coordinated through the WTO. Already the WTO has done considerable work in bringing together steel producers from around the world to develop Steel Standards Principles for common emissions measurement methodologies.[15] The WTO Secretariat has also worked to ensure awareness of the TBT's Code of Good Practice and its Six Principles for the Development of International Standards, Guides and Recommendations (transparency, openness, impartiality and consensus, effectiveness and relevance, coherence, and the development dimension).[16] Engagement with the WTO and its Secretariat would significantly enhance the likelihood that any methodologies for measuring GHGs in traded goods are interoperable, transparent, and adoptable by others, sparing countries the difficulty of developing their own methodologies or of having to comply with multiple competing quantification systems.

c) Items Listed in the WTO's Trade Policy Tools for Climate Action

The WTO's *Trade Policy Tools for Climate Action*,[17] presented at the COP28 in December 2023, are voluntary but would be more effective with continued

---

14   European Commission, "Carbon Border Adjustment Mechanism" (last modified 17 January 2025), online: europa.eu [perma.cc/7MYM-7CFD].

15   WTO, "Steel Standards Principles" (2025), online (pdf): wto.org [perma. cc/99DB-2ZKG].

16   See WTO, *Decisions and Recommendations Adopted by the WTO Committee on Technical Barriers to Trade Since 1 January 1995*, WTO Doc G/TBT/1/Rev.15 (2022), online (pdf): docs.wto.org [perma.cc/D3G7-AJQA].

17   *Trade Policy Tools for Climate Action*, above note 8.

engagement from the WTO Secretariat. For example, one of the suggested tools is the use of international standards around energy efficiency for consumer goods such as appliances or EVs in order to avoid regulatory fragmentation when upgrading energy efficiency regulations. For all the reasons noted above regarding GHG measurement standards, the WTO TBT Committee could play a very helpful role in limiting regulatory fragmentation. Similarly, the recommendation to speed up customs clearance, thereby reducing GHGs associated with trucks sitting in long lines waiting for customs officials, would be more effective if the WTO Secretariat did all it could to promulgate best practices for how to do so and used aspects of the *Trade Facilitation Agreement* to help in the expediting of border controls.

2) Climate-Related Actions the Secretariat Could Take Itself but Which Would Work Better with Member Support

a) Separately Report Subsidy Notifications with a Climate Change or Decarbonization Purpose

The WTO *Agreement on Subsidies and Countervailing Measures* (SCM Agreement) requires Members to annually notify specific subsidies they have granted or maintained, including their form, amount, duration, and objective or purpose.[18] Despite this requirement, in practice, notifications are sparse and often late. For those that do notify, the subsidy's designated purpose typically only identifies the project or product being built with the subsidy. However, if the WTO Secretariat created an additional distinction for Members to self-identify subsidies that are designed to address climate mitigation or adaptation, this could reshape the subsidy notification system at the WTO while encouraging the increased disclosure of subsidies with a clear climate change or decarbonization purpose.

Such an addition would allow for cross references between the EDB and subsidy notifications and could enhance the accuracy of the subsidies being

---

18   *Agreement on Subsidies and Countervailing Measures* (entered into force 1 January 1995), in Annex 1A of the *Marrakesh Agreement Establishing the World Trade Organization*, 15 April 1994, 1867 UNTS 14 art 25 [*SCM Agreement*]. "25.2 Members shall notify any subsidy as defined in paragraph 1 of Article 1, which is specific within the meaning of Article 2, granted or maintained within their territories. 25.3 The content of notifications should be sufficiently specific to enable other Members to evaluate the trade effects and to understand the operation of notified subsidy programmes."

disclosed. A separate report would also create an incentive to notify climate change related subsidies, thereby improving the current lackluster rate of subsidy notifications. While such designations would not create a formal safe harbor under SCM Article 25.7—as the act of notification does not prejudge the legal status of the subsidy—specific notifications would serve to put other countries on notice that the subsidizing Member considers the subsidies to be "climate change subsidies" which likely could be justifiable under Article XX (General Exceptions) of the *General Agreement on Tariffs and Trade* (GATT). Finally, this addition could prompt questions about the efficacy of the subsidies to be raised during Trade Policy Reviews (TPRs).

b) Include a Dedicated Section on Climate Measures—Positive and Negative—in Trade Policy Reviews

A MAIN OBJECTIVE OF TPRS is to increase transparency and understanding of countries' trade policies and practices through regular monitoring. These "peer reviews" by WTO Members encourage Members to align more closely with WTO rules and to fulfill their commitments. All WTO Members are subject to these reviews, with the rules mandating that the four Members with the largest shares of world trade be reviewed every three years, with other countries reviews every five or seven years. While Members are already raising climate change in some TPRs and the EDB already catalogues environmental measures and policies mentioned during a TPR, creating a dedicated section in each TPR report, covering both desirable and undesirable trade-related climate measures, would provide added benefits. It would establish a baseline for assessing progress in subsequent reports, contribute to highlighting activity at the intersection of trade and climate, and provide a comprehensive set of best—and possibly worst—practices, furthering the prevalence of climate policies and encouraging positive climate action by Members.

3) Climate Actions Taken Pursuant to Existing WTO Mechanisms

a) Definitive Interpretation of PPMs to Expressly Allow Distinctions Based on GHG Levels or High-Versus Low-GHG Emissions Processes

Traditionally, the rules of the WTO were seen as focused on final products rather than the conditions under which they are produced. Both the GATT rules and the TBT Agreement provisions relating to most-favoured-nation and national treatment prohibit discrimination against imported "like" products. But whether governments may differentiate between otherwise like products based on their process of production remains an unsettled question, particularly if there is no physical trace of any differences left in the end-product (known as non-product related production and process methods (NPR PPMs)).[19] This lack of certainty has had a chilling effect on governments' proactive use of PPM-based trade measures to green trade.[20] Moreover, developing countries have long opposed NPR PPM measures on the grounds that they could easily be used by developed nations to discriminate against developing country exports that are unable to comply with production process mandates or costly reporting requirements.[21] The ambiguity over whether and when countries may draw distinctions between products based on PPMs heightens many developing country concerns that measures making such distinctions have been adopted largely for protectionist reasons.

One way to address the ongoing uncertainty would be an interpretative statement or declaration on PPMs by the WTO Ministerial Conference. Article IX:2 of the WTO Agreement allows the Ministerial Conference and the General Council to adopt authoritative interpretations of the WTO agreements. This power can be used to clarify the treatment of PPMs under WTO provisions, such as GATT Article I (Most-Favoured-Nation Treatment), Article III (National Treatment), and Article XX (General Exceptions). By providing a clear interpretation of how and when nations can distinguish "like" products based on the process by which they were made (including the amount of GHGs used), the WTO can provide a useful guardrail for Members wishing

---

19 While the early GATT cases (*Tuna-Dolphin I & II*) suggested that differences in PPMs not affecting a product's physical properties, end uses, or consumer preferences were not a basis for trade distinctions, subsequent WTO cases (*Shrimp Turtle*) indicate that PPM-based distinctions could be justified under the general exceptions in GATT Article XX, despite finding that PPMs were not a valid basis for distinctions. These rulings confirm that trade measures that differentiate products based on their PPMs are not prohibited *per se*, but make it clear that their justification requires meeting strict and not precisely specified conditions. See Ricardo Meléndez-Ortiz, "Cracking the Hard Nut: Differentiated Treatment of Products Under Existing Trade Law" in Daniel C Esty & Susan Biniaz, eds, *Cool Heads in a Warming World: How Trade Policy Can Help Fight Climate Change* (New Haven: Yale Center for Environmental Law & Policy, 2020).

20 Carolyn Deere Birkbeck, *Greening International Trade: Pathways Forward*, Global Governance Centre and the Forum on Trade, Environment and the SDGs (2021) at 39.

21 *Ibid.*

to adopt climate-based trade measures and forestall unnecessary discrimination disputes. Such an interpretation should also address the need for a flexible approach that focuses on climate change outcomes rather than the use of specific processes or technologies, especially those that may be unaffordable or unavailable in developing countries.[22]

4) Climate Actions Needing Changes to Existing Rules

a) New Disciplines on Fossil Fuel Subsidies

Despite the growing threat of climate change and the need for action to prevent further warming, governments continue to dedicate significant and increasing resources to subsidizing fossil fuels, even though fossil fuels account for more than 90 percent of global carbon emissions.[23] The vast majority of such fossil fuel subsidies are directed to consumers to keep the costs for heating and transportation fuels affordable, but significant support continues to be provided to fossil fuel producers, with $42 billion in production subsidies reported across the G7 countries in 2022.[24] According to the International Energy Agency, global consumption subsidies for fossil fuels reached over $1 trillion in 2022, doubling from 2021 levels.[25] While much of the dramatic increase in subsidies can be attributed to market instability from Russia's invasion of Ukraine, fossil fuel subsidies have been consistently high. From 2016 to 2021, $422 billion in international public finance has gone towards fossil fuels, compared to only $173 billion for clean energy.[26] Despite their harmful effects on the environment, many of these subsidies remain permissible under the current WTO framework, hindering progress in the fight against climate change. When the WTO's SCM Agreement was created, its rules were primarily devoted to removing commercial trade distortions.

---

22 *Ibid* at 40.

23 United Nations, "Causes and Effects of Climate Change" (2025), online: un.org [perma.cc/M6E4-JAHQ].

24 Jonas Kuehl, Megan Darby, & Ivetta Gerasimchuk, "What the G7 Ministerial Could Have Delivered on Fossil Fuel Subsidies Reform" (30 April 2024), online: iisd.org [perma.cc/R5R6-PT2X].

25 IEA, *Fossil Fuels Consumption Subsidies 2022* (Paris: International Energy Agency, 2023), online: iea.org [perma.cc/5L4V-P2QZ].

26 Oil Change International, *Promise Breakers: Assessing the Impact of Compliance with the Glasgow Statement Commitment to End International Public Finance for Fossil Fuels* (Washington, DC: Oil Change International, 2023), online (pdf): oilchange.org [perma. cc/2GGF-ZPU8].

Only export and import-substitution subsidies were expressly prohibited within the trading system.

However, in the wake of overwhelming evidence of the harmful contribution subsidies were making to overfishing and the depletion of the oceans, in 2022 WTO Members reached a pathbreaking *Agreement on Fisheries Subsides*. In effect, this Agreement added to the category of prohibited subsidies—those that Members agree not to grant or maintain—subsidies concerning illegal, unreported, and unregulated fishing of overfished stock. It provides a model that can be applied in the context of fossil fuel subsidies, while demonstrating that WTO Members can agree to discipline subsidies on the basis of environmental concerns.

A new fossil fuel subsidies agreement should build on the Fisheries Agreement model of defining additional prohibited subsidies, along with the work of the Fossil Fuel Subsidy Reform initiative—an effort designed to "rationaliz[e] . . . and phase out inefficient fossil fuel subsidies that encourage wasteful consumption."[27] It should either amend the existing list of prohibited subsidies (Article 3 of SCM Agreement) or, like the Fisheries Agreement, create a new agreement with equivalent effect and will need to include gradual phase-out timelines, along with special and differential treatment for developing countries. But reaching such an agreement would make a very substantial contribution to global climate goals and the transition to a cleaner energy future.

b) Explicit Carve Out for Green Subsidies

When the SCM Agreement was established, there was an effort to include a list of permitted ("non-actionable") subsidies for certain research activities or adaptions to new environmental requirements.[28] Non-actionable subsidies would be immune from challenge at the WTO. This approach of safeguarding certain subsidies from dispute settlement and countervailing duty action was only temporary for the first five years of enforcement of the SCM Agreement. Since its expiration, WTO Members have failed to agree on any extensions, with no subsidy programs explicitly protected as non-actionable.[29]

---

27 WTO, *Ministerial Statement on Fossil Fuel Subsidies*, WTO Doc WT/MIN(21)/9/Rev.2 (2022) at para 8, online (pdf): docs.wto.org [perma.cc/9QGF-XHT2].

28 Jennifer A Hillman & Inu Manak, *Rethinking International Rules on Subsidies* (New York: Council on Foreign Relations, 2023), online (pdf): cfr.org [perma.cc/JU8F-HG64].

29 Robert Howse, *Climate Mitigation Subsidies and the WTO Legal Framework* (Winnipeg: International Institute for Sustainable Development, 2010), online (pdf): iisd.org [perma.cc/AUC2-7ZDS].

Today, many countries are independently moving forward with various programs that provide financial support to renewable energy and green technologies. Examples include the United States' $369 billion *Inflation Reduction Act* (IRA), which provides massive subsidies for greening the US economy and tax credits for everything from renewable energy to nuclear power to electric vehicles, and the EU's Green Deal, which seeks to increase funding for renewable energy and clean technology sectors. However, because none of these subsidies can currently be deemed as "non-actionable," they continue to be subject to scrutiny at the WTO, with many potential findings that various aspects of these subsidy programs run afoul of the SCM Agreement. In particular, a number of the programs contain various local content requirements that limit the subsidy to goods that are made or sourced locally. Such local content requirements quite likely transform such subsidies into "prohibited" subsidies that WTO Members have pledged not to grant or maintain.[30]

The lack of consideration for "green" subsidies underscores the need for a more targeted approach that strikes a better balance between addressing trade distortions and promoting climate action and sustainable development. Reviving and updating the SCM Agreement's Article 8 approach and specifically carving out green subsidies would align the WTO subsidy regime with modern climate goals. But such a carve out would need to maintain some of the current guardrails around prohibited subsidies, as permitting Members to completely mix up the objective of developing and promoting green technology with the goal of favouring domestic industry would in most instances tip the balance too far in favour of protectionism over green goals. The advantage of a multilateral approach to green subsidies is that it could address one of the subsidy regime's key challenges—the lack of a shared definition of what constitutes a green subsidy—while enhancing the effectiveness of any agreed-upon commitments. Providing a safe haven for subsidies for products that help combat climate change, like solar panels or other renewable energy technologies, is a first step. These technologies are critical to combat climate change, yet they can still be cost-prohibitive and uncompetitive. Subsidies to such products could help offset the high costs of research, production process development, technology transfer and human capital development,

---

30   *SCM Agreement*, above note 18 at art 3 provides that subsidies "contingent, whether solely or as one of several other conditions, upon the use of domestic over imported goods" are prohibited and that WTO members "shall neither grant nor maintain" such subsidies.

while providing the security and predictability that investors in cutting-edge green technology need.

E. Conclusion

AS THE WORLD LOOKS TOWARDS harnessing trade policy in the urgent battle against climate change, Valerie Hughes's legacy of proactive problem-solving and trust in institutional capacity resonates deeply. Her unwavering commitment to the WTO reminds us of the pivotal role it can play in shaping a sustainable future. By embracing measures outlined in this chapter, from harmonizing GHG measurement standards to green-lighting green subsidies, the WTO can catalyze global efforts towards decarbonization while ensuring equitable outcomes for developed and developing countries alike.

CHAPTER 30

Emerging into the Light: Fossil Fuel Subsidies at the WTO

Ronald Steenblik[*]

FOSSIL FUEL PRODUCTION, CONSUMPTION, OR both, have been subsidized in many countries of the world for decades. Globally, these subsidies have ranged in recent years from around USD 450 billion to almost USD 1.7 trillion. Controlling them has been a topic of discussion in several inter-governmental bodies since at least the early 1980s, including the World Trade Organization (WTO) and its predecessor, the *General Agreement on Tariffs and Trade* (GATT). Numerous individual governments have pledged to reduce their fossil fuel subsidies, and some have, mainly to reduce their burdens on budgets. But the concern that the subsidies are undermining efforts to address global climate change has given new impetus to efforts to coordinate action at the plurilateral and multilateral level, on the assumption that many countries might find it easier to reform their subsidies if others do too. The WTO, as the inter-governmental forum with the most experience with multilateral subsidy reform, seems an obvious choice for such joint action. This chapter reviews briefly the pathways that have brought fossil fuel subsidies to the WTO, progress made by the forty-eight WTO Members of the

---

[*] Senior technical advisor to the Sustainable and Just Economic Systems program of the Quaker United Nations Office, Geneva. Former (retired) OECD Special Counselor for Fossil Fuel Subsidy Reform (2016–18). The author acknowledges with gratitude Henok Asmelash for his thorough and helpful comments on an earlier unpublished paper by the author from which this chapter draws heavily.

Fossil Fuel Subsidy Reform (FFSR) Initiative to date and how the recently concluded quadrilateral Agreement on Climate Change, Trade and Sustainability (ACCTS) could help guide the FFSR's work in the future.

A. Introduction

GOVERNMENTS IN MANY COUNTRIES HAVE been providing financial benefits to fossil fuel producers or consumers for decades, if not longer.[1] Globally, fossil fuel subsidies have ranged in recent years from around USD 450 billion to almost USD 1.7 trillion a year—increasing when energy prices rise, and declining when they fall.[2] Oil and natural gas producers have typically benefitted from special tax provisions; coal producers, especially those that have struggled to compete with cheaper fossil alternatives or imports, from more traditional subsidies. Consumers of petroleum fuels and natural gas have been subsidized through administrative pricing and in some cases government assistance for purchasing particular fuels.[3] Variation in rates of excise taxes, and sometimes value-added taxes (VAT), across different fuels and user categories is common.[4]

The impetus for reforming fossil fuel subsidies, particularly at the multilateral level, was initially on reducing unfair international competition in sales of like fuels (especially coal) and in eliminating the advantage conferred

---

1   See, e.g., Mark Kosmo, *Money to Burn? The High Costs of Energy Subsidies* (Washington, DC: World Resources Institute, 1987); IEA, *Coal Prospects and Policies of IEA Countries: 1987 Review* (Paris: International Energy Agency, 1988); Nancy Pfund & Ben Healey, *What Would Jefferson Do?: The Historical Role of Federal Subsidies in Shaping America's Energy Future* (San Francisco: DBL Investors, 2011); Bjorn Larsen & Anwar Shah, *World Fossil Fuel Subsidies and Global Carbon Emissions* (1992), World Bank, Working Paper No 1002.

2   IISD & OECD, "Country Data" (last visited 29 March 2025), online: fossilfuelsubsidytracker.org [perma.cc/V7AG-QZ76]. Note: there are many gaps in the data, both in terms of country and policy coverage. For example, the Organisation for Economic Co-operation and Development (OECD) estimates budgetary support and tax expenditures benefitting fossil fuel production or consumption for only fifty-one countries. See OECD, "Fossil Fuel Support – Detailed Indicators" (last visited 29 March 2025), online: data-explorer.oecd.org [perma.cc/K2CA-XKGK]; IEA, "Tracking the Impact of Government Support: Fossil Fuel Subsidies" (last visited 29 March 2025), online: iea.org [perma.cc/JS6G-BK3U].

3   For examples, see the OECD database and the IEA database.

4   See OECD, *Taxing Energy Use for Sustainable Development: Opportunities for Energy Tax and Subsidy Reform in Selected Developing and Emerging Economies* (Paris: OECD, 2021).

to energy-intensive industries of artificially low-priced fuel inputs. Since the early 1990s, however, environmental arguments for phasing out fossil fuel subsidies have become dominant. The combustion of fossil fuels is the leading source of carbon-dioxide (CO_2) emissions, which contribute to global climate change,[5] as well as of airborne pollutants. Air pollution from the burning of fossil fuels is credited with causing over eight million premature deaths in 2018.[6] Subsidizing fossil fuels favours their consumption, hence phasing out those subsidies should help efforts to constrain their use.

Arguments within countries for fossil fuel subsidy reform point to many of the same benefits—particularly a more level playing field for renewable forms of energy and cleaner air—but also the idea that funds allocated to fossil fuel subsidies could be better spent in support of more socially desirable goals. Analysis has shown that untargeted fossil fuel consumption subsidies, which governments have often justified as necessary to protect low-income households from high fuel prices, tend to favour high-income and middle-income households—i.e., those can afford larger homes or vehicles.[7]

The biggest barriers to reform, as with most industries, is the power of vested interests. Within countries, these include fossil fuel producers but also industries that rely heavily on fossil fuels as feedstocks, such as producers of petrochemicals. So far, economically viable ways of meeting the needs fulfilled by these products have yet to emerge at scale. Producers of biofuels (ethanol, biodiesel, and bio-jet, which are in most cases blended with equal or larger volumes of petroleum fuels), while not usually supporters of fossil fuel subsidies, have called for "levelling the playing field" between liquid fuels and subsidies to industries that would render liquid fuels obsolete.[8] Similarly,

---

5   Shukla et al, eds, "Emissions Trends and Drivers" in Shukla et al, eds, *Climate Change 2022: Mitigation of Climate Change* (Cambridge: Cambridge University Press, 2022) 215.

6   Vohra et al, "Global Mortality from Outdoor Fine Particle Pollution Generated by Fossil Fuel Combustion: Results From GEOS-Chem" (2021) 195 *Environmental Research* 110754.

7   Cecile Couharde & Sara Mouhoud, "Fossil Fuel Subsidies, Income Inequality, and Poverty: Evidence from Developing Countries" (2020) 34:5 *Journal of Economic Surveys* 34.

8   Dan Morgan, "We Can Love Electric Cars, But Let's Not Spurn Biofuels" (16 July 2021), online: theglobalist.com [perma.cc/6GYN-HZ53] ("[the] American Farm Bureau Federation has joined an alliance with the U.S. oil industry to fight federal and state electric car subsidies seen as discriminating against biofuels").

car manufacturers and vendors have often benefitted from subsidized gasoline and diesel, creating a drag on reform.[9]

Consumers—particularly low-income consumers—pose an obstacle to reform of a different sort, especially in the short run, as can be seen from the many outbreaks of civil unrest in countries with low levels of distributive justice that have tried to raise prices for fossil fuels.[10] Over the longer run, however, most consumers do not care about having access to fossil fuels *per se* but rather about the share of their income they spend on the services that energy enables: mobility, heating, cooling, and cooking. By contrast, the fossil fuel industry and its suppliers know that the long-run goal of civil society, and increasingly of governments, is to phase out fossil fuel use entirely.[11]

B. Early Efforts at the International Level to Discipline Fossil Fuel Subsidies

INTERNATIONAL EFFORTS TO CURB FOSSIL fuel subsidies, mainly because of their adverse trade effects, can be traced back to the 1950s.[12] Several Parties to the *General Agreement on Tariffs and Trade* (GATT), the predecessor body to the WTO, raised the issue of "dual pricing"—the practice by mainly net energy-exporting countries of charging their domestic consumers less than the full market value of their fossil fuels—in the 1970s and even tried to get fossil fuel subsidies into the Uruguay Round of multilateral trade negotiations. But all attempts to curb the practice were successfully thwarted by oil producing and exporting countries.[13]

Since 1995, subsidies to fossil fuels have been governed at the WTO by its *Agreement on Subsidies and Countervailing Measures* (SCM Agreement), an

---

9   See IEA, *Fossil Fuel Subsidy Reform in Mexico and Indonesia* (Paris: International Energy Agency, 2016) at 72.

10   Margherita Belgioioso & Edward Newman, "Fossil Fuel Subsidy Reform, Distributive Justice and Civil Unrest" (2025) 119 *Energy Research & Social Science* 103868.

11   See, e.g., Mike Scott, "Why Aren't We Reducing Our Reliance on Fossil Fuels Faster?" (12 August 2024), online: weforum.org [perma.cc/A6YT-CHFX].

12   See *Treaty Establishing the European Coal and Steel Community*, 18 April 1951, art 4(c), online: eur-lex.europa.eu [perma.cc/U9CD-BWTK].

13   Anna Marhold, *Fossil Fuel Subsidy Reform in the WTO: Options for Constraining Dual Pricing in the Multilateral Trading System* (Geneva: International Centre for Trade and Sustainable Development, 2017) at 6.

outcome of the Uruguay Round of multilateral trade negotiations.[14] The SCM Agreement contains a definition of subsidies; rules for determining which are prohibited, which are actionable, and for a brief period which ones were non-actionable;[15] and actions that a WTO Member can take to remedy the adverse effects of another Member's subsidies. Export subsidies and subsidies contingent upon the use of domestic over imported goods are prohibited. An actionable subsidy, by contrast, must meet a specificity standard—i.e., it must be demonstrated to be specific to "certain enterprises" or an industry or small group of industries that operate within the jurisdiction of the granting authority—and cause harm to the trade interests of the complaining Member. The available remedies include bringing the offending subsidy to the WTO for arbitration by a dispute panel or applying countervailing duties (if the subsidized product is being imported).

To date, the trade-related disciplines of the SCM Agreement have never been applied to fossil fuel subsidies alleged to be benefiting foreign producers directly. (There have, however, been at least two indirect challenges involving allegations that producers of steel[16] or aluminum[17] had benefitted from cheap energy inputs, among other forms of support). One likely reason is the structure of the international oil and gas industry. It takes support from a domestic industry to challenge a subsidy or impose a countervailing duty, but

---

14 *Agreement on Subsidies and Countervailing Measures* (entered into force 1 January 1995), in Annex 1A of the *Marrakesh Agreement Establishing the World Trade Organization*, 15 April 1994, 1867 UNTS 14 [*SCM Agreement*].

15 *Ibid*, art 8.

16 In 2009, China imposed anti-dumping (AD) and countervailing duties (CVD) on imports from the United States of grain-oriented flat-rolled electrical steel, after a finding that, among other countervailable subsidies, subsidies to the US natural gas industry were being "passed-through" to the US steel industry. The United States challenged this action at the WTO, however, and the Appellate Body upheld the Panel's finding that China had provided insufficient evidence to support its claims. See Thomas J Prusa & Edwin Vermulst, "China – Countervailing and Anti-Dumping Duties on Grain Oriented Flat-rolled Electrical Steel from the United States: Exporting US AD/CVD Methodologies Through WTO Dispute Settlement?" (2014) 13:2 *World Trade Review* 229.

17 In January 2017, the United States filed a "request for consultations" at the WTO, alleging that China was undercutting global prices for primary aluminum and artificially expanding its market share through, among other practices, providing coal to one of the producers for less than adequate remuneration. The case never proceeded past the consultations stage, however. See *China—Subsidies to Producers of Primary Aluminum (Complaint by the United States)* (2017), WTO Doc WT/DS519/1 (Request for Consultations), online (pdf): docs.wto.org [perma.cc/4YUR-KYBZ].

typically the dominant players in an industry are large, multinational enterprises that benefit from the particular or similar foreign subsidies. Another reason may be that countries that produce oil and natural gas often use similar policies—namely special tax breaks—to encourage domestic production.

A more fundamental problem is the concept of "likeness." Subsidies that lower the end-user price of a fossil fuel, or of a facility that uses the fossil fuel as an input to generate district heat or electric power, make it harder for alternative technologies that do not use fossil fuels, such as wind turbines, to compete. However, because any resulting injury affects sellers of products that are not "like" the subsidized fossil fuel or technology, there is no remedy available currently under the SCM Agreement.

Subsidies favouring the consumption of fossil fuels are also difficult to challenge but for other reasons. Many take the form of policies that set prices for all domestic consumers of petroleum products or natural gas that are lower than what a country charges for exports of those products, a practice called "dual pricing." Such subsidies, if economy-wide, would likely be considered non-specific, hence not actionable. Accordingly, WTO Members have tried to rein in such subsidies when new Members have acceded to the WTO. The WTO accession agreements for Saudi Arabia (2005) and Russia (2012), for example, obtained promises from those Members to curb some practices that supported dual pricing.[18]

Meanwhile, discussions have at various times taken place at the WTO outside of negotiations or of the dispute settlement mechanism. In 1997, for example, the WTO Secretariat produced a study in response to a request by members of the WTO's Committee on Trade and Environment (CTE) that, among other topics, discussed subsidies to energy, including fossil fuels.[19] At the CTE's meeting in October 2002, Saudi Arabia was highly critical of OECD members' energy taxes and subsidies, asserting that removing subsidies to producers of oil and natural gas provided by OECD countries "would be beneficial not only for environment and development, but also for trade."[20] Fossil fuel subsidies thereafter fell off the CTE's agenda until 2014

---

18   Marhold, above note 13 at 7.

19   WTO, *Environmental Benefits of Removing Trade Restrictions and Distortions*, WTO Doc WT/CTE/W/67 (1997) at paras 58–63, online (pdf): docs.wto.org [perma. cc/5M2B-YRVD].

20   WTO, *Report of the Meeting Held on 8 October 2002*, WTO Doc WT/CTE/M/31 (2002) at 18, online (pdf): docs.wto.org [perma.cc/LB69-RYK6]. Text between quotation marks is not necessarily verbatim.

(unlike fisheries subsidies),[21] though at least one WTO Member tried to raise the issue in discussions relating to subsidy disciplines during the Doha Round of multilateral trade negotiations.[22]

What ignited and has kept alive the current wave of interest in addressing fossil fuel subsidies at the international level were the dual commitments, first by the Leaders of the Group of Twenty (G20)[23] and then of the Asia-Pacific Economic Cooperation (APEC)[24] economies, both in 2009, to "Rationalize and phase out over the medium term inefficient fossil fuel subsidies that encourage wasteful consumption."[25] The Group of Seven (G7) economies—all of which are members of the G20—followed suit, setting a specific target date for ending such subsidies by 2025.[26] In September 2015 the United Nations (UN), at its Sustainable Development Summit, included a goal to phase out "inefficient" fossil fuel subsidies (12.c) as part of its set of seventeen Sustainable Development Goals (SDGs) for 2030;[27] and in November 2022 the Conference of Parties to the UN Framework Convention on Climate Change (UNFCCC) for the first time called upon all Parties to accelerate "efforts towards . . . the phaseout of inefficient fossil fuel subsidies."[28] All of these statements contained additional caveats that allowed governments to, for example, provide citizens with essential energy services, target support at the poorest, take into

---

21 Henok Asmelash, "The Regulation of Environmentally Harmful Fossil Fuel Subsidies: From Obscurity to Prominence in the Multilateral Trading System" (2022) 33:2 *European Journal of International Law* 993 at 999.

22 See, e.g., WTO, *Communication from the United States*, WTO Doc TN/RL/W/78 (2003) at 3, online (pdf): docs.wto.org [perma.cc/4PG8-KFY2].

23 G20 Research Group, "G20 Leaders Statement: The Pittsburgh Summit" (2009) at paras 24 and 29, online: g20.utoronto.ca [perma.cc/W559-A7QD] [G20 Research Group, "G20 Leaders Statement"].

24 APEC, "2009 Leaders' Declaration" (14 November 2009), online: apec.org [perma.cc/AC77-GJH5].

25 G20 Research Group, "G20 Leaders Statement," above note 23 at para 29. The 2009 APEC Leaders' Declaration initially omitted the word "inefficient" but inserted it into all subsequent reiterations of the commitment.

26 Ministry of Foreign Affairs of Japan, "G7 Ise-Shima Leaders' Declaration" (2016) at 28, online (pdf): mofa.go.jp [perma.cc/ R9AH-KJVB].

27 See United Nations, "Transforming Our World: the 2030 Agenda for Sustainable Development" (last visited 29 March 2025), online: sdgs.un.org [perma.cc/8FFG-WHKS].

28 See the *Report of the Conference of the Parties Serving as the Meeting of the Parties to the Paris Agreement on its Third Session, Held in Glasgow from 31 October to 13 November 2021 (Glasgow Climate Pact)*, UNFCCC, 2022, UN Doc PA/CMA/2021/10/Add.1, at 5, online (pdf): unfccc.int [perma.cc/5LML-4G3Z].

account the specific needs and conditions of developing countries and, in the case of SDG 12.c, to minimize "the possible adverse impacts" on developing countries' ability to develop "in a manner that protects the poor and the affected communities," or more generally, as in the Glasgow Climate Pact, to recognize "the need for support towards a just transition."

All these commitments are non-binding, however, with no formal sanctions for non-attainment. Unsurprisingly, therefore, not long after the G20 and APEC Leaders' issued their initial statements, various legal scholars and activist groups started calling for the WTO to launch negotiations on developing a new, legally binding instrument that would address energy broadly (e.g., a Sustainable Energy Trade Agreement or SETA[29]), trade and climate change more narrowly,[30] or fossil fuel subsidies specifically.[31] This community was and remains mainly concerned about the effects of fuel combustion on emissions of carbon dioxide and of local air pollutants, but it wants the WTO to take the lead because the Organization offers enforceable rules on subsidies, whereas other intergovernmental institutions do not.

C. The Emergence of the Fossil Fuel Subsidies Reform (FFSR) Initiative at the WTO

MUCH OF THE CREDIT FOR getting fossil fuels back onto the WTO agenda can be accorded to the Government of New Zealand. In June 2010 it led the formation of an informal Friends of Fossil Fuel Subsidy Reform (FFFSR) group, initially with the purpose of building political consensus on the importance of fossil fuel subsidy reform, especially but not exclusively within the G20

29 Gary C Hufbauer, Ricardo Meléndez-Ortiz, & Richard Samans, "Introduction: Setting the Horse Before the Cart to Preserve a Viable World" in Gary C Hufbauer, Ricardo Meléndez-Ortiz, & Richard Samans, eds, *The Law and Economics of a Sustainable Energy Trade Agreement* (Cambridge: Cambridge University Press, 2016) 1 at 5.

30 Robert Howse, *Climate Mitigation Subsidies and the WTO Legal Framework: A Policy Analysis* (Geneva: International Institute for Sustainable Development, 2010).

31 See, e.g., Ronald Steenblik, "Subsidies in the Traditional Energy Sector" in Joost Pauwelyn, ed, *Global Challenges at the Intersection of Trade, Energy and the Environment* (Geneva: Centre for Trade and Economic Integration, 2010) 183; Joel P Trachtman, *Fossil Fuel Subsidies Reduction and the World Trade Organization* (Geneva: International Centre for Trade and Sustainable Development, 2017); Simon Happersberger, Eleanor Mateo, & Selcukhan Ünekbas, "How to rein in fossil fuel subsidies? Towards a New WTO Regime" (Geneva: Centre for Trade and Economic Integration, 2021).

and APEC.[32] As pointed out by Asmelash,[33] during the mid-2010s members of the Friends revived discussions on fossil fuel subsidies in the WTO's CTE, organized roundtables at the WTO on the topic[34], and raised questions about other countries' subsidies in the Committee on Subsidies and Countervailing Measures (CSCM) and in the WTO's Trade Policy Reviews.

At the 11th Ministerial Conference (MC11) of the WTO (Buenos Aires, 10–13 December 2017), six of the non-European Union members of the Friends group plus six other non-European Union members of the WTO supported a "Fossil Fuel Subsidies Reform Ministerial Statement" that, among other "shared understandings," stated that the signatories sought "to advance discussion in the [WTO] aimed at achieving ambitious and effective disciplines on inefficient fossil fuel subsidies that encourage wasteful consumption."[35] Three years would pass before another Ministerial Statement on FFSR was issued (six months in advance of MC12), this time signed by forty-five WTO Members, *including* the European Union and its twenty-seven Member States, plus the United Kingdom.[36] The crucial difference between the 2017 Ministerial Statement and the December 2021 statement was that the latter one dropped any reference to explicitly seeking disciplines on fossil fuel subsidies and instead *confirmed* that the WTO "can play a central role in the reduction of trade and investment distortions caused by fossil fuel subsidies by achieving effective disciplines on inefficient fossil fuel subsidies" and sought with less urgency "the rationalization and phase out of inefficient fossil fuel subsidies that encourage wasteful consumption *along a clear timeline*" (italics added), encouraging other WTO Members to join them in

---

32   The Friends' group membership has evolved over the years but has always included only countries that are not members of the G20. Having started with five members (indicated by asterisks), its current members are Costa Rica, Denmark*, Ethiopia, Finland, New Zealand*, Norway*, Sweden*, Switzerland*, and Uruguay. See Friends of Fossil Fuel Subsidy Reform, "About FFFSR" (last visited 29 March 2025), online: fffsr.org [perma.cc/5WV3-MFGE].

33   See Asmelash, above note 21 at 1000.

34   See, e.g., WTO, *New Zealand Report on Key Points from a Recent Roundtable on Fossil Fuel Subsidy Reform*, WTO Doc RD/CTE/36 (2014) [on file with author].

35   WTO, *Fossil Fuel Subsidies Reform Ministerial Statement*, WTO Doc WT/MIN(17)/54 (2017), online (pdf): docs.wto.org [perma.cc/BNE5-2XU5].

36   WTO, *Ministerial Statement on Fossil Fuel Subsidies*, WTO Doc WT/MIN(21)/9 (2022), online (pdf): docs.wto.org [perma.cc/674X-KCYN]; *Ministerial Statement on Fossil Fuel Subsidies (Revision 1)*, WTO Doc WT/MIN(21)/9/Rev.1 (2022), online (pdf): docs.wto. org [perma.cc/U2LR-X442].

those efforts. It also enjoined its signatories to "elaborate concrete options to advance this issue at the [WTO] in advance of MC13."

The second revision to the December 2021 "Ministerial Statement on Fossil Fuel Subsidies," which was submitted on 10 June 2022—two days before the start of the MC12 (Geneva, 12–15 June 2022)—was identical to the December document, except that it included two more "co-sponsors:" Paraguay and Samoa.[37] In a separate statement the Ministers established an informal Fossil Fuel Subsidies Reform (FFSR) working group, to be coordinated and chaired by New Zealand, and agreed a work plan for the remainder of 2022 and 2023 that focused on: (1) taking stock of activities related to FFSR by WTO Members and international bodies and gaining a better understanding of definitions and relevant concepts, (2) hearing from cosponsors about their priorities under the initiative, (3) discussing lessons learned from past reforms, (4) exploring ways to improve transparency into fossil fuel subsidies; and (5) planning next steps following MC13.[38] The work plan seemed to envisage working group meetings taking place every two months, but on average since the first one, in October 2022, they have occurred three times a year. These meetings are open to all other WTO Members and to a set of approved observers from inter-governmental (IGOs) and non-governmental organizations (NGOs).[39]

During MC13 (Abu Dhabi, 26–29 February 2024), the forty-eight co-sponsors[40] of the FFSR Initiative issued an updated Ministerial Statement[41] that included a work plan for 2024–25 organized under three themes,

---

37   *Ministerial Statement on Fossil Fuel Subsidies (Revision 2)*, WTO Doc WT/MIN(21)/9/ Rev.2 (2022), online (pdf): docs.wto.org [perma.cc/FJF7-UH43].

38   WTO, *Ministerial Statement on Fossil Fuel Subsidies: High-Level Work Plan*, WTO Doc WT/MIN(22)/8 (2022), online (pdf): docs.wto.org [perma.cc/WGS6-6EPV]. See also WTO, *Fossil Fuel Subsidy Reform (FFSR): Summary Report, Meeting Held on 24 November 2023*, WTO Doc INF/TE/FFSR/R/2 (2024), online (pdf): docs.wto.org [perma.cc/ M5DV-TL5Y].

39   See WTO, "Fossil Fuel Subsidy Reform" (last visited 29 March 2025), online: wto.org [perma.cc/CEY9-BHS8]. Among the IGOs that participate in the meetings, besides the WTO Secretariat, are the secretariats of the IEA, the OECD, the World Bank, the UN Conference on Trade and Development (UNCTAD), the UN Development Program (UNDP), and the UN Environment Program (UNEP). The NGOs most active in the meetings have been the Forum on Trade, Environment, and the SDGs (TESS); the International Institute for Sustainable Development (IISD); and the Quaker United Nations Office (QUNO).

40   Colombia became the forty-eighth co-sponsor of the Initiative in February 2023.

41   WTO, *Ministerial Statement on Fossil Fuel Subsidies*, WTO Doc WT/MIN(24)/19 (2024), online (pdf): docs.wto.org [perma.cc/LW32-7N7R] [WTO, *Statement on FFS*].

or "pillars:" (1) enhancing transparency, (2) developing guidelines for improving the targeting of, and transparency into, temporary crisis support measures (such as those used by many WTO Members during 2022 and 2023), and (3) elaborating ways to identify and address the most harmful fossil fuel subsidies. The FFSR working group convened three meetings in 2024 and one off-site "informal dialogue."[42] In addition, as part of the first pillar, the Ministerial Statement envisaged the co-sponsors increasing their engagement with other WTO Members on issues related to fossil fuel subsidies and fossil fuel subsidy reform and so provided sample questions to guide them during the WTO's Trade Policy Reviews.[43]

D. Getting to Disciplines

DURING 2025 AND UP UNTIL MC14 (scheduled to take place in Yaoundé, Cameroon, on 26–29 March 2026) one of the tasks assigned by Ministers of the forty-eight FFSR Initiative economies is for "[c]o-sponsors and other interested Members to work on the development of a timetable for phased reduction pathways on [those fossil fuel subsidies that are most harmful to the environment and to trade] for possible pledges at MC14."[44] The term "pledges" suggests that the Ministers would accept a soft-law approach in lieu of a hard-law instrument that would establish binding disciplines on the use of fossil fuel subsidies. The key phrase, even for a voluntary "phased reduction" of those fossil fuel subsidies determined to be most harmful, is "the development of a timetable," which if it were synchronized with the UN's Sustainable Development Goals would mean by the end of 2030. Obtaining a set of voluntary "phased reduction commitments" would not be too heavy a lift for the FFSR Initiative to achieve (with the usual caveats) considering that Initiative's co-sponsors include:

- all the current members of the Friends of Fossil Fuel Subsidy Reform informal group;

---

42 Since the beginning of 2024, the FFSR Initiative has issued Summary Reports of its meetings, which can be found at the initiative's dedicated web page. See WTO, "Fossil Fuel Subsidy Reform," above note 39. For a summary of the informal dialogue, see WTO, *Fossil Fuel Subsidy Reform (FFSR): Summary Report, Meeting Held on 24 November 2024*, WTO Doc INF/TE/FFSR/R/5 (2025), online (pdf): docs.wto.org [perma.cc/AM3V-HZA5].

43 WTO, *Statement on FFS*, above note 41 at 6.

44 *Ibid* at 5.

- all but one (the exception being Antigua and Barbuda) of the sixteen-member Coalition on Phasing Out Fossil Fuel Incentives Including Subsidies (COFFIS), which was established in 2024 to work "to remove fossil fuel subsidies both collectively and through domestic action;"[45]
- six of the seventy members (Colombia, Costa Rica, Fiji, Paraguay, Samoa, and Vanuatu) of the Vulnerable Twenty (V20) Group of economies that consider themselves systematically vulnerable to climate change and have called for repurposing fossil fuel subsidies;[46]
- five of the governments (Colombia, Fiji, Samoa, Tonga, and Vanuatu) participating in the Fossil Fuel Non-Proliferation Treaty Initiative, "a growing bloc of 17 countries [that] are seeking a negotiating mandate for a Fossil Fuel Treaty" to end the expansion of coal, oil and natural gas and manage a just transition to renewable energy;[47] and
- all four of the recent signatories (Costa Rica, Iceland, New Zealand, and Switzerland) to the plurilateral Agreement on Climate Change, Trade and Sustainability (ACCTS)—an international trade agreement that, among other things, imposes disciplines on harmful fossil fuel subsidies with a view ultimately to eliminate them.[48]

Considering the proliferation of non-binding international commitments to reform fossil fuel subsidies that have been promulgated in recent years, and the limited progress that they have made,[49] it is reasonable to question the added value of yet another constellation of countries promulgating yet another set of promises. What if, instead, the co-sponsors of the FFSR Initiative were to decide to develop binding disciplines on fossil fuel subsidies?

---

45   IISD, "Coalition on Phasing Out Fossil Fuel Incentives Including Subsidies" (last visited 29 March 2025), online: iisd.org [perma.cc/G7K8-QEZY].

46   V20, "Ministerial Communique VIII" (21 April 2022), online: v-20.org [perma. cc/9D6Q-VRYT].

47   See Fossil Fuel Non-Proliferation Treaty, "Governments Participating in Discussions on a Fossil Fuel Treaty" (last visited 22 June 2025), online: fossilfueltreaty.org [perma. cc/9CAF-5JK3].

48   See *Agreement on Climate Change, Trade and Sustainability*, Costa Rica, Iceland, New Zealand and Switzerland, 15 November 2024, ch 4, online: mfat.govt.nz [perma.cc/ F3T4-ACQJ] [ACCTS].

49   Setenay Hizliok, Giorgia Monsignori, & Antonina Scheer, "Are We Getting Any Closer to Ending Fossil Fuel Subsidies?" (22 November 2024), online (blog): blogs.lse.ac.uk [perma.cc/ERM8-QG8V].

Two broad options present themselves: negotiating a new WTO multilateral Agreement on Fossil Suel Subsidies[50] or a plurilateral one. As of mid-2025, the GATT or the WTO has successfully negotiated three separate subsidy agreements: one general (the SCM Agreement), and two sector-specific (the Agreement on Agriculture and the Agreement on Fisheries Subsidies). All three are multilateral—i.e., they apply to all WTO Members. One common critique of the most recently negotiated agreement, the WTO Agreement on Fisheries, is that it took more than twenty years between when WTO Ministers approved a negotiating mandate and a final agreement was reached in June 2022.[51] Such a lengthy negotiation would be unacceptable to repeat again, at least to those seeking to transition away from fossil fuels.

Yet to negotiate a multilateral agreement would mean winning over the net fossil-fuel exporting countries, particularly members of OPEC.[52] Some, such as the members of the Gulf Cooperation Council (GCC), have said they intend to reduce their fossil fuel subsidies and have already undertaken tangible reforms to raise prices and implement more targeted support systems for their citizens but without fundamentally altering the social contract.[53] With 5 percent to 12 percent of total (fossil-fuel generated) electricity in the region used for desalinating water,[54] and an even larger share used for air

---

50 See Kasturi Das et al, *Making the International Trade System Work for Climate Change: Assessing the Options* (London, UK: Climate Strategies, 2018) at 45–46. Kasturi Das et al also suggest the possibility of amending the SCM Agreement to address the specificities of fossil fuel subsidies; however, they note, the advantage of pursuing a separate agreement would be that it would limit the risk that other issues and subsidies would enter into the same discussion.

51 Nonetheless, considering that the WTO *Agreement on Fisheries Subsidies* is aimed primarily at the environmental effects of those subsidies, and only secondarily at their trade effects, it is likely the best-suited model for fossil fuel subsidies.

52 There are also numerous middle-income countries that subsidize producers of particular fossil fuels, such as coal, or fuel used for particular uses, such as diesel for running irrigation pumps or to generate electricity in remote regions and that may seek to protect those subsidies from deep cuts or at least provide time to phase them out over many years. There is also a "fairness" argument for many developing countries, who point out that richer ones have benefitted at earlier stages in their development from cheap fossil fuels and do not want to foreclose that opportunity for themselves.

53 Mohammad Al-Saidi, "Instruments of Energy Subsidy Reforms in Arab Countries— The Case of the Gulf Cooperation Council (GCC) Countries" (2020) 6:S1 *Energy Reports* 68 at 72.

54 Afreen Siddiqi & Laura Diaz Anadon, "The Water–Energy Nexus in Middle East and North Africa" (2011) 39:8 *Energy Policy* 4529.

conditioning,[55] these countries can be expected to resist external pressures for more radical pricing reforms until sufficient non-fossil electric power plants are in place.[56] Moreover, during meetings of the CTE during the mid-2010s, not just GCC members but also other oil-producing and oil-exporting countries argued that fossil fuel subsidies fell outside of the CTE's mandate.[57]

That argues for pursuing an "open plurilateral" agreement which essentially means working with a coalition of the willing while at the same time convincing recalcitrant members to join the plurilateral over time. That appears to be the strategy being pursued by the FFSR Initiative, judging from the language of their 2024–25 program of work instruction, in which co-sponsors are tasked with working with "other interested Members" on "the development of a timetable for phased reduction pathways."[58] A major obstacle to pursuing such an approach *within* the WTO, however, is that some WTO Members, such as India and South Africa, have been highly critical of "Joint Statement Initiatives" (JSIs) that then lead to negotiations and ultimately plurilateral agreements. As they point out, the negotiating Members who then seek to have a plurilateral agreement formalized as a legal instrument, by adding it to Annex 4 to the *Marrakesh Agreement Establishing the WTO* (which would then allow it to make use of the WTO's dispute settlement mechanism, for one), can do so only if during a WTO Ministerial Conference the WTO Members agree to do so by consensus.[59] The implied subtext is: "Don't count on it."

55   M Asif, "Growth and Sustainability Trends in the Buildings Sector in the GCC Region with Particular Reference to the KSA and UAE" (2016) 55 *Renewable & Sustainable Energy Review* 1267.

56   Currently, the contribution of renewable energy to electricity production in the GCC region is less than 5 percent. See Enerdata, "Share of Renewables in Electricity Production" (2024), online: yearbook.enerdata.net [perma.cc/P9PR-NYJZ]; the United Arab Emirates is the only GCC member with nuclear power plants. By 2050 it plans to be generating 6 percent of its electric power from those plants, and 44 percent from renewable energy sources. See Dania Saadi, "UAE's ENEC May Develop More Nuclear Power Plants Locally, Internationally in Future" (3 March 2022), online: spglobal.com [perma.cc/W27M-23KD].

57   Asmelash, above note 21 at 1004.

58   WTO, *Statement on FFS*, above note 41 at 5.

59   See WTO, *The Legal Status of 'Joint Statement Initiatives' and Their Negotiated Outcomes*, WTO Doc WT/GC/W/819 (2021), online (pdf): docs.wto.org [perma.cc/QR5X-7VEK].

E. Building on ACCTS

THE ALTERNATIVE TO PURSUING A plurilateral agreement *within* the WTO is to conclude one outside of it. That is where the ACCTS could provide a template for a "phased reduction pathway" for fossil fuel subsidies. Once the ACCTS enters into force—likely by early 2026[60]—it will be open to requests for accessions from any WTO Member.[61] However, the ACCTS also reduces import barriers to trade in environmental goods and services and provides guidelines for voluntary ecolabelling programs: it is likely that some FFSR Initiative members or other WTO Members who would be willing to be bound by ACCTS' rules pertaining to fossil fuel subsidies might not be willing to be bound by the whole rest of the Agreement. At the least, therefore, the ACCTS provides ideas that could be built upon.

The basic elements included in the ACCTS that pertain to fossil fuel subsidies are set out in Chapter 4, which include its objective and scope, definitions, disciplines, specific exceptions, transparency requirements, and procedures for reviewing the Chapter. Dispute Settlement is addressed in a separate chapter (Chapter 7) that applies to the whole Agreement. Neither the ACCTS nor Chapter 4 include specific language on special and differential treatment, but Chapter 4 does encourage technical cooperation and capacity building related to fossil fuel subsidies.

The objective of ACCTS Chapter 4 (Fossil Fuel Subsidies) is "to discipline and eliminate harmful fossil fuel subsidies in order to mitigate their adverse impact on the environment and contribute to global efforts to rapidly reduce greenhouse gas emissions resulting from production and consumption of fossil fuels." Its scope applies to subsidies as described in Article 4.3 (Definitions)—which are based on Article 1 of the SCM Agreement—that confer a benefit to producers or consumers of goods considered as fossil fuels (as set out in Annex VII to Chapter 4) or energy products considered as fossil fuels (as set out in Annex VIII to Chapter 4). Notably, the latter category excludes products made from fossil fuels that are not "used as a source of energy," such as nitrogenous fertilizers and plastics.

---

60   *ACCTS*, above note 48, art 8.3(2) (providing that "the Agreement shall enter into force on the first day of the third month following the date on which at least three signatories to the Agreement have notified the Depositary (New Zealand) in writing that they have completed their applicable legal procedures").

61   *Ibid*, art 8.6.

The Agreement prohibits Parties from introducing or maintaining subsidies for the production or consumption of peat, lignite, coal, or any coke or semi-coke made from those solid fuels; pitch or pitch coke obtained from coal tar or other mineral tars; and several types of bitumen and asphalt.[62] It also prohibits "subsidies for the exploration, extraction, refining, processing, manufacturing, storage and pipeline transportation, transport, distribution, trade, and marketing of oil and gas" derived from coal, petroleum or other gaseous hydrocarbons.[63] It sets *de minimis* limits on any new subsidies that a Party to the Agreement may introduce, provided that the subsidies are not of the type that are prohibited.[64] In addition, each Party is required to "eliminate or schedule" its existing fossil fuel subsidies "and shall not introduce any policy changes that increase an existing scheduled fossil fuel subsidy or enlarge its eligible group of recipients."[65] Each Party's schedule forms part of the Agreement. Notably, these various obligations do not apply to production subsidies for oil or natural gas "when such subsidies are granted in the form of tax revenue foregone".[66] This carve-out relates, essentially, to tax breaks, which are the most common form of support provided to the oil and gas industry.[67]

Most of the specific exceptions listed in Article 4.6 of the Agreement allow for fossil fuel subsidies that either do not benefit current production (e.g., support for decommissioning of fossil fuel infrastructure and research and development into ways to reduce greenhouse gas emissions or pollution resulting from the production or use of fossil fuels) or that provide targeted support to vulnerable groups or temporary support, such as in response to a natural disaster.

ACCTS also gives a Party the option to undertake its commitments using what the Agreement calls a "Standardized Carbon Rate Mechanism" (SCRM). The SCRM refers to the net total price applying to carbon dioxide (CO_2) emissions from the use of fossil fuels as a result of one or more policy instruments—such as a carbon tax or tradable carbon credit but not value-added

---

62 *Ibid*, art 4, Annex IX.

63 *Ibid*.

64 *Ibid*, art 4.5 at para 2.

65 *Ibid* at para 3.

66 *Ibid* at para 5.

67 See, e.g., the descriptions of individual policies contained in the OECD's Detailed FFS data, online: data-explorer.oecd.org [perma.cc/HD3K-6GH7] (last visited 24 March 2025).

taxes or the price effects of product or production regulations—that increases or decreases the effective CO_2 price. The Agreement deems a benefit to be conferred if, as a consequence of a financial contribution from its government or income or price support, the SCRM for a fossil fuel or energy product falls below the Party's commitment as set out in its appendix to Annex X of the Agreement.[68]

The Chapter's transparency provisions are set out in Article 4.9 (Transparency) and are similar to those set out in Article 25 of the SCM Agreement.[69] Each Party is required to notify the other Parties to the Agreement of any fossil fuel subsidy that is not prohibited, including production subsidies granted in the form of tax revenue and subsidies covered under Article 4.6 (Specific Exceptions). The information to be furnished on each notified subsidy include its legal basis, policy objective, form, rate (e.g., subsidy per unit), target recipient(s), and intended duration. These notifications are in addition to whatever notifications on the same subsidies each Party may furnish to the WTO.

Finally, Article 4.10 of the ACCTS calls on the Joint Commission, a body created to monitor and review the implementation of the overall Agreement,[70] at an unspecified date to undertake a review of various issues that have relevance to the implementation and operation of Chapter 4. Among the topics listed for review are the possible future inclusion of export restrictions or dual-pricing schemes as part of the measures covered under Article 4.3 (Definitions) and "the application of Article 4.5 (Prohibition and Scheduling of Fossil Fuel Subsidies) to production subsidies in the form of tax revenue forgone."[71]

As the topics identified for attention in the first Joint Commission review reveal, there remain outstanding issues that have not been fully resolved in the ACCTS. Besides dual-pricing and tax subsidies to production, the question of what benchmarks to use when measuring tax expenditures related to excise taxes or VAT has been a perennial issue in discussions of fossil fuel subsidies.[72] Another issue is financing, such as that provided by multilateral financial institutions and national development banks, through conces-

---

68   *ACCTS*, above note 48, art 4.5 at paras 2(b)(iii), 3.

69   *SCM Agreement*, above note 14, art 25.

70   *ACCTS*, above note 48 art 6.2.

71   *Ibid*, art 4.10.

72   Government of the Netherlands, "Joint Statement on Fossil Fuel Subsidies" (9 December 2023), online (pdf): government.nl [perma.cc/QA8K-T73C].

sional loans, loan guarantees, and equity injections, the subsidy values of which are difficult to estimate.[73] Still, that several countries have concluded an agreement on fossil fuel subsidies that both disciplines some subsidies and provides a review process strengthening it is a positive development.

Whatever might be the theoretically optimal path to reform, it is likely that the countries that are committed to phasing out fossil fuel subsidies will continue to probe multiple pathways in the hope that a breakthrough will take place that will reveal the one that is some compromise between smoothest and fastest.

---

73   Yuki Matsumoto, Chloé Papazian, & Jegan Sauvage, *Quantifying the Role of State Enterprises in Industrial Subsidies* (Paris: OECD, 2024).

CHAPTER 31

#TradeForWomen: A Quest for Mainstreaming Gender Considerations in WTO Agreements

Margaret M. Kim[*]

Les petits ruisseaux font les grandes rivières.
It is from small streams that big rivers rise.

VALERIE HUGHES HAS BEEN A model advocate for women's empowerment in international trade in her multiple roles as a counsel, adjudicator, teacher, and mentor. This chapter is a tribute to her pioneering achievements, which have paved numerous paths for women in trade, and it seeks to build on her thought leadership on inclusive trade, particularly in the sphere of trade and gender.

A. Introduction

SINCE THE WORLD TRADE ORGANIZATION (WTO)'s inception, global trade has surged, reaching over USD 30.4 trillion in 2023—a fivefold increase

---

[*] The views expressed in this chapter are my own and do not necessarily reflect those of the Government of Ontario.

from 1995.[1] Despite its pivotal role in driving trade liberalization and consequential global economic growth, the WTO—the institution responsible for making and operating a global system of trade rules—has historically remained "gender neutral" or "gender blind" to the uneven distributional impacts of trade[2] and the barriers women face in participating in global trade.[3]

The WTO made a marked departure from gender-blind trade in December 2017 with the signing of the Joint Declaration on Trade and Women's Economic Empowerment at the margins of the 11th WTO Ministerial Conference in Buenos Aires, Argentina. The Buenos Aires Declaration signified the first occasion in WTO history, where WTO Members and observers collectively endorsed an initiative to increase the participation of women in trade, remove trade barriers that limit women's economic opportunities, and identify a framework for collaborating on making trade and development policies more gender-responsive at the WTO.[4] Currently, 127 WTO Members and observers—over two-thirds of Member and observer states—have endorsed the Declaration.[5]

Since that watershed event, recent efforts by the WTO and its Members to promote trade and gender suggest that the WTO is "at the vanguard" of gender-inclusive trade.[6] Yet, the rapidly evolving global trade landscape—

---

1   WTO, "Thirty Years of Trade Growth and Poverty Reduction" (24 April 2024), online (blog): wto.org [perma.cc/GU4L-BK3S].

2   See Katrin Kuhlmann & Amrita Bahri, "Gender Mainstreaming in Trade Agreements: 'A Potemkin Façade'?" in WTO, *Making Trade Work for Women: Key findings from the 2022 World Trade Congress on Gender* (Geneva: WTO, 2023) 234 at 235–36, online (pdf): wto.org [perma.cc/WS86-3H3V]; for a broader discussion on narratives that identify the "winners" and "losers" of economic globalization, see Anthea Roberts & Nicolas Lamp, *Six Faces of Globalization: Who Wins, Who Loses, and Why It Matters* (Cambridge, MA: Harvard University Press, 2021).

3   World Bank Group, *Women, Business and the Law 2024* (Washington, DC: World Bank Group, 2024), online (pdf): openknowledge.worldbank.org [perma.cc/64JZ-XJZ8].

4   See WTO, *Joint Declaration on Trade and Women's Economic Empowerment on the Occasion of the WTO Ministerial Conference in Buenos Aires in December 2017* (2017), online (pdf): wto.org [perma.cc/UVL6-PD22] [WTO, *Buenos Aires Declaration*]; Rohini Acharya et al, "Trade and Women—Opportunities for Women in the Framework of the World Trade Organization" (2019) 22:3 *Journal of International Economics* 323.

5   WTO, "Women and Trade: Buenos Aires Declaration on Trade and Women's Economic Empowerment" (last visited 11 June 2025), online: wto.org [perma.cc/J87X-2MPV].

6   WTO, "World Trade Congress on Gender: Remarks by Deputy Director-General Angela Ellard" (7 December 2022), online: wto.org [perma.cc/G3KU-JR33] ("With more than 80 speakers and 15 sessions, this is the first time in the history of the WTO that we have held discussions on trade and gender of such magnitude . . . I'm so glad to see the WTO at the vanguard of work on such a significant topic."); for a list of

propelled by digital transformation, technological innovation, rise in services, and geopolitical fragmentation—demands a multi-pronged approach to mainstreaming gender considerations and promoting women's economic empowerment. Despite its fair share of challenges, this topic undeniably warrants continued focus at the WTO, as it aligns with the organization's founding objectives of sustainable and inclusive trade[7] and can enhance shared prosperity among its Members.[8]

This chapter contends that the WTO's gender mainstreaming efforts should incorporate a gender lens into its trade rules. It examines the integration of women-related considerations into select WTO agreements, particularly those aligned with the key discussion themes of the Buenos Aires Declaration: trade facilitation, e-commerce and digital trade, small and medium-sized enterprises (SMEs), and public procurement. The chapter adopts both reflective and prospective approaches to assess successes, missed opportunities, and future prospects for achieving this consideration. The increasing adoption of explicit gender provisions on these key themes by bilateral and plurilateral trade agreements suggests that the time is ripe for the WTO and its Members to evaluate the merits of embedding a gender perspective into trade negotiations within these disciplines.

The remainder of the chapter is structured as follows. Section B provides an overview of the gender-specific barriers women face in international trade. Section C examines current gender mainstreaming trends in bilateral and regional free trade agreements, which serve as laboratories for trade rulemaking, as well as in plurilateral agreements such as the *Global Trade and Gender Arrangement* and the *Digital Economy Partnership Agreement*. Section D surveys how and why the WTO has—and has not—integrated women's perspectives into its agreements related to services, trade facilitation, public

---

recent initiatives at the WTO on women's empowerment in trade, see Amrita Bahri, "Can WTO Laws and Institutions Empower Women?" in Amrita Bahri, *Trade Agreements and Women: Transcending Barriers* (Oxford: Oxford University Press, 2025) 64 at 64–65 (citing Anoush der Boghossian, "Gender-Responsive WTO: Making Trade Rules and Policies Work for Women" in Amrita Bahri, Dorotea López, & Jan Yves Remy, eds, *Trade Policy and Gender Equality* (Cambridge, UK: Cambridge University Press, 2023) 21).

7 See *Marrakesh Agreement Establishing the WTO*, 15 April 1994, 1867 UNTS 154, Preamble at para 1 [*Marrakesh Agreement*].

8 World Bank & WTO, *Women and Trade: The Role of Trade in Promoting Gender Equality* (Washington, DC: World Bank Group, 2020), online (pdf): openknowledge.worldbank. org [perma.cc/35HS-JULS] [*World Bank & WTO, 2020 Report*].

procurement, and e-commerce and digital trade. Section E offers concluding thoughts.

B. Barriers to Women's Participation in Trade

TRADE POLICIES AND AGREEMENTS CAN affect women and men differently due to a combination of social, economic, and cultural factors,[9] as well as industry-specific, country-specific, regional contexts, and wealth disparities. Women engage in international trade in various capacities, including as workers, producers, consumers,[10] traders and entrepreneurs, and decisionmakers. In these roles, women often face constraints that either do not apply to men or apply to them to a lesser degree.[11]

Recent data-driven and comprehensive studies have provided deeper insights into the systemic and structural barriers faced by women in trade. These challenges are multi-faceted and intertwined. According to the World Bank and WTO's 2020 Report on the Role of Trade in Promoting Gender Equality, these barriers can be classified into two categories.[12]

The first category includes barriers directly related to the movement of goods and services across international borders. These barriers encompass higher trading costs (e.g., tariffs[13] and non-tariff measures[14]), burdensome

---

9   United Nations, "Gender Equality & Trade Policy" (2011), online (pdf): un.org [perma. cc/P3KB-F2EJ].

10   See United Nations, "Addis Ababa Action Agenda of the Third International Conference on Financing for Development" (2015) at 90, online (pdf): sustainabledevelopment.un.org [perma.cc/3GYA-ZXQ9] (recognizing the critical role of women as producers and traders and addressing their specific challenges in order to facilitate women's equal and active participation in domestic, regional, and international trade).

11   World Bank & WTO, *2020 Report*, above note 8 at 83–84.

12   *Ibid* at 82.

13   Sectors that employ more women (e.g., textiles and apparel, food, and beverage) face higher tariffs on input than other sectors. They are often referred to as "pink tariffs," which can increase trade costs and hinder the competitiveness of sectors in which women are more heavily represented. See also, Nadia Rocha & Roberta Piermartini, "Trade and Development Chart: Pink Tariffs Burden Women's Employment" (23 October 2023), online (blog): blogs.worldbank.org [perma.cc/8E8W-WZ93].

14   Non-tariff measures (NTMs) can incur high trade costs, which are disproportionately borne by women. These costs include information costs (identifying requirements), compliance costs (meeting product requirements), costs to demonstrate compliance (e.g., certification), as well as indirect time costs associated with demonstrating compliance (e.g., delays at borders). See United Nations, *Neutral Policies, Uneven Impacts:*

customs requirements,[15] bureaucratic measures, and gender-based discrimination that women may face at border crossings, which can compromise women's physical security.[16] The second category consists of "beyond-the-border" constraints. These include limited access and control over resources, such as land and other assets, credit, information, and technology.[17] Social constraints—which are more intrinsic—are also significant, as women often bear more social responsibility involving informal, unpaid domestic work (e.g., childcare and eldercare)[18] and face discriminatory cultural norms[19] and legal barriers that impede their meaningful participation in international trade.[20] Notably, the World Bank's Women, Business, and the Law (WBL) 2024 Report identifies 504 legal provisions across 145 economies that hinder

---

Non-tariff Measures through a Gender Lens (Geneva: United Nations, 2022), online (pdf): unctad.org [perma.cc/T5QK-BTC9].

15   Customs duties tend to be particularly high for products essential to women, such as hygiene items and reproductive health goods. For example, these goods are subject to significantly high tariffs in a number of countries, including the Bahamas (30 percent), Djibouti (26 percent), and Mexico (15 percent). See Hannelore Maria Leona Niesten & Lolita Laperle-Forget, "Equal Rights, Unequal Import Tariffs: How Women Pay the Price" (21 November 2023), online (blog): blogs.worldbank.org [perma. cc/3MDW-3WDC].

16   See Mila Malavoloneque & Ankur Huria, "Making Trade Safer for Women Cross-Border Traders in Mozambique and Malawi" (8 March 2023), online (blog): blogs.worldbank.org [perma.cc/3NE5-S9PH] (observing small-scale women cross-border traders are victims of verbal, physical, and sexual harassment and face discriminatory border passing practices).

17   World Bank & WTO, *2020 Report*, above note 8 at 92–94.

18   *Ibid*; see also, Ally Brodsky, Jasmine Lim, & William Reinsch, *Women and Trade: How Trade Agreements Can Level the Gender Playing Field* (Washington, DC: Center for Strategic & International Studies, 2021), online (pdf): csis.org [perma. cc/6U6F-CMQY].

19   World Bank & WTO, *2020 Report*, above note 8 at 105 ("Even if all discriminatory laws and practices were addressed overnight, women would still face challenges to playing a more active role as traders. Many of the barriers that prevent them from accessing the benefits of trade are rooted in social, cultural, and behavioral phenomena that legal and regulatory reforms can affect only over time").

20   Lolita Laperle-Forget & Alev Gürbüz Cuneo, *Women, International Trade, and the Law: Breaking Barriers for Gender Equality in Export-Related Activities* (Washington, DC: World Bank Group, 2024), online (pdf): worldbank.org [perma.cc/S6GN-M7LW]; United Nations, *Gender and Trade – Assessing the Impact of Trade Agreements on Gender Equality: Canada-EU Comprehensive Economic Trade Agreement* (Geneva: United Nations, 2020), online (pdf): unctad.org [perma.cc/U2JZ-J9PU]; and *Trade as a Tool for the Economic Empowerment of Women*, UNCTAD, 2016, UN Doc B/C.I/ EM.8/2, online (pdf): unctad.org [perma.cc/P4SZ-JCCP].

women's participation in global trade.[21] Examples of such legal restrictions include limitations on women's ownership and property rights, the inability to sign export contracts or register a business, and prohibitions on working in certain industries, thereby preventing equal participation in the workforce of exporting firms.[22]

Addressing these barriers is not only a moral imperative but also can enhance women's participation in international trade, thereby fostering greater global economic growth.[23] The 2015 McKinsey Global Institute Report projects that if women participated in the economy identically to men to their "full potential," the global Gross Domestic Product (GDP) in 2025 would increase by 26 percent—to USD 28 trillion,[24] a figure that is almost equivalent to the 2023 GDP of the United States of America.[25]

Gender mainstreaming[26] in trade agreements is a "top-down" legal approach that can influence domestic laws and policies, societal frameworks, and the workplace and economic sectors to promote women's economic

---

21   Laperle-Forget & Gürbüz Cuneo, above note 20.

22   Lolita Laperle-Forget, "The Power of Gender Equality Laws to Shape Inclusive Trade" (26 March 2024), online (blog): blogs.worldbank.org [perma.cc/CP66-MQ3Z] (offering the example of the Russian Federation, where women are prohibited from employment in oil production, and thus being excluded from an industry that constitutes 42 percent of Russian exports and is valued at over USD 7.3 trillion).

23   See, e.g., World Bank, *Gender Strategy 2024-2023: Accelerate Gender Equality for a Sustainable, Resilient, and Inclusive Future (Consultation draft)* (Washington, DC: World Bank Group, 2023) at 4–5, online (pdf): worldbank.org [perma.cc/KK6H-EZMN].

24   McKinsey Global Institute, *The Power of Parity: How Advancing Women's Equality Can Add $12 Trillion to Global Growth* (New York: McKinsey & Company, 2015) at 3, online (pdf): mckinsey.com [perma.cc/BY2E-T4VV].

25   US Department of Commerce, "Gross Domestic Product, Fourth Quarter and Year 2023 (Second Estimate)" (28 February 2024), online: bea.gov [perma.cc/CC4P-ZFGZ].

26   "Gender mainstreaming" can be defined as the "(re)organization, improvement, development, and evaluation of policy process so that a gender equality perspective is incorporated in all policies at all levels at all stages, by the actors normally involved in policymaking. The aim of gender mainstreaming is to take into account differences in policymaking, so that they benefit both women and men and do not increase inequality but enhance gender equality." See Council of Europe, "What is Gender Mainstreaming?" (last visited 30 March 2025), online: coe.int [perma.cc/469Y-XMRP]. For a more in-depth explanation of gender mainstreaming from a human rights perspective, see United Nations, *Handbook on Gender Mainstreaming for Gender Equality Results* (Geneva: United Nations, 2022), online (pdf): unwomen.org [perma.cc/ RPX9-6DYX].

empowerment and gender equality.[27] The aim of this strategy is to ensure that trade policies and agreements address the specific needs and challenges faced by women in global trade and promote gender equality.[28] Section C examines the recent trends in incorporating gender considerations into bilateral and regional trade agreements, as well as a couple of plurilateral agreements.

C. Recent Trends of Mainstreaming Gender Considerations in Trade Agreements

1) Evolution of Gender-Related Provisions in Regional Trade Agreements

INCORPORATING GENDER CONSIDERATIONS INTO TRADE agreements has become increasingly commonplace, but this was not always the case. Before the 1990s, only a few trade agreements included gender-related provisions, such as the 1957 *Treaty of Rome establishing the European Economic Community* (EEC) and the 1983 *Treaty establishing the Economic Community of Central African States* (ECCAS).[29] It was not until 2016 that the number and share of bilateral and regional trade agreements (RTAs) with gender-related provisions significantly surged.[30] The WTO Database on gender provisions in RTAs, last updated in September 2022, indicates that approximately one-third (106 out of 353) of in-force RTAs—both notified and unnotified to the WTO—contain at least one explicit reference to women.[31]

In the absence of updated data from the WTO Database, the author examined gender provisions in RTAs from 2022 to February 2025. This analysis revealed that at least fifteen new RTAs with one or more gender-related

---

27   Amrita Bahri, Dorotea López, & Jan Yves Remy, "Introduction" in Bahri, López, & Remy, above note 6 at 5.

28   International Trade Centre, *Mainstreaming Gender in Free Trade Agreements* (Geneva: International Trade Centre, 2020) at 2, online (pdf): intracen.org [perma.cc/L4F6-2VQG] [ITC, *2020 She Trades Report*].

29   See José-Antonio Monteiro, "Gender-Related Provisions in Regional Trade Agreements" (2018) WTO, Working Paper ERSD 2018-15 at 4 and 7, online (pdf): wto.org [perma.cc/QE3F-6CWL].

30   *Ibid*; see also ITC, *2020 She Trades Report*, above note 28; WTO, *Informal Working Group on Trade and Gender: Trade and Gender-Related Provisions in Regional Trade Agreements*, WTO Doc INF/TGE/COM/4/Rev.1 (2023), online (pdf): docs.wto.org [perma.cc/8N2T-FARK] [WTO, *IWGTG Report 2023*]. See also Monteiro, *ibid*, for a more in-depth account on the evolution of gender-related provisions in RTAs.

31   WTO, *IWGTG Report 2023*, above note 30 at 2.

provisions have come into force, alongside at least nine additional RTAs that have been signed but are not yet effective.[32] This emerging trend highlights the growing integration of gender mainstreaming within RTAs, indicating that explicit women-related provisions in RTAs are "here to stay."[33]

RTAs offer fertile ground for piloting and advancing innovative trade policies that address women's welfare concerns and promote economic empowerment.[34] The following key insights are derived from observations of recently implemented and signed RTAs that incorporate gender considerations.

Observation 1: An Increasing Number of Trade Agreements Have Incorporated Dedicated Chapters and Articles on Trade and Gender Equality

Prior to 2022, only a limited number of RTAs featured dedicated chapters on gender equality, exemplified by the modernized *Canada–Chile Free Trade Agreement* (2019),[35] *Chile–Argentina Free Trade Agreement* (2019),[36] and the modernized *Canada–Israel Free Trade Agreement* (2019).[37] However, since then, new signatories—including Brazil, Ecuador, Paraguay, New Zealand, Australia, the United Kingdom, and the European Union—have adopted standalone gender chapters in their trade agreements. This trend signals the growing utilization of trade agreements to advance women's economic empowerment and the increasing recognition of the benefits associated with gender-inclusive

---

32 *European Union–Malaysia Framework Agreement on Partnership and Cooperation*, 14 December 2022; *Organisation of African, Caribbean and Pacific States (OACPS)–European Union Samoa Agreement*, 15 November 2023 (provisionally applied to the signatories since January 2024, effective date pending ratification of two thirds of OACPS members) [OACPS–EU Samoa Agreement]; *MERCOSUR–Singapore Free Trade Agreement*, 7 December 2023; *European Free Trade Association–India Trade and Economic Partnership Agreement*, 10 March 2024; *Australia–United Arab Emirates Comprehensive Economic Partnership Agreement*, 11 June 2024 [Australia–UAE CEPA]; *European Union–Kyrgyzstan Enhanced Partnership and Cooperation Agreement*, 24 June 2024; *Chile–United Arab Emirates Comprehensive Economic Partnership Agreement*, 28 July 2024; *European Free Trade Association–Kosovo Free Trade Agreement*, 21 January 2025; and *New Zealand–United Arab Emirates Comprehensive Economic Partnership Agreement*, 13 January 2025 [New Zealand–UAE CEPA].

33 ITC, *2020 She Trades Report*, above note 28 at 2.

34 Amrita Bahri, "Gender Mainstreaming in Trade Agreements: Best Practice Examples and Challenges in the Asia-Pacific" in Bahri, López, & Remy, above note 6 at 294.

35 Modernized *Canada–Chile Free Trade Agreement*, 5 June 2017 (entered into force 5 February 2019) [CCFTA].

36 *Chile–Argentina Free Trade Agreement*, 2 November 2017 (entered into force 1 May 2019) [Chile–Argentina FTA].

37 Modernized *Canada–Israel Free Trade Agreement*, 28 May 2018 (entered into force 1 September 2019) [CIFTA].

trade rules. Furthermore, some of these RTAs' standalone gender chapters also reiterate commitments to advancing women's economic empowerment and promoting gender equality in SMEs/micro, small and medium-sized enterprises (MSMEs), financial services, labour, public procurement, and digital trade.[38] Accordingly, these new agreements exemplify more specific and robust gender mainstreaming in trade agreements.

Observation 2: More Parties Have Reaffirmed Their Commitments to Women's Economic Empowerment and Gender Equality Within International Frameworks, Including Those Articulated in the Buenos Aires Declaration

Standalone gender chapters in RTAs typically include general provisions (such as objectives) and provisions related to international agreements,[39] recognizing women's pivotal role in trade and reaffirming adherence to international frameworks such as the *United Nations' Sustainable Development Goal (SDG) 5*[40] and the *Convention on the Elimination of All Forms of Discrimination Against Women* (CEDAW), widely regarded as the international bill of rights for women.

Among the fifteen RTAs enforced since 2022, nine explicitly incorporate the WTO Buenos Aires Declaration, with varying placements.[41] For instance, the *UK–Australia FTA* (2023)[42] includes it in its objectives provision, while the

---

38 See *United Kingdom–Australia Free Trade Agreement*, 17 December 2021, arts 16.22.2(f) and 24.1.4 [*UK–Australia FTA*]; *United Kingdom–New Zealand Free Trade Agreement*, 28 February 2022, arts 16.22.2(e) and 25.5.3(g) [*UK–New Zealand FTA*].

39 See Valerie Hughes, "Gender Chapters in Trade Agreements: Nice Rhetoric or Sound Policy?" (9 October 2019), online: cigionline.org [perma.cc/R472-7JQ8].

40 United Nations, "Sustainable Development Goals – Goal 5: Gender Equality" (last visited 30 March 2025), online: un.org [perma.cc/9J9F-PYZH].

41 *Brazil–Chile Free Trade Agreement*, 21 November 2018, art 18.1.4 [*Brazil–Chile FTA*]; *Chile–Ecuador Economic Complementation Agreement*,13 August 2020, art 18.1.6 [*Chile–Ecuador ECA*]; *Iceland–Liechtenstein–Norway–United Kingdom Free Trade Agreement*, 8 July 2021, art 13.17.3 [*Iceland–Liechtenstein–Norway–UK FTA*]; *UK–New Zealand FTA*, above note 38, art 25.4.2; *UK–Australia FTA*, above note 38, art 24.1.3; *Chile–Paraguay Free Trade Agreement*, 1 December 2021, art 13.3(d) [*Chile–Paraguay FTA*]; *Modernized Canada–Ukraine Free Trade Agreement*, 22 September 2023, art 23.2.5 [*Modernized Canada–Ukraine FTA*]; *European Union–New Zealand Free Trade Agreement*, 9 July 2023, art 19.4.2 [*EU–New Zealand FTA*]; *European Union–Chile Interim Trade Agreement*, 13 December 2023, art 27.1.5 [*Interim EU–Chile FTA*].

42 *UK–Australia FTA*, above note 38, art 24.1.3. Interestingly, the parties also acknowledge the work of *other* multilateral fora, such as the Organization for Economic Co-operation and Development, in advancing the evidence base on women's economic empowerment and trade.

Chile–Paraguay FTA (2024),[43] *UK–New Zealand FTA* (2024),[44] *Iceland–Liechten-stein–Norway–UK FTA* (2023),[45] and *Chile-Ecuador Economic Complementation Agreement* (ECA) (2022)[46] incorporate it within their international agreements provisions. In the latter two agreements, the parties explicitly reference the fourth preamble in the Buenos Aires Declaration, which acknowledges the need to develop evidence-based interventions to address barriers limiting women's economic opportunities.[47]

Among the nine RTAs with gender provisions signed but not yet in force since 2022, the *Australia–UAE CEPA* (2024)[48] and the *New Zealand–UAE CEPA* (2024)[49] affirm the parties' commitments made in the Buenos Aires Declaration. The inclusion of the Buenos Aires Declaration in RTAs with gender provisions, along with references to specific commitments the parties wish to prioritize, is becoming increasingly common. In the case of the *United Kingdom–Japan Free Trade Agreement* (2021), the parties go beyond merely acknowledging their commitments by agreeing to undertake cooperation activities related to the Buenos Aires Declaration.[50]

Although the Buenos Aires Declaration is a soft law instrument, its increasing citation in recent RTAs indicates that the WTO remains the recognized forum for addressing issues related to women and trade. This observation is echoed in the context of the stand-alone plurilateral agreements analyzed in subsection 2 below.

Observation 3: An Increasing Number of Trade Agreements Now Include Specific Cooperation-Based Provisions to Promote Women's

---

43   *Chile–Paraguay FTA*, above note 41, art 13.3(d) (International Agreements): "Each Party reaffirms its commitment to implement ... the WTO Joint Declaration on Trade and Women's Economic Empowerment, adopted at the WTO Ministerial Conference in Buenos Aires in December 2017."

44   *UK–New Zealand FTA*, above note 38, art 25.4.2 (International Instruments).

45   Iceland-Liechtenstein-Norway-UK FTA, above note 41, art 13.17.3 International Commitments: "The Parties recognise the commitments made in the Joint Declaration on Trade and Women's Economic Empowerment on the occasion of the WTO Ministerial Conference in Buenos Aires in December 2017, including acknowledgement of the need to develop evidence-based interventions to address the barriers that limit opportunities for women in the economy."

46   *Chile–Ecuador ECA*, above note 41, art 18.1.6.

47   WTO, *Buenos Aires Declaration*, above note 4.

48   *Australia–UAE CEPA*, above note 32, art 19.2.

49   *New Zealand–UAE CEPA*, above note 32, art 14.6.2.

50   *United Kingdom–Japan Free Trade Agreement*, 23 October 2020, art 21.2(d).

Empowerment in the Areas of SMES, Public Procurement, and E-Commerce and Digital Trade

As Valerie Hughes observed in her 2019 article, "Gender Chapters in Trade Agreements: Nice Rhetoric or Sound Policy?", traditional gender provisions have typically been declarative, affirming principles such as gender equality, equal pay for equal work, the elimination of workplace discrimination, and similar principles.[51] Hughes further observed that the new gender chapters found in the three RTAs—CCFTA, Chile–Argentina FTA, and CIFTA—include "considerably more content," such as provisions regarding cooperation activities, specific commitments to establish a trade and gender committee, and, in one case, a dispute settlement provision.[52]

The recently enforced or signed RTAs follow the trend of incorporating more specific and robust cooperation activities.[53] Notably, aligning with emerging trends in global trade—such as the rise in services,[54] the growth of digital economy,[55] and the proliferation of SMEs[56]—the newly implemented RTAs contain cooperation provisions focused on women's empowerment in SMEs and MSMEs, as well as in e-commerce and digital trade and public procurement obligations. Each of these areas is examined below.

---

51 Hughes, above note 39.

52 *Ibid.*

53 For additional actions to address gender issues and implement gender provisions, see Lolita Laperle-Forget, "WTO Database on Gender Provisions in RTAs" (last visited 30 March 2025), online (pdf): wto.org [perma.cc/FZZ4-2WZ2].

54 See United Nations Trade and Development, "Services are Powering Growth. Here's How Developing Nations Can Catch Up" (23 December 2024), online: unctad.org [perma.cc/3N3V-WUFG] (noting that service exports now represent 25 percent of world trade). See also, WTO & World Bank, *Trade in Services for Development: Fostering Sustainable Growth and Economic Diversification* (Geneva: WTO, 2023) at 13, online (pdf): wto.org [perma.cc/YB64-H79T].

55 See United Nations Trade and Development, "Digital Economy Report 2024" (last visited 30 March 2025), online: unctad.org [perma.cc/E63N-M97Y] (observing that new data from forty-three countries, representing 75 percent of global GDP, show business e-commerce sales grew nearly 60 percent from 2016 to 2022, reaching $27 trillion).

56 See World Bank, "Small and Medium Enterprises (SMEs) Finance" (16 October 2019), online: worldbank.org [perma.cc/5PV6-73JC] (stating that SMEs account for the majority of businesses worldwide, representing about 90 percent of businesses and more than 50 percent of employment worldwide).

a) Commitments Pertaining to Women's Empowerment and the Advancement of SMEs or MSMEs

Of the fifteen RTAs that have come into force since 2022 and incorporate women's considerations, ten agreements include provisions explicitly aimed at improving women's opportunities in SMEs or MSMEs.[57] The *India–United Arab Emirates Comprehensive Economic Partnership Agreement* (India–UAE CEPA) (2022) notably includes several substantive commitments to promote women's empowerment pertaining to SMEs.[58]

Firstly, India and the UAE established an SME Committee (Article 13.4). Among the activities that are mandated for the SME Committee is the facilitation of information exchange on entrepreneurship education and awareness programs for women, thereby promoting an entrepreneurial environment in the territories of the parties.[59] Secondly, Article 13.2, titled "Cooperation to Increase Trade and Investment Opportunities for SMEs", enumerates five actions through which each party shall seek to increase trade and investment opportunities. One such action involves strengthening collaboration on activities that promote women-owned SMEs and startups, fostering partnerships among these SMEs, and encouraging their participation in international trade.[60]

The inclusion of these provisions represents a significant advancement for India, which has not previously negotiated gender-related provisions

---

57 *Brazil–Chile FTA*, above note 41, art 10.15(a); *India–United Arab Emirates Comprehensive Economic Partnership Agreement*, 18 February 2022, art 13.2(b) [India–UAE CEPA]; *Chile–Ecuador ECA*, above note 41, art 10.14; *United Arab Emirates–Israel Comprehensive Economic Partnership Agreement*, 31 May 2022, art 13.2(b); *UK–New Zealand FTA*, above note 38, arts 24.3.1(c) and 25.5.3(h); *UK–Australia FTA*, above note 38, arts 19.1.4 and 24.1.4; *Turkiye–United Arab Emirates Comprehensive Economic Partnership Agreement*, 3 March 2023, art 15.2(b); *Indonesia–United Arab Emirates Comprehensive Economic Partnership Agreement*, 1 July 2022, art 13.2(b); *Chile–Paraguay FTA*, above note 41, art 13.5.5(b); Interim EU–Chile FTA, above note 41, art 27.4.5.

58 The India–UAE CEPA is the first bilateral trade agreement signed by the UAE and the first trade agreement in the MENA region signed by India. See United Arab Emirates Ministry of Economy, *The India-UAE Comprehensive Economic Partnership Agreement* (Abu Dhabi: United Arab Emirates Ministry of Economy, 2012), online (pdf): moec.gov. ae [perma.cc/7D7U-J88V].

59 India–UAE CEPA, above note 57, art 13.4(l) (this provision includes youth in addition to women).

60 India–UAE CEPA, above note 57, art 13.2(b) (this provision also includes youth in addition to women).

in its RTAs[61] nor endorsed the Buenos Aires Declaration. According to the International Finance Corporation (IFC), Indian women entrepreneurs lead nearly 15 million MSMEs, predominantly in manufacturing, out of 63 million Indian MSMEs, contributing 30 percent of the national GDP and over 40 percent of exports.[62] Future studies would benefit from examining the impact of these MSME provisions in unlocking more opportunities for women-owned and women-led SMEs in bilateral trade between the UAE and India. Additionally, it would be valuable to track whether India and the UAE continue to adopt more gender-related provisions in their future trade agreements.

b) Enhancing Women Entrepreneurs' Participation in Public Procurement

The Buenos Aires Declaration underscores the importance of enhancing women entrepreneurs' participation in public procurement markets as a key discussion theme for achieving gender equality in trade. Despite the global public procurement market for goods, services, and construction work being valued at approximately USD 13 trillion, only 1 percent of this amount is awarded to women-owned businesses.[63]

Among the fifteen RTAs that have come into force since 2022, four include explicit provisions to promote women-owned businesses in public procurement markets.[64] Additionally, of the nine RTAs signed but not yet in force, one contains a cooperation provision aimed at encouraging women's greater participation in government procurement.[65] Two agreements show leadership in mainstreaming gender considerations in this regard: the *UK–Australia FTA* and the *UK–New Zealand FTA* reinforce this commitment by

---

61 Monteiro, above note 29 at 11 (observing that the inclusion of comprehensive gender-related provision is a relatively recent phenomenon and countries such as India, Pakistan, and Switzerland have not negotiated gender-related provisions in their respective RTAs).

62 International Finance Corporation, "Small Business, Big Impact: Empowering Women SMEs for Success" (27 June 2024), online: ifc.org [perma.cc/T45P-GYD6].

63 International Trade Centre, *WTO Government Procurement Agreement: A Gender Lens for Action* (Geneva: International Trade Centre, 2023), online (pdf): intracen.org [perma.cc/2Z7M-YSQ8] [ITC, *WTO GPA Gender*].

64 *UK–New Zealand FTA*, above note 38, arts 16.22.2(e) and 25.5(g); *UK–Australia FTA*, above note 38, art 16.22.2(f); *Chile–Paraguay FTA*, above note 41, art 13.5.5(i); and Modernized Canada–Ukraine FTA, above note 41, art 23.4(g).

65 *Australia–UAE CEPA*, above note 32, art 15.25.1(g).

including provisions in their government procurement chapters[66] and then referencing this commitment again in their standalone gender chapters. The *UK–New Zealand FTA* takes a further step by establishing a Government Procurement Working Group to facilitate women's participation in government procurement, in line with the objectives of the Chapter on Trade and Gender Equality.[67]

The timing of these RTAs' commitments regarding women's participation in public procurement is particularly significant in the context of post-pandemic recovery. According to UN Women, there has been a notable increase in policy-building initiatives aimed at leveraging public procurement processes as a strategic tool to support the post-COVID-19 recovery of women-led enterprises, for example, in the Latin American and Caribbean (LAC) region. This region has faced unparalleled challenges, making these efforts crucial for fostering economic resilience and gender equality.[68] Chile, one of the pioneering countries in the LAC region to implement a robust procurement and contracting system, is among the signatories in the recently enforced RTAs that commit to enhancing women entrepreneurs' participation in public procurement. It remains to be seen how the public procurement rules embedded in RTAs will serve as catalysts for domestic public procurement changes, fostering greater access for women-owned and women-led businesses.

c)   Advancing Inclusive Electronic Commerce & Digital Trade for Women

Digital trade—often used interchangeably with electronic commerce (e-commerce)—is a cornerstone of modern commerce,[69] offering numerous

---

66   *UK–New Zealand FTA*, above note 38, art 16.22.2(e); and *UK–Australia FTA*, above note 38, art 15.22.2(f).

67   *UK–New Zealand FTA*, above note 38, art 16.22.2(e).

68   See UN Women, *Public Procurement with a Gender Perspective: Achievements and Challenges in the Revitalization of Women-Led Enterprises in Latin America as a Driver of the Post-COVID-19 Recovery* (New York: UN Women, 2022), online (pdf): unwomen. org [perma.cc/D8YE-6B3K].

69   According to WTO estimates, digitally delivered services (via Mode 1) have recorded an almost fourfold increase in value since 2005, rising 8.1 percent on average per year over the period 2005–22, outpacing goods (5.6 percent) and other services exports (4.2 percent) to account for 54 percent of total services exports. See WTO, *Handbook on Measuring Digital Trade* (Geneva: WTO, 2023) at 74, online (pdf): wto.org [perma. cc/2ALJ-KRTS].

potential benefits.[70] Studies suggest that women's deeper involvement in e-commerce can drive inclusive growth and support their economic empowerment.[71] E-commerce can facilitate the entry of women entrepreneurs into trade by mitigating supply-side barriers that disproportionately affect them, particularly in areas such as access to finance, business networks, and market opportunities.[72] Bridging a substantial digital gender divide that exists at the global level also remains a monumental task,[73] one that requires multi-level solutions beyond what trade agreements alone can offer.

There is an increasing number of recently enforced or signed RTAs that aim to advance inclusive e-commerce and digital trade for women. Among the RTAs enforced since 2022, seven agreements contain provisions that explicitly link gender with e-commerce and digital trade.[74]

These provisions focus on capacity building and collaboration in establishing best practices, employing both macro and micro approaches. Some agreements emphasize solutions that cater to individual women's skill-building and access to information. For example, the *UK–New Zealand FTA* promotes business development services for women to enhance their digital skills and access online business tools. Conversely, other agreements adopt a more macro approach by establishing and implementing legal and institutional frameworks.

The *Chile–Paraguay FTA*'s robust digital inclusion provision includes a non-exhaustive list of cooperative activities designed to achieve digital inclusion for women.[75] The list encompasses the exchange of experiences and best practices, including the exchange of experts, addressing barriers to accessing

---

70   For a thorough discussion on the statistical definitions of digital trade and e-commerce, see IMF, OECD, UN, WB & WTO, *Digital Trade for Development* (Geneva: WTO, 2023) at 18, online (pdf): wto.org [perma.cc/PR8V-HYXS].

71   United Nations Trade and Development, *The Impact of Non-Tariff Measures on Women's E-Commerce Businesses in Developing Countries* (Geneva: UNCAD, 2024) at 3, online: unctad.org [perma.cc/Z64X-HSLM].

72   *Ibid* at 6; See also World Bank & WTO, *2020 Report*, above note 8 at 136–41 ("Opportunities for women in trade through digital technology").

73   See, e.g., Jan Yves Remy, "Closing the Digital Gender Divide through Trade Rules" (9 October 2019), online: cigionline.org [perma.cc/C2NW-44Q2].

74   *Brazil–Chile FTA*, above note 41, art 10.15(a); *Chile–Ecuador ECA*, above note 41, art 10.14(a); *UK–New Zealand FTA*, above note 38, arts 15.2(d), 15.20, and 25.5.3(b) and (d); *UK–Australia FTA*, above note 38, arts 14.21(h) and 24.1.4; *Chile–Paraguay FTA*, above note 41, art 13.5.5(c); *EU–New Zealand FTA*, above note 41, art 19.4; and *Interim EU-Chile FTA*, above note 41, art 27.4.5(c).

75   *Chile–Paraguay FTA*, above note 41, art 7.22.2–3.

digital economy opportunities, and sharing methods and procedures for data collection related to participation in the digital economy.[76] Another example is found in the *Organisation of African Caribbean and Pacific States–European Union Samoa Agreement*: "The Parties shall cooperate to create an enabling environment, specifically through the establishment and adaptation of appropriate legal and institutional frameworks, to unlock the potential of the digital economy, including e-commerce, in job creation and economic development, with a particular focus on women and youth."[77]

In summary, these recent RTAs serve as model provisions that can be considered for promoting women's digital inclusion and bridging the digital gender divide.

2) Gender Mainstreaming in Plurilateral Agreements

In addition to RTAs, countries are increasingly exploring the mainstreaming of gender equality considerations on a plurilateral basis by negotiating supplementary or independent instruments that integrate trade and gender equality concerns.[78] Two recent plurilateral agreements exemplify distinct approaches to mainstreaming women's considerations: the *Global Trade and Gender Arrangement*, which centers on empowering women to engage in international trade, and the *Digital Economy Partnership Agreement*, which, while addressing a specific set of issues on the digital economy, incorporates women-related concerns as part of its broader effort to promote inclusive trade.

a) Global Trade and Gender Arrangement (GTAGA)
The *Global Trade and Gender Arrangement* (GTAGA), a non-binding plurilateral arrangement,[79] was founded by Canada, Chile, and New Zealand in

---

76 *Chile–Paraguay FTA*, above note 41, art 7.22.3 (a), (c), and (e).

77 *OACP–EU Samoa Agreement*, above note 32, art 25.3.

78 See Amrita Bahri, "Making Trade Agreements Work for Women Empowerment: How Does It Help, What Has Been Done, and What Remains Undone?" (2021) 4:11 *Latin American Journal of Trade Policy* 12 at 12.

79 Government of Canada, "Global Trade and Gender Arrangement" (last modified 13 March 2025), online: international.gc.ca [perma.cc/5A5E-YH5E] [GTAGA]; see also Yin-Jun Lin, "The Role of Regional Governance on Shaping Trade and Gender Nexus Policy in the Pandemic and Recovery: Asia-Pacific Practices and Perspectives" in WTO above note 2 at 181 (noting that the GTAGA "implicates the efforts to promote international governance of the trade and gender nexus").

2020.[80] In the words of the Inclusive Trade Action Group, while not linked to any specific trade agreement, the GTAGA is "similar to a Trade and Gender chapter or article in an FTA as it is designed to assist in removing barriers that women face when participating in trade, and proposes cooperation activities."[81] Specifically, it aims to foster mutually supportive trade and gender policies, enhancing women's participation in trade and investment, and advancing women's economic empowerment and sustainable development. Since its inception, its membership has expanded to include Mexico, Colombia, Peru, Argentina, Brazil, Costa Rica, Ecuador, and Australia.[82]

One interesting observation is that among the thirteen GTAGA participants, six countries—Canada, Chile, Australia, Brazil, New Zealand, and Ecuador—are signatories to the recently enforced or signed RTAs that include gender-related provisions, as examined in Section C. The overlap underscores the deliberate and sustained efforts of these nations in integrating women's considerations into their trade agreements. Former Chilean Foreign Minister Andrés Allamand, who played a role in developing the Arrangement, aptly captures this sentiment: the Arrangement "[draws] inspiration from trade and gender chapters, reinforcing and complementing countries' commitments to gender issues and encouraging them to work together."[83]

While its provisions are not legally binding, the GTAGA offers a vital framework for its participants to consider the nexus between gender and trade. It includes commitments from governments and business stakeholders to promote responsible business conduct by integrating internationally recognized standards, guidelines, and principles addressing gender equality into their internal policies. Additionally, it encourages collaboration

---

80 The idea of the GTAGA was conceived by Canada, Chile, and New Zealand at the margins of the 2018 Asia-Pacific Economic Cooperation (APEC) Leaders Summit, with the establishment of the Inclusive Trade Action Group (ITAG). The three participants signed the Arrangement on 4 August 2020. The participants' list has expanded to include Mexico (2021), Colombia and Peru (2022), Costa Rica and Ecuador (2023), and Australia and Brazil (2024).

81 New Zealand Ministry of Foreign Affairs and Trade, "Inclusive Trade Action Group" (last visited 30 March 2025), online: mfat.govt.nz [perma.cc/XET4-LGRM].

82 Australian Department of Foreign Affairs and Trade, "Inclusive Trade Action Group and the Global Trade and Gender Arrangement" (last visited 29 March 2025), online: dfat.gov.au [perma.cc/D29E-GCDP].

83 See Caroline Dommen, "GTAGA: The Global Trade and Gender Arrangement, Decoded" (1 March 2023), online: iisd.org [perma.cc/K8R6-Q3JG] (citing Former Chilean Foreign Minister Andrés Allamand).

with businesses to develop initiatives that promote gender equality *within* businesses.[84]

Similar to some gender chapters in the recent RTAs, the GTAGA outlines extensive possibilities for cooperation among its participants. Articles 8 and 9 enumerate activities such as improving women's access to innovation, e-commerce and any other trade-related fields,[85] promoting digital skills development,[86] increasing women entrepreneurs' participation in government procurement markets,[87] and fostering women's entrepreneurship, including promoting the internalization of women-led SMEs.[88] Many of these activities align with the discussion themes outlined in the Buenos Aires Declaration.

Another feature linking the GTAGA to the WTO is its transparency provision, which states that participants will endeavour to share experiences related to policies and programs that encourage women's participation in the economy through their voluntary reports to the WTO Trade Policy Review Mechanism (TPRM).[89] It is conceivable that the Buenos Aires Declaration influenced this design, given that using the TPRM to share experiences related to policies and programs promoting women's participation in national and international economies is a notion originally included in the Declaration.[90] Although the discussion of the efficacy of the GTAGA is beyond the scope of this chapter, its connection to the TPRM for sharing Participants' domestic progress is significant in that it underscores the WTO's pivotal role in monitoring and facilitating discussions on gender mainstreaming in trade within a multilateral framework.

b) Digital Economy Partnership Agreement (DEPA)

Another pioneering trade agreement signed in 2020 is the *Digital Economy Partnership Agreement* (DEPA), initially involving Chile, New Zealand, and Singapore. The DEPA is a digital-only trade agreement that focuses on digital

---

84 GTAGA, above note 79, art 9.a.vii.

85 GTAGA, above note 79, art 9.a.ii.

86 GTAGA, above note 79, art 9.a.iv.

87 GTAGA, above note 79, art 9.a.v.

88 GTAGA, above note 79, art 9.a.ix.

89 GTAGA, above note 79, art 7.

90 WTO, *Buenos Aires Declaration*, above note 4, art 1: "Sharing our respective experiences relating to policies and programs to encourage women's participation in national and international economies through World Trade Organization (WTO) information exchanges, as appropriate, and voluntary reporting during the WTO trade policy review process."

economy issues, such as data flows, e-commerce, Artificial Intelligence governance, and fintech. Similar to the GTAGA, it is a stand-alone plurilateral agreement open for other WTO Members to join. Substantively, the DEPA addresses several new issues that are rarely covered in digital trade chapters in other trade agreements, such as the *Comprehensive and Progressive Agreement for Trans-Pacific Partnership* (CPTPP) or the *Canada—United States-Mexico Agreement* (CUSMA).[91]

Notably, the agreement includes a commitment to cooperate on matters relating to digital inclusion, including the participation of women, and improving access for women in the digital economy by removing barriers. A unique feature of the DEPA is its expansive cooperation framework, which extends beyond intergovernmental collaboration. The provision explicitly lists a non-exhaustive array of stakeholders including enterprises, labour unions, civil society, academic institutions, and non-governmental organizations, with whom the parties may coordinate to advance digital inclusion.[92] This broad-based approach, coupled with its status as an open plurilateral agreement, positions the DEPA parties to lead discussions on digital trade agreements in multilateral forums such as the WTO. Some experts view the DEPA as a template for a much larger agreement, possibly within the WTO itself.[93] As the DEPA attracts more signatories who are also WTO Members,[94] including China—one of the top three leaders in global digital trade alongside the European Union and the United States—[95] it remains to be seen how its model for digital inclusion, particularly for women, will shape future digital trade negotiations. A glimpse of the DEPA's influence is evident in the *Chile-Paraguay FTA* discussed above, which also adopts comprehen-

---

91 See Economic and Social Commission for Asia and the Pacific, "Digital Economy Partnership Agreement – Summary" (last visited 30 March 2025), online: digitalizetrade. org [perma.cc/M8F7-9ML6].

92 *Digital Economy Partnership Agreement*, 12 June 2020, art 11.1.4 [DEPA].

93 Dan Ciuriak & Robert Fay, "The Digital Economy Partnership Agreement: Should Canada Join?" (31 January 2022) at 2, online (pdf): cigionline.org [perma.cc/F8YH-DX4M].

94 South Korea has already been added as the DEPA's first new member, and Costa Rica's accession is imminent. The list of other countries who have expressed interest in joining is growing and includes China, Canada, Peru, the United Arab Emirates, El Salvador, and Ukraine. See Organization of American States, "Foreign Trade Information System – Digital Economy Partnership Agreements (DEPA)" (last visited 30 March 2025), online: sice.oas.org [perma.cc/C2VQ-YES3].

95 Global Digital Trade Expo, "Global Digital Trade Volume Surges to \$7.13 Trillion in 2023, According to the Global Digital Trade Development Report 2024" (3 December 2024), online: globalnewswire.com [perma.cc/3W5E-S46T].

sive cooperative activities under the "MSME Digital Dialogue" and "Digital Inclusion" provisions. These provisions include the beyond-the-party cooperation framework featured in the DEPA.[96]

In summary, much like the French adage cited at the beginning of this chapter—*les petits ruisseaux font les grandes rivières*—although the incorporation of women's considerations in trade agreements began modestly and slowly, these initial efforts have now converged to form significant currents within the gender mainstreaming movement and demonstrate an accelerating impact on promoting gender equality and women's empowerment in trade.

D. Mainstreaming Gender Considerations in WTO Agreements

THE PRECEDING DISCUSSIONS ILLUMINATE THAT specific gender provisions in RTAs and plurilateral agreements are becoming a normative phenomenon. Furthermore, the frequent references to the WTO—particularly its Buenos Aires Declaration and mechanisms such as the TPRM—underscore the WTO's standing as a recognized multilateral forum for leading trade and gender discussions. The WTO has the potential to create synergy with RTAs' gender mainstreaming and women's empowerment efforts.

However, pursuing gender mainstreaming in WTO agreements encounters significant institutional challenges, such as the consensus requirement, which demands unanimous agreement of the Members, and the "Single Undertaking" principle, where nothing is agreed upon until everything is agreed upon. These factors pose substantial obstacles to implementing formal changes that represent women's interests in the WTO agreements.[97]

In light of these challenges, there is growing interest in exploring how plurilateral initiatives can offer an alternative path to revitalize the WTO's negotiating function. As WTO Members increasingly consider a "critical mass" approach to negotiations and rule-making, future opportunities to mainstream gender considerations in the WTO agreements would likely need to be considered on a plurilateral basis.[98] The remainder of this sec-

---

96   See *Chile–Paraguay FTA*, above note 41, arts 7.21.1 (MSME Digital Dialogue) and 7.22.4 (Digital Inclusion).

97   Judit Fabian, "Global Economic Governance and Women: Why is the WTO a Difficult Case for Women's Representation" in Bahri, López, & Remy, above note 6 at 72–75.

98   The most recent example is the *Investment Facilitation for Development (IFD) Agreement*, 25 February 2024, which has at least 125 participating members of the WTO.

tion surveys the successes, missed opportunities, and future prospects for mainstreaming gender considerations in its current agreements, the *Trade Facilitation Agreement* and the *Revised Agreement on Government Procurement*. These evaluations are presented with the premise that explicit women-related provisions in trade agreements represent a case of success. However, it is crucial to recognize that gender-neutral trade rules can also foster trade policies that are more globally beneficial, including for women.

1) A Success Case: The Joint Statement Initiative on Services Domestic Regulation

The Joint Statement Initiative on Domestic Regulation (JSI DR) marked the first outcome on services negotiations at the WTO in more than twenty years. The JSI DR disciplines contain new rules aimed at improving the regulatory environment for trade in services, making procedures services exporters have to comply with more transparent, predictable, and non-discriminatory. Currently, seventy-four WTO Members are committed to implementing the disciplines on services domestic regulation,[99] with fifty-three having implemented them, potentially reducing global trade costs by over US$125 billion.[100]

The JSI DR marks the first binding gender equality provision in a WTO plurilateral agreement. Situated in the provision titled "development of measures," which governs the approach governments must take in developing their rules, regulations, and requirements governing the sale of services, Article 22(d) requires Members to ensure no service authorization measures discriminate between men and women.[101] Accordingly, the provision aims to

---

The IFD Agreement could be incorporated into Annex 4 of the *Marrakesh Agreement Establishing the World Trade Organization* as a plurilateral agreement. See WTO, "Investment Facilitation for Development (IFD)" (last visited 30 March 2025), online: wto.org [perma.cc/YPL8-6RNM].

99 This is an increase from the original sixty-seven WTO members who adopted the Declaration in December 2021.

100 WTO, "Services Domestic Regulation" (last visited 30 March 2025), online: wto.org [perma.cc/3LPF-PRJD].

101 WTO, *Declaration on the Conclusion of Negotiations on Services Domestic Regulation*, WTO Doc WT/L/1129 (2021) at 14, fn 33, online (pdf): docs.wto.org [perma.cc/2TXX-MRHS] (clarifying that "differential treatment that is reasonable and objective, and aims to achieve a legitimate purpose, and adoption by Members of temporary special measures aimed at accelerating de facto equality between men and women, shall not be considered discrimination for the purpose of this provision").

ensure non-discrimination in authorization processes, supporting women's economic empowerment and boosting their participation in services trade.[102]

Even though this development lays a promising foundation for future discussions on including gender equality provisions in trade rules, some scholars lament the reality that the JSI DR is the "only [WTO agreement] to include a reference to gender-responsible trade policy."[103]

2) A Missed Opportunity: Joint Statement Initiative on E-Commerce

The JSI on e-commerce, involving ninety-one WTO Members, culminated in the release of the "stabilized" text on 26 July 2024, following protracted negotiations spanning over five years.[104] Unlike the JSI on Domestic Regulation or the DEPA, this initiative lacks gender-related provisions, despite the growing participation of women-owned and women-led businesses in e-commerce and the gender-specific barriers previously discussed.

During the negotiations, Canada proposed two texts that referenced women and gender, although not in a substantial manner. The first proposal included preambular language aimed at fostering improved economic opportunities and access to information and communications technologies for MSMEs, as well as disadvantaged and under-represented groups, including women.[105] The second proposal, presented three months later as a concept paper, focused on preventing the use of personal information for discrimination or persecution.[106]

---

102 WTO, "Services Domestic Regulation Factsheet" (February 2024) at 2, online (pdf): wto.org [perma.cc/2GU9-EBQW].

103 See, e.g., Mia Mikic, "Advances in Feminizing the WTO" in Bahri, López, & Remy, above note 6 at 63.

104 WTO, *Joint Statement Initiative on Electronic Commerce*, WTO Doc IJF/ECOM/87 (2024), online (pdf): docs.wto.org [perma.cc/NX2Q-TKBY].

105 Government of Canada, "Joint Statement on Electronic Commerce – Text Proposal" (last modified 3 July 2019), online: international.gc.ca [perma.cc/H6HB-WS4L].

106 Government of Canada, "Concept Paper: Preventing the Use of Personal Information from Being Used for the Discrimination or Persecution of Natural Persons" (last modified 5 September 2019), online: international.gc.ca [perma.cc/2LHQ-YF8N] (The proposed provision reads, "No Party/Member shall use the personal information of users of digital trade to persecute or discriminate against a natural person on the basis of race, colour, sex, sexual orientation, gender, language, religion, political or other opinion, national or social origin, property, birth or other status, or disability" (footnote omitted)).

The International Trade Centre's report notes that "the absence of substantive gender commitments in the JSI on e-commerce may reflect the fact that advanced e-commerce work at the WTO remains a relatively new phenomenon."[107] Canada's summary of the negotiating history simply states, "other WTO Members have also tabled text proposals on issues of importance to them, which formed the basis of negotiating text."[108]

The JSI represents a missed opportunity to explicitly promote women's access to e-commerce through a text-based approach. Nevertheless, the JSI holds significant potential to advance the e-commerce initiative through a gender lens. The WTO's Information on the Agreement on Electronic Commerce document, albeit informal, underscores that the agreement "supports inclusion" by providing new opportunities to those with limited access to international markets, including women.[109]

Furthermore, the co-conveners have established the E-Commerce Capacity Building Framework as part of the JSI initiative.[110] The Framework supports developing and least-developed countries harnessing digital trade opportunities through programs. Examples include the EU-led Digital Economy and Society for Sub-Saharan Africa, which focuses on increasing internet access, supporting digital startups, and enhancing digital literacy and job creation, particularly for women and youth.[111] Another example is UNCTAD's E-commerce and Digital Economy Program (ECDE), which includes UNCTAD's eTrade for Women initiative. This program fosters gender-inclusive digital economies by amplifying women's voices in digital leadership, empowering women entrepreneurs in developing countries with knowledge, skills, recourses, and opportunities to scale their businesses, and ensuring their active participation in digital policy-making.[112] In this regard, the JSIs

---

107 International Trade Commission, *E-commerce Negotiations at the WTO: A Gender Lens for Action* (Geneva: International Trade Commission, 2023), online (pdf): intracen.org [perma.cc/9PYC-ND56] [ITC, *2023 E-Commerce Report*].

108 Government of Canada, "World Trade Organization Joint Statement Initiative on Electronic Commerce" (last modified 21 June 2024), online: international.gc.ca [perma.cc/RFT6-ZVR6].

109 WTO, "Information on the Agreement on Electronic Commerce" (last visited 30 March 2025) at para 3.11, online (pdf): wto.org [perma.cc/N8EP-NKHH].

110 WTO, "Joint Statement Initiative on E-commerce – Capacity Building Framework" (last visited 30 March 2025), online: wto.org [perma.cc/AK7A-ZZCT].

111 WTO, "Capacity Building Framework for the WTO Agreement on Electronic Commerce" (last visited 30 March 2025), online (pdf): wto.org [perma.cc/K5M6-6ZPT].

112 *Ibid* at 15–16. The contributing WTO Members include Australia, Germany, the Netherlands, Sweden, Switzerland, and the United Kingdom.

serve as useful nodes for WTO Members who would like to mainstream gender considerations in this discipline through the work programs.

3) Applying A Gender Lens to WTO Agreements

This part examines two WTO agreements—on trade facilitation and public procurement—both of which encompass gender-neutral provisions. While these agreements include rules that have the potential to empower women, their intended policy objectives may be rendered ineffective due to adverse gendered impacts and the inherent barriers women face within these domains. To that end, this subsection canvasses a number of possibilities within the respective agreements to incorporate gender considerations and mitigate their effects.

a) Trade Facilitation Agreement

The *Agreement for Trade Facilitation* (TFA) is a WTO agreement that aims to expedite the movement, release, and clearance of goods across borders.[113] It also establishes measures for effective cooperation between customs and other relevant authorities on trade facilitation and customs compliance. Additionally, the agreement contains provisions for technical assistance and capacity building in this domain. According to the WTO, the full implementation of the TFA could reduce trade costs by an average of 14.3 percent and increase global trade by up to USD 1 trillion annually, with the poorest countries experiencing the most significant benefits.[114]

The TFA is gender-neutral in its design and does not contain any provisions related to women. However, many believe its trade facilitation measures have strong potential for gender lens implementation and recommend incorporating a women's perspective to maximize benefits for women in both formal and informal trade.[115]

113　The *Agreement for Trade Facilitation*, 22 February 2017 [TFA]. Note: this is not a plurilateral agreement but a full WTO agreement, representing the first multilateral trade agreement concluded since the WTO's establishment in 1995. To date, the TFA has been ratified by 160 countries. See WTO, "Trade Facilitation Agreement Database – Ratifications" (last visited 30 March 2025), online: tfadatabase.org [perma.cc/D5Z7-H2PN].

114　WTO, "Trade Facilitation" (last visited 30 March 2025), online: wto.org [perma.cc/JR9H-EWXH].

115　See United Nations Trade and Development, *Policy Brief No 98: Integrating a Gender Perspective into Trade Facilitation Reforms* (Geneva: UNCTAD, 2022), online (pdf): unctad.org [perma.cc/ZS8P-GCZP].

An analysis of select TFA provisions reveals that while gender-neutral trade facilitation measures can aid women traders and their businesses in overcoming barriers, they may also produce negative gendered effects or fail to address structural shortcomings, thereby undermining the provisions' intended objectives.

Article 1 mandates the parties publish easily accessible trade-related information about import, export, and transit procedures on the Internet. Bahri observes that this provision "deals directly with information access problems faced by many cross-border women traders."[116] The publication and availability of such information are particularly beneficial for women traders who often lack preparedness and knowledge of relevant trade rules, have lower confidence levels when interacting with officials, or lack support networks.[117]

However, despite Article 1.1's requirement for Members to publish trade-related information in a "non-discriminatory and easily accessible manner," women traders with low literacy levels and limited access to the Internet or digital devices may not benefit from these arrangements. Consequently, the ITC asserts that solutions relying on the internet and the publication of legal texts are unlikely to bridge the information gaps faced by women traders.[118]

To address these negative gendered effects, Members could undertake gender-sensitive actions such as assessing the information gaps and the quality of information displayed on existing platforms and subsequently addressing any inconsistencies.[119]

Another example is found in Article 7, which facilitates the expedited release and clearance of goods, as well as the acceptance of electronic payments for duties, taxes, and other customs charges.[120] Additionally, mechanisms such as post-clearance audits and the establishment of average release times for goods further support the expedited release of goods. Bahri identifies two benefits that this provision offers to women traders: first, a monetary benefit that saves women traders and their businesses the investments they would have had to make in the release of goods without such procedures

---

116 Amrita Bahri, "Trade Facilitation Agreement" in *Trade Agreements and Women: Transcending Barriers*, above note 6 at 81.

117 ITC, *2023 E-Commerce Report*, above note 107 at 9.

118 *Ibid.*

119 Global Alliance for Trade Facilitation, "The World Trade Organization's Trade Facilitation Agreement Through a Gender Lens" (2020) at 1, online (pdf): tradefacilitation.org [perma.cc/C8FM-7ZSG].

120 TFA, above note 113, art 7.2.

and second, protection against discrimination they might have faced from customs officials at the border in the release process.[121]

Moreover, the ITC identifies an additional benefit, namely the reduction of personal safety risks for women traders who would otherwise need to carry and handle cash, making them vulnerable to theft. However, this provision may also increase transaction costs for women and compel them to use a third-party payment service, thereby weakening their financial control.[122]

As the above analysis demonstrates, applying a gender lens to understand the impact of gender-neutral trade rules would be crucial to ensure that their intended policy objectives are fully realized. This can be achieved in tandem with the WTO Informal Working Group on Trade and Gender, whose agenda involves exchanging views on how to apply a gender lens to the work of the WTO.[123]

b) The Revised Agreement on Government Procurement

In the words of the former WTO Director-General Pascal Lamy, the WTO *Agreement on Government Procurement* (GPA) is a plurilateral accord that "has the potential to open up significant economic opportunities for under-represented social groups, including Women Business Enterprises, in this important market segment."[124] The Agreement leverages the principles of non-discrimination, transparency, and predictability to establish a framework for public procurement among its signatory countries. Although public procurement is excluded from the coverage of the *General Agreement on Tariffs and Trade 1947* (GATT), the *Agreement on Government Procurement* (GPA) was negotiated in 1996 and revised in 2012 (GPA 2012).[125]

The GPA 2012 includes several gender-neutral provisions that can help signatories foster conducive procurement conditions for women-owned and

---

121 Bahri, above note 116 at 81.

122 ITC, *2023 E-Commerce Report*, above note 107.

123 WTO, "Informal Working Group on Trade and Gender" (last visited 30 March 2025), online: wto.org [perma.cc/YBX5-3GPD].

124 Pascal Lamy, "Opening Government Procurement to Women's Enterprises" (1 July 2012), online: intracen.org [perma.cc/PR3F-6VPS].

125 *Agreement on Government Procurement*, 30 March 2012 [GPA 2012]. WTO, "Agreement on Government Procurement" (last visited 30 March 2025), online: wto.org [perma.cc/P6CF-S5TF]. Currently, GPA 2012 comprises twenty-two parties representing forty-nine WTO Members, with thirty-five WTO Members and observers participating in the Committee on Government Procurement (CGP) as observers. Additionally, a few WTO Members are seeking accession negotiations.

women-led businesses. Amrita Bahri's recent book titled, *Trade Agreements and Women: Transcending Barriers*, provides a thorough analysis of such benefits, which are summarized below:

- Article XVI: encourages e-procurement tools to enhance accessibility and efficiency of procurement systems;
- Articles VI and VII: mandate prompt publication and notice requirements, ensuring businesses, including women-owned ones, receive timely bidding information;
- Articles VIII, IX and X: streamline and standardize participation conditions, supplier qualification requirements, technical specifications, and tender documentation to mitigate complex and burdensome procedures that deter women-owned businesses from participating;
- Article XI: sets a forty-day general minimum period for tender submission, providing sufficient time for suppliers, particularly women-owned businesses, to prepare their applications;
- Article XV: may also be helpful as it ensures that the treatment of tenders and awarding of contracts are handled in a simple, fair, and impartial manner; and
- Article XVIII: establishes domestic review requirements, offering women business owners a platform to address any unfair or discriminatory treatment that puts them at a disadvantage in the procurement market.[126]

These provisions collectively indicate that the GPA 2012 is crucial for levelling the procurement playing field for women-owned businesses, enabling them to capitalize on new opportunities in the public procurement sector.

The GPA 2012 has the potential to enhance gender perspectives within the agreement. Similar to the RTAs examined in Section C above, it could include women-specific references to increase women's participation in public procurement. This could be achieved through aspirational language in the preamble or by negotiating specific exceptions in party-specific schedules and/or Annex 7 (General Notes). For instance, the United States has included an exception in its Annex 2 for state entities, allowing preferences for programs promoting businesses owned by women, in addition to minorities and disabled veterans.[127]

---

126 Amrita Bahri, "Can WTO Laws and Institutions Empower Women?" in *Trade Agreements and Women: Transcending Barriers*, above note 6 at 84–86.

127 WTO, "Agreement on Government Procurement: United States of America – Sub-Central Government Entities" (last visited 30 March 2025), online: e-gpa.wto.org [perma.cc/F8DX-B3KB], Annex 2, n 2.

Additionally, the GPA 2012 provisions on work program items offer pathways to promote women's economic empowerment. Article XXII (Final Provisions) Paragraph 7 permits the adoption of "additional items" to improve the agreement and reduce discriminatory measures.[128] Another possible avenue is by adding gender-specific components to existing work programs, such as the SME work program (analyze women-owned SMEs, their participation in bids, supply chains, and gendered market segmentation); sustainable procurement program (examine gender-responsive procurement practices aligned with *UN SDG 5*); and data collection and statistical reporting program (develop methodologies for gender impact assessments and gather gender-disaggregated data on women-owned businesses, unsuccessful bidders, and joint tendering; monitor gender equality in access to public services like health, education, and transportation).[129]

E. Conclusion

TO DATE, MAINSTREAMING GENDER CONSIDERATIONS into WTO agreements has been a rare occurrence, contrasting sharply with the prolific efforts observed in the context of RTAs and other plurilateral agreements outside the WTO. Nevertheless, as emphasized by former German Chancellor Angela Merkel on the eve of International Women's Day 2025, it is crucial to "preserve and improve multilateralism as a key tool to foster international collaboration and expand women's participation in international trade."[130] In this endeavour, Dr. Merkel underscored the importance of establishing rules and standards to ensure women have equal access to economic opportunities.[131]

In 2025, the WTO faces numerous challenges, including the currently non-operational Appellate Body. Nevertheless, the global trade rulemaking function is an essential role of the WTO. Looking ahead to the next thirty years, making continued—albeit incremental—progress in the quest to mainstream gender considerations within the WTO, particularly in its agreements, will be a worthy challenge to pursue.

---

128 GPA 2012, above note 125, art 7.
129 See ITC, *WTO GPA Gender*, above note 63 at 16.
130 WTO, "Presidential Lecture Series: Angela Merkel Highlights Multilateralism's Role in Global Cooperation, Women's Participation in Trade" (7 March 2025), online: wto.org [perma.cc/VY97-MUUB].
131 *Ibid.*

CHAPTER 32

The End of the "Single Undertaking" in WTO Negotiations

Andrew Stoler

A. Introduction

ANYONE WHO KNOWS THE HISTORY of the multilateral trading system of the *General Agreement on Tariffs and Trade* (GATT) and the World Trade Organization (WTO) was not surprised by the failure of the Doha Round. A critical mistake was made when it was decided that the outcomes of the Doha Round should be decided by consensus and that all Members should be bound by those outcomes (the "single undertaking" approach). Trying to make progress on this basis was bound to fail, and it also reflected a misunderstanding of the origins of the Uruguay Round "single undertaking." After twenty years of wasted time, it seems that Members of the WTO who want to make progress in the multilateral system have finally realized that they need to go back to the way progress was made in the past. The path to this progress is through what WTO Members are today calling "Joint Statement Initiatives." Essentially, these are plurilateral agreements among those WTO Members that want to see progress in particular trade areas. For an old timer like me, it is encouraging, and it is about time.

B. Background

INITIALLY, NEGOTIATIONS HELD UNDER THE auspices of the GATT focused exclusively on the reduction and elimination of customs tariffs.

Reciprocity was more or less determined by whether a government considered the opportunities represented by its trading partners' tariff reductions justified reduction of its own tariff barriers to trade. Participation in these early rounds of tariff negotiations was limited by today's standards, and non-tariff barriers were not on the table.

Progress in the GATT and WTO has almost never been possible on the basis of all Member countries being bound by the same rules. Way back in the 1950s, only a limited number of governments undertook to be bound by the export subsidy disciplines of GATT Article XVI:4. The Kennedy Round produced the limited-membership Anti-Dumping Code.

The Tokyo Round resulted in a number of limited-membership agreements that were implemented as "codes."[1] I would argue that even with their limited membership, the codes represented a big step forward in rulemaking for important trade issues. Many of the Tokyo Round codes were applied on a most-favoured-nation (MFN) basis so that even non-code members received the benefits of the agreements. Several were non-MFN in their application.[2]

Bringing the codes into the GATT system was problematic. The developing countries refused (initially) to have the GATT Secretariat administer the codes to which few of them were members. They blocked agreement and funding for this to happen. This led to a negotiation whereby, in order to get the codes into the system, two important decisions were negotiated and agreed in late 1979. The first of these two decisions, agreed on 28 November 1979, was the decision on "Differential and More Favourable Treatment Reciprocity and Fuller Participation of Developing Countries."[3] Perhaps the most important part of this Decision is found in its paragraph 5, which reads:

> 5. The developed countries do not expect reciprocity for commitments made by them in trade negotiations to reduce or remove tariffs and other barriers to trade of developing countries, i.e., the developed countries

---

1   They included a revised Anti-Dumping Code, a code on Subsidies and Countervailing Duties, a code on Technical Barriers to Trade (the Standards Code), the Government Procurement Code, the Customs Valuation Code, and the *Agreement on Trade in Civil Aircraft*.

2   The Codes on Government Procurement, Technical Barriers to Trade and Subsidies and Countervailing Measures were applied in ways that provided benefits only to members of the agreements.

3   GATT, *Differential and More Favourable Treatment Reciprocity and Fuller Participation of Developing Countries*, GATT Dec L/4903 (1979), online (pdf): docs.wto.org [perma. cc/695D-9HBN].

do not expect the developing countries, in the course of trade negotiations, to make contributions which are inconsistent with their individual development, financial and trade needs. Developed contracting parties shall therefore not seek, neither shall less-developed contracting parties be required to make, concessions that are inconsistent with the latter's development, financial and trade needs.

The other outcome of this negotiation—brought on by the perceived need to make the codes GATT agreements—was the Decision of 28 November 1979 entitled "Action by the Contracting Parties on the Multilateral Trade Negotiations."[4] It was this decision that allowed the codes to be brought into the GATT and administered by the GATT Secretariat. In my view, the key parts of this decision are found in paragraphs 3 and 5, which read:

> 3. The CONTRACTING PARTIES also note that existing rights and benefits under the GATT of contracting parties not being parties to these Agreements, including those derived from Article I, are not affected by these Agreements . . .
> 5. Further, the CONTRACTING PARTIES understand that interested non-signatory contracting parties will be able to follow the proceedings of the Committees or Councils in an observer capacity, and that satisfactory procedures for such participation would be worked out by the Committees or Councils.

So, there was a price to pay for gaining the Contracting Parties' agreement to bring the Tokyo Round codes under the GATT umbrella. Also, it was clear from these decisions that if non-signatories wished over time to join the codes they could do so. Certain countries also joined the Code on Subsidies and Countervailing Measures on a nonvoluntary basis.[5]

---

4   GATT, *Action by the Contracting Parties on the Multilateral Trade Negotiations*, GATT CP Dec L/4905 (1979), online (pdf): docs.wto.org [perma.cc/T3D7-FR3P].

5   Depending upon whether goods subject to a countervailing duty investigation were dutiable or duty-free, the United States applied the injury test selectively. Countries affected by this policy and who wished to have their exports to the United States protected by the application of an injury test in countervailing duties (CVD) cases had to first negotiate "subsidies commitments" with the United States and join the Code. This was the case, for example, with both New Zealand and Australia when the American National Wool Growers Association brought a CVD case against those countries' lamb exports to the United States.

C. The Uruguay Round

GETTING THE NEXT MULTILATERAL TRADE negotiation off the ground
proved difficult because of disagreements between developed and developing
countries over which subjects should be taken up in new talks. The first step
was the 1982 GATT Ministerial in Geneva where actual negotiations were
not launched but a follow-on work program was eventually agreed.[6] In its
initial stages, the work program focused on future subjects for negotiations,
including agriculture, safeguards, and dispute settlement. After two years,
services were added as an issue. Discussions on services were particularly contentious. I can recall that, in an effort to slow progress, delegations like India
insisted that before a next session could be held, the secretariat was required
to produce verbatim records of a session's deliberations—and in the three
official GATT languages. This was extremely time-consuming and costly.

A preparatory committee (PrepCom) was eventually established to plan
for a new round of multilateral trade negotiations and began work in January 1986.[7] The Americans added investment and intellectual property to the
list of subjects they wanted covered. This stimulated fierce opposition from
developing countries. Delegations arrived in Uruguay in September ready for
a gunfight over what would be the negotiating agenda for the next round.

When one revisits the Punta del Este Declaration that launched the
Uruguay Round negotiations, it is clear that there were a number of subjects,
such as trade in services and protection of intellectual property rights, listed
for negotiation where it was never expected that all of the GATT Contracting
Parties would participate in the negotiations and be bound by the outcomes.
In the Ministerial Declaration,[8] Part I was addressed to trade in goods and
Part II was addressed to trade in services. Technically, the services negotiations were not even under GATT auspices. General Principle B. (2) stated in
part: "The launching, the conduct and the implementation of the outcome
of the negotiations shall be treated as parts of a <u>single undertaking</u>." How

---

6   GATT, *Ministerial Declaration*, GATT Doc L/5424 (1982), online (pdf): docs.wto.org
     [perma.cc/E2HY-Y9YU].

7   GATT, *Decision by the Contracting Parties Establishing the Preparatory Committee*,
     GATT Dec CP L/5925 (1985), online (pdf): docs.wto.org [perma.cc/VLY7-WP8W].

8   GATT, *Ministerial Declaration on The Uruguay Round*, GATT Dec GATT/1396 (1986),
     online (pdf): docs.wto.org [perma.cc/8PP7-MNC5].

these outcomes would be implemented was left open for decision at the end of the talks.[9]

Subject-wise, in addition to the new subjects proposed for negotiation, the existing GATT plurilateral codes were also on the table for revision and improvement. Certain agreements attracted the attention of more than the original members. The focus was on fine-tuning the codes (this was the third time the *Anti-Dumping Agreement* was negotiated). The Uruguay Round also expanded the talks in areas where the GATT rules had been ineffective—particularly in the case of dispute settlement. Anyone who has studied dispute settlement under GATT knows how poorly the system performed when guilty parties were able to block adoption of dispute settlement panel reports. The new Dispute Settlement Understanding and the creation of the Appellate Body were designed to fix these issues. In almost all of the Uruguay Round negotiations, only a limited number of GATT Contracting Parties were active participants.

It was the creation of a new organization in the form of the WTO at the end of the Uruguay Round that made it possible to broaden membership in what had been the limited-membership codes and other agreements resulting from the round. But the idea of creating a new organization to administer the results of the Uruguay Round was not agreed until the very last days of the negotiations in December 1993. Some countries backed the creation of a Multilateral Trade Organization. The United States resisted this until the last moment, arguing instead to create a new agreement to replace GATT, which would be called the General Agreement on Trade (GAT). Up until the point where the pieces fell into place to create a WTO, participants in the negotiations were free to agree or not to agree to the negotiated results of the round.

In discussions among the Quad countries (the Unites States, European Communities, Canada, and Japan), the question arose about how the round might be ended. So long as participants enjoyed the protection of the GATT, they had little to lose by not agreeing to all or parts of the Uruguay package. The idea came up that we could force countries to accept all of the package if the Quad countries quit the GATT and thereby broke our MFN obligations to those that refused to go into all of the new agreements. Of course, the Quad itself did not want to just junk the GATT and all of its provisions, so

9   The Ministerial Declaration specified that: "[w]hen the results of the Multilateral Trade Negotiations in all areas have been established, Ministers meeting also on the occasion of a Special Session of Contracting Parties shall decide regarding the international implementation of the respective results."

it was decided that a new GATT—GATT 1994—would be created to replace GATT 1947. The Quad countries did in fact quit GATT 1947 and agree to GATT 1994. Any country that did not want to lose MFN and other benefits then also had to join GATT 1994—but this was only possible if they accepted all of the other Uruguay results. All of these results were packaged in the creation of the WTO.

Article XI of the *Marrakesh Agreement Establishing the World Trade Organization* therefore specified that "the Contracting Parties to the GATT 1947 as of the date of entry into force of this Agreement, and the European Communities, which accept this Agreement and the Multilateral Trade Agreements and for which Schedules of Concessions and Commitments are annexed to GATT 1994 and for which Schedules of Specific Commitments are annexed to GATS shall become original Members of the WTO."

Thus, the creation of the new organization not only ended the long-standing practice of treating post-colonial countries as "*de facto*" GATT members but also set off a somewhat frantic negotiation of specific commitment negotiations under the *General Agreement on Trade in Services* (GATS) (which many developing countries had not expected as a price to pay for entry into the WTO).

D. Post-WTO Developments

THE LIMITATIONS OF A "SINGLE undertaking" approach became apparent shortly after the completion of the Uruguay Round and the creation of the WTO. The blackmail approach only works once, and after that only willing participants will be part of a negotiation.

After the advent of the WTO, trade liberalization progress on the "multilateral" front came with limited-membership agreements for telecommunications services, financial services, and high technology products. Generally, these are called "critical mass agreements" because enough of a percentage of global trade was covered that participants did not mind that others did not sign up. Non-participants did not object because they received the benefits of the agreements on an MFN basis. In the case of the *Information Technology Agreement* (ITA), the Agreement was concluded by twenty-nine participants at the Singapore Ministerial Conference in 1996. Since then, the number of participants has grown to eighty-two, representing about 97 percent of world trade in information technology (IT) products. The participants are committed to completely eliminating tariffs on IT products covered by the

Agreement. At the Nairobi Ministerial Conference in December 2015, over fifty Members concluded the expansion of the Agreement, which now covers an additional 201 products valued at over $1.3 trillion per year.[10]

E. Post-WTO and Post-Doha

I WAS THERE IN DOHA when the Ministerial Declaration was adopted and the Doha Round was launched. It was a fatal mistake to agree that the new round could only be concluded through the "single undertaking" approach. We were blind to history. By forcing all of the developing countries (and all of the countries that had enjoyed "de facto CP" status) to join the WTO and accept all of the agreements, we also forced all of them to be part of the decision-making process in the WTO. It only took a couple of years (and the so-called "implementation" debate) to see that the one-size-fits-all approach was not going to work, and that the system was never going to be a one-tier system. In fact, things got much worse in the period between Marrakesh and Doha with a proliferation of groups getting special treatment and having to undertake less than full obligations. We now have all these countries (many of whom care very little about the trading system and international trade, and I put India in this group) who are intent on being very participative in the WTO decision-making process frequently with the objective of making sure nothing happens.

Fast forward to the post-Doha period where we find ourselves now. Over the past twenty years, all significant trade rule-making and liberalization has taken place in the context of bilateral and regional trade agreements outside of the WTO. WTO rule-making has been largely frozen in the 1990s while important trade issues have been subject to updated rules in these preferential agreements.

In recent years, some WTO Members have moved to update WTO rules through new "critical mass" agreement efforts called Joint Statement Initiatives (JSIs). JSIs have addressed electronic commerce, services domestic regulation, and investment facilitation. Certain countries—chief among them India and South Africa—evidently do not want to see progress in these areas

---

10   WTO, "Information Technology Agreement" (last visited 11 June 2025), online: wto.org [perma.cc/5JF2-5YDS].

and have opposed JSIs. In February 2021, India and South Africa circulated a paper arguing against the "legality" of JSIs.[11]

There are a number of points made in this paper that I agree with. If a subset of WTO Members negotiate an agreement that would modify <u>rules</u> and then want to "add that agreement to Annex 4" or formalize the agreement "into the WTO framework of rules" or bring the results of their agreement "under the umbrella of the WTO," this cannot be done outside of the accepted framework of WTO rules and decision-making procedures. In another part of their paper, they correctly suggest that a proposed Trade in Services Agreement (TISA) involves rule-making and would need to be implemented outside the framework of WTO rules. I do not see a problem here as it was always my understanding that TISA would have been an agreement concluded pursuant to GATS Article V.

Where I disagree with India and South Africa is with some of the things they put forward in the Annex to their paper. For example, I disagree with their assertion that "even changes to schedules cannot be made unilaterally, as other members have the right to protect the existing balance of rights and obligations." This is true if you want to make your schedule more trade restrictive but not if you unilaterally modify your schedule to make it more liberal. The certification procedure they refer to in connection with the ITA was not a negotiation with all other WTO Members. The ITA was essentially negotiated as an early JSI only among a subset of members on a critical mass basis.

So where are we as I write this in early 2024? There is some good news and some bad news. On 25 February 2024, Ministers representing 123 WTO Members issued a joint ministerial declaration marking the finalization of the *Investment Facilitation for Development (IFD) Agreement* which they hope to incorporate into Annex 4 of the *Marrakesh Agreement* as a WTO plurilateral agreement. The agreement would help its signatories attract the foreign direct investment they want to drive growth, productivity gains, job creation, and integration into global supply chains. Participants believe that the IFD agreement incorporated into the WTO would create clear and consistent global benchmarks for investment facilitation.

---

11   WTO, *The Legal Status of "Joint Statement Initiatives" and Their Negotiated Outcomes*, WTO Doc WT/GC/W/819 (2021), online (pdf): docs.wto.org [perma.cc/6QV6-JQBD].

But can this agreement be incorporated into Annex 4 of the *Marrakesh Agreement*? On 1 March 2024, India issued a Ministerial statement[12] that reads in part: "We further emphasize that given the lack of consensus, any issue relating to investment facilitation is not a matter for consideration and action within the agenda of, or as an agenda or sub-agenda item of the 13th session of the WTO Ministerial Conference." The Indian position is of course disappointing to those who want to see multilateral progress on issues like this.

India's opposition to the IFD agreement is two-fold. First, the Indians argue that investment *per se* is different from trade and investment has no part to play in the WTO. I disagree and I believe that most WTO Members that are serious international traders recognize that investment questions are in fact closely related to trade performance. India's second argument—that plurilaterals are "illegal" in the WTO—is without legal foundation. Stranger still is that India has itself participated in the ITA and has dropped its opposition to the JSI on domestic regulations for services—a plurilateral agreement that is currently being implemented through modification of members' services schedules. It would seem that the Indians have no problem with JSIs like the ITA and the services domestic regulation agreement when they can see that due to MFN implementation there are benefits for India in the agreements.

India and its cohorts[13] were of course central to the termination of work in the WTO on investment and competition policy in the years after the Singapore Ministerial. In my view, it is very disappointing that the WTO was not allowed to continue work in these areas which are clearly closely related to trade policy.

There are still other areas where WTO Members have got the message and are advancing work on a JSI basis. The JSI on E-Commerce looks very promising. Hopefully, these initiatives will help the WTO move forward in the twenty-first century.

So, as long as a JSI only involves changes in schedules (making them more liberal) and does not seek to modify WTO rules or bring the resulting agreement into Annex 4, I do not see any conflict between JSIs and WTO. With Members like India and South Africa blocking progress at the multilateral

---

12   WTO, *Ministerial Statement by India*, WTO Doc WT/MIN(24)/29 (2024), online (pdf): docs.wto.org [perma.cc/N749-E3BG].

13   India's "cohorts" in opposition have changed over the years. Brazil formerly frequently sided with India in opposition to developed country initiatives but has now gone over to the other side. Today, India's staunch allies are normally South Africa and Namibia.

level in the WTO,[14] other Members have no recourse other than to pursue the JSI route, either as critical mass agreements within the WTO framework or where rule-making is involved, outside the WTO as plurilateral agreements.

14 It is a fair point that India and South Africa are not the only reason the Doha Round failed. The US position on agricultural subsidies and China's lack of enthusiasm for sectoral agreements are other examples of blockages in the system. However, in almost all cases, the negotiating problem can be traced back to the idea that all agreements should be agreed as a single undertaking with all participants expected to participate in the outcome.

Part IV:

Concluding Reflections

CHAPTER 33

Reforming the WTO's Dispute Settlement System—Putting the Cart Before the Horse

Ujal Singh Bhatia

A. Introduction

THE ORIGINS OF THE WORLD Trade Organization (WTO) crisis lie in its nearly comatose legislative function, which since the WTO was established, has largely failed to negotiate new multilateral trade rules for a rapidly changing global economy. The WTO's vibrantly active dispute resolution function has paid the price for the legislative paralysis. The resolution of the WTO's crisis requires Members to fix the legislative backlog with new rules for a global trading system that has changed dramatically since its last major overhaul in the Uruguay Round. It is then that the need and direction of dispute settlement system (DSS) reform will be clear.

The present urgency for DSS reform arises from the disablement of the Appellate Body by a United States veto. The fact that 130 WTO Members have been regularly approaching the Dispute Settlement Body (DSB) for sanctioning the process for selection of new Appellate Body Members suggests that the problem with the DSS is more political than substantive. At the 12th Ministerial Conference of the WTO, the Ministers resolved to conduct discussions with the view to having a fully functioning dispute settlement system by 2024. This commitment was reiterated in the 13th Ministerial

Conference in early 2024. An informal process on dispute settlement reform was convened in February 2023 and the DSB has been receiving reports on the progress of discussions regularly. The discussions have now been formalized. It is premature at this stage to speculate on the possibility and nature of the outcome, especially when the most contentious issue, the appellate review function, does not seem to have figured in the discussions so far. But the real issue is whether a revived DSS can perform its mandated function in a global trading system that has undergone very significant changes in the thirty years since the WTO came into existence.

B. The Crisis of the WTO

AND THAT BRINGS US BACK to the crisis around the WTO's legislative function. Since the Uruguay Round, WTO Members have failed to conclude any fresh multilateral agreement except the *Trade Facilitation Agreement* and the (incomplete) *Agreement on Fisheries Subsidies*. The failure of the Doha Development Round hovers like the ghost of Banquo on the WTO, with little collective introspection about the reasons for its collapse or on how consensus can be built around a new agenda that can revitalize the organization and reposition it as the pre-eminent provider of rules for the global trading system.

A multilateral organization is built around the idea of common purpose and consequently, its decision-making typically proceeds through consensus, a principle that is reiterated in Article IX of the *Marrakesh Agreement Establishing the World Trade Organization*. In its earlier years, the *General Agreement on Tariffs and Trade* (GATT) found it quite easy to obtain consensus around its agenda and outcomes, with the strong role played by the United States and its allies. After the WTO was created in 1995 however, the tectonic plates of global economic power have shifted in many ways, with consensus becoming more elusive. There are a host of reasons for this, and they have to do with geopolitical changes, the emergence of China as the largest trading Member, technological developments which are transforming the nature and composition of trade, and frequent supply shocks induced by climate change, conflicts, and pandemics. Unequal access to resources and technology has created a two-track world, and inequalities are on the rise, both domestically in many countries as well as across the world. And underlying all this is the question of trust. The lack of agreement between Members on shaping the new agenda of the organization is a reflection of the absence of trust after the failure of the Doha Round and its Development Agenda and the absence of any meaningful initiatives to rebuild that trust.

In terms of their global significance, the effects of recent developments in the United States on the WTO have been the most important. Since the beginning of GATT negotiations in 1947, the United States has provided unswerving leadership for the development of the rules-based trading system based on the idea that it could only prosper if the rest of the world shared its prosperity. It can safely be said that the extensive and much admired (and envied) corpus of rules built within a range of agreements in the GATT/WTO would not have been possible without US leadership. It is not much of an exaggeration to call the United States, as some have, "the original architect and guarantor of the trading system."[1]

However, recent years have witnessed a remarkable change in US positions on multilateral rules as a consequence of changes in domestic politics brought on by a more open trading regime. This has combined with geopolitical concerns, of which the stand-off with China is the most significant. The priorities of the United States have clearly shifted from seeking global trade expansion to addressing imbalances. The changes in domestic politics, which demand greater attention to issues like reviving manufacturing in several sectors, workers' welfare, national security, and related goals, weigh more heavily on its international positions than in the past.

It would be incorrect however, to view the changes in US policies purely in political terms, or merely as a reflection of geopolitical developments. It is important to bear in mind that the global economy and the trading system are undergoing a structural transformation which is primarily driven by technological changes. New technologies are building intelligent machines, changing the nature of manufacturing, and driving changes in critical sectors like data management, biotechnology, environment, communication, and other areas. Global competitiveness is increasingly being defined by innovation and what may seem like trade wars often have their basis in technology competition. Such technologies are commonly of a dual use nature and therefore often bring in considerations of national security. For these reasons, geopolitical and economic objectives are being increasingly aligned, involving a greater role for the state in building competitiveness and resilience.

---

1   Alan W Wolff, *Revitalizing the World Trading System* (Cambridge: Cambridge University Press, 2023).

China's clean energy and electric vehicles industries are examples of these developments. China now produces nearly 80 percent of the world's solar photovoltaic (PV) modules, 60 percent of wind turbines, and 60 percent of electric vehicles and batteries.[2] China invested very early in these sectors, and the high competitiveness built by its industries through innovation and subsidies enabled it to achieve global dominance in their export,[3] inviting a range of trade defense actions in several countries.

Other developments requiring a greater role for the state are the multiple supply shocks caused by factors like climate change, pandemics, and conflicts. The increasing frequency of such events has focused attention on resilience strategies. The impact of shocks caused by climate change on supply chains for food is well documented. The COVID-19 pandemic revealed the risks inherent in depending on a few suppliers of critical medicines and equipment, as well as food. The large number of export restrictions imposed by several countries was a reminder that open markets cannot always be relied upon in crisis situations. The conflict in Ukraine has led to rerouting of energy supply chains away from Russia for several countries. In most cases, such resilience strategies involve an active role for governments.

The ongoing digital transformation is another major arena for global competition requiring state capacity and coordination in areas like data processing, super computers, 5G networks etc. The rush to invest in semiconductors in several countries reflects the critical importance of digital technologies in advancing competitiveness and strengthening national security. Technologies like generative AI are likely to have a transformative effect on the world—on labour markets, trade, medicine, education, environment, and various other kinds of human activity. They also have an obvious strategic dimension requiring some oversight by the state.

C. The Return of the State

THERE ARE SEVERAL COMMON FEATURES of these developments which underscore the return of the state. The most important is the interface between the emerging strategic technologies and geopolitics. But there is also the dual-use nature of these technologies which brings in considerations

---

2   Dani Rodrik, "Don't Fret About Green Subsidies" (10 May 2024), online: project-syndicate.org [perma.cc/Z3EU-NY5J].

3   Paolo Gerbaudo, "The Electric Vehicle Developmental State" (11 April 2024), online: phenomenalworld.org [perma.cc/S2LU-9AUF].

of national security. The need felt for strategic autonomy in these sectors in several countries also spurs public investments. These developments together help to explain the re-emergence of industrial policy around the world.

WTO disciplines are not built around any normative principles regarding the relationship between the market and the state and indeed provide appropriate flexibilities to states to pursue various domestic objectives. As Howse and Langille point out:

> Instead, by and large, the WTO's legal disciplines attempt to preserve the ability of states to organize their domestic economic and political structures as they see fit. They are rooted in a procedure that in principle is suited to preserve pluralism at the domestic level: state consent and the requirement of consensus. Substantively, they protect the right of states to regulate, even in ways that restrict trade, for reasons that they consider to be important—including economic, scientific, moral, or religious reasons.[4]

However, the guardrails established by fundamental GATT principles like non-discrimination and various rules like those on subsidies set the boundaries for acceptable conduct.

The changes in global dynamics in recent years, however, effectively constitute a shift in the global trade paradigm, with several important countries moving decidedly towards one end of the market-state spectrum. While it is important to mention the United States in this regard, it is by no means alone—several others like the European Union (EU), Japan, and India seem to be emulating China by moving towards a greater role of the state in their trade policies to often achieve non-trade objectives. In several ways, these developments constitute a challenge to the liberal rules-based order as an organizing principle for global trade. The crucial question that needs to be asked in the context of DSS reform initiatives is whether this challenge can be resolved within the existing rules, or whether the departures from WTO rules require fresh rule-making in a vastly changed global economy.

---

4   Robert Howse & Joanna Langille, "Continuity and Change in the World Trade Organization: Pluralism Past, Present, and Future" (2023) 117:1 *American Journal of International Law* 1.

D. Industrial Policy in 2023

IT IS USEFUL TO PROVIDE a factual basis for a discussion on recent industrial policy interventions around the world to fully understand the nature, scope, and dimensions of this development. The International Monetary Fund (IMF)'s New Industrial Policy Observatory (NIPO) data set tracks the emergent patterns of policy interventions associated with industrial policy across the world. In a recent paper,[5] the authors track the wave of new industrial policies introduced during 2023, and their conclusions are striking:

- New industrial policy interventions increased by over 2500 during 2023, and around 1800 of these measures (71 percent) were trade distorting. The bulk of such measures (70.9 percent) were introduced by Advanced Economies.
- China, EU, and the United States accounted for 47.7 percent of the trade distorting measures.
- The most often-stated objectives of such interventions were national security, geopolitical concerns, resilience/security of supply (nonfood), and domestic competitiveness in strategic sectors.
- The most common policy measures involved export barriers, import barriers, domestic subsidies, export incentives, foreign direct investment (FDI) measures, procurement policies, and localization incentives/requirements.
- In Advanced Economies, subsidies are the most employed instrument, while the Emerging Market and Developing Economies usually employ trade restrictions on imports and exports.
- Strategic competitiveness is the dominant motive for such measures, but other objectives include climate change mitigation and adaptation, resilience, and national security.
- An interesting conclusion of the study was regarding tit-for-tat measures. Implemented measures are often correlated to past use of similar measures in the same sectors by other governments.

The findings from this study merit reflection. The sheer number of industrial policy interventions in 2023 makes it clear that this is not a passing phenomenon. The bulk of such measures were in Advanced Economies. The infant industry argument has indeed come a long way. The fact that

---

5 Simon Evenett et al, "The Return of Industrial Policy in Data" (2024) International Monetary Fund, Working Paper No 2024/001, online: imf.org [perma.cc/55X6-B92Y].

the United States, EU, and China accounted for almost half of the trade distorting measures is important in the context of potential disputes before the DSS, as is the large correlation in tit-for-tat measures. The often-stated objective of national security for industrial policy measures is also important in view of the differences between WTO Members regarding how GATT Article XXI should be read.

E. Are WTO Disciplines Strong Enough?

IN A RECENT PAPER, SIMON Evenett examines some recent events in which trade measures either involve a *prima facie* violation of multilateral trade rules or which involve rules that are not tightly defined to act as deterrents against inconsistent behaviour.[6] In this connection, he discusses the United States-China "trade war" between 2018 and 2020 and the "the apparent 'weaponization' of medical goods and food exports in recent years."

In 2018, the United States imposed import tariffs of 25 percent on 1333 products sourced from China.

The next day China threatened to retaliate with 25 percent import tariffs on 106 products. President Trump instructed his officials to consider imposing higher tariffs on $100 billion more of Chinese imports. These tit-for-tat actions were repeated by both sides till a "phase one deal" was signed in January 2020. The deal did not lead to withdrawal of the additional tariffs.

Evenett draws some stark conclusions from this episode—Membership of the WTO did not deter the US from revoking most-favoured-nation (MFN) status from China or from exceeding bound tariffs. In its retaliatory actions, China was similarly undeterred on both counts. Moreover, "these import tariff changes have not been reversed, may be permanent, and are at minimum, non-transitory."[7]

The second episode relates to GATT Article IX:2(a) which allows Members to levy temporary export prohibitions or restrictions "to prevent or relieve critical shortages of foodstuffs or other products essential to the exporting contracting party."[8] Evenett points out that there is no agreed list of which

---

6   Simon J Evenett, "Can the World Trade Organization Act as a Bulwark Against Deglobalization?" (2024) 19:1 *Asian Economic Policy Review* 1.

7   *Ibid.*

8   *General Agreement on Tariffs and Trade 1994*, Annex 1A of the *Marrakesh Agreement Establishing the World Trade Organization*, 15 Apr 1994, 1867 UNTS 187 art IX:2(a).

products are deemed essential. Moreover, the application of the exception is self-judging.

On the outbreak of the COVID-19 pandemic, a large number of export restrictions/prohibitions were imposed on a range of medical equipment and medical consumables. For 31 percent of the measures introduced in 2020, the Global Trade Alert could not gather evidence that they had been removed. There is a similar situation regarding restrictions on exports of foodstuffs that were imposed in the wake of the COVID-19 pandemic as well as Russia's invasion of Ukraine.

Lack of the required transparency regarding export restrictions and the fact that there is no mechanism within the WTO to ensure their removal raises the possibility that "a sequence of systemic crises could result in a permanent reduction of cross-border trade in 'essential goods.'"[9]

There is another dimension to this. Since the beginning of 2022, a growing number of import restrictions have been imposed in the food and medical sectors around the world. These restrictions are often accompanied by large subsidies to local producers. Evenett notes that WTO rules have not prevented Members from reducing dependence on imports.

F. A Changed Ethos

THESE DEVELOPMENTS HELP TO UNDERSCORE the fact that "new industrial policy" constitutes a significant departure from the trade liberalization ethos that has so far guided rulemaking in the GATT/WTO. Its implications need to be discussed and debated by WTO Members before a common understanding can be reached on whether the existing rules in the relevant areas remain fit-for-purpose in the changed environment, or whether new disciplines are needed. Judging from several submissions made in the WTO in recent months on issues related to industrial policy, it is clear that the path forward requires engagement of all Members in such an exercise.

The need for and content of DSS reform has to be discussed in this broad context. While it is undisputable that the DSS could do with reform in some areas, especially in timelines for dispute resolution, requiring it to adjudicate disputes arising from measures being introduced by Members to address new policy priorities, on the basis of existing rules, may create very difficult challenges for adjudicators. Rulings are likely to be contested more

---

9   Evenett, above note 6.

than before, and issues are likely to be raised regarding the credibility and legitimacy of the adjudicatory processes.

G. National Security

A GOOD EXAMPLE OF THIS likely contestation relates to the national security exception in GATT Article XXI. The WTO panel report for *Russia—Measures Concerning Traffic in Transit*[10] contained the first formal analysis of Article XXI(b)(iii) which relates to actions taken by a Member which it considers necessary for the protection of its essential security interests "in time of war or other emergency in international relations."[11] Russia argued that Article XXI was entirely self-judging and the Panel lacked jurisdiction. The Panel did not agree with Russia's interpretation of the provision and ruled that WTO panels have jurisdiction to review aspects of a Member's invocation of Article XXI(b)(iii). The Panel further rejected the argument of the United States that Russia's invocation of Article XXI(b)(iii) is "non-justiciable."[12]

Despite the adoption of the panel report in the DSB, the US position remains unchanged. In 2018, the United States imposed additional tariffs on steel and aluminum products against several countries on grounds of national security. In December 2022, a WTO Panel found against the United States.[13] This prompted a sharp retort from the US. In the January 2023 meeting of the DSB, the US Permanent Representative to the WTO clearly stated the US position—"For over 70 years, the United States has held the clear and unequivocal position that issues of national security cannot be reviewed in WTO dispute settlement and the WTO has no authority to second-guess the ability of a WTO Member to respond to a wide-range [sic] of threats to its security."[14]

---

10 *Russia—Measures Concerning Traffic in Transit (Complaint by Ukraine)* (2019), WTO Doc WT/DS512/R (Panel Report), online (pdf): docs.wto.org [perma.cc/C738-YZSR] [*Russia—Measures Concerning Traffic in Transit*].

11 *General Agreement on Tariffs and Trade 1994*, above note 8, art XXI(b)(iii).

12 *Russia—Measures Concerning Traffic in Transit*, above note 10 at paras 7.102–7.103.

13 *United States—Certain Measures on Steel and Aluminum Products (Complaint by China)* (2022), WTO Doc WT/DS544/R (Panel Report), online (pdf): docs.wto.org [perma.cc/FX4G-VZ6Q].

14 U.S. Mission to International Organizations in Geneva, "U.S. Statements by Ambassador María Pagán at the WTO Dispute Settlement Body Meeting" (27 January 2023), online (pdf): usmission.gov [perma.cc/C7TM-JGPZ].

The battle lines are clearly drawn on this issue, and this will not go away. We can reasonably expect several more disputes on the national security exception to be filed involving trade measures by the United States as well as by other Members. While there may not be broad support for the US position regarding the jurisdiction of WTO panels to adjudicate such disputes, the more frequent recourse to an Article XXI defense by respondents in such disputes should lead WTO Members to consider the existing scope of the exception. This would warrant a political discussion rather than leaving it to the dispute resolution process alone.

H. Trade Related Climate Measures and Policies

ANOTHER EXAMPLE OF AN IMPORTANT issue which is likely to increasingly feature in the DSS in the near future is that of trade related climate measures and policies. In view of the escalating urgency of the climate change issue, several WTO Members are enacting such measures through a range of approaches. There is growing concern about the impact of such measures on the trading system. These concerns include fears that such measures will fragment trade, undermine collective international climate action, and adversely impact the trade competitiveness of developing countries.

In the WTO, disputes regarding departures from the non-discrimination provisions for environmental purposes have largely been dealt with under the exception of GATT Article XX.[15] With the sharp increase in trade-related climate measures, the "likeness" of products will be a prominent issue in disputes because of the role of Processes and Production Methods in carbon emissions.[16] There is the even more sensitive issue of Special and Differential Treatment (S&DT) for developing countries.

---

15   See *United States—Import Prohibition of Certain Shrimp and Shrimp Products (Complaint by India et al)* (1998), WTO Doc WT/DS58/AB/R (Appellate Body Report), online (pdf): docs.wto.org [perma.cc/Z2XE-C59K]; *United States—Import Prohibition of Certain Shrimp and Shrimp Products: Recourse to Article 21.5 of the DSU by Malaysia (Complaint by India et al)* (2001), WTO Doc WT/DS58/AB/RW (Appellate Body Report), online (pdf): docs.wto.org [perma.cc/5P2W-2E2D].

16   See *Philippines—Taxes on Distilled Spirits (Complaint by United States)* (2011), WTO Doc WT/DS403/AB/R (Appellate Body Report), online: docs.wto.org [perma.cc/856T-L68Y]; *European Communities—Measures Affecting Asbestos and Products Containing Asbestos (Complaint by Canada)* (2001), WTO Doc WT/DS135/AB/R (Appellate Body Report), online: docs.wto.org [perma.cc/V2HV-BHA6].

At a broader level, the issue of coherence between commitments and flexibilities under different international agreements has to be addressed. For instance, under the *Paris Agreement*, the signatories have agreed to reduce their emissions through Nationally Determined Contributions, and flexibilities have been provided under the principle of Common but Differentiated Responsibilities and Respective Capabilities.

It is clear that trade related climate measures need to be seen as legal hybrids as they implicate several areas of international law. "[T]he rationale, design, and debates about these measures draw from different international law regimes, including those relating to the environment generally, climate change specifically, and international trade, along with the rules and principles of general international law, international human rights law, and international commitments to sustainable development."[17]

The WTO will need to consider how such "legal hybrids" should be dealt with under WTO rules. Given the several dimensions of the climate change crisis, there is a clear need for a harmonious view which reconciles the various dimensions. A sustainable reconciliation is more likely to emerge from a political process rather than through litigation.

I. Rebuilding Consensus

IN BRIEF, THE CRISIS OF the DSS is actually a crisis of the WTO itself and needs to be viewed holistically to enable a sustainable resolution. One cannot be resolved without the other. An exercise to reform the DSS, without addressing the fundamental asymmetry between new global priorities and existing trade rules can hardly be expected to resolve the WTO's crisis in a lasting manner. WTO Members would be well advised to first address the issue of legislative paralysis. For this to happen, it is essential that they arrive at a shared understanding on how the global situation has changed and what changes are called for in the rules as a consequence. Given the legislative record of the WTO, that is not an easy task. Consensus is a rare commodity in a fragmenting world order.

Recent discussions in the WTO have focused on the legality of a number of plurilaterals (the so-called Joint Statement Initiatives) being negotiated,

---

17   TESS Forum on Trade, Environment & the SDGs, *Principles of International Law Relevant for Consideration in the Design and Implementation of Trade-Related Climate Measures and Policies* (TESS, 2023).

as well as on the consensus principle. This is a discussion eminently worth having. There can be no doubt that while the primary concern of the WTO has to be to negotiate multilateral agreements, there should also be space for subsets of Members to pursue other agreements through plurilateral initiatives. There are others who believe that in a fractured system, the pursuit of consensus is futile, and plurilaterals should be the preferred route for fresh commitments.

It is important to situate this discussion beyond binaries. While the objections of Members like India and South Africa to plurilaterals are based formally on legal grounds, they essentially reflect the lack of trust flowing from the failure of the Doha Round and the pick-and-choose follow-up on the Doha agenda. A broad negotiating agenda which reflects a balance between the interests of all Members is what the WTO requires to restore the multilateral process. The Single Undertaking approach has been pronounced dead by some, but the underlying principle of the Single Undertaking, the trade-offs between different interests, is what can help to rebuild consensus and galvanize the multilateral process.

For the restoration of trust, several things need to fall in place—a deliberative process, along the lines suggested by the EU but without a pre-agreed agenda, involving off-campus discussions between capitals; a supportive US Administration; and active engagement by systemically important countries like Brazil, China, and India in shaping a new agenda. As far as India is concerned, it has remained on the sidelines for too long and needs to engage in such discussions based on a clearer understanding of its emerging place in the world order. For instance, the long-stalled permanent solution to the public stock holding for food security requires new negotiating energy. Similarly, India has done very well on clean energy initiatives but also needs to protect its exports from unilateral actions in importing countries. An understanding on integrating commitments and flexibilities in multilateral environment agreements with WTO rules could provide an acceptable framework. On investment, India is a major player both on the inward and outward sides and needs to put forward its perspectives in the WTO rather than questioning whether investment is within the WTO's mandate.

J. Conclusion

TO SUMMARIZE, THE WTO NEEDS a major reboot in a world in transition. The return of the state and of industrial policy are factors that cannot be wished away and need to be frontally addressed. Global issues like climate change, the digital transformation, public health, and food security require the participation of all Members. For this to happen, trust has to be restored and good faith efforts made to build consensus. This is not an easy task given the present political uncertainties, increasing confrontations, and lack of leadership. But other options, while more convenient and necessary, do not constitute a lasting solution to the WTO's crisis. Once Members arrive at common understandings on how to deal with the key challenges that have emerged, the consequential changes required in the DSS will be an easy stroll. It is important to get the sequence right.

CHAPTER 34

Valerie Hughes as a Model and as a Leader

Nadia Theodore

THE PURPOSE OF THIS BOOK is to reflect on the history of the World Trade Organization (WTO) and its dispute settlement system but also look forward into its future. Valerie Hughes has made tremendous contributions to the system over the past decades, but I want to suggest that she can also serve as a guiding light for thinking about the system's future. For me, she represents that future. To explain why I think so, I first need to go back into my own past.

I have been fascinated by international trade ever since I was a child. Walking through the aisles of a grocery store with my dad, I could not help but wonder where all the products were made. What added to the fascination was the fact that I myself am the product of people who came from a different country, who immigrated to Canada and built a life in Canada but who were always very dedicated to making sure that their country of birth was also set up for success. I came from a very globally minded family, which gave me a natural affinity for trade.

At the time, I was of course not aware that there was such a thing as trade policy, and it was not until much later, when I was a student at Carleton University in Ottawa, that I started thinking about trade policy as a possible career. It was while I was searching for someone whom I could relate to as a model for what such a career might look like that I heard the name Valerie Hughes for the first time. Everyone said to me: you have to go talk to this woman, Valerie Hughes. At the time, there were very few women working in international trade and even fewer who were not just trying to make it through the day but who were willing and able to give back and serve as mentors to younger women. I started reading about Valerie and talking to people who knew her, and I was in awe of who she was and what she was doing, including the fact that she had worked in other government departments before joining (what was then) the Department of Foreign Affairs and International Trade and had not always worked directly in trade policy. For me, as someone who had been trying to decide between law and the policy world, her career path provided an inspiration for how you could contribute to the world of trade policy with experience from different fields.

I went on to encounter Valerie at various points over the course of my career and sometimes, as when I was visiting Geneva while she was working at the WTO, we also saw each other in social contexts. However, I want to emphasize that I do not think that Valerie's impact on me and others as a mentor depended on having a close personal relationship with her. This is important for students and young professionals to know. In order for someone to be a model and a mentor for you, you do not need to have a deep and direct personal relationship with that person over a long period of time. In fact, I believe that Valerie's impact on others was mostly due to what people saw of her almost from afar.

What, then, is that impact, and why do I say that Valerie has not just made enormous contributions to Canada's trade policy and the multilateral trade regime in the past but also represents the system's future?

The first aspect I want to mention is Valerie's drive for excellence, which I think is extremely important. We do not talk about it enough anymore—the importance of being unapologetically just extremely good at your job, showing up prepared, being ready to give it your all, having pride in your work as a leader. As public servants, we have a responsibility for people's faith in the system, for people's trust in the institution. You cannot meet that responsibility without a commitment to doing your best and giving your best, and Valerie is the epitome of excellence in the job. And we have to acknowledge the challenges for women in a field dominated by men. Sometimes when you reach a certain level, it gets even more difficult. Instead of celebrating the achievements, the narrative can be: don't get too big for your boots. And as a result, people, and especially women, will sometimes pull back. Valerie has never done that, and that is an amazing testament to her leadership. With her example, she showed people what is possible, how to take up space and how to master your craft.

The second way in which Valerie represents the future is in her recognition, from very early on, that there is no tension between excellence and inclusion. She always understood the importance of having many voices at the table, and she was never afraid to double down on that insight. One reason I think that is spectacular is that she comes from a generation when it was much easier not to do that.

One of the clearest expressions of her commitment to diversity for me was the speech she gave in 2019 when she received the Award for Excellence in International Law from the Ontario Bar Association. She dedicated her speech to the importance of inclusiveness in the system and of gender diversity among trade lawyers and officials working in trade policy. For me, the choice to devote her acceptance speech to this topic made sense of every interaction I had had with her ever since I first met her. In that speech, she articulated what she had always valued. And it is these values that we need to extrapolate to the scale of the multilateral trading system. We must honour Valerie's example especially today, as it is getting harder to be loud about the fact that the system must work for everybody in order to be successful and sustainable.

Finally, Valerie is someone who, in speaking about trade law and policy, was always able to weave in the *why* with the *what* and the *how*, and in that way, she also points the way to where we need to go with the multilateral trading system. We do have to think a little bit more about the *why* than practitioners have been used to. For a very long time in trade policy and global economic governance, we have almost prided ourselves in not having to worry too much about the *why*. We had the rules, and we worked within the rules. If you followed the rules, everybody was going to be better off, the thinking went. But given the challenges that the system confronts today, we will need people who understand that we always have to keep the *why* front of mind. Valerie is a woman who exudes excellence with regards to the *what* and the *how*—knowing the law, knowing the policy, knowing the way that it all works together—but she has also been a very loud champion around the *why*.

Canada's prosperity depends on a functioning multilateral trading system. And that requires us to be very heavily committed and involved in the building and maintaining of the system. That requires a multifaceted effort. The trade negotiators are a part of that, but a huge part of that is also taking your best people and putting them out there in the world, to help build and maintain those institutions. Valerie has been at the pinnacle of that effort. There are few people who have done more for Canada and its leadership in the multilateral system—both in terms of what it is today and what it will be tomorrow. And that has made her into one of our legends.

Notes on Contributors

Editor

NICOLAS LAMP is an Associate Professor at the Faculty of Law at Queen's University, where he teaches and writes primarily in the areas of international trade law and policy. At Queen's, he is also cross-appointed to the School of Policy Studies and serves as the Director of the Queen's Institute on Trade Policy, a professional training course for Canadian trade officials. His 2021 book *Six Faces of Globalization: Who Wins, Who Loses, and Why It Matters* (co-authored with Anthea Roberts and published by Harvard University Press) was named as one of the best books of 2021 by the *Financial Times* and *Fortune Magazine*. Professor Lamp is also a co-author (with Henry Gao, Jennifer Hillman, and Joost Pauwelyn) of a free online casebook on international trade law entitled *International Trade Law. A Casebook for a System in Crisis* (published by the Geneva Trade Platform since 2023). Before joining Queen's University in 2014, Professor Lamp worked for two years as a Dispute Settlement Lawyer in the Appellate Body Secretariat of the World Trade Organization, where he advised the Members of the Appellate Body on legal issues arising in disputes before the Appellate Body. Professor Lamp holds a PhD in Law and an LLM in Public International Law from the London School of Economics and Political Science and degrees in International Relations from the Universities of Bremen and Dresden in Germany.

Contributors

DANIEL ARI BAKER is a Dispute Settlement Lawyer in the Legal Affairs Division of the WTO Secretariat.

UJAL BHATIA is a former member and chair of the Appellate Body of the WTO and former ambassador of India to the WTO.

JAN BOHANES is a Counsellor in the Advisory Centre on WTO Law in Geneva.

RAMBOD BEHBOODI is a Senior Counsel at Borden Ladner Gervais LLP and Adjunct Professor at the Faculty of Law, University of Ottawa.

KATHLEEN CLAUSSEN is Anne Fleming Research Professor and Professor of Law at Georgetown University Law Center. She also serves as Managing Co-Director of Georgetown's Institute of International Economic Law. Among other leadership roles, she has served on the Executive Council and Executive Committee of the American Society of International Law and is co-Editor-in-Chief of the Journal of International Economic Law. Prior to joining the academy, Professor Claussen was Associate General Counsel at the Office of the US Trade Representative.

CHRIS COCHLIN is founding Partner at Cassidy Levy Kent LLP in Ottawa, where he advises businesses and governments on a wide range of international trade matters, including antidumping and countervailing duty litigation, trade policy and trade negotiations, bilateral investment, and market access strategies to challenge or defend foreign and domestic government measures. Mr. Cochlin also advises Canadian and international companies in the defense, energy, materials, high technology, and communications sectors extensively on customs compliance and on compliance with Canada's export controls, economic sanctions and the controlled goods regime.

MATEO DIEGO-FERNÁNDEZ ANDRADE is a founding Partner at Agon, an arbitrator under the Multi-Party Interim Appeal Arbitration Arrangement (MPIA) of the World Trade Organization, and on the roster of panelists of *Canada-United States-Mexico Agreement* (CUSMA) Chapter 31.

ADEET DOBHAL is a Trade Policy Analyst in the Market Access Division of the WTO Secretariat.

ANGELA ELLARD is a Deputy Director-General at the World Trade Organization.

SCOTT FALLS is an associate at Lévy Kaufman-Kohler in Geneva, where he practises international commercial and investment arbitration and public international law as counsel and tribunal secretary. Prior to joining LKK, Scott was assistant legal counsel at the Permanent Court of Arbitration. He holds an LLM from the Graduate Institute and University of Geneva (MIDS), JD from Queen's University, and BA from the University of Western Ontario.

MALLORY FELIX is an International Trade Counsel at Cassidy Levy Kent LLP in Ottawa, where she represents and advises clients on multiple aspects of Canada's trade remedies, export controls and sanctions regimes. Ms. Felix earned her Juris Doctor from Queen's University and her Master of Arts in Economics from the University of British Colombia, writing her final thesis on international trade and development.

MATEO FERRERO is a Counsellor at the Trade and Environment Division of the WTO Secretariat.

JAMES FLETT is a Deputy Director in the Legal Service of the European Commission.

JONATHAN FRIED is a Senior Advisor with the Albright Stonebridge group and senior associate at the Centre for Strategic and International Studies. He was previously senior advisor at Bennett Jones LLP and served in several high-level positions in the Canadian government, including as Canada's Ambassador and Permanent Representative to the World Trade Organization.

A.V. GANESAN is a former member and chair of the Appellate Body of the World Trade Organization.

HENRY GAO is a Professor at Singapore Management University.

MARIA GEORGE is a PhD Candidate at the Graduate Institute, Geneva, and was formerly an intern at the World Trade Organization.

MARISA GOLDSTEIN is a Counsellor in the Legal Affairs Division of the WTO Secretariat.

JENYA GRIGOROVA is a Dispute Settlement Lawyer in the Legal Affairs Division of the WTO Secretariat.

JENNIFER HILLMAN is a Professor of Practice at Georgetown Law, Georgetown University in Washington, DC. She was formerly a member of the Appellate Body of the World Trade Organization.

ALEXANDER HOBBS is an International Trade Counsel at Cassidy Levy Kent LLP in Ottawa. He advises businesses and governments on trade remedies, government procurement, economic sanctions and export controls, and competition law. Mr. Hobbs has worked with public and private clients on international trade, procurement, and investment issues and disputes under many of Canada's international trade treaties.

RODD IZADNIA is a Counsellor in the Legal Affairs Division of the WTO Secretariat.

MARK JEWETT is a Senior Fellow at the Centre for International Governance Innovation (CIGI). He was formerly Counsel at Bennett Jones LLP, Senior Assistant Deputy Minister at the Departments of Justice and Finance (Canada), and General Counsel and Corporate Secretary at the Bank of Canada.

MARGARET M. KIM is Trade Counsel for the Government of Ontario, Canada.

SIMON LESTER is the co-founder of WorldTradeLaw.net and China Trade Monitor and a non-resident fellow for the Baker Institute International Economics Program. Previously, he was the associate director of the Cato Institute's Herbert A. Stiefel Center for Trade Policy Studies, focusing on WTO disputes, regional trade agreements, and international trade law history. He began his career at a Washington, DC, law firm advising on WTO matters and later served as a legal affairs officer at the WTO's Appellate Body Secretariat. He has taught international trade law at various universities and is the co-author of a leading textbook in the field. He has published scholarly articles in the *Stanford Journal of International Law*, the *Journal of International Economic Law*, and the *World Trade Review*.

GABRIELLE MARCEAU has held several high-level positions in the WTO, including as senior counsellor in the Legal Affairs Division. She is an Honorary Professor at the Université de Genève and Visiting Professor at University of Ottawa.

DONALD MCRAE is a Professor Emeritus at the University of Ottawa.

NIALL MEAGHER is the Executive Director of the Advisory Centre on WTO Law in Geneva.

LIZZIE MEDRANO is a Training Officer in the WTO Institute for Training and Technical Cooperation; she was previously Dispute Settlement Registrar of the WTO Secretariat.

MARCO TULIO MOLINA TEJEDA is an international trade and investment expert, founder of Molina & Associates LLC, and former Minister Counsellor and Deputy Permanent Representative of Guatemala to the WTO.

MARÍA J. PEREYRA is Senior Counsellor in the Legal Affairs Division of the WTO, member of the Executive Council of the Society of International Economic Law (SIEL) (2018–24) and of the Advisory Board of the Master on International Legal Studies at IE Law School.

PENELOPE RIDINGS is a member of the International Law Commission for New Zealand and former arbitrator under the Multi-Party Interim Appeal Arbitration Arrangement (MPIA) of the World Trade Organization. She chaired the MPIA arbitration in *China—Enforcement of Intellectual Property Rights* (DS611) and the arbitration under the Trade and Cooperation Agreement between the European Union and United Kingdom (PCA Case No. 2024-45: *UK-Sandeel (European Union v United Kingdom)*. She has been a WTO panelist and has served on ICSID Annulment Committees, including as President.

IAIN SANDFORD is a Partner at Foley Hoag in Geneva.

ROY SANTANA is a Counsellor in the Market Access Division of the WTO Secretariat.

SIVAN SHLOMO-AGON is an Associate Professor at Bar-Ilan University.

MICHAEL SOLURSH is General Counsel and leads the Trade Law Practice Group for the Government of Ontario, Canada.

RONALD STEENBLIK is a Senior Technical Advisor to the Quaker United Nations Office (QUNO), Geneva. He was formerly the Organization for Economic Cooperation and Development's Special Counselor for Fossil Fuel Subsidy Reform.

ANDREW STOLER is a former trade negotiator with the Office of the US Trade Representative and a former Deputy-Director General of the World Trade Organization. In 2003 he established the Institute for International Trade at the University of Adelaide.

NADIA THEODORE is Ambassador and Permanent Representative at the Permanent Mission of Canada to the World Trade Organization in Geneva.

J. ANTHONY VANDUZER is a Professor Emeritus of the Common Law Section at the University of Ottawa.

GERALDO VIDIGAL is Associate Professor in the Faculty of Law, University of Amsterdam.

WENHUA JI is a Professor at the School of Law of the University of International Business and Economics (UIBE) in Beijing, China.

MÜSLÜM YILMAZ is a Senior Dispute Settlement Lawyer in the Legal Affairs Division of the WTO Secretariat. He previously worked for the Turkish Ministry of Trade. He taught WTO Law at Bilkent University, Ankara, and will be teaching International Trade Law at the University of Mannheim as from the 2025–26 academic year.